Handbook of Research on Developing Circular, Digital, and Green Economies in Asia

Patricia Ordóñez de Pablos
The University of Oviedo, Spain

IGI Global
PUBLISHER of TIMELY KNOWLEDGE

A volume in the Advances in Finance, Accounting, and Economics (AFAE) Book Series

Published in the United States of America by
IGI Global
Business Science Reference (an imprint of IGI Global)
701 E. Chocolate Avenue
Hershey PA, USA 17033
Tel: 717-533-8845
Fax: 717-533-8661
E-mail: cust@igi-global.com
Web site: http://www.igi-global.com

Library of Congress Cataloging-in-Publication Data

Names: Ordóñez de Pablos, Patricia, 1975- editor.
Title: Handbook of research on developing circular, digital, and green economies in Asia / Patricia Ordonez de Pablos.
Description: Hershey : Business Science Reference, 2021. | Includes bibliographical references and index. | Summary: "This book explores new and emerging business and management practices to support companies and economies in the digital transformation in Asia, with special emphasis on success and failure experiences and analyzing the role of digital skills and competences, green issues and technological disruptors in these emerging practices in Asia and how they can contribute to the creation of new business opportunities, more jobs and growth for the recovery of Asian economies after the pandemic"-- Provided by publisher.

Identifiers: LCCN 2021019275 (print) | LCCN 2021019276 (ebook) | ISBN 9781799886785 (hardcover) | ISBN 9781799886808 (ebook)
Subjects: LCSH: Managerial economics--Asia. | Technological innovations--Economic aspects--Asia. | Sustainable development--Economic aspects--Asia.
Classification: LCC HD30.22 H36 2021 (print) | LCC HD30.22 (ebook) | DDC 338/.064095--dc23
LC record available at https://lccn.loc.gov/2021019275
LC ebook record available at https://lccn.loc.gov/2021019276

This book is published in the IGI Global book series Advances in Finance, Accounting, and Economics (AFAE) (ISSN: 2327-5677; eISSN: 2327-5685)

British Cataloguing in Publication Data
A Cataloguing in Publication record for this book is available from the British Library.

All work contributed to this book is new, previously-unpublished material. The views expressed in this book are those of the authors, but not necessarily of the publisher.

For electronic access to this publication, please contact: eresources@igi-global.com.

Advances in Finance, Accounting, and Economics (AFAE) Book Series

Ahmed Driouchi
Al Akhawayn University, Morocco

ISSN:2327-5677
EISSN:2327-5685

Mission

In our changing economic and business environment, it is important to consider the financial changes occurring internationally as well as within individual organizations and business environments. Understanding these changes as well as the factors that influence them is crucial in preparing for our financial future and ensuring economic sustainability and growth.

The **Advances in Finance, Accounting, and Economics (AFAE)** book series aims to publish comprehensive and informative titles in all areas of economics and economic theory, finance, and accounting to assist in advancing the available knowledge and providing for further research development in these dynamic fields.

Coverage

- Theoretical Issues in Economics, Finance, and Accounting
- Economic Downturn
- Economics of Risks, Uncertainty, Ambiguity, and Insurance
- Wages and Employment
- Risk Analysis and Management
- Economic Theory
- Economic Indices and Quantitative Economic Methods
- Borrowing and Lending
- Economics of Intellectual Property Rights
- Health Economics

IGI Global is currently accepting manuscripts for publication within this series. To submit a proposal for a volume in this series, please contact our Acquisition Editors at Acquisitions@igi-global.com or visit: http://www.igi-global.com/publish/.

The Advances in Finance, Accounting, and Economics (AFAE) Book Series (ISSN 2327-5677) is published by IGI Global, 701 E. Chocolate Avenue, Hershey, PA 17033-1240, USA, www.igi-global.com. This series is composed of titles available for purchase individually; each title is edited to be contextually exclusive from any other title within the series. For pricing and ordering information please visit http://www.igi-global.com/book-series/advances-finance-accounting-economics/73685. Postmaster: Send all address changes to above address.

Titles in this Series

For a list of additional titles in this series, please visit: www.igi-global.com/book-series/advances-finance-accounting-economics/73685

Handbook of Research on Climate Change and the Sustainable Financial Sector
Odunayo Magret Olarewaju (Durban University of Technology, South Africa) and Idris Olayiwola Ganiyu (University of KwaZulu-Natal, South Africa)
Business Science Reference • © 2021 • 573pp • H/C (ISBN: 9781799879671) • US $295.00

CSR and Management Accounting Challenges in a Time of Global Crises
Ionica Oncioiu (Titu Maiorescu University, Romania)
Business Science Reference • © 2021 • 278pp • H/C (ISBN: 9781799880691) • US $215.00

Impact of Global Issues on International Trade
Ahu Coşkun Özer (Marmara University, Turkey)
Business Science Reference • © 2021 • 325pp • H/C (ISBN: 9781799883142) • US $215.00

Handbook of Research on the Empirical Aspects of Strategic Trade Negotiations and Management
Nuno Crespo (ISCTE – Instituto Universitário de Lisboa, Portugal) and Nadia Simoes (ISCTE – Instituto Universitário de Lisboa, Portugal)
Business Science Reference • © 2021 • 446pp • H/C (ISBN: 9781799875680) • US $265.00

Handbook of Research on Financial Management During Economic Downturn and Recovery
Nuno Miguel Teixeira (Center for Research in Business and Administration, School of Business Sciences, Polytechnic Institute of Setúbal, Portugal) and Inês Lisboa (CARME, School of Management and Technology, Polytechnic of Leiria, Portugal)
Business Science Reference • © 2021 • 566pp • H/C (ISBN: 9781799866435) • US $295.00

Understanding the Active Economy and Emerging Research on the Value of Sports, Recreation, and Wellness
David J. Finch (Mount Royal University, Canada) and David Legg (Mount Royal University, Canada)
Business Science Reference • © 2021 • 312pp • H/C (ISBN: 9781799879398) • US $225.00

Applied Doughnut Economics and Neuroeconomic Psychology for Business and Politics
Torben Larsen (DEALs Online Collaborative Platform, Denmark)
Business Science Reference • © 2021 • 257pp • H/C (ISBN: 9781799864240) • US $195.00

IGI Global
PUBLISHER of TIMELY KNOWLEDGE

701 East Chocolate Avenue, Hershey, PA 17033, USA
Tel: 717-533-8845 x100 • Fax: 717-533-8661
E-Mail: cust@igi-global.com • www.igi-global.com

Editorial Advisory Board

List of Reviewers

List of Contributors

Table of Contents

Detailed Table of Contents

The low supply of vaccines for COVID-19 has disrupted tourism development in Asia. The question is if the vaccine may change cultural divergence into cultural convergence at the tourist destination. The purpose of this study is to examine the culture and price elasticity of hotel demand to find the cultural convergence. The study has conducted autoregressive distributed lag model to test whether the vaccine would change the price and income elasticities of hotel demand to find the cultural transformation from divergence to convergence through tourism. Findings indicate that the impact of the vaccine on transferring culture from divergence to convergence was confirmed. Tourists from the divergent cultures specified by less levels of Hofstede's cultural dimensions will visit the country destination with high levels of Hofstede's cultural dimensions after COVID vaccination. Japan and the US that possess divergent levels of power will visit Vietnam for power convergence. China, Korea, and Russia that possess divergent levels of indulgence will visit Vietnam for indulgence convergence.

It is crucial for business organizations to maintain sustainability within the globalized market environment. However, the organizational ability of micro, small, and medium enterprises (MSMEs) is inadequate to generate sustainable competitive advantage. Moreover, strategic management theories are developed based on large business organizations which cannot be fully applied in MSMEs. From this knowledge gap, this research study addressed the core question of "Does strategic human resource management (SHRM) and organizational learning impact the sustainability of service-based MSMEs in Brunei Darussalam, with competitive strategy as mediator?" From a questionnaire survey of 275 service-based MSMEs, this research study confirmed SHRM and organizational learning to yield significant impact on organizational performance of service-based MSMEs. These results are partial significantly mediated by competitive strategy. From these findings, this research study extended the knowledge on resource-based view, contingency theory, and organizational alignment theory within the MSME context.

The main purpose of this study is to seek industrial players' inputs on fiscal and monetary policies necessary to enhance SME export performance. The authors use survey data from 215 small and medium enterprises having export markets. They report the most essential governmental export support policies from the perspective of the industry players. The study revealed that accessing to financing is the top request to the government. Other policy recommendations are related to market access, human capital development, tax regimes, infrastructure and technology adoption, legal and regulatory environment, and

employees of Punjab emergency service (Rescue 1122) through questionnaires. The partial least square structural equation modeling (PLS-SEM) has been employed to draw the results. The final results have shown a positive and significant relationship between supervisor feedback, customer employee exchange, creative personal identity and innovative behaviour of employees, while interpersonal trust was found to play an intermediary role between customer employee exchange, creative personal identity, and innovative behaviour.

Organic food is becoming popular among today's millennial consumers because of increased awareness of healthy lifestyles. Scholars and practitioners attempt to understand what drives consumers to purchase organic foods toward developing market domination strategies and tactics. Since organic food tends to be more expensive than non-organic, this study aims to analyze the impact of consumer values on their tendency to buy organic food. Consumption values are an important factor that could drive consumer behavior and their preferences for goods or services. Consumption values are defined in terms of the required benefits from the purchase and consumption of the preferred products. Sheth, Newman, and Gross defined consumption values in terms of practical, social, emotional, epistemic, and conditional values.

Circularity concept is not just recycling. It is basically a system that is restorative in the industrial processes that treat waste as a resource. It implies that once a product reaches the end of life, attempts should be made to utilize them by creating a value out of it. The present study is an exploratory study that aims at exploring the lessons of circular economy, which India can share with others through the analysis of business models of companies for the three paradigms: reduce, reuse, and recycle. For understanding the take-make-dispose model to take-make-reduce model, the analysis of business model of El Rhino has been carried out. For take-make-recycle model, business model of Saahas Zero Waste and Goonj as unique business models displaying an outstanding effect of share-reuse-prolong model has been studied.

The Indian film industry has consistently performed well across years and has emerged as the largest in the world in terms of the number of movies it produces annually. However, the year 2020 presented a crude shock to the prospects and promises of the industry. The catastrophic effect of the pandemic in the year 2020 led to the drop in the global box office by as much as 72% with a mere $12 billion collections across the world in the form of ticket sales. To understand the factors facilitating the Indian film industry to go beyond theatres during the pandemic and to explore the key challenges faced by the industry in light of its advancement, secondary data was collected from available publications, industry reports, and official websites of various bodies. The chapter aims at exploring the factors which contribute to the recent trends of the Indian film industry, attempts to identify the new and emerging challenges that plague its growth and how this transition can speed the recovery of Indian film industry as this would provide ample input to the various stakeholders of the industry.

This research studies the case of KT to see how a mobile operator expanded beyond its existing offerings to new smart energy business based on digital technology. Details were analysed specifically on how the business was developed, why the smart energy service was started, and what the success factors were. KT's smart energy business (KT-MEG: KT Micro Energy Grid) utilizes ICT to resolve energy issues such as global climate change and energy consumption growth. It also provides growth opportunities for KT with its KT-MEG platform. The authors analyze that KT was able to leverage sustainability as a new growth engine by developing new businesses to differentiate customer experience, create effective organization structure, and generate business impact in addition to application of latest ICT technologies such as artificial intelligence, IoT (internet of things), and big data. The results provide a good guideline for business transformation of ICT firms in the era of Industry 4.0.

The idea of the circular economy is gaining steam in academia through the green economics of human resources policies in Asia. A high performance model delivers superior outcomes but does not deter praiseworthy professors from biased human interference. Using the computerized-based geometric performance base incentive model (CGPBI) is particularly beneficial in encouraging faculty who have achieved superior outcomes in all areas of science, academia, and other contributions. To fill this gap, the author proposed a geometric hybrid reward policy model that includes a number of fictitious variables such as topic tolerance, the effects of subject matter, and the average outcome across all subjects. This model uses Python to construct a standardized framework to gather data on the success of faculty. It provides a robust indication of comparative success and motivates workers to achieve more transparent performance outcomes. The author proposes the use of a multi-source assessment (MSA) to evaluate the faculty's annual results.

Preface

INTRODUCTION

The COVID-19 outbreak has caused unprecedented disruptions in societies, companies and nations across the globe. Companies need to develop innovative business models and management practices to answer new challenges and speed the recovery of economies, create new jobs and simultaneously achieve more sustainable growth (Almunawar, Islam and Ordóñez, 2021; European Commission, 2021a).

The transition to digital economies and greener economies brings enormous challenges as well as opportunities for people, companies, and governments. For example, the new Circular Economy Action Plan of the European Commission addresses actions to make sustainable products the norm in the EU or focus on specific sectors that use most resources and that have potential for circularity (for example, electronics, food, textiles, vehicles, water) (European Commission, 2021b, c). Governments need develop digital infrastructure and connectiveness to promote research and innovation, boost the development of strategic networks of international collaboration, invest in digital technologies and smart education and cities and nurture human capital with the needed skills for the new jobs demanded by the labour market, among other key actions (Lytras *et al.,* 2018; Ordóñez, 2004, 2005; Ordóñez and Edvinsson, 2020).

There are not many publications that address these topics and even less, that explore the topics in the Asian region (Ordóñez *et al.,* 2021). This book bridges the gap offering a collection of chapters discussing major issues on digital, circular, and green economies in Asia and ASEAN, sharing lessons from different countries, like Brunei Darussalam, India and Malaysia.

OBJECTIVE

The book will explore new and emerging business and management practices to support companies and economies in the digital transformation in Asia, with special emphasis on success and failure experiences. It will analyze the role of digital skills and competences, green issues and technological disruptors in these emerging practices in Asia and how they can contribute to the creation of new business opportunities, more jobs and growth for the recovery of Asian economies after the pandemic. For example, resource-efficient and greener economies can foster the creation of eco-friendly innovative businesses and eco-innovation and waste prevention can generate important savings for economies and regions.

TARGET AUDIENCE

Professors in academia, deans, heads of departments, director of masters, students (undergraduate and postgraduate level), politicians, policy makers, corporate heads of firms, senior general managers, managing directors, information technology directors and managers, libraries, etc.

CONTENTS OF THE BOOK

The handbook presents a collection of 21 chapters that address crucial topics for companies in the circular, digital and green economy.

Chapter 1, titled "Circular Economy for Plastics and Digitally-Enabled Community Towards ASEAN Halal Hub in Asia" (by Khairunnisa Musari), focuses on "the significant economic opportunities from the implementation of the circular economy paradigm for plastics as a requirement for halal industry in the ASEAN region. If this can be realized, the ASEAN halal industry will have a comparative advantage and all at once leads radically in reducing plastic pollution in halal market. ASEAN has opportunities for influencing the value to halal market in Asia. All the more, Asia also has opportunities for influencing the value to halal market around the world. With support from the digitally-enabled community, this circular economy best practice may spread and influence another region or another industry in Asia. This not only opens up opportunities of ASEAN for leading a Halal Hub in Asia, but it can also be encouraging the collaboration between community groups, businesses, industry, local and national governments, international donors, and world-class experts seeking meaningful actions to defeat plastic pollution."

Chapter 2, titled "Digital Leadership Competencies in Malaysian Context: A Study in Managers' Level" (by Sree Maruthuvellu, Yashar Salamzadeh and Christopher Richardson), explores "the most important digital leadership competencies for managers in Malaysia and to develop the profile of digital leadership competencies among managers in Malaysia. This study adopted quantitative research method and cross-sectional study. In order to provide a better understanding of the digital leadership competencies in Malaysia, the researcher uses Exploratory Factor Analysis and Fuzzy Topsis method in interpreting results. The importance of each dimension was determined and compared with current performance. Hence, Importance-Performance Charts were provided to elaborate the research results. This study will inspire managers to embrace change, to develop new competencies needed in order to guide their organizations into the uncertain future of the digital age. This study being the first in its kind will extends the knowledge of digital leadership competencies particularly in Malaysian context. Further, it enhances the literature by provided empirical evidence on the importance and how to develop the profile among managers."

Chapter 3, titled "Impacts of COVID-19 Vaccines on Tourism Demand and Cultures" (by Xuan Tran), states that "the low supply of vaccines for COVID-19 has disrupted tourism development in Asia. The question is if the vaccine may change cultural divergence into cultural convergence at the tourist destination. The purpose of this study is to examine the culture and price elasticity of hotel demand to find the cultural convergence. The study has conducted Autoregressive Distributed Lag Model to test whether the vaccine would change the price and income elasticities of hotel demand to find the cultural transformation from divergence to convergence through tourism. Findings indicate that the impact of the vaccine on transferring culture from divergence to convergence was confirmed. Tourists from the divergent cultures specified by less levels of Hofstede's cultural dimensions will visit the country destination with high levels of Hofstede's cultural dimensions after COVID-vaccination. Japan and the US that possess divergent levels of power will visit Vietnam for power convergence. China, Korea, and Russia that possess divergent levels of indulgence will visit Vietnam for indulgence convergence."

Chapter 4, titled "Quantitative Analysis of Strategic Human Resource Management and Organizational Learning: The Sustainability of MSMEs in Brunei Darussalam" (by Chin Wuen, Fahmi Ibrahim and Kabiru Ringim), affirms that "it is crucial for business organizations to maintain sustainability within the globalized market environment. However, the organizational ability of micro, small and medium enterprises (MSMEs) is inadequate to generate sustainable competitive advantage. Moreover, strategic management theories are developed based on large business organizations which cannot be fully applied in MSMEs. From this knowledge gap, this research study addressed the core question of "Does strategic human resource management (SHRM) and organizational learning impact the sustainability of service-based MSMEs in Brunei Darussalam, with competitive strategy as mediator?" From a questionnaire survey of 275 service-based MSMEs, this research study confirmed SHRM and organizational learning to yield significant impact on organizational performance of service-based MSMEs. These results are partial significantly mediated by competitive strategy. From these findings, this research study extended the knowledge on Resource-Based View, Contingency Theory and Organizational Alignment Theory within MSMEs context."

Chapter 5, titled "Policies for Promotion of Malaysian SMEs Go Global in Digital Economy: SMEs Go Global From Malaysia" (by Hui Nee Au Yong and Ke Xin Liew), aims to "seek industrial players' inputs on fiscal and monetary policies necessary to enhance SMEs' export performance. We use survey data from 215 small and medium enterprises having export markets. We report the most essential governmental export support policies from the perspective of the industry players. The study revealed that Accessing to Financing is the top request to the Government. Others policy recommendations are related to market access, human capital development, tax regimes, infrastructure and technology adoption, legal and regulatory environment and monetary policies Implications & Recommendations: This study gives implications for Malaysia External Trade Development Corporation (MATRADE) policymakers and export-oriented Small and Medium Enterprises (SMEs).The study contributes to the Malaysian SMEs in relation to inputs to the Government to improve in their export performance especially using E-commerce."

Chapter 6, titled "A Study on the Internet Usage Pattern of Youths in Sikkim" (by Saibal Saha and Sangita Saha), states that "internet is being used by people all over the world. It has become a part of their day to day activity. The smartness brought my internet and its related devices have made life of people easy. Sharing knowledge, researching and reaching out to people are now within the reach of fingertips. This study aims to find the internet usage pattern of youth in Sikkim, India. Fourteen internet activities have been identified and through a survey the usage of these activities were analysed for the youth population in Sikkim, India. It has been found that more or less, all the activities are used by the youth population of Sikkim. The most popular activity is use of emails and social networking sites while blogging and video calling is not too popular. In addition, it has been found that 67% of the users use internet for more than 3 hours per day. Hence, there also is a serious risk of "internet addiction."

Chapter 7, titled "Influence of Industry 4.0 on Asia, Motives and Cultures in the Post-COVID-19 Era" (by Xuan Tran), states that "as the challenge of big data impacts how we understand cultural differences, a motive-integrated model of culture is becoming an effective strategy to study current culture divergence by the fourth industrial revolution called "Industry 4.0." This study examines the impact of Industry 4.0 with COVID-19 vaccines on motives and cultures of the world and Asia in the post COVID-19 era. Structure Equation Modelling has been conducted on the data in 38 countries during the period of 2006-2021. Findings indicate that Industry 4.0 has enhanced the achievement motive in the reactive culture and the power motive in the multi-linear culture, but it has decreased the affiliation motive in the linear active culture. In addition, Industry 4.0 has enhanced the gross domestic product per capita (GDP) in the linear active and reactive cultures but it has decreased the GDP in the multi-linear cultures. Finally, Industry 4.0 has made the power and affiliation motives in Asia decreased, but it has increased the achievement motive in Asia."

Chapter 8, titled "Impact of Supervisors Feedback, Customer Employee Exchange, Creative Personal Identity on Innovative Behavior" (by Muhammad Imran and Iqra Akhtar), focuses on employee innovative behaviour and affirms that it is "crucial for any firm success in term of generation, promotion and realization of new ideas which can benefit to organization positive performance. The main purpose of this study is to examine the relationship between supervisor's feedback, customer employee exchange, creative personal identity and innovative behaviour with mediating role of interpersonal trust.The three hundred and seventy (370) responses have been collected from employees of Punjab emergency service (Rescue 1122) through questionnaires. The partial least square structural equation modeling (PLS-SEM) has been employed to draw the results. The final results have shown a positive and significant relationship between supervisor feedback, customer employee exchange, creative personal identity and innovative behaviour of employees, while interpersonal trust found an intermediary role between customer employee exchange, creative personal identity and innovative behaviour."

Chapter 9, titled "Propensity to Purchase Organic Food: an Integrative Model of Consumption Values in Malaysia" (by Khairul Mahmud and Asmat-Nizam Abdul-Talib), states that "organic food is becoming popular among today's millennial consumers because of increased awareness of healthy lifestyles. Scholars and practitioners attempt to understand what drives consumers to purchase organic foods toward developing market domination strategies and tactics. Since organic food tends to be more expensive than non-organic one, this study aims to analyze the impact of consumer values on their tendency to buy organic food. Consumption values are an important factor that could drive consumer behavior and their preferences for goods or services. Consumption values are defined in terms of the required benefits from the purchase and consumption of the preferred products. Sheth, Newman, and Gross (1991) defined consumption values in terms of practical, social, emotional, epistemic, and conditional values."

Chapter 10, titled "Practicing Circular Economy in India: Insights of Business Models on the Three Paradigms – Reduce, Reuse, and Recycle" (by Namita Kapoor, Sangeeta Jauhari and Deepti Maheshwari), addresses the concept of circularity and states that it "is not just recycling it is basically a system which is restorative in the industrial processes which treats the waste as a resource. It implies that once a product reaches the end of life, attempts should be made to utilize them by creating a value out of it. The present study is an exploratory study that aims at exploring the lessons of Circular Economy which India can share with others through the analysis of Business Models of companies for the three paradigms: Reduce, Reuse and Recycle. For understanding the Take-Make-Dispose Model to Take-Make-Reduce model, the analysis of business model of El Rhino has been carried out. For Take- Make- Recycle Model, business model of Saahas Zero Waste and Goonj as a unique business model displaying an outstanding effect of Share-Reuse -Prolong Model has been studied."

Chapter 11, titled "Reconfiguration of the Indian Film Industry During the COVID-19 Pandemic: The Enablers and the Impeders" (by Selvalakshmi M and Kabila Ramanthan), states that "Indian film industry has consistently performed well across years and has emerged as the largest in the world in terms of the number of movies it produces annually. However, the year 2020 presented a crude shock to the prospects and promises of the industry. The catastrophic effect of the Pandemic in the year 2020 lead to the drop in the global box office by as much as 72% with a mere 12$ billion collections across the world in the form of ticket sales. To understand the factors facilitating the Indian film industry to go beyond theatres during the pandemic and to explore the key challenges faced by the industry in light of its advancement, secondary data was collected from available publications, industry Reports and official websites of various bodies. The chapter aims at exploring the factors which contribute to the recent trends of Indian film Industry, attempts to identify the new and emerging challenges which plague its growth and how this transition can speed the recovery of Indian film Industry as this would provide ample inputs to the various stakeholders of the industry."

Chapter 12, titled "New Business Development Strategy of Telecommunication Operator based on Smart Energy System - Case of KT-MEG: Telco New Business Development Strategy – KT-MEG" (by Junghwan Lee and Dongwook Kim), presents a "research studies the case of KT to see how a mobile operator expanded beyond its existing offerings to new smart energy business based on digital technology. Details were analysed specifically on how the business was developed, why the smart energy service was started, and what the success factors were. KT's smart energy business (KT-MEG: KT Micro Energy Grid) utilizes ICT to resolve energy issues such as global climate change and energy consumption growth. It also provides growth opportunities for KT with its KT-MEG platform. We analyze that KT was able to leverage sustainability as a new growth engine by developing new businesses to differentiate customer experience, create effective organization structure, and generate business impact in addition to application of latest ICT technologies such as artificial intelligence, IoT (Internet of Things) and big data. The results provide good guideline for business transformation of ICT firms in the era of Industry 4.0."

Chapter 13, titled "An Automated Geometric Appraisal Model: A Computerized Performance-Based Incentive Policy Suitable for HEIs in India" (by Hari Govinda Rao chukka and Sampath Dakshina Murthy Achanta), states that "the idea of the circular economy is gaining steam in academia, through the green economics of human resources policies in Asia. A high performance model delivers superior outcomes but does not deter praiseworthy professors from biased human interference. Using the Computerized based geometric performance base incentive model (CGPBI) model is particularly beneficial in encouraging faculty who have achieved superior outcomes in all areas of science, academia and other contributions. To fill this gap, the author proposed a geometric hybrid reward policy model that includes a number of fictitious variables such as topic tolerance, the effects of subject matter, and the average outcome across all subjects. This model uses python to construct a standardized framework to gather data on the success of faculty. It provides a robust indication of comparative success and motivates workers to achieve more transparent performance outcomes. The author proposes the use of a Multi-Source Assessment (MSA) to evaluate the faculty's annual results."

Chapter 14, titled "Exploratory Study on User Satisfaction of E-HRM: Evidence From Brunei Government Employee Management System (GEMS)" (by Fahmi Ibrahim, Hazimah Suhip, Kabiru Kura and Liana HM Noor), affirms that "with the high demands to provide service quality, growing workforce and globalization of economy, HR has transformed into an inevitable power of technology that transform HRM into Electronic Human Resource Management (E-HRM) system. Brunei Darussalam without exception is also practicing E-HRM in the government sector called Government Employee Management System (GEMS). This chapter investigates the user satisfaction of E-HRM by examining the current status of GEMS in Brunei Darussalam. The user satisfaction was studied through seven elements: the implementation of E-HRM, training, user-friendliness, infrastructure, data security, technical support and user support. Qualitative interview and descriptive quantitative method were conducted on HR officers from the public organization. Findings revealed that the GEMS not able to provide satisfactory system.

This paper has developed a theoretical framework as a recommendation to integrate relevant elements, together with the influence of age, gender and years of service that impact the user satisfaction."

Chapter 15, titled "Green Consumerism in Brunei Darussalam: Exploratory Study on Purchasing Behaviour" (by Fahmi Ibrahim, Siti Abd Rahman and Nurul Jefri), explores "the relationship of the demographic and socio-psychological determinants on consumers' green purchase behaviours in Brunei Darussalam, with the application framework of the Affect-Behaviour-Cognition (ABC) model. A total of 119 consumers from different background participated in this study, whereby 113 respondents participated in the online questionnaire, and the other 6 respondents were interviewed. It is discovered that consumers who are more environmentally conscious are not necessarily likely to purchase green products, but are actually involved in green behaviours. However, in the environmental aspects of awareness, concern and knowledge, the other factors; monthly income and educational level did not possess major significance. The product attributes such as price and availability of the green products played a significant role in consumer's buying decisions which will lead to the value-action gap phenomenon. Moreover, this study discovered the government is needed to promote and encourage green purchase behaviours in Brunei Darussalam."

Chapter 16, titled "Prospect of Promoting Sikkim as a Smart Tourism Destination: A Descriptive Analysis" (by Supriya Dam), discusses how "since 2006, Sikkim progressively switching to a full fledged tourism centred state having declared it a predominant industry as an engine for its economic growth. The State accounted for highest influx of foreign tourists' amongst the eight North Eastern States of India during the last twenty years or so. The Smart City Mission was commissioned by Government of India as a Centrally Sponsored Scheme destined to provide financial support for the allotted cities to the extent of INR. 100 Crore per city per year spanning over five years'. Studies suggest that induction of smart city concept will act as precursor for growth of smart tourism destinations (STDs) across the country. The STD as a concept revolves around "6A's", an essential ingredient for promoting smart tourism in destinations. Incidentally, two cities in Sikkim have been enlisted amongst top 100 cities in India for promoting smart city, instrumental in promoting STD in tourism driven State. Present paper delves into the concept of smart city as an antecedent for promoting STD along with conditions with respect to Sikkim."

Chapter 17, titled "An Explanatory Study of Users' Satisfaction: Evidence from Brunei Health Information and Management System (Bru-HIMS)" (by Fahmi Ibrahim, Nurhidayatu Aqilah Gulihana and Heru Susanto), discusses that "in achieving one of Brunei Vision 2035 which is to be among the top 10 in the world for quality of life, Ministry of Health (MOH) Brunei Darussalam has responded by implementing Brunei Healthcare Information and Management System (Bru-HIMS) that is equivalent to international best practices. Bru-HIMS has been implemented for about eight years since its first launched on 11 September 2012 where the outcome to user's experience is unknown. Hence, this paper is to investigate user's satisfaction on Bru-HIMS specifically at RIPAS hospital and to study area for improvement towards providing quality healthcare in Brunei. DeLone and McLean Information System framework is applied to evaluate Bru-HIMS users satisfaction based on the six variables; information quality, system quality, service quality, intention to use and usage, perceived net benefits and user satisfaction. Questionnaire survey was conducted to obtain primary data from Bru-HIMS. The findings demonstrate positive relationships between the six variables which indicate Bru-HIMS has positively influenced Bru-HIMS users."

Chapter 18, titled "Employee Motivation for Training and Development: A Study on a Pharmaceutical Company in Sikkim" (by Sangita Saha, Saibal Saha, Jaya Pandey and Ajeya Jha), states that "training and development is an important function of Human Resource Management. Employees need to regularly undergo training and development programmes to update themselves with the latest technologies and skills, which help to increase the efficiency of the organization. Motivating employees to undergo a training programme is often a challenge faced by employees. This study aims to find the motivating factors for employees to undertake a training and development programme. With a sample size of 172 employees from a leading pharmaceutical company in Sikkim, India, responses were collected and analysed. It was found that interest for updating oneself with the latest technology, better chance of career exploration, commitment to train from the company's end and encouragement provided from subordinates play significant role in motivating employees in undertaking a training and development programme."

Chapter 19, titled "The Employee Performance in the Fast Food Industry: A Mediating Role of Happiness" (by Muhammad Imran and Hammad Wajid), studies "the relationship of role overload (RO), love of money (LOM), empowerment (EMP) and work engagement (WE) on employee performance (EP) in the fast food industry and also to find out the mediating effect of happiness (HAP) between RO, LOM, EMP and WE on employee performance and moderating effect of the spirit of work (SOW) on Happiness and employee performance (EP). The data was gathered using the online survey method through questionnaires from the employees of Fast Food Restaurants of South Punjab, Pakistan. The sample size was 297. Smart PLS 3 was used to analyze data. The result findings show that LOM, WE and HAP has an influence on EP while RO and EMP have no influence on EP. There was a mediating effect of HAP between EMP and EP whereas there was no mediating influence of HAP between RO, LOM, WE and EP. No moderating influence of SOW between HAP and EP was found. This study findings are very useful for manager/owner of the restaurant the increase their employee performance, which leads to firm high performance."

Chapter 20, titled "The Influence of Training, Performance Appraisal and Organizational Support on Employee Service Behavior with Compensation as Mediator" (by Muhammad Imran and Tehmina Ambreen), addresses training, performance appraisal, organizational support, and compensation and the role they pay "in enhancing employee service behavior in the police department. The main objective of this study is to examine the impact of training, performance appraisal, and organizational support on employee service behavior, with the mediating role of compensation. Data was collected from the employees of Punjab police through the questionnaire. The partial least square structural equation modeling (PLS-SEM) has employed for data analysis. The results of the study found a positive and significant relationship between training, performance appraisal, organizational support, and employee service behavior. Furthermore, compensation plays the mediating role between training, performance appraisal, organizational support, and employee behavior in Punjab police, Pakistan. As per the findings of the study, employee behavior can be improved with the help of training, performance appraisal, organizational support, compensation."

Finally, the last chapter of this handbook is titled "Technology Gap, Information and Communication Technology Trade and Sustainability Issues in India". Its authors, Ritu Rana, Manoj Sharma and Ajay Singh, focus on the "examination of causality between foreign direct investment (FDI), economic growth (GDP) and the environment [CO2 emissions and energy consumption (EC)] in Indian context. Two more important variables i.e., trade openness and technology gap were also added. The chapter further examines the effects of information and communication technology (ICT) trade on both GDP and the environment of India. The results of previous model show that FDI is neither causing GDP nor is it bridging the technology gap. The results also indicate the existence of Pollution Haven Hypothesis (PHH) in India as FDI is causing both CO2 and EC. Also FDI is, though not causing the GDP directly, but is doing so indirectly through CO2 validating the existence of PHH. FDI is causing trade openness in India but that openness is again causing more FDI which is doing no good for India. The results of ICT trade model indicate that both GDP and ICT exports cause CO2 in India. Also, both the GDP and ICT exports are consuming energy in India."

Patricia Ordóñez de Pablos
The University of Oviedo, Spain

REFERENCES

Almunawar, M. N., Islam, Z., & Ordóñez de Pablos, P. (2021). *Digital Transformation Management: Challenges and Futures in the Asian Digital Economy. Routledge.*

European Commission. (2021a). *Commission to maximise job opportunities in green economy.* Available at https://ec.europa.eu/environment/europeangreencapital/opportunities-green-economy

European Commission. (2021b). *A European Green Deal. Striving to be the first-climate neutral continent.* Available at https://ec.europa.eu/info/strategy/priorities-2019-2024/european-green-deal_en

European Commission. (2021c). *Green growth and circular economy.* Available at https://ec.europa.eu/environment/green-growth/index_en.htm

Lytras, M. D., Visvizi, A., Daniela, L., Sarirete, A., & Ordóñez de Pablos, P. (2018). Social networks research for sustainable smart education. *Sustainability, 10*(9), 2974. doi:10.3390u10092974

Ordóñez de Pablos, P. (2004). The nurture of knowledge-based resources through the design of an architecture of human resource management systems: Implications for strategic management. *International Journal of Technology Management, 27*(6/7), 533–543.

Ordóñez de Pablos, P. (2005). Western and eastern views on social networks. *The Learning Organization- International Journal, 12*(5), 436–456.

Ordóñez de Pablos, P., & Edvinsson, L. (Eds.). (2020). Intellectual capital in the digital economy. Routledge.

Ordóñez de Pablos, P., Zhang, X., Almunawar, M. N., & Gayo Labra, J. E. (2021). *Big Data, Green Growth, and Technology Disruption in Asian Companies and Societies.* IGI-Global.

Chapter 1
Circular Economy for Plastics and Digitally Enabled Community Towards ASEAN Halal Hub in Asia

Khairunnisa Musari
https://orcid.org/0000-0003-0525-9903
Kiai Haji Achmad Shiddiq State Islamic University, Jember, Indonesia

ABSTRACT

This chapter highlights the significant economic opportunities from the implementation of the circular economy paradigm for plastics as a requirement for halal industry in the ASEAN region. If this can be realized, the ASEAN halal industry will have a comparative advantage that will all at once leads radically in reducing plastic pollution in halal market. ASEAN has opportunities for influencing the value to halal market in Asia. All the more, Asia also has opportunities for influencing the value to halal market around the world. With support from the digitally enabled community, this circular economy best practice may spread and influence another region or another industry in Asia. This not only opens up opportunities of ASEAN for leading a halal hub in Asia, but it can also be encouraging the collaboration between community groups, businesses, industry, local and national governments, international donors, and world-class experts seeking meaningful actions to defeat plastic pollution.

INTRODUCTION

Plastic is an overwhelming driver of the economy. Without a doubt, plastic leads plentiful merits to society and is often viewed as environmentally friendly than other materials, at least for its lightweight. However, plastic explosion brings in fact not only severe impacts on human health and environment but also detonates a tremendous volume of greenhouse gas effect. Ellen MacArthur Foundation (2016, 2017), Europe Commission (2019), Hisham and Florent (2019), Heinrich Böll Foundation and Break Free From Plastic (2019), Son (2020) confirmed the abundance of evidence that plastics have serious

DOI: 10.4018/978-1-7998-8678-5.ch001

effects on human health and environment, particularly to marine ecosystems and coastal environments. Three percent of all plastic leaks into the ocean every year. Without immediate undertaking, marine debris pollution may negatively impact marine biodiversity, society, and the global economy.

Ellen MacArthur Foundation (2017) declared the use of plastics has increased twentyfold in the past half-century. More than 40 years after the launch of the first universal recycling symbol, that only 14% of plastic packaging is collected for recycling globally. Each year, US$80-120 billion plastic packaging material value is lost to the economy. As a part of daily life around the globe, Son (2020) justified the production of plastic has been continually escalating since 1950. Because of plastic's ubiquitous use, incomparabled properties, and low production costs, production is predicted to enlarge in the next two decades. Figure 1 shows the global plastic production during 1950 until 2019. PlasticsEurope (2020) reported global plastics production in 2019 reached 368 million tonnes and covered as much as 51% in Asia with composition 31% of China, 3% of Japan, and 17% rest of Asia.

Prior to 2018, Tiseo (2020a, 200b) and Arkin (2019) explained that China was the leading destination for plastic waste exports. However, at the beginning of that year, China decided on much stricter standards, only accepting plastic waste with less than 0.5 percent contamination by non-recyclable materials. This put pressure on major exporting countries such as the United States (US), Germany, and the United Kingdom (UK) to find new waste destinations. With China no longer an option, other nations, especially in Southeast Asia (SEA), began to increase plastic waste imports. Between January and November 2018, Malaysia was the leading nation to import plastic waste worldwide. Its shares of imports were twice that of Thailand's, which was ranked second and Vietnam was the third. However, in 2018, Malaysia and Thailand also have announced bans on imports of plastic scrap by 2021 and Vietnam in 2019 followed suit with their own plastic import bans, whilst Indonesia and Cambodia have earlier restricted imports of non-recyclable waste.

Furthermore, Akenji, Bengtsson, Kato, Hengesbaugh, Hotta, Aoki-Suzuki, Gamaralalage, and Liu (2019) mentioned SEA has emerged as a global hotspot for tackling plastic-related issues. Major economies in the region have been found to be among the largest contributors to marine plastic pollution globally. Hisham and Florent (2019) announced eight of the world's most polluted rivers flow through the Association of Southeast Asian Nations (ASEAN) countries and six of the top 20 countries based on the percentage of waste that is littered or inadequately disposed are located in ASEAN. Refer to Jambeck, Geyer, Wilcox, Siegler, Perryman, Andrady, Narayan, and Law (2015), five of the top 10 countries ranked by mass of mismanaged plastic waste in 2010 were ASEAN countries. Table 1 shows the ASEAN countries ranked by mass of mismanaged plastic waste.

In the face of growing public pressure to address a plastic pollution crisis, research and investigations by Changing Market Foundation (2020) in over 15 countries across five continents reported that industries have obstructed and undermined legislative solutions for decades. The voluntary initiatives by industries failed to contain the plastics crisis. The industries even have used these initiatives as a tactic to delay and derail progressive legislation and distracting consumers and governments with empty promises and false solutions. In ASEAN, Akenji et al (2019) wrote all national governments of the ASEAN Member States recognize the need to address the issues of plastics. Although all governments in the region agree with the need for more and better recycling, few countries have policies that effectively contribute towards these objectives. That's why the rationale of member states for taking action to address the issues of plastics varies in the ASEAN.

However, referring to Yates (2017), ASEAN has proved its capability as the 'primary manager' in SEA and the 'regional conductor' of the order of Asia Pacific in negotiating the social roles. By considering

Figure 1. Global plastic production (1950-2019)
Source: Statista.Com (2021), Processed

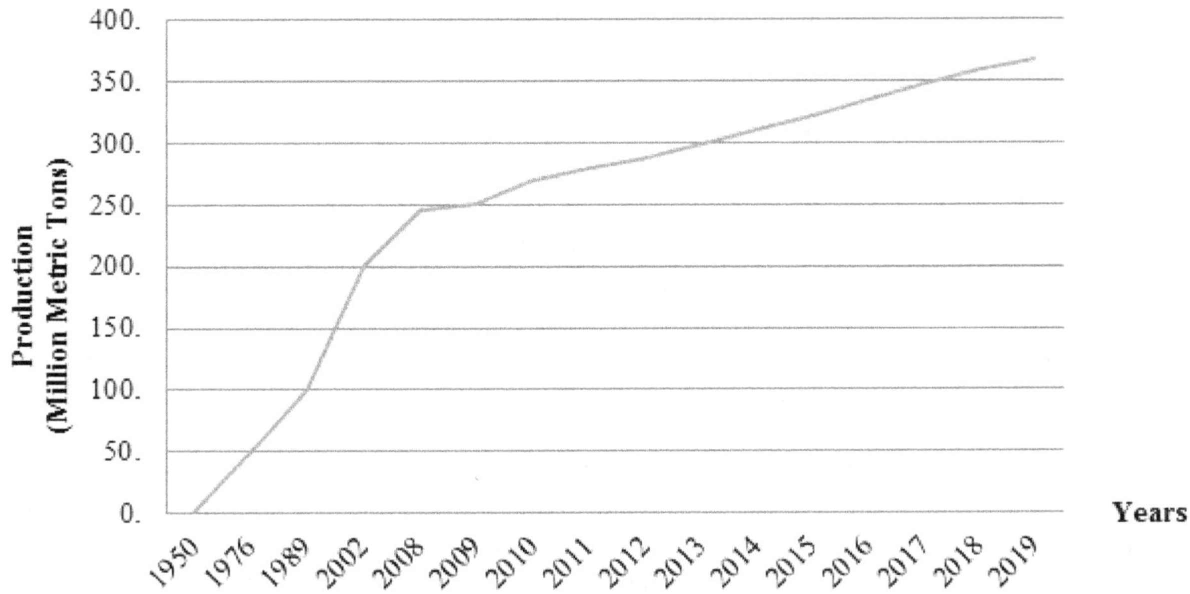

the prominence in regional order negotiation and management in SEA and the Asia Pacific through the lens of social role negotiation, this chapter becomes a preliminary study to explore a circular economy paradigm for plastics as a requirement for the halal industry in ASEAN region for accelerating the opportunities of ASEAN for leading a halal hub in Asia through support of a digitally-enabled community.

In line with Anbumozhi and Kim (Eds.) (2016), in view of circular economy's systematic nature and its overarching importance to emerging Asia's sustainable growth, the creation of an ASEAN-wide circular economy platform bringing together the ASEAN Social-Cultural Community and ASEAN Economic Community merits further research for mobilizing the effect for the industries, countries, and region. Therefore, this chapter purposes to address the circular economy paradigm for plastics as a requirement for ASEAN halal industry for becoming the comparative advantage and leads radically in reducing plastic pollution in halal market and influence this circular economy best practice to Asia.

Table 1. The ASEAN countries ranked by mass of mismanaged plastic waste

Rank	Country	Waste Generate [kg/ppd]	% Plastic Waste	% Mismanaged Waste	Mismanaged Plastic Waste [MMT/year]	% of Total Mismanaged Plastic Waste	Plastic Marine Debris [MMT/year]
2	Indonesia	0.52	11	83	3.22	10.1	0.48-1.29
3	Philippines	0.5	15	83	1.88	5.9	0.28-0.75
4	Vietnam	0.79	13	88	1.83	5.8	0.28-0.73
6	Thailand	1.2	12	75	1.03	3.2	0.15-0.41
8	Malaysia	1.52	13	57	0.94	2.9	0.14-0.37
17	Burma/Myanmar	0.44	17	89	0.46	1.4	0.07-0.18

Source: Jambeck et al (2015); Note: ppd = person per day; MMT = million metric tons.

Through literature review, this chapter addresses the key topics by focusing on three issues. *First,* gaps in addressing circular economy for plastics. *Second,* a digitally-enabled community, facts and figures. *Third,* the opportunities for ASEAN towards a halal hub in Asia.

GAPS IN ADDRESSING CIRCULAR ECONOMY FOR PLASTICS

Tanakasempipat (2019) from Reuters reported that SEA is a major contributor to land-based plastic waste leaking into the world's oceans, with more than half of it coming from four nations - Indonesia, the Philippines, Vietnam and Thailand - along with China, the top single polluter. Many countries in the region struggle with poor waste sorting and disposal systems, and their growth in population and explosive demand for consumer products mean more single-use plastic ends up in landfill or leaks into the environment. To battle the growing crisis, SEA as home to 641 million people across 10 countries, needs to develop region-wide policies to regulate plastic packaging.

Akenji et al (2019) explained that preventing and reducing plastic pollution is about more than waste management. It needs a circular economy perspective to plastics and presents frameworks for addressing related sustainability challenges. A shift to a circular economy will require coordinated policy interventions at all stages of the life-cycle of plastics, including: resource extraction and refining, design and manufacture of products, trade and retail, use and reuse, recycling, and final disposal when necessary. However, at the implementation level, there is a gap between expectations and reality. Table 2 shows the four main types of gaps common to addressing plastics in ASEAN region, namely: Information and Knowledge, Policy and Governance, Technical Capacity and Markets and Finance.

To head for the New Plastics Economy as a new wave from a circular economy for plastics, ASEAN region should eliminate the gaps common in addressing plastics. Ellen MacArthur Foundation (2016) mentioned that the New Plastics Economy builds on and aligns with the principles of the circular economy with three main missions. *First,* establish an effective after-use plastics economy by improving the economics and uptake of recycling, reusing and controlling the biodegradation for targeted applications. This is the cornerstone of the New Plastics Economy and its first priority which helps realize the two following missions. *Second,* drastically minimize the plastic leakage into natural systems, particularly to the ocean, and other negative externalities. *Third,* separate plastics from fossil raw materials by exploring and adopting renewably sourced raw materials.

To increase reuse and recycling of plastic packaging to 70%, from today's recycling rate of just 14%, Ellen MacArthur Foundation (2017) offered three key transition strategies and related priority action areas. *First,* without fundamental redesign and innovation, about 30% of plastic packaging will never be reused or recycled. *Second,* for at least 20% of plastic packaging, reuse provides an economically attractive opportunity. *Third,* with concerted efforts on design and after-use systems, recycling would be economically attractive for the remaining 50% of plastic packaging. The all three are distinct strategies to drive the transition toward the road ahead.

Furthermore, considering the three global trends which create opportunities to transform SEA by 2030, one of them is deploying disruptive technologies. Woetzel, Tonby, Thompson, Burtt, and Lee (2014) and ASEAN Secretariat (2016) reported that these disruptive technologies are predicted up to $625 billion in annual economic value for SEA by 2030. There are five related deploying disruptive technologies ---mobile internet, big data, the internet of things (IoT), the automation of knowledge work, and cloud technology--- which could modernize sectors across the economy and drive major productivity

Table 2. The four types of gaps common to addressing plastics in ASEAN region

	Items
Information and knowledge	1. Data on use patterns and trends, as well as on waste handling and recycling routes. 2. Understanding of types of plastics and their properties, applications and benefits, associated issues at different life cycle stages, and sustainable alternatives. 3. Knowledge on the relative merits of different recycling options, including 'down-cycling' and 'closed-loop' recycling. 4. Awareness on issues associated with hazardous chemicals and substances of concern found in plastics. 5. A life-cycle understanding of plastics and of how global value chains can both amplify and help in addressing issues concerning plastics.
Policy and governance	1. Clarity on mandates, roles and responsibilities at different levels of and agencies of government. 2. Comprehensive frameworks with policy packages and instruments to turn national strategies and plans into action on the ground. 3. Effective approaches for governments to engage and coordinate with diverse stakeholders. 4. Tools and guidelines to support actions by stakeholders.
Technical capacity	1. Limited technical training of responsible personnel in the complexities of plastics, including chemical, supply chain, and environmental aspects of different types of plastics. 2. Technological and human-resource constraints associated with managing post-use plastics, often including lack of infrastructure for preventing environmental leakage of plastics 3. Low capacity for innovation, especially among SMEs. 4. Few initiatives to encourage innovation, including social innovation to reduce plastic use as well as technical innovation on sustainable alternatives.
Markets and finance	1. Access to financing for eco-solutions, including development of alternatives to plastics and efficient post-use processing. 2. Shared and accepted standards for recyclables to ensure quality control and bring trust to the market. 3. Access to markets for recyclables. 4. High perceived market uncertainty, hampering investments. 5. Uncertainty on how to effectively transition from fully market-driven (and largely informal) recycling systems to more regulated and formalised systems.

Source: Akenji et al (2019)

improvements. Therefore, to degrade the gaps in addressing circular economy for plastics, these disruptive technologies can be a driver to make a leap forward.

DIGITALLY-ENABLED COMMUNITY, FACTS AND FIGURES

Digitalization trends are bringing unprecedented disruptions for all traditional business models and hastening the need for a redesign and digitalize many activities. Musari and Zaroni (2021) reminded that everyone must be a partner with the disrupters. At the macroeconomic level, Box and Lopez-Gonzalez (2017) mentioned these trends hold the potential for new sources of productivity and economic growth. In order to the transition to an inclusive, fair, and science-based circular economy, Bigum and Oposa (2020) confirmed that technology innovation is a key enabler. Thus, regarding digitally-enabled community in ASEAN, this economic-social-cultural organization is also believed to present opportunities to create new value and economic growth from the circular economy paradigm for plastics as a requirement for ASEAN halal industry.

Through a digitally-enabled community, the digital network platforms which are developed to support the circular economy paradigm for plastics as a requirement for ASEAN halal industry may become a driver to facilitate buyers and sellers be economically viable find each other to collect plastic waste at the best prices, easily, and quickly. Although these platforms help to create a level of certainty around agreements, bargains, and contract arrangements between industry and market but the endorsement by the digitally-enabled community in varying degrees and leveraging them for economic and social advancement becomes a key to enlarge and impress these best practices to another region or another industry in Asia and around the world.

In order to capitalize on digitalization, Burns (2018) emphasized that one of the most fundamental challenges for the ASEAN region to overcome will be the skills gap. It is a stumbling block for many economies around the world. If ASEAN successfully harnesses the benefits of disruptive technologies, it is set to become a major force in the global digital economy, it will bring benefits not just to SEA but to all those who help it on its digital journey. Therefore, ASEAN Secretariat (2015) and Box and Lopez-Gonzalez (2017) declared that ASEAN stands on the cusp of a historic transition and information and communications technology (ICT) stands to play a transformative role in fostering an integrated and inclusive digitally-enabled community. A new era for ASEAN requires the successful implementation of a new ICT vision to address and inspire the growing aspirations of ASEAN citizens. As comparison, Table 3 shows the connectivity of ASEAN, Asia, and around the world.

Table 3. The comparison of connectivity to ASEAN, Asia, and the world

	ASEAN	Asia	All The World
Population (Per 1 July 2020)	667,301,395	4,641,054,775	7,860,797,900
Population (% World; Per 1 July 2020)	8.56%	59.54%	100%
Internet User (31 December 2020)	430,505,159*	2,707,088,121	5,102,758,282
Internet User (%)	64.5*	53.1%	100%
Penetration (% Population)	-	62.6%	64.8 %

Source: Akenji et al (2019), internetworld stats.com (2021), worldometers.info (2021)
*Forecasting by Author

In order to realize the vision of ASEAN Connectivity 2025, *"To achieve a seamlessly and comprehensively connected and integrated ASEAN that will promote competitiveness, inclusiveness, and a greater sense of Community",* ASEAN Secretariat (2016) and Box and Lopez-Gonzalez (2017) highlighted that one of five strategies is digital innovation. This is indeed a must. As stated by Hoppe, May, and Lin (2018), ASEAN is a key global economy but not yet a key digital economy. ASEAN is ranked third in the world in population, sixth in the gross domestic product (GDP), and fourth in trade value. However, ASEAN's digital economy lags, only representing 7% of GDP, while in China reached 16%, in Europe reached 27%, and the US reached 35%.

ASEAN Secretariat (2016) claimed that digital technologies in ASEAN could potentially be worth up to US$625 billion by 2030 or equal 8% of ASEAN's GDP in that year. It will be achieved from increased efficiency, new products and services, etc. Capturing this opportunity requires the establishment of regulatory frameworks for the delivery of new digital services (including data management and digital financial services); support for the sharing of best practices on open data; and equipping micro, small and medium enterprises (MSMEs) with the capabilities to access these new technologies.

Without a doubt, in order to drive and speed intraregional trade and growth through digital integration in the ASEAN region, a digitally-enabled community is one of the engines. As deduced by Ahmedov (2020), the global economy and digitalization in international trade are growing rapidly and digital space is becoming a major sphere for global trade. Regarding the existence of ASEAN as a halal community and the commitment to developing the digital-enabled economy, study by Hidayat & Musari (2022) found ASEAN digitally-enabled community and chances for ASEAN becoming a global halal logistics have positively and statistically significant relationship. Therefore, a digitally-enabled community will be critical for the ASEAN region to realize the digital innovation and open the opportunities for becoming a halal hub in Asia.

THE OPPORTUNITIES FOR ASEAN TOWARDS A HALAL HUB IN ASIA

Digitalization and new technologies change what and how trade works, but not the economic fundamentals of why trade works. Referring to Box and Lopez-Gonzalez (2017), trade is still subject to comparative advantage, informational asymmetries and barriers to trade both at-the-border and behind-the-border. However, the existence of new technologies help to minimize the cost of sharing ideas across borders and connecting different actors along the value chain, help surmount some of the constraints associated with engaging with international markets and may shift sources of comparative advantage.

The implementation of the circular economy for plastics as a requirement for ASEAN halal industry can be a comparative advantage for this region. Apart from being responsible for various plastic waste generated by ASEAN member states, it is also for developing new sources of economic growth through the halal industry which has the opportunity to influence Asia. Musari and Zaroni (2021) mentioned Asia has the opportunity to become a leader of halal logistics. By considering ASEAN is home to 25% of the world's Muslims and more than 42% of SEA Muslims, also Asia is home to 65% of the world's Muslims, all of them are real markets potential to fill the halal logistics. This is of course also an opportunity for the halal industry in general. Referring to worldometers.info, the current population of Asia is 7,860,797,900 as of 1 July 2020. This is equivalent to 59.54% of the world's total population.

Referring to State of the Global Islamic Economy Report, there are four ASEAN member states which often within Top 15 Countries in the Global Islamic Economy Indicators (GIEI), namely Malaysia, Indonesia, Brunei, and Singapore. Malaysia has always been in the top ranking and has not been overtaken. In GIEI 2020, Indonesia ranks the fourth for the first time. There is also Thailand which is in the Top 10 Countries for Muslim Friendly-Travel sector. Table 4 shows the four contries of ASEAN as the Top 15 Countries in the GIEI since 2014.

No doubt, the existence of Malaysia, Indonesia, Singapore, Brunei Darussalam, and Thailand are recognized as the world's foremost countries driving the global halal industry. According to Hidayat and Musari (2022), most ASEAN Member States also have established halal institutions in their jurisdictions especially to issue halal certification and develop halal industry. Considering it, the ASEAN region has the opportunity for leading a halal hub in Asia through this comparative advantage. With support from the digitally-enabled community in varying degrees and leveraging them for economic and social advancement, the best practice of circular economy for plastics as a requirement for ASEAN halal industry may expand and affect another region or another industry in SEA and the Asia Pacific through the lens of economic-social-cultural role negotiation.

Table 4. Top 15 countries in the GIEI

No.	2014-2015	2015-2016	2016-2017	2017-2018	2018-2019	2019-2020	2020-2021
1	Malaysia	Malaysia	Malaysia	Malaysia	Malaysia	Malaysia	Malaysia
4							Indonesia
5						Indonesia	
9				Brunei			
10	Indonesia	Indonesia	Indonesia		Indonesia		
11	Brunei	Singapore	Singapore	Indonesia	Brunei	Brunei	
12			Brunei				
13	Singapore			Singapore			
15							Singapore

Source: State of the Global Islamic Economy Report 2014-2015, 2015-2016, 2016-2017, 2017-2018, 2018-2019, 2019-2020

One best practice that brings together the variables of circular economy for plastics, digitalization, and halal industry is Albéa Indonesia. Albéa Indonesia is a global halal cosmetic packaging wholesaler and manufacturer. Refer to the https://www.albea-group.id, along with some partners and customers, Albéa engages the New Plastics Economy Global Commitment brought up by Ellen MacArthur Foundation to raise a circular economy for plastics. Albéa has commitment to supporting customers by producing products that are safe for the environment, reduce the use of carbon footprints, and contribute to the economic growth of local communities. Since 2002, business strategy of Albéa concerns to sustainability for inventing the packaging through Life-Cycle Analysis software. Albéa also implements plastic weight reduction, eco-design guidelines, development of recyclable packaging, use of bio-based plastics and post-consumer recycled as well as alliances with recycling associations and industries.

Regarding the halal, Albéa Indonesia has certification from The Assessment Institute for Foods, Drugs, and Cosmetics- Indonesian Council of Ulama (LPPOM-MUI) for all material in producing the packaging. Albéa Indonesia serves halal packaging with various types such as bottle, tube, pump, compact, jars, lip cream, palette, lipstick, beauty accessories, face powder case, packs with formula and many more by continuously innovating, capability in design and development using modern technology. In unifying the concept of halal and the concern to circular economy for plastics, Albéa engages in 2025 to produce 100% of plastic packaging reusable or recyclable, decides for using recycled content target of 10% across all plastic packaging used, leading action to move towards relevant reuse models, and carrying action to abolish the problematic or unnecessary plastic packaging.

Related to the use of Polyethylene Terephthalate (PET) as plastic material into Recycled Polyethylene (r-PET) in Indonesia, a sweet soy sauce brand 'Bango' from Unilever becomes the first product with packaging from recycled content (100% rPET) which received halal approval by Indonesia's National Food & Drug Agency (BPOM). This also prompted Malaysia to push halal approval for the use of r-PET in the packaging industry. In Malaysia, refer to World Bank Group (2021), packaging with recycled content is not allowed to be marketed as a 'Halal packaging' as the current Malaysian standard for halal packaging, MS2565:2014, which disallows the use of recycled material. However, Noor (2020) confirmed that Malaysia today best prepared to provide end-to-end halal services, from halal product traceability to Islamic finance facilities. Malaysia has created a halal value chain with high technology, knowledge-based and capital-intensive powerhouses, integrating design as well as research and development activities.

Furthermore, digitally-enabled community supports for the halal industry in Malaysia is also very great. This, for one, is indicated by the creation of The Global Halal Data Pool (GHDP). Deloitte (2020) wrote that GHDP is an information depository that links halal manufacturers to suppliers, buyers, and retailers to synchronise the listing of their halal-certified products globally. Connected to 1.4 million global traders and 40,000 organisations, this data pool bolsters Verify Halal, a halal certification verification application, launched in 2017. Then, in 2019, Serunai Commerce, which established the Verify Halal and GHDP, started a blockchain-enabled halal digital records system which sophisticating of its whole suite of products that complete a halal digital ecosystem so as providing better supply chain traceability and data integrity.

Therefore, adopted the results of the factor analysis for setting up a business environment to introduce a new material for packaging in Indonesia by Oktariani, Tirdasari, Hasanah, and Indrawan (2018), the advocacy factor for implementing the circular economy for plastics as a requirement for halal industry in the ASEAN region and the new logistic infrastructure factor supported by institutional networks should be established. And, refer to Bigum and Oposa (2020), there are five approaches can drive the shift toward circular economy for a sustainable plastic future, ie. (1) Increase investments in effective integrated solid waste management systems and infrastructure; (2) Strengthen governmental policies, regulations, and commitments for a circular plastics economy; (3) Boost stakeholder engagement and value chain commitments to combat plastic pollution and introduce circular economy practices; (4) Rethink current delivery models and invest in innovation, pilots, and demonstration projects; and (5) Learn from others.

Overall, it can be seen how the relationship between circular economy for plastics, digitally-enabled community, and the opportunities for ASEAN towards a halal hub in Asia. Along support from the digitally-enabled community, this best practice of circular economy for plastics may spread and influence another region or another industry in Asia. This is not only opening up opportunities of ASEAN for leading a Halal Hub with its comparative advantages in Asia, but it can also encourage the collaboration between community groups, businesses, industry, local and national governments, international donors, and world-class experts seeking meaningful actions to defeat plastic pollution.

REFERENCES

Ahmedov, I. (2020, July). The Impact of Digital Economy on International Trade. *European Journal of Business and Management Research*, *5*(4), 1–7. doi:10.24018/ejbmr.2020.5.4.389

Akenji, L., Bengtsson, M., Kato, M., Hengesbaugh, M., Hotta, Y., Aoki-Suzuki, C., Gamaralalage, P. J. D., & Liu, C. (2019). Circular economy and plastics: A gap-analysis in ASEAN member states. Brussels: European Commission Directorate General for Environment and Directorate General for International Cooperation and Development, Jakarta: Association of Southeast Asian Nations (ASEAN).

Anbumozhi, V. (2019, September 11*). Circular economy for plastics: What is at stake for Asean?* Retrieved from https://www.nationthailand.com/opinion/30376083

Anbumozhi, V., & Kim, J. (Eds.). (2016). Towards a circular economy: Corporate management and policy pathways. Jakarta: Economic Research Institute for ASEAN and East Asia (ERIA).

Anbumozhi, V., & Kimura, F. (Eds.). (2018). Industry 4.0: Empowering ASEAN for the circular economy. Jakarta: Economic Research Institute for ASEAN and East Asia (ERIA).

Arkin, C. (2019, November 4). Waste exports: The rubbish dump is closed. *Heinrich Böll Foundation*. Retrieved from https://www.boell.de/en/2019/11/04/waste-exports-rubbish-dump-closed

ASEAN Secretariat, . (2015). *The ASEAN ICT masterplan 2020*. ASEAN Secretariat.

ASEAN Secretariat, . (2016). *Master plan on ASEAN connectivity 2025*. ASEAN Secretariat.

ASEAN Secretariat, . (2020a). *ASEAN Sustainable Development Goals Indicators Baseline Report 2020*. ASEAN Secretariat.

ASEAN Secretariat, . (2020b). *ASEAN Statistical Yearbook 2020*. ASEAN Secretariat.

Asia Society. (2018). *Disruptive Asia 2018*. Asia Society Australia.

Bigum, M., & Oposa, A. (2020, November 17). *A circular economy for a sustainable plastic future*. Retrieved from https://www.adb.org/news/features/circular-economy-sustainable-plastic-future

Box, S., & Lopez-Gonzalez, J. (2017). The future of technology: Opportunities for ASEAN in the digital economy. In S. S. C. Tay & J. P. Tijaja (Eds.), *Global megatrends: Implications for the ASEAN economic community* (pp. 37–60). ASEAN Secretariat.

Buchholz, K. (2020, June 2). Asia produces half the plastic in the world. *Statista*. Retrieved from https://www.statista.com/chart/17564/annual-per-capita-production-of-plastic-by-region/

Burns, D. (2018). A connected South-East Asia. In *Asia Society, Disruptive Asia 2018* (pp. 43–45). Asia Society Australia.

Changing Market Foundation. (2020). *Talking trash, the corporate playbook of false solutions to the plastic crisis*. Changing Market Foundation.

Deloitte (2020). *Edges of southeast asia*. The Deloitte Center for the Edge US-ASEAN Business Council, and the Singapore Economic Development Board (EDB).

Dinar Standard. (2020). *State of the global islamic economy report 2020/2021*. Dinar Standard, Dubai Islamic Economic Development Center, and Salam Gateway.

Dinard Standard. (2014). *State of the Global Islamic Economy Report 2014/2015*. Dinar Standard, Dubai Islamic Economic Development Center, and Salam Gateway.

Dinard Standard. (2015). *State of the Global Islamic Economy Report 2015/2016*. Dinar Standard, Dubai Islamic Economic Development Center, and Salam Gateway.

Dinard Standard. (2016). *State of the Global Islamic Economy Report 2016/2017*. Dinar Standard, Dubai Islamic Economic Development Center, and Salam Gateway.

Dinard Standard. (2017). *State of the Global Islamic Economy Report 2017/2018*. Dinar Standard, Dubai Islamic Economic Development Center, and Salam Gateway.

Dinard Standard. (2018). *State of the Global Islamic Economy Report 2018/2019*. Dinar Standard, Dubai Islamic Economic Development Center, and Salam Gateway.

Dinard Standard. (2019). *State of the Global Islamic Economy Report 2019/2020.* Dinar Standard, Dubai Islamic Economic Development Center, and Salam Gateway.

Ellen MacArthur Foundation. (2012). *Towards the circular economy vol. 1: An economic and business rationale for an accelerated transition.* Retrieved from https://www.ellenmacarthurfoundation.org/publications/towards-the-circular-economy-vol-1-an-economic-and-business-rationale-for-an-accelerated-transition

Ellen MacArthur Foundation. (2013). *Towards the circular economy vol. 1: Opportunities for the consumer goods sector.* Retrieved from https://www.ellenmacarthurfoundation.org/assets/ downloads/publications/TCE_Report-2013.pdf

Ellen MacArthur Foundation. (2016, January 19). *The new plastics economy: Rethinking the future of plastics.* Retrieved from https://www.ellenmacarthurfoundation.org/publications/the-new-plastics-economy-rethinking-the-future-of-plastics

Ellen MacArthur Foundation. (2017, January 20). *The new plastics economy catalysing action.* Retrieved from https://www.ellenmacarthurfoundation.org/publications/new-plastics-economy-catalysing-action

European Commission. (2019). *A circular economy for plastics: Insights from research and innovation to inform policy and funding decisions.* European Commission.

Heinrich Böll Foundation and Break Free From Plastic. (2019). *The plastic atlas 2019.* Druckhaus Kaufmann.

Hidayat, S. E., & Musari, K. (2022). ASEAN towards a global halal logistics through the digitally-enabled community. *International Journal of Asian Business and Information Management, 13*(2).

Hisham, M., & Florent, Z. (2019). Briefing note ASEAN inter-parliamentary assembly: Overview of plastic issues in ASEAN, focusing on marine debris and microplastics in the region. Phnom Penh: Parliamentary Institute of Cambodia (PIC).

Hoppe, F., May, T., & Lin, J. (2018). *Advancing towards ASEAN digital integration empowering SMEs to build ASEAN's digital future.* Report of Bain & Company.

Jambeck, J. R., Geyer, R., Wilcox, C., Siegler, T. R., Perryman, M., Andrady, A., Narayan, R., & Law, K. L. (2015). Plastic waste inputs from land into the ocean. *Science, 347*(6223), 768–771. doi:10.1126cience.1260352 PMID:25678662

Musari, K., and Zaroni. (2021). Reverse logistics in the age of digital transformation for circular economy and halal logistics through the leadership of Asia. In P. O. de Pablos, X. Zhang, & M. N. Almunawar (Eds.), *Handbook of research on disruptive innovation and digital transformation in Asia* (pp. 83-103). Hershey, PA: IGI Global. . doi:10.4018/978-1-7998-6477-6

Noor, R. (2020). *Percepatan pembangunan ekosistem industri halal di Indonesia melalui intervensi teknologi.* A presentation material at Webinar 'Digitalisasi New Normal Industri Halal di Indonesia' held by Sucofindo.

Oktariani, A., Tirdasari, N. L., Hasanah, N., & Indrawan, D. (2020). Setting up a business environment to introduce a new material for packaging in Indonesia. *Indonesian Journal of Business and Entrepreneurship*, *6*(3), 302–310. doi:10.17358/ijbe.6.3.302

PlasticsEurope. (2019). *Plastics – the Facts 2019*. PlasticsEurope.

PlasticsEurope. (2020). *Plastics – the Facts 2020*. PlasticsEurope.

RitchieH.RoserM. (2018, September). *Plastic pollution*. Retrieved from https://ourworldindata.org/plastic-pollution#total-plastic-waste-by-country

Son, N. T. X. (2020). Policy on marine plastic waste in ASEAN and Viet Nam. *Environmental Claims Journal*, 1–13. doi:10.1080/10406026.2020.1775347

Tanakasempipat, P. (2019, November 13). *Southeast Asian countries need tougher plastic policies to curb pollution: U.N.* Retrieved from https://www.reuters.com/article/us-asia-plastic-idUSKBN1XN1QL

The ASEAN Post Team. (2019). *Southeast Asia's Internet Economy Booming*. Retrieved from https://theaseanpost.com/article/southeast-asias-internet-economy-booming

Tiseo, I. (2020a, June 22). Leading plastic waste importers worldwide 2018. *Statista*. Retrieved from https://www.statista.com/statistics/1127268/plastics-waste-import-shares-by-country-worldwide/

Tiseo, I. (2020b, September 4). Plastic waste worldwide - statistics & facts. *Statista*. Retrieved from https://www.statista.com/topics/5401/global-plastic-waste/

UNCRD. (2019). *State of plastics waste in Asia and the Pacific: Issues, challenges and circular economic opportunities*. United Nations Centre for Regional Development (UNCRD).

Woetzel, J., Tonby, O., Thompson, F., Burtt, P., & Lee, G. (2014). *Southeast Asia at the crossroads: Three paths to prosperity*. McKinsey Global Institute.

World Bank Group. (2021). *Market study for Malaysia: Plastics circularity opportunities and barriers*. Marine Plastics Series, East Asia and Pacific Region.

Yates, R. (2017). ASEAN as the 'regional conductor': Understanding ASEAN's role in Asia-Pacific order. *The Pacific Review*, *30*(4), 443–461. doi:10.1080/09512748.2016.1264458

Chapter 2
Digital Leadership Competencies in the Malaysian Context:
A Study in Manager Levels

Sree Gayithri Maruthuvellu
Graduate School of Business, Universiti Sains Malaysia, Malaysia

Yashar Salamzadeh
https://orcid.org/0000-0002-6917-2754
Graduate School of Business, Universiti Sains Malaysia, Malaysia

Christopher Richardson
https://orcid.org/0000-0002-0371-6085
Graduate School of Business, Universiti Sains Malaysia, Malaysia

ABSTRACT

The purpose of this chapter is to investigate the most important digital leadership competencies for managers in Malaysia and to develop the profile of digital leadership competencies among managers in Malaysia. This study adopted quantitative research method and cross-sectional study. In order to provide a better understanding of the digital leadership competencies in Malaysia, the researcher uses exploratory factor analysis and fuzzy topsis method in interpreting results. The importance of each dimension was determined and compared with current performance. Hence, importance-performance charts were provided to elaborate the research results. This study will inspire managers to embrace change and to develop new competencies needed in order to guide their organizations into the uncertain future of the digital age. This study being the first in its kind will extend the knowledge of digital leadership competencies particularly in Malaysian context. Further, it enhances the literature by provided empirical evidence on the importance and how to develop the profile among managers.

DOI: 10.4018/978-1-7998-8678-5.ch002

INTRODUCTION

The advancement of technology in today's world, especially in Industrial Revolution 4.0 (IR 4.0), greatly influences every aspect of our lives including leaderships and education settings across the world (Schwab & Davis, 2018). In this current era, people's daily lives and businesses have been highly transformed by digital technologies in the last years. However, the concept of digital competence is considered important tool which covers many areas and is rapidly evolving as new technologies appear. Digitalization helps to connect more than 8 billion devices worldwide (World Economic Forum, 2018) and started to change the nature of organizations, their boundaries, relationships, and work processes (Lorenz *et al.*, 2015; Vidgen *et al.*, 2017). Digital transformation simply means the adoption of a portfolio of technologies that, at varying degrees have been employed by many firms such as social media, digital platforms, artificial intelligence, machine learning and big data (Harvard Business Review Analytic Services, 2017).

Malaysia is among the countries which is working hard on technology-driven economic growth using IR 4.0 (Bujang et al, 2020). By interconnection of technologies the digitalization process is experiencing a paradigm shift and this change proposes many new opportunities for different industries (Maskuriy et al., 2019). Here is the point that we need to think twice on the readiness of Malaysian leaders in different industries to be successful digital leaders. This is why Malaysia's Minister of Youth and Sports, Khairy Jamaluddin, said that "rapidly developing digital economy is increasing the demand for highly skilled technical workers, and digital business skills" (Khan et al, 2021).

Over the years, leadership scholars have been trying to monitor the effects of digitalization processes (Kirkland 2014). The focus was on the role of manager's ability to integrate the digital transformation into their companies and inspire employees to embrace the change, which is often perceived as a threat to the current status quo (Gardner *et al.,* 2010). Digitalization has changed the way companies communicate, manufacture, and organize themselves. The use of modern technologies in organizations influences the interpersonal expectations, competencies, and self-awareness of the workforce (Colbert *et al.,* 2016). Many companies mainly focus on the increase of productivity, efficiency, and profitability through the integration of new technology to connect devices and machines, digital tools such as platforms and digitalized distribution channels. Thereafter, they realize that it is not only the machines and methods to be adapt to the changes resulting from digitalization, but also the ways of leadership within the company and its culture. This means that the communication, working methods and standards must be set. Adequate leadership is essential to react to the changing customer demands and determines the success of a company.

There are remarkable differences between traditional leadership and leadership in the digital age as these mainly contributes to a changing work environment with computer-mediated communication playing a pivotal role (Phelps, 2014). Therefore, it is crucial to understand how both traditional settings differ from one another and to recognise the importance of digital technology for leadership concepts, to identify challenges and to finally derive necessary leadership skills. It can be difficult to find people or organizations that are not engaged in several aspects of digitalization daily (Phelps, 2014). The limitations are due to lack of skills among employees, ineffective leadership competencies, limited access to finance and slow adoption of digital technologies (Matzler *et al.,* 2008).

The Fourth Industrial Revolution (4IR), the Industry4WRD, which was launched on 31st October 2018 is the next phase of evolution in Malaysia. According to Ministry of International Trade and Industry (2019), the objective is to drive digital transformation of many related sectors in Malaysia. Technology can be useful only with the knowledge of application or it will not be helpful for any improvement. The industry 4.0 will be helpful to address number of issues in health and safety of human labour, efficiency and skills in managing supply chains and saves time in efficient management of delivery systems. In Malaysia, it is time to change to digitalisation, advance technologies with efficiency and competencies to move forward (Ministry of International Trade and Industry, 2019). By having a strong sector would encourage way to enhanced productivity, innovation capability, job availability, skilful talents, and good economy. Malaysia being a trading nation should continuously find ways to become greater in the market. This will technically make the country to become primary leader globally and attract more high-tech investments.

Besides that, e-competencies plays strong role in strengthening innovation and competitiveness (Martin, 2018). These changes make it compulsory for leaders to adapt to new skills and appoint digital tools to align their business as per the other large organizations which has implement this (Li *et al.,* 2016). Companies must develop adaptive capability and build innovation to create dynamic capability (Swanson *et al.,* 2017). In this digital era, innovation management plays important role too as it helps companies to remain competitive in the long run. An organization attitude in implementing a good market concept with both cultural and behavioural concept is known as market orientation, which focuses on customers' needs and wants (Gaur *et al.,* 2011). Digital leadership connect leaders with the use of latest technology and is known as the new construction of leadership. Besides that, the number of active internet users in Malaysia has now exceeded 20 million, with 16.8 million being active on social media (MCMC, 2017). Technology advancement has made people utilize technology in their daily life where the digital competencies is defined as one of the central competences and the uses of digital tools as a basic skill needed in the future (Ilomaki *et al.,* 2016).

There are many reasons as to why changes cannot be implemented easily. According to Rafferty and Jimmieson (2016), some employees are resistant to adapt to these new digitalised changes in their organization. Today, Digitalization and digital transformation is known as global megatrend as it changes the existing value chains across many industries and sectors (Collin *et al.,* 2015). The current trends are the data and machines learning, application programme learning interfaces (APIs) and mobile connectivity has cause difficulties for the traditional barriers to increase the speed of change (Ismail, 2017). Further, more focus has been given on managing digital transformation and leading the digital change although there are still insufficient information and exploratory at this moment (Andervin and Jansson, 2016; Soon and Salamzadeh, 2021). About 80% of the world's major business companies are forced to implement for digital transformation of their own business and develop a new digital strategy in ahead of their competitors with latest IT-technologies in business (Grabchak *et al.,* 2018). Malaysian managers need to adapt to the current digitisation, engage for more self-development skills and accept the challenge to shift their thinking on the role of leader (Korn Ferry Institute, 2018). The research aims to focus on the changes that can takes place in managerial leadership practices with the shift to the digital, virtual world. To address the problems accordingly, the objectives of this research was twofold. First, to investigate the most important digital leadership competencies for managers in Malaysia. Next, to develop the profile of digital leadership competencies among managers in Malaysia. By fulfilling the aim and objectives stated above, this study will be able to address the gap in the context of a developing country (Malaysia) and to provide practical and theoretical contributions.

This study makes several contributions. Firstly, on the competencies needed specifically on digital leadership skills for managers in Malaysia. The study is also expected to add types of characteristics and competencies required in the digital age and how organization will support the digitalisation through adequate leadership skills. It further provides broader overview on managers that has managerial experiences to understand how digital transformation is implemented across different organizations, community and teams. In addition to that, this study will enhance the knowledge and future leaders may use this research as an initiative to engage in more digitalization with leadership skills and practices in future. There are not many studies have been conducted to investigate the competencies of digital leadership in the context of managers in Malaysia, although there is a general agreement on the importance of implementing digital leaderships. However, this research will add to the literature on areas knowledge about digital leadership, list of competencies which are important for leaders, characteristics and qualities required for digital leadership. Since there are limited studies on digital leadership competencies in the Malaysian context particularly on managers, this study will fill the research gap. Therefore, this study will find the most important and relevant digital leadership competencies among Malaysian managers.

LITERATURE REVIEW

Digital Leadership is defined as implementing the right things for a successful digitalization of organization (El Sawy *et al.,* 2016) and being a digital leader whom able to find ways to lead and build their teams (Bawany, 2019). According to Avolio *et al.,* (2014), digital leadership is defined as a social influence process embedded in both proximal and distal contexts that can produce a change in attitudes and performance. The variants of digital leadership include virtual, ICT, technology and e-leadership. Innovative approaches to leadership that relate to this technology take-up include distributed, collaborative, shared and disruptive (Jameson, 2013). Digital competencies are classified as the knowledge, skills and digital literacy that needed by every leader to develop and manage digital information systems in their respective organization (Ferrari, 2012). Van Laar *et al.,* (2017) pointed that digital competency is essential for managers and organizations to keep track of developments and innovations of processes and products. Further, Capgemini (2018) defines digital competencies as a technology that helps change how the organization communicate with their customers and internal technologies. Digital skills mean a capability in using digital information systems like software and hardware to apply appropriate measures and protect digital information in working place (Trepanier, 2012). To keep up with latest trends and technologies, the aspect of leadership must shift towards digital leadership (Legner *etal,* 2017). However, there is currently no consensus on the definition of digital leadership, resulting in different concepts in respect of digital competencies.

In Malaysia, leadership has been identified as one of the key drivers in building a successful and sustainable digital ecosystem for the country (Digital Malaysia, 2013). By having Digital Malaysia initiative, it is safe to say that there will be more leaders who are directly involved in technology and lead digital based organizations. This also signifies that, Malaysian leaders need to be prepared to respect the different backgrounds of people that their organization may work with and redefine the boundaries of team as well as what it means to collaborate in achieving performance (Digital Malaysia, 2013). According to the Dell Technologies Digital Transformation Index, there are only 3% of Malaysian businesses are categorised as digital leaders, 18% as digital adopters who has innovations and advance digital plans to implement transformation, 51% does not have any digital plans in place or moving slowly and 28% are those whom still embracing the digital transformation (www.marketinginteractive.com, 2018).

There are many managers in Malaysia that understand the need for change, but they are struggling to balance current performance expectations, against innovating for the future. According to New Korn Ferry Institute (2018), 7 per cent of Malaysia's gross domestic product came from digital products and services which was created through digital technologies in the year 2017 as shown in table 1. Further, it was found that a lack of communication among Malaysian managers inhibits them from engaging, inspiring, and empowering their followers. In addition to that, they need to develop better capacity for self-development, face challenges and practice more self-confidence to drive this vision forward. The institute pointed out that managers must be risk taker, agents of change, to view leadership through a different lens, to collaborate with their teams and understands that everyone has a role to play in the organization. Therefore, it is crucial among Malaysian managers to adapt this change for a successful future (New Korn Ferry Institute, 2018).

Table 1. The digital leadership characteristics (New Korn Ferry Institute, 2018)

TRAITS	COMPETENCIES	DRIVERS
Curiosity Risk Taking Adaptability Tolerance of Ambiguity Confidence	Cultivate Innovation Manage Ambiguity Strategic Vision Engage and inspire. Drive Results	Independence Structure Challenge

Digital Transformation in an Organization and Challenges

The current trends such as Big Data, Internet of Things (IoT) and Artificial Intelligence is transforming existing industries, and this makes it challenging for many companies to survive in the digital age. For an industry to be successful, it needs to improve its operation, create a digital business, establish new key performance indicator (KPI) and adopt new skills and knowledge (New Korn Ferry Institute, 2018). Dahlstrom *et al.,* (2017) pointed out that the implementation of digital transformation practices does requires companies to be prepared with disruptions to current routine activities and processes which usually takes months to years, it can effectively streamline processes, improve efficiency, and support sustainable activities to achieve growth and stability. In this context, it is managers responsibility to view some elements where the organization can succeed with this effort and accomplish its goals effectively (Dahlstrom *et al.,* 2017).

ASEAN countries display notable differences in their mindsets about digital experience and maturity. As for Malaysia, it has started to shift its focus to the innovation divide since the 10th Malaysia Plan (now moving to 12th Malaysia Plan), whereas in the case of the less developed ASEAN nations, the focus may still be on the digital divide. According to Katz (1974), technical skills is defined as the specialized knowledge using tools and techniques of the specific discipline, human skills as the ability to work together and build cooperative effort within the team and conceptual skills as the ability to see the enterprise including recognising how the various functions depend on one another and how changes in one part can affect all the others. Additionally, Liu *et al.,* (2016) highlighted that every organization should adapt to the e-leadership model in place to promote successful change related to digital transformation and provide much-needed stability during the change process. Manager's duty in an organization is to ensure to achieve companies' objectives as they have managerial skills and experiences (Kostic, 2017). As organizations plan to digitize, the challenge of recruiting skilled managers will increase. Digital leadership is an important tool to be practice by managers in every organization because the changes that it made in organization patterns facilitated by the digital transformation. (Anthopoulos *et al.,* 2007).

The digital transformation in an organization is important, however it has its costs and consequences (Gruman, 2016). Managers in every organization has difficulty in making choices among the initiatives and potential disruptive in implementing digital transformation (Westerman, *et al.,* 2014). There are some issues that managers need to consider before undertaking these initiatives in their company. Westerman *et al.,* (2014) pointed that, managers are focusing in changing three key areas in their organization namely the operation department, customer experience and business models. Digital leadership implementation does have its major management challenges in which managers has to cope. These challenges include the priorities, more resources required, employees and machines and security with accessibility. Tiersky (2017) reveals whether increasing the efficiency of current operations or focusing on the customer needs should be the priority. It is common that non-IT employees and those from IT department needs more resources for their work purposes (Panetta, 2016). However, it is difficult to access trainings provided for IT employees compared to other employees in functional areas. The computing machines have and will continue to replace unskilled and semi-skilled workers (Davenport & Kirby, 2016). The confidential data should be accessible by authorised individuals who has authorised access in their respective department. Nevertheless, it is managers responsibility to ensure safeguard the data importance and sensitivity with accessibility concerns (Filkins *et al.,* 2016)

The Digital Leadership Competencies

Competencies is an ability to perform any task with good effort which involves knowledge, ability, and skills (Sultana, 2009), whereas digital competencies are defined as having a good knowledge, skills and attitude to be efficient in using digital processes and devices (Ala-Muta, 2011). Knowledge is an important resource for the function of professional in an information driven society. It includes principles, theories, and acts of a specific field of work or study which derived from learning (Bohlinger, 2008). In terms of e-competencies, the required knowledge is an understanding of main computer applications, the risks of the internet and online communication and the role of technologies in supporting creativity and innovation as a collaborative tool (Ferrari *et al.,* 2012). The word skill is referred to the ability to use one's knowledge effectively in any job performance and power of doing something competently (Shah, 2008). In addition to that, skills also define as the combination of characteristics includes knowledge, attitudes and behaviours. In today's digital era, an individual need to have good mind-set to adapt to the changes and requirements by the evolving technology (Romani, 2009). It requires an attitude to apply the right knowledge and skills as per to the environments.

The following are the essential competencies required for managers for managing and adapting to new changes and processes in their organizations. The competencies include teamwork, corporate social responsibility, enterprise architecture, behavioural competence, ethical competence, intercultural competence, social competence, meta competence, and talent management. Detailed descriptions of each competency is listed in Table 2 below.

Table 2. Essential competencies for digital leadership

Essential Competencies	Descriptions
Teamwork	According to Kelchner (2013), teamwork is defined as a group of different types of people who brings in diverse attributes to the team. This diversity within a team is important to allow different skill sets and share ideas for the best solution possible. Managers should understand the company culture and work together in team to strengthen the natural dynamics of the team and its members. A creative approach needs to be taken to drive the strategic vision of the organization through effective leadership.
Corporate Social Responsibility (CSR)	Companies are encouraged to consider corporate social responsibility (CSR) initiatives for economic, social and environmental duties to their stakeholders for sustainable development (Smith, 2003). According to Strand (2011), there are limited research examining the role of leadership in corporate social responsibility. Hence, a manager should increase their participation in CSR activities and share their belief in the values of such actions to their employees.
Enterprise Architecture Knowledge	In current business practice, it is absolute necessary to have an integrated approach towards business and information technology. The enterprise architecture knowledge involves the new methods, models and principles designed to use in implementing business processes and organizational structure for daily operations (Jonkers *et al.*, 2006).
Behavioural Competence	According to Wilson *et al.*, (2006), behavioural competency is increasingly being used by organisations to evaluate leadership potential and assess the differences between individuals. It simply means how an activity or situation is approached and it plays an important role in planning, training and development for both managers and employees.
Ethical Competence	Winterton *et al.*, (2005) stated that ethical competence means possession of appropriate personal and professional values, ability to make sound judgements in work-related situations and interacting with information and communication technology (ICT) in a responsible way (Ng and Salamzadeh, 2020).
Intercultural Competence	The intercultural competency refers to the ability of one to operate in different cultural settings. This competency not only provides managers a better understanding of their workplace and employees, but also helps to adapt to new working environment (Davies *et al.*, 2011).
Social Competence	It defines as the willingness to connect with people in a direct way, stimulate reactions and desired interactions (Mitrovic *et al.*, 2013). Socially intelligent employees can quickly assess the emotions of those around them and adapt their words and gestures accordingly to foster strong relationship building.
Meta Competence	This is the overarching competencies that applicable to wide range of work which helps in adaptation and flexibility of the organization. These skills are the higher-order abilities which have to do with ability to learn and adapt instead to demonstrate that one can do it (Bezuidenhou, 2011).
Talent Management	A leader in an organization need to focus on talent management, because the process is expected to create an environment to develop skills in preparation for a range of future possibilities (Innovation & Growth, 2013). Moreover, talented people will thrive and progress if they meet the competency and performance requirements of this process (Elsalanty, 2007).

E-Skills Competencies

Ravesteijn & Ongena (2019) have mentioned that definitions of e-leadership (also referred to as digital leadership) are derived commonly from definitions of leadership in general. This is supported further by Lander (2020) that links Digital Leadership as Technology leadership. In her literature review it is stated that Technology Leadership (and digital leadership) is another term for e-leadership. According to Lanvin & Passman (2008), e-skills competencies refers to the ability to use information and communication technology (ICT) efficiently. The following table consists of six skill-based competencies that successful e-leaders should aim to master. The competencies are e-communication, e-social skills, e-team building skills, e-change management, e-technological skills, and e-trustworthiness. Detailed descriptions of each competency is listed in Table 3 below.

Table 3. Defining e-leadership as six e-competencies (Van Wart et al., 2019)

E-skills	Descriptions
e-communications skills	Communication clarity: Communication in electronic settings is clear, organized and allows for feedback to avoid errors and untested assumptions. Lack of miscommunication: Communication in electronic settings is especially careful not to convey unintended messages that leave the receiver feeling insulted or angry because of tone or misunderstandings. Management of communication flow: Ensures that the ease of communications does not invite excessive communications impeding the ability of employees/leaders to get their work done.
e-social skills	Good leader support: Ensures that all employees in ICT-mediated environments are provided with customized communication from time to time. Uses richer media such as face-to-face meetings, telephone and virtual conferencing when appropriate. Ensures that teams use robust interaction methods that are inclusive.
e-team building skills:	Team motivation: Ensures that team building occurs in virtual teams which includes introductory activities, sense of their purpose, and occasional encouragement. Makes sure that new virtual members are properly introduced and integrated. Team accountability: Ensures that individuals in virtual teams are held accountable for participating and contributing. Team and team member recognition: Make sure that members of virtual teams get as much opportunity for recognition, rewards, development, and advancement as face-to-face team members.
e-change management skills	Change management: Provides change management techniques by preplanning transitions, monitoring implementation, and refining technology practice with experience.
e-technological skills	Currency with relevant ICTs: Stays abreast of new ICTS and new enhancements of ICTs. Investigates and compares ICTs to ensure that those in use are optimally effective given a cost–benefit analysis including financial and transaction costs. Blending traditional and virtual methods: Use of adopted ICTs is practiced in a sensible mix with other ICTs and traditional communication methods. Basic technological savvy: Has sufficient skills and inclination to deal with various types of technology breakdowns in both personal and enterprise settings, either directly or with the aid of technology specialists in a timely manner. Can support subordinates and others when there are technology breakdowns or underperformance issues. Technological security: Provides assurance of safe storage of information for privacy. Is vigilant against hacking and systems breaches.
e-trustworthiness	Trustworthiness in a virtual environment: Creates a sense of trust in the leader about honesty, consistency, follow-through, fairness, and general integrity. Work–life balance: Does not allow virtual technologies to intrude into employees' lives excessively. Ensures demands for client responsiveness do not overwhelm employees. Diversity management: Ensures that support of diversity is as well monitored in virtual settings as it is in face-to-face settings.

Leading for Change and Learning Competencies

In another research by (Kin & Kareem, 2019) stated there are twelve competencies which illustrates the core focus for a manager leading for a change and learning. The Figure 1 below shows the twelve competencies.

The first circle in the above model includes collaboration, ability to manage change, entrepreneurship, and communication. Collaboration is a way of managing people in an organization across functional and boundaries. In this working environment, managers not only oversee the projects but also work along with their employees in collaboration with other teams and departments to accomplish shared goals (Waugh *et al.*, 2006). Ability to manage change is getting others to change and upholding constant change in their respective company. The process of leading and managing an organization in this era of digitisation has

Figure 1. Proposed leadership competency model (Kim & Kareem, 2019)

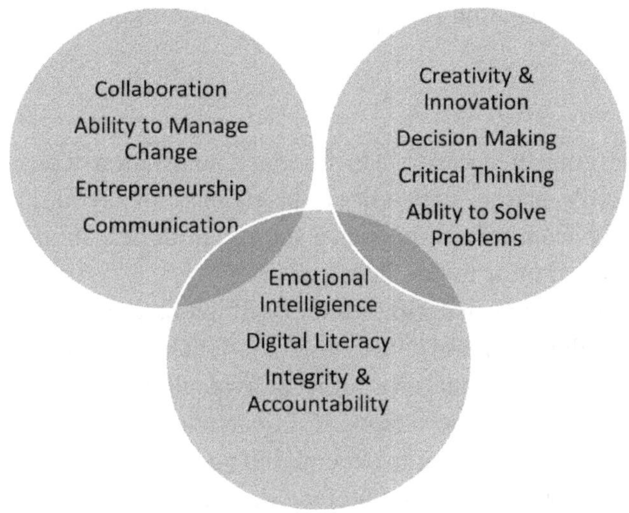

become more complex as the manage is fully accountable and responsible for the implementation of these changes (Holmes *et al.,* 2013). According to Akbar & Obaid (2014), entrepreneurship defines as the ability to manage and organize with good initiative and taking risk for creating better opportunities for the betterment of the organization. Communication is core leadership function as both are closely intertwined. A leader must be able to communicate effectively with various group within an organization to achieve the company goals. Further, communication is important when comes to decision making process as it is increasingly interactive (Smoliar & Sprague, 2003).

The second circle includes creativity and innovation, decision making, critical thinking and ability to solve problems. Creative and innovation skills is the ability to think outside the box and create new ideas or methods whereas innovation involves the creation of new knowledge or combinations of old insights to make it useful contribution in enhancing organization effectiveness (Mainemelis *et.al.,* 2015). Decision making is making a choice among alternative courses of action and use it to support their decision (Brunsson, 2007). An excellent leader needs to optimize their most valued beliefs, responsibilities, and obligations to make good decision that minimize adverse consequences. Critical thinking refers to the ability to evaluate and analyse using various types of methods to form a judgement (Joe, 2011). Generally, this form of competencies is needed by managers to lead their organizations rationally, reasonably, and empathetically. According to Angeli & Valanides (2012), ability to solve problems is to develop new ideas and solution or turn problems into opportunities. A leader must know more than others about how to manage different problem solvers in respect of the issues at hand.

The last circle includes emotional intelligence, digital literacy, integrity and accountability. Emotional intelligence is a set of abilities involved in reasoning about emotions and using emotions to inform cognitive activities such as reasoning and problem solving (Omar & Tai, 2018). This is the basic competency that leaders need to apply across the complete terrain of the organization. Considering the rapid and continual development of digital technology, individuals are required to use a growing variety of technical skills in order to perform tasks and solve problems in digital environments which known as digital literacy (Gilster, 1997). Organizations should emphasize in a culture of ethics that makes quality initiatives works as it is helps in organization performance. There should be a culture of ethics to ensure quality work as it is important in sustaining the performance of the organization (Maguad & Krone, 2009).

E-Competencies

The clarification of the term competence assists in the conceptualisation of e-competence. Digital leadership requires knowledge, skills, and the capability to be efficient in anything they do. There are several components related to the concept of e-competence such as e-participation skills, technology literacy, media literacy, data literacy and information literacy.

E-participation is the basis by which digital leaders will interact to share information, discuss issues and help formulate policy in digital cities (Dutta *et al.,* 2015). This competency is useful for supporting communication and interaction of individuals with other individuals. Given the imperative of e-participation in the digital city, more research on how various ICTs can support citizen participation in the digital city is needed. In today's world, everything is dependable on internet and thing get digitized on almost every division in an organization. Technology literacy defines as ability to use appropriate technology tools to communicate, access, collect and evaluate information (Mitrovic, 2015). It also consists of the efficient use of ICT tools for the storage and management of information and understanding potential risks. Everybody has a smart phone and able to send messages to many online users at any time by on touch of a button.

Media literacy simply means the ability to identify types of media and understand the messages they send (Romani, 2009). No matter how media literacy is introduced, it is important to develop this competency and understand to have media literacy and understand the concept. Data literacy means finding, managing, manipulating, and interpreting data which also includes reading graphs and charts, and to draw correct conclusions from data for decision making in an organization (Romani 2009). Everyone in an organization must understand the concept of data literacy and its importance. This is because this data will be useful in daily job and by using it, it contributes to overall company performance. The ability to read and understand the meaning, to evaluate and to connect different type of information is knows as information literacy (Romani, 2009). Since todays working environment are global, competitive, and digital, managers capability to navigate information is important for organization's success.

Digital Leadership Characteristics

Managers in an organization must lead the digital transformation through industry 4.0 together with their employees and managing the disruptive changes (Staffen & Schoenwald, 2016). In this era of digital transformation, it is important for a manager to be equipped with most distinguished digital leadership characteristics such as innovative visionary, networking intelligence, digital intelligence, digital talent scout, complexity management skill and business intelligence.

Many companies are challenging to be innovative visionary. A manager should have the entrepreneurial mindset (Sikora, 2017), to have an inspiring digital vision for the future and has to be innovative (Toduk, 2014). Besides that, they should create more room for innovations, implement innovation orientated culture in their organization as it is learnable (Oberer & Erkollar, 2018) and ascertain that it is conformed to the overall organization business strategy (Bawany, 2019). It is important to build networks both from technical and organizational perspective. Hence, networking intelligence is said to be an important characteristic in digital leadership. According to Herder-Wynne, Amato & Uit de Weerd

(2017), networking intelligence is defined as an ability to coordinate and build a networked team. The manager must be able to combine skills, knowledge resources and execute the task together as a team by delegating task based on each team competency (Bauer *et al.,* 2015; Oberer & Erkollar, 2018). However, there is challenges in leading the teams in the network and motivate the team members to create the vision together (Lindner & Greff, 2019). A manager must be first able to understand the possibilities of digital technologies in business, failing which it is impossible to lead organization's digital transformation. Therefore, digital intelligence is expected characteristics of digital leadership. Digital intelligence is defined as having information technology skills, technical skills and detail information about digital technologies (Raza, 2016). The manager in an organization should have good understanding as how things can be transformed and feel eager for the digitization (Hanschke, 2018). Further, it is crucial to employ the right employee for the right job that has suitable capabilities.

Managers should act as a digital talent scout, who search ways to attract new high digital capabilities (Durmus, 2019). Investing in talent development is critical element to ensure sustainable growth. And the best way is to invest in flexible talent recruitment and management systems (Kofler, 2018). Digital transformation does involve disruptive changes in organization and transformation process which usually involves high complexity. Hence, managers must be a complexity master whom able to interpret in difficult situation, understand the problems that arise and solve it (Hammermann & Stettes, 2017). Another important digital leadership characteristic is business intelligence. The managers in their organization should have the ability to create own business models, to have an ecosystem-centeredness, establish external customer focus and business understanding (Durmus, 2019). These insights help organization to make strategic business decisions that increase productivity, improve revenues, and enhance growth.

Research Theory: Dynamic Capabilities Theory

In this section, the suggested theory for this study is dynamic capabilities. For an organization to implement dynamic capabilities, digital leadership should be taken into consideration because it helps to ensure the dynamic capabilities of an organization aligns with the market (Racela, 2014). The widely accepted theoretical framework were resource-based view (RBV) which explains how a firm can achieve a competitive advantage and sustain their organization capabilities (Barney, 1997). The dynamic capabilities focus more on the existing resources and reconfiguration including new competencies arise due to the demand from rapid environmental changes (Eisenhardt & Martin, 2000). Pulley and Sessa (2001), identified that the impact on digital technology on leadership and e-leadership as a complex challenge for a manager to make individuals to work together to accomplish company goals.

Griffith *et al.,* (2006) suggest that developing dynamic capabilities can lead to a better performance in an organization. Managers of an organization must be bold enough to adapt knowledge resources and learning mechanisms that helps the development of dynamic capabilities. Once managers recognize the value of knowledge resources, they will take a leading role in the enhancement of the firm's dynamic capabilities. Likewise, Morgan *etal.* (2009) found that dynamic capabilities facilitate the business performance of a firm. Roberts and Grover (2011) provide evidence of a positive relationship between dynamic capabilities and performance. The strength of a manager's dynamic capabilities determines the degree to which firm can adapt to the latest digital transformation or no. In short, dynamic capabilities serve as the bridge between the present and future. Without them, an organization is stuck and will likely be deeply disrupted by change (Schoemaker *et al.,* 2018). Dynamic capabilities are central to a firm's business model and innovation process. It is also put forward that the role of leadership, especially

Table 4. The 5-step exploratory factor analysis protocol (Brown et.al., 2010)

Step 1: Is the data suitable for factor analysis?
Step 2: How will be the factors extracted?
Step 3: What criteria will assist in determining factor extraction?
Step 4: Selection of rotational method
Step 5: Interpretation and labelling

digital leadership, has a significant, direct and indirect effect in building innovations in the development of dynamic capabilities.

RESEARCH METHODS

Data Collection and Sampling Methods

This research is a quantitative, cross-sectional study with data gathered a structured questionnaire (Sekaran & Bougie, 2010). Malaysian managers that have managerial experiences with varied responsibilities in an organization who are aged above 18 years are used as the unit of analysis. The questionnaire was distributed to all managers that works in any field or company in Malaysia. A self-administered questionnaire was distributed online to managers in Malaysia and 167 were returned. Electronic surveys are the most convenient way to collect information quickly and conveniently (Sekaran & Bougie, 2016). The questionnaire comprised of three sections. There are three stages involved in data collecting process. Firstly, data were collected using online survey tools which is Google Form using the convenient sampling method. Next, the data is gathered and updated into the SPSS (Statistical Package for Social Sciences). Lastly, the data gathered need to be tested using the fuzzy topsis method, exploratory factor analysis and performance-importance charts in interpreting results.

Exploratory Factor Analysis

According to Tucker & MacCallum (1997), exploratory factor analysis is a statistical method that attempts to identify the smallest number of hypothetical constructs (known as factors, dimensions, latent variables or internal attributes) that can explain the covariation observed among a set of measured variables (known as observed variables, manifest variables, effect indicators or surface attributes). In simple words, it is to identify the common factors that explain the order and structure among measured variables. As described by Brown (2015), a factor is an unobservable variable that influences more than one observed measure and that accounts for the correlations among these observed measures. The following five step exploratory factor provides researchers with starting reference point in developing clear decision pathways. Each of these steps explained in more detail as follows in table 4:

The purpose of an exploratory factor analysis is to describe a multidimensional data set using fewer variables. The items which make up these factors (or components) should generally be more correlated to each other than the factors are to each other. The exploratory factor analysis was performed using the statistical package for social sciences (SPSS). The researcher performed the analysis by using Q-type factor analysis because the factors are calculated from the individual respondent. In factor analysis rotation, the varimax method was chosen to simplify the column of the factor matrix so that the factor extracts are clearly associated and there should be some separation among the variables. The researcher used to summarise data by grouping together all 31 variables and the findings shows that all these variables can be classified under one group.

The Fuzzy Topsis Method

In this study, Fuzzy Topsis method is used to rank all competencies to recognize the most important ones from overall list and also in each cluster. Fuzzy theory method provides a proper tool to encounter with uncertainties and complex environment (Lin & Sun, 2009; sooreh et al., 2011). The method consists of the steps used in previous research done by Sevkli et al., (2010).

Importance-Performance Analysis

The Importance-Performance Analysis was introduced by (Martilla & James, 1977) to examine the customer satisfaction, to determine what is important and how it works. Figure 3 shows a typical Importance-Performance Chart. The four quadrants are typically identified as keep up the good work (Q1), possible overkill (Q2), low priority (Q3) and concentrate here (Q4). The first quadrant represents the strengths and advantages of a product or service. The second quadrant attributes of low importance to customers which are performing strongly and indicates possible waste of limited resources that are inefficiently used and could be reallocated elsewhere. The attributes that fall into the third quadrant are not performing exceptionally well but are relatively unimportant to customers. Therefore, managers should not be overly concerned with these attributes. The most crucial region in the plot is fourth quadrant. The attributes situated in this quadrant are underperforming and represent the product's major weaknesses and threats to its competitiveness. Figure 2 shows above explanations.

DATA ANALYSIS AND RESULT

Respondent Profile

By November 2020, the researcher has received 167 returned questionnaires. The screening process was carried out and showed that 105 responses was manager and valid for data analysis. Based on the filtering question, the researcher has removed the non-managers which were 62 respondents. The data were analysed using SPSS (Statistical Package for Social Sciences) using 105 samples. The demographic profile of the respondents is shown in Table 5.

Importance Performance Matrix

A crucial stage in the formulation of operations strategy is the derivation of a ranked (or rated) list of competitive factors such as quality, flexibility, and cost. This list is used either to infer an appropriate set of strategic operations decisions or alternatively it is used in conjunction with an independently derived list of the organization's performance to prioritize each of the competitive factors. Typically,

Figure 2. Importance-performance chart (Ivan, 2015)

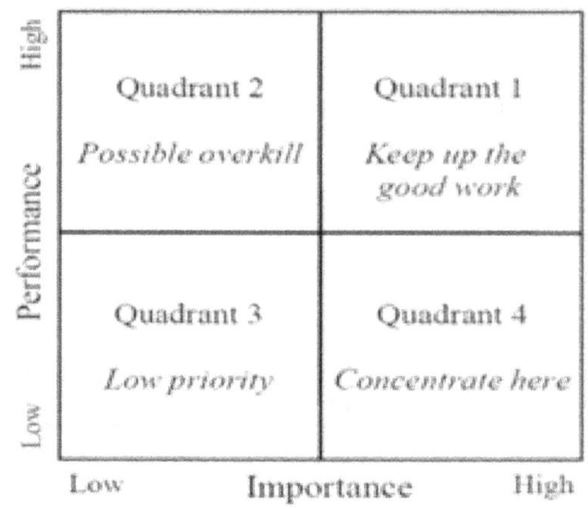

such a list ranks or rates those factors which the operations function contributes to the competitiveness of the organization (Martilla & James, 1977). The objective of using importance performance matrix is determine whether managers who were leading an improvement initiative in their own company could modify the importance performance matrix to provide improvement priorities which were seen as credible within the company.

Table 6 below list down 31 variables which is categorised in one group. The average value for all 31 competencies stated below was calculated in excel sheet using average formula for both importance and performance level for managers. The output of a cross analysis of these two data sets is shown in the importance-performance matrix chart in figure 3 below.

The finding shows that all 31 competencies needed for a manager are located in one dimension which is above 3 and below 5. The average value for each importance and performance value shows the place on this axis.

Fuzzy Topsis

In this study, the researcher attempted to explain the importance of 31 competencies for a manager in Malaysia. In order to do so, the researcher first reviewed the existing literature and then proposed list of competencies in order to develop the profile of digital leadership among Malaysian managers. After distributing questionnaires and collecting data, the researcher conducted exploratory factor analysis which was the first step of analysis. Next, fuzzy Topsis method and Importance-Performance Analysis were used to rank, determine, and measure the 31 competencies for managers in Malaysia. Fuzzy Topsis's initial analysis is shared in table 7.

Table 8 below shows ranking of competencies using their distance from positive Ideal and negative ideal. The first ten competencies (competency 4 to competency 8) indicate a good situation and managers must keep the good work on them. The elements include ability to solve problem, decision making, teamwork, ability to manage change, collaboration, critical thinking, communication, integrity and accountability, behavioural competence, and emotional intelligence. The ten competencies in the middle (competency 24 to competency 26) indicate that managers need to get improved on these items. The elements include meta competence, technology literacy, creativity and innovation, e-participation,

Table 5. Demographic characteristics of the sample

Demographic	Category	Respondent	Percentage
Are you currently working/ have worked as a manager in an organization?	Manager	Yes (105)	62.9%
Gender	Male Female	78 27	46.8% 16.2%
Age	20 – 30 31 – 40 41 – 50 51 – 60 > 61	15 52 26 10 2	9% 31.2% 15.6% 6% 1.2%
Marital Status	Single Married Widowed	31 71 3	18.6% 42.6% 1.8%
Race	Malay Chinese Indian Other	13 23 65 4	7.8% 13.8% 39% 2.4%
Level of Education	Diploma Bachelor's Degree Master's Degree Doctor of Philosophy Degree Other: Certificate SPM	9 42 46 6 1 1	5.4% 25.2% 27.6% 3.6% 0.6% 0.6%
formal education	Science Arts Social Sciences Engineering Medical, Dental & Health Other: Logistics & Supply Chain Management	11 27 26 34 2 5	6.6% 15.6% 15.6% 20.4% 1.2% 3%
Industry	Service Manufacturing Other: Logistics	66 36 3	39.6% 9.6% 1.8%
working experience	Less than 5 years 5 – 10 years 11 – 15 years More than 15 years	7 25 31 42	4.2% 15% 18.6% 25.2%
managerial experience	Less than 5 years 5 – 10 years 11 – 15 years More than 15 years	45 28 14 18	27% 16.8% 8.4% 10.8%
Total monthly salary	Below RM3000 RM3001 – RM5000 RM5001 – RM7000 RM7001 – RM9000 RM9001 – above	3 17 23 13 49	1.8% 10.2% 13.8% 7.8% 29.4%

ethical competence, intercultural competence, complexity management skill, social competence, business intelligence and innovative visionary. Lastly, the remaining eleven competencies (competency 1 to competency 8) are found to be problematic for most of the managers and they need further improve-

Table 6. Average result of each variable for 105 respondents

Rank	Abbreviation	Variable	Average Value (Importance)	Average Value (Performance)
1	Comm. 1	Entrepreneurship	4.36	4.01
2	Comm. 2	Communication	4.89	4.38
3	Comm. 3	Ability to Manage Change	4.8	4.4
4	Comm. 4	Ability to Solve Problem	4.86	4.55
5	Comm. 5	Collaboration	4.76	4.36
6	Comm. 6	Critical Thinking	4.77	4.44
7	Comm. 7	Decision Making	4.90	4.48
8	Comm. 8	Emotional Intelligence	4.53	4.23
9	Comm. 9	Digital Literacy	4.34	3.97
10	Comm. 10	Creativity and Innovation	4.47	4.19
11	Comm. 11	Integrity and Accountability	4.75	4.35
12	Comm. 12	E-Participation	4.34	4.05
13	Comm. 13	Technology Literacy	4.52	4.06
14	Comm. 14	Media Literacy	4.04	3.89
15	Comm. 15	Data Literacy	4.45	3.96
16	Comm. 16	Information Literacy	4.09	3.86
17	Comm. 17	Teamwork	4.82	4.44
18	Comm. 18	Corporate Social Responsibility	4.15	3.98
19	Comm. 19	Enterprise Architecture Knowledge	3.98	3.96
20	Comm. 20	Behavioural Competence	4.50	4.24
21	Comm. 21	Ethical Competence	4.6	4.33
22	Comm. 22	Intercultural Competence	4.37	4.17
23	Comm. 23	Social Competence	4.37	4.16
24	Comm. 24	Meta Competence	4.49	4.24
25	Comm. 25	Talent Management	4.45	4.06
26	Comm. 26	Innovative Visionary	4.41	4.04
27	Comm. 27	Networking Intelligence	4.45	4.02
28	Comm. 28	Digital Intelligence	4.16	3.95
29	Comm. 29	Complexity Management Skill	4.49	4.23
30	Comm. 30	Digital Talent Scout	4.04	3.90
31	Comm. 31	Business Intelligence	4.37	4.12

ments. The elements include digital literacy, talent management, media literacy, data literacy, digital intelligence, networking intelligence, information literacy, enterprise architecture knowledge, digital talent scout and corporate social responsibility.

Figure 3. Importance-performance matrix chart

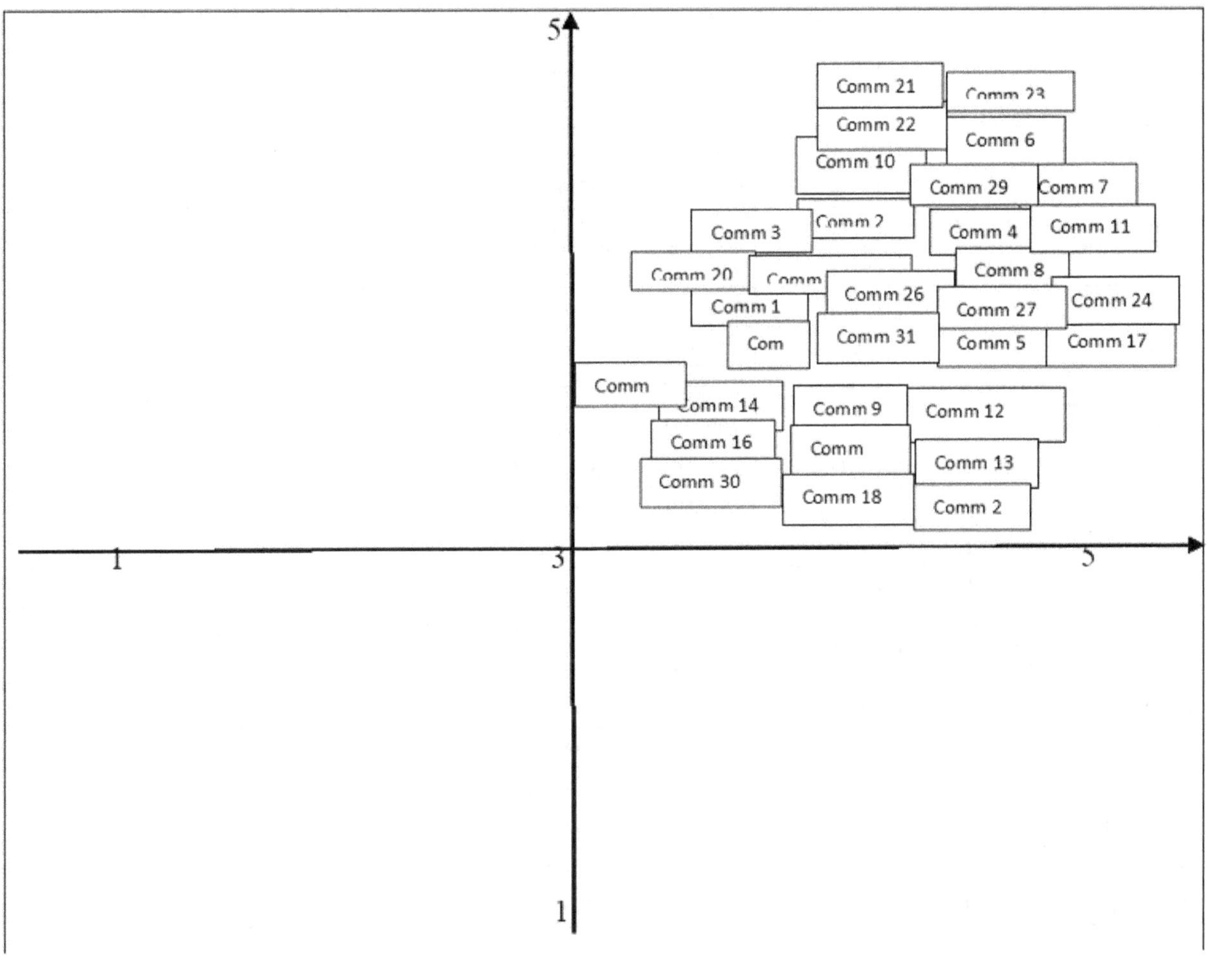

DISCUSSION

In this study, the findings were discussed based on research objective. Firstly, to identify the most important competencies of digital leadership for managers in Malaysia. Secondly, to develop the profile of digital leadership competencies among managers in Malaysia. 31 competencies are identified and investigated which is important and considered relevant among Malaysian managers.

The result shows the top ten competencies are found to be in good situation and managers must keep up the good work on them. The elements are ranked as follows: ability to solve problem, decision making, teamwork, ability to manage change, collaboration, critical thinking, communication, integrity and accountability, behavioural competence, and emotional intelligence. This is a good outcome and necessary to ensure that the organization can undergo digital transformation and changes can be accomplished. The middle ten competencies need slight improvement because a manager has to be equipped with these competencies for managing and adapting to new changes and processes in their organizations. These elements include meta competence, technology literacy, creativity and innovation, e-participation, ethical competence, intercultural competence, complexity management skill, social competence, busi-

Table 7. Values and normalized values for each competency

	LFi	MFi	UFi		NLFi	NMFi	NUFi
Comm. 1	9.209524	9.304762	9.27619	**Comm. 1**	0.945259	0.955034	0.952102
Comm. 2	9.533333	9.628571	9.6	**Comm. 2**	0.978495	0.98827	0.985337
Comm. 3	9.580952	9.67619	9.647619	**Comm. 3**	0.983382	0.993157	0.990225
Comm. 4	9.67619	9.771429	9.742857	**Comm. 4**	0.993157	1.002933	1
Comm. 5	9.561905	9.657143	9.628571	**Comm. 5**	0.981427	0.991202	0.98827
Comm. 6	9.561905	9.657143	9.628571	**Comm. 6**	0.981427	0.991202	0.98827
Comm. 7	9.647619	9.742857	9.714286	**Comm. 7**	0.990225	1	0.997067
Comm. 8	9.4	9.495238	9.466667	**Comm. 8**	0.964809	0.974585	0.971652
Comm. 9	9.142857	9.238095	9.209524	**Comm. 9**	0.938416	0.948192	0.945259
Comm. 10	9.361905	9.457143	9.428571	**Comm. 10**	0.960899	0.970674	0.967742
Comm. 11	9.438095	9.533333	9.504762	**Comm. 11**	0.968719	0.978495	0.975562
Comm. 12	9.361905	9.457143	9.428571	**Comm. 12**	0.960899	0.970674	0.967742
Comm. 13	9.380952	9.47619	9.447619	**Comm. 13**	0.962854	0.97263	0.969697
Comm. 14	9.114286	9.209524	9.180952	**Comm. 14**	0.935484	0.945259	0.942326
Comm. 15	9.114286	9.209524	9.180952	**Comm. 15**	0.935484	0.945259	0.942326
Comm. 16	9.009524	9.104762	9.07619	**Comm. 16**	0.924731	0.934506	0.931574
Comm. 17	9.6	9.695238	9.666667	**Comm. 17**	0.985337	0.995112	0.99218
Comm. 18	8.914286	9.009524	8.980952	**Comm. 18**	0.914956	0.924731	0.921799
Comm. 19	9.009524	9.104762	9.07619	**Comm. 19**	0.924731	0.934506	0.931574
Comm. 20	9.438095	9.533333	9.504762	**Comm. 20**	0.968719	0.978495	0.975562
Comm. 21	9.342857	9.438095	9.409524	**Comm. 21**	0.958944	0.968719	0.965787
Comm. 22	9.32381	9.419048	9.390476	**Comm. 22**	0.956989	0.966764	0.963832
Comm. 23	9.304762	9.4	9.371429	**Comm. 23**	0.955034	0.964809	0.961877
Comm. 24	9.390476	9.485714	9.457143	**Comm. 24**	0.963832	0.973607	0.970674
Comm. 25	9.142857	9.238095	9.209524	**Comm. 25**	0.938416	0.948192	0.945259
Comm. 26	9.219048	9.314286	9.285714	**Comm. 26**	0.946237	0.956012	0.953079
Comm. 27	9.047619	9.142857	9.114286	**Comm. 27**	0.928641	0.938416	0.935484
Comm. 28	9.07619	9.171429	9.142857	**Comm. 28**	0.931574	0.941349	0.938416
Comm. 29	9.314286	9.409524	9.380952	**Comm. 29**	0.956012	0.965787	0.962854
Comm. 30	8.971429	9.066667	9.038095	**Comm. 30**	0.920821	0.930596	0.927664
Comm. 31	9.285714	9.380952	9.352381	**Comm. 31**	0.953079	0.962854	0.959922

ness intelligence and innovative visionary. However, the last eleven competencies in the ranking were found to be problematic for most of the managers and they need further improvements. These elements are digital literacy, talent management, media literacy, data literacy, digital intelligence, networking intelligence, information literacy, enterprise architecture knowledge, digital talent scout and corporate social responsibility. Hence, managers need to be prepared to adapt, learned and practice to overcome their limitations in order to lead their organization better.

Table 8. Ranking of the fuzzy topsis

Rank	d+	d-	CCi
Comm. 4	0.004298	0.998705	0.995715
Comm. 7	0.005892	0.995773	0.994118
Comm. 17	0.010001	0.990885	0.990008
Comm. 3	0.011811	0.98893	0.988197
Comm. 5	0.013662	0.986975	0.986347
Comm. 6	0.013662	0.986975	0.986347
Comm. 2	0.016483	0.984042	0.983526
Comm. 11	0.026065	0.974267	0.973944
Comm. 20	0.026065	0.974267	0.973944
Comm. 8	0.029933	0.970357	0.970076
Comm. 24	0.030901	0.96938	0.969107
Comm. 13	0.031871	0.968402	0.968138
Comm. 10	0.03381	0.966447	0.966198
Comm. 12	0.03381	0.966447	0.966198
Comm. 21	0.035752	0.964492	0.964257
Comm. 22	0.037695	0.962537	0.962314
Comm. 29	0.038667	0.96156	0.961342
Comm. 23	0.039639	0.960582	0.96037
Comm. 31	0.041584	0.958627	0.958425
Comm. 26	0.048398	0.951785	0.951611
Comm. 1	0.049372	0.950807	0.950637
Comm. 9	0.056194	0.943965	0.943815
Comm. 25	0.056194	0.943965	0.943815
Comm. 14	0.059119	0.941032	0.94089
Comm. 15	0.059119	0.941032	0.94089
Comm. 28	0.06302	0.937122	0.936989
Comm. 27	0.065947	0.934189	0.934062
Comm. 16	0.06985	0.930279	0.930159
Comm. 19	0.06985	0.930279	0.930159
Comm. 30	0.073753	0.926369	0.926256
Comm. 18	0.07961	0.920504	0.920399

This study adopts fuzzy Topsis method as the analytical tool that determines the ranking of each competency. This technique provides novelty and a mellow contribution in this study. According to Schoemaker *et al.,* (2018), the global vision, reflectiveness, collaboration, and in-depth knowledge are crucial aspect of digital leadership. The finding found that there are limited studies on digital leadership competencies in the Malaysian context, particularly on managers. Thus, this study fills in the research gap.

Implication

Theoretical Implications

As a theoretical contribution, the researcher focused on the competencies needed specifically on digital leadership skills for managers in Malaysia. The significance and importance are value-added information to many organizations. As of now, the research on digital leadership were focus more on management such as the characteristics needed for leaders, to prioritise what is important, to start recruiting and developing the mindset of leaders as well create symbols of change that align to the company's goals. Malaysian leaders need to see this change as a great platform for opportunities and embrace a new vision of leadership.

Practical Implications

Organizations have changed the way they do business in this digital age and managers are the ones who must lead by example. This study will inspire managers to embrace change, to develop new competencies needed in order to guide their organizations into the uncertain future of the digital age. Moreover, organizations can never fully embrace the digital age if their managers are not willing to change the way they work and manage their employees. Although there are still few managers lack these competencies, but most of them have started to develop them.

The National Policy on Industry 4.0 (Industry 4wrd) has its plan to transform the Malaysian manufacturing industry and its related services to be more systematic, smarter, and resilient. As the year 2020 marks the end of Vision 2020 and the Eleventh Malaysia Plan (2016-2020) period, the post-2020 development plan with a clear strategic direction will be formulated to set the way forward for national development agenda over the next decade along with the implementation framework (www.rmke12.epu.gov.my). The Human Resources Development Fund (HRDF) National Workforce Human Capital Development Blueprint (2018 – 2025) helps in upgrading our Malaysian talent. It outlines the steps that HRDF is committed to take and to catalyse the preparation of Malaysian talent for this digital reality (www.hrdf.com.my). All these respective policy makers may consider use this result to fill the gaps in their strategies in digital transformation.

As developing digital leadership competencies is one of the ways for managers, the findings of this study will enable them to focus more on identify trends, understand the importance of technology and how to be implemented to drive the bottom line. Further, this study will enhance the knowledge and future leaders may use this research as an initiative to engage in more digitalization with leadership skills and practices in future.

Limitation and Recommendation for Future Research

There are some limitations in this study that could be an opening for future research. Firstly, the researcher focused exclusively on managers in the Malaysian context only. Therefore, the result cannot be generalised to other position or countries, and it is limited on the global context. Different countries may have different points of view in terms of knowledge, characteristics and qualities required for a digital leader. Secondly, the technology background information of which the managers work. The survey did not include questions that addressed whether manager's organization were Tech-savvy or not. This information may provide additional information from the manager as to how they view the importance of digital leadership competencies in their organization. Finally, the response rate was moderate. Although 350 questionnaires were distributed, only 167 managers had responded. Some managers refused to participate in the survey because they do not prefer to share their personal information's, their knowledge on this subject matter and their company policy did not allow them to participate in any surveys.

Recommendation for future research is to study a greater sample than the one focused in this research. The current study is limited to only managers that works in companies in Malaysia, the future researchers may choose other countries for the purpose of study and additional items of digital leadership practices can be suggested. Another direction for future research is to investigate how managers demographics can affect attitudes toward digital leadership. Because this study was delivered to Malaysian managers teachers randomly, to the researcher could not control the balance of managers demographics. Future research is recommended to adjust the sampling strategies and obtain samples with more balanced demographics. Also we may suggest future researchers to do a comparison study between Malaysia and other countries to give a better comparative view about their status on digital leadership competencies.

CONCLUSION

Manager competencies can improve management skills and influence the behaviour of others which can result in a positive impact on the bottom line. To find the energy to confront the change required, managers in Malaysia need to engage their strong capacity for self-development and embrace the challenge to fundamentally shift their thinking on the role of leader. The managers should also build on their innate confidence to expand their leadership capacity. This study successfully examined the importance and level of the competencies in each manager. The research objective of this study was successfully achieved.

REFERENCES

Adler, N. J. (2008). Global leadership: giving oneself for things far greater than oneself. In International Dimensions of Organizational Behavior (5th ed.). Thomson.

Akbar, F., & Haitham Obaid, A. A. (2014). Explaining the relationship between creativity, Explaining the relationship between creativity, Innovation and entrepreneurship. *International Journal of Economy. Management and Social Sciences*, *3*(12), 1–4.

Ala-Mutka, K. (2011). *Mapping digital competence: Towards a conceptual understanding*. Academic Press.

Andervin, M., & Jansson, J. (2016). Att leda digital transformation. California Management Review, 61, 15–42.

Angeli, C., & Valanides, N. (2012). Epistemological beliefs and ill-structured problem-solving in solo and paired contents. *Journal of Educational Technology & Society*, *15*(1), 2–14.

Anthopoulos, L., Siozos, P., & Tsoukalas, I. (2007). Applying participatory design and collaboration in digital public services for discovering and re-designing e-government services. *Government Information Quarterly*, *24*(2), 353–376. doi:10.1016/j.giq.2006.07.018

Avolio, Sosik, Kahai, & Baker. (2014). *E-leadership: Re-examining transformations*. Academic Press.

Barney, J. B. (1997). *Gaining and sustaining competitive advantage*. Addison-Wesley.

Bauer, W., Hammerle, M., Schlund, S., & Vocke, C. (2015). Transforming to a hyper-connected society and economy–towards an "Industry 4.0". *Procedia Manufacturing*, *3*, 417–424. doi:10.1016/j.promfg.2015.07.200

Bawany, S. (2019). Leadership 4.0: How Ready Are You to Be A Digital Leader? *Leadership Excellence*, *36*(2), 28–30.

Bezuidenhout, M. (2011). *The development and evaluation of a measure of graduate employability in the context of the new world of work* (Doctoral dissertation). University of Pretoria.

Bohlinger, S. (2008). Competences as the Core Element of the European Qualifications Framework. *European Journal of Vocational Training*, *42*(1), 96–112.

Brown, T. A. (2015). *Confirmatory factor analysis for applied research* (2nd ed.). Guilford Press.

Brunsson, N. (2007). *The consequences of decision making*. Oxford University Press.

Bujang, S. D. A., Selamat, A., Krejcar, O., Maresova, P., & Nguyen, N. T. (2020). Digital Learning Demand for Future Education 4.0—Case Studies at Malaysia Education Institutions. *Informatics (MDPI)*, *7*(2), 13. doi:10.3390/informatics7020013

Capgemini. (2018). *Understanding digital mastery today*. Digital Transformation Institute.

Colbert, A., Yee, N., & George, G. (2016). The digital workforce and the workplace of the future. *Academy of Management Journal*, *59*(3), 731–739. doi:10.5465/amj.2016.4003

Collin, J., Hiekkanen, K., Korhonen, J. J., Halen, M., Itala, T., & Helenius, M. (2015). IT Leadership in Transition-The Impact of Digitalization on Finnish Organizations. *The Academy of Management Annals*, *9*(1), 393–482.

Dahlstrom, P., Desmet, D., & Singer, M. (2017). *The seven decisions that matter in a digital transformation: a CEO's guide to reinvention*. McKinsey.

Davenport, T., & Kirby, J. (2016). *Only humans need apply: Winners and losers in the age of smart machines*. Harper Business.

Davies, A., Fidler, D., & Gorbis, M. (2011). *Future work skills 2020*. Institute for the Future for University of Phoenix Research Institute.

Durmuş, A. (2019). Endustri 4.0 Egitim 4.0 Liderlik 4.0 Toplum 5.0 (1st ed.). İstanbul: Efe Akademi Yayınları.

Dutta, S., Geiger, T., & Lanvin, B. (2015). *The Global Information Technology Report 2015: ICTs for Inclusive Growth.* Geneva: World Economic Forum and INSEAD. Available at: http://www3.weforum.org/docs/WEF_Global_IT_Report_2015.pdf

Eisenhardt, K. M., & Martin, J. A. (2000). Dynamic capabilities: What are they? *Strategic Management Journal, 21*(10-11), 1105–1121. doi:10.1002/1097-0266(200010/11)21:10/11<1105::AID-SMJ133>3.0.CO;2-E

El Sawy, O. A., Kræmmergaard, P., Amsinck, H., & Vinther, A. L. (2016). How LEGO Built the Foundations and Enterprise Capabilities for Digital Leadership. *MIS Quarterly Executive, 15*(2), 141–166.

Elsalanty, L. E. (2011). The Mediating Methods of Leadership Development in the Relationship between Talent Management and Job Performance. *International Journal of Innovation & Human Resources Management, 1*(1).

Ferrari, A. (2012). *Digital competence in practice: an analysis of frameworks. JRC Technical Reports, European Commission, Joint Research Centre.*

Filkins, B. L., Kim, J. Y., Roberts, B., Armstrong, W., Miller, M. A., Hultner, M. L., & Steinhubl, S. R. (2016). Privacy and security in the era of digital health: What should translational researchers know and do about it? *American Journal of Translational Research, 8*(3), 1560–1580. PMID:27186282

Gardner, W. L., Lowe, K. B., Moss, T. W., Mahoney, K. T., & Cogliser, C. C. (2010). Scholarly leadership of the study of leadership: A review of the leadership quarterly's second decade, 2000–2009. *The Leadership Quarterly, 21*(6), 922–958. doi:10.1016/j.leaqua.2010.10.003

Gaur, S. S., Vasudevan, H., & Gaur, A. S. (2011). Market orientation and manufacturing performance of Indian SMEs: Moderating role of firm resources and environmental factors. *European Journal of Marketing, 45*(7), 1172–1193. doi:10.1108/03090561111137660

Gilster, P. (1997). *Digital literacy.* Wiley.

Grabchak, E.P., Medvedev, E.A., & Vasilyeva, I.G. (2018). How to make digitalization successful. *Energetic Keskaya Politika, 5*, 25-29.

Griffith, D. A., Noble, S., & Chen, Q. (2006). The performance implications of entrepreneurial firm performance. *Strategic Management Journal, 30*(8), 909–920.

Gruman, G. (2016). What digital transformation really means. *InfoWorld.* Available online at: https://www.infoworld.com/article/3080644/what-digital-transformation-really-means.html

Hair, J. F., Ringle, C. M., & Sarstedt, M. (2011). PLS-SEM: Indeed a silver bullet. *Journal of Marketing Theory and Practice, 19*(2), 139–151. doi:10.2753/MTP1069-6679190202

Hammermann, A., & Stettes, O. (2017). Does digitization make new demands on leadership and performance management? *IW Trends Quarterly on Empirical Economic Research, 44*(4), 93-111.

Hanscheke, I. (2018). *Digitization and Industry 4.0 – simple and effective: Mastering the digital transformation systematically and lean.* Carl Hanser Verlag.

Harvard Business Review Analytic Services. (2017). *Operationalizing Digital Transformation: New Insights into Making Digital Work*. Available online at: https://hbr.org/sponsored/2017/05/operationalizing-digital-transformation-new-insights-into-making-digital-transformation-work

Herder-Wynne, F., Amato, R., & Uit de Weerd, F. (2017). *Leadership 4.0 A review of the thinking*. Oxford Leadership.

Holmes, K., Clement, J., & Albright, J. (2013). The complex task of leading educational Change in schools. *School Leadership & Management, 33*(3), 270–283. doi:10.1080/13632434.2013.800477

Human Capital Development Blueprint. (2019). *National Workforce Human Capital Development Blueprint 2018 – 2025*. Available online at: https://www.hrdf.com.my

Ilomaki, L., Paavola, S., Lakkala, M., & Kantosalo, A. (2016). Digital competence–an emergent boundary concept for policy and educational research. *Education and Information Technologies, 21*(3), 655–679. doi:10.100710639-014-9346-4

Innovation & Growth. (2013). *Talent Management: Process Guide*. Retrieved from: http://novascotia.ca/psc/pdf/ hrCentre/resources/talentManagement/TM_Process_Guide.pdf

Interactive, M. (2018). *Study finds that only 3% of Malaysian businesses are digital leaders*. Available online at: https://www.marketing-interactive.com/study-finds-that-only-3-of-malaysian-businesses-are-digital-leaders

Ismail, N. (2017). *The game has changed: adapting to digitalisation necessary to stay ahead of the pack*. Assess on 10.4.2020. https://www.information-age.com/game-changed-adapting-digitalisation-necessary-stay-ahead-pack-123466799/

Jameson, J. (2013). e-leadership in higher education: The fifth "age" of educational technology research. *British Journal of Educational Technology, 44*(6), 889–915. doi:10.1111/bjet.12103

Joe, Y. F.L. (2011). *An introduction to critical thinking and creativity: Think more, think better.* John Wiley & Sons.

Jonkers, H., Lankhorst, M. M., ter Doest, H. W. L., Arbab, F., Bosma, H., & Wieringa, R. J. (2006). Enterprise architecture: Management tool and blueprint for the organisation. *Information Systems Frontiers, 8*(2), 63–66. doi:10.100710796-006-7970-2

Katz, R. L. (1974). Skills of an Effective Administrator. *Harvard Business Review*, (Sep-Oct), 91–93.

Kelchner, L. (2013). *Strengths and weaknesses of cross-functional teams*. Retrieved from: https://smallbusiness.chron.com/strengths-weaknesses-cross-functional-teams-24653.html

Khan, N., Khan, S., Tan, B. C., & Loon, C. H. (2021). Driving Digital Competency Model Towards IR 4.0 In Malaysia. *Journal of Physics: Conference Series, 1793*(1), 12–49. doi:10.1088/1742-6596/1793/1/012049

Kin, T. M., & Kareem, O. A. (2019). School leaders' Competencies that make a difference in the Era of Education 4.0: A Conceptual Framework. *International Journal of Academic Research in Business & Social Sciences, 9*(4). Advance online publication. doi:10.6007/IJARBSS/v9-i4/5836

Kin, T. M., & Kareem, O. A. (2019). School leaders' Competencies that make a difference in the Era of Education 4.0: A Conceptual Framework. *International Journal of Academic Research in Business & Social Sciences*, *9*(4). Advance online publication. doi:10.6007/IJARBSS/v9-i4/5836

Kirkland, R. (2014). Artificial Intelligence Meets the C-suite. *McKinsey Quarterly*. Available onlineat: https://www.mckinsey.com/insights/strategy/artificial_intelligence_meets_the_c-suite

Kofler, T. (2018). Digitale Transformation in Unternehmen. In N. Hohne, D. Méndez, K. B. Zimmer (Ed.), ZD. B Digital Dialogue Positions papier.

Korn Ferry Institute. (2018). *Digital Leadership in Malaysia*. Available online at: https://focus.kornferry.com/wp-content/uploads/2015/02/Korn-Ferry-Digital-leadership-in-Malaysia.pdf

Kostic, M. (2017). Challenges of Agile Practices Implementation in The Medical Device Software Development Methodologies. *European Project Management Journal.*, *7*(2), 36–44.

Lander, J. (2020). *The relationship between principals' pillars of digital leadership aligned values and actions and teacher technology use*. St. John's University.

Lanvin, B. & Passman, P. (2008). *Building E-skills for the Information Age*. Academic Press.

Legner, C., Eymann, T., Hess, T., Matt, C., Bohmann, T., Drews, P., Madche, A., Urbach, N., & Ahlemann, F. (2017). Digitalization: Opportunity and Challenge for the Business and Information Systems Engineering Community. *Business & Information Systems Engineering*, *59*(4), 301–308. doi:10.100712599-017-0484-2

Li, W., Liu, K., Belitski, M., Ghobadian, A., & O'Regan, N. (2016). E-Leadership through Strategic Alignment: An Empirical Study of Small and Medium-Sized Enterprises in the Digital Age. *Journal of Information Technology*, *31*(2), 185–206. doi:10.1057/jit.2016.10

Lindner, D., & Greff, T. (2019). Fuhrung im Zeitalter der Digitalisierung–was sagen Fuhrungskrafte? *HMD Praxis der Wirtschaftsinformatik*, *56*(3), 628–646. doi:10.136540702-018-00447-9

Lorenz, M., Rubmann, M., Strack, R., Lueth, K. L., & Bolle, M. (2015). *Man and Machine in Industry 4.0. How Will Technology Transform the Industrial Workforce Through 2025?* The Boston Consulting Group.

Maguad, B. A., & Krone, R. M. (2009). Ethics and moral leadership: Quality linkages. *Total Quality Management*, *20*(2), 209–222. doi:10.1080/14783360802623043

Mainemelis, C., Kark, R., & Epitropaki, O. (2015). *Creative Leadership: A Multi-Context*. Academic Press.

Malaysia, D. (2013). *Empowering Malaysia towards a digital economy*. Available online at: http://www.digitalmalaysia. my/ebook/

Malaysian Communications and Multimedia Commission. (2017). https://skmm.gov.my/skmmgovmy/media/General/pdf/InternetUsersSurvey2016.pdf

Martilla, J. A., & James, J. C. (1977). Importance-performance analysis. *Journal of Marketing*, *41*(1), 77–79. doi:10.1177/002224297704100112

Martin, J. (2018). *Skills for the 21st Century: Findings and Policy Lessons from the OECD Survey of Adult Skills*. Working Papers 201803, Geary Institute, University College Dublin.

Maskuriy, R., Selamat, A., Ali, K. N., Maresova, P., & Krejcar, O. (2019). Industry 4.0 for the construction industry—How ready is the industry? *Applied Sciences (Basel, Switzerland)*, *9*(14), 2819. doi:10.3390/app9142819

Matzler, K., Schwarz, E., Deutinger, N., & Harms, R. (2008). The Relationship between Transformational Leadership, Product Innovation and Performance in SMEs. *Journal of Small Business & Entrepreneurship*, 21(2): 139–151. Available online at: . doi:10.1080/08276331.2008.10593418

Ministry of International Trade and Industry. (2019). *Industry 4wrd.* Assess on 19.4.2020. https://www.miti.gov.my/index.php/pages/view/industry4WRD?mid=559

Mitrovic, Z. (2015). Strengthening the evidence-base for open government in developing countries: Building Open Data Capacity through e-Skills Acquisition. (March):1–38.

Morgan, N. A., Vorhies, D. W., & Mason, C. H. (2009). Market orientation, marketing capabilities, and firm performance. *Strategic Management Journal*, *30*(8), 909–920. doi:10.1002mj.764

Ng, Y. N., & Salamzadeh, Y. (2020). The Impact of Ethical Leadership on the Intention to Stay among the Generation-Y Workforce of MNCs in Penang, Malaysia: Mediating Role of Employee Rewards. *International Journal of Business Science and Applied Management*, *15*(2).

Oberer, B., & Erkollar, A. (2018). Leadership 4.0: Digital Leaders in the Age of Industry 4.0. *International Journal of Organizational Leadership*, *7*(4), 404–412. doi:10.33844/ijol.2018.60332

Panetta, K. (2016). Analyst answers: The CIO's biggest digital transformation challenges. Available online at: https://www.gartner.com/smarterwithgartner/cios-biggest-digital-transformationchallenges/. Assessed on 30.4.2020.

Phelps, K. C. (2014). 'So much technology, so little talent'? Skills for harnessing technology for leadership outcomes. *The Journal of Leadership Studies*, *8*(2), 51–56. doi:10.1002/jls.21331

Pulley, M. L., & Sessa, V. I. (2001). E-leadership: Tackling complex challenges. Industrial and Commercial Training, 33(6/7). proclivity: a dynamic capabilities approach. *Journal of Retailing*, *82*(1), 51–62.

Racela, O. C. (2014). Customer orientation, innovation competencies, and firm performance: A proposed conceptual model. *Procedia: Social and Behavioral Sciences*, *148*, 16–23. doi:10.1016/j.sbspro.2014.07.010

Rafferty, A. E., & Jimmieson, N. L. (2016). Subjective Perceptions of Organizational Change and Employee Resistance to Change: Direct and Mediated Relationships with Employee Well-being. *British Journal of Management*, *28*(2), 248–264. doi:10.1111/1467-8551.12200

Ravesteijn, P., & Ongena, G. (2019). The role of E-leadership in relation to IT capabilities and digital transformation. IADIS Proceedings.

Raza, B. (2016). Leadership 4.0. Module: Management Competencies 1 (MC1) (Master's thesis, Frankfurt University of Applied Sciences, Frankfurt, Germany).

Roberts, N., & Grover, V. (2011). Investigating firm's customer agility and firm performance. the importance of aligning sense and respond capabilities. *Journal of Business Research, 64*(3), 1–7.

Romani, J. (2009). *Strategies to promote the development of e-competencies in the next generation of professionals: European and international trends.* Available online at: http://www.cardiff.ac.uk/socsi/research/researchcentres/skope/publications/monograp hs/monograph13.pdf

Schoemaker, P. J., Heaton, S., & Teece, D. (2018). Innovation, dynamic capabilities, and leadership. *California Management Review, 61*(1), 15-42.

Schwab, K., & Davis, N. (2018). *Shaping the Fourth Industrial Revolution* (1st ed.). Crown Publishing Group.

Sekaran, U., & Bougie, R. (2010). *Research Methods for Business: A Skill Building Approach* (5th ed.). John Wiley & Sons.

Sekaran, U., & Bougie, R. (2016). *Research methods for business: A skill building approach.* John Wiley & Sons.

Sever, I. (2015). Importance-performance analysis: A valid management tool? *Tourism Management, 48*, 43–53. doi:10.1016/j.tourman.2014.10.022

Sevkli, M., Zaim, S., Turkyilmaz, A., & Satir, M. (2010, July). An application of fuzzy Topsis method for supplier selection. In *International Conference on Fuzzy Systems* (pp. 1-7). IEEE. 10.1109/FUZZY.2010.5584006

Shah, N. Z. (2008). Are graduates to be blamed? Unemployment of computer science graduates in Malaysia. *Computer Science, 3*, 19–5.

Sikora, H. (2017). Digital Age Management: Leadership in the Digital Age. *E & I Electrical Engineering and Information Technology, 134*(7), 344-348.

Smith, N. C. (2003). Corporate social responsibility: Whether or how? *California Management Review, 45*(4), 52–76. doi:10.2307/41166188

Smoliar, S. W., & Sprague, R. (2003). Technology Support for Communication and Understanding. *Journal of Decision Systems, 2*(2), 123–139. doi:10.3166/jds.12.123-139

Soon, C. C., & Salamzadeh, Y. (2021). The impact of Digital Leadership Competencies on Virtual Team Effectiveness in MNC companies in Penang, Malaysia. Journal of Entrepreneurship. *Business Economics (Cleveland, Ohio), 8*(2), 219–253.

Sooreh, L. K., Salamzadeh, A., Safarzadeh, H., & Salamzadeh, Y. (2011). Defining and measuring entrepreneurial universities: A study in Iranian context using importance-performance analysis and TOPSIS technique. *Global Business and Management Research, 3*(2), 182–199.

Staffen, S., & Schoenwald, L. (2016). *Leading in the Context of the Industrial Revolution.* https://www.capgemini.com/consulting-de/wp-content/uploads/sites/32/2017/08/resouces_leader_40_industrial_revolution.pdf

Strand, R. (2011). Exploring the role of leadership in corporate social responsibility: *A review. Journal of Leadership, Accountability and Ethics*, *8*(4), 86–96.

Sultana, R. G. (2009). Competence and competence frameworks in career guidance: Complex and contested concepts. *International Journal for Educational and Vocational Guidance*, *9*(1), 15–30. doi:10.100710775-008-9148-6

Sun, C. C., & Lin, G. T. (2009). Using fuzzy TOPSIS method for evaluating the competitive advantages of shopping websites. *Expert Systems with Applications*, *36*(9), 11764–11771. doi:10.1016/j.eswa.2009.04.017

Swanson, D., Jin, Y. H., Fawcett, A. M., & Fawcett, S. E. (2017). Collaborative process design: A dynamic capabilities view of mitigating the barriers to working together. *International Journal of Logistics Management*, *28*(2), 571–599. doi:10.1108/IJLM-02-2016-0044

Tiersky, H. (2017*). 5 top challenges to digital transformation in the enterprise*. Available online at:<https://www.cio.com/article/3179607/e-commerce/5-top-challenges-to-digitaltransformation

Toduk, Y. (2014). *2023 Lideri Dijital Çagın Liderlik Sırları* (1st ed.). Dogan Egmont Yayıncılık.

Trepanier, D. (2012). *Define Digital Skills*. Available online at: www.ymcaimpact.ca/content/define-digitalskills#sthash.usCOWpvO.pdf

Tucker, L. R., & MacCallum, R. C. (1997). *Exploratory factor analysis*. Retrieved from https://www.unc.edu/~rcm/book/factor.pdf

Twelfth Malaysia Plan. (2019). *Preparation of the Twelfth Malaysia Plan*. Available online at: http://rmke12.epu.gov.my/

Van Laar, E., Van Deursen, A. J. A. M., Van Dijk, J. A. G. M., & De Haan, J. (2017). The relation between 21st-century skills and digital skills: *A systematic literature review. Computers in Human Behavior*, *72*, 577–588. doi:10.1016/j.chb.2017.03.010

Van Wart, M., Roman, A., Wang, X., & Liu, C. (2019). Operationalizing the definition of e-leadership: Identifying the elements of e-leadership. *International Review of Administrative Sciences*, *85*(1), 80–97. doi:10.1177/0020852316681446

Vidgen, R., Shaw, S., & Grant, D. B. (2017). Management challenges in creating value from business analytics. *European Journal of Operational Research*, *261*(2), 626–639. doi:10.1016/j.ejor.2017.02.023

Waugh, W. L. Jr, & Streib, G. (2006). Collaboration and leadership for effective emergency management. *Public Administration Review*, *66*(s1), 131–140. doi:10.1111/j.1540-6210.2006.00673.x

Westerman, G., Bonnet, D., & McAfee, A. (2014). *Leading digital: turning technology into business transformation*. Harvard Business Press.

Williams, B., Onsman, A., & Brown, T. (2010). Exploratory factor analysis: A five-step guide for novices. *Australasian Journal of Paramedicine, 8*(3).

Wilson, A., Lenssen, G., & Hind, P. (2006). *Leadership qualities and management competencies for corporate responsibility*. Academic Press.

Winterton, J., Delamare-Le Deist, F., & Stringfellow, E. (2005). *Typology of knowledge, skills and competences: clarification of the concept and prototype*. Office for Official Publications of the European Communities.

World Economic Forum. (2018). *Digital Transformation Initiative - Unlocking $100 Trillion for Business and Society from Digital Transformation*. Available online at: http://reports.weforum.org/digitaltransformation/wpcontent/blogs.dir/94/mp/files/pages/files/dti-executive-summary-

Chapter 3
Impact of COVID-19 Vaccines on Tourism Demand and Culture

Xuan Tran
https://orcid.org/0000-0001-9521-5722
University of West Florida, USA

ABSTRACT

The low supply of vaccines for COVID-19 has disrupted tourism development in Asia. The question is if the vaccine may change cultural divergence into cultural convergence at the tourist destination. The purpose of this study is to examine the culture and price elasticity of hotel demand to find the cultural convergence. The study has conducted autoregressive distributed lag model to test whether the vaccine would change the price and income elasticities of hotel demand to find the cultural transformation from divergence to convergence through tourism. Findings indicate that the impact of the vaccine on transferring culture from divergence to convergence was confirmed. Tourists from the divergent cultures specified by less levels of Hofstede's cultural dimensions will visit the country destination with high levels of Hofstede's cultural dimensions after COVID vaccination. Japan and the US that possess divergent levels of power will visit Vietnam for power convergence. China, Korea, and Russia that possess divergent levels of indulgence will visit Vietnam for indulgence convergence.

INTRODUCTION

COVID-19 has negatively affected tourism that brings different cultures together. Previous tourism demand models have not caught the exogenous variables of vaccines and cultures. It is necessary to have an updated model of tourism demand with COVID vaccines.

COVID-19, a pandemic caused by severe acute respiratory syndrome coronavirus 2, emerged in January 2020 in China and spread to the world quickly. More than 30 million people are infected and people from different cultures have worked to develop the vaccines for the coronavirus. As a result, there have been 165 coronavirus vaccines (Corum, Wee, & Zimmer, 2020). As of today, around 748 million (9.6%)

DOI: 10.4018/978-1-7998-8678-5.ch003

people have been fully vaccinated (OurWorldData, 2021) and most of them are from US, China, and Russia (Figure 1). The big question is whether or not the different cultures of the wealthiest countries such as the US, China, and Russia will converge even though they have been competing in producing the vaccines recently.

Figure 1.

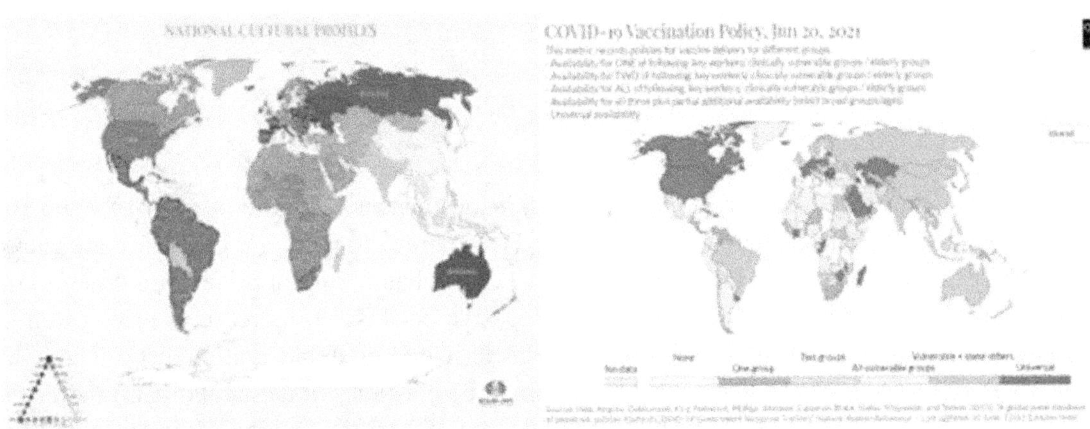

Source: Hammer, 2014 and Our World in Data, 2021.

The American, Chinese, and Russian tourists are now safe to travel to the most controllable countries in the world in handling the COVID-19 outbreak. According to Minh (2021), Vietnam is the second-top country in the world in handling the COVID-19 outbreak after New Zealand. The purpose of this study is thus to examine the vaccinated tourists' behavior of American, Chinese, Russian, Japanese, and Korean who are the top tourist arrivals in Vietnam in 2020 through the price and income elasticities of demand to see the trend of the cultures.

Elasticity is a measurement of preference for utility of people based on their limit income versus market price. The preference for utility of people including the need for personal and cultural satisfaction must be assessed after the damage of the COVID-19 using the elasticity. The vaccines that have recovered the damage of tourism connections can enhance human cultural understanding. Therefore, elasticity can be used to measure the impacts of COVID-19 vaccines on cultural understanding.

Price elasticity of demand (PED) indicates the relative change of tourism demand when a unit price of a tourist product changes. The absolute PED will be elastic if it is greater 1 and inelastic if it is <1. If the PED is nearly 0, the price will not affect the demand. Income elasticity of demand (YED) shows the relative change of tourism demand when a tourist's income changes. If the YED is positive, the tourism product will be normal or luxury. If the YED is negative, the tourism product will be inferior and obsolete. If the YED is nearly 0, the income will not affect the demand; a change in tourists' income does not affect their visits. Coefficients of variance (CV) that indicates a level of difference from the culture shows the level of change in tourists' behavior will be smaller (culture convergence) or bigger (culture divergence) after COVID-19 than before.

LITERATURE

Price and Income Elasticities of Tourists' Demand

Price elasticity of demand (PED) indicates the relative change of tourism demand when a unit price of a tourist product/service changes. It is measured by the following formula:

$$PED = \frac{\Delta Q / Q}{\Delta P / P}$$

where: PED: Price elasticity of demand Q_i: Tourist demand measured by the number of hotel rooms sold at time *i*. ΔQ: $Q_j - Q_i$ The change of tourist demand from time *i* to time *j* P_i: Unit price measured by the average daily rate of hotel rooms at time *i*. ΔP: $P_j - P_i$ The change of unit price from time *i* to time *j*

The price elasticity of demand (PED) is usually negative because an increase in price often leads to a decrease in demand. The absolute PED will be elastic if it is greater 1 and inelastic if it is <1. If PED is nearly 0, the price will not affect the demand. Income elasticity of demand (YED) indicates the relative change of tourism demand when an average income of a tourist changes. It is measured by the following formula:

$$YED = \frac{\Delta Q / Q}{\Delta y / y}$$

Where: YED: Income elasticity of demand Q_i: Tourist demand measured by the number of hotel rooms sold at time *i*. ΔQ: $Q_j - Q_i$ The change of tourist demand from time *i* to time *j*

Y_i: *Tourist income measured by gross domestic product per capita (GDPpc) of the original at time* i.
ΔY: $Y_j - Y_i$ The change of tourist income from time *i* to time *j*

Income elasticity of demand shows the relative change of tourism demand when a tourist's income changes. If it is positive, the good will be normal or luxury. If it is negative, the good will be inferior. If YED is nearly 0, the visit package will be sticky and the change in income has no effect on the visit package purchased.

During the pandemic, when vaccinated tourists decide to visit a destination, they really want to meet their need for travel. As a result, the price of the package or the change in their income will not affect their demand. That is, the price elasticity of their demand and the income elasticity of their demand are nearly zero (Aguiló, Riera, and Rosselló, 2005; Uner, Kose, and Gokten, 2008; Brida, Risso, and Carrera, 2008; Garin-Munoz, 2009; Bonham, Gangnes, and Zhou, 2009; Dritsakis and Gialetaki, 2004; Fernandes and Karnik, 2010; Görmüs and Göçer, 2010; Hanim, Osman, Noor, & Hasim, 2010; Thompson and Thompson, 2010; Veloce, 2004; Yang, Lin, & Han, 2010).

Convergence of Gene Evolution and Social Learning Culture

Boyd and Richerson (1985) and Cavalli-Sforza and Feldman (1981) report that human affective and cognitive mechanisms are a combination between genes and social learning culture. During the COVID-19 pandemic. Hill and Boyd (2021) found that "places where hunter-gatherers are more polygynous, there also tend to be more polygynous birds and mammals" (p. 236).

Tourist Behavioural and Cultural Convergence

Culture is the growth of personality traits (Lynn, 2000). Hofstede and McCrae (2004) studied that personality scores from 33 countries were significantly and substantially correlated with culture dimension scores in which traits are predictors of cultures. High Neuroticism trait is a predictor for Uncertainty Avoidance and Masculinity cultures. Low Agreeableness is a predictor for Uncertainty Avoidance culture. Low Extraversion is a predictor for Power Distance culture. High Conscientiousness is a predictor for Power Distance. High Extraversion is a predictor of Individualism. High Neuroticism and Openness are predictors of Masculinity (Hofstede & McCrae, 2004).

Hofstede (1991) divided culture into uncertainty avoidance, power distance, individualism, masculinity, indulgence, and long term. Based on the theories of human needs from Maslow (1943) and McClelland (1961), According to Hofstede (2001), individualism is the culture in which human needs balance between individual goals and company goals. Indulgence is the culture in which human needs attempt to avoid restriction to relax. Power Distance is the culture in which human needs seek protection from a superior. Masculinity is the culture in which human needs seek out career and money, rather than social values and environment. Uncertainty Avoidance is the culture in which human needs rigidly follow rules to avoid nervous stress. Long-term orientation is the culture in which human needs look for future rewards.

Culture or national character is "relatively enduring personality characteristics and patterns that are modal among adult members of the society" (Inkeles & Levinson, 1969). Hofstede (1991) has used factor analysis to cluster the six culture dimensions from a matrix of 32 values questions for 40 countries, surveying a wide variety of individuals including country elites, employees, managers, consumers, and civil servants through IBM data between 1990 and 2002. In this study, Hofstede's (1991, 2001) cultural dimensions have been used as a tool given its validity and reliability across multiple countries. Hofstede (1991) has combined the empirically statistical findings to name two top values in one dimension related with people for Eastern and Western cultures, which are Power distance (Safety and the need for power) and Individualism (Actualization), respectively. In the other dimension related with traits, Hofstede identified Uncertainty Avoidance and Masculinity. Finally, Hofstede (2010) has added Indulgence (happiness) for the East.

In sum, the convergence of six cultural dimensions becomes the East and the West. The East psychology including Indulgence, Long-term orientation, and Power Distance. (Hofstede, 2001). The West culture "transformed human psychology into that observed today in "WEIRD" (Western, educated, industrialized, rich, democratic) societies, where individualism is paramount, rather than the psychology of traditional societies" (Hill and Boyd, 2021, p. 235). During the COVID-19 vaccination, the tourists might seek for what they lack of; that is, the East tourists might seek for indulgence whereas the West tourists might seek for power. Figure 2 and Table 1 indicate the convergence of cultures in the top 3 inbound tourist countries (France, the US, and Spain) as well as Vietnam.

France with Switzerland, US, and China. Each of the top five arrival countries has one Hofstede's score less than France in terms of Uncertainty Avoidance (France (86)> Switzerland (58) > US (46)>China (30)).

Spain with UK, Germany, and France. Each of the top five arrival countries has one Hofstede's score less than Spain in terms of Power (Spain (57)> Germany (35), UK(35)) and Uncertainty Avoidance (Spain (86)>Germany (65)>UK (35))

US with Mexico, Canada, Japan. Each of the top five arrival countries has one Hofstede's score less than the US in terms of Individualism (US (91)> Canada (80) > Japan (46> Mexico (30)).

VN with US, China, Russia, Japanese and Korean. Each of the top five arrival countries has one Hofstede's score less than Vietnam in terms of Power (Vietnam (70)> Japan (54) > US (40)) and Indulgence (Vietnam (35)>Korea (29)>China (24)>Russia (20))

Figure 2.

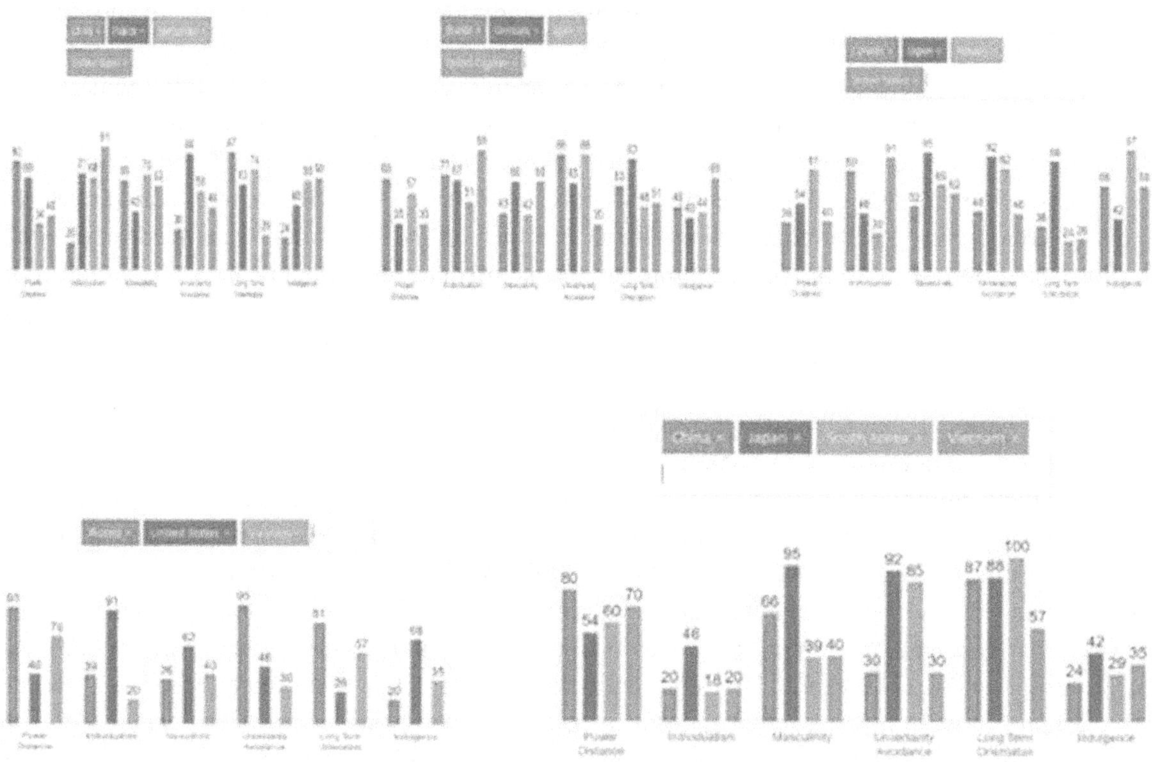

Previous literature has suggested that globalization has resulted in a converged income (Bullmore, 2000; Assael, 1998) resulting in tourist demands growing increasingly. Aguiló, Riera, and Rosselló (2005), Uner, Kose, and Gokten (2008), Brida, Risso, and Carrera, (2008), Garin-Munoz (2009), Bonham, Gangnes, and Zhou (2009), Dritsakis and Gialetaki, (2004), Fernandes and Karnik (2010), Görmüs and Göçer (2010), Hanim, Osman, Noor, and Hasim (2010), Thompson and Thompson, (2010), Veloce (2004), and Yang, Lin, and Han (2010) report that tourists from the US, China, Russia, Japan, and South Korea were not affected by income or price when they travel in critical circumstances.

Table 1.

	France	US	Spain	Vietnam
UA	86>Sw(58), US(46),CN(30)		86>Ger(65), UK(35)	
Individualism		91>Ca(80),Jp(46),Me(30)		
PD			57>Ger(35), UK(35)	70>US(40), JP (54), KR(60)
Indulgence				35>KR(29), CN(24)

Therefore, the present study has assumed vaccinated tourists tend to visit Vietnam for cultural convergence and they would be driven by ecological developing pattern, especially COVID-19 control. During the pandemic, the vaccinated tourists from the above five countries visit Vietnam to meet their lack of cultures will be assumed to have the price and income elasticities of demand are nearly zero.

Hypothesis 1: The price elasticity of vaccinated Chinese tourists' demand in Vietnam would be nearly zero.

Hypothesis 2: The income elasticity of vaccinated Chinese tourists' demand in Vietnam would be nearly zero.

Hypothesis 3: The price elasticity of vaccinated Japanese tourists' demand in Vietnam would be nearly zero.

Hypothesis 4: The income elasticity of vaccinated Japanese tourists' demand in Vietnam would be nearly zero.

Hypothesis 5: The price elasticity of vaccinated South Korean tourists' demand in Vietnam would be nearly zero.

Hypothesis 6: The income elasticity of vaccinated South Korean tourists' demand in Vietnam would be nearly zero.

Hypothesis 7: The price elasticity of vaccinated American tourists' demand in Vietnam would be nearly zero.

Hypothesis 8: The income elasticity of vaccinated American tourists' demand in Vietnam would be nearly zero.

Hypothesis 9: The price elasticity of vaccinated Russian tourists' demand in Vietnam would be nearly zero.

Hypothesis 10: The income elasticity of vaccinated Russian tourists' demand in Vietnam would be nearly zero.

Hypothesis 11: The price elasticity of vaccinated resident Vietnamese tourists' demand in Vietnam would be nearly zero.

Hypothesis 12: The income elasticity of vaccinated resident Vietnamese tourists' demand in Vietnam would be nearly zero.

Hypothesis 13: At the tourist destination in Vietnam, the vaccinated tourists from the East would prefer indulgence but the tourists from the West would prefer power.

METHODOLOGY

Sample

The present study has selected Vietnam as a sample for this study during COVID-19 vaccination because of the following reasons:

1. Vietnam is the second-best performer around the world in handling the COVID-19 outbreak (after New Zealand) (Minh, 2021).
2. It includes InterContinental (World's Best Awards, 2017)
3. It is selected as the top ten beaches by TripAdvisor (2017)
4. The top tourist arrivals in Danang are from US, Russia, Korea, Japan, and China, that have been most related to Vietnam in culture during the last 65 years (1954-2019) and are the top 20 richest countries in the world.
5. Each of the top five arrival countries has one Hofstede's score less than Vietnam in terms of Power (Vietnam (70)> Japan (54) > US (40)) and Indulgence (Vietnam (35)>Korea (29)>China (24)>Russia (20))
6. Four of the five countries are positioning as the top score in Hofstede's cultural dimensions in the world (Korea: Long term (100), Russia: Uncertainty Avoidance (95), US: Individualism (91), Japan: Masculinity (95)).

Data were retrieved daily during the COVID-19 from January 31, 2020, till March 21, 2021. This is the secondary data. The participants are the guests in 5,241 guestrooms during the 420-day period from Jan 2013- to March 2021 including Chinese, Korean, American, Japanese, and Russian from 24 properties; about 16% of total hotel class number of guestrooms and 11,965 upscale guestrooms from 38 properties; about 36% of total hotel class number of guestrooms in the four big cities: Hanoi (HN), Ho Chi Minh (HCM), Danang (DN), and Nhatrang (NT).

The secondary data of COVID-vaccination were retrieved from Center for Disease Control and Prevention (CDC) (2021) and the World bank (2021). Data of tourists' incomes were gross domestic product per capita of the tourists' countries retrieved from World bank (2021). The data from CDC include the COVID-19 cases and vaccines of 6 countries during the 420 days. They are the United States, China, Japan, South Korea, Russia, and Vietnam. The assumption of the study is the hotel guests are vaccinated.

Data of hotel price were average daily rate at the destination and original country of the tourists retrieved from Smith Travel Research (2021). As of January 2020, the hotel prices (average daily rates) for Vietnam and substitutes are (1) $134.97 in Vietnam from 115,265 guestrooms in 967 properties, (2) $125.45 in the US from 5,333,882 guestrooms in 55,661 properties, (3) $69.74 in China from 2,987,050 guestrooms in 19,389 properties, (4) $126.09 in Japan from 733,949 guestrooms in 4,582 properties, (5) $82.48 in Russia from 181,569 guestrooms in 1,816 properties, and (6) $108.72 in the South Korea from 95,285 guestrooms in 380 properties.

Hotel price elasticity (PED_d) for Vietnam is the coefficient of the hotel price *P* measured by average daily rate. Hotel price elasticity (PED_k) for country *k* is the coefficient of the hotel substitute price RP_k in the hotel demand. Income elasticity (YED_k) is the coefficients of the income of guests from country *k* in the following hotel log demand retrieved from Tran (2015).

$$Qt = F(Ykt\text{-}j, Pt\text{-}j, RPkt\text{-}j) \quad (1)$$

$$lnQ_t = \gamma 0 + \mathring{a}\ PED_d\ lnP_{t-j} + \mathring{a}YED\ lnY_{kt-j} + \mathring{a}PED_k\ lnRP_{kt-j} + dummies + u_t \quad (2)$$

where *Qt* is the number of hotel room nights sold in Vietnam every day from January 31, 2020 till March 21, 2021. *PEDd* is the price elasticity of demand for Vietnamese. *PEDk* is the price elasticity of demand for country *k*. YED_k is the income elasticity of demand for country *k*. *Ykt-j* is the per capita income of a country kth at time *t-j (t lag j)*, including the US, China, Russia, South Korea, Japan, and domestic Vietnamese tourists. *Pt-j* is the average daily rate of hotels in Vietnam at time t lag j. *RPkt-j* is the average daily rate of hotels in country *k* at time *t-j*. u_t is the error term that captures all other factors that may influence the number of rooms sold at time t.

Auto Regressive Distributed Lag (ARDL)

This paper uses an ARDL model on data from a number of daily macroeconomic variables between Jan 2020 to March 2021. Tourism and lodging demand relates to time series behavior of consumers that varies over time. As a result, the relationships among time series variables may cause spurious regression, which shows relationship much more than they should at the nominal test level.

This study has used ADLM bound and F-tests proposed by Pesaran, Shin, and Smith (2001). This test does not require unit root tests nor a large sample size (Narayan, 2005). In addition, it removes omitted variables and autocorrelation.

Equation (1) is tested by ADLM as follows:

$$\Delta\ lnQ_{kt} = \alpha_0 + \mathring{a}^p\ \Psi_Q \Delta\ lnQ_{kt-j} + \mathring{a}^p\Psi_Y \Delta\ lnY_{kt-j} + \mathring{a}^p\Psi_{RP} \Delta\ lnRP_{kt-j} + \mathring{a}^p\ \Pi_j\ lnQ_{kt-j} + \mathring{a}^p\Pi_j\ lnY_{kt-j} + \mathring{a}^p\ \Pi_j\ lnRP_{kt-j} + dummies + \varepsilon t \quad (2)$$

where Δ is the first difference ($\Delta X_t = X_t - X_{t-1}$). Lag p is obtained using Akaike Information Criterion (AIC).

Equation (2) describes the short and long-run relationships between the hotel demand and its determinants. The Ψ coefficients in equation (2) describe the short-run relationships. The Π coefficients describe long run relationships.

In order to test the long run relationships, F-test is employed to test the null hypotheses of no cointegration among variables. Pesaran and Shin (1998), Pesaran, Shin, and Smith (2001) provide the critical values of the lower and the upper bounds. If the F-statistic is higher than the upper bound, there will be long-run relationships. If the F-statistic is below the lower bound, there is no long-run relationship. If it is between these bounds, the result is inconclusive. When there is a long-run relationship, t-test is applied with the null hypothesis $\Pi_1 = 0$. If the null hypothesis is rejected, there will be long term relationships among the hotel luxury and independent demands in HoChiMinh, Hanoi, and Danang and 5

Table 2.

	Vietnam	China	Japan	Russia	US	Korea
Uncertainty Avoidance (UA)	30	30	92	95	46	85
Individual (INDV)	20	20	46	39	91	18
Masculine (MAS)	40	66	95	36	62	39
Power to Distance (PD)	70	80	54	93	40	60
Long term (LT)	57	87	88	81	26	100
Indulgence (INDU)	35	24	42	20	68	29

Source: Hofstede (2001)

origin countries (US, Russia, China, Korea, and Japan). After confirming there are short and long run relationships, the cofficients for short and long run will measure the elasticity that reflects the level of demand change by price or income.

In measuring convergence of the convergence, we used De Mooij's method (2003) with the formula of Williamson and Fleming (1996, 349-350), in which

$$MC/year = 100^* \ (CVt_1 - CVt_2)/\ [CVt_1{}^*(t_2 - t_1)]$$

Where *MC/year* is percent mean of convergence per year, CVt_1—coefficient of variation at the earlier date, CVt_2—coefficient of variation at the later date, t_1—the earlier date, and t_2—the later date.

The coefficient of variation is measure by $CV = \sigma/\mu$ *100 where CV is the percentage reflecting the convergence level, σ is the standard deviation and μ is the mean.

The interpretation of the CV of the process is that if the CV decreases after vaccination, it means convergence of the variable.

RESULTS

The top six hotel guest countries in Vietnam whose demand represents one of Hofstede's cultural dimensions in Table 2 are described as follows.

1. Vietnam hotel guest residents possess higher score of indulgence (its score of 35) than other three countries in the sample (Russia, China, and Korea).
2. US hotel guests possess the highest score of individualism (its score of 91) of all countries in the sample.
3. Russia hotel guests possess the highest score of uncertainty avoidance (its score of 95) of all countries in the sample.
4. China hotel guests possess a higher score of power distance orientation (its score of 80) than four countries in the sample (US, Vietnam, Korea, and Japan).
5. South Korea hotel guests possess the highest score of long-term orientation (its score of 100) of all countries in the sample.

6. Finally, Japan hotel guests possess the highest score of masculinity (its score of 95) of all countries in the sample.

The study has conducted E-VIEWS 11 to find the significant long run relationships. Table 3 summarized the results of the six tests for tourist demand functions from equation 4 as follows.

Table 3.

Vietnam Hotels	China	Russia	VN	US	Japan	Korea
R^2	.708	.702	.805	.712	.74	.713
Adjusted R^2	.607	.601	.704	.611	.71	.682
F-stat	32.2	32.6	32.7	32.5	32.1	32.3
Prob (F-stat)	0.00	0.00	0.00	0.00	0.00	0.00
Durbin-Watson	1.74	1.89	1.85	1.73	1.82	1.82
AIC (lag 2)	-7.82*	-7.96*	-8.30*	-8.15*	-8.12*	9.40*
RESET	13.3*	12.65*	13.22*	15.4*	13.9*	13.5*

Note: (1)** and * represent 1% and 5% significance levels, respectively. (2) Durbin-Watson test for autocorrelation (3) AIC: Akaike information criterion test for serial correlation at lag 2; RESET: Ramsey's Regression Equation Error Test with one augmentation term

Table 4 indicates the convergence of the process. Data were divided into two stages. Stage 1 (Jan 31, 2020, to Nov 30, 2020) and Stage 2 (Dec 1, 2020, to Mar 25, 2021) based on the date of available vaccination in the last country of the six country participants. We assumed all the hotel guests in the study were vaccinated after December 1, 2020.

The coefficients of variance in Table 4 and the mean of convergence in Table 5 confirm the convergence of power and indulgence cultures of tourists in Vietnam. Table 5 shows that the absolute values of the price and income elasticities of tourists' demand ranges from 0 to 0.05. Therefore, all hypotheses 1-13 were confirmed.

DISCUSSION

In this study, elasticity index is used to measure vaccinated tourists' preferences for their selections to visit Vietnam during the pandemic. The price and income elasticities of tourists' demand are almost zero reflecting they really want to explore and meet their cultural needs no matter what the change in prices and income.

Tourists from the divergent cultures specified by less levels of Hofstede's cultural dimensions will visit the country destination with high levels of Hofstede's cultural dimensions after COVID-vaccination. Japan and the US that possess divergent levels of power will visit Vietnam for power convergence.

Table 4.

Item	Mean (1)	Mean (2)	SD (1)	SD (2)	CV (1)	CV (2)
China Case	87045	101415	11454	153	0.1	0.0
China Vaccine	4516935	66412427	12002368	12796069	2.7	0.2
Japan Case	107108	450543	131754	6860	1.2	0.0
Japan Vaccine	1289	450262	7002	231509	5.4	0.5
S. Korea Case	27964	97069	25660	2331	0.9	0.0
S. Korea Vaccine	4627	637416	35741	87316.2	7.7	0.1
Russia Case	1355554	4364183	1333892	49999	1.0	0.0
Russia Vaccine	119899	8487954	848556	1407123	7.1	0.2
US Case	8545200	29584223	9096113	296289	1.1	0.0
US Vaccine	6464510	114785824	18057887	12983181	2.8	0.1
Vietnam Case	862	2557	668	18	0.8	0.0
Vietnam Vaccine	1	22710	18	14654	20.1	0.6
US ADR	94.1	95.8	17.5	9.1	0.2	0.1
China ADR	56.5	63.8	6.9	1.4	0.1	0.0
Japan ADR	105.2	102.4	17.7	14.3	0.2	0.1
Vietnam ADR	98.9	94.6	10.6	2.7	0.1	0.0
Korea ADR	103.3	118.0	11.1	5.3	0.1	0.0
Russia ADR	63.0	67.3	10.6	5.0	0.2	0.1
US Income	64312.7	63023.9	567.6	177.4	0.0	0.0
China Income	10490.7	10847.8	157.3	49.2	0.0	0.0
Japan Income	39721.8	39034.0	302.9	94.7	0.0	0.0
Vietnam Income	3453.0	3500.0	20.7	6.5	0.0	0.0
Korea Income	31319.7	30630.0	303.8	95.0	0.0	0.0
Russia Income	10878.2	9952.8	407.6	127.4	0.0	0.0
US Demand	1849189.4	1913885.9	721571.4	371769.5	0.4	0.2
China Demand	42508239.3	43969579.6	15467621.0	8225763.0	0.4	0.2
Japan Demand	8256551.2	7768777.4	3539741.3	1607368.8	0.4	0.2
Vietnam Demand	793606.4	773570.3	314458.9	82653.5 0.4	0.1	0.0
Korea Demand	1044826.1	990278.0	269553.7	64510.4 0.3	0.1	0.0
Russia Demand	1827983.0	2414236.2	940369.6	243587.1	0.5	0.1

Source: CDC (2021), STR (2021), & Author's Calculations

Table 5.

Elasticity	Period 1	Period 2	Mean	Standard Deviation	Mean of convergence/day
VNYED	-0.00035	-0.001	-0.000670	.000461	0
VNPED	0.006	-0.001540	.00223	0.005332	0
USYED	-0.00014	3.60E-05	-5.1E-05	0.000122	0
USPED	0.05	0.005	0.0275	0.03182	0
CNYED	0.000169	-6.61E-05	5.15E-05	0.000166	0
CNPED	0.00117	-0.000989	.35E-05	0.001522	0
JPYED	1.80E-05	-1.36E-05	2.2E-06	2.23E-05	0
JPPED	-0.0014	-0.00056	-0.000980	.000593	0
KRYED	-0.00011	-0.00021	-0.00016	7.35E-05	0
KRPED	0.00135	-0.0002	0.000575	0.001096	0
RUYED	-0.0001	0.000126	1.15E-05	0.000162	0
RUPED	0.013	-0.008	0.0025	0.014849	0
VN Vac			0.20	0.03	0
US Vac			0.07	0.02	0
CN Vac			0.04	0.01	0
JP Vac			0.03	0.01	0
KR Vac			0.07	0.08	0
RU Vac			0.09	0.06	0

Source: Author's Calculations

China, Korea, and Russia that possess divergent levels of indulgence will visit Vietnam for indulgence convergence. The empirical study has supported the discovery of the convergence of gene evolution and social learning culture (Hill & Boyd, 2021). Thanks to vaccinated tourists' behaviour, different cultures have been proved to converge in a tourism demand model controlling for vaccination.

Without identifying the difference and forecasting the cultural convergence in tourism during the post epidemic of COVID-19, hotel marketers could make a big loss for the hospitality, tourism, and travel in the country. Globalization has resulted in an increasingly convergent income and power as well as indulgence. This paper has extended Hofstede's findings about wealth correlates not only to power distance but also to indulgence. Prediction of cultural dimensions in hotel demand is important for hotel marketing and management.

In this paper, Autoregressive Distributed Lag Model has been used to forecast a long-run relationship.

A limitation of this study is in the relatively small scope of the hotel sample in Vietnam, which may limit the applicability of these findings to other hotel markets. This study also develops theory of motivation (McClelland, 1961) in Hofstede's (1991) factor analyses in seeing the association between need for power and achievement for indulgence. Finally, the paper has contributed to hotel investment when forecasting target markets through culture; the two cultural dimensions: Power Distance and Indulgence are correlated. The findings of this paper have contributed to the understanding of price and income elasticities in microeconomics, and thereby further emphasizing its role as key tools to explain cultural perspectives to maximize future business revenue.

REFERENCES

Abrate, G., Fraquelli, G., & Viglia, G. (2012). Dynamic pricing strategies: Evidence from European hotels. *International Journal of Hospitality Management*, *31*(1), 160–168. doi:10.1016/j.ijhm.2011.06.003

Aguilo, E., Riera, A., & Rossello, J. (2005). The Short-Term Price Effect of a Tourist Tax through a Dynamic Demand Model: The Case of the Balearic Islands. *Tourism Management*, *26*(3), 359–365. doi:10.1016/j.tourman.2003.07.005

Assael, H. (1998). *Consumer Behavior and Marketing Action* (6th ed.). South Western College Publishing.

Blodgett, J. G., Bakir, A., & Rose, G. (2008). A test of the validity of Hofstede's cultural framework. *Journal of Consumer Marketing*, *25*(6), 339–349. doi:10.1108/07363760810902477

Bonham, C., Gangnes, B., & Zhou, T. (2009). Modeling Tourism: A Fully Identified VECM Approach. *International Journal of Forecasting*, *25*(3), 531–549. doi:10.1016/j.ijforecast.2008.11.014 PMID:32287620

Boyd, R., & Richerson, P. (1985). *Culture and the Evolutionary Process*. Univ. of Chicago Press.

Brida, J. G., Risso, W. A., & Carrera, E. J. S. (2008). A Long-Run Equilibrium Demand Function: Tourism in Mexico. *Tourismos*, 3.

Bullmore, J. (2000). Alice in Disneyland, a creative view of international advertising. In J. P. Jones (Ed.), *International Advertising, Realities and Myths*. Sage. doi:10.4135/9781452231334.n4

Burt, S. (1989). Trends and management issues in European retailing. *International Journal of Retailing*, *4*(4), 2–22. doi:10.1108/EUM0000000002924

Cavalli-Sforza, L., & Feldman, M. (1981). *Cultural Transmission and Evolution*. Princeton Univ. Press.

Corum, J., Wee, S., & Zimmer, C. (2020). Coronavirus vaccine tracker. *New York Times*. Available online as of 23 September 2020: https://www.nytimes.com/interactive/2020/science/coronavirus-vaccine-tracker.html

Crampon, L. J., & Tan, K. T. (1973). A Model of Tourism Flow into the Pacific. *Tourism Review*, *28*(3), 98–104.

De Mooij, M. (2004). *Consumer behavior and culture: Consequences for global marketing*. Sage.

De Mooij, M. (2009). *Global marketing and advertising: Understanding cultural paradoxes* (3rd ed.). Sage.

De Mooij, M., & Hofstede, G. (2002). Convergence and divergence in consumer behavior: Implications for international retailing. *Journal of Retailing*, *78*(1), 61–69. doi:10.1016/S0022-4359(01)00067-7

Dritsakis, N., & Gialetaki, K. (2004). Cointegration Analysis of Tourism Revenues by the Member Countries of European Union to Greece. *Tourism Analysis*, *9*(3), 179–186. doi:10.3727/1083542042781258

Du, F., Yang, F., Liang, L., & Yang, M. (2016). Do service providers adopting market segmentation need cooperation with third parties?: An application to hotels. *International Journal of Contemporary Hospitality Management*, *28*(1), 136–155. doi:10.1108/IJCHM-01-2014-0014

Fernandes, C., & Karnik, A. V. (2010). Estimating Elasticity of Demand for Tourism in Dubai. *Tourism Analysis*, *15*(1), 57–69. doi:10.3727/108354210X12724734223630

Garin-Munoz, T., & Montero-Martin, L. F. (2007). Tourism in the Balearic Islands: A Dynamic Model for International Demand Using Panel Data. *Tourism Management*, *28*(5), 1224–1235. doi:10.1016/j.tourman.2006.09.024

Google. (2020). *COVID-19 Community Mobility Reports*. As of 23 September 2020:https://www.google.com/covid19/mobility/

Gormus, S., & Gocer, I. (2010). The Socio-economic Determinants of Tourism Demand in Turkey: A Panel Data Approach. *International Research Journal of Finance and Economics*, *55*, 88–99.

Guizzardi, A., Emanuele, F., & Ranieri, E. (2017). Advance booking and hotel price variability online: Any opportunity for business customers? *International Journal of Hospitality Management*, *64*, 85–93. doi:10.1016/j.ijhm.2017.05.002

Hagist, C., & Kotlikoff, L. (2009). *Who's going broke? Comparing growth in public healthcare expenditure in ten OECD countries*. Hacienda Pública Española.

Halliburton, C., & Hunerberg, R. (2005). Pan-European marketing ten years after 1993—A current appraisal and proposed conceptual framework. In E. Kaynak & F. Jallat (Eds.), *Marketing issues in Western Europe —Changes and developments* (pp. 16–29). Routledge. doi:10.1300/J037v14n01_02

HammerJ. (2014). Available online at https://www.youtube.com/watch?v=wKydlMWHwSc

Hanim, N., Osman, R., Noor, A. H. A. M., & Hasim, M. S. (2010). Malaysian Tourism Demand from the Middle East Market: A Preliminary Analysis. *Journal Antarabangsa Kajian Asia Barat*, *2*(1), 37–52.

Hill, K., & Boyd, R. (2021). Behavioral convergence in humans and animals. *Science*, *271*(6526), 235–236. doi:10.1126cience.abf7572 PMID:33446544

Hofstede, G. (1991). Cultures and Organizations, Software of the Mind. London: McGraw Hill.

Hofstede, G. (2001). *Culture's Consequences* (2nd ed.). Sage.

Hofstede, G., & McCrae, R. (2004). Personality and Culture Revisited: Linking Traits and Dimensions of Culture. *Cross-Cultural Research*, *38*(1), 52–88. doi:10.1177/1069397103259443

Inkeles, A., & Levinson, D. J. (1969). National character: The study of modal personality and sociocultural systems. The Handbook of Social Psychology, 4, 418-506.

Ivanov, S., & Zhechev, V. (2012). Hotel revenue management-a critical literature review. *Tourism (Zagreb), 60*(2), 175–197.

Kaynak, E., & Jallat, F. (2005). *Marketing in Western Europe: A monolith or a multidimensional market?* In E. Kaynak & F. Jallat (Eds.), *Marketing issues in Western Europe—Changes and developments* (pp. 4–9). Routledge.

Leeflang, P. S. H., & van Raaij, W. F. (1995). The changing consumer in the European Union: A "metaanalysis. *International Journal of Research in Marketing, 12*(5), 373–387. doi:10.1016/0167-8116(95)00031-3

Lemmens, A., Croux, C., & Dekimpe, M. G. (2005). The European consumer: United in diversity? ERIM Report Series Research in Management. Reference No. ERS- 2005-022-MKT, Erasmus University, Rotterdam, The Netherlands.

Levitt, T. (1983). The globalization of markets. *Harvard Business Review, 61*(3), 92–102.

Lim, C., & McAleer, M. (2002). A Cointegration Analysis of Annual Tourism Demand by Malaysia for Australia. *Mathematics and Computers in Simulation, 59*(1-3), 197–205. doi:10.1016/S0378-4754(01)00408-6

Lim, C., Min, J. C. H., & McAleer, M. (2008). Modelling Income Effects on Long and Short Haul International Travel from Japan. *Tourism Management, 29*(6), 1099–1109. doi:10.1016/j.tourman.2008.02.012

Lynn, M. (2000). National Personality and Tipping Customs. *Personality and Individual Differences, 28*(2), 395–404. doi:10.1016/S0191-8869(99)00109-9

Manrai & Manrai. (2001). Cultural issues in the cross-cultural and cross-national consumer research in the new millennium. *Journal of East-West Business, 7*(1), 1–10.

Maslow, A. H. (1943). A theory of human motivation. *Psychological Review, 50*(4), 370–396. doi:10.1037/h0054346

McClelland, D. (1961). *A scoring manual*. Cambridge University Press. doi:10.1017/CBO9780511527937.011

Minh, N. (2021). Vietnam ranks second in world Covid-19 response. *VietnamExpress.* Available online at https://e.vnexpress.net/news/news/vietnam-ranks-second-in-world-covid-19-response-4227749.html

Njegovan, N. (2005). A Leading Indicator Approach to Predicting Short-Term Shifts in Demand for Business Travel by Air to and from the UK. *Journal of Forecasting, 24*(6), 421–432. doi:10.1002/for.961

Njegovan, N. (2006). Elasticities of Demand for Leisure Air Travel: A System Modelling Approach. *Journal of Air Transport Management, 12*(1), 33–39. doi:10.1016/j.jairtraman.2005.09.003

Our World Data. (2021). Available online at https://ourworldindata.org/covid-vaccinations?country=OWID_WRL

Parker, P. (1992). Price elasticity dynamics over the adoption life cycle. *JMR, Journal of Marketing Research, 24*(3), 358–367. doi:10.1177/002224379202900306

Pesaran, M. H., & Shin, Y. (1998). An autoregressive distributed-lag modelling approach to cointegration analysis. *Econometric Society Monographs*, *31*, 371–413. doi:10.1017/CCOL0521633230.011

Pesaran, M. H., Shin, Y., & Smith, R. J. (2001). Bounds testing approaches to the analysis of level relationships. *Journal of Applied Econometrics*, *16*(3), 289–326. doi:10.1002/jae.616

Schmidt, R. A. (1996). Serving the Euro-consumer: A marketing challenge or a case for intervention? *Marketing Intelligence & Planning*, *14*(5), 14–19. doi:10.1108/02634509610127527

Sciglimpaglia, D., & Saghafi, M. (2005). Marketing consequences of European internal market unification: An executive perspective. *Journal of Euromarketing*, *14*(1/2), 35–57. doi:10.1300/J037v14n01_03

Smith Travel Research. (2019). https://www.str.com/

Smith Travel Research. (2021). https://www.str.com/

Su, X. (2007). Intertemporal pricing with strategic consumer behavior. *Management Science*, *53*(5), 726–741. doi:10.1287/mnsc.1060.0667

Suh, T., & Kwon, L.-W. (2002). Globalization and reluctant buyers. *International Marketing Review*, *19*(6), 663–680. doi:10.1108/02651330210451962

Talluri, K., & Ryzin, G. (2004). The Theory and Practice of Revenue Management. Springer. doi:10.1007/b139000

Thompson, A., & Thompson, H. (2010). The Exchange Rate, Euro Switch and Tourism Revenue in Greece. *Tourism Economics*, *16*(3), 773–780. doi:10.5367/000000010792278338

Tran, X. (2015). Effects of economic factors on demand for luxury hotel rooms in the U.S. *Advances in Hospitality and Tourism Research*, *3*(1), 1–17.

TripAdvisor. (2017). *Top ten Beaches*. https://tripadvisor.mediaroom.com/press-releases?item=125343

Uner, M. M., Kose, N., & Gokten, S. (2008). An Econometric Model of Tourism Demand and Room Rates: A Study in Belek, Antalya. *Anatolia*, *19*(1), 41–50. doi:10.1080/13032917.2008.9687052

Veloce, W. (2004). Forecasting Inbound Canadian Tourism: An Evaluation of Error Corrections Model Forecasts. *Tourism Economics*, *10*(3), 262–280. doi:10.5367/0000000041895049

Vives, A., Jacob, M., & Payeras, M. (2018). Revenue management and price optimization techniques in the hotel sector. *Tourism Economics*, *64*(6), 720–752. doi:10.1177/1354816618777590

Williamson, J. B., & Fleming, J. J. (1996). Convergence theory and the social welfare sector: A cross-national analysis. In A. Inkeles & M. Sasaki (Eds.), *Comparing nations and cultures* (pp. 349–354). Prentice Hall.

Willis, G. (1991). The single market and national marketing thinking. *European Journal of Marketing*, *25*(4), 148–156.

World Bank Data. (2021). Available at https://data.worldbank.org/

World Data. (2021). Available online at https://ourworldindata.org/covid-vaccinations?country=OWID_WRL

World's Best Award. (2017). Available at http://www.danang.intercontinental.com/top-100-hotels-in-the-world-by-travel-leisure-world-s-best-awards-2017

World's Best Award. (2017). Available at http://www.danang.intercontinental.com/top-100-hotels-in-the-world-by-travel-leisure-world-s-best-awards-2017

Yang, C., Lin, H., & Han, C. (2010). Analysis of International Tourist Arrivals in China: The Role of World Heritage Sites. *Tourism Management*, *31*(6), 827–837. doi:10.1016/j.tourman.2009.08.008 PMID:32287732

Chapter 4
Quantitative Analysis of Strategic Human Resource Management and Organizational Learning:
The Sustainability of MSMEs in Brunei Darussalam

Chin Han Wuen
Universiti Teknologi Brunei, Brunei

Fahmi Ibrahim
https://orcid.org/0000-0001-5016-7755
Universiti Teknologi Brunei, Brunei

Kabiru Jinjiri Ringim
Ahmadu Bello University, Nigeria

ABSTRACT

It is crucial for business organizations to maintain sustainability within the globalized market environment. However, the organizational ability of micro, small, and medium enterprises (MSMEs) is inadequate to generate sustainable competitive advantage. Moreover, strategic management theories are developed based on large business organizations which cannot be fully applied in MSMEs. From this knowledge gap, this research study addressed the core question of "Does strategic human resource management (SHRM) and organizational learning impact the sustainability of service-based MSMEs in Brunei Darussalam, with competitive strategy as mediator?" From a questionnaire survey of 275 service-based MSMEs, this research study confirmed SHRM and organizational learning to yield significant impact on organizational performance of service-based MSMEs. These results are partial significantly mediated by competitive strategy. From these findings, this research study extended the knowledge on resource-based view, contingency theory, and organizational alignment theory within the MSME context.

DOI: 10.4018/978-1-7998-8678-5.ch004

INTRODUCTION

The survivability of any business organizations to adapt with the globalized business environment stemmed from their sustainability to compete within their market industry (Bilan et al., 2015). This requires the business organizations to be flexible towards allocating their strategic resources to outperform their competitors (Gelhard & Delft, 2016; Hindasah & Nuryakin, 2020). Thus, the importance of sustainable development, within strategic management context, has been highlighted by various researchers and practitioners (Macke & Genari, 2018; Maletic et al., 2018; Varadarajan, 2015).

In line with the above discussion, micro, small and medium enterprises (MSMEs) have been receiving attentions due to their impact towards the country's economic growth (Abubakar et al., 2018; Hindasah & Nuryakin, 2020; L'Ecuyer & Raymond, 2017; Matthews et al., 2017; Yanuarti & Murwatiningsih, 2019; Yu et al., 2017). This is apparent in Asian region, in which, 30% to 60% of the gross domestic product and 40% to 80% of the country's employment is contributed by the MSMEs (Abubakar et al., 2018; Chen, 2016; Matthews et al., 2017). In Brunei Darussalam, the importance of MSMEs is also well-documented. The Brunei Government has emphasized on service-based MSMEs development to gain sustainable development for competing with global market (Brunei Ministry of Development, 2019; Ministry of Finance, 2017). However, the organizational ability of MSMEs is not adequate to cope with the dynamic competitive environment (Hindasah & Nuryakin, 2020). Moreover, the prevalence of strategic management theories is based on the sophisticated management structure of large business organizations which cannot be wholly applied to the simplicity and transparency of MSMEs (L'Ecuyer & Raymond, 2017; Shirokova et al., 2013). Thus, this research study focused the investigation of the research phenomenon on the service-based MSMEs in Brunei Darussalam.

Within the strategic management literature, Resource-Based View has been incorporated to explain business growth (Hitt et al., 2016; Nason & Wiklund, 2018). Particularly, the Resource-Based View reasoned the differences in organizational performance derived from the allocation of resources and capabilities (Castrogiovanni et al., 2011; Tan et al., 2014). It is necessary to clarify how sustainability can be achieved through articulating the strategic resources in the business organizations (Hindasah & Nuryakin, 2020; Maletic et al., 2018). In view of this, organizational performance is frequently incorporated as dependent variable for evaluating the sustainability of business organizations within a specific timeframe (Gharakhani & Mousakhani, 2012; Hooi & Ngui, 2014; Ramawickrama et al., 2017). Therefore, this research study adopted Resource-Based View to explain the sustainability of service-based MSMEs in Brunei Darussalam by examining their organizational performance.

The Resource-Based View highlights the aspects of valuable, rare, inimitable and non-substitutability (VRIN) in strategic resources to be responsible for achieving sustainable competitive advantage (Bilan et al., 2020; Donnellan & Rutledge, 2019; Hitt et al., 2016; Nason & Wiklund, 2018; Yuen et al., 2019). Drawing from this ideology, the current study critically assessed the impact of strategic human resource management (SHRM) and organizational learning, particularly the development of employees' skills and knowledge as strategic VRIN resources, towards the performance of service-based MSMEs in Brunei Darussalam.

SHRM is essential for achieving sustainable competitive advantage by aligning human resource management with organizational goals (Harrison & Bazzy, 2017; L'Ecuyer & Raymond, 2017; Martinson & Leon, 2018) to adapt with the globalized market industry (Cunningham & Rowley, 2007; Saha et al., 2016). Despite the importance of SHRM being well-established, majority of these discussions stemmed from large business organizations which are often assumed to be applicable in MSMEs context at a smaller scale (Newman & Sheikh, 2014; Hooi & Ngui, 2014; McEvoy & Buller, 2013). Furthermore, MSMEs are observed to implement non-systematic SHRM by combining personal experience and mixed strategies (McEvoy & Buller, 2013; Woschke et al., 2017). Therefore, this research study followed the recommendations of Hooi and Ngui (2014) and L'Ecuyer and Raymond (2017) by focusing on the SHRM investigation within MSMEs context.

Organizational learning is another vital aspect which strengthens the sustainability of business organizations (Altinay et al., 2015; Chung et al., 2019; Kalmuk & Acar, 2015; Saha et al., 2016). This is due to organizational learning reflects how business organizations adapt with the dynamic market industry by facilitating appropriate learning environment (Hooi & Ngui, 2014; Matthews et al., 2017). Without adequate knowledge, business organizations become "brittle and unchangeable" in the long-run (Matthews et al., 2017). Furthermore, there is limited information which details how organizational learning contributes to sustainable competitive advantage (Chaston et al., 2001; Matthews et al., 2017). Hence, this research study examined the impact of organizational learning towards the service-based MSMEs in Brunei Darussalam.

Despite SHRM and organizational learning being well-established to achieve sustainability, some findings have revealed organizational performance to be not significantly impacted by SHRM (Ologunde et al., 2015; Singh, 2018; Sojka, 2015) and organizational learning (Altinay et al., 2015; Gomes & Wojahn, 2017). This is due to the lack of clarity and distinction under the ideology of Resource-Based View (Hitt et al., 2016). This can be resolved by utilizing a mediating variable to explain the relationship between the variables in the theoretical model (Aliyu et al., 2015; Koopman, 2015; Ozdil & Kutlu, 2019; Sekaran & Bougie, 2016). The inclusion of mediating variable can be justified with theoretical discussion (Cooper & Schindler, 2014). As such, this research study included a mediating variable based on the ideology of Contingency Theory and Organizational Alignment Theory. Contingency Theory highlights how sustainable orientated practices stemmed from achieving fit between organizational factors (Omotosho & Anyigba, 2019; Maletic et al., 2018; Tamayo-Torress et al., 2016) while Organizational Alignment Theory emphasized the integration between people and process to be necessary for achieving sustainability (Alagaraja et al., 2015; Andrade & Goksel, 2017; Martinson & Leon, 2018).

Although the intuitive appeal for Contingency Theory and Organizational Alignment Theory has been well-established, there is limited information on the impact of mediator towards the sustainability practices in strategic management literature (Alagaraja et al., 2015; Maletic et al., 2018). Moreover, the cause and effect relationship between SHRM, organizational learning and organizational performance is not straightforward as often perceived (Altinay et al., 2015; Karami et al., 2004). The integration of sustainability aspects to enhance performance can be traced to the inherent connection of competitive strategy (Alagaraja et al., 2015; Harrison & Bazzy, 2017; Maletic et al., 2018). As such, it is possible to assess how MSMEs addressed the perceived gaps in their strategic resources to outperform their rival competitors (Donnellan & Rutledge, 2019). Thus, this research study deemed competitive strategy to be an appropriate mediator.

Drawing from the above discussion, this research study aimed to address the core questions of "Does SHRM and organizational learning impact the sustainability of service-based MSMEs in Brunei Darussalam, with competitive strategy as the mediating variable?"

LITERATURE REVIEW

Underpinning and Contemporary Theories

The strategic management theories describe the system of ideas which are developed from examining the evolution of business organizations from operating in the dynamic business environment (Omalaja & Eruola 2011; Tan & Tan, 2005). Among the strategic management theories, Resource-Based View is adopted as the underpinning theory for this research study to explain the significance of developing VRIN aspects in employees through SHRM and organizational learning process towards the sustainability of service-based MSMEs. Subsequently, Contingency Theory and Organizational Alignment Theory are incorporated in this research study by introducing competitive strategy as the mediator for explaining the relationship between SHRM, organizational learning and organizational performance. The relationship between the variables is illustrated in the conceptual framework as Figure 1.

Figure 1. Conceptual framework

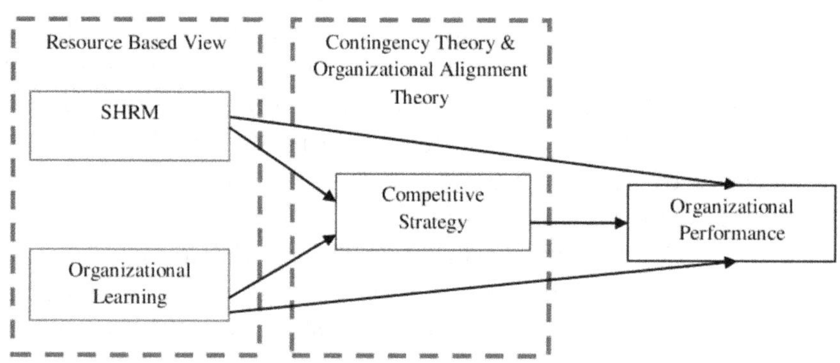

Following this, the ideology of Resource-Based View, Contingency Theory and Organizational Alignment Theory are further discussed in the following sections respectively.

Resource-Based View

The Resource-Based View highlights the internal pool of resources, i.e. employees, to be the main aspects for the success in business organizations (Tan et al., 2014; Rockwell, 2019; Yuen et al., 2019). From this ideology, Resource-Based View serves as the dominant strategic management paradigm for explaining how business organizations addressed their weakness to gain sustainable competitive advantage (Cabrales & Cabrera, 2020; Donnellan & Rutledge, 2019; Hitt et al., 2016). In view of this, it is necessary for business organizations to develop their strategic resources to adapt with the globalized market industry (Liao et al., 2016).

Various researchers have agreed the development of VRIN aspects in strategic resources to be the key components for achieving sustainable competitive strategy over rival competitors. For instance, Matlay et al. (2005) and Newbert (2008) affirmed VRIN aspects of strategic resources significantly contributed to sustainable competitive advantage. This is supported by findings from Gruber et al. (2010) which clarified firms with higher resources capabilities outperformed firms with lower resources capabilities. Additionally, Dubey et al. (2019) reported the combination of normative, mimetic and coercive pressure significantly impact tangible human resource development. From these findings, it implies how different resource implementations and capabilities reduce the chances of resource replication by rival firms.

The main assumptions of Resource-Based View depicted the strategic resources to be heterogeneous and immobile (Donnellan & Rutledge, 2019; Rockwell, 2019). As such, the strategic resources required configuration and development to achieve sustainable competitive advantage (Costa et al., 2012; Lim et al., 2012). Past findings by Castrogiovanni et al. (2011) and Tan et al. (2014) affirmed the efficient managerial allocation of resources and capabilities significantly impact overall organizational performance. Therefore, this research study incorporated Resource-Based View as the underpinning theory to explain the impact of SHRM and organizational learning (through acquisition, management and development of employees as VRIN resources) towards the sustainability of service-based MSMEs in Brunei Darussalam.

Contingency Theory

Contingency Theory is applicable for various research contexts to explain a research phenomenon, i.e. competitive strategy (Maletic et al., 2018; Marchini et al., 2018; Oltra & Flor, 2010; Smith et al., 2019). The core focus of Contingency Theory highlights how a singular best management for all types of business organizations to be non-existent (Dearnaley, 2013; Marchini et al., 2018; Oltra & Flor, 2010). Furthermore, the Contingency Theory recommends each business organizations to achieve fit by incorporating best strategic choices to create sustainable competitive advantage, based on the current globalized market environment (Maletic et al., 2018; Marchini et al., 2018; Schuler, 2000; Smith et al., 2019).

Past studies, which incorporated Contingency Theory, reported how achieving fit in competitive strategy has resulted in business organizations to generate sustainable competitive advantage. For instance, Liao (2005) reported (i) behavior-control based management is a significant predictor for cost reduction firms; and (ii) output-control based management is a significant predictor for quality-enhancement firms. Meanwhile, Azmi (2011) also affirmed (i) human resource management fit and cross-functional fit to have significant impact on organizational performance; and (ii) roles-position fit and intra-functional fit have significant impact on organizational performance. In a different context, Tamayo-Torress (2016) reported organizational learning has significant and positive indirect impact on organizational performance through strategic fit. As for Maletic et al. (2018), the findings revealed sustainability exploration and exploitation practices significantly impact organizational performance.

From the above findings, it implies the implementation of SHRM and organizational learning is based on the strategic orientation of the business organizations. This is attributed to the successful experiences gained by business organizations following the adjustments of their strategic choices by assessing their favorable and unfavorable performance (Chung et al., 2019). In view of the empirical support for Contingency Theory to achieve sustainability, this research study aimed to broaden the knowledge of sustainability practices within SHRM and organizational learning process by incorporating competitive strategy as the mediating variable.

Organizational Alignment Theory

Organizational Alignment Theory emphasized the importance of structuring the internal components (i.e. strategy, people and performance) of business organizations to achieve optimal effectiveness (Andrade

& Goksel, 2017; Harrison & Bazzy, 2017; Nadler & Tushman, 1980; Semler, 1997). The key aspects for achieving sustainability derived from the degree of alignment between policies and practices (Martinson & Leon, 2018). This highlights the importance of coherency and complementary planning within the business organizations to achieve the expected results (Cabrales & Cabrera, 2020). As such, alignment is described as a resource adapting capability which allows shared understanding of organizational goals among employees (Alagaraja et al., 2015; Andrade & Goksel, 2017).

A comprehensive review of past studies has incorporated Organizational Alignment Theory to explain the impact of alignment towards achieving sustainability. For instance, Parisi (2012) confirmed top management commitment yield indirect significant impact on sustainability through structural alignment, social alignment and strategic performance measurement system. Similarly, Gibb and Wallace (2014) affirmed alignment between organizational strategic priorities significantly impact human resource development effectiveness. Meanwhile, Gerow et al. (2016) reported (i) high level of intellectual alignment significantly impact customer benefits; (ii) operational alignment significantly impact productivity; and (iii) social alignment significantly impact intellectual alignment. As for Yousaf and Majid (2016), the findings revealed strategic alignment to be a significant mediating variable for strategic performance. Drawing from these empirical evidences which incorporated Organizational Alignment Theory, this research study aimed to reduce the knowledge gap on sustainability within Organizational Alignment Theory, by introducing a mediating variable.

Organizational Performance

Sustainability is an essential concept within strategic management literature which strengthens competitive advantage of business organizations (Hammadi & Hussain, 2018). However, past studies which investigate sustainable organizational performance within service industry are not comprehensive (Hammadi & Hussain, 2018). As such, several past studies incorporated organizational performance as a dependent variable to examine the sustainability of business organizations (Gharakhani & Mousakhani, 2012; Hooi & Ngui, 2014; Ramawickrama et al., 2017). Drawing from the above discussion, organizational performance is defined as the degree of past, present and future accomplishments by business organizations based on various efficiency and effectiveness assessments (Gharakhani & Mousakhani, 2012; Wadongo & Abel-Kader, 2014; Yousaf & Majid, 2016). However, the reasoning to implement specific measurement indicators based on strategic priorities has remained vague (Hammadi & Hussain, 2018; Valmohammadi, 2011).

Financial measurement indicators have been deemed acceptable to measure organizational performance in different field of studies (Abubakar et al., 2018; Bilal et al., 2017; Chereau & Meschi, 2019; Waiganjo et al., 2012; Yanuarti & Murwatiningsih, 2019). However, financial measurement indicators have been critiqued to be poor indicator for intangible assets (Parnell, 2010; Waiganjo et al., 2012) and deemed insufficient to explain long-term sustainability of business organizations (Cabrales & Cabrera, 2020). The assessment of sustainability requires a set of vital measurement indicators (Hammadi & Hussain, 2019; Radzi, Jenatabadi & Hasbullah, 2015). As such, Waiganjo et al. (2012) recommended business organizations to incorporate multiple measurement indicators instead of single financial measurement indicators. Moreover, non-financial measurement indicators are deemed essential to evaluate learning and growth of key stakeholders (i.e. managers and employees) (Jusoh & Parnell, 2008; Kaplan & Norton, 1996; Parnell, 2010; Roca-Puig & Bon Llusar, 2007). As such, the combination of financial and non-financial measurement indicators are essential to articulate long-term planning with short-term actions based on the strategic objectives (Chen et al., 2016; Hammadi & Hussain, 2019; Jusoh & Parnell, 2008; Roca-Puig & Bon-Llusar, 2007). Hence, this research study incorporated the combination of financial and non-financial measurement indicators to examine the performance of service-based MSMEs in Brunei Darussalam, in relation to their sustainability.

Strategic Human Resource Management

SHRM is deemed essential for business organizations to secure vital resources by developing employees' skills to achieve organizational sustainability (Manzoor et al., 2019; Podgorodnichenko et al., 2020). However, Cabrales and Cabrera (2020) identified the lack of conceptual explanations of SHRM towards the sustainability of business organizations. Drawing from the Resource-Based View, SHRM highlights the employees to be the VRIN resources for achieving sustainable competitive advantage (Martinson & Leon, 2018). Moreover, SHRM is considered as a reactive or proactive function by serving as structural mechanism for employees' development through delegating work tasks and responsibilities to the appropriate employees (Al-Ayed, 2019; Sanchez et al., 2015). Based on the above discussion, SHRM is operationally defined as the systematic management process and dynamic architecture for acquiring, developing and deploying human resources to accomplish the main objectives (Floren et al., 2016; L'Ecuyer & Raymond, 2017; Martinson & Leon, 2018).

SHRM has been reported to be necessary for achieving sustainable competitive advantage by developing employees' skill to create additional value for business organizations (Dabic et al., 2011; McEcoy & Buller, 2013; Schuler & Jackson, 2014; Yao & Chang, 2017). Moreover, past findings by Fabi et al. (2009) observed world-class SMEs placed heavy emphasis on informing and training aspects. Similarly, Zheng et al. (2009) also affirmed (i) innovative SMEs focused on training and development, performance evaluation and employee involvement; and (ii) transitional SMEs emphasized on free market selection, performance-based pay and employee participation. As for, Seong, (2011) and Manzoor et al. (2019), both studies reported high performance and sustainable human resource management have positive significant impact on job performance. Drawing from the above findings and analysis, this research study expected similar findings between SHRM and sustainability by examining the impact of SHRM towards the organizational performance of service-based MSMEs in Brunei Darussalam. Thus, this research study proposed the following hypothesis:

H1: SHRM has a significant positive impact on organizational performance of service-based MSMEs in Brunei Darussalam.

Organizational Learning

Organizational learning is a crucial process which equips the employees with relevant knowledge and understanding for achieving sustainable organizational performance to adapt within the dynamic market industry (Fiol & Lyles, 1985; Kordab et al., 2020; Oelze et al., 2014). This is attributed to organizational learning process which highlights the capability of business organizations by examining the dynamic process of creation, acquisition and integration of knowledge to achieve superior organizational performance (Hindasah & Nuryakin, 2020; Oelze et al., 2014). As such, Pedler et al. (1988) described learning company as "an organization which facilitate the learning of all its members and continuously transform itself". A learning organization has the ability to act on the ideas it generated, evaluate its ideas as well as reject those which are unsuitable (Denton, 1998). Based on this description, the operational definition of organizational learning for this research study is defined as the managerial characteristics of business organizations to process knowledge, as well as facilitates learning process for improving organizational performance (Chiva et al., 2007; Gomes & Wojahn, 2017). It is important to note that knowledge is claimed to be significant source of sustainable competitive advantage (Drucker, 1998; Carlucci & Schiuma, 2006; Ibrahim & Reid, 2009).

Organizational learning has been reported to yield significant impact on a wide range of performance under different context. For instance, Hooi and Ngui (2014), Kordah et al. (2020) and Liao et al. (2017) confirmed organizational learning to yield significant positive impact on sustainable competitive advantage, organizational performance and organizational innovativeness. Garcia-Morales et al. (2006) also reported the significant impact of organizational learning towards organizational performance stemmed from personal mastery, transformational leadership, shared vision, proactivity and environment. In addition, Michna (2009) observed dialogue and empowerment of employees, leader's attitude, collaboration, team learning and key results as the main facilitators for organizational learning. In recent studies, Bilan et al. (2020) reported organizational learning to serve as a significant mediator for the relationship between organizational capabilities and firm's sustainability. In view of the above past findings, this research study also expected similar results between organizational learning and sustainability by observing the impact of organizational learning towards the performance of service-based MSMEs in Brunei Darussalam. Therefore, this research study proposed the following hypotheses:

H2: Organizational learning has a significant impact on organizational performance of service-based MSMEs in Brunei Darussalam.

Competitive Strategy

Competitive strategy is one of the paradigms which clarify the main objectives of business organizations before any crucial decision making of key resources (Donnellan & Rutledge, 2019; Karami et al., 2004; Yanuarti & Murwatiningsih, 2019; Yuliansyah et al., 2017). Due to the key characteristics of strategic resource being heterogeneous and imperfectly immobile, strategic position of key resource is necessary for achieving sustainable competitive advantage (Donnellan & Rutledge, 2019). In other words, the aim of competitive strategy is guiding the business organizations towards achieving their specified objectives. As such, the operational definition of competitive strategy can be described as the comprehensive plan implemented by business leaders to obtain sustainable competitive advantage for accomplishing their main objectives (Anwar & Hasnu, 2017; Harrison & Bazzy, 2017; Shavarini et al., 2013; Teeratansirikool et al., 2013).

In line with the above discussion, competitive strategy has been reported as an appropriate mediating variable by past findings. For instance, Gates and Langevin (2010) reported similar findings by confirming (i) innovative measurement is significant predictor for differentiation based managers; and (ii) cost efficient measurement is significant predictor for cost-leadership based managers. Moreover, findings from Parnell (2015) affirmed firms with high strategic clarity significantly outperformed firms with moderate or low strategic clarity. In another study, Chi (2015) reported significant difference in strategy responses between high and low performers within different business environment. This is supported by findings from Wuen et al. (2021) which reported competitive strategy to be a significant mediator for SHRM and organizational performance. Based on the findings, this research study believes the sustainability of service-based MSMEs in Brunei Darussalam can be explained by examining the mediating impact of competitive strategy towards the relationship between SHRM, organizational learning and organizational performance. Thus, the following hypotheses are proposed:

H3: Competitive strategy mediates the relationship between SHRM and organizational performance of service-based MSMEs in Brunei Darussalam

H4: Competitive strategy mediates the relationship between organizational learning and organizational performance of service-based MSMEs in Brunei Darussalam

METHODOLOGY

The measurement items of this questionnaire survey, which were adapted from past studies, incorporated Likert scale to allow the evaluation of favorable and non-favorable responses towards the research topic (Cooper & Schindler, 2014; Sekaran & Bougie, 2016). Additionally, this research study conducted validity testing on the questionnaire survey by obtaining feedback from university experts and specialists of the field, as recommended by Bryman (2012), Cooper and Schindler (2014) and Sekaran and Bougie (2016). Subsequently, reliability testing was conducted with Cronbach's coefficient alpha on 38 collected questionnaires from the pilot study. The result, in Table 1, revealed the measurement items have satisfied the minimum reliability requirement of 0.70 (Ringim & Reni, 2018; Wuen et al., 2021).

Table 1. Result of Cronbach's alpha from pilot study

	Variable	No of items	No of items deleted	Cronbach's Alpha
1	Organizational Performance	8	0	.707
2	SHRM	7	0	.777
3	Organizational Learning	4	0	.713
4	Competitive Strategy	8	0	.849

This research study followed Sekaran and Bougie's (2016) sampling sequence by detailing the research population and sampling frame. This research study aimed to investigate the sustainability of service-based MSMEs in Brunei Darussalam. The MSMEs in Brunei Darussalam are defined by the number of employees, in which their sizes are categorized into micro (1-4 employees), small (5-19 employees) and medium (20-99 employees) (Department of Economic Planning and Development, 2017). The questionnaire survey targeted the service-based MSME owners/managers to achieve high degree of data validity due to their knowledge and multiple responsibilities (Ibrahim et al., 2020). In line with the definition of MSMEs in Brunei Darussalam, the criteria for selecting the service-based MSMEs consisted of (i) having less than 100 employees; (ii) registered in Brunei Darussalam; and (iii) being the private sector.

From the above selection criteria, this research study adopted simple random sampling to guarantee equal probability for the individual participants to be selected to generalize the research population (Bryman, 2012; Cooper & Schindler, 2014; Sekaran & Bougie, 2016). This research study calculated the minimum sample size for the research population of 3,477, based on the confidence level of 95% and 5% margin of error as recommended by Saunders et al. (2009), to be 346. From the recommended sample size, this research study was able to achieve statistical generalization on the research population by maintaining standard level of accuracy and confidence from the research findings (Creswell, 2012; Saunders et al., 2009; Sekaran & Bougie, 2016; Yin, 2011). The questionnaire survey was distributed personally to the MSME owners/managers between June 2018 and August 2018. The MSME owners/managers were also reminded to complete the survey with short message services and self-visit. In doing so, 296 out of 346 questionnaires were collected. However, only 275 questionnaires were considered appropriate for further analysis, which still yielded a high response rate of 79.3%.

RESULT AND ANALYSIS

This research study incorporated SPSS software version 23 and SmartPLS software version 3.0 to conduct the data analysis on the questionnaire survey. Firstly, the SPSS software is utilized to provide descriptive and inferential statistical analysis. Secondly, the SmartPLS software was run to conduct the Structural Equation Modeling as a means to remove variables with measurement errors, create a model to illustrate the relationship between the variables, testing hypotheses with empirical data and evaluating loading of observed items (Hair et al., 2011; Ringim & Reni, 2018). Lastly, the Preacher and Hayes mediation test was conducted via SPSS software to examine the impact of competitive strategy as the mediating variable.

Demographic Profile of Service-Based MSMEs in Brunei Darussalam

The demographic profile of the service-based MSMEs in Brunei Darussalam, as depicted in Table 2, is categorized based on (i) number of operating years; (ii) number of employees; and (iii) types of industry.

The number of operating years for the participating service-based MSMEs is categorized into (i) less than 2 years (2.9%); (ii) 2 to 5 years (28.0%); (iii) 6 to 10 years (22.2%); (iv) 11 to 15 years (13.1%); and (v) more than 15 years (33.8%). In terms of the number of employees, 22.5% of the participating service-based MSMEs employed 1 to 4 employees; 52.4% of the participating service-based MSMEs employed 5 to 19 employees whereas 25.1% of the participating service-based MSMEs employed 20 to 99 employees. Meanwhile, the participating service-based MSMEs in Brunei Darussalam serves as (i) retails (14.9%); (ii) import and export representative (3.6%); (iii) transportation services (1.1%); (iv) packaging services (0.7%); (v) food and beverages (13.5%); (vi) hotel and travel (4.7%); (vii) financial institutions (4.0%); (viii) professional services (12.4%); (ix) engineering, architecture and technical services (11.6%); (x) maintenance and repair services (4.7%); (xi) education services (6.9%); (xii) health services (1.1%); (xii) personal care services (1.1%); and (xiii) others (19.6%).

Structural Equation Model: Measurement Model

The SmartPLS software version 3.0 was utilized to ensure the reliability and validity requirements are met in this research study. The PLS algorithm was run and it revealed the AVE of organizational learning and competitive strategy to be above the required value of 0.5. However, organizational performance and SHRM, having AVE value of less than 0.5, required further treatment. The OP02 was found to have

Table 2. Demographic profile of service-based MSMEs in Brunei Darussalam

	Frequency	Percentage (%)
Number of operating years		
Less than 2 years	8	2.9
Between 2 to 5 years	77	28.0
Between 6 to 10 years	61	22.2
Between 11 to 15 years	36	13.1
More than 15 years	93	33.8
Number of employees		
Between 1 to 4	62	22.5
Between 5 to 19	144	52.4
Between 20 to 99	69	25.1
More than 100	0	0
Type of industry		
Retail	41	14.9
Import and export representative	10	3.6
Transportation services	3	1.1
Packaging services	2	.7
Food and beverages	37	13.5
Hotel and travel	13	4.7
Financial institution	11	4.0
Professional services	34	12.4
Engineering, architecture and technical services	32	11.6
Maintenance and repair services	13	4.7
Education services	19	6.9
Health services	3	1.1
Personal care services	3	1.1
Others	54	19.6

the lowest loading (-0.408), was deleted to increase the AVE of organizational performance (0.501). To ensure the AVE of organizational performance far exceeded the required value of 0.5, OP07 was deleted due to being the lowest loading (0.530). This further increased the AVE of organizational performance to be 0.561.

The PLS algorithm indicated the AVE of SHRM to be 0.411. As such, SHRM04 was deleted due to having the lowest loading (0.531). Following the deletion, the AVE of SHRM was increased to 0.458. This research study further increased the AVE of SHRM by deleting SHRM01 due to having the lowest loading of 0.591. This increased the AVE of SHRM to be 0.485. With SHRM02 being the lowest loading of 0.480, this research study deleted SHRM02 which increased the AVE of SHRM to be 0.580. With the AVE of the research variables reaching above the required value of 0.5, as indicated in Figure 2 and Table 3, this research study has established convergent validity.

Although the AVE of competitive strategy is shown to be above 0.5, it is necessary to delete CS08 with the loading value of 0.270 to meet the requirements of discriminant validity. In turn, this increased the AVE of competitive strategy to 0.614.

Following the above procedure, this research study assessed the composite reliability value. The analysis revealed all the variables in model to have satisfied the recommended value of 0.7, as indicated in Table 3. Subsequently, the outer factor loadings were examined. Majority of the factor loadings indicated to be above 0.70, in Table 3. Although some of the outer factor loading were shown to be lower than 0.70, Hair et al. (2011) and Ringim and Reni (2018) affirmed any factor loading below 0.70 can still be used for further analysis when their composite reliability value is above 0.70. In view of this, the

Figure 2. Remaining items of SHRM, organizational learning, competitive strategy and organizational performance after items deletion process

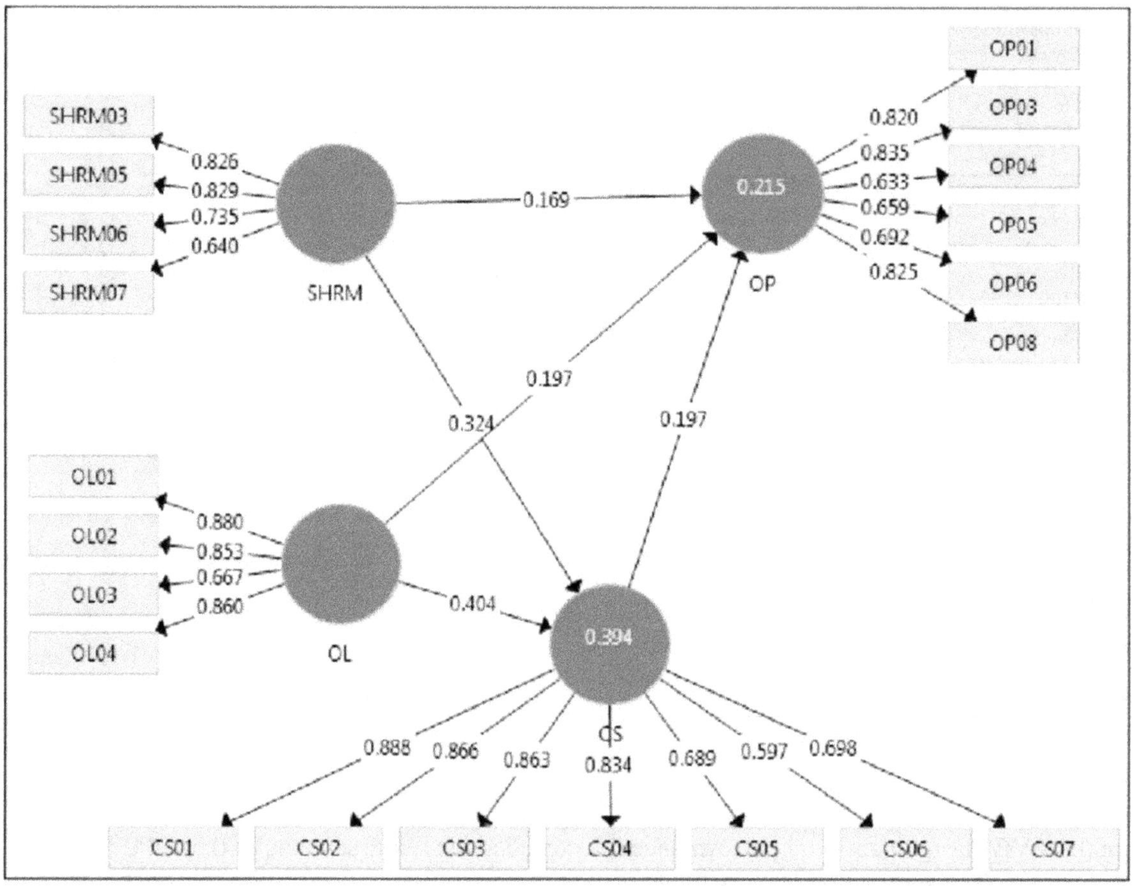

outer factor loadings with value less than 0.70 for this research study remain useful for further analysis due to the composite reliability value being above the required value of 0.7. Additionally, this research study established the unidimensionality of the research variables by ensuring the factor loading to be above 0.5, as stipulated by Nazim and Ahmad (2013). Hence, the indicator reliability has been satisfied for this research study.

In regards to discriminant validity analysis, the Fornell-Larcker criterion was incorporated in this research study by ensuring the square root of AVE to be higher than other latent value. The result, presented in Table 4, indicated the square root of AVE to be higher than the remaining correspondent latent constructs, as recommended by Abubakar et al. (2018), Hair et al. (2018), Ringim and Reni (2018) and Shrafat (2018). Therefore, the discriminant validity of this research study is confirmed.

The results in Figure 2, Table 3 and Table 4 have established the validity and reliability of the questionnaire survey in this research study. As such, this research study proceeds with structural model assessment to test the research hypotheses in the following section.

Table 3. Composite reliability values, AVE and outer factor loading here

	SHRM	Organizational Learning	Competitive Strategy	Organizational Performance	Composite Reliability	AVE Values
SHRM03 SHRM05 SHRM06 SHRM07	0.826 0.829 0.735 0.640				0.845	0.580
OL01 OL02 OL03 OL04		0.880 0.853 0.667 0.860			0.890	0.672
CS01 CS02 CS03 CS04 CS05 CS06 CS07			0.888 0.866 0.863 0.834 0.689 0.597 0.698		0.916	0.614
OP01 OP03 OP04 OP05 OP06 OP08				0.820 0.835 0.633 0.659 0.692 0.825	0.883	0.561

Structural Equation Model: Structural Model

As recommended by Hair et al. (2011), Hair et al. (2019) and Ringim and Reni (2018), this research study examined the coefficient of determination (R^2) to explain the percentage of variance in the endogenous variable being explained by the exogenous variable. The R^2 obtained for organizational performance is indicated to be 0.215 (weak). This means SHRM, organizational learning and competitive strategy collectively explained 21.5% of the variance in organizational performance.

The SmartPLS software assumed the used data are not normally distributed, which in turn, applied non-parametric bootstrap procedure to obtain the significance of inner weights (Hair et al., 2011; Ringim & Reni, 2018). In other words, this involves the bootstrap sample being created from repeated random sampling from the original sample to achieve the standard errors for hypothesis testing (Hair et al., 2011; Ringim & Reni, 2018). As such, this research study followed the recommendations by Abubakar et al.

Table 4. Discriminant validity values (Fornell-Larcker criterion)

	Competitive Strategy	Organizational Learning	SHRM	Organizational Performance
Competitive Strategy	0.783			
Organizational Learning	0.559	0.820		
SHRM	0.518	0.478	0.761	
Organizational Performance	0.394	0.387	0.364	0.749

(2018), Hair et al. (2011) and Ringim and Reni (2018) by setting the number of bootstrap to be 5,000. Following this, the path coefficient results are presented in Figure 3 and Table 5.

Figure 3. Structural model

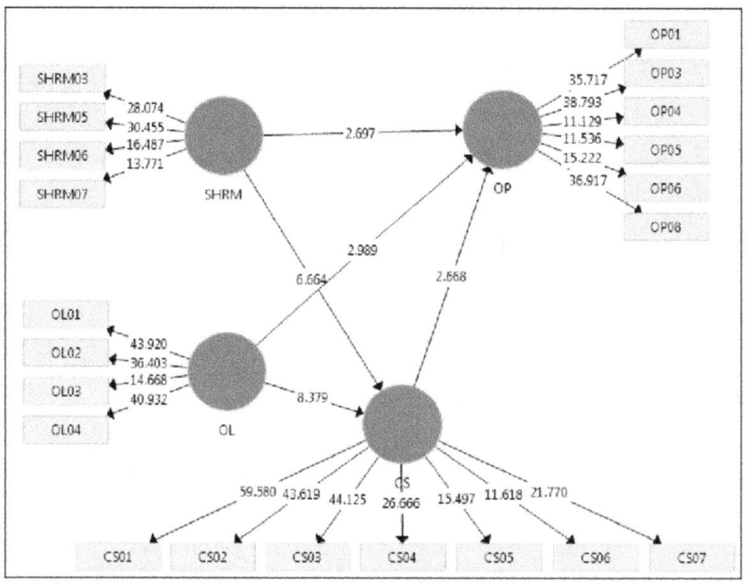

The relationship between SHRM, organizational learning and organizational performance are examined based on the t-value and p-value. As shown in Table 5, H1 and H2 are shown to be significant with t-value greater than 2.58 and p-value lower than 0.01. The results are in accordance with Resource-Based View as SHRM and organizational learning served as the foundation for employees' skill development into VRIN resources to gain sustainable competitive advantage (Al-Ayed, 2019; McEvoy & Buller, 2013).

Table 5. Results of path coefficient

Hypothesis	Correlation between dimension	Original sample	T-Statistics	P-value	Result
H1	SHRM -> Organizational Performance	0.169	2.697	0.007	Supported
H2	Organizational Learning -> Organizational Performance	0.197	2.989	0.003	Supported

In line with the above analysis, the effect size (f^2) indicated the impact of *SHRM* and *organizational learning* on *organizational performance* yielded 0.025 and 0.032 respectively. Based on rules of thumbs by Hair et al. (2011), Hair et al. (2019) and Ringim and Reni (2018), the reported effect size (f^2) for SHRM and organizational learning are deemed to be minimal. However, following the Q^2 testing via cross-validated redundancy approach, the result revealed the Q^2 value to be 0.105, which exceeded the recommended value of 0.02 as recommended by Hair et al. (2011), Hair et al. (2019) and Ringim and Reni (2018). In other words, despite the small effect size, this research study affirmed the small effect size of SHRM and organizational learning on organizational performance still yield significant predictive relevance.

Preacher and Hayes Mediation Test

As recommended by Preacher and Hayes (2004) and Ringim and Reni (2018), the mediation testing was assessed based on the p-value and z-value. Furthermore, this research study determined the mediation types based on the sequence by Demming, Jahn and Boztug (2017). The result of the mediation test and types are summarized in Table 6 and 7.

Table 6. Results of indirect effect and significant using normal distribution

H	Value	S.E.	LL95CI	UL95CI	Z	Sig(two)	Remark
H3	.1113	.0246	.0630	.1596	4.5155	.0000	Significant
H4	.1163	.0276	.0623	.1704	4.2206	.0000	Significant

H3 described competitive strategy to be the mediator for the relationship between SHRM and organizational performance. As shown in Table 6, the mediation result of indirect effect is shown to be significant based on the normal distribution, in which is z-value =4.5155 and p-value = 0.0000. Subsequently, the direct and total effect for H3 is also significant when evaluating the t-value and sig (two) column. Drawing from these observations, H3 is supported in this research study, in which, competitive strategy is deemed to have significant partial mediation impact on the relationship between SHRM and organizational performance.

Table 7. Direct and total effect results of mediation analysis

		Coeff	S.E.	t	Sig(two)
(X) SHRM (Y) Organizational Performance (M) Competitive Strategy	b(YX) b(MX) b(YM,X) b(YX,M)	.2324 .4409 .2524 .1211	.0379 .0442 .0496 .0423	6.1374 9.9637 5.0910 2.8614	.0000 .0000 .0000 .0045
(X) Organizational Learning (Y) Organizational Performance (M) Competitive Strategy	b(YX) b(MX) b(YM,X) b(YX,M)	.2473 .4925 .2363 .1310	0.373 .0419 .0521 .0442	6.6319 11.7595 4.5382 2.9622	.0000 .0000 .0000 .0033

H4 highlighted competitive strategy to be the mediator for the relationship between organizational learning and organizational performance. As depicted in Table 6, the mediation result of indirect effect for H4 is significant based on the normal distribution, where z value = 4.2206 and p = 0.0000. Furthermore, the direct and total effect for H4 is also significant when assessing the t-value and sig (two) column.

Based on these observations, H4 is supported in this research study, in which, competitive strategy is observed to have significant partial mediation impact on the relationship between organizational learning and organizational performance.

DISCUSSION

This research paper addressed the core question of "Does SHRM and organizational learning impact the sustainability of service-based MSMEs in Brunei Darussalam, with competitive strategy as the mediating variable?" In doing so, the current study contributes to the research context of sustainability within strategic management literature.

The Impact of SHRM and Organizational Learning on Organizational Performance

Based on the result and analysis from the structural equation model, SHRM and organizational learning is confirmed to yield significant positive impact on organizational performance of service-based MSMEs in Brunei Darussalam. This is further evident from the number of operating years by the service-based MSMEs in Brunei Darussalam, in which, 97.1% have been in operation for 2 to 15+ years. It should be noted SHRM and organizational learning yielded small effect size ($f^2 = 0.025$ and 0.032 respectively) towards organizational performance. The small effect size can be attributed to the statistical analysis being generated from a broad range of service-based MSMEs in Brunei Darussalam which employed a small number of employees. However, this research study asserted SHRM and organizational learning to have significant predictive relevance ($Q^2 = 0.105$) towards the organizational performance, and thus, appropriate explanation for the sustainability within the service-based MSMEs in Brunei Darussalam.

The results and analysis also clarified the implemented SHRM and organizational learning is mainly based on the structural aim of the MSMEs and requirements of the intended objectives which, in turn, impact the overall organizational performance. This is expected as SHRM is considered as the foundation for developing the employee's essential capabilities and skills towards achieving sustainable organizational performance (Al-Ayed, 2019; Huang, 2001; McEvoy & Buller, 2013; Salaheldin, 2009). Meanwhile, organizational learning is the key process to convert relevant knowledge into VRIN resource for achieving sustainable organizational performance (L'Ecuyer & Raymond, 2017; Matlay et al., 2005; Newbert, 2008; Rockwell, 2019; Yuen et al., 2019). However, specific SHRM and organizational learning aspects may not be compatible and inefficient with the sustainability objective. Hence, this research study reaffirmed the ideology of Resource-Based View by establishing the service-based MSMEs in Brunei Darussalam achieved sustainable competitive advantage by strengthening the VRIN aspects of the employees.

Competitive Strategy as the Mediator for the Relationship between SHRM, Organizational Learning and Organizational Performance

This research study established competitive strategy to have partial significant mediating impact on the relationship between SHRM, organizational learning and organizational performance. However, it should be noted the statistical analysis is generated from a broad range of service-based MSMEs in Brunei

Darussalam which employed a small number of employees. This, in turn, generated a weak coefficient of determination ($R^2 = 21.5\%$) for the endogenous variables (namely, SHRM, organizational learning and competitive strategy) to explain the organizational performance of service-based MSMEs in Brunei Darussalam. Despite the weak coefficient of determination, this research study established the predictive relevance ($Q^2 = 0.105$) of competitive strategy towards the organizational performance of service-based MSMEs in Brunei Darussalam. Hence, competitive strategy remains as a significant mediating variable to explain the sustainability of service-based MSMEs in Brunei Darussalam.

The results and analysis clarified the implemented competitive strategy is mainly based on the current objectives and characteristics of the MSMEs which, in turn, explain the impact of SHRM on organizational performance. In doing so, this research study reaffirmed the concept of Contingency Theory and Organizational Alignment Theory. In terms of the Contingency Theory, it suggests the employees are necessary physical resource to achieve balance via the selection of asset and resource orchestration process (Simon & Hitt, 2009) towards achieving the main objectives. As for Organizational Alignment Theory, the MSMEs are required to consider the importance of accurate alignment, namely strategy and employees, as the precondition for organizational effectiveness (Parisi, 2012). In particular, business organizations should select the best strategic choice to achieve the main objectives (Parisi, 2012; Schuler, 2000; Simon & Hitt, 2009). In doing so, this reduces the chances of VRIN resource within the service-based MSMEs in Brunei Darussalam to be replicated as the result of configuration and alignment procedures.

CONCLUSION

In conclusion, the findings from this research study reduced the knowledge gap found in the Resource-Based View. As mentioned earlier, Resource-Based View describes business organizations as an organized combination of competencies for achieving sustainable competitive advantage (Ho et al., 2013; Tan et al., 2014). In other words, Resource-Based View suggests the main component for achieving sustainable competitive advantage over rival business organizations is developing the VRIN aspects of the strategic resources (Donnellan & Rutledge, 2019; Harrison & Bazzy, 2017; L'Ecuyer & Raymond, 2017; Rockwell, 2019; Yuen et al., 2019). Hence, this research study identified SHRM and organizational learning as the VRIN development process in strategic resources for achieving sustainable competitive advantage.

This research study also provided further understanding on the ideology of Contingency Theory and Organizational Alignment Theory. Contingency Theory emphasized the organizational performance derived from achieving best fit among organizational factors to achieve sustainable competitive advantage (Marchini et al., 2018; Smith et al., 2019). Meanwhile, Organizational Alignment Theory highlighted organizational performance stemmed from the interdependence between internal aspects of the business organization (Kaplan & Norton, 2004; Nissen, 2014). Drawing from the findings of this research study, the implemented competitive strategy directs the implementation of SHRM and organizational learning towards sustainable organizational performance stemmed from maintaining cooperation and shared understanding among the employees.

However, there are a few limitations which merit discussion to defend the reliability and validity in this research study. The questionnaire survey targeted mainly MSME owners/managers to gain understanding how they derived their decision making processes. However, many MSME owners/managers lacked interest to be involved in the questionnaire survey. As such, the overall research findings derived mainly from the availability of the MSME owners/managers to share their experience as valid and reliable information.

This research study also did not utilize any control variable to investigate the research phenomenon. The control variable aims to ensure consistency for ruling out alternative explanations on the research findings and reducing error terms (Schjoedt & Sanghoon, 2015; Spector, 2020). However, control variable serves could also provide explanations for the dependent variables which are uncorrelated with the hypothesized independent variable (Klarmann & Feurer, 2018). Hence, this research study excluded control variables due to not being linked to Resource-Based View, Contingency Theory and Organizational Alignment Theory.

REFERENCES

Abubakar, R. A., Kura, K. M., & Ringim, K. J. (2018). Total quality management, firm performance and the moderating role of competitive intensity. *Journal of International Business. Economics and Entrepreneurship*, *3*(1), 10–20.

Al-Ayed, S. I. (2019). The impact of strategic human resource management on organizational resilience: An empirical study on hospitals. *Business: Theory and Practice*, *20*(1), 179–186. doi:10.3846/btp.2019.17

Alagaraja, M., Rose, K., Shuck, B., & Bergman, M. (2015). Unpacking organizational alignment: The view from theory and practice. *Journal of Organizational Learning and Leadership.*, *13*(1), 18–31.

Aliyu, M. S., Rogo, H. B., & Mahmood, R. (2015). Knowledge management, entrepreneurial orientation and firm performance: The role of organizational culture. *Asian Social Science*, *11*(23), 140–152.

Altinay, L., Madanoglu, M., De Vita, G., Arasli, H., & Ekinci, Y. (2015). The interface between organizational learning capability, entrepreneurial orientation, and SME growth. *Journal of Small Business Management*, *54*(3), 871–891. doi:10.1111/jsbm.12219

Andrade, M. S. O., & Göksel, A. (2017). Organizational alignment case study of Ministry of Justice of Cape Verde. *International Journal of Business and Management Invention*, *6*(4), 25–35.

Anwar, J., & Hasnu, S. (2017a). Strategic patterns and firm performance: Comparing consistent, flexible and reactor strategies. *Journal of Organizational Change Management*, *30*(7), 1015–1029. doi:10.1108/JOCM-03-2016-0053

Becker, T. E. (2005). Potential problems in the statistical control of variables in organizational research: A qualitative analysis with recommendations. *Organizational Research Methods*, *8*(3), 274–289. doi:10.1177/1094428105278021

Bilal, A. R., Naveed, M., & Anwar, F. (2017). Linking distinctive management competencies to SMEs' growth decisions. *Studies in Economics and Finance*, *34*(3), 302–330. doi:10.1108/SEF-10-2015-0236

Bilan, Y., Hussain, H. I., Haseeb, M., & Kot, S. (2020). Sustainability and economic performance: Role of organizational learning and innovation. *The Engineering Economist*, *31*(1), 93–103. doi:10.5755/j01.ee.31.1.24045

Brunei Ministry of Development. (2019). *Strategic planning 2018 – 2023*. Retrieved on 08/12/2019, from http://www.mod.gov.bn/_layouts/15/osssearchresults.aspx?u=http%3A%2F%2Fwww%2Emod%2Egov%2Ebn&k=strategic%20plan%202018%2D2023

Bryman, A. (2012). *Social Research Methods* (4th ed.). Oxford University Press.

Carlucci, D., & Schiuma, G. (2006). Knowledge Value Spiral: Linking Knowledge Assets to Company Performance. *Knowledge and Process Management, 13*(1), 35–46. doi:10.1002/kpm.243

Castrogiovanni, G. J., Urbano, D., & Loras, J. (2011). Linking corporate entrepreneurship and human resource management in SMEs. *International Journal of Manpower, 32*(1), 34–47. doi:10.1108/01437721111121215

Chaston, I., Badger, B., Mangles, T., & Sadler-Smith, E. (2001). Organisational learning style, competencies and learning systems in small, UK manufacturing firms. *International Journal of Operations & Production Management, 21*(11), 1417–1432. doi:10.1108/EUM0000000006224

Chen, Y., Jaw, Y., & Wu, B. (2016). Effect of digital transformation on organisational performance of SMEs. *Internet Research, 26*(1), 186–212. doi:10.1108/IntR-12-2013-0265

Chereau, P., & Meschi, P. (2019). The performance implications of the strategy–business model fit. *Journal of Small Business and Enterprise Development, 26*(3), 441–463. doi:10.1108/JSBED-04-2018-0122

Chiva, R., Alegre, J., & Lapiedra, R. (2007). Measuring organisational learning capability among the workforce. *International Journal of Manpower, 28*(3/4), 224–242. doi:10.1108/01437720710755227

Chung, H., Ding, Z., & Ma, X. (2019). Organisational learning and export performance of emerging market entrepreneurial firms. *European Journal of Marketing, 53*(2), 257–278. doi:10.1108/EJM-08-2017-0496

Cooper, D., & Schindler, P. (2014). *Business Research Methods* (12th ed.). McGraw-Hill/Irwin.

Costa, L. A., Cool, K., & Dierickx, I. (2012). The competitive implications of the deployment of unique resources. *Strategic Management Journal, 34*(4), 445–463. doi:10.1002mj.2018

Creswell, J. W. (2012). *Educational research: Planning, conducting and evaluating quantitative and qualitative research* (4th ed.). Pearson Education.

Cunningham, L. X., & Rowley, C. (2007). Human resource management in Chinese small and medium enterprises. *Personnel Review, 36*(3), 415–439. doi:10.1108/00483480710731356

Dabic, M., Ortiz-De-Urbina-Criado, M., & Romero-Martínez, A. M. (2011). Human resource management in entrepreneurial firms: A literature review. *International Journal of Manpower, 32*(1), 14–33. doi:10.1108/01437721111121206

Dearnaley, P. (2013). Competitive advantage in the new contrived social care marketplace: Do we need a new theoretical framework? *Housing. Care and Support, 16*(3/4), 126–135. doi:10.1108/HCS-08-2013-0013

Demming, C. L., Jahn, S., & Boztug, Y. (2017). Conducting mediation analysis in marketing research. *Marketing ZFP, 39*(3), 76–98. doi:10.15358/0344-1369-2017-3-76

Department of Economic Planning and Development. (2017). Statistics on micro small and medium enterprises (MSMEs). Seminar presented at Department of Economic Planning and Development, Brunei Darussalam, Bandar Seri Begawan.

Donnellan, J., & Rutledge, W. L. (2019). A case for resource-based view and competitive advantage in banking. *Managerial and Decision Economics*, *40*(6), 728–737. doi:10.1002/mde.3041

Drucker, P. F. (1998). The Coming of the New Organization. In *Harvard Business Review on Knowledge Management*. Harvard Business School Press.

Floren, H., Rundquist, J., & Fischer, S. (2016). Entrepreneurial orientation and human resource management: Effects from HRM practices. *Journal of Organizational Effectiveness: People and Performance*, *3*(2), 164–180. doi:10.1108/JOEPP-03-2016-0029

Gelhard, C., & Von Delft, S. (2016). The role of organizational capabilities in achieving superior sustainability performance. *Journal of Business Research*, *69*(10), 4632–4642. doi:10.1016/j.jbusres.2016.03.053

Gharakhani, D., & Mousakhani, M. (2012). Knowledge management capabilities and SMEs organizational performance. *Journal of Chinese Entrepreneurship*, *4*(1), 35–49. doi:10.1108/17561391211200920

Gomes, G., & Wojahn, R. M. (2017). Organizational learning capability, innovation and performance: Study in small and medium-sized enterprises (SMES). *Revista ADM*, *52*(2), 163–175. doi:10.1016/j.rausp.2016.12.003

Gruber, M., Heinemann, F., Brettel, M., & Hungeling, S. (2010). Configurations of resources and capabilities and their performance implications: An exploratory study on technology ventures. *Strategic Management Journal*, *31*(12), 1337–1356. doi:10.1002mj.865

Hair, J., Wolfinbarger, M., & Money, A. (2011). *Essentials of Business Research Methods* (2nd ed.). M.E. Sharpe.

Hair, J. F., Risher, J. J., Sarstedt, M., & Ringle, C. M. (2019). When to use and how to report the results of PLS-SEM. *European Business Review*, *31*(1), 2–24. doi:10.1108/EBR-11-2018-0203

Hammadi, F. A., & Hussain, M. (2019). Sustainable organizational performance. *The International Journal of Organizational Analysis*.

Harrison, T., & Bazzy, J. D. (2017). Aligning organizational culture and strategic human resource management. *Journal of Management Development*, *36*(10), 1260–1269. doi:10.1108/JMD-12-2016-0335

Hindasah, L., & Nuryakin, N. (2020). The relationship between organizational capability, organizational learning and financial performance. *The Journal of Asian Finance, Economics, and Business*, *7*(8), 625–633. doi:10.13106/jafeb.2020.vol7.no8.625

Hitt, M. A., Xu, K., & Carnes, C. M. (2016). Resource-Based View in operations management research. *Journal of Operations Management*, *100*(41), 77–94. doi:10.1016/j.jom.2015.11.002

Ho, T. C. F., Ahmad, N. H., & Thurasamy, R. (2013). Learn and thou shall thrive: Advancing a model of workplace familism and organizational learning capability in small and medium enterprise (SMEs) manufacturers in Malaysia. *Business Strategy Series*, *14*(5/6), 151–159. doi:10.1108/BSS-08-2012-0045

Hooi, L. W., & Ngui, K. S. (2014). Enhancing organizational performance of Malaysian SMEs. *International Journal of Manpower, 35*(7), 973–995. doi:10.1108/IJM-04-2012-0059

Huang, T. C. (2001). The effects of linkage between business and human resource management strategies. *Personnel Review, 30*(2), 132–151. doi:10.1108/00483480110380316

Ibrahim, F., & Reid, V. (2009). What is the Value of Knowledge Management Practices? *Electronic Journal of Knowledge Management, 7*(5), 567–574.

Ibrahim, I., Ali, D. N. H., & Besar, N. S. A. (2020). Accounting information system (AIS) in SMEs: Towards an integrated framework. *International Journal of Asian Business and Information Management, 11*(2), 51–67. doi:10.4018/IJABIM.2020040104

Joo, B. K., & Park, S. (2010). Career satisfaction, organizational commitment, and turnover intention: The effects of goal orientation, organizational learning culture and developmental feedback. *Leadership and Organization Development Journal, 31*(6), 482–500. doi:10.1108/01437731011069999

Jusoh, R., & Parnell, J. A. (2008). Competitive strategy and performance measurement in the Malaysian context: An exploratory study. *Management Decision, 46*(1), 5–31. doi:10.1108/00251740810846716

Kalmuk, G., & Acar, A. Z. (2015). The mediating role of organizational learning capability on the relationship between innovation and firm's performance: A conceptual framework. *Procedia: Social and Behavioral Sciences, 210*, 164–169. doi:10.1016/j.sbspro.2015.11.355

Kaplan, R. S., & Norton, D. P. (1996). Using balanced scorecard as a strategic management system. *Harvard Business Review, 74*(1), 75–85.

Kaplan, R. S., & Norton, D. P. (2004). The strategy map: Guide to aligning intangible assets. *Strategy and Leadership, 32*(5), 10–17. doi:10.1108/10878570410699825

Karami, A., Analoui, F., & Cusworth, J. (2004). Strategic human resource management and resource-based approach: The evidence from the British manufacturing industry. *Management Research News, 27*(6), 50–68. doi:10.1108/01409170410784202

Kaya, N. (2015). Corporate entrepreneurship, generic competitive strategies, and firm performance in small and medium-sized enterprises. *Procedia: Social and Behavioral Sciences, 207*(20), 662–668. doi:10.1016/j.sbspro.2015.10.136

Klarmann, M., & Feurer, S. (2018). Control Variables in Marketing Research. *Journal of Research and Management, 40*(2), 26–40.

Koopman, J. (2015). Pulling the Sobel test up by its bootstraps. In C. E. Lance & R. J. Vandenberg (Eds.), *More Statistical and Methodological Myths and Urban Legends* (pp. 224–244). Routledge.

Kordab, M., Raudeliūnienė, J., & Meidutė-Kavaliauskienė, I. (2020). Mediating Role of Knowledge Management in the Relationship between Organizational Learning and Sustainable Organizational Performance. *Sustainability, 12*(23), 10061. doi:10.3390u122310061

L'Ecuyer, F., & Raymond, L. (2017). Aligning the e-HRM and strategic HRM capabilities of manufacturing SMEs: A "gestalts" perspective. In *Electronic HRM in the Smart Era (The Changing Context of Managing People, Volume)* (pp. 137–172). Emerald Publishing Limited. doi:10.1108/978-1-78714-315-920161006

Liao, S. H., Chen, C. C., Hu, D. C., Chung, Y. C., & Liu, C. L. (2017). Assessing the influence of leadership style, organizational learning and organizational innovation. *Leadership and Organization Development Journal*, *38*(5), 590–609. doi:10.1108/LODJ-11-2015-0261

Liao, S. H., Chen, C. C., Hu, D. C., Chung, Y. C., & Yang, M. J. (2017). Developing a sustainable competitive advantage: Absorptive capacity, knowledge transfer and organizational learning. *The Journal of Technology Transfer*, *42*(6), 1431–1450. doi:10.100710961-016-9532-1

Liao, Y. S. (2005). Business strategy and performance: The role of human resource management control. *Personnel Review*, *34*(3), 294–309. doi:10.1108/00483480510591444

Lim, D. S. K., Celly, N., Morse, E. A., & Rowe, W. G. (2012). Rethinking the effectiveness of asset and cost retrenchment: The contingency effects of a firm's rent creation mechanism. *Strategic Management Journal*, *34*(1), 42–61. doi:10.1002mj.1996

Lopez-Cabrales, A., & Valle-Cabrera, R. (2020). Sustainable HRM strategies and employment relationships as drivers of the triple bottom line. *Human Resource Management Review*, *30*(3), 100689. doi:10.1016/j.hrmr.2019.100689

Macke, J., & Genari, D. (2019). Systematic literature review on sustainable human resource management. *Journal of Cleaner Production*, *208*, 806–815. doi:10.1016/j.jclepro.2018.10.091

Maletic, M., Maletic, D., & Gomiscek, B. (2018). The role of contingency factors on the relationship between sustainability practices and organizational performance. *Journal of Cleaner Production*, *171*, 423–433. doi:10.1016/j.jclepro.2017.09.172

Manzoor, F., Wei, L., Bányai, T., Nurunnabi, M., & Subhan, Q. A. (2019). An examination of sustainable HRM practices on job performance: An application of training as a moderator. *Sustainability*, *11*(8), 2263. doi:10.3390u11082263

Marchini, P. L., Mazza, T., & Medioli, A. (2018). Related party transactions, corporate governance and earnings management, *Corporate Governance. The International Journal of Business in Society*, *18*(6), 1124–1146. doi:10.1108/CG-11-2017-0271

Martinson, M., & Leon, J. D. (2018). Testing horizontal and vertical alignment of HR practices designed to achieve strategic organizational goals. *Journal of Organizational Effectiveness: People and Performance*, *5*(2), 158–181. doi:10.1108/JOEPP-10-2016-0057

Matlay, H., Khandekar, A., & Sharma, A. (2005). Organizational learning in Indian organizations: A strategic HRM perspective. *Journal of Small Business and Enterprise Development*, *12*(2), 211–226. doi:10.1108/14626000510594610

Matthews, R. L., MacCarthy, B. L., & Braziotis, C. (2017). Organisational learning in SMEs: A process improvement perspective. *International Journal of Operations & Production Management*, *37*(7), 970–1006. doi:10.1108/IJOPM-09-2015-0580

McEvoy, G. M., & Buller, P. F. (2013). Human resource management practices in mid-sized enterprises. *American Journal of Business*, *28*(1), 86–105. doi:10.1108/19355181311314789

Meehl, P. E. (1971). High School Yearbooks: A Reply to Schwarz. *Journal of Abnormal Psychology*, *77*(2), 143–148. doi:10.1037/h0030750

Ministry of Finance. (2017). *Budget speech financial year 2015/2016*. Retrieved on 06-03-2017, from http://www.mof.gov.bn/attachments/article/223/BUDGET%20SPEECH%20FY%202015%202016.pdf

Nadler, D., & Tushman, M. (1980). A model for diagnosing organizational behavior. *Organizational Dynamics*, *9*(2), 35–51. doi:10.1016/0090-2616(80)90039-X

Nason, R. S., & Wiklund, J. (2018). An assessment of resource-based theorizing on firm growth and suggestions for the future. *Journal of Management*, *44*(1), 32–60. doi:10.1177/0149206315610635

Naz, F., Aftab, J., & Awais, M. (2016). Impact of human resource management practices (HRM) on performance of SMEs in Multan, Pakistan. *International Journal of Management. Accounting & Economics*, *3*(11), 699–708.

Nazim, A., & Ahmad, S. (2013). Assessing the unidimensionality, reliability, validity and fitness of influential factors of 8th grades student's mathematics achievement in Malaysia. *International Journal of Advanced Research*, *1*(2), 1–7.

Newbert, S. L. (2008). Empirical research on the resource-based view of the firm: An assessment and suggestions for future research. *Strategic Management Journal*, *28*(2), 121–146. doi:10.1002mj.573

Newman, A., & Sheikh, A. Z. (2014). Determinants of best HR practices in Chinese SMEs. *Journal of Small Business and Enterprise Development*, *21*(3), 414–430. doi:10.1108/JSBED-05-2014-0082

Nissen, M. E. (2014). Organization design for dynamic fit: A review and projection. *Journal of Organization Design*, *3*(2), 30–42. doi:10.7146/jod.8196

Oelze, N., Hoejmose, S. U., Habisch, A., & Millington, A. (2016). Sustainable development in supply chain management: The role of organizational learning for policy implementation. *Business Strategy and the Environment*, *25*(4), 241–260. doi:10.1002/bse.1869

Ologunde, A. O., Monday, J. U., & James-Unam, F. C. (2015). The impact of strategic human resource management on competitiveness of small and medium-scale enterprises in the Nigerian hospitality industry. *African Research Review*, *9*(4), 264–276. doi:10.4314/afrrev.v9i4.20

Oltra, M. J., & Flor, M. L. (2010). The moderating effect of business strategy on the relationship between operations strategy and firms' results. *International Journal of Operations & Production Management*, *30*(6), 612–638. doi:10.1108/01443571011046049

Omalaja, M. A., & Eruola, O. A. (2011). Strategic management theory: Concepts, analysis and critiques in relation to corporate competitive advantage from the resource-based philosophy. *Strategic Management Theory*, *44*(1-2), 59–77.

Omotosho, S., & Anyigba, H. (2019). Conceptualising corporate entrepreneurial strategy: A contingency and agency collaborative approach. *Journal of Strategy and Management*, *12*(2), 256–274. doi:10.1108/JSMA-05-2018-0046

Ozdil, S. O., & Kutlu, O. (2019). Investigation of the mediator variable effect using BK, Sobel and Bootstrap methods (Mathematical literacy case). *International Journal of Progressive Education*, *15*(2), 30–43. doi:10.29329/ijpe.2019.189.3

Parisi, C. (2012). The impact of organizational alignment on the effectiveness of firms' sustainability strategic performance measurement systems: An empirical analysis. *The Journal of Management and Governance*, *17*(1), 71–97. doi:10.100710997-012-9219-4

Parnell, J. A. (2010). Strategic clarity, business strategy and performance. *Journal of Strategy and Management*, *3*(4), 304–324. doi:10.1108/17554251011092683

Podgorodnichenko, N., Edgar, F., & McAndrew, I. (2020). The role of HRM in developing sustainable organizations: Contemporary challenges and contradictions. *Human Resource Management Review*, *30*(3), 100685. doi:10.1016/j.hrmr.2019.04.001

Polit, D. F., & Beck, C. T. (2010). Generalization in quantitative and qualitative research: Myths and strategies. *International Journal of Nursing Studies*, *47*(11), 1451–1458. doi:10.1016/j.ijnurstu.2010.06.004 PMID:20598692

Preacher, K. J., & Hayes, A. F. (2004). SPSS and SAS procedures for estimating indirect effects in simple mediation models. *Behavior Research Methods, Instruments, & Computers*, *36*(4), 717–731. doi:10.3758/BF03206553 PMID:15641418

Radzi, C. W. J. B. W. M., Jenatabadi, H. S., & Hasbullah, M. B. (2015). Firm Sustainability Performance Index Modeling. *Sustainability*, *7*(12), 16196–16212. doi:10.3390u71215810

Ramawickrama, J., & Opatha, H. H. P., & PushpaKumari, M. (. (2017). A Synthesis towards the construct of job performance. *International Business Research*, *10*(10), 66–81. doi:10.5539/ibr.v10n10p66

Ringim, K. J., & Reni, A. (2018) Mediating effect of Social Media on the Consumer Buying Behaviour of Cosmetic Products. In *The 3rdInternational Conference on Accounting Management and Economics (ICAME) 1- 23*. Hassanuddin University.

Roca-Puig, V., & Bou-Llusar, J. C. (2007). Organizational fit and performance in Miles and Snow's configurational Theory: A covariant analysis. *Management Research*, *5*(1), 17–28. doi:10.2753/JMR1536-5433050102

Rockwell, S. (2019). A resource-based framework for strategically managing identity. *Journal of Organizational Change Management*, *32*(1), 80–102. doi:10.1108/JOCM-01-2018-0012

Saha, N., Chatterjee, B., Gregar, A., & Sáha, P. (2016). The impact of SHRM on sustainable organizational learning and performance development. *International Journal of Organizational Leadership, 5*(1), 63–75. doi:10.33844/ijol.2016.60291

Sanchez, A. A., Marin, G. S., & Morales, A. M. (2015). The mediating effect of strategic human resource practices on knowledge management and firm performance. *Revista Europea de Dirección y Economía de la Empresa, 24*(3), 138–148. doi:10.1016/j.redee.2015.03.003

Saunders, M., Lewis, P., & Thornhill, A. (2009). *Research Methods for Business Students* (5th Edition). Financial Times/Prentice Hall.

Saunders, M. N. K., Gray, D. E., & Goregaokar, H. (2013). SME innovation and learning: The role of networks and crisis events. *European Journal of Training and Development, 38*(2), 136–148. doi:10.1108/EJTD-07-2013-0073

Schjoedt, L., & Sangboon, K. (2015). Control Variables: Problematic Issues and Best Practices. In The Palgrave Handbook of Research Design in Business and Management (pp. 239-261). Palgrave Macmillan.

Schuler, R., & Jackson, S. E. (2014). Human resource management and organizational effectiveness: Yesterday and today. *Journal of Organizational Effectiveness: People and Performance, 1*(1), 35–55. doi:10.1108/JOEPP-01-2014-0003

Schuler, R. S. (2000). The internationalization of human resource management. *Journal of International Management, 6*(3), 239–260. doi:10.1016/S1075-4253(00)00025-9

Sekaran, U., & Bougie, R. (2016). *Research Methods for Busines: A Skill Building Approach* (7th ed.). Wiley.

Semler, S. W. (1997). Systematic agreement: A theory of organizational alignment. *Human Resource Development Quarterly, 8*(1), 23–40. doi:10.1002/hrdq.3920080105

Seong, J. Y. (2011). The effects of high performance work systems, entrepreneurship and organizational culture on organizational performance. *Seoul Journal of Business, 17*(1), 3–36. doi:10.35152nusjb.2011.17.1.001

Shavarini, S. K., Salimian, H., Nazemi, J., & Alborzi, M. (2013). Operations strategy and business strategy alignment model (case of Iranian industries). *International Journal of Operations & Production Management, 33*(9), 1108–1130. doi:10.1108/IJOPM-12-2011-0467

Shirokova, G., Vega, G., & Sokolova, L. (2013). Performance of Russian SMEs: Exploration, exploitation and strategic entrepreneurship. *Critical Perspectives on International Business, 9*(2), 173–203. doi:10.1108/17422041311299941

Singh, R. (2018). Formal human resource management (HRM) Practices and the performance of small & medium-sized enterprises (SMEs): A study of SMEs in the Caribbean nation of Trinidad. *Journal of Elasticity, 42*(2), 53–80.

Smith, B. (2018). Generalizability in qualitative research: Misunderstandings, opportunities and recommendations for the sport and exercise sciences. *Qualitative Research in Sport, Exercise and Health, 10*(1), 137–149. doi:10.1080/2159676X.2017.1393221

Smith, J. S., Jayaram, J., Ponsignon, F., & Wolter, J. S. (2019). Service recovery system antecedents: A contingency theory investigation. *Journal of Service Management*, *30*(2), 276–300. doi:10.1108/JOSM-01-2018-0026

Smith, K. A., Vasudevan, S. P., & Tanniru, M. R. (1996). Organizational learning and resource-based theory: An integrative model. *Journal of Organizational Change Management*, *9*(6), 41–53. doi:10.1108/09534819610150512

Sojka, L. (2015). Investigation the relationship between human resource management practices and firm's finance performance. *European Scientific Journal*, *11*(34), 87–105.

Sousa, H. P., & Leite, J. C. S. (2014). Modeling Organizational Alignment. In E. Yu, G. Dobbie, M. Jarke, & S. Purao (Eds.), Lecture Notes in Computer Science: Vol. 8824. *Conceptual Modeling*. Springer. doi:10.1007/978-3-319-12206-9_34

Spector, P. E. (2020). Mastering the Use of Control Variables: The Hierarchical Iterative Control (HIC) Approach. *Journal of Business and Psychology*, 1–14. doi:10.100710869-020-09709-0

Tamayo-Torres, I., Gutiérrez-Gutiérrez, L. J., Llorens-Montes, F. J., & Martínez-López, F. J. (2016). Organizational learning and innovation as sources of strategic fit. *Industrial Management & Data Systems*, *116*(8), 1445–1467. doi:10.1108/IMDS-12-2015-0518

Tan, C. L. T., Smyrnios, K. X., & Xiong, L. (2014). What drives learning orientation in fast growth SMEs? *International Journal of Entrepreneurial Behaviour & Research*, *20*(4), 324–350. doi:10.1108/IJEBR-02-2013-0032

Tan, J., & Tan, D. (2004). Environment-strategy co-evolution and co-alignment: A staged model of Chinese SOEs under transition. *Strategic Management Journal*, *26*(2), 141–157. doi:10.1002mj.437

Teeratansirikool, L., Siengthai, S., Badir, Y., & Charoenngam, C. (2013). Competitive strategies and firm performance: The mediating role of performance measurement. *International Journal of Productivity and Performance Management*, *62*(2), 168–184. doi:10.1108/17410401311295722

Twomey, D. F., & Harris, D. L. (2000). From strategy to corporate outcomes: Aligning human resource management systems with entrepreneurial intent. *International Journal of Commerce and Management*, *10*(3/4), 43–55. doi:10.1108/eb047408

Valmohammadi, C. (2011). The impact of TQM implementation on the organizational performance of Iranian manufacturing SMEs. *The TQM Journal*, *23*(5), 496–509. doi:10.1108/17542731111157608

Wadongo, B., & Abdel-Kader, M. (2014). Contingency theory, performance management and organisational effectiveness in the third sector. *International Journal of Productivity and Performance Management*, *63*(6), 680–703. doi:10.1108/IJPPM-09-2013-0161

Waiganjo, E. W., Mukulu, E., & Kahiri, J. (2012). Relationship between strategic human resource management and firm performance of Kenya ' s corporate organizations. *International Journal of Humanities and Social Science*, *2*(10), 62–70.

Woschke, T., Haase, H., & Kratzer, J. (2017). Resource scarcity in SMEs: Effects on incremental and radical innovations. *Management Research Review*, *40*(2), 195–217. doi:10.1108/MRR-10-2015-0239

Wuen, C. H., Ibrahim, F., & Ringim, K. J. (2021). Mediating effect of competitive strategy in the relationship between strategic human resource management and performance of small and medium enterprises in Brunei Darussalam. *Middle East Journal Management, 8*(2/3), 254–277. doi:10.1504/MEJM.2021.114010

Yanuarti, D. W., & Murwatiningsih, M. (2019). Mediating role of competitive strategy and marketing capability on the relationship between entrepreneurial orientation and market performance. *Management Analysis Journal, 8*(2), 188–195.

Yao, F. K., & Chang, S. (2017). Do individual employee's learning goal orientation and civic virtue matter? A micro-foundations perspective on firm absorptive capacity. *Strategic Management Journal, 38*(10), 2041–2060. doi:10.1002mj.2636

Yin, R. K. (2011). *Qualitative Research from Start to Finish.* The Guilford Press.

Yousaf, Z., & Majid, A. (2016). Strategic performance through inter-firm networks: Strategic alignment and moderating role of environmental dynamism. *World Journal of Entrepreneurship, Management and Sustainable Development, 12*(4), 282–298. doi:10.1108/WJEMSD-03-2016-0015

Yu, C., Zhang, Z., & Shen, H. (2017). The effect of organizational learning and knowledge management innovation on SMEs' technological capability. *Eurasia Journal of Mathematics, Science and Technology Education, 13*(8), 5475–5487. doi:10.12973/eurasia.2017.00842a

Yuen, K. F., Wang, X., Ma, F., Lee, G., & Li, X. (2019). Critical success factors of supply chain integration in container shipping: An application of resource-based view theory. *Maritime Policy & Management, 46*(6), 653–668. doi:10.1080/03088839.2019.1597289

Yuliansyah, Y., Gurd, B., & Mohamed, N. (2017). The significant of business strategy in improving organizational performance. *Humanomics, 33*(1), 56–74. doi:10.1108/H-06-2016-0049

Ziyae, B. (2016). Presenting an evaluation model of human resource management's effect on corporate entrepreneurship. *World Journal of Entrepreneurship, Management and Sustainable Development, 12*(3), 228–242. doi:10.1108/WJEMSD-03-2016-0013

Chapter 5
Policies for Promotion of Malaysian SMEs Go Global in the Digital Economy:
SMEs Go Global From Malaysia

Hui Nee Au Yong
https://orcid.org/0000-0002-3337-213X
Universiti Tunku Abdul Rahman, Malaysia

Ke Xin Liew
Universiti Tunku Abdul Rahman, Malaysia

ABSTRACT

The main purpose of this study is to seek industrial players' inputs on fiscal and monetary policies necessary to enhance SME export performance. The authors use survey data from 215 small and medium enterprises having export markets. They report the most essential governmental export support policies from the perspective of the industry players. The study revealed that accessing to financing is the top request to the government. Other policy recommendations are related to market access, human capital development, tax regimes, infrastructure and technology adoption, legal and regulatory environment, and monetary policies. This study gives implications for Malaysia External Trade Development Corporation (MATRADE) policymakers and export-oriented small and medium enterprises (SMEs). The study contributes to the Malaysian SMEs in relation to inputs to the government to improve their export performance especially using e-commerce.

INTRODUCTION

Regional Comprehensive Economic Partnership (RCEP) is the world's biggest free trade, aiming` to facilitate trade and cooperation throughout the Asia-Pacific regions in 15 countries. The RCEP's member countries are willing to accept e-commerce/digital trade provisions that adopt digitalized solutions. The

DOI: 10.4018/978-1-7998-8678-5.ch005

RCEP will significantly accelerate the digitalization of the cross-border e-commerce. Asian e-commerce is growing rapidly. Many countries in the ASEAN countries have demonstrated a strong commitment to the digital trade e-commerce. The ASEAN Digital Masterplan (ADM) 2025 has a vision that 2021-2025 could see the ASEAN make giant strides towards becoming both a digital economy and a digital society, with the ASEAN population now own broadband devices and cloud services while the COVID-19 pandemic has inadvertently allowed people to engage in digital-oriented economic activities (ASEAN Secretariat, 2021). A regional market of ASEAN and RCEP can help SMEs pilot their exports.

SMEs have always been important in the development of the economy. SMEs contribute significantly to the nation building especially in terms of employment and GDP. Based on SME Corporation Malaysia (2013), the manufacturing process is defined as the conversion of components as well as materials into new products. The meaning associated with services indicates all services. In addition, mining & quarrying, construction along with primary agriculture are also included. According to SME Corporation Malaysia (2019), SMEs contributed 66.2% of employment, 38.3% of GDP and 17.3% of export in 2018. In comparison, countries such as Germany recorded 57% share of GDP (Small and Medium Industries Development Corporation Malaysia, 2006). In other words, there is still the lack of global expansion activities among SMEs.

According to Department of Statistics Malaysia, DOSM (2018), the total amount of SMEs is 907,065, which converts to around 98.5% of business establishments in Malaysia. In terms of SMEs establishment by Sector by 2016, SMEs consist of a sizeable amount of service sector SMEs which adds up to 89% SMEs in the entire Malaysia. The list is consecutively followed by manufacturing (6%), construction (4%), agriculture (1%), and mining sector (<1%). According to Key Statistics on SMEs 2016/17, the main SMEs establishment states in Malaysia that represent 19.8%, 14.7%, 10.8%, 8.3% and 7.4% of the total establishments are Selangor, Kuala Lumpur, Perak, Johor and Pulau Pinang. Digital Trade Free Zone is also a significant milestone in globalization. Malaysia External Trade Development Corporation (MATRADE) indicates that SMEs should reduce their dependency on the domestic market and start looking for their expansion beyond Malaysia. Despite all the merits of expanding abroad, Malaysian SMEs need to be alert and to amplify their horizons so that this move will improve their performance, but also to mitigate risk. The export performance of SMEs in 2018 remained 17.3% in 2018. SME exports increased to RM171.9 billion in 2018. Despite making up 98.5% of business establishments in Malaysia, only 17.3% of export rate was contributed by SMEs. However, only 50,197 or 5.53% of Malaysian SMEs involve exporting activities. The export share of SMEs was more than 20 percent less than that in countries such as the Philippines, Hong Kong, Taiwan and even the USA (World Bank Group, 2020). Exporting is the most used mode of entry while increasing profit is the main cause for internationalization (Abdullah and Zain, 2011).

Globalization and digitalization are unavoidable trends for businesses. Rapid updates have been brought by disruptive innovations. These challenges were mentioned by MATRADE which highlighted that more international companies are entering the local market, propelling SMEs to move on to greener pastures in overseas markets. With more export, Malaysia can also benefit from it with faster economic development, and faster rate of employment. The government is encouraging the SMEs to increase their export to expand their markets overseas as part of their business growth. The Government's commitment is to drive the nation's digital economy agenda. It will serve to expand the e-Commerce sector by facilitating SMEs to enhance their online presence and entering third country markets. Malaysia's SMEs using e-Commerce are offered the opportunity of global expansion via export to grow exponentially. Change in the mindset among leaders of SMEs is necessary to move forward. Malaysia and Alibaba Group opened the Digital Free Trade Zone (DFTZ) in 2017. DFTZ is a project to make cross-border trade easier via e-commerce. It is a milestone that nurtures SMEs through e-commerce. DFTZ gives a simpler route for Malaysian SMEs to involve in the export trade. Malaysia's SMEs and e-Commerce players have offered global expansion opportunities through DFTZ. For the digital technologies, Malaysia has become quite prominent in terms of its E-commerce activities. Malaysian Government had also participated in the ASEAN Agreement on Electronic Commerce in 2018. Companies using this platform for export expanded from 1,800 to 27,000, with their investment totaled RM1.5 billion for setting-up regional e-Fulfilment hubs (MDEC, 12 May 2021).

One of the main problems faced by many SMEs is its risk adverse nature. These risk-adverse SMEs avoid taking on risk in the overseas market which will unavoidably impact the performance of the company. Risk management is the practice of managing risks. Due to high-risk strategies, it may produce either a high return or serious failure, so effective companies have exhibited a commitment toward calculated risk-taking. The export-oriented companies pursue opportunities with their tolerance of risk. To sustain the business growth, SMEs are encouraged to determine the risk appetite for their businesses without being fearful of economic and regulatory changes to which they are exposed. Overall risk appetite relates to the degree of tolerance of an enterprise to the risk. In pursuing the export performance of the enterprise, it is of the interest of the society to be aware of the risks an enterprise is willing to take as well as the ethical behavior the enterprise needs to adopt, and elements that influence the risk appetite of an enterprise. In Malaysia, most of the small and medium enterprises are considered risk averse since more than 98.5% of them without the willingness to conduct global business. At the same time, around half of the Malaysian SMEs still prefer the traditional method instead of digitalization when doing business. Ironically, about 33% of SMEs confront a threat to be out of business without additional help in one month, and up to half within three months (Islam et al., 2021). This may lead to a sluggish economy.

According to MATRADE, the key issue faced by the government is that many SMEs are risk averse as only around 5% of SMEs had allocated resources to conduct business globally. Therefore, this global mindset change process involves risks from an investment's financial risks to the risks of the lack of technology and IT skills in facing international markets. The performance of the SME sector represents the economic environment in a country since SMEs occupy integral parts of business trading activities in a country. In Taiwan, 97% of the businesses fall under the SME sector which contributed 50% of total GDP in Taiwan. Other than that, SMEs in Singapore make up 99% of the entire business industry, making up to around 50% of the total GDP, and accommodating 67% of the workforce via employee hiring. In fact, there are 98.50% of established business entities in Malaysia's SME sector yet they only make up 38.3% of contribution rate towards the total GDP, with an amount of 66.20% employment rate and 17.3% export rate. The intended target in the Master Plan 2012-2020 is to achieve 41% of GDP and 23% of the share of export. When a company decides to expand through globalization, it is important to establish an expansion strategy to overcome the risks. This can be achieved with a business specific risk appetite to foster a corporate cultural change ensuring that the risk appetite has a linkage with the business objectives. In order to adapt to an entry to a foreign market, the company has to create a win-win tactic to contribute to its growth and the foreign market's prosperity. It allows the firm's risk to be reduced when it demonstrates the market behaviors that adapt to foreign markets.

Based on the data collected from SMEs, the usage of ICT tool is shown to go below the expectation. Meanwhile, there are only 44% of SMEs using cloud service and merely 35% of SMEs have utilized IOT solutions. This improvement brought upon by DFTZ brings changes in connection. The status of Malaysia is a turning point for e-commerce improvement which must be accelerated together with higher awareness of the SME's. The purpose of this study is to collect suggested policies necessary to improve the SMEs' export performance. This study adds values to SMEs studies in Malaysia. The importance of this research is to clarify several factors which can be instrumental, other than contributing useful insights to SMEs, and policymakers upon its completion. This study gives an opportunity for SMEs to be aware about the risk of global expansion. By understanding the risk, such action will be able to provide a broader perspective for SMEs. Other than that, suggestions on the enhancement of government policies to promote export commitment, and technology adoption such as e-commerce with the alertness of the underlying risk towards the improvement of export performance will create value to SMEs. This study will serve as an alternative perspective to policymakers, on the global dealings of SMEs. Policymakers can implement policies based on the recommendation of this study. The study's findings can also be reference for the policymakers in providing support to SMEs more effectively.

This chapter proceeds as follows. The next section discusses past literature and methodology. Next, the main findings will be established and elaborated. Finally, the last section sets forth our conclusions.

Background

Involvement in digital economy is encouraged by the government, as it is the latest driver of economy growth. Alm et al. (2016) opine that Europe will be surpassed by these more digitally inclined economies, Hong Kong, China, Taiwan, South Korea. Similarly, weaknesses in digital infrastructure and financial credits are the major problems in developing countries (Arbache, 2019) including Malaysia. The results from Tseng and Johnsen (2011) show that the technological advancement level is essential for SMEs that have adopted the Internet in their internationalisation effort. According to Mazzarol (2015), what will determine SMEs to adopt ICT is the mindset, who will need to better understand the investment in ICT. SMEs are typically more dependent on their business ecosystem and are more vulnerable to market failures, policy inefficiencies and inconsistencies (OECD, 2017).

Zailani, Dahlan and Jallaludin (2009) affirm that knowledge sources do positively influence the adoption of electronic business (e-business), and the speed of international market entry by e-business is positively affected by entrepreneurs' international experience, business innovation capability, and marketing capability (Ziyae et al., 2014). Eventually, the firm performance in global markets has been better for those that have adopted more e-business tools (Lal, 2004).

SMEs with a strong growth motivation have more international orientation and growth mindset (Moen, Heggeseth and Lome. 2016). Potential challenges and uncertainties in making profit are the major excuse for non-internationalization (Abdullah & Zain, 2011). The main influence upon the foreign market entry was the level of cost involved and the amount of risk occurred at the company/brand (Hutchinson, Quinn & Alexander, 2006). Firms are motivated to expand overseas when their Porter's Diamond attributes in their local market seem to be deficient (Yang et al., 2009). In addition, more willingness on taking risk will also be reflected in better management commitment (Chugan and Singh, 2015). Rosnan et al. (2014) also highlight that early preparation is needed before going to export against risk, but not many manufacturing SMEs in Malaysia will turn it to action.

The government needs to fully recognize the potential to capture export opportunities (HeinrichÃ, 2014). In other words, given the low take-up rate of government support programmes, governments should proactively promote these programmes (OECD 2008).

Theoretically, Karavdic et al., (2005) put forward a contingency approach for a relationship between marketing strategies and export performance, and further extend the theory by introducing the factor of e-commerce into export theories. On the other hand, the mindset theory is a decision-making process to achieve organization objectives (Dominguez & Mayrhofer (2017). According to Felício, Meidutė and Kyvik (2016), global mindset is linked to the strategic and cultural dimensions of an organization (Kedia & Mukherji, 1999; Paul, 2000).

Government's SMEs Supporting Policies

Past literature shows that the government has intervened in several ways to help the firm, for instance in financial funds (Cull, Li, Sun, & Xu, 2015; Owenvbiugie, 2017), policy (Lazzarini, 2015) and fiscal policies such as tax reductions or exemptions an important role (Alhnity, Mohamad, & Ishak, 2016). SMEs in both servicing and manufacturing industries have more access and eligibility to funds (Van Auken and Carter, 1989). The grants shield SMEs mainly the manufacturing sector, from the fund imbalance (Madrid-Guijarro et al., 2009). Furthermore, SMEs in the manufacturing sector allocate most of these grants to the production process (Hosamane and Alroaia, 2009) that reduces their operational risks. According to Yatim, Rusuli and Yatim (2019), many SMEs are of the opinion that government intervention is important to gain competitive advantage and success of SMEs in a sustainable way. In contrast, Cheong and Lee and Weissmann (2020) found that (1) debt funding is not conducive to company performance; (2) access to non-bank credit and tax incentives enhances the performance of SME; (3) tax structures restrain SME growth; and (4) SMEs are more conservative on accounting and taxation.

Export Commitment

Export commitment refers to the owner or manager's willingness to involve in export related activities by devoting adequate managerial, financial, and human resources. Companies involved in international trade have to allocate necessary resources in order to reap the fruits from the success in the export market. Wee et al. (2019) show that human capital is found to be the challenge for Malaysian SMEs in export. SMEs rely heavily on the information collected by the personal contacts for their internationalisation process (Altnaa, Vasa, Neszmélyi, 2021). Chugan and Singh (2015), and Walter, Nique and Bischoff (2018) argue that export commitment influences export performance among SMEs. There is another perspective that export performance is an antecedent of export commitment among small and medium-sized exporters (Lages & Montgomery, 2004). There is also a positive effect of adaptation, cooperation and communication on export performance mediated by trust and commitment (Hasaballah et al., 2019). In another study, Ismail, Alam and Hamid (2017) show that trust is linked to commitment and export performance, while commitment positively affects competitive advantage, and trust affects competitive advantage through commitment. In contrast, Bloemer, Pluymaekers, and Odekerken, (2013) conclude on the indirect impact of commitment towards performance.

Electronic Experience

Export experience is company experience in exporting operations. Findings of Felício, Meidutė, and Kyvik (2016), Forsgren (2002), Leonido (2004), and Sinkovics, Kurt, and Sinkovics (2018) on SMEs highlight that export experience is the main factor in minimizing export-related risks. Through learning and gaining the export experience from exporting operations, SMEs will be able to grow their overseas markets knowledge and thus implement better exporting activities (Forsgren, 2002; Katsikeas et al., 1994;

Felício, Meidutė, and Kyvik, 2016; Sinkovics, Kurt and Sinkovics, 2018). The finding of Altıntaş et al. (2007) ascertains a positive relationship between export experience and export performance. Therefore, sufficient export experience will contribute to more company capacities.

Electronic Commerce (E-Commerce)

E-commerce is the level of access in multi-level networking gadget which merges a logistic platform with an e-commerce-based network. Internet was opened for use by the public since early 1990s. The Internet will help SMEs in dealing with the challenges that come with the market risks (Ajdari, 2007). In turn, when the Internet is used to reduce cost and as a competitive weapon, this will have a positive impact on export marketing performance (Lu and Julian, 2007). In short, when SMEs deploy Internet capabilities, these firms will benefit with performance gains (Mathews et al., 2018). The findings of Savrul, Incekara and Sener (2014) show that for SMEs to compete in a global platform, e-commerce can help them although their size is a disadvantage. Specifically, results from Ramanathan, Ramanathan and Hsiao (2012) suggest that e-commerce's operations and marketing aspects can lead to SMEs giving solid performance. Improvement in export performance is influenced by export orientation, logistic supports, and adoption of e-commerce (Handayani, Ferdinand, Sugiono, 2017). E-commerce adoption has a positive influence on SMEs' performance measured by the average sales growth rate (Abebe, 2014).

Risk Appetite

Risk is the probability of an event and its consequences. Risk appetite is defined as the total risk one wishes to undertake. Risk is inevitable in the business environment. Risk appetite also provides an awareness to restrain overflowing risks which might lead to detrimental consequences in the organization. Global economic risks and geopolitical risks are of main concern for SMEs (Asgary, Ozdemir & O¨ zyu¨rek, 2020). On the other hand, managed risks may bring benefits to companies. According to Aftab and Rehman (2017), in terms of exchange rate risk, the exchange rate volatility can expedite the demand for the gas and plastic industries. It was suggested that risk-taking had impacted directly (Felício, 2016 and Epetimehin, 2013) and in positive way (García-Granero et al., 2015, Gilson & Shalley, 2004, Lawal et al., 2018, Wambugu et al., 2015 and Yuan & Woodman, 2010) the performance of enterprises. Specifically, SMEs focus mainly on the Control Environment and Risk Appetite components of enterprise risk management (Yap, Angeline & Yap, 2018). Risk appetite indicates the risk level that the company decides to pursue. The identification of the risk appetite is one of the crucial procedures of running an effective risk control system in enterprises (Gontarek (2016). Besides, a risk-identifying process will be able to set priorities for allocating resources and effective communication within a competitive environment (Gontarek, 2016; Gorzeń-Mitka, 2013). That said, the perception of risk taking, and the industry are key factors to leverage Internet-related capabilities for firms (Mathews et al., 2018).

Export Performance

Export performance can be explained as the outcome of selling locally made goods and services to other countries. Export performance can also be described in terms of profit and customer satisfaction. Ultimately, companies involved in international trade aim to expand globally to gain external market share and achieve performance positively in export. However, Wijayarathne and Perera (2018) suggest that financial barriers, governmental barriers and economic barriers are the main barriers to export. Specifically, the government barriers related to taxes and customs delays tend to affect exporters (Knox, 2020). In terms of trade in goods, the retail trade sector is the sector reporting the greatest peculiarities regarding export barriers (Silva, Franco & Magrinho, 2016). Altıntas, Tokol and Harcar (2007) suggest that procedural barriers and foreign competition are negatively affecting export performance. Furthermore, Jalali (2012) identifies the operational dimension, environmental dimension, financial dimension, source dimension, legal dimension and logistic dimension as export barriers to the export performance. Externally, procedural and foreign exchange are the top barriers for companies in pursuing internationalization due to foreign exchange know-how (Roy, Sekhar & Vyas, 2016). SMEs' performance is negatively related to the external exporting barriers (Al-Hyari et al., 2011). Vivekanandan et al. (2006) suggest that the perception of export barriers declines with the business growth. Sinkovics, Kurt and Sinkovics (2018) put their focus of the study on export performance.

These empirical results allow the following research hypotheses:

Hypothesis One: Export commitment affects risk appetite positively.
Hypothesis Two: Export experience affects risk appetite positively.
Hypothesis Three: Electronic commerce affects risk appetite positively.
Hypothesis Four: Risk appetite affects export performance positively.

In this study, the chapter would like to find out the main drivers promoting SMEs to adopt digital service in the scope of the use of e-commerce. Meanwhile, the study further extends the contingency model of export marketing strategy and performance so as to contribute to Malaysian SMEs and researchers. The conceptual framework of this study is demonstrated in Figure 1 below.

METHODS

The ethical approval for this research project/protocol was approved on 6 September 2018 with the approval reference number U/SERC/103/2018. The targeted population for this study is a total of 1,326 SMEs registered to Malaysia's Digital Free Trade Zone (DFTZ) for export business or for the plan to expand to overseas markets. Most of the questionnaires for this study are distributed in export related exhibitions and seminars to SMEs, the industrial players. The data was collected using survey questionnaires (Appendix) during export-oriented exhibitions. Therefore, a lot of information is collected from a very specific group of respondents. A total of 215 useful pieces of data have been collected. At the end, 16% of the response rate was recorded. The statistical software utilized is SmartPLS 3 version 3.2.8. This study looks into a two-stage analysis which is the measurement model (validity and reliability), and then the structural model to test the hypothesis relationships.

RESULTS

Figure 2 shows the location of the respondents. The top five Malaysian states include 35% in Selangor, 26% in Johor, 14% in Kuala Lumpur, 9% Pulau Pinang and 5% in Perak among the DFTZ companies. Other states comprise of 11% of the respondents.

Figure 1. Conceptual framework

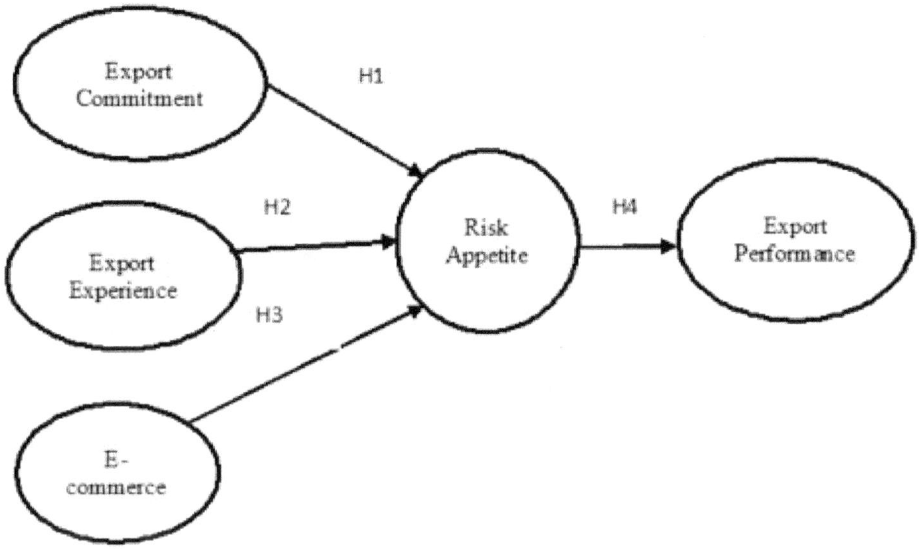

Figure 2. Respondent location by state

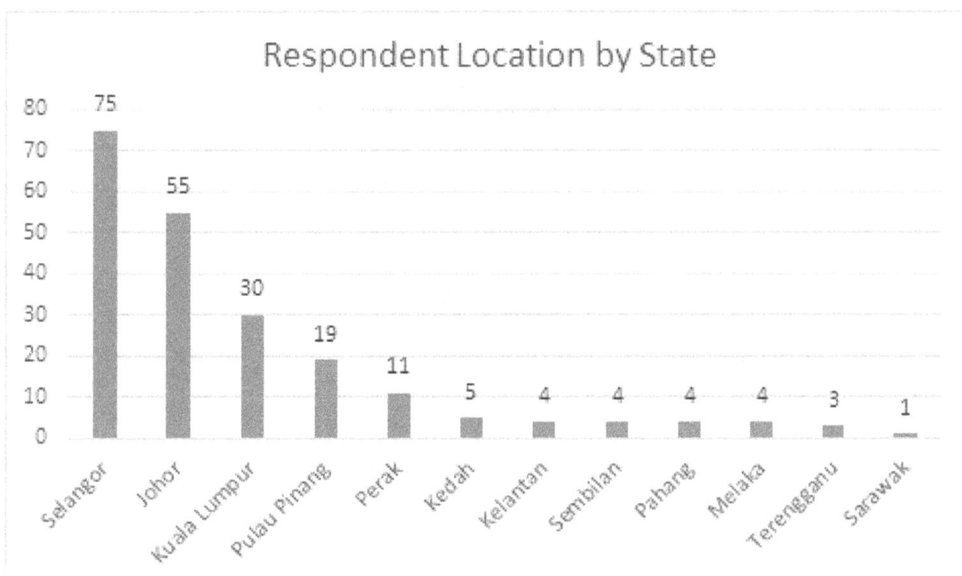

Referring to Figure 3, in terms of percentage, 30% of the respondents are owners or directors, while 22% are managers, indicating that 52% of the respondents are middle to top management of the company, 34% of the respondents are officers / executive, and 14% are non-executive staff.

Referring to Figure 4, most (53%) of the companies have over 12 months of export experience, 16% have less than one month of experience, and the rests are between one and twelve months.

Figure 3. Position of respondents, by frequency

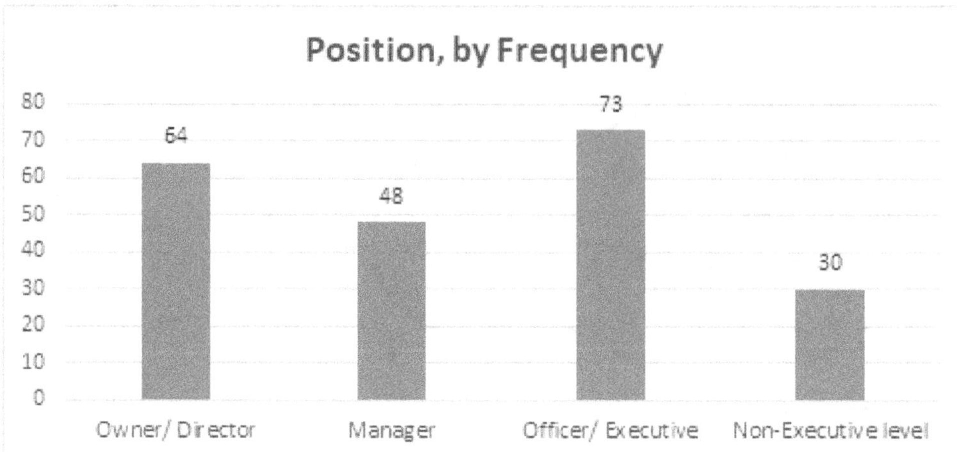

Figure 4. Months involved in export activities

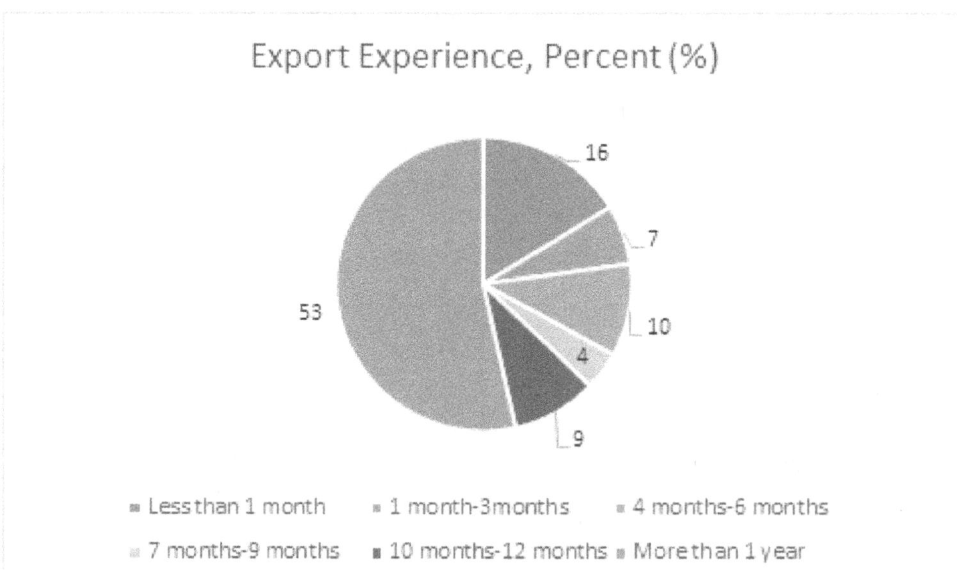

The assessment of the measurement model was conducted; the Cronbach Alpha values for the measurement of the model range between 0.865 and 0.911 for all the variables. Composite reliability yields results between 0.901 and 0.931, exceeding the recommended 0.70 threshold value, with the AVE values being higher than 0.5. Refer Table 1.

Positive relationships were found between independent variable and dependent variable. Other than that, all the p-values of hypothesis are less than 0.05 significance level and therefore they support all hypotheses in the study. The study has identified that there are positive relations between E-Commerce and risk appetite ($\beta = 0.245$, ρ-value below 0.01), Export Commitment and risk appetite ($\beta = 0.172$, ρ-value

Table 1. Measurement model

Constructs	No. of Items	Cronbach's Alpha	Composite Reliability	Average Variance Extracted
E-Commerce	4	0.909	0.927	0.647
Export Commitment	4	0.877	0.916	0.732
Export Experience	7	0.895	0.927	0.760
Export Performance	6	0.865	0.901	0.647
Risk Appetite	5	0.911	0.931	0.693

below 0.05), Export Experience and risk appetite (β = 0.104, ρ-value below 0.05) and risk appetite and Export Performance (β = 0.460, ρ-value below 0.01). Thus, H1, H2, H3 and H4 were supported for this study. The R2 for this study which is 20.8%, shows a weak impact towards the endogenous construct.

Based on the result of the study, export commitment has shown a significant impact on the willingness of risk-taking and pursuing the export performance. Other than that, the importance of digitalization is also confirmed by the study. The result further indicates that higher level of adoption of e-commerce will bring along higher level of effectiveness when conducting global business. Refer to Table 2.

Table 2. Path coefficients analysis

Independent Variable	Path Coefficients	T-Statistics	P-Values
Electronic commerce	0.245	3.170	0.002*
Export Commitment	0.172	2.028	0.043*
Export Experience	0.104	1.992	0.046*
Risk Appetite	0.460	7.254	0.000*

*P-value<0.05 significance level

Respondents' Inputs

There are close to one hundred SME's suggestions of government policies provided by the respondents. Refer to Figure 5. The respondents' suggestions are grouped into seven categories: Access to Financing, Market Access, Human Capital Development, Tax Regimes, Infrastructure and Technology Adoption, Legal and Regulatory Environment, and Monetary Policies.

Access to Financing

Financing is the main concern of the SMEs. Most of the suggestions are for the government to increase export credits / funds / grants / support / subsidies / low interest loans to entrepreneurs / SMEs, provide grants for promotional activities for manufacturers to provide product overseas, provide allowances / incentives to SMEs, provide extra incentive to those players in the market, provide funds to entrepreneurs to join the foreign market, provide logistics and taxes clearance subsidy, provide incentive for certification and training courses for companies on export businesses, increase incentives e.g. tax cost, subsidies on transportation and sponsor business matching events, provide more financing for SMEs interested to export, and provide subsidies against costs.

Market Access

For market access, SMEs suggest many initiatives for the government's consideration. The government can consider assisting the SMEs in foreign product registration, getting support from the diplomat to get official channel, ease of contact and to ask for foreign market information, helping SMEs to gain a breakthrough in exporting and identifying the rules of regulation for each country, especially on custom regulations.

Others include increase in the quality of the product export and price efficiency, increase in export oversea promotional tours, provide more platforms and provide export information, more exposition and exhibition to introduce the product to other countries, and promote local products to the export market.

Furthermore, the government can intensify the promotion of the advantages of export, promote products' export markets and opportunities, promote export of halal products, promote matching to bring delegates from overseas to meet the locals, provide better exposure to the companies, and provide exhibition / event / summit opportunities to expose companies to the export market.

Human Capital Development

Human capital development is very important for the sustainable development of the export trade. The SMEs suggest that the government conduct more training / workshops / seminars / forums on e-commerce and expand export opportunities and publish guidance for the SMEs to grow their businesses.

Tax Regimes

In terms of taxation, the SMEs suggest reduction in export duties and tax rates, cancellation of Sales and Services Tax (SST) and this is to be replaced with a lower Goods and Services Tax (GST) rate, tax incentives for the use of latest technology and rebate for exporting companies.

Infrastructure and Technology Adoption

On infrastructure and technology adoption, the respondents suggest the expansion of warehouse facilities and enhancement of e-commerce, logistics management system and supply chain management. Besides, the SMEs expect that the third-party platform and Digital Free Trade Zone (DFTZ) area are enabled for easy access of tax, permits with simplified process and open one-step center for documentation.

Legal and Regulatory Environment

The respondents highlight their desire to have a legal and regulatory environment, which is transparent and open-minded in policymaking for proper procedure for export, reduced red-tape and efficient custom-clearing that provide a better solution for SMEs.

Monetary Policy

For the nature of cross-border trade, in terms of monetary policy, the respondents suggest the importance for the government to maintain a stable and favorable foreign exchange rate.

Figure 5. Summary of policy recommendations

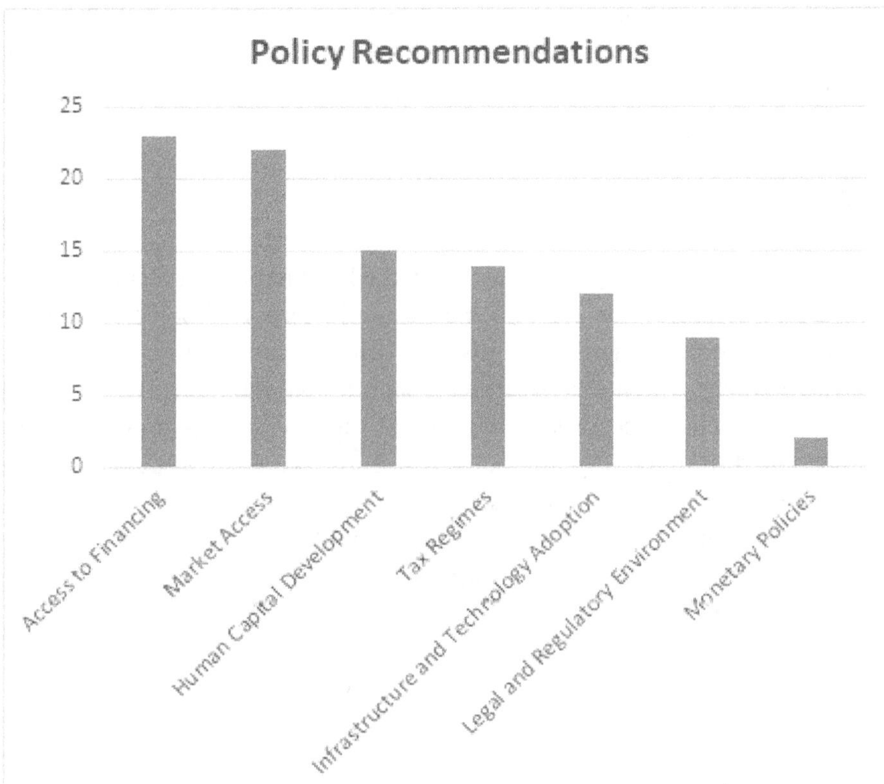

SOLUTIONS AND RECOMMENDATIONS

Research findings reveal the relationships of export commitment and electronic commerce with risk appetite, and the latter with export performance. Respondents believed that their export commitment may influence their export performance. This is consistent with the findings from (Hasaballah et al., 2019). Furthermore, respondents emphasized that risk-taking is important because it can contribute positively to export performance. The findings show that the use of electronic commerce by SMEs makes significant contributions to control risk. The finding is consistent with Ajdari (2007) which highlighted that the Internet would help SMEs in handling market risks. The findings are in line with researchers advocating the role of risk-taking in enhancing SMEs' export demand (Aftab & Rehman, 2017) and subsequently their performance (Lawal et al., 2018).

This chapter also collected SMEs' inputs on the required financial sector policies, monetary policies and other polices for the government's consideration. Firstly, it was found that e-commerce and globalization are pushing the SMEs to advanced business level. Secondly, financial constraint is one the main obstacles that demotivate SMEs from expanding overseas.

FUTURE RESEARCH DIRECTIONS

Nevertheless, one restriction of this research is the number of respondents. More respondents should be considered in future studies. At the same time, the Malaysian government also launched many SME development and financing programmes to encourage SMEs to venture into digitalization. Thus, SMEs are suggested to work closely and obtain more useful information provided by government agencies.

CONCLUSION

This study contributes that it provides information about the key factors that influence Malaysian SME's future global expansion for policy makers and managers. In terms of policy recommendations, the government is recommended to strengthen the dissemination of information of funding programmes. Some respondents give feedback that the government should maintain a stable foreign exchange rate. The practical contribution of the necessary governmental support policies especially access to financing and markets is obtained from the SMEs directly. Currently, there is a limited theoretical framework which comprises risk appetite in the marketing strategy-export performance relationship. Positive relations between export commitment and export performance with risk appetite were detected. This study significantly contributes to the integration of risk appetite in the contingency model of export marketing strategy and the performance model.

ACKNOWLEDGMENT

This research was supported by the Universiti Tunku Abdul Rahman Research Fund (UTARRF) under Grant Project No.: IPSR/RMC/UTARRF/2018-C1/A03.

REFERENCES

Abdullah, N. A. H. N., & Zain, S. N. M. (2011). The Internationalization Theory and Malaysian Small Medium Enterprises (SMEs). *International Journal of Trade. Economics and Finance*, *2*(4), 318–322.

Abebe, M. (2014). Electronic commerce adoption, entrepreneurial orientation and small- and medium-sized enterprise (SME) performance. *Journal of Small Business and Enterprise Development*, *21*(1), 100–116. doi:10.1108/JSBED-10-2013-0145

Adam, C. S., & Bevan, D. L. (2005). Fiscal deficits and growth in developing countries. *Journal of Public Economics*, *4*(1), 571–597. doi:10.1016/j.jpubeco.2004.02.006

Aftab, M., & Rehman, I. U. (2017). Exchange rate risk and the bilateral trade between Malaysia and Singapore. *Studies in Economics and Finance*, *34*(3), 407–426. doi:10.1108/SEF-08-2015-0188

Al-Hyari, K., Al-Nasour, M., Alnsour, M., Al-Weshah, G., & Abutayeh, B. (2011). Exporting Performance and Manufacturing Activities in Jordanian SMEs: External Barriers and Relationships. *International Journal of Global Business*, *4*(1), 44–72.

Alesina, A., de Broeck, M., Prati, A., & Tabellini, G. (1992, Oct.). Default risk on government debt in OECD Countries. *Economic Policy: A European Forum*, 427-463.

Alhnity, H., Mohamad, A., & Ishak, A. K. (2016). Impact of Entrepreneurial Orientation on Small Business Performance: Moderating Role of Government Intervention. *International Review of Management and Marketing*, *6*(S7), 95–100.

Alm, E., Colliander, N., Deforche, F., Lind, F., Stohne, V., & Sundstrom, O. (2016). *Digitizing Europe: Why Northern European Frontrunners Must Drive Digitalization of the EU Economy*. The Boston Consulting Group (BSG).

Altıntas¸, M. H., Tokol, T., & Harcar, T. (2007). The effects of export barriers on perceived export performance: An empirical research on SMEs in Turkey. *EuroMed Journal of Business*, *2*(1), 36–56. doi:10.1108/14502190710749947

Altnaa, U., Vasa, L., & Neszmelyi, G. I. (2021). The Role of Network Ties on SMEs Internationalization Process in the Developing Countries/Emerging Markets: A Comparison between Mongolia, China, and Malaysia. *International Journal of Economics and Business Administration*, *9*(1), 274–291. doi:10.35808/ijeba/672

Arbache, J. (2018) Seizing the Benefits of the Digital Economy for Development. *International Centre of Trade and Sustainable Development*. https://www.ictsd.org/opinion/seizing- the-benefits-of-the-digital-economy-for- development

ASEAN Secretariat, . (2021, January). *ASEAN Digital Masterplan 2025*. ASEAN.

Asgary, A., Ozdemir, A. I., & Özyürek, H. (2020). Small and Medium Enterprises and Global Risks: Evidence from Manufacturing SMEs in Turkey. *Int J Disaster Risk Sci*, *11*(1), 59–73. doi:10.100713753-020-00247-0

Bloemer, J., Pluymaekers, M., & Odekerken, A. (2013). Trust and affective commitment as energizing forces for export performance. *International Business Review*, *22*(2), 363–380. doi:10.1016/j.ibusrev.2012.05.002

Cheong, C. W. H., Lee, M. H., & Weissmann, M. A. (2020). Credit access, tax structure and the performance of Malaysian manufacturing SMEs. *International Journal of Managerial Finance*, *16*(4), 433–454. doi:10.1108/IJMF-08-2019-0308

Chugan, P. K., & Singh, S. (2015). Export Commitment and Its Impact on Firm-level Export Performance: Evidence from SMEs Cluster of Ahmedabad, India, *Journal of Behavioural Economics, Finance, Entrepreneurship. Accounting and Transport*, *3*, 90–95.

Cull, R., Li, W., Sun, B., & Xu, L. C. (2015). Government Connections and Financial Constraints Evidence from a Large Representative Sample of Chinese Firms. *Journal of Corporate Finance*, *32*(June), 271–294. doi:10.1016/j.jcorpfin.2014.10.012

Dominguez, N., & Mayrhofer, U. (2017). Internationalization stages of traditional SMEs: Increasing, decreasing and re-increasing commitment to foreign markets. *International Business Review*, *26*(6), 1051–1063. doi:10.1016/j.ibusrev.2017.03.010

Epetimehin, F. M. (2013). Cross-border insurance marketing and the corporate implications. *European Scientific Journal*, *9*(1), 152–162.

Felício, J. A., Meidutė, I., & Kyvik, Ø. (2016). Global mindset, cultural context, and the internationalization of SMEs. *Journal of Business Research*, *69*(11), 4924–4932. doi:10.1016/j.jbusres.2016.04.054

Forsgren, M. (2002). The concept of learning in the Uppsala internationalization process model: A critical review. *International Business Review*, *11*(3), 257–277. doi:10.1016/S0969-5931(01)00060-9

García-Granero, A., Llopis, Ó., Fernández-Mesa, A., & Alegre, J. (2015). Unraveling the link between managerial risk-taking and innovation: The mediating role of a risk-taking climate. *Journal of Business Research*, *68*(5), 1094–1104. doi:10.1016/j.jbusres.2014.10.012

Gilson, L. L., & Shalley, C. E. (2004). A little creativity goes a long way: An examination of teams' engagement in creative processes. *Journal of Management*, *30*(4), 453–470. doi:10.1016/j.jm.2003.07.001

Gontarek, W. (2016). Risk governance of financial institutions: The growing importance of risk appetite and culture. *Journal of Risk Management in Financial Institutions*, *9*(2), 120–129.

Gorzeń-Mitka, I. (2013). Risk Identification Tools – Polish MSMES Companies Practices. *Problems of Management in the 21stcentury*, *7*, 6-11.

Handayani, E., Ferdinand, A. T., & Sugiono, S. (2017). Analysis of Factors Affecting the Performance of SME Exports in Central Java through Export Marketing Strategies. *Jurnal Sains Pemasaran Indonesia*, *16*(2), 103–116. doi:10.14710/jspi.v16i2.103-116

Hasaballah, A. H. A., Genc, O. F., Mohamada, O., & Ahmed, Z. U. (2019). How do relational variables affect export performance? Evidence from Malaysian exporters. *Asia Pacific Journal of Marketing and Logistics*, *31*(1), 128–156. doi:10.1108/APJML-12-2017-0345

HeinrichÃ, S (2014). Socio-Economic Consequences of Digital Transformation: Socio-ekonomske posledice digitalne transformacije. *Socioeconomica – The Scientific Journal for Theory and Practice of Socio-economic Development. Procia CIRP*, *3*(6), 179-202. DOI: doi:10.12803/ SJSECO.369814

Hosamane, M. D., & Alroaia, Y. V. (2009). Entrepreneurship and development of small-scale industries in Iran: Strategic management tools and business performance assessment. *The IUP Journal of Entrepreneurship Development*, *6*(1), 27.

Hutchinson, K., Quinn, B., & Alexander, N. (2006). SME retailer internationalisation: Case study evidence from British retailers. *International Marketing Review*, *23*(1), 25–53. https://doi.org/10.1108/02651330610646287

Islam, A., Jerin, I., Hafiz, N., Tali Nimfa, D., & Abdul Wahab, S. (2021). Configuring a blueprint for Malaysian SMEs to survive through the COVID19 crisis: The reinforcement of Quadruple Helix Innovation Model. *Journal of Entrepreneurship. Business Economics (Cleveland, Ohio)*, *9*(1), 32–81.

Jalali, S. H. (2012). Export Barriers and Export Performance: Empirical Evidence from The Commercial Relationship Between Greece and Iran. *South-Eastern Europe Journal of Economics*, *1*, 53–66.

Karavdic, M., & Gregory, G. (2005). Integrating e-commerce into existing export marketing theories: A contingency model. *Marketing Theory*, *5*(1), 75–104. doi:10.1177/1470593105049602

Katsikeas, C. S., & Morgan, R. E. (1994). Differences in perceptions of exporting problems based on firm size and. *European Journal of Marketing*, *28*(5), 17–35.

Kedia, B. L., & Mukherji, A. (1999). Global managers: Developing a mindset for global competitiveness. *Journal of World Business*, *34*(3), 230–251. doi:10.1016/S1090-9516(99)00017-6

Knox, J. L. (2020). *Mitigating Perceived External Export Barriers for Small and Medium-Sized Enterprises that Manufacture and Sell "Made in the USA" Consumer Apparel Products in Washington State* (DBA dissertation). City University of Seattle.

Kyvik, O., Saris, W., Bonet, E., & Augusto Felício, J. (2013). The internationalization of small firms: The relationship between the global mindset and firms' internationalization behavior. *Journal of International Entrepreneurship*, *11*(2), 172–195.

Lages, L. F., & Montgomery, D. B. (2004). Internet resources and capabilities: Japanese SME risk-taking, industry and performance. *European Journal of Marketing*, *38*(9/10), 1186–1214. doi:10.1108/03090560410548933

Lal, K. (2004). E-Business and Export Behavior: Evidence from Indian Firms. *World Development*, *32*(3), 505–517. doi:10.1016/j.worlddev.2003.10.004

Lawal, F. A., Adegbuyi, O. A., Iyiola, O. O., Ayoade, O. E., & Taiwo, A. A. (2018). Nexus Between Informal Networks and Risk-Taking: Implications for Improving the Performance of Small and Medium Enterprises (SMEs) In Nigeria. *Academy of Strategic Management Journal*, *17*(2), 1–13.

Lazzarini, S. G. (2015). Strategizing by the Government: Industrial Policy and Sustainable Competitive Advantage. *Strategic Management Journal*, *36*(1), 96–112. https://doi.org/10.1002/smj.2204

Leonidou, C. L. (2004). An analysis of the barriers hindering small business export development. *Journal of Small Business Management*, *42*(3), 279–302.

Lu, V. N., & Julian, C. C. (2007). The internet and export marketing performance: The empirical link in export market ventures. *Asia Pacific Journal of Marketing and Logistics*, *19*(2), 127–144. doi:10.1108/13555850710738480

Madrid-Guijarro, A., Garcia, D., & Van Auken, H. (2009). Barriers to innovation among Spanish manufacturing SMEs. *Journal of Small Business Management*, *47*(4), 465–488.

Mathews, S. W., Maruyama, M., Sakurai, Y., Bebenroth, R., Luck, E., Chen, H. L., & Franco, E. (2018). Internet resources and capabilities: Japanese SME risk-taking, industry and performance. *Asia Pacific Business Review*, *24*(5), 675–692. https://doi.org/10.1080/13602381. 2018.1492690

Mazzarol, T. (2015). SMEs engagement with e-commerce, e-business and e-marketing. *Small Enterprise Research*. Advance online publication. doi:10.1080/13215906.2015.1018400

MDEC. (2021). *MDEC Confident Growth of Digital Economy Will Continue to Strengthen, In Line with GDP Performance*. https://mdec.my/news/mdec-confident-growth -of-digital-economy-will- continue-to-strengthen-in- line-with-gdp-performance/

Moen, Ø., Heggeseth, A. G., & Lome, O. (2016). The Positive Effect of Motivation and International Orientation on SME Growth. *Journal of Small Business Management*, *54*(2), 659–678. https://doi.org/10.1111/jsbm.12163

Organisation for Economic Co-Operation and Development. (2008). *Removing Barriers to SME Access to International Markets*. The 30th Small and Medium Enterprises Working Group Meeting, Hong Kong, China.

Organisation for Economic Co-Operation and Development. (2017). *Enhancing the Contributions of SMEs in a Global and Digitalised Economy*. Meeting of the OECD Council at Ministerial Level. Paris.

Owenvbiugie, R. O. (2017). Role of Finance on the Growth of Small and Medium Scale Enterprises in Edo State of Nigeria. *Journal of Educational and Social Research*, *5*(1), 241. https://doi.org/10.5901/jesr.2015.v5n1p241

Paul, H. (2000). Creating a mindset. *Thunderbird International Business Review*, *42*(2), 187–200.

Ramanathan, R., Ramanathan, U., & Hsiao, H. L. (2012). The Impact of e-commerce on Taiwanese SMEs: Marketing and operations effects. *International Journal of Production Economics*, *140*, 934–943. https://dx.doi.org/10.1016/ j.ijpe.2012.07.017

Rosnan, H., Saihani, S., Yusoff, N., & Norzaidi, M. D. (2014). Export Readiness Among Small- and Medium-Sized Enterprises in Malaysia. *AAGBS International Conference on Business Management*, 57–64.

Roy, A., & Sekhar, C., & Vyas, V. (2016). Barriers to internationalization: A study of small and medium enterprises in India. *Journal of International Entrepreneurship*, *14*, 513–538. doi:10.100710843-016-0187-7

Savrul, M., Incekara, A., & Sener, S. (2014). The Potential of E-commerce for SMEs in a Globalizing Business Environment. *Procedia: Social and Behavioral Sciences*, *150*, 35–45.

Siddiqui, S., & Rakesh, S. (2018). Digitalization and E-Commerce in India: An Employment Generation Initiative. *Intl. J. Adv. Res. Comm & Mgmt*, *4*(2), 1–11.

Silva, J. R., Franco, M., & Magrinho, A. (2016). Empirical investigation of the effects of industry type and firm size on export barriers. *Journal of Business. Economics and Management*, *17*(6), 1052–1065. doi:10.3846/16111699.2016.1143874

Sinkovics, R. R., Kurt, Y., & Sinkovics, N. (2018). The effect of matching on perceived export barriers and performance in an era of globalization discontents: Empirical evidence from UK SMEs. *International Business Review*, *27*(5), 1065–1079. https://doi.org/10.1016/ j.ibusrev.2018.03.007

Small and Medium Industries Development Corporation Malaysia. (2006). *SME Performance Report 2005*. Author.

Tseng, K. K. M., & Johnsen, R. E. (2011). Internationalisation and the internet in UK manufacturing SMEs. *Journal of Small Business and Enterprise Development*, *18*(3), 571–593. doi:10.1108/14626001111155718

Van Auken, H. E., & Carter, R. B. (1989). Acquisition of capital by small business. *Journal of Small Business Management*, *27*(2), 1.

Vivekanandan, K., & Rajendran, R. (2006). Export Marketing and The World Wide Web: Perceptions of Export Barriers Among Tirupur Knitwear Apparel Exporters- An Empirical Analysis. *Journal of Electronic Commerce Research*, *7*(1), 27–40.

Wambugu, A. W., Gichira, R., Wanjau, K. N., & Mung'atu, J. (2015). The Relationship Between Risk Taking and Performance of Small and Medium Agro-Processing Enterprises In Kenya. *International Journal of Economics. Commerce and Management*, *3*(12), 1–13.

Wee, M., Zaki, K. M., Sadik, M. Z., Marmaya, N. H., & Razak, N. A. (2019). The challenges faced by Malaysian Small Medium Entrepreneurs (SMEs) in export initiatives. *ASEAN Entrepreneurship Journal*, *5*(2), 14–19.

Wijayarathne, J. M. D. S., & Perera, M. P. S. R. (2018). Sri Lankan SMEs and Perceived Export Barriers: Evidence from Manufacturing Sector. *Asian Journal of Economics Business and Accounting*, *7*(3), 1–10.

World Bank Group. (2020). *Malaysia's experience with the SME Masterplan: Lessons Learnt*. Author.

Yang, X. H., Lim, Y. T., Sakurai, Y., & Seo, S. Y. (2009). Internationalization of Chinese and Korean Firms. *Thunderbird International Business Review*, *51*(1), 37–51. doi:10.1002/tie.20243

Yap, K.H., & Yap, S.T. (2018). COSO Enterprise Risk Management: Small-Medium Enterprises Evidence. *Asia-Pacific Management Accounting Journal*, *13*(2), 83–111.

Yatim, N. H. M., Rusuli, M. S. C., & Yatim, N. A. M. (2019). The Effect of Government Intervention on The Sustainable Competitive Advantage Among SMEs In Malaysia. *International Journal of Modern Trends in Business Research*, *2*(8), 15–22.

Yuan, F., & Woodman, R. W. (2010). Innovative behavior in the workplace: The role of performance and image outcome expectations. *Academy of Management Journal*, *53*(2), 323–342.

Zailani, S., Dahlan, N., & Jallaludin, Y. H. (2009). E-business adoption among SMEs in Malaysia: Investigation from the supply chain perspective. *Problems and Perspectives in Management*, *7*(4), 46–57.

Ziyae, B., Sajadi, S. M., & Mobaraki, M. H. (2014). The deployment and internationalization speed of e-business in the digital entrepreneurship era. *Journal of Global Entrepreneurship Research.*, *4*(15), 1–11. http://www.journal-jger.com/content/4/1/15

APPENDIX

UNIVERSITI TUNKU ABDUL RAHMAN
Kampar Campus
Determining the Risk Appetite to Go Global: Evidence from Malaysian Small and Medium Enterprises

Dear valued respondent,

My name is Liew Ke Xin, a postgraduate student currently pursuing my Master of Philosophy at University Tunku Abdul Rahman (UTAR). In partial fulfillment of my dissertation entitled "Determining the risk appetite to go global: evidence from Malaysian small and medium enterprises". I am required to conduct a survey questionnaire to discover the extent of globalization of Malaysian SMEs. Your company have been invited to participant to this research is because your company is currently involved in the exporting activities or the member of Digital Free Trade Zone (DFTZ).

I would be extremely grateful if you could spend about ten minutes of your precious time to complete this survey questionnaire. The validity of this research highly depends on your truthful response. Hence, it is of utmost important for you to fully complete the survey questionnaire. Please rest assured that information collected in this survey questionnaire will strictly be kept confidential and would be used for academic purposes only. Your cooperation is highly appreciated. Thank you.

If any require addition information or have questions, please do not hesitate to contact the project supervisor: Asst. Prof. Dr. Au Yong Hui Nee for further information on Tel: 05-46 88 888 Ext: 1034 or via email: auyonghn@utar.edu.my. Thank you.

Yours sincerely,

Liew Ke Xin
Student ID: 17ABM06831
Faculty of Business and Finance
University Tunku Abdul Rahman (UTAR)
Contact number: 0167482254
Email: nikkiliew0814@gmail.com

***Your information and responses will be kept private and confidential. ***

(NOTE: Please (√) tick your answers.)

Section A: Demographics Information

The following questions are intended to solicit information that will be used to determine the profile of respondents. Please tick [√] the most appropriate option in the relevant column for each statement below:

1) Where is your company based in?

[ ] Perlis
[ ] Pulau Pinang
[ ] Kedah
[ ] Perak
[ ] Selangor
[ ] Kuala Lumpur
[ ] Sembilan
[ ] Putrajaya
[ ] Melaka
[ ] Johor
[ ] Kelantan
[ ] Terengganu
[ ] Pahang
[ ] Sabah
[ ] Sarawak
[ ] Labuan

2) What is the sector of economy of your organization?
[ ] Services
[ ] Manufacturing
[ ] Construction
[ ] Agriculture
[ ] Mining & quarrying

3) How many months have your company involved in Digital Free Trade Zone?
[ ] Less than 1 month
[ ] 1 month-3months
[ ] 4 months-6 months
[ ] 7 months-9 months
[ ] 10 months-12 months
[ ] More than 1 year
[ ] Planning in future

4) What is your current position in company?
[ ] Owner/ Director
[ ] Manager
[ ] Officer/ Executive
[ ] Other: ________________

Section B

Instruction: Indicate the extent that you agree with each statement in Section B. Please refer to the ratings provided and tick [√] the most appropriate option in the relevant column for each statement below.

Rating: 1= Strongly Disagree 2= Disagree 3= Neutral (Neither Agree nor Disagree) 4= Agree 5= Strongly Agree

Table 3. Export Commitment-The degree to which organizational and managerial resources are allocated to exporting ventures.

No	Statement	1	2	3	4	5
1	Our company has committed significant resources to the export venture					
2	Our company is demonstrating commitment to the export venture					
3	Our company develops a specific commercial program to conduct our export business					
4	Our company dedicates more resources to export activity than to the local market					
5	Our company invests time in getting to know the export venture					

Table 4. Export Experience- Experience involve by the manager in exporting activities and also experience in the handling the process of export.

No	Statement	1	2	3	4	5
1	Our company employs staff with experience in export operations					
2	Our company has current knowledge of the export market					
3	Our company has information on conducting business in export markets					
4	Our company employs highly qualified staff to address the demands of international clients					

Table 5. Risk Appetite- Amount and type of risk that an organization is willing to take in order to meet their strategic objectives.

No	Statement	1	2	3	4	5
1	Our company plans in advance before entering our main export country					
2	Our company communicates expectations for risk-taking in meetings					
3	Our company sets limits for risk-reward trade-offs					
4	Our company understands of the concept of risk appetite					
5	Our company has the ability to integrate risk appetite with operational activities					
6.	Our company has developed suitable quantitative risk measurements					

Table 6. E-commerce- Business model that allows individual or a firm to conduct business over an electronic network.

No	Statement	1	2	3	4	5
1	Our company develops technologies by investing in R&D					
2	Our company employs advanced technologies in marketing					
3	Our company identifies and applies technological trends abroad					
4	Our company utilizes new sales channels abroad					
5	Our company applies new techniques to promote products abroad					
6	Our company acquires new technologies					
7	Key vendors or service providers of our company required to notify customer information if needed					
8	Our company's data access is assigned based on user need					
9	Our company is confident on securing the information received by customer or vendors					
10	User accounts and passwords are unique for each user and kept private					

Table 7. Export Barrier- Defined as barriers firms face in export

No	Statement	1	2	3	4	5
1	Our company feels difficulty in identifying foreign business opportunities					
2	Our company feels difficulty in warehousing facilities abroad					
3	Our company feels difficulty in developing new products for foreign markets					
4	Our company is not familiar in handling exporting procedures/documentation					
5	Our company feels challenging in contact overseas customers					

Table 8. Export Performance- The result of the company's international activities

No	Statement	1	2	3	4	5
1	Customer abroad has the awareness of our product/company					
2	Export increased the profitability of the company					
3	Our main product-market export venture has been very profitable					
4	Our main product-market export venture has generated a high volume of sales					
5	Our main product-market export venture has achieved rapid growth					
6	Our main product-market export venture has improved our global competitiveness					
7	Our main product-market export venture has contributed to the achievement of strategic export goals					

Section C

Instruction: Please [√] tick your answers.

1) What is your company's annual gross sales or revenues?
   [ ] Less than RM50, 000
   [ ] RM50, 000-RM100, 000
   [ ] RM100, 000-RM200, 000
   [ ] RM 200, 000-RM300, 000
   [ ] RM300, 000-RM500, 000
   [ ] RM500, 000-RM900, 000
   [ ] RM1 million-RM4.9 million
   [ ] RM5 million-RM9.9 million
   [ ] RM10 million-RM24.9 million
   [ ] RM 25 million-RM49 million
   [ ] RM 50 million or over
2) What is your company's performance in terms of export sales as percentage of total sales?
   [ ] 0%-10%
   [ ] 11%-20%
   [ ] 21%-30%
   [ ] 31%-40%
   [ ] 41%-50%
   [ ] 51%-60%
   [ ] 61%-70%
   [ ] 71%-80%
   [ ] 81%-90%
   [ ] 91%-100%

Suggestion:
What will you suggest to government policies that are important to encourage companies to export?
************End of Questionnaire, Thank You!!************

Your information and responses will be kept private and confidential.
Thank you for your kind assistant

Chapter 6

A Study on the Internet Usage Pattern of Youths in Sikkim

Saibal Kumar Saha
https://orcid.org/0000-0002-7842-698X
Sikkim Manipal Institute of Technology, Sikkim Manipal University, India

Sangita Saha
https://orcid.org/0000-0002-4676-5370
Sikkim Manipal Institute of Technology, Sikkim Manipal University, India

ABSTRACT

Internet is being used by people all over the world. It has become a part of their day-to-day activity. The smartness brought by internet and its related devices have made life of people easy. Sharing knowledge, researching, and reaching out to people are now within the reach of fingertips. This study aims to find the internet usage pattern of youth in Sikkim, India. Fourteen internet activities have been identified and through a survey. The usage of these activities was analysed for the youth population in Sikkim, India. It has been found that, more or less, all the activities are used by the youth population of Sikkim. The most popular activity is use of emails and social networking sites while blogging and video calling is not too popular. In addition, it has been found that 67% of the users use internet for more than 3 hours per day. Hence, there also is a serious risk of "internet addiction."

INTRODUCTION

The evolution of internet and technology has changed the lives of people in many ways. The challenges of speed, time, cost and distance have been overcome to a great extent with the advancement of technology and its widespread use in the modern era. The availability and affordability of high end, technologically advanced devices are possible due to cheap data plans and wide scale adoption of mobile devices among the masses. People have been using internet and technology for many purposes (Saha, 2016) like communication with each other by email, text messages, telephone calls, video conferencing, sending pictures and videos, research, writing and reading blogs, booking tickets, shopping, searching for colleges, doctors, hobbies, playing games and many more things (Saha, 2015). This has become a part of every individual in this high tech world. The wide scale availability of a number of robust and

DOI: 10.4018/978-1-7998-8678-5.ch006

multi device compatible, user friendly applications have increased the popularity of internet. The use of internet has not only been adopted for high end competition in the business world but has diffused into the lives of individuals.

LITERATURE REVIEW

College students are a perfect blend of work and leisure, childhood and adulthood, are the futures of tomorrow. Internet is a part of their daily routine as they are habituated of using computers and mobiles since their childhood (Unnikrishnan et al., 2008). College students use internet as a supplement of their formal education and use the same to enhance their social lives (Jones, 2002).

One of the most important scientific developments in the field of technology is internet which is an ocean of information (Lal et al., 2006). Its advantage over paper based diffusion of information is cost and easy instant accessibility. Today internet is the biggest global digital information library. It is the most widely used information source for today's generation (Kumar & Kaur, 2005). The popularity of internet databases for accessing journals was highlighted in the study of (Asemi, 2005). A study conducted by Voorbij (1999) in Netherlands revealed that students and academicians used internet to search a wide variety of information including factual, ephemeral and specific information. According to Kooganurmath and Jange (1999) majority of users used internet for communication, followed by information access. The study also reported that 70% of users used internet for higher studies while 39% used it for deliberations with friends. The study of Mahajan and Patil (1999) reveals that researchers used internet for literature search, students used internet for more information on curriculum while teachers used internet to find secondary information for writing articles. The study of Kaur (2000) reveals that 75.6% of the respondents faced problems due to slow internet connectivity, more than 80% felt internet saved time, it is easy to use, provides extra information, is useful and is widely preferred over other medium. The study of Bavakutty & TK, (1999) confirms that students primarily use internet for their study, research scholars for research and academicians for teaching. Internet was also used for e-mail services, finding library catalogues and downloading images.

All good things are bundled with some negative and bad elements. Internet is no exception. Although there are numerous benefits of internet, there is an inherent problem of addiction (Carbonell et al., 2018; Menon et al., 2018). The possible inclusion of addictive usage of internet and mobile phones in the list of mental disorder has become a topic of great concern in the scientific fraternity (Carbonell et al., 2009). The term "technological addiction" has been given to the possible addiction of use of technology and technology enabled devices like television, mobiles, virtual gaming and internet (Griffiths, 2000). This problem is mainly seen among youth and adolescents (Lepp et al., 2015). Due to this there is increase in the stress and anxiety levels while there is lack of communication and sleep disorders (Thomée et al., 2012). It also affects psychological and mental health leading to numerous problems like loss of social skills, extreme obsession with websites, mobile apps, social networks and internet (Ghassemzadeh et al., 2008; Liu & Potenza, 2007).

Although technology of internet and mobile services has disseminated into the metros and other cities of India, it is yet to penetrate into the rural areas due to low population density and low paying capacity of users (Raman & Chebrolu, 2007). With rapid popularity of 4G technology and cheap data plans, Digital India is all set to change the scenario of technology adoption in the rural areas of India.

With an area of 7096 sq.kms, Sikkim is the second smallest state of India and holds the record of having the least population. The population of the state is 6.1 lakhs which is about .05% of total population of

India. Lepchas, Bhutia and Nepalese are the three major ethnic groups of the state. The State is divided into only four Districts: North, South, East and West. Around 60% of the population is in the working age group while around 35% is in the age-group of 0-14. This paper aims to find out the internet usage habit of youths in the state of Sikkim, India. How do the young people of this state use internet? What are the activities they pursue in their virtual world? How do they perceive the technology of internet? Are they becoming internet addicted?

METHODOLOGY

To achieve the objectives of this research, a structured questionnaire was framed. The questionnaire was divided into three broad section: i) demographics, ii) activities done over internet and iii) attitude towards internet. The demographic section had questions related to gender, age, education, employment status, mode of internet usage, and daily internet usage duration of the respondents. The section for "activities done over internet", was further divided into four sub sections: "entertainment", "research", "work", and "communication". The sub section "entertainment" had questions related to "chatting", "social networking", "playing online games", and "watching movies and videos". The sub section "research" had questions related to "research about studies", "blogging", "reading news", and "research about hobbies and topics of interests". The sub section "work" had questions related to "downloading softwares and files", "online shopping", "ticket booking", and "payment of bills". The sub section "communication" had questions related to "video calling" and "e-mails". The section for "attitude towards Internet", was further divided into three sub sections: "usefulness", "familiarity with internet", and "perception about internet". The sub section "usefulness" had questions related to "usefulness of internet for study purposes", "increase in efficiency of work", "learning new things" and "use of internet in classrooms". The sub section "familiarity with internet" had questions related to "level of difficulty in use of internet", "enjoyment in internet usage" and "knowledge about internet". The sub section "perception about internet" had questions related to "stability of internet connection", "integration of internet with life events or works", "how internet had affected them" and "whether respondents try to reduce dependency on internet".

A pilot survey was conducted to test the questionnaire. Face validity of the questionnaire was conducted by taking feedback from five experts. The target population for the research were the youths residing in the state of Sikkim in India. With the help of random sampling method 211 samples were collected through an online questionnaire. 4 responses were discarded as the respondents did not answer all the questions. 3 samples were discarded due to data entry error by the respondents. So the sample size used for analysis was 204. The data was coded and analysed in MS excel 2016. Percentage analysis and correlation was done to get more insights about the research.

RESULTS AND DISCUSSION

Sample Characteristics

The survey constituted of 89.2% male and 10.8% female respondents. 60% of the respondents were between the age group of 18 to 25 years while 40% were above 25 years. 33.8% of the survey respondents were students, 40% were employed and working in some organization while 20% were unemployed.

80% of the respondents had University level education while for 20% the level of education was up to school. The survey revealed that smart phone was the most preferred mode of internet access. 92.3% of the respondents used this mode for internet access. 30.8% of the respondents used internet for less than 3 hours per day, 30.8% for less than 5 hours per day but more than 3 hours while 36.9% used internet for more than 5 hours per day.

Activities Done Over Internet

Entertainment

Internet has emerged as one of the most influential technologies. People all over the world use this technology for various purposes (Tripathi & Ahad, 2017). Internet provides various sources of entertainment for its users. There are numerous alternatives available catering to the needs of different individuals. People spend their time chatting with their friends, staying connected to various social networking sites, playing online games and watching videos and movies for their entertainment.

Figure 1. Entertainment

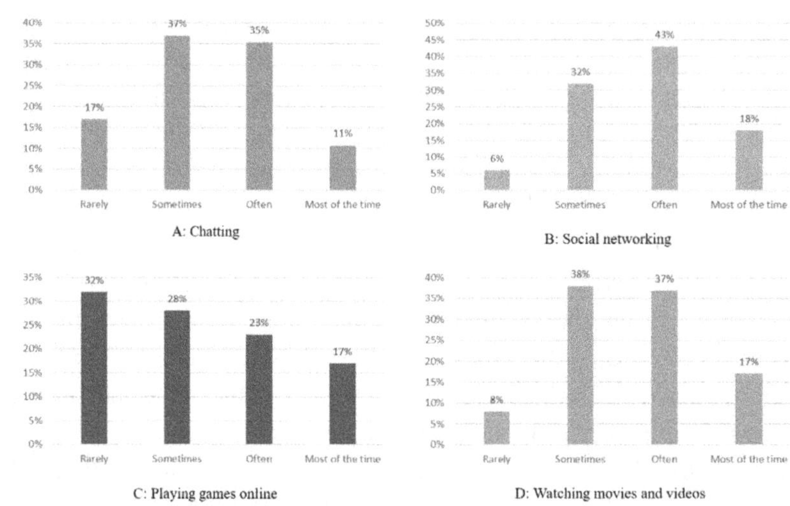

From figure 1 (A): 17% of the respondents confirmed that they rarely use chatting, 37% use it sometimes, 35% use it often while 11% use this activity most of the time. The study conducted by Tripathi & Ahad, (2017) in New Delhi India found that 86% of the respondents use internet for chatting. On comparing the two studies we find that the youths of Sikkim have comparatively lesser chatting habits than the youths of New Delhi, the capital of India. Figure 1 (B) reveals that social networking sites was rarely accessed by 6% of the respondents, sometimes by 32%, often by 43% and most of the time 18%. Similar results were obtained in a study conducted in Hong Kong, China where it was reported that the screen time spent by respondents were 0 (hour) = 7.1%, 0 to <1 (hour) = 29.9%, ^{3}1 to < 2 (hour) = 27%, ^{3}2 to <3 (hour) = 12.6% and ^{3}3 (hour) = 22.8% (Guo et al., 2021). From figure 1 (C) we find that online gaming is rarely done by 32% of the respondents, 28% do it sometimes, 23% use this activity often and 17% use do it most of the time. The study of identifies 18.5 as the average weekly hours spent by Italian online gamers (Caselli et al., 2021). In the 11th "Revision of the International Classification of Diseases" (ICD-11) World Health Organization included gaming sickness allied to addictive behaviours (*ICD-11 - ICD-11 for Mortality and Morbidity Statistics*, n.d.). From figure 1 (D) it is evident that 8% respondents watch movies and videos online rarely, 38% do it sometimes, 37% do it often and only 17% do it most of the time. A study conducted in the US with children reported screen time to be associated with 3.7% rise in thought problems, 5% rise in social problems, 5.9% rise in rule-breaking behaviour and 4% rise in aggressive behaviour and.

Numerous problems have been identified associated with increased online behaviour of people. As people spend more time over internet, their time for physical activities reduce, they spend lesser time on personal interacts. This affects their personal life as reduced quality time with friends, family and relatives creates a distance between them. The increased virtual presence creates a sense of second identify among the youths which they may find it different from the actual world.

Research

Researchers, academicians and common people look upon inter as a source of information from where they can get explicit knowledge on any subject of their choice. Academicians get easy access to different libraries, forums, blogs and user experiences from different sites. Easy accessibility to numerous educational websites providing video and audio lectures help people to learn new things and get knowledge about the subject of their choice.

Figure 2. Research

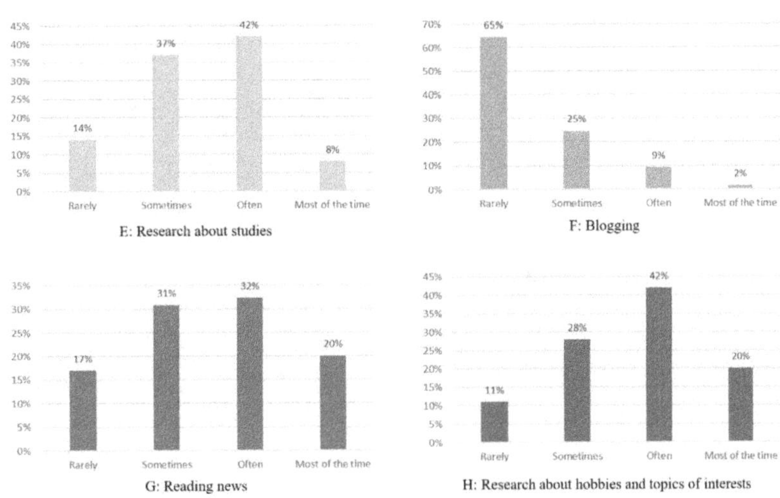

From figure 2 (E) we find that 14% of the respondents rarely use internet for research about studies while 37% use it sometimes, 42% use it often and only 8% use it most of the time. The percentage in use of internet for academic is higher among the youths in Sikkim as compared to a study in Ghana (70.2%) (Yebowaah, 2018). The activity of blogging was rarely performed by 65% of the respondents, sometimes by 25%, often by 9% and most of the time by 2% (as shown in figure 2 (F)). In figure 2 (G) it is seen that 17% of the respondents rarely read news over the internet, 31% sometimes, 32%, often 32% and 20% most of the time. On comparing other studies related to news reading habits of young people it is found that the percentage of Sikkimese youth that use internet for reading news is higher. Similar study conducted in Ghana reported only 39.9% of the respondents spent time reading online news (Yebowaah, 2018). From figure 2 (H) it is found that 1% of the respondents confirmed that they rarely research about hobbies and topics of interests over the net while 28% perform this activity sometimes, 42% do it often and it is done most of the time by 20% of the respondents.

As every good technology as a negative side, internet is no different. Although internet provides an enormous source of information, there are fake and counterfeit websites which is a kind of trap, waiting for innocent visitors to execute. Unexperienced youths often fall prey to these websites and are easily lured by the fake news and even created to cheat these individuals. Hence, it is very important to educate the youths about the use of trusted websites and their usage.

Work

Use of internet for daily requirements has become indispensable. The ease of information and variety of options for purchase of items, payment of bills and booking tickets have made the lives of people easy. The survey reveals that the youth of Sikkim are making progressing usage of these facilities and are becoming a part of digital India.

Figure 3. Work

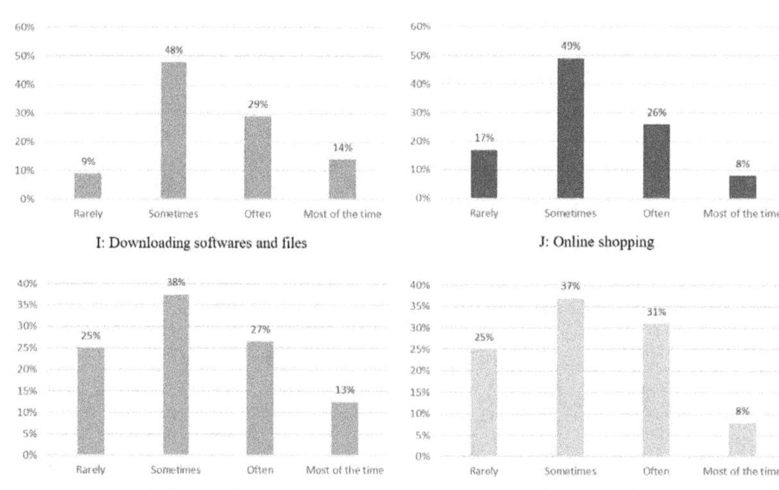

When one starts using any electronic device, usage of software and downloading of the same becomes necessary. From the survey it was seen that 9% of respondents used internet for downloading softwares and files rarely, 48% used it sometimes, 29% used it often and only 14% used it most of the time (as shown in figure 3 (I)). As shown in figure 3 (J), the activity of online shopping was rarely used by 17% of the respondents, sometimes by 49%, often by 26% and most of the time by 8%. The activity of ticket booking was rarely used by 25%, sometimes by 38%, often by 27% and most of the time by 13% of the respondents (as shown in figure 3 (K)). From figure 3 (L) it is evident that the activity of payment of bills was rarely used by 25%, sometimes by 37%, often by 31% and most of the time by 8% of the respondents.

Communication

Communication is one of the most important usage of internet. Documents, letters can be easily sent to people without the limitations of time, space and availability synchronization. This facility has been accepted by the youths of Sikkim and a good number of them are using them in their day to day life. From figure 4 (N) it is found that email was rarely used by 17%, sometimes by 22%, often by 41% and most of the time by 22% of the respondents. However, there is lack of popularity for video calling usage. It is rarely used by 43% of the respondents while 43% use it sometimes and only 14% use it often. None of the respondents reported its usage for most of the time (as shown in figure 4 (M)).

Figure 4. Communication

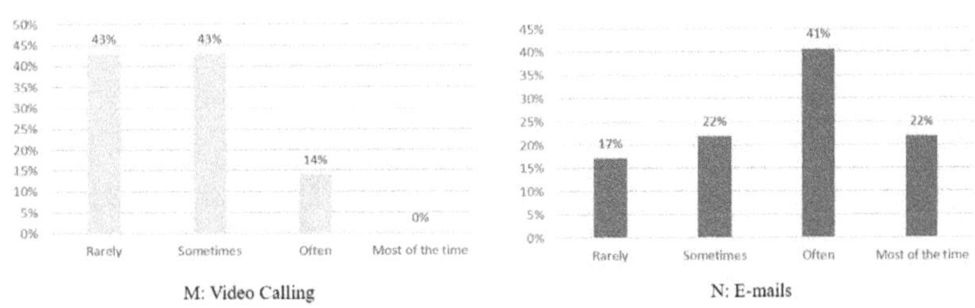

Attitude towards Internet

Usefulness

Internet is useful for many tasks. The availability of e-books, video lectures, research articles and journals have opened immense opportunities for its users to gain knowledge. Figure 5 (O) shows that 97% of the respondents agreed that internet is useful for their study purposes. Figure 5 (P) also shows that 92% of the respondents believe that use of internet helps to increase the efficiency of their work. 95% of the respondents agree that internet helps to learn new things (as shown in figure 5 (Q)). In figure 5 (R) it is seen that 75% of the respondents were of the opinion that internet and technology should be used in classrooms. Although internet has bridged the gap of distance and time with easy access of materials form distant places and from different times, but this has also lead to issues like less attention during class hours and lesser interaction among the peers.

Familiarity with Internet

93% of the respondents confirmed that they find internet easy to use (as shown in figure 6 (S)). From figure 6 (T) it is seen that 92% of the respondents confirmed that they enjoyed using internet. Figure 6 (U) reveals that 89% of the respondents affirmed that they want to learn more about the uses and benefits of internet.

Figure 5. Usefulness

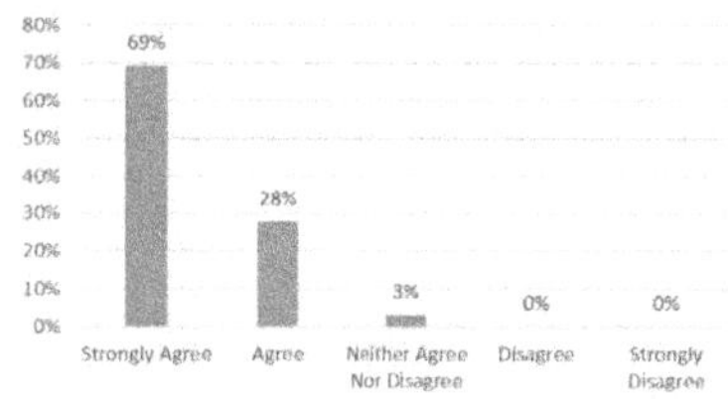

O: Useful for study purposes

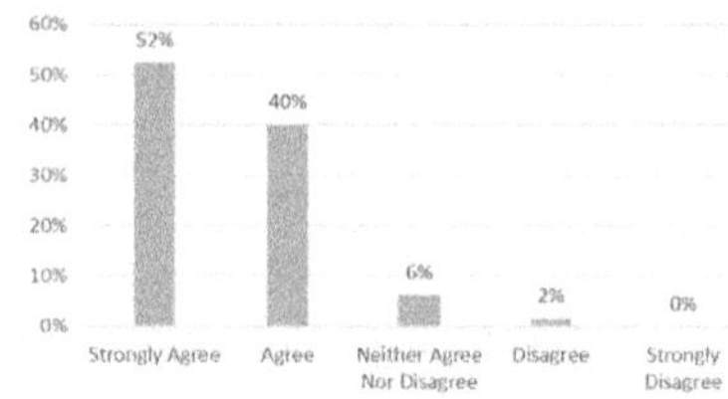

P: Increase in efficiency of work

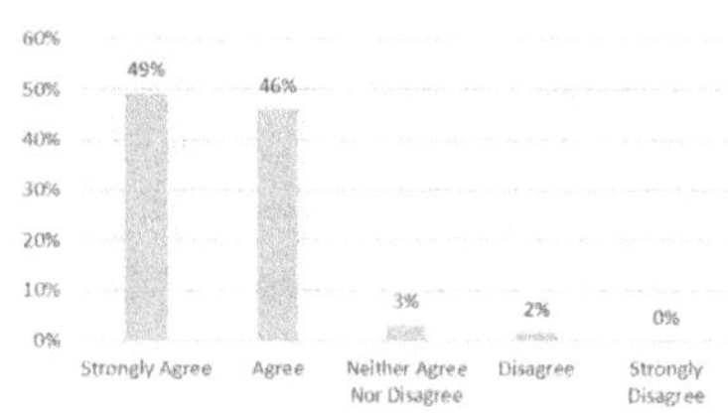

Q: Internet helps to learn new things

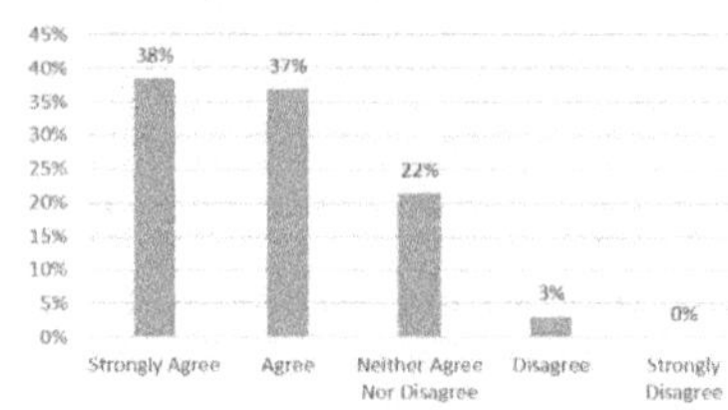

R: Use of internet and technology in classrooms

Figure 6. Familiarity with internet

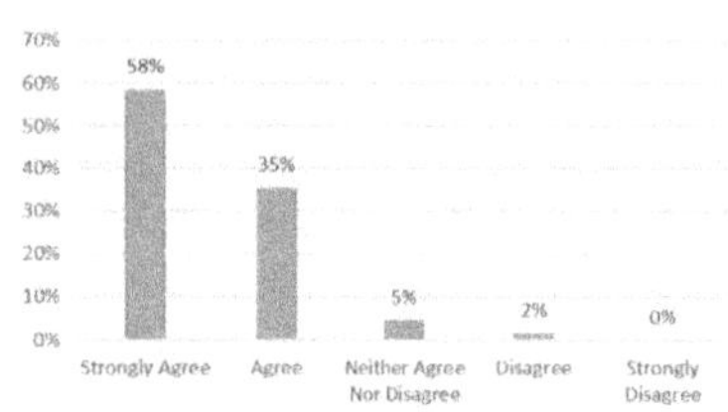

S: Internet is easy to use

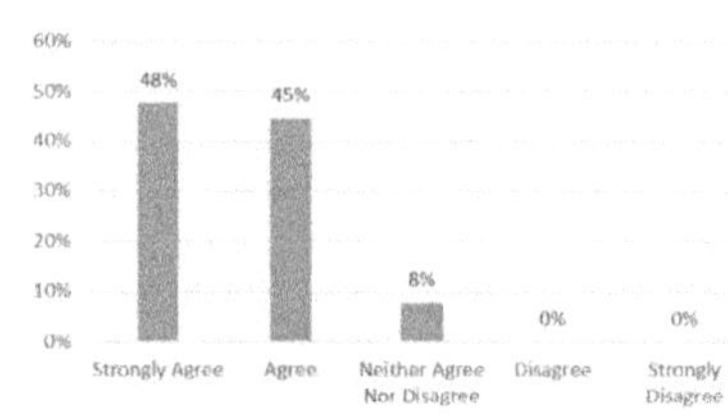

T: Enjoy using internet

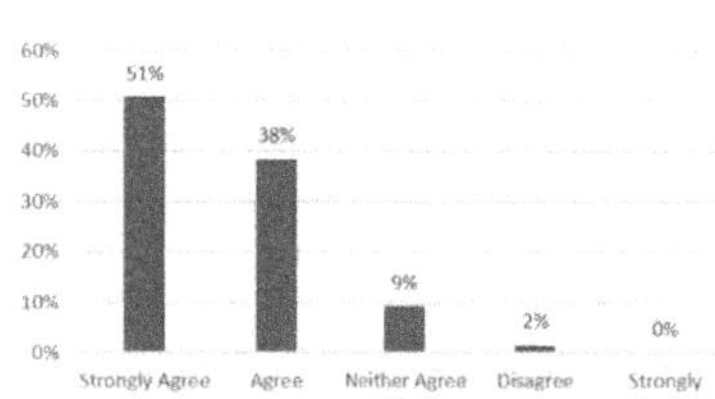

U: Knowledge about internet

Perception about Internet

On examining figure 7 (V) it can be seen that 68% of the respondents agrees with the statement that technology breaks down too often to be of much use. Sikkim has a hilly terrain and there are frequent landslides, rainfall and power cuts. These problems lead to frequent disruption in internet and telephone services. Hence, the people of this region face problems of seamless internet and other technological connectivity. Figure 7 (W) shows that 91% of the respondents are of the opinion that internet and technology has made our lives easier and more convenient. The evidence of this reflects in the other figures where it is found that the youths use internet for different purposes of work. From figure 7 (X) it can be inferred that 86% of the respondents believe that internet and technology has made us smarter. 56% of the respondents confirmed that they try to reduce dependency on internet and technology while 6% disagree with the statement (as shown in Figure 7 (Y)).

Figure 7. Perception about internet

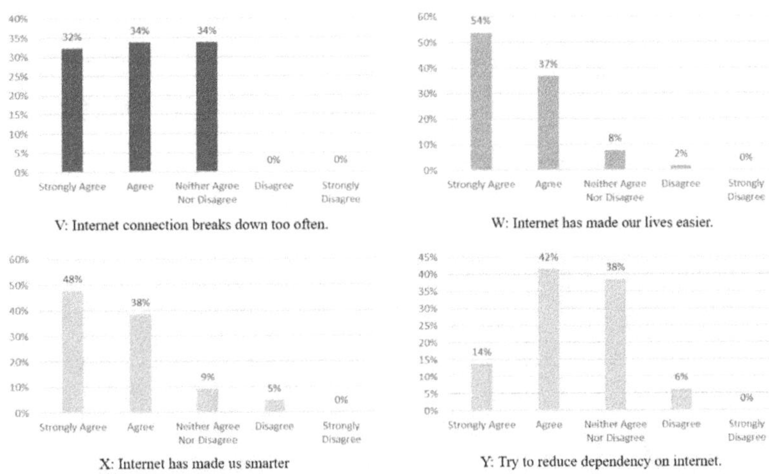

Correlation

A correlation analysis was done for the different activities that were identified for being most commonly used over the internet. The correlation coefficient which are higher than 0.5 and lower than -0.5 have been highlighted as these values represent strong correlation.

Correlation analysis was conducted for the different variables taken in the study. Highlighted cells in table 1 indicate the correlation values which are above 0.35. A detailed analysis of the correlation matrix portrays that respondents who engage themselves with "chatting" activity have positive moderate correlation with the activities: "video Calling" (0.39) and "social networking" (0.39). This is evident as some of the social networking platforms have integrated chatting and video calling facilities in it. "Research about studies" has positive moderate correlation with "research about hobbies" (0.48) and "ticket booking" (0.36). As search engines have become smart and have starting advertising based on search history of internet users, people who visit different websites automatically get advertisements through google ads. "Research about hobbies" has positive moderate correlation with "social networking" (0.43), "reading news" (0.40) and accessing "e-mails" (0.45). When people research about their hobbies, they often do it in congruence with others and discuss the same with friends and like-minded people over social media. "Playing games online" has positive moderate correlation with "downloading softwares" (0.36) and "blogging" (0.36). Gamers generally need to download supporting softwares and patches to have a better gaming experience. They also actively engage in downloading game updates. It is also common among the gamers to discuss about the problems faced in games and look for solutions through blogs.

The correlation matrix also revealed that "Downloading softwares" has positive moderate correlation with "social networking" (0.35), "online shopping" (0.41), "payment of bills" (0.39), "reading news" (0.58) and accessing "e-mails" (0.41). "Social networking" has positive moderate correlation with "online shopping" (0.57), "reading news" (0.36), accessing "e-mails" (0.51) and "ticket booking" (0.47). "Online Shopping" has positive moderate correlation with "payment of bills" (0.45), accessing "e-mails" (0.44) and "ticket booking" (0.54). "Payment of bills" has positive moderate correlation with "reading news" (0.45), accessing "e-mails" (0.61) and "ticket booking" (0.66). "Reading news" has positive moderate correlation with accessing "e-mails" (0.58) and "ticket booking" (0.46). Accessing "e-mails" has positive moderate correlation with "ticket booking" (0.59).

Table 1. Correlation

	Chatting	Video Calling	Research about studies	Research about hobbies	Watching movies & videos	Playing games online	Downloading softwares	Social networking	Online Shopping	Payment of bills	Reading news	E-mails	Ticket booking	Blogging
Chatting	1.00													
Video Calling	0.39	1.00												
Research about studies	0.16	0.27	1.00											
Research about hobbies	0.07	-0.01	0.48	1.00										
Watching movies & videos	0.28	-0.03	-0.06	0.16	1.00									
Playing games online	-0.05	0.03	-0.02	0.17	0.28	1.00								
Downloading softwares	0.16	0.00	0.26	0.32	0.20	0.36	1.00							
Social networking	0.39	0.27	0.21	0.43	0.19	0.11	0.35	1.00						
Online Shopping	0.26	0.21	0.25	0.28	0.26	0.19	0.41	0.57	1.00					
Payment of bills	0.20	0.12	0.27	0.10	0.22	0.18	0.39	0.28	0.45	1.00				
Reading news	0.11	-0.01	0.35	0.40	0.19	0.12	0.58	0.36	0.30	0.45	1.00			
E-mails	0.12	0.21	0.33	0.45	0.11	0.12	0.41	0.51	0.44	0.61	0.58	1.00		
Ticket booking	0.16	0.21	0.36	0.25	0.10	0.13	0.32	0.47	0.54	0.66	0.46	0.59	1.00	
Blogging	0.06	0.34	-0.11	-0.02	0.21	0.36	0.26	0.16	0.32	0.20	0.17	0.16	0.26	1.00

CONCLUSION

The objective of the paper was to find the internet usage habit of youths in the state of Sikkim, India. An effort was made to find answers to four questions: How do the young people of Sikkim use internet? What are the activities they pursue in their virtual world? How do they perceive the technology of internet? And are they becoming internet addicted? From the study conducted it can be seen that the youth of Sikkim are internet savvy and participate in many activities over the internet. The feature of video calling is not very popular and blogging is rarely used. However, the youth are active users of emails, social networking sites, online videos and research activities.

Around 92% of the users use internet through smartphone and 98% of the users have been using internet for more than one year. 67% of the users use internet for more than 3 hours per day. Which means that they may be under "internet addiction". It is a matter of great concern that people are unknowingly getting into internet addiction and are unaware about its consequences. 92% of the youth enjoy using internet and technology. Only 14% of the respondents strongly agree that they try to reduce dependency on internet and technology. Similar results were found in a study conducted among medical students in Malaysia and was reported that internet addiction was frequent among male students who used internet for surfing and entertainment purposes (Ching et al., 2017).

The threat of smart phone addiction is enhanced due to the fact that it is a very handy device, it is used as a leisure activity (Carbonell et al., 2012) and is a part of the user. The addictive behaviour is enhanced with the addiction to internet and virtual social networking activities (Carbonell & Panova, 2017), creating or joining existing groups, messaging, blogging and using emails (Anderson, 2001). The psychosocial well-being of the youths are challenged on prolonged usage of internet, games, social media and other applications (van Rooij et al., 2017). A study conducted across nine European countries reported that around 14 to 55% people are addicted to internet usage (Laconi et al., 2018). When youths spend more time over the internet, it leads to problems of negative emotions, loss of relationships, school opportunities, career and higher levels of self-regulation failures.

It is very important that the youth are made aware about the concepts of internet addiction and its consequences. The internet regulatory authorities should make sure that the major players in this business provide information about "internet addition" to its users and warn them about the serious consequence of it.

REFERENCES

Anderson, K. J. (2001). Internet use among college students: An exploratory study. *Journal of American College Health*, *50*(1), 21–26. doi:10.1080/07448480109595707 PMID:11534747

Asemi, A. (2005). Information searching habits of Internet users: A case study on the Medical Sciences University of Isfahan, Iran. *Webology*, *2*(1), 10.

Bavakutty, M., & TK, M. S. (1999). *Internet services in Calicut University*. Academic Press.

Carbonell, X., Chamarro, A., Oberst, U., Rodrigo, B., & Prades, M. (2018). Problematic use of the internet and smartphones in university students: 2006–2017. *International Journal of Environmental Research and Public Health*, *15*(3), 475. doi:10.3390/ijerph15030475 PMID:29518050

Carbonell, X., Fuster, H., Chamarro, A., & Oberst, U. (2012). Internet and mobile cell phone addiction: A review of Spanish empirical studies. *Papeles del Psicólogo*.

Carbonell, X., Guardiola, E., Beranuy, M., & Bellés, A. (2009). A bibliometric analysis of the scientific literature on Internet, video games, and cell phone addiction. *Journal of the Medical Library Association: JMLA*, *97*(2), 102–107. doi:10.3163/1536-5050.97.2.006 PMID:19404500

Carbonell, X., & Panova, T. (2017). A critical consideration of social networking sites' addiction potential. *Addiction Research & Theory, 25*(1), 48–57.

Caselli, G., Marino, C., & Spada, M. M. (2021). Modelling Online Gaming Metacognitions: The Role of Time Spent Gaming in Predicting Problematic Internet Use. *Journal of Rational-Emotive & Cognitive-Behavior Therapy*, *39*(2), 172–182. doi:10.100710942-020-00365-0

Ching, S. M., Hamidin, A., Vasudevan, R., Sazlyna, M. S., Wan Aliaa, W. S., Foo, Y. L., Yee, A., & Hoo, F. K. (2017). Prevalence and factors associated with internet addiction among medical students-A cross-sectional study in Malaysia. *The Medical Journal of Malaysia*, *72*(1), 7–11. PMID:28255133

Ghassemzadeh, L., Shahraray, M., & Moradi, A. (2008). Prevalence of Internet addiction and comparison of Internet addicts and non-addicts in Iranian high schools. *CyberPsychology & Behavior, 11*(6), 731–733.

Griffiths, M. (2000). Internet addiction-time to be taken seriously? *Addiction Research*, *8*(5), 413–418. doi:10.3109/16066350009005587

Guo, N., Luk, T. T., Wang, M. P., Ho, S. Y., Fong, D. Y. T., Wan, A., Chan, S. S., & Lam, T. H. (2021). Self-Reported Screen Time on Social Networking Sites Associated With Problematic Smartphone Use in Chinese Adults: A Population-Based Study. *Frontiers in Psychiatry*, *11*, 614061. doi:10.3389/fpsyt.2020.614061 PMID:33519554

ICD-11 - ICD-11 for Mortality and Morbidity Statistics. (n.d.). Retrieved July 2, 2021, from https://icd.who.int/browse11/l-m/en#/http://id.who.int/icd/entity/1448597234

Jones, S. (2002). The Internet Goes to College. Pew Internet & American Life. *USDLA Journal, 16*(10).

Kaur, A. (2000). Internet facility at GNDU: A survey. *National Seminar on Academic Libraries in the Modern Era*, 119–124.

Kooganurmath, M. M., & Jange, S. (1999). Use of Internet by social science research scholars: A study in academic libraries in the Internet era. *National Convention Academic Libraries in the Internet Era*, 478–483.

Kumar, R., & Kaur, A. (2005). Internet and its use in the engineering colleges of Punjab, India: A case study. *Webology*, *2*(4), 1–22.

Laconi, S., Kaliszewska-Czeremska, K., Gnisci, A., Sergi, I., Barke, A., Jeromin, F., Groth, J., Gamez-Guadix, M., Ozcan, N. K., Demetrovics, Z., Király, O., Siomos, K., Floros, G., & Kuss, D. J. (2018). Cross-cultural study of Problematic Internet Use in nine European countries. *Computers in Human Behavior*, *84*, 430–440. doi:10.1016/j.chb.2018.03.020

Lal, P., Malhotra, R., Ahuja, C., & Ingle, G. K. (2006). Internet use among medical students and residents of a medical college of North India. *Indian Journal of Community Medicine*, *31*(4), 293–294.

Lepp, A., Li, J., Barkley, J. E., & Salehi-Esfahani, S. (2015). Exploring the relationships between college students' cell phone use, personality and leisure. *Computers in Human Behavior*, *43*, 210–219. doi:10.1016/j.chb.2014.11.006

Liu, T., & Potenza, M. N. (2007). Problematic Internet use: Clinical implications. *CNS Spectrums*, *12*(6), 453–466. doi:10.1017/S1092852900015339 PMID:17545956

Mahajan, S. G., & Patil, S. K. (1999). Internet: Its use in university libraries in India. *National Convention on Academic Libraries in the Internet Era*, 483–488.

Menon, S., Narayanan, L., & Kahwaji, A. T. (2018). Internet addiction: A research study of college students in India. *Journal of Economics and Business*, *1*(1), 100–106. doi:10.31014/aior.1992.01.01.9

Raman, B., & Chebrolu, K. (2007). Experiences in using WiFi for rural internet in India. *IEEE Communications Magazine*, *45*(1), 104–110. doi:10.1109/MCOM.2007.284545

Saha, S. K. (2015). A study on the Internet Usage Pattern of Doctors. *CBS Journal of Management Practices*, *2*(1), 113–122.

Saha, S. K. (2016). What are Medical Students Doing Online. *A Study in Kolkata, India. Arabian J Bus Manag Review*, *6*(214), 2.

Thomée, S., Härenstam, A., & Hagberg, M. (2012). Computer use and stress, sleep disturbances, and symptoms of depression among young adults—A prospective cohort study. *BMC Psychiatry*, *12*(1), 1–14. doi:10.1186/1471-244X-12-176 PMID:23088719

Tripathi, G., & Ahad, M. A. (2017). Impact of excessive use of internet on cognitive development of youngsters. *International Journal of Information Technology (Singapore)*, *9*(3), 281–286. doi:10.100741870-017-0028-5

Unnikrishnan, B., Kulshrestha, V., Saraf, A., Agrahari, A. C., Prakash, S., Samantaray, L., & Parida, A. (2008). Pattern of computer and internet use among medical students in Coastal South India. *South East Asian Journal of Medical Education*, *2*(2), 18–25.

van Rooij, T., Ferguson, C. J., de Mheen, D., & Schoenmakers, T. M. (2017). *Time to abandon internet addiction? Predicting problematic internet, game, and social media use from psychosocial well-being and application use*. Clinical Neuropsychiatry.

Voorbij, H. J. (1999). Searching scientific information on the Internet: A Dutch academic user survey. *Journal of the American Society for Information Science*, *50*(7), 598–615. doi:10.1002/(SICI)1097-4571(1999)50:7<598::AID-ASI5>3.0.CO;2-6

Yebowaah, F. A. (2018). Internet use and its effect on senior high school students in Wa municipality of Ghana. *Library Philosophy & Practice*.

Chapter 7
Influence of Industry 4.0 on Asia:
Motives and Cultures in the Post-COVID-19 Era

Xuan Tran
https://orcid.org/0000-0001-9521-5722
University of West Florida, USA

ABSTRACT

As the challenge of big data impacts how we understand cultural differences, a motive-integrated model of culture is becoming an effective strategy to study current culture divergence by the fourth industrial revolution called "Industry 4.0." This study examines the impact of Industry 4.0 with COVID-19 vaccines on motives and cultures of the world and Asia in the post-COVID-19 era. Structure equation modelling has been conducted on the data in 38 countries during the period of 2006-2021. Findings indicate that Industry 4.0 has enhanced the achievement motive in the reactive culture and the power motive in the multi-linear culture, but it has decreased the affiliation motive in the linear active culture. In addition, Industry 4.0 has enhanced the gross domestic product per capita (GDP) in the linear active and reactive cultures, but it has decreased the GDP in the multi-linear cultures. Finally, Industry 4.0 has made the power and affiliation motives in Asia decrease, but it has increased the achievement motive in Asia.

INTRODUCTION

Failure to examine the effects of industrial revolutions on motives and cultures creates critical issues in maintaining and developing cultures in the world. Arguably, World War 1 and 2 could be attributed in part to the negative impacts of the first two industrial revolutions on human motives and cultures. Motives are concerns over starting, maintaining, and directing (1) evaluated performance of human activities (achievement motive), (2) the means of influencing a person (power motive), and (3) positive affective relationships with another person (affiliation motive) (McClelland, 1985). In this study, motives are

DOI: 10.4018/978-1-7998-8678-5.ch007

specific implicit behavior, so they are different from needs and traits. Needs generate response tendency and traits are the surface of motives (McClelland, 1951). Cultures are the growth of national personality traits (Lynn, 1991). Traits are the motives' channels (Winter, John, Stewart, Klohnen, and Duncan, 1998), so cultures are the channels of motives. Culture or national character is "relatively enduring personality characteristics and patterns that are modal among adult members of the society" (Inkeles & Levinson, 1954,1969). In sum, how cultures and motives that are consistent variables over time will be changed by the fourth industrial revolution or Industry 4.0 in the world and Asia in this study.

To thoroughly analyze the strengths of Industry 4.0, the study will examine how the preceding three industrial revolutions affected motives and cultures. The first industrial revolution in 1784 changed agriculture to industry based on the discovery of coal. The sedentary human society became diverged into urban and country society. The human motive of power in agriculture was enhanced in urban cities. Cultures are mostly the polychronic culture in which people pursue multiple goals simultaneously and let one project influence another. They solicit first-hand information from people and use body language. The second industrial revolution in 1867 transformed industry from mechanic to electricity based on the discovery of gas. Every high-power country is searching for rich natural resources to enhance power resulting in the two World Wars in 1914-1918 and 1939-1945. The third industrial revolution transformed industry from electricity to nuclear based on the discovery of uranium. The polychronic culture has been changed to a monochronic culture in which people just do one thing at one time. Thus, the affiliation motive focusing on the institution rules and avoiding human critics is very important. Then international trades among countries were based on the competitive advantage or excellent performance. The achievement motive is the key in each country. The two world superpowers US and Russia competed in technology in the Cold War 1947-1991 by the three implicit motives: achievement, power, and affiliation (McClelland & Winter, 1969, 1971). In sum, the first three industrial revolutions focused on discovering, controlling, and distributing natural resources for the country.

The fourth industrial revolution called Industry 4.0 has transformed industry from physical to virtual based on the Internet of things and automation with renewable resources. The most significant discovery from Industry 4.0 in 2021 is the invention of COVID-19 vaccines and their impact is certainly very critical to human lives represented by motives, cultures, and economy.

Implicit motives of people or countries including achievement, power and affiliation will operate human behaviors through the three channels called linear active, multi-linear active and reactive cultures under the impacts of COVID-19 vaccines. For example, Vietnam, China, and Japan representing the reactive culture should create environments for people to perform their excellent services during the post of COVID-19 era. Vietnam was ranked as the second top country in the world to control COVID-19 cases. China was ranked as the frontier in producing COVID-19 vaccines. Japan was ranked as the top achievement of economics under the control of COVID-19.

In sum, the discovery of COVID-19 vaccines has critically affected the motives and cultures of human society in the economy, but little research has focused on their impacts on motives and cultures across countries, especially Asia. This paper is thus to examine the effects of the fourth industrial revolution with COVID-19 vaccines on the changes of motives and cultures in 38 worldwide countries and then on Asian countries.

The remaining sections of the present paper are organized as follows. Section 2 provides the history of Industry 4.0 affecting cultures, motives, and Asia. Section 3 examines Structure Equation Modelling to find coefficients of three motives and three cultural dimensions with the mediation of Industry 4.0.

Section 4 focuses on the discussions of the study findings. Section 5 concludes the contributions of the paper and highlights potential future research.

LITERATURE REVIEW

History of Industry 4.0 and Cultures

In the first Industrial Revolution in 1765 (Industrial Revolution, 2021), people used mechanics to produce products from coal. The processes included the steam engine for railroad transportation, the metal forging for production, the spinning machine for fabric, the boat for canal transportation, and the mules for ground transportation. The processes have changed agricultural society into nonegalitarian social relationships. As a result, productivity has increased and divided a society into upper and lower social classes. The cultures in each class are different; one is more individual, and the other is more collective.

In the second Industrial Revolution in 1870 (Industrial Revolution, 2021), people used the combustion engine with oil. There was mass production from the appearance of steel and chemical products, telegraph and telephone for communication, and planes and cars for transportation. As a result, jobs are more specialized, and cultures were divided into more task or social oriented. The two World Wars were incurred by divergent cultures.

The third Industrial Revolution transformed the electrical industry using nuclear technology invented in 1969 (Industrial Revolution, 2021). The discovery of nuclear resources has divided cultures by time either monochronic in present and future or polychronic cultures in the past.

The fourth Industrial Revolution or Industry 4.0 has transformed the nuclear industry into digital technology. The industrial internet, cloud technology and artificial intelligence created a physical and virtual environment for people. In addition, the growth trend of Industry 4.0 has been changed by disruptive technology (Dont, 2021). As a result, the cultures are divided not only by time but also by performance. There appear thus three types of culture: linear active or monochronic culture, multi-linear culture or polychronic culture, and reactive culture or performance culture in the fourth industrial revolution.

In this study, we will use data from the most magnificent discovery in Industry 4.0 called COVID-19 vaccines to reflect the most contribution of Industry 4.0 to the world in 2021. The COVID-19 pandemic was caused by severe acute respiratory syndrome coronavirus 2 in January 2020 and spread to the world quickly. More than 30 million people are infected and people from different cultures have worked to develop the vaccines for the coronavirus. As a result, there have been 165 coronavirus vaccines (Corum, Wee, & Zimmer, 2020). As of today, around 748 million (9.6%) people have been fully vaccinated (OurWorldData, 2021) and most of them are from the US, China, and Russia. The study model thus examined the impact of Industry 4.0 on behavioral cultures in the world and Asia.

Cultures Across Countries – Linear Active, Multi-Linear Active, and Reactive

Culture is the growth of country personality traits (Lynn, 1971/1991). Traits are different from motives. Motives are expressed in behavior implicitly, that is, not accessible to consciousness and therefore measurable only by indirect means (Greenwald & Banaji, 1995). Traits are the motives' channels (Winter, John, Stewart, Klohnen, and Duncan, 1998). Motives are future ends of the traits in a particular way in time and traits are the life outcomes (McAdams, 1995). McClelland (1951) defines traits as "surface or stylistic manifestations of personality only". Therefore, motives are complementary to traits and traits are subsuming of motives (Winter, John, Stewart, Klohnen, & Duncan, 1998).

Culture or national character is "relatively enduring personality characteristics and patterns that are modal among adult members of the society" (Inkeles & Levinson, 1954,1969). Based on Eysenck's (1966) theory of personality including psychoticism, extraversion, and neuroticism, Lynn (1971/1991) showed results of a factor analysis of national medical indicators in 18 developed countries and identified the dimension of "anxiety." Lynn and Hampson (1975) extended this to two dimensions, "neuroticism" and "extraversion." Lynn (1981) added "psychoticism." Lynn and Martin (1995) have studied the national differences for 37 nations and found that extraversion, neuroticism, and psychoticism were related to economics of these countries.

Hall (1966) has integrated culture into the three dimensions of architecture by adding time as the fourth dimension.

In his book "Beyond Culture", Hall (1976) has grouped countries into cultures based on specific types of communication. There are two dimensions: the first based on perception and organization of time, and the second based on contextualization of information. There are monochronic and polychronic types in terms of time. In the culture of monochronic, people work on schedules and promptness. In the culture of polychronic, people do several things at the same time (p.17). In terms of contextualization, the culture related to the meaning of the message is called low context and the culture related to the way in which information is transmitted is called high context. Hall (1983) identified that polychronic culture is used to repetition and past experiences whereas the monochronic culture is toward the present and the future.

Therefore, Hall (1983) identified three types of culture: monochronic culture, polychronic culture, and contextualization culture.

Lewis (2006) has revised the combinations of Hall's monochronic and polychronic types with high and low contextualization to create three types of cultures: linear active, multi active, and reactive. The countries in the linear active culture in Northern Europe and North America are the monochronic type with low contextualization in which punctuation is very important. People think logically to plan and compartmentalize projects. They get information from scratch and separate the social and professional. The linear-active culture might be thus fit for the affiliation motive.

The countries in the multi active culture in Southern Europe, Latin, African, and Middle East are the polychronic type with high contextualization in which punctuation is not important. People think of relationships rather than logistics. They pursue multiple goals simultaneously and let one project influence another. They solicit first-hand information from people and use body language. The multi-linear culture might be thus fit for the power motive.

Combining the linear and multilinear, the reactive people in East Asia are friendly to harmonize both data and people sources. They do not plan step by step or grand outline, they look at the general principles and strictly must not lose face. If the truth to linear and multilinear is priority and flexibility, respectively, it is the second after diplomacy in reactive. If the communication of linear and multilinear is written and spoken, respectively, the face-to-face is the key communication to the reactive. When the linear and multilinear set up the mission by compartmentalizing and one affecting another, the reactive sees the whole picture in reactive. If the linear and multilinear respect officialdom and pulling strings, the reactive respect networks. The reactive culture might be thus fit for the achievement motive.

Lewis's (2006) cultures in Figure 1 includes 56 countries and groups of countries in the world. "The several hundred national and regional cultures of the world can be roughly classified into three groups: task-oriented, highly organized planners (linear-active); people-oriented, loquacious inter-relators (multi-active); and introverted, respect-oriented listeners (reactive). Italians see Germans as stiff and time-dominated; Germans see Italians gesticulating in chaos; the Japanese observe and quietly learn from both." (Lewis, 2006).

Figure 1. Lewis's (2006) model with 56 countries and groups of countries.

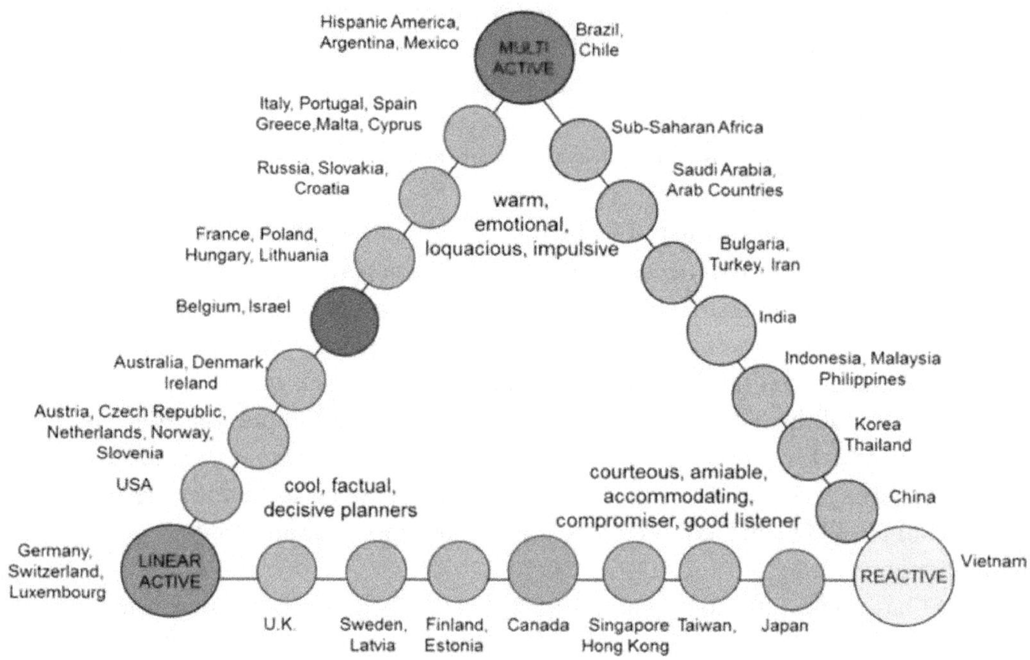

Bacik and Turakova (2018) have applied the three cultural dimensions of linear-active, multi-active and reactive cultures to corporate culture in their empirical studies. Chandarana (2011) has elaborated the 3 dimensions of Lewis's (2006) model in terms of trust hierarchy as follows: (1) Family only, (2) School only, and (3) Institution only. He indicates the relationship between schoolmates' performance and the reactive culture, family control and the multi-linear culture, and institution law and the linear active culture. Lewis (2019) reports how the Western culture and economic power dominate the world. He also identifies the role of Asian countries in this era. Guiso, Sapienza, and Zingales (2006) report the relationships between culture and economics. Gardner (2021) examines the impacts of Industry 4.0 on cultures and economy. He posts, "The key to getting it right is to prioritize adoption rather than change for changes sake (i.e., linear active culture). A phased approach (i.e., Industry 4.0) will be beneficial for everyone in the long term (i.e., GDP per capita)." (p. 1).

Asia Culture: East and West

Asia culture or the culture in the East is different from the Western culture. The key differences between East and West cultures are one is hardworking and the other is adventurous; one is group interest first and the other is self-interest first; one is low profile and the other is high profile. Leung and Bozionelos

(2004) used the five-factor model of personality to examine the Asian culture affected mostly by Confucius, a Chinese philosopher 2500 years ago. They forecasted extraversion related to high profile and openness associated with low conservatism would be low in the Asian culture because they are opposite with the Confucius principles "industriousness, sacrifice of personal interests over group interest, concealment of emotions, and low profile" (Leung and Bozionelos, 2004, p. 31). Judge, Bono, Ilies, and Gerhardt (2002) found that extraversion, conscientiousness, and openness had the strongest influence in the leadership for western culture. However, the interactions between East and West have been changed by industrial revolutions especially the Industry 4.0. Ishibashi and Kottke (2009) also found that Japanese culture highly appreciates extraversion in leadership for Japan culture. To thoroughly understand the roots of cultures, we have examined the human motivation theory (McClelland, 1985) through the implicit motives of people and countries.

Motives: Achievement, Power, and Affiliation

In this study, we will use the three implicit motives (Achievement, Affiliation, and Power) of the motivation theory of McClelland (1985). The three motives are implicit because they are measured by Thematic Apperception Test (TAT) (Vane, 1981) to measure the unconscious motives of human beings. In the TAT, participants will write their imagination based on the ambiguous TAT pictures and the professional raters will score the writings in three motives: achievement, power, and affiliation. The TAT approach is considered as an "X-ray" technology to reflect people's motivation (McClelland, 1985). The reason for this study is to use the three implicit motives for the 24 countries because the unconscious motives are more consistent than the explicit motives in the changing environment and the three motives are embedded in the fairy tales of each country (McClelland, 1985).

The achievement motive is the need for a standard of excellence in competition. Motivation theory (McClelland, 1985) states that high need for achievement (n Ach) persons or countries tend to be competitive and strive to do better than others and the direction of that striving is toward an excellence performance. High need for achievement (n Ach) appears to lead people or countries toward performance goals rather than toward influencing others or obtaining large profits (McClelland & Winter, 1969/1971). McClelland (1961/1976) used Thematic Apperception Tests to score the three motives in 24 countries in the 1950s to compare the economic development of these countries. Since then, researchers have applied this approach to examine the economic growth of countries (Hay Group, 2003; Spangler, 1992; Tuerlinckx, De Boeck, & Lens, 2002; Vane, 1981). Lynn (1991) administered a survey of university students in 43 countries between 1986 and 1989 and found that "The innovations on which economic growth depends are made by individuals who need to have the motivation to make these innovations". In addition, Lynn (1991) also sees the high scores on competitiveness in the five countries in Asia: Korea, Taiwan, Hong Kong, Japan, and Singapore that contribute to the development of their economies significantly.

The first assumption is thus the achievement motive of a country would be a future end of the channel or culture targeting on performance.

The power motive is the need to influence, teach, or encourage others to achieve, with little interest in doing things alone (Chusmir, 1985). Countries or people with a high need for power (n Pow) like to work with other countries or people who have disciplines and self-respects (McClelland, 1985). Managers who are n Pow appear to be more concerned with the maintenance of the system rather than expansion (Winter, 1973). While high n Ach managers look to become professionals with new and alternative means, n Pow managers generally stay with available means and fight for a greater share of existing limited resources (McClelland & Winter, 1969/1971).

The second assumption is thus that the power motive might be a future end of the culture of interaction among people or countries, i.e., the polychronic culture.

The affiliation motive is the need for positive friendship with other persons. Individuals with high need for affiliation (n Aff) tend to worry about disappointing others (Winter, 1982), leading them to avoid making decisive or unkind comments or criticism (McClelland, 1985; Winter, 1982). They tend to avoid conflict and competition with others (McClelland, 1985). They are thus overly sensitive under risk-taking situations (Winter & Stewart, 1977). The affiliation-motivated managers/leaders are reluctant to monitor subordinates' behavior, to convey negative feedback, or to discipline subordinates (McClelland, 1985). Therefore, high affiliation people prefer to avoid people's conflicts by doing one thing at one time.

The third assumption is thus the affiliation motive might be a future end of the monochronic culture.

Hypotheses

The above literature has reviewed the findings of the empirical studies on theory of motivation (McClelland, 1985) and indicated some assumptions for the present study. Before setting up hypotheses, we looked up the secondary historical data regarding cultures, motives, and economies across countries in the world affected by the impact of industrial revolutions as follows.

During Industry 2.0 and Industry 3.0, McClelland (1961/1976) has measured the three motives of achievement, affiliation, and power across 31 countries (Australia, Austria, Belgium, Brazil, Bulgaria, Canada, Chile, Denmark, England, Finland, France, Germany, Greece, Hungary, India, Iran, Iraq, Ireland, Israel, Italy, Japan, Netherland, Norway, Pakistan, Poland, Portugal, Spain, Sweden, Switzerland, Turkey, and Russia) in 1925 and in 1950 during the second and third industrial revolutions in Table 1. Data in 1925 is affected by the second industrial revolution due to the discovery of the oil fields in Texas and Persian Gulf; Data in 1950 is affected by nuclear power in 1945.

During Industry 4.0, Emmerik, Gardner, and Wendt (2010) have applied McClelland's (1976) approach to measure the three motives across 24 countries (Argentina, Australia, Brazil, Canada, France, Germany, Greece, Hong Kong, India, Indonesia, Italy, Japan, Malaysia, Mexico, Netherlands, Nordic countries, Philippines, South Africa, South Korea, Spain, Taiwan, Turkey, United Kingdom, and United States) which are illustrated in Table 1.

In Table 1, we also calculated the average data of motives, cultures, gross domestic product per capita in the world and Asia. We found that Industry 4.0 has changed (1) the average cultures of linear active, multi-linear active, and reactive, (2) the average motives of achievement, affiliation, and power of Asia countries, and (3) the average gross domestic product per capita of 41 countries. Therefore, we come up with the hypotheses and sub hypotheses as follows.

- *Hypothesis 1: The relationships between the three motives (Achievement, Affiliation, and Power) and three cultures (Linear Active, Multi-linear Active, and Reactive) would be changed by Industry 4.0.*
    - *Hypothesis 1a*: There would be a significant relationship between the reactive culture and the achievement motive.
    - *Hypothesis 1b*: There would be a significant relationship between the multi-linear active culture and the power motive.

  - *Hypothesis 1c:* There would be a significant relationship between the linear active culture and the affiliation motive.
- *Hypothesis 2: Industry 4.0 would change the impact of cultures (Linear Active, Multi-linear Active, and Reactive) on the GDP per capita.*
  - *Hypothesis 2a*: The Multi-linear active culture with Industry 4.0 would reduce the GDP per capita.
  - *Hypothesis 2b*: The linear-active culture with Industry 4.0 would enhance the GDP per capita.
  - *Hypothesis 2c*: The Reactive culture with Industry 4.0 would enhance the GDP per capita.
- *Hypothesis 3: Technology would increase the impact of motives (Achievement, Affiliation, and Power) on Asia.*
  - *Hypothesis 3a:* The power motive will decrease in Asia through Industry 4.0.
  - *Hypothesis 3b*: The achievement motive will increase in Asia through Industry 4.0.
  - *Hypothesis 3c:* The affiliation motive will decrease in Asia through Industry 4.0.

METHODOLOGY

Sample

The study sample is the motives and cultures of 38 countries selected from 24 countries in the two periods 1925 and 1950 in McClelland's (1961/1976) book, 56 countries from Lewis's model (2006), and 25 countries in the research of Emmerik, Gardner, Wendt, and Fischer (2010). These countries include Algeria, Argentina, Australia, Austria, Belgium, Brazil, Bulgaria, Canada, Chile, Denmark, England, Finland, France, Germany, Greece, Hong Kong, Hungary, India, Indonesia, Iran, Iraq, Ireland, Israel, Italy, Japan, Malaysia, Mexico, Netherland, Norway, Pakistan, Russia, South Africa, South Korea, Spain, Sweden, Switzerland, Taiwan, Turkey, and US.

Method

This study first used Canonical Correlation analysis to find 3 significant relationships among 9 possible pairs of the relationships between 3 motives and 3 cultures. Then we used Structure Equation Modeling (SEM) to build six models for the three hypotheses of the study. Each hypothesis has two models: one with Industry 4.0 and the other without it. Lewis' (2006) three culture types including Linear-active, Multi-active, and Reactive are endogenous and the three motives Achievement, Affiliation, and Power are exogenous variables. Industry 4.0 is as an endogenous variable measured by a dummy variable with 1 representing the presence of vaccinations and 0 representing a lack of vaccinations from Jan 31, 2020 to June 30, 2021. Data of vaccinations was retrieved from Our World Data (2021). Similarly, the dummy variable ASIA is used for Asian countries as an endogenous variable. Motives for the 24 countries in 1925 and 1950 are the secondary data of McClelland (1976). If there are a missing one for the country, we will leave it blank. Motives for the 24 countries in 2010 are the secondary data of the study of Emmerik et al. (2010). Total of countries involved in the study sample is 38 countries because of the country overlap of the two previous samples. The cultures of 56 countries in Lewis's (2006) model are measured as follows. We have measured three vector scalars for each of 56 countries based on the assumption that (1) each

Table 1. Effects of industrial revolutions (1.2, I.3, I.4) on motives across 41 countries

		Achievement			Affiliation				Power
Asia***	1.7	1.29	1.7	0.7	1.7	1.3	1.3	1.14	1.1
Linear(L)***	1.7	1.7	1.6	1.8	1.7	1.3	1	0.9	1.1
Multilinear (M)***	0.8	1.9	1.7	1.3	1.3	1.3	1.3	1	1
Reactive (R)***	1.8	1.8	1.8	0.8	1.7	1.5	1.2	1	1.1
GDPpc/Motives	1419	1991	19228	1384	2488	24883	1833	3736	30108
Argentina (M)	NA	NA	1.6	NA	NA	1.5	NA	NA	1.1
Australia (L)	2.8	2.4	1.8	1.8	1.2	1.3	1.2	0.5	1.1
Austria (L)	1.6	1.9	NA	1.2	1.1	NA	1.2	0.4	NA
Belgium (L)	1	0.4	NA	1.6	1.5	NA	0.8	0.9	NA
Brazil (M)	0.3	1.1	1.6	1	0.1	1.2	0.8	0.9	1.1
Bulgaria (M)	NA	2.2	NA	NA	1.2	NA	NA	1.1	NA
Canada (L)	2.7	2.3	1.6	2.4	2.2	1.1	1.1	1.2	0.9
Chile (M)	1.3	1.2	NA	0.9	2.2	NA	1.4	0.8	NA
Denmark (L)	2	1.1	1.5	2.2	1.8	1.3	1.7	0.9	1.2
England (L)	2.1	1.7	1.8	2.4	2.5	1.3	1.1	1.1	1
Finland (L)	1.2	1.5	1.5	1	1.7	1.3	1.3	1.1	1.2
France (M)	0.8	2.4	1.8	1.4	1.2	1.3	1.7	0.5	1.2
Germany (L)	1.4	2.1	1.7	1.6	1.3	1.2	1.3	1.3	1.2
Greece (M)	0.4	2.3	2.1	2.8	2.1	1.4	0.7	0.8	1.1
Hong Kong (R)**	NA	NA	1.5	NA	NA	1.2	NA	NA	1.1
Hungary (M)	1.3	1.8	NA	0.9	1.2	NA	1.5	0.5	NA
India (M)**	NA	2.7	1.7	NA	1.2	1.4	NA	1.2	1.1
Indonesia (R)**	NA	1.7	NA	NA	1.1	NA	NA	1.1	NA
Iran (M)	NA	1.2	NA	NA	0.2	NA	NA	0.9	NA
Iraq (M)	NA	2	NA	NA	0.6	NA	NA	2.7	NA
Ireland (L)	3.2	2.3	1.5	2	1.4	1.3	1.3	0.9	1.2
Israel (L)	NA	2.3	NA	NA	2.9	NA	NA	0.2	NA
Italy (M)	NA	1.3	1.9	NA	2	1.4	NA	1	1
Japan (R)**	1.8	1.3	1.9	0.8	2.2	1.4	1.3	1	1.2
Malaysia (R)**	NA	NA	1.8	NA	NA	1.3	NA	NA	1
Mexico (M)	NA	1.6	1.5	NA	1.6	1.2	NA	1.2	0.8
Netherland (L)	0.3	1.5	1.8	2.1	2.1	1.2	0.4	0.7	1.1
Norway (L)	1.3	1.7	1.5	0.6	2	1.3	0.8	0.6	1.2
Pakistan (M)**	NA	2.3	NA	NA	1.2	NA	NA	0.5	NA
Russia (M)	1	2.1	NA	1	1.3	NA	1.6	1.2	NA
South Africa (M)	NA	NA	1.9	NA	NA	1.2	NA	NA	1.3
South Korea (M)**	NA	NA	2.1	NA	NA	1.6	NA	NA	1.3
Spain (M)	0.8	2.3	1.5	1.1	0.6	1.3	1.6	1.9	0.8
Sweden (R)	2.2	1.6	1.5	1.1	1.5	1.3	0.6	0.8	1.2
Switzerland (L)	NA	1	NA	NA	1.1	NA	NA	1.6	NA
Taiwan (L)**	NA	NA	1.6	NA	NA	1.5	NA	NA	1
Turkey (L)	NA	3.6	1.6	NA	0.9	1.2	NA	0.6	0.7
United States (M)	1.9	2.2	1.7	2.3	2.1	1.3	0.9	1.4	1

Source: McClelland (1976), Emmerik et al. (2010), & Author's calculation based on Lewis (2006)
(*) (1) 1925 (Industry 2.0), (2) 1950 (Industry 3.0), (3) 2010 (Industry 4.0)
(**) Asian countries (***) Three motive averages of Asia, Linear, Multi-Linear, and Reactive

country possesses three vector dimensions (Linear, Multi-linear, and Reactive) and (2) its relative distance to each cultural dimension in Lewis's (2006) model, on a scale of 25-100 (Table 2). All data were transferred into log to avoid any spurious regressions before conducting structure equation modelling.

In Table 2, the linear active culture is the culture people plan, schedule, organize, pursue action chains, and do one thing at a time. The multi active culture is the culture in which people "do many things at once, planning their priorities not according to a time schedule, but according to the relative thrill or importance that each appointment brings with it." (Lewis, 2006). The reactive culture is the culture which "prioritize courtesy and respect, listening quietly and calmly to their interlocutors and reacting carefully to the other side's proposals." (p.34).

Findings

1. The study has conducted canonical correlation analysis to find the pair of variates in the relationships between the three motives (Achievement, Affiliation, and Power) and three cultures (Linear Active, Multi-linear Active, and Reactive) under Industry 4.0. Results indicate that (1) affiliation motive and linear active culture are the first pair with highest canonical correlations (.74/.90). (2) achievement motive and reactive are the second pair with second highest canonical correlation (.25/.61). (3) Finally, power motive and multi-linear active are the third pair with significant canonical correlation (.23/.34) in the first variate. Hypothesis 1 was confirmed. There are 3 significant relationships between motives and cultures in Industry 4.0. In other words, Industry 4.0 affects the three relationships as follows: Achievement motive fits for reactive culture, Affiliation motive fits for linear active culture, and Power motive fits for multi-linear active culture. Hypotheses 1a, 1b, and 1c were supported.
2. Regarding the impacts of Industry 4.0 on the motives and cultures, The study has conducted AMOS SPSS 27 to set up two following models: one with Industry 4.0 and the other without it, the study has found the following equations retrieved from Figure 2. The two models "with Industry 4.0" and "without Industry 4.0" in figure 2 are well-fit models with composite reliability of .94 and .95, respectively and variance extracted of 70% and 72% (CMINs/df=1.03/1.05; ps=.406/.50; GFIs=.93/.96; CFIs=.99/.99; RMSEAs=.04/.05, AICs=43.82/45.1)

The following equations for Model 1 with Industry 4.0 (eq.1.1, eq.1.2, eq.1.3, and eq.1.4) and for Model 2 without Industry 4.0 (eq.2.1, eq.2.2, and eq.2.3) and figure 2 are the outcome of Structure Equation Modelling of SPSS AMOS 27.

$$LLinear = (-.85)\ LAffiliation + (.06)\ LIndustry\ 4.0 + e1.1 \tag{1.1}$$

$$LMultilinear = (-1.02)\ LPower + (-.02)\ LIndustry\ 4.0 + e1.2 \tag{1.2}$$

$$LReactive = (.76)\ LAchievement + (-.09)\ LIndustry\ 4.0 + e1.3 \tag{1.3}$$

$$LIndustry\ 4.0 = (2.92)\ LAchievement + (-2.29)\ LAffiliation + (-1.44)\ LPower + e1.4 \tag{1.4}$$

Table 2. The scores of three cultural dimensions of 56 countries in Lewis's (2006) model

Country	Multi-linear Active	Linear Active	Re-Active
Hispanic America	100	25	25
Argentina	100	25	25
Mexico	100	25	25
Italy	85	30	30
Portugal	85	30	30
Spain	85	30	30
Greece	85	30	30
Malta	85	30	30
Cyprus	85	30	30
Russia	75	40	35
Slovakia	75	40	35
Croatia	75	40	35
France	65	65	40
Poland	65	65	40
Hungary	65	65	40
Lithuania	65	65	40
Belgium	50	75	50
Israel	50	75	50
Australia	40	80	40
Denmark	40	80	40
Ireland	40	80	40
Austria	35	85	35
Czech Republic	35	85	35
Netherlands	35	85	35
Norway	35	85	35
Slovenia	35	85	35
USA	30	90	30
Germany	25	100	25
Switzerland	25	100	25
Luxembourg	25	100	25
UK	30	90	30
Sweden	35	85	40
Latvia	35	85	40
Finland	40	80	45
Estonia	40	80	45
Canada	50	70	50
Singapore	40	50	65
Taiwan	35	40	85
Hong Kong	35	40	85
Japan	30	30	90
Vietnam	25	25	100
China	30	30	90
Korea	40	40	80
Thailand	40	40	80
Indonesia	45	45	65
Malaysia	45	45	65
Philippines	45	45	65
India	50	50	60
Bulgaria	70	45	55
Turkey	70	45	55
Iran	70	45	55
Saudi Arabia	85	30	40
Arab Countries	85	30	40
South Saharan Africa	90	25	30
Brazil	100	25	25
Chile	100	25	25

Source: Author's calculations based on Lewis's (2006) model on a scale of 25-100.

$$LMultilinear = (-1.00)\ LPower + e2.1 \tag{2.1}$$

$$LReactive = (.65)\ LAchievement + e2.2 \tag{2.2}$$

$$LLinear = (-.98)\ LAffiliation + e2.3 \tag{2.3}$$

Figure 2. Model 1 with industry 4.0 and Model 2 without industry 4.0

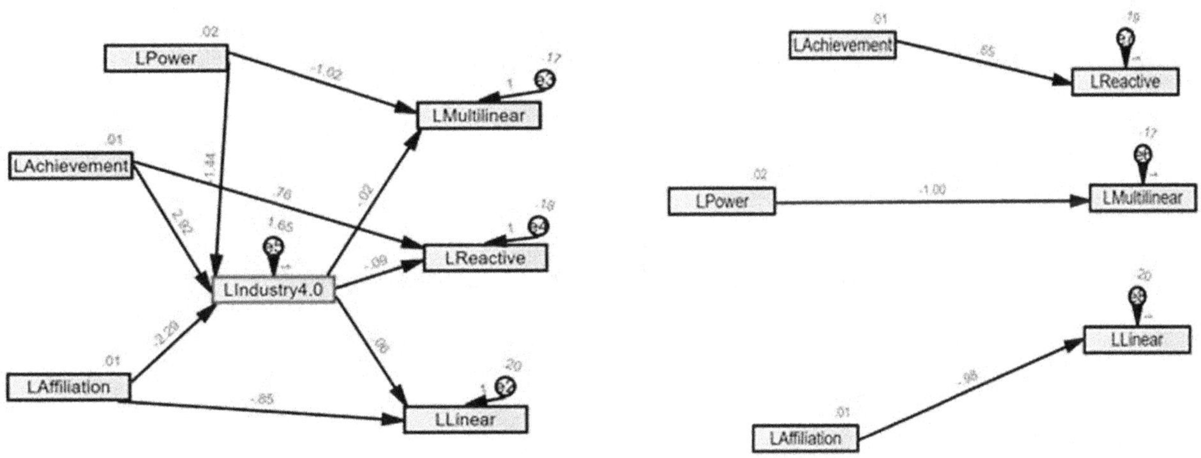

The mediator of Industry 4.0 has enhanced the relationship between achievement motive and reactive culture as follows. Figure 2 indicates that the coefficient of achievement motive on reactive culture is bigger with the mediator Industry 4.0 than without it (.76>.65). Industry 4.0 enhances the effects of achievement motive on reactive culture.

The mediator of Industry 4.0 has enhanced the relationship between power motive and multi-linear active culture as follows. Figure 2 indicates that the coefficient of power motive on multi-linear active culture is bigger with the mediator Industry 4.0 than without it (1.02>1). Industry 4.0 enhances the effects of power motive on multi-linear active culture.

The mediator of Industry 4.0 has enhanced the relationship between affiliation motive and linear active culture as follows. Figure 2 indicates that the coefficient of affiliation motive on linear active culture is smaller with the mediator Industry 4.0 than without it (.85<.98). Industry 4.0 reduces the effects of affiliation motive on linear active culture.

3. Regarding the impacts of Industry 4.0 on the motives and cultures, The study has conducted AMOS SPSS 27 to set up two following models: one with Industry 4.0 and the other without it, the study has found the following equations retrieved from Figure 3. The two models "with Industry 4.0" and "without Industry 4.0" in figure 2 are well-fit models with composite reliability of .94 and .95, respectively and variance extracted of 70% and 72% (CMINs/df=1.03/1.05; ps=.406/.50; GFIs=.93/.96; CFIs=.99/.99; RMSEAs=.04/.05, AICs=43.82/45.1).

The following equations for Model 3 with Industry 4.0 (eq.3.1, eq.3.2) and for Model 4 without Industry 4.0 (eq.4) and figure 3 are the outcome of Structure Equation Modelling of SPSS AMOS 27.

$$LGDPpc = (.29)\ LLinear + (-.67)\ LMultilinear + (-.40)\ LReactive + (-.12)\ LIndustry\ 4.0 + e3.1 \quad (3.1)$$

$$LIndustry\ 4.0 = (.84)\ LLinear + (.35)\ LMultilinear + (-.57)\ LReactive + e3.2 \quad (3.2)$$

$$LGDPpc = (.18)\ LLinear + (-.71)\ LMultilinear + (-.33)\ LReactive + e4 \quad (4)$$

Figure 3. Industry 4.0 has changed the impacts of cultures on GDP per capita.

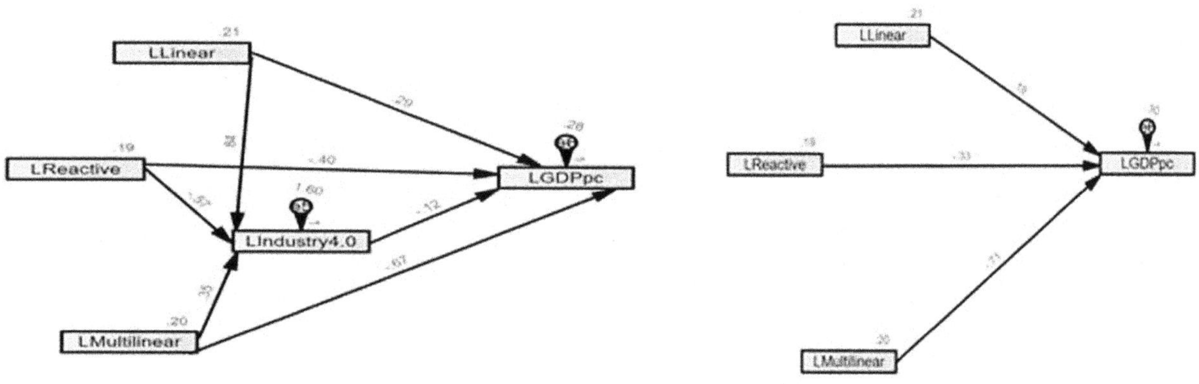

The mediator of Industry 4.0 has enhanced the relationship between reactive culture and GDP per capita as follows. Figure 3 indicates that the coefficient of reactive culture on the GDP per capita is bigger with the mediator Industry 4.0 than without it (.40>.33). Industry 4.0 enhances the effects of reactive culture on the GDP per capita.

The mediator of Industry 4.0 has enhanced the relationship between multi-linear active culture on the GDP per capita as follows. Figure 3 indicates that the coefficient of multi-linear active culture on GDP per capita is smaller with the mediator Industry 4.0 than without it (.67<.71). Industry 4.0 reduces the effects of multi-linear active culture on the GDP per capita.

The mediator of Industry 4.0 has enhanced the relationship between linear active culture and the GDP per capita as follows. Figure 3 indicates that the coefficient of linear active culture on the GDP per capita is bigger with the mediator Industry 4.0 than without it (.29<.18). Industry 4.0 enhances the effects of linear active culture on the GDP per capita.

4. Regarding the impacts of Industry 4.0 on the motives and Asian countries, The study has conducted AMOS SPSS 27 to set up two following models: one with Industry 4.0 and the other without it, the study has found the following equations retrieved from Figure 4. The two models "with Industry 4.0" and "without Industry 4.0" in figure 3 are well-fit models with composite reliability of .94

and .95, respectively and variance extracted of 75% and 76% (CMINs/df=0.99/1.03; ps=.49/.50; GFIs=.93/.96; CFIs=.99/.96; RMSEAs=.04/.05, AICs=48.82/49.1).

The following equations for Model 5 with Industry 4.0 (eq.5.1, eq.5.2) and for Model 6 without Industry 4.0 (eq.6) and figure 4 are the outcome of Structure Equation Modelling of SPSS AMOS 27.

$$Asia = (.17)\ LAchievement + (1.45)\ LAffiliation + (.31)\ LPower + (-.04)\ LIndustry\ 4.0 + e5.2 \tag{5.1}$$

$$LIndustry\ 4.0 = (2.92)\ LAchievement + (-2.29)\ LAffiliation + (-1.44)\ LPower + (1)\ e5.1 \tag{5.2}$$

$$Asia = (.06)\ LAchievement + (1.53)\ LAffiliation + (.36)\ LPower + e6 \tag{6}$$

Figure 4. Industry 4.0 has changed the impacts of motives in Asia.

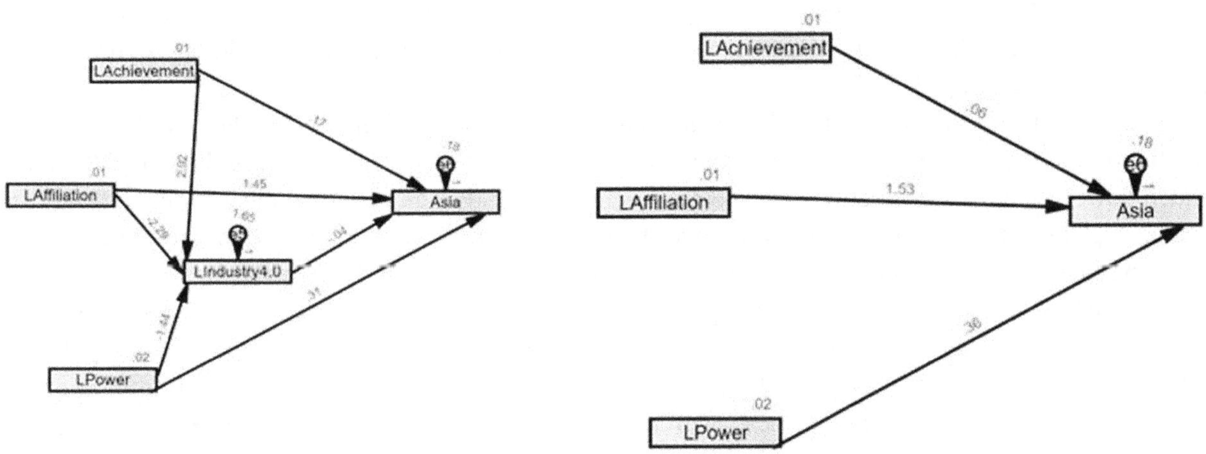

The mediator of Industry 4.0 has enhanced the relationship between achievement motive and Asian countries as follows. Figure 4 indicates that the coefficient of achievement motive in Asian countries is bigger with the mediator Industry 4.0 than without it (.17>.06). Industry 4.0 enhances the effects of achievement motive in Asia.

The mediator of Industry 4.0 has reduced the relationship between power motive and Asia as follows. Figure 4 indicates that the coefficient of power motive on Asia is smaller with the mediator Industry 4.0 than without it (.31<.36). Industry 4.0 reduces the effects of power motive in the Asian countries.

The mediator of Industry 4.0 has reduced the relationship between affiliation motive and Asian countries as follows. Figure 4 indicates that the coefficient of affiliation motive in Asia is bigger with the mediator Industry 4.0 than without it (1.53<1.45). Industry 4.0 enhances the effects of affiliation motive in Asian countries.

DISCUSSION

The study findings are applicable to practice. Firstly, the impact of Industry 4.0 with COVID-19 vaccines on motives and cultures of the world and Asia in the post COVID-19 era has enhanced the achievement motive in the reactive culture and Asia and the power motive in the multi-linear culture, but it has decreased the affiliation motive in the linear active culture. In the 6-step process of Industry 4.0 presented by Gardner (2021), the study findings are consistent with the process summary as follows. Step 1 regarding "Be Realistic" indicates the digital transformation may attract many people at first, Gardner suggests not to "take everything on at once". It implies the linear active culture should decrease affiliation motive. Step 2 regarding "get stakeholders on board" indicates it is impeccable for increasing power motive in multi-linear culture in Industry 4.0. Step 3 regarding "Keep talking" indicates Industry 4.0 communications to increase information for achievement motives to increase in Asia is very critical.

Secondly, Industry 4.0 has enhanced the gross domestic product per capita (GDP) in the linear active and reactive cultures but it has decreased the GDP in the multi-linear cultures. In step 4 of Gardner's (2021) Industry 4.0 process, it is necessary for people to keep "comprehensive training and ongoing support" in Industry 4.0. It implies that the linear active culture and reactive culture countries who invest most in COVID-19 vaccines will get increasing payoffs (The Guardian, 2021). On the contrary, the multi-linear culture countries who cannot invent COVID-19 vaccines suffer a decrease in the GDP per capita in 2020.

Thirdly, Industry 4.0 has enhanced the achievement motive in Asia but reduced the power motive and affiliation motive. In step 5 regarding "Take your time", it implies the investment in Industry 4.0 using much power motive "too quickly could be detrimental" even though Asian countries are successful in increasing the achievement motive to discover COVID-19 vaccines and apply them first in China. In step 6 regarding "Undertaking regular reviews," Gardner (2021) warns the regular reviews are critical because the achievement motive is often opposite to the affiliation motive (McClelland, 1985) resulting in the reduction of affiliation motive in Asia while achievement motive increasing in Industry 4.0. In addition, Peng (2018) and Qin (2015) reports the unique culture of Asia will be the fit integration of East and West. This reflects the Japanese, Korean, and Chinese trendy dramas to create the re-imagined Asian-ness.

CONCLUSION

The study has compiled the two famous books: "The Achieving Society" by McClelland (1961/1976) and "When Cultures Collide: Leading across cultures" by Lewis (2006) and reviewed recent research findings of motives, cultures, and Asia. Although the limit of study is a small sample of 36 countries, the study has contributed to the academia and practice in providing the significant relationships between motives and cultures under the impact of Industry 4.0 and the changes in Asia.

REFERENCES

Bacik, R, & Turakova, A. (2018). The analysis of culture differences defined in Lewis's model and impact on corporate culture. *Journal of Global Science,* 1-6.

Chandarana, A. (2011). *Crossroads of Culture – How to do business effectively in the global marketplace*. Available online at https://www.slideshare.net/prturner/avinash-chandaranacrossroads-of-culture-cesse-2011

Chusmir, L. (1985). Motivation of managers: Is gender a factor? *Psychology of Women Quarterly*, *9*(1), 153–159. doi:10.1111/j.1471-6402.1985.tb00868.x

Corum, J., Wee, S., & Zimmer, C. (2020). Coronavirus vaccine tracker. *New York Times*. Available online as of 23 September 2020: https://www.nytimes.com/interactive/2020/science/coronavirus-vaccine-tracker.html

Dont, E. (2021). *Why EHRs are not disruptive?* Available online at http://captaindont.blogspot.com/2014/05/why-ehrs-are-not-yet-disruptive.html?m=1

Emmerik, I., Gardner, W., & Wendt, H. (2010). Associations of Culture and Personality with McClelland's Motives: A Cross-Cultural Study of Managers in 24 Countries. *Group and Organization Management*, *35*(3), 329-367.

Eysenck, H. J. (1966). Personality and experimental psychology. *Bulletin of the British Psychological Society*.

Gardner, A. (2021). The importance of creating the right 'culture' in Industry 4.0. *Business Insights: Essentials*. Available online at http://bi.gale.com.ezproxy.lib.uwf.edu/essentials/article/GALE%7CA616135591/a122f7264ff04c67475a42a51429c96b?u=pens49866

Greenwald, A. G., & Banaji, M. R. (1995). Implicit social cognition: Attitudes, self-esteem, and stereotypes. *Psychological Review*, *102*(1), 4–27. doi:10.1037/0033-295X.102.1.4 PMID:7878162

Guiso, L., Sapienza, P., & Zingales, L. (2006). Doeas culture affect economic outcomes. *The Journal of Economic Perspectives*, *20*(2), 23–48. doi:10.1257/jep.20.2.23

Hall, E. T. (1966). *Hidden Dimension*. Doubleday & Company Inc.

Hall, E. T. (1976). *Beyond Culture*. Anchor Books.

Hall, E. T. (1983). *The Dance of Life*. Anchor Books.

Hay Group. (2003). *Picture Story Exercise (PSE): Technical manual*. The McClelland Center for Research and Innovation, Hay Group.

Industrial Revolution. (2021). Retrieved online at https://www.britannica.com/event/Industrial-Revolution

Inkeles, A., & Levinson, D. J. (1969). National character: The study of modal personality and sociocultural systems. In G. Lindzey & E. Aronson (Eds.), *The handbook of social psychology IV* (pp. 418–506). McGraw-Hill. (Original work published 1954)

Ishibashi, Y., & Kottke, J. (2009). Confucianism, personality traits, and effective leaders in Japan and the United States. *Annual Conference of the Association for Psychological Science*.

Judge, T. A., Bono, J. E., Ilies, R., & Gerhardt, M. W. (2002). Personality and leadership: A qualitative and quantitative review. *The Journal of Applied Psychology*, *87*(4), 765–780. doi:10.1037/0021-9010.87.4.765 PMID:12184579

Leung, S. L., & Bozionelos, N. (2004). Five-factor model traits and the prototypical image of the effective leader in the Confucian culture. *Employee Relations*, *26*(1), 62–71. doi:10.1108/01425450410506904

Lewis, R. (2006). *When Cultures Collide: Leading Across Cultures*. Nicholas Brealey International. Retrieved online at http://www.utntyh.com/wp-content/uploads/2011/11/When-Cultures-Collide.pdf

Lewis, R. (2019). The cultural imperative: Global trends in the 21st century. *Training. Language and Culture*, *3*(3), 8–20. doi:10.29366/2019tlc.3.3.1

Lynn, R. (1971). *Personality and national character*. Pergamon Press.

Lynn, R. (1981). Cross-cultural differences in neuroticism, extraversion and psychoticism. In R. Lynn (Ed.), *Dimensions of personality: Papers in honour of H. J. Eysenck* (pp. 263–286). Pergamon Press.

Lynn, R. (1991). *The secret of the miracle economy: Different national attitudes to competitiveness and money*. The Social Affairs Unit.

Lynn, R., & Hampson, S. L. (1975). National differences in extraversion and neuroticism. *The British Journal of Social and Clinical Psychology*, *14*(3), 223–240. doi:10.1111/j.2044-8260.1975.tb00175.x PMID:1182404

Lynn, R., & Martin, T. (1995). National differences for 37 nations in extraversion, neuroticism, psychoticism and economic, demographic and other correlates. *Personality and Individual Differences*, *19*(3), 403–406. doi:10.1016/0191-8869(95)00054-A

McAdams, D. P. (1995). What do we know when we know a person? *Journal of Personality*, *63*(3), 365–396. doi:10.1111/j.1467-6494.1995.tb00500.x

McClelland, D., Winter, D. (1971). *Motivating Economic Achievement*. Free Press-Collier-Macmillan.

McClelland, D. C. (1951). *Personality*. Sloane. doi:10.1037/10790-000

McClelland, D. C. (1976). The achieving society. New York: Irvington.

McClelland, D. C. (1985). *Human motivation*. Scott, Foresman.

Our World Data. (2021). Available online at https://ourworldindata.org/covid-vaccinations?country=OWID_WRL

Peng, H. (2018). Global shift of the TV landscape and popular culture in East Asia: From Cultural imperialism to the rise of regionalization. *The 7th Annual International Conference on Journalism and Mass Communications (JMCommm 2018)*. doi:10.5176/2301-3710_JMComm18.131

Qin, A. (2015). China's Love Affair With Irresistible Korean TV. *New York Times Style*. http://cn.nytstyle.com/culture/20150721/t21koreatv/en-us/

Spangler, W. D. (1992). Validity of questionnaire and TAT measures of need for achievement: Two meta-analyses. *Psychological Bulletin*, *112*(1), 140–154. doi:10.1037/0033-2909.112.1.140

The Guardian. (2021). *From Pfizer to Moderna: who's making billions from Covid-19 vaccines?* Available online at https://www.theguardian.com/business/2021/mar/06/from-pfizer-to-moderna-whos-making-billions-from-covid-vaccines

Tuerlinckx, F., De Boeck, P., & Lens, W. (2002). Measuring needs with the Thematic Apperception Test: A psychometric study. *Journal of Personality and Social Psychology*, *82*(3), 448–461. doi:10.1037/0022-3514.82.3.448 PMID:11902627

Vane, J. R. (1981). The Thematic Apperception Test (TAT): A review. *Clinical Psychology Review*, *1*(3), 319–336. doi:10.1016/0272-7358(81)90009-X

Winter, D. (1973). *The Power Motive*. Free Press.

Winter, D. (1982). A motivational model of leadership: Predicting long-term management success from TAT measures of power motivation and responsibility. *The Leadership Quarterly*, *2*(2), 67–80. doi:10.1016/1048-9843(91)90023-U

Winter, D., John, O., Stewart, A., Klohnen, E., & Duncan, L. (1998). Traits and motives: Toward an integration of two traditions in personality research. *Psychological Review*, *105*(2), 230–250. doi:10.1037/0033-295X.105.2.230 PMID:9577238

Winter, D. G., & Stewart, A. J. (1977). Power motive reliability as a function of retest instructions. *Journal of Consulting and Clinical Psychology*, *45*(3), 436–440. doi:10.1037/0022-006X.45.3.436

Chapter 8
Impact of Supervisor Feedback, Customer-Employee Exchange, and Creative Personal Identity on Innovative Behavior

Muhammad Imran
https://orcid.org/0000-0001-7126-2831
The Islamia University of Bahawalpur, Pakistan

Iqra Akhtar
The Islamia University of Bahawalpur, Pakistan

ABSTRACT

Employee innovative behaviour is crucial for any firm success in terms of generation, promotion, and realization of new ideas, which can increase the organisational performance to organizational positive performance. The main purpose of this study is to examine the relationship between supervisor feedback, customer employee exchange, creative personal identity, and innovative behaviour with the mediating role of interpersonal trust. The three hundred and seventy (370) responses have been collected from employees of Punjab emergency service (Rescue 1122) through questionnaires. The partial least square structural equation modeling (PLS-SEM) has been employed to draw the results. The final results have shown a positive and significant relationship between supervisor feedback, customer employee exchange, creative personal identity and innovative behaviour of employees, while interpersonal trust was found to play an intermediary role between customer employee exchange, creative personal identity, and innovative behaviour.

INTRODUCTION

The Punjab emergency service (Rescue 1122) is the top emergency humanitarian service of Pakistan started in 2004 from Lahore which is providing services in the 36 districts of Punjab. Moreover, it is

DOI: 10.4018/978-1-7998-8678-5.ch008

expanded in tehsils level as well. The Punjab emergency service (Rescue 1122) has deal the 2660222 road traffic accidents emergencies, 3993224 medical emergencies, 152348 fire emergencies, 251676 crime incidents, 9475 structure collapse and 13118 drowning emergencies since 14th October 2004 and maintaining the seven minutes response time (Naseer, 2018). Hence, the main point is, to sustain these seven minutes response time, high level of employee's innovative behavior, skills and expertise are required to deal with the emergencies and maintain the maximum customer satisfaction. Employees of rescue 1122 have usually a direct interaction with the patients, their behavior matters in talking with people and in giving treatment to them. Hence, the question is that how innovatively they behave in both things (interaction and treatment). Given the significance of employee innovative behaviour for organizations, experts and researchers attempt to respond to the question how to improve employee interactions with victim and treatment of victims innovatively?

Rescue 1122 is a government organization. However, private sectors have given more attention as compare to the public sector in past researches regarding innovation (Aghion, Dewatripont, & Stein, 2008; Lin, Lin, Song, & Li, 2011). Since, these organizations are frequently risk averse, they will in general follow past practices instead of investigation with new thoughts (Verhoest, Verschuere, & Bouckaert, 2007). According to the researchers, employees of public sector can only bring innovation when they are permitted to experiment and are motivated to make improvements (Demircioglu & Audretsch, 2017). The importance of innovation is widely important for organization effectiveness (Woodman, Sawyer, & Griffin, 1993). Particularly, employees' innovative behavior (IB) (e.g., generating, adopting and applying new ideas for work and product procedures) is considered as key asset and source for firm success (Shalley & Gilson, 2004). The individuals can improve performance of the organizations when they create and apply fresh ideas to fulfill their duties efficiently (Xerri, 2013).

There are different factors that have been considered and examined as important antecedents of employee innovative behavior separately in different context in the recent researches such as organization's climate and culture (Scott & Bruce, 1994), connection with supervisor (Janssen, Van de Vliert, & West, 2004), characteristics of job, individual differences (Bunce & West, 1995), group or social context (Munton & West, 1995).

The impact of different factors i.e. supervisor's feedback (SF), customer- employee exchange (CEX) and creative personal identity (CPI) on innovative behavior (IB) of rescue 1122 employees will be has examined in current study considering mediating role of interpersonal trust (IT). These all variables are separately examined in different studies in relationship with employee innovative behaviour such as, (Dhar, 2016; Li & Hsu, 2016a; Uddin, Priyankara, & Mahmood, 2019) with different mediating variables like, creative climate, creative process engagement (Uddin et al., 2019), furthermore, work engagement, psychological contract breach (Eva, Meacham, Newman, Schwarz, & Tham, 2019). However, there is a limited study by considering interpersonal trust as mediator between supervisor feedback, customer employee exchange, creative personal identity, and employee innovative behaviour. However, these all variables are not tested into one research framework in context of Punjab emergency service (Rescue1122) (Pakistan). SHRM specialists place an enduring importance on features of the organization that urge workers to participate in innovative behavior, for example, the provision of feedback from supervisors (Ma Prieto & Pilar Perez-Santana, 2014). Prior study has assumed the immediate supervisors as the important agents of organization who characterize the firm in psychological contract among employees and firm (Lester, Turnley, Bloodgood, & Bolino, 2002).

The innovative behaviour of employees generally enhances by the getting ideas from others, having participation and exchange from others such as, CEX. It is impacted by not exclusively individual's intellectual abilities, yet additionally social capital, which refers to the potential advantages, which employees get from the interaction with others (Shalley & Gilson, 2004). Further, employee innovative behaviour of employee may also be affected by the opinions of people about his creative personality. People take an interest in an creative practice to guarantee that such job will profit them personally and publicly in organizational context (Jaussi, Randel, & Dionne, 2007; A. C. Wang & Cheng, 2010). This is the reason that, role performances of the employees having creative identity have an element of innovativeness and they find fresh approaches to the problems (Song, Yu, Zhang, & Jiang, 2015; Zhu, Ritter, Müller, & Dijksterhuis, 2017). Moreover, this study introduces the interpersonal trust as a mediating variable between supervisor feedback, creative personal identity, customer employee exchange and employee innovative behaviour. According to Social exchange theory that if there is an excessive level of interpersonal trust then it will create a mind of positive attitude towards others. e.g. support and acceptance (L. Wang, Law, Hung, & Guillet, 2014). In return of this, that person will take interest which will give benefits to other party (e.g., providing information and sharing knowledge) (Nunkoo & Ramkissoon, 2012).

Moreover, past literature found that there are limited studies on employee innovative behaviour more specifically in public sector such as Punjab emergency service (Rescue1122) Pakistan. Although some of studies have been conducted in context of Punjab emergency service (Rescue1122) such as job stress (Amin, 2018), public relations (Ali & Iftikhar). Therefore, on the basis of above discussion, this study is presenting the following questions;

1. Is there any relationship between supervisor's feedback and innovative behavior of employee?
2. Is there any relationship between customer employee exchange and innovative behavior of employee?
3. Is there any relationship between creative personal identity and innovative behavior of employee?
4. Does interpersonal trust mediate the relationship between supervisor's feedback, customer employee exchange, creative personal identity, and innovative behavior?

LITERATURE REVIEW

Innovation has become root of the success for every organization, in this dynamic environment (Cankar & Petkovšek, 2013). This is need for any organization to sustain their competitive advantage through innovative behavior their employees (Y. Chen, Tang, Jin, Xie, & Li, 2014). In this regard of public sector, they are keen to learn new methods, solutions of issues innovatively, and promote the innovation culture (Bani-melhem, Abukhait, Shamsudin, & Al-hawari, 2021; Mulgan & Albury, 2003). However, the public sectors organizations are less innovative than private sector, basically, the public sector are facing hurdles in promoting innovative behaviour among employees due rigid hierarchical settings, risk avoidance and Government rules & regulations (Micheli, Schoeman, Baxter, & Goffin, 2012). According to the past researchers, public sector is taking serious steps towards promoting innovation culture into the organization for reducing the cost (Cankar & Petkovšek, 2013; Mu & Wang, 2020). Hence, current study examines the impact of supervisor feedback, customer employee exchange, creative personal identity, interpersonal trust, and employee innovative behaviour in Punjab emergency services (Rescue 1122).

Supervisor's Feedback and Employee Innovative Behavior

The performance of employee would enhance if they realized that management of organization or supervision is supporting. According to job demands resources (JD-R) model that, resources such as, rewards, training and feedback helps the employees to improve their work (Boon & Kalshoven, 2014). As well as, whereas found the absence of supervisor feedback, employees are de-motivated and more opposed to participate in innovative behaviour (Eva et al., 2019). Supervisor's remarks and supportive feedback about the performance of the employee has a positive impact on the working interest of the employees. Employees can get better idea about their performance in the organization by having supportive feedback from their supervisor which helps them to improve their innovative way of working (Zhou, 1998). According to the previous researches, direct supervisors are the important agents of organization who characterize the firm in psychological contract between employees and firm (Lester et al., 2002). The supportive feedback environment is very helpful in enhancing the employees' well-being as well as positive performance (Gabriel, Frantz, Levy, & Hilliard, 2014; Lee, Choi, & Kang, 2021). Drawing on social exchange theory this research argue that Employees feel psychological contract breach when there is absence of cooperative and informative feedback from the supervisors (Restubog, Bordia, & Tang, 2007). Employee's proactive behavior is negatively affected by the perception of psychological contract breach which they feel from the organization side (Robinson, Kraatz, & Rousseau, 1994) and it ultimately leads the employees to neglect their work (Bak, 2020; Lemire & Rouillard, 2005). Thus, this study examines the impact of supervisor's feedback on the innovative behavior of employees in Punjab emergency services (Rescue 1122).

H1: There is a significant relationship between supervisor's feedback and innovative behavior.

Customer Employee Exchange and Innovative Behavior

Idea generation and its implementation need the support and resources from others. Worker's exchange with others is also an element required for having innovation behavior (Li & Hsu, 2016a). CEX may also consider important for employee innovative behavior. It may affect the IB in a different way from other interactions e.g., LMX (Li & Hsu, 2016a). Due to social network opportunities, exchange of ideas with others may be the possible innovation facilitator for the employees (Li & Hsu, 2016a). IB is impacted by not exclusively individual's intellectual abilities, yet additionally by sharing thoughts in social gatherings that suggests the potential benefit workers get from the connection with others (Shalley & Gilson, 2004). CEX is very crucial in services, as services are produced and consumed at the same time (Ma & Qu, 2011). According to social exchange theory, employees who get profits by customers have incredible goals to return back (Lawler, 2001). Rescue is also a service providing organization and in service dominant firms, expectation of the organization from its employees about innovation is more prominent because in this job employees needs a frequent decision to fulfill client's requirements with higher innovative behavior (Bani-Melhem, Zeffane, & Albaity, 2018; Xu & Wang, 2020). Due to the social connections, exchange of thoughts with someone else particularly the immediate customers may provide the important chance to innovate (Li & Hsu, 2016a). From the past studies, it is cleared that innovation in behavior of employees is different in service sector as compare to manufacturing sector (Li & Hsu, 2016b; Mohamed, 2020). Hence, present study examines the impact of CEX on the employee's innovative behavior.

H2: There is a significant relationship between customer-employee exchange and innovative behavior

Creative Personal Identity and Innovative Behavior

CPI may also a driver for the innovative behavior of employees. Individual innovativeness is seen as impacted by various individual factors, for example, creative personality (Zhou & George, 2003). People who have the well-built creative identity have a tendency to behave according to their role identities, and to maintain an inner self-consistency (Callero, Howard, & Piliavin, 1987). Personal identity means what we think about our self that "who we are" and what another think about us that "what we are". It attributes a job in the creative procedure that is spontaneously bred through the images seen by oneself and by others (Karwowski, Lebuda, Wisniewska, & Gralewski, 2013; C.-J. Wang, Tsai, & Tsai, 2014). One study says that employees who have creative personal identity engage themselves in creative process and ultimately they show the innovative behavior (Uddin et al., 2019). Researcher defines the personal identity as one that any person holds basic to their self-idea (Brewer, 1991). CPI plays a vital role in making creativity at work when an individual try to apply the problem solving strategy (Jaussi et al., 2007). People take an interest in an creative practice to guarantee that such activity will benefit them personally as well as publicly in hierarchical setting (Jaussi et al., 2007; A. C. Wang & Cheng, 2010). Subsequently, they are bound to display an elevated level of creativity to check and keep up their innovative character (Fisher, 1997). Therefore, this study examines, innovative behavior of rescue employees is affected by the feelings that they are known creative person by themselves and others.

H3: There is a significant relationship between creative personal identity and innovative behavior of employees.

Mediating Role of Interpersonal Trust

Trust really matters in any organization to have good bound between parties. It is a mental state where in a trustier believes on a trustee and can acknowledge hazards along with helplessness of a specific conduct of the trustee (Hassan, Toylan, Semerciöz, & Aksel, 2012). Social exchange theory states that if there is an excessive level of interpersonal trust then it will create a mind of positive attitude towards others e.g support and acceptance (L. Wang et al., 2014). In return of this, that person will take interest in a conduct which will give benefits to second party (e.g., providing information and sharing facts) (Nunkoo & Ramkissoon, 2012). Therefore, this study examines the mediating role of interpersonal trust between SF, CEX, CPI and IB. Trust can be an efficient predictor of employees' optimistic attitude and behaviors, for instance cooperative behavior in an organizational context (Hansen, Dunford, Boss, Boss, & Angermeier, 2011), organizational dedication (Cho & Park, 2011) and employee devotion (X.-P. Chen, Eberly, Chiang, Farh, & Cheng, 2014). On the workplace, the relationship with the supervisors, customers, employees generally become stable and cooperative due to the interpersonal trust. The job requests a high level of interpersonal cooperation alongside the capacity to bargain with the heterogeneous needs and needs of client (Seo, Kim, Chang, & Kim, 2016). Trust on the supervisor is viewed as vital for pioneer viability and work unit efficiency (Kouzes & Posner, 2006). In addition, the supervisor's conduct is the key in deciding the degree of interpersonal trust in a work unit (Deluga, 1994). Organizations have to bear direct and indirect cost, due to the reason that employees mistrust each other (Schindler & Thomas, 1993).

Further, attributable to social network opportunities, exchange of ideas with others may be the possible innovation facilitator for the employees (Li & Hsu, 2016a). Interpersonal trust may also have a mediating role between customers and employees because when customer share about the innovative ideas and employees behaves in positive manner then it creates the interpersonal trust between them. When customer provide additional knowledge, measures, or emotions that are related to service procedures can enhance the interpersonal trust between employees and customer (Johnson & Grayson, 2005). Therefore, interpersonal trust involving the two parties has been considered most importance factor in the previous research. CPI is a person's conviction or the level to which he or she identifies as being creative person (Farmer, Tierney, & Kung-Mcintyre, 2003) and this CPI of individual may also affect the interpersonal trust and then ultimately innovative behavior of employee. The role identity empowers association among the people, commitment in IB and job support (Amabile & Pratt, 2016). Following three hypotheses are formulated to examine the mediating role of IT.

H4: Interpersonal trust mediates the relationship between supervisor's feedback and innovative behavior
H5: Interpersonal trust mediates the relationship between customer employee exchange and innovative behavior
H6: Interpersonal trust mediates the relationship between creative personal identity and innovative behavior of employee

Research Framework

Figure1. Research framework

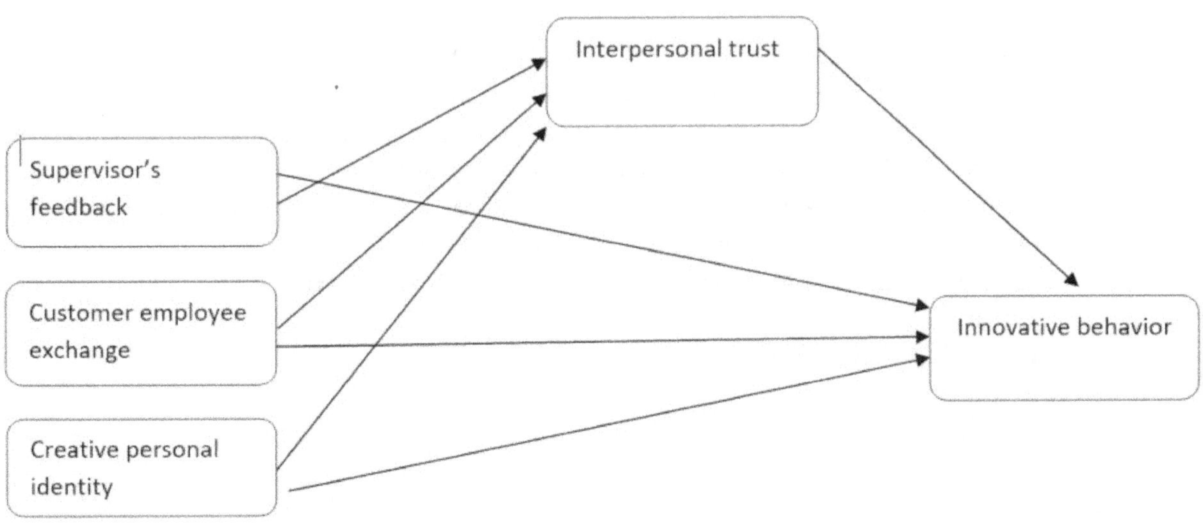

RESEARCH METHODOLOGY

The target population of this study is employees of Punjab emergency service (Rescue 1122), Punjab, Pakistan. The sampling frame of the study consider the 10k employees of Rescue 1122 (Imran, Hamid, Aziz, & Wan, 2019). Krejcie and Morgan (1970) table has used to find the sample size, which is 370.

Furthermore, the random sampling strategy has used to collect the responses from Rescue 1122 employees. However, the Microsoft excel (RAND) function was used to select the respondents randomly (Thornhill, Saunders, & Lewis, 2009). The seven-point Likert scale was taken such as strongly disagree **(SD)**, Disagree **(D)**, Somewhat disagree **(SWD)**, Neutral **(N)**, Somewhat agree **(SWA)**, Agree **(A)**,Strongly agree **(SA).**

SF (independent variable) is measured by using supervisor's developmental feedback scale by (Eva et al., 2019), consists of three items, such as "My immediate supervisor often gives me developmental feedback". A seven point Likert scale is adopted to measures the CEX (independent variable) consist of five items developed by (W.-J. Chen, 2016), such as "Most of our patients are polite". To measure the CPI (independent variable) a scale developed by the Karwowski et al. (2013) is adopted based on the five items. To measure mediator variable (IT) scale based on ten items is adopted developed by Li and Hsu (2018), There are six items of IB (dependent variable) that are considered to measure the innovative behavior of employees and this scale is adopted from (Eva et al., 2019). The first item is "I am creating new ideas for improvements''

ANALYSIS AND FINDINGS

For the analysis of the data collected from the employees of rescue 1122, SPSS v 20 and smart PLS is used in this study. For the descriptive analysis SPSS v 20 is used i;e missing data analysis, outlier's examination, and normality of the data and smart PLS SEM, is used for the reliability and validity analysis and hypothesis testing. The data collected for the analysis has some missing values and according to the author, when there are less than 5% missing value per item then it can be replaced using mean (Hair, Sarstedt, Ringle, & Mena, 2012). Hence, all the items have missing values less than 5% therefore they were replaced through SPSS v20 using mean replacement. There were some outliers in the data, hence, by using Mahala Nobis d^2 test (Tabachnick & Fidell, 2013), out of 370 responses 20 responses have the value less than 0.01, therefore that were deleted and the final analysis is conducted on the 350 responses. In this study, to test the normality of the data, skewness and kurtosis analysis is conducted (Tabachnick & Fidell, 2013). According to the author, the value of skewness should be between -3 to +3 and kurtosis should be -10 to+10, which shows that the data is normally distributed (Kline, 2011). The table 1 shows that, the skewness value of each variable is between (-3+3) and value of kurtosis is also between (-10+10). Hence, the result shows, data is normally distributed.

Assessment of PLS Path Model Results

Testing of Hypothesis

There are two parts of the research models in SMART PLS one is called measurement model (outer model) and other is structural model (inner model). Structural model relates one latent variable to another statistically, while the measurement model examines that how well the indicators (items) load theoretically and related to their respective construct. Thus, this model make certain that the indicators and constructs are reliable and valid (Aminu, 2015)

Table 1. Normality analysis

	Skewness		Kurtosis	
	Statistic	**Std. Error**	**Statistic**	**Std. Error**
Supervisor's feedback	-1.344	.130	3.421	.260
Customer employee exchange	-1.145	.130	1.570	.260
Creative personal identity	-1.483	.130	2.110	.260
Interpersonal Trust	-.619	.130	.657	.260
Innovative Behavior	-1.768	.130	4.109	.260
Valid N (listwise)				

The Measurement Model

The assessment of measurement model is the first step in the smart PLS SEM. To evaluate the outer model, reliability and validity are the two main criteria used in the smart PLS (Ramayah, Lee, & In, 2011). Outer model's suitability can be measured by looking at the 1) Indicator reliability and internal consistency reliability by using loading values and composite reliability (CR); 2) Convergent validity of the measures associated with individual constructs using average variance extracted (AVE). 3) Discriminant validity using Fornell-Larcker criterion and the indicator's outer loadings (Aminu, 2015).

Figure 2. Measurement model

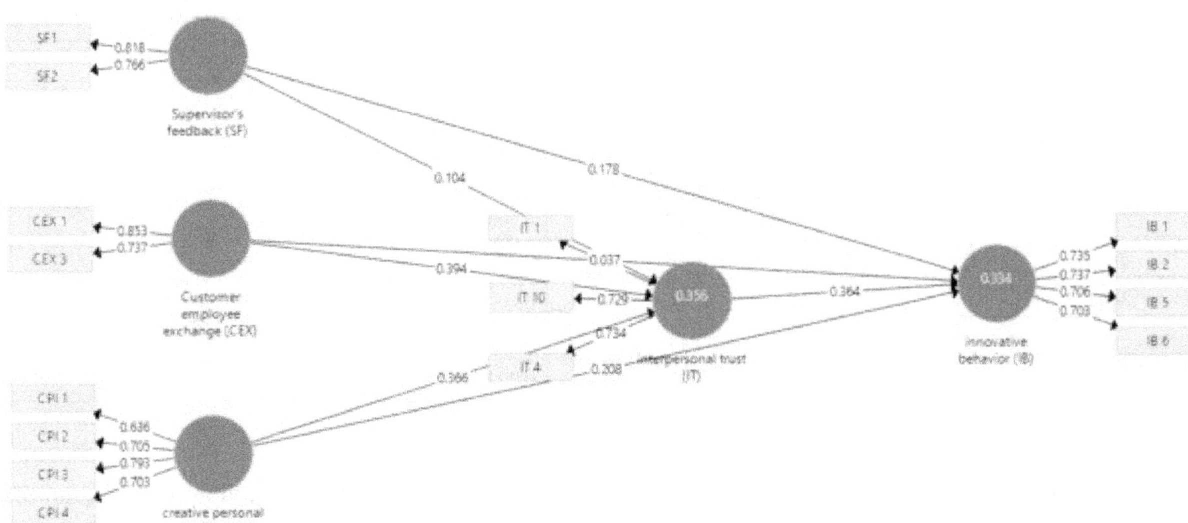

Checking Reliability and Validity

Validity and reliability test are conducted to ensure the goodness of the measures of the adopted items. There is a need to make certain that the items that are adopted to measure the concept are actually and correctly measuring the concept and variable. Reliability measures the consistency and validity of the adapted or adapted measures in measuring the concept (Cavana, Delahaye, & Sekeran, 2001). Reliability shows that the particular item that is adapted or adopted in the study will yield the same result on different occasion (Greener, 2008). Validity relates to the extent to which measures, instrument and methods that are being used in the research actually measures what it is supposed to measure or describe (Lancaster, 2005).

There are many types of validity, but this research has used the construct validity and the indicators validity. To make certain that the items which are adopted in this study measuring the concepts for which the study has been conducted construct validity is used. There are two ways that are used in this study to determine the construct validity i.e., discriminant validity and convergent validity (Vanderstoep & Johnson, 2008).

Table 2. Internal consistency reliability and convergent validity

Constructs	Indicators	Outer loading (indicators)	Composite reliability (CR)	Average variance extracted (AVE)
Supervisor's feedback(SF)	SF1	0.818	0.776	0.627
	SF2	0.766		
Customer employee exchange(CEX)	CEX1	0.853	0.776	0.636
	CEX3	0.737		
Creative personal identity(CPI)	CP1 1	0.636	0.803	0.506
	CP1 2	0.705		
	CPI 3	0.793		
	CPI 4	0.703		
Innovative behavior(IB)	IB 1	0.735	0.812	0.519
	IB 2	0.737		
	IB 5	0.706		
	IB 6	0.703		
Interpersonal trust(IT)	IT 1	0.660	0.751	0.501
	IT 4	0.734		
	IT 10	0.729		

In the table 2, it can be observed that all the indicators have loading values equal and more than the standard value 0.7 except two indicator which have loading value around 0.6 but still it is reliable because AVE is 0.5 of those constructs. Hence, this shows that all the indicators are reliable. Some indicators were deleted due to the low loading values to set the data and reliability. Traditionally, in the social sciences research "Cronbach's alpha" is used to measure the internal consistency reliability but it tends to provide conservative measurement in PLS-SEM. The use of "Composite reliability" is suggested by the prior literature as a replacement of "Cronbach alpha" (Bagozzi & Yi, 1988; Hair et al., 2012). In this research, the researcher uses the composite reliability to measure the internal consistency and reliability than Cronbach alpha. According to the research **CR** is a less biased estimate of reliability than Cronbach Alpha, the acceptable value of CR is 0.7 and above (Alarcón, Sánchez, & De Olavide, 2015). However, table 2 shows that all the latent variables have high level of internal consistency as the value of CR is equal to and more than 0.7 and AVE is equal and more than 0.5 (Fornell & Larcker, 1981).

According to author convergent validity shows the level of confidence that we have the indicators have measured the specific trait well (Campbell & Fiske, 1959). Convergent validity shows that theoretically related measures of the same construct are actually related (Henseler, Ringle, & Sinkovics, 2009). Convergent validity of the measurement model can be assessed by the Composite Reliability (CR) and Average Variance Extracted (AVE). AVE measures the level of variance captured by a construct versus the level due to measurement error, 0.7 is the standard value of AVE which is considered very good, while, the 0.5 is also the acceptable value of AVE. same as, CR is also used to assess the convergent validity having standard value of 0.7 and above (Fornell & Larcker, 1981). The table 2 shows that, all the constructs have the value of AVE Equal to or more than 0.5. Moreover, all the constructs have CR equal to or more than 0.7. This shows that this measurement model and constructs has a high level of convergent validity (Alarcón et al., 2015).

Discriminant Validity

Discriminant validity is the degree to which measures of different traits are unrelated (Campbell & Fiske, 1959). In other words, it is theoretically explained that measures of constructs are not related to each other actually not related to each other (Churchill Jr, 1979). Campbell and fiske say that to establish the discriminant validity the square root of AVE of each latent variable is taken. The correlation values of each row and column is less than the first value of each column and row then it shows that all the constructs have well established discriminant validity. The most conventional approach in assessing discriminant validity is Fornell-Larcker criterion (Hair Jr, Hult, Ringle, & Sarstedt, 2016). Following is the table 3, which shows the square root of all the Ave's of construct.

Table 3. Discriminant validity

Constructs	Customer employee exchange (CEX)	Supervisor's feedback (SF)	creative personal identity (CPI)	innovative behavior (IB)	interpersonal trust (IT)
Customer employee exchange (CEX)	**0.797**				
Supervisor's feedback (SF)	0.181	**0.792**			
creative personal identity (CPI)	0.095	0.185	**0.711**		
innovative behavior (IB)	0.251	0.311	0.398	**0.720**	
interpersonal trust (IT)	0.447	0.243	0.422	0.512	**0.708**

Hence, the latent variable customer employee exchange has the AVE 0.636 mentioned in table 2, hence the square root of value is taken out to check the discriminant validity of this construct. The value is 0.797 after the square root which larger than the correlation values in the column of CEX and larger than those in the row of CEX. The value of supervisor feedback is also larger than all correlation value in the column of SF and also larger than the values in the row of SF. Subsequently, it can be easily seen in that table 3, all the construct has the larger value on the top as compared to the all correlation values that are present in their column and rows. Thus, result indicates that discriminant validity of all latent variables is well established.

After the evaluation of the measurement model (outer model) and having the good results about the validity and reliability of the indictors and construct now, evaluation of the inner model (structural model) is the next important step.

Structural Model

As it is mentioned above that after outer model reliability analysis the next important step is examining the structural model but before assessing this inner model, collinearity should be examined (Hair Jr et al., 2016) between exogenous variable and endogenous variables. In table 4, all the outer values of predictor construct are less than threshold of 5.(Hair Jr et al., 2016). Therefore, it is cleared that there is no collinearity problem between latent variable and their indicators. Therefore, it is concluded that there is no collinearity problem between all the predictor constructs. Hence, the further analysis can be carried out

Inner Value (VIF)

After assessing the collinearity problem and having good results the next step is to assess the structural model, the results can see in below table.

Table 4. VIF values

Constructs	Customer employee exchange (CEX)	Supervisor's feedback (SF)	creative personal identity (CPI)	innovative behavior (IB)	interpersonal trust (IT)
Customer employee exchange (CEX)				1.279	1.038
Supervisor's feedback (SF)				1.082	1.065
creative personal identity (CPI)				1.247	1.040
innovative behavior (IB)					
interpersonal trust (IT)				1.552	

Direct Relationship

To provide a detailed picture of result and testing of hypothesis from H1 to H6 comprehensively, systemic model analysis of structural model is carried out; this evaluation of structural model begins with the direct relationship between independent variables and dependent variables. The significance of the relationship is examined with the bootstrapping using smart PLS and the size of path coefficient is examined with the smart PLS algorithm. 5000 used as the bootstrapping samples but otherwise original sample is used as the number of cases (Henseler et al., 2009). Firstly, this analysis focused on the direct relationship between the independent variable and dependent variable (H1 to H3). Secondly the relationship between the independent variable and mediator and dependent variable will be examined, in other words mediation analysis took place (H4 TO H6).

Figure 3.

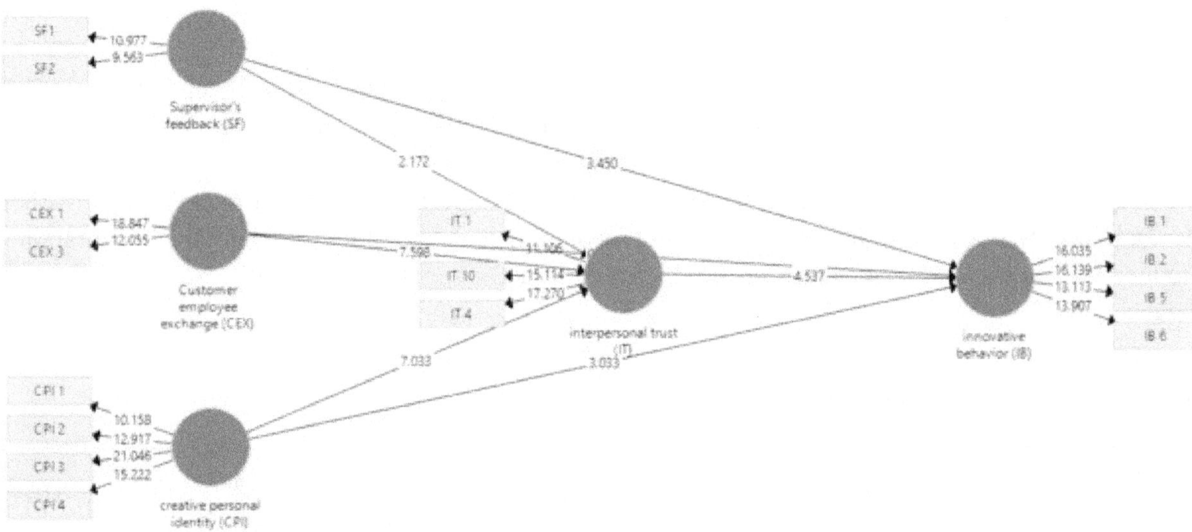

PLS SEM Bootstrapping

There were 3 hypotheses that were proposed in the previous chapter to examine the direct relationship. H1, relationship between supervisor feedback and innovative behavior.H2, between customer employee exchange and innovative behavior and H3, between creative personal identity and innovative behavior. According to the table 5, bootstrapping analysis shows that, the relationship between SF, CEX, CPI AND IB is significant because p value is less than 0.01

Table 5. Bootstrapping (total effect)

	Hypothesis	BETA	Standard Deviation (STDEV)	TStatistics (lO/ STDEVl)	P Values
H1	**Supervisor's feedback (SF) -> innovative behavior (IB)**	0.216	0.050	4.356	**0.000**
H2	**Customer employee exchange (CEX) -> innovative behavior (IB)**	0.180	0.060	3.007	**0.003**
H3	**creative personal identity (CPI) -> innovative behavior (IB)**	0.341	0.056	6.041	**0.000**

H1, shows that, supervisors feedback has the significant plus positive impact on the innovative behavior of employees ($p<0.01$ and t value 4.356, Beta 0.216), therefore H1 is supported. H2 is also supported and has significant as well as positive relationship with DV because ($p<0.01$, T value is 3.007 and beta is 0.180). For the third hypothesis, result shows significant as well as positive impact of creative personal identity on the IB of employees ($p<0.01$, t value, 6.041), it is also supported.

Mediation Analysis

With the intervening variable researcher can easily assess the indirect effect of independent variable on dependent variable. However, there are many techniques to assess the mediation affects (Preacher & Hayes, 2008), which include: Causal steps strategy or serial approach (Hoyle & Robinson, 2004). Other approaches for mediation analysis include product of coefficient method or Sobel test (Sobel, 1982). However, bootstrapping is the most recent mediation analysis technique where the bootstrapping produce an empirical representation of the distribution of the sample of the indirect effect (Hayes & Preacher, 2010).

Table 6. Specific indirect effects

	HYPOTHESIS	BETA	Standard Deviation (STDEV)	T Statistics (|O/STDEV|)	P Values
H4	**Supervisor's feedback (SF) -> interpersonal trust (IT) -> innovative behavior (IB)**	0.038	0.020	1.882	**0.060**
H5	**Customer employee exchange (CEX)->interpersonal trust (IT) -> innovative behavior (IB)**	0.143	0.040	3.562	**0.000**
H6	**creative personal identity (CPI) -> interpersonal trust (IT) -> innovative behavior (IB)**	0.133	0.036	3.728	**0.000**

There were 3 hypotheses (H4 TO H6) which were proposed to examine the mediating effect of interpersonal trust between IV's and DV. In this above bootstrapping analysis, one mediating hypotheses is rejected and other two is accepted. H4, is not accepted because $p>0.01$. Hence, there is no mediating effect of interpersonal trust between supervisor's feedback and innovative behavior. H5 is accepted, has significant plus positive mediating effect on the relationship between customer employee exchange and innovative behavior of employees ($p<0.01$, t, 3.562, beta 0.143). H6, is also accepted and is shows that IT mediate the relationship between creative personal identity and innovative behavior ($P<0.01$, t, 3.728, beta 0.133).

Coefficient of Determination (R^2)

For assessing structural model, coefficient of determination (R2) of endogenous latent variables is one of the most commonly used criteria (Hair Jr et al., 2016). R2 values of .27, .13 and .02 indicate substantial, moderate, and weak R2 values, respectively (cohen1988). The table 7 shows that R^2 value of IT is 0.356 (35.6%) is substantial and IB is also substantial 0.334 (33.4%). it means that all the exogenous variables

(SF, CEX, CPI) together explain the 35.6% variance in mediating variable (IT) and similarly all of the 4 variables (SF, CEX, CPI and IT) together explain the 46.4% variance in the endogenous variable (innovative behavior. On the basis on R^2 of endogenous latent variable it can be concluded that, model has substantial predictive validity.

Table 7. Coefficient of determination

Constructs	R Square	R Square Adjusted
innovative behavior (IB)	0.334	0.326
interpersonal trust (IT)	0.356	0.350

Effect Sizes (f^2)

After assessing the coefficient of determination R^2 Value of endogenous variable (IB and IT), the next criteria is effect size (Hair Jr et al., 2016). Effect size shows that what effect will be on model if the construct in the model is omitted. Basically, it shows the difference between the presence and omission of the construct in the model. This analysis is done purposely to check that whether that particular omitted construct has influence on the endogenous latent variable or not (Hair Jr et al., 2016). While calculating the effect size for the exogenous construct 0.02 shows the small effect, 0.15 shows moderate effect, and 0.35 shows large effect (Cohen, 2013).

Table 8, shows that, some exogenous constructs have small and some have moderate effect size on their respective endogenous construct in this study.

Table 8.

Construct	Effect size(F^2)	Effect size
CEX- IB	0.002	SMALL
SF-IB	0.044	SMALL
CPI-IB	0.052	SMALL
CEX-IT	0.232	MODERATE
SF-IT	0.016	SMALL
CPI-IT	0.200	MODERATE
IT-IB	0.128	MODERATE

Model Fit

In current study, the standard root mean square residual (SRMR) and normal fit index (NFI) is considered to examine the model fit. A model which have the value of SRMR, less than 0.1 is considered as a good fit (Hu & Bentler, 1999). This model has the value of SRMR less than 0.1, which shows a good model fit. In previous study, SRMR is used as goodness of fit measure that is used to avoid misspecification in smart PLS SEM (Henseler et al., 2014). The value of NFI ranges between 0.0 to 1.0 (Iacobucci, 2010). Hence, this model has the value of NFI in the given range (0 to 1.0) which shows the good model fit.

Table 9.

Criteria	Saturated Model	Estimated Model
SRMR	0.096	0.096
NFI	0.386	0.386

DISCUSSION AND CONCLUSION

The main purpose of this study was to examine the link between supervisor's feedback, customer employee exchange, creative personal identity and innovative behavior of employees having interpersonal trust as mediator. 4 objectives were made to examine the relationship between variables and the study has achieved almost all the objectives. The research provides the meaningful conclusion.

The first, second and third objective and hypothesis (H1, H2, H3) were formulated to examine the direct relationship between SF, CEX, CPI and IB respectively. H1, was hypothesized that, there is a significant relationship between SF and IB. The finding shows that, H1 is supported. Hence, SF has a significant and positive relationship with IB. Therefore, in promoting innovative performance supportive feedback from supervisor has a significant and positive role which is consistent with the previous theoretical analyses and studies (Davidson & De Stobbeleir, 2011). Further this research reveals that, exchange of information between employees and customer (patients) also enhances the innovative behavior. H2 was, there is a significant relationship between CEX and IB. In line with the previous study, H2 is supported. The result of this study also shows the positive and significant relationship between customer employee exchange and innovative behavior of employees (Li & Hsu, 2017). Cognitive skills are not only way to enhance innovative behavior, the social capital also matters, which deals with potential advantage employees receives from the contacts with others (Shalley & Gilson, 2004). According to the social exchange theory, employees who receive benefits from customers have great intentions to return back (Lawler, 2001). Moreover, the innovative behavior of employees also increases when the employees have creative personal identity. H3 was, there is a significant relationship between CPI and IB. Hence, result shows significant and positive relationship of creative personal identity with IB. The employees who feel himself as creative person and also known as a creative personality among other employees and people working with him puts a very positive impact on innovative behavior of that employee. Past Study supports this finding, those employee who have CPI are more engage in creative process which leads to innovative behavior (Uddin et al., 2019). This result is also consistent with (Farmer et al., 2003), therefore indicating that CPI is an important antecedent of IB.

The fourth objective was to examine the link between the supervisor feedback, customer employee exchange, creative personal identity and innovative behavior considering interpersonal trust as mediator. This research reveals that, interpersonal trust act as mediator between two links only i;e customer employee exchange and IB, secondly, creative personal identity and IB. H4 was, interpersonal trust mediates the relationship between supervisor feedback and innovative behavior. H5 was, IT mediates the relationship between CEX and IB and H6 was, interpersonal trust mediates the relationship between

CPI and IB. Results shows that, H5 and H6 has supported while H4 is not supported. Trust between customer and employees is very important because it motivate the employee to provide best services to its customer and ultimately employee perform innovatively (Slåtten & Mehmetoglu, 2011). Hence, current study shows that IT plays a mediating role between CEX and IB. Social exchange theory also says that, before conducting any act or behavior, a person first measures the cost and benefit of that conduct (Xerri, 2013). Previous study also supports the result, customer employee exchange enhances the level of IB by increasing level of interpersonal trust (Li & Hsu, 2018). Interpersonal trust also mediates the relationship between creative personal identity and innovative behavior. Creative personality makes the trust among people in the organization about performance of a person and this interpersonal trust ultimately increases the innovative behavior of employee. CPI is the social image together with the self-image, as well as drives the self to perform or not to behave according to the role identities that are attributed to the employees (Farmer et al., 2003). This study does not show the mediation of interpersonal between supervisor feedback and innovative behavior. In consistent with the previous studies, feedback from the supervisor directly affects the innovative behavior (Davidson & De Stobbeleir, 2011). Hence, this study shows the importance of all of discussed factors in enhancing the level of innovative behavior in employees.

Theoretical Implication

The findings of this study lead to several theoretical implications. In the research framework, this study has incorporated the concept of individual innovative behavior and the different factors that put influence on this behavior. There was a limited study on the innovative behavior of government employees of rescue 1122 in Pakistan. Therefore, this, study has focused on this topic by examining impact of different factors on IB. The finding of this research supports the theoretical explanation, which have been given about the relationship between the variables. The result reveals that, SF, CEX and CPI has a significant and positive relationship with IB and mediating role of IT between two links. However, between one relation, IT does not have any impact. The finding of this result is consistent with the previous studies and with theory (social exchange theory). This theory explains that the behavior of one person based on the behavior of other and cost benefit analysis in this exchange (Homans, 1961). This study has highlighted the importance and direction of SF, CEX, CPI and IT in enhancing innovative behavior in rescue 1122.

Practical Implication

As study shows that, supervisor feedback, customer employee exchange and creative personal identity has significant and positive relationship with innovative behavior. Innovative behavior of employees really matters in service organization. The results reveal that if supervisor give the feedback to the employees, it will increase their innovative behavior because the employees will be able to know about their performance time to time. Therefore, supervisors should focus on the feedback environment to enhance the IB of employees. Further, the interaction and exchange of information between the patients and employees enhances the level of innovative behavior. Customer employee exchange not just help in increasing product and service quality but also innovative behavior (Gremler, Gwinner, & Brown, 2001). Hence, the exchange of information between employees and customer should be encouraged in the service firms. In line with previous study, the employees who have creative personal identity then it will also boost up the innovative behavior (Zhou & George, 2003). This study reveals that, organization should focus on developing the sense CPI in the existing employees as well as select and hire the new employees with high CPI. Moreover, trust really matters in any organization to achieve success. This finding also supporting most of the hypotheses, in which interpersonal trust is acting as a mediator. Therefore, organization should focus on enhancing the level of interpersonal trust between different parties which are in contact with organization (customer, employees and supervisor).

Methodological Implication

Together with practical and theoretical implication, this study also provides the methodological implications. Previous studies on innovative behavior have mainly used SPSS, AMOS. But, some have used smart PLS SEM 3.0 (Henseler et al., 2009). This study has used SPSS as well as smart PLS SEM model for analysis of the data. Questionnaire was designed on the bases of seven-point Likert scale, self-administered questionnaire method was used. However, in previous studies 5 point Likert scale is used (Li & Hsu, 2018; X. H. Wang, Fang, Qureshi, & Janssen, 2015). Moreover, Convergent validity, discriminant validity and composite reliability were assessed and achieved satisfactory according to the required threshold. Hence, the current research contributes to the methodology and literature of innovative behavior of employees by establishing reliability and validity of adopted measures in the context of rescue 1122 Punjab (Pakistan).

Limitations and Future Recommendations

There are several limitations of this study, which can inform and direct future studies. First one is, cross sectional study is conducted due to the short period of time, hence, future study can focus on the longitudinal study to have better results (consistency). Secondly, this study is conducted, and the framework is examined only in government organization rescue 1122 Punjab (Pakistan). However, in future this model can also be assessed in any private service firm or in any other government organization. In future research, other factors can also be examined on innovative behavior of employee in rescue 1122 having different mediating factor. Further, this study has only examined the relationship with mediating effect; however, future research should add the moderating effect also to examine this model.

REFERENCES

Aghion, P., Dewatripont, M., & Stein, J. C. (2008). Academic freedom, private-sector focus, and the process of innovation. *The RAND Journal of Economics*, *39*(3), 617–635. doi:10.1111/j.1756-2171.2008.00031.x

Alarcón, D., Sánchez, J. A., & De Olavide, U. (2015). *Assessing convergent and discriminant validity in the ADHD-R IV rating scale: User-written commands for Average Variance Extracted (AVE), Composite Reliability (CR), and Heterotrait-Monotrait ratio of correlations (HTMT).* Paper presented at the Spanish STATA Meeting.

Ali, M. K., & Iftikhar, I. (n.d.). *An Empirical Study of the Effectiveness of Public Relation Campaigns of Rescue 1122*. Academic Press.

Amabile, T. M., & Pratt, M. G. (2016). The dynamic componential model of creativity and innovation in organizations: Making progress, making meaning. *Research in Organizational Behavior*, *36*, 157–183. doi:10.1016/j.riob.2016.10.001

Amin, M. (2018). Effects of job stress on employee engagement and organizational commitment: a study on employees of emergency rescue service rescue 1122 district Peshawar. *City University Research Journal, 8*(2).

Aminu, I. M. (2015). *Mediating role of access to finance and moderating role of business environment on the relationship between strategic orientation attributes and performance of small and medium enterprises in Nigeria*. Universiti Utara Malaysia.

Bagozzi, R. P., & Yi, Y. (1988). On the evaluation of structural equation models. *Journal of the Academy of Marketing Science*, *16*(1), 74–94. doi:10.1007/BF02723327

Bak, H. (2020). Supervisor feedback and innovative work behavior: The mediating roles of trust in supervisor and affective commitment. *Frontiers in Psychology*, *11*, 11. doi:10.3389/fpsyg.2020.559160 PMID:33041923

Bani-melhem, S., Abukhait, R., Shamsudin, F. M., & Al-hawari, M. A. (2021). How and when does job challenge promote the innovative behaviour of public sector employees? *International Journal of Innovation Management*, 2150069. doi:10.1142/S1363919621500699

Bani-Melhem, S., Zeffane, R., & Albaity, M. (2018). Determinants of employees' innovative behavior. *International Journal of Contemporary Hospitality Management*, *30*(3), 1601–1620. doi:10.1108/IJCHM-02-2017-0079

Boon, C., & Kalshoven, K. (2014). How high-commitment HRM relates to engagement and commitment: The moderating role of task proficiency. *Human Resource Management*, *53*(3), 403–420. doi:10.1002/hrm.21569

Brewer, M. B. (1991). The social self: On being the same and different at the same time. *Personality and Social Psychology Bulletin*, *17*(5), 475–482. doi:10.1177/0146167291175001

Bunce, D., & West, M. A. (1995). Self perceptions and perceptions of group climate as predictors of individual innovation at work. *Applied Psychology*, *44*(3), 199–215. doi:10.1111/j.1464-0597.1995.tb01076.x

Callero, P. L., Howard, J. A., & Piliavin, J. A. (1987). Helping behavior as role behavior: Disclosing social structure and history in the analysis of prosocial action. *Social Psychology Quarterly*, *50*(3), 247–256. doi:10.2307/2786825

Campbell, D. T., & Fiske, D. W. (1959). Convergent and discriminant validation by the multitrait-multimethod matrix. *Psychological Bulletin*, *56*(2), 81–105. doi:10.1037/h0046016 PMID:13634291

Cankar, S. S., & Petkovšek, V. (2013). Private and public sector innovation and the importance of cross-sector collaboration. *Journal of Applied Business Research*, *29*(6), 1597–1606. doi:10.19030/jabr.v29i6.8197

Cavana, R., Delahaye, B., & Sekeran, U. (2001). *Applied business research: Qualitative and quantitative methods*. John Wiley & Sons.

Chen, W.-J. (2016). The model of service-oriented organizational citizenship behavior among international tourist hotels. *Journal of Hospitality and Tourism Management*, *29*, 24–32. doi:10.1016/j.jhtm.2016.05.002

Chen, X.-P., Eberly, M. B., Chiang, T.-J., Farh, J.-L., & Cheng, B.-S. (2014). Affective trust in Chinese leaders: Linking paternalistic leadership to employee performance. *Journal of Management*, *40*(3), 796–819. doi:10.1177/0149206311410604

Chen, Y., Tang, G., Jin, J., Xie, Q., & Li, J. (2014). CEO s¢ transformational leadership and product innovation performance: The roles of corporate entrepreneurship and technology orientation. *Journal of Product Innovation Management*, *31*, 2–17. doi:10.1111/jpim.12188

Cho, Y. J., & Park, H. (2011). Exploring the relationships among trust, employee satisfaction, and organizational commitment. *Public Management Review*, *13*(4), 551–573. doi:10.1080/14719037.2010.525033

Churchill, G. A. Jr. (1979). A paradigm for developing better measures of marketing constructs. *JMR, Journal of Marketing Research*, *16*(1), 64–73. doi:10.1177/002224377901600110

Cohen, J. (2013). *Statistical power analysis for the behavioral sciences*. Academic press. doi:10.4324/9780203771587

Davidson, T., & De Stobbeleir, K. E. (2011). Shaping environments conducive to creativity: the role of feedback, autonomy and self-concordance. *Academy of Management Proceedings*. 10.5465/ambpp.2011.65869660

Deluga, R. J. (1994). Supervisor trust building, leader-member exchange and organizational citizenship behaviour. *Journal of Occupational and Organizational Psychology*, *67*(4), 315–326. doi:10.1111/j.2044-8325.1994.tb00570.x

Demircioglu, M. A., & Audretsch, D. B. (2017). Conditions for innovation in public sector organizations. *Research Policy*, *46*(9), 1681–1691. doi:10.1016/j.respol.2017.08.004

Dhar, R. L. (2016). Ethical leadership and its impact on service innovative behavior: The role of LMX and job autonomy. *Tourism Management*, *57*, 139–148. doi:10.1016/j.tourman.2016.05.011

Eva, N., Meacham, H., Newman, A., Schwarz, G., & Tham, T. L. (2019). Is coworker feedback more important than supervisor feedback for increasing innovative behavior? *Human Resource Management*, *58*(4), 383–396. doi:10.1002/hrm.21960

Farmer, S. M., Tierney, P., & Kung-Mcintyre, K. (2003). Employee creativity in Taiwan: An application of role identity theory. *Academy of Management Journal*, *46*(5), 618–630.

Fisher, T. (1997). The Designer's Self-Identity—Myths of Creativity and the Management of Teams 1. *Creativity and Innovation Management*, *6*(1), 10–18. doi:10.1111/1467-8691.00044

Fornell, C., & Larcker, D. F. (1981). Evaluating structural equation models with unobservable variables and measurement error. *JMR, Journal of Marketing Research*, *18*(1), 39–50. doi:10.1177/002224378101800104

Gabriel, A. S., Frantz, N. B., Levy, P. E., & Hilliard, A. W. (2014). The supervisor feedback environment is empowering, but not all the time: Feedback orientation as a critical moderator. *Journal of Occupational and Organizational Psychology*, *87*(3), 487–506. doi:10.1111/joop.12060

Greener, S. (2008). *Business research methods*. BookBoon.

Gremler, D. D., Gwinner, K. P., & Brown, S. W. (2001). Generating positive word-of-mouth communication through customer-employee relationships. *International Journal of Service Industry Management*, *12*(1), 44–59. doi:10.1108/09564230110382763

Hair, J. F. Jr, Hult, G. T. M., Ringle, C., & Sarstedt, M. (2016). *A primer on partial least squares structural equation modeling (PLS-SEM)*. Sage Publications.

Hair, J. F., Sarstedt, M., Ringle, C. M., & Mena, J. A. (2012). An assessment of the use of partial least squares structural equation modeling in marketing research. *Journal of the Academy of Marketing Science*, *40*(3), 414–433. doi:10.100711747-011-0261-6

Hansen, S. D., Dunford, B. B., Boss, A. D., Boss, R. W., & Angermeier, I. (2011). Corporate social responsibility and the benefits of employee trust: A cross-disciplinary perspective. *Journal of Business Ethics*, *102*(1), 29–45. doi:10.100710551-011-0903-0

Hassan, M., Toylan, N. V., Semerciöz, F., & Aksel, I. (2012). Interpersonal trust and its role in organizations. *International Business Research*, *5*(8), 33. doi:10.5539/ibr.v5n8p33

Hayes, A. F., & Preacher, K. J. (2010). Quantifying and testing indirect effects in simple mediation models when the constituent paths are nonlinear. *Multivariate Behavioral Research*, *45*(4), 627–660. doi:10.1080/00273171.2010.498290 PMID:26735713

Henseler, J., Dijkstra, T. K., Sarstedt, M., Ringle, C. M., Diamantopoulos, A., Straub, D. W., Ketchen, D. J. Jr, Hair, J. F., Hult, G. T. M., & Calantone, R. J. (2014). Common beliefs and reality about PLS: Comments on Rönkkö and Evermann (2013). *Organizational Research Methods*, *17*(2), 182–209. doi:10.1177/1094428114526928

Henseler, J., Ringle, C. M., & Sinkovics, R. R. (2009). *The use of partial least squares path modeling in international marketing New challenges to international marketing*. Emerald Group Publishing Limited.

Homans, G. (1961). Social behavior: Its elementary forms. New York: Harcourt, Brace.

Hoyle, R. H., & Robinson, J. C. (2004). Mediated and moderated effects in social psychological research. Handbook of methods in social psychology, 213-233.

Hu, L., & Bentler, P. M. (1999). Cutoff criteria for fit indexes in covariance structure analysis: Conventional criteria versus new alternatives. *Structural Equation Modeling*, *6*(1), 1–55. doi:10.1080/10705519909540118

Iacobucci, D. (2010). Structural equations modeling: Fit indices, sample size, and advanced topics. *Journal of Consumer Psychology*, *20*(1), 90–98. doi:10.1016/j.jcps.2009.09.003

Imran, M., Hamid, S. N. B. A., Aziz, A. B., & Wan, C. Y. (2019). *The Effect of Performance Appraisal Politics on Employee Performance in Emergency Services of Punjab*. Academy of Strategic Management Journal.

Janssen, O., Van de Vliert, E., & West, M. (2004). The bright and dark sides of individual and group innovation: A special issue introduction. *Journal of Organizational Behavior*, *25*(2), 129–145. doi:10.1002/job.242

Jaussi, K. S., Randel, A. E., & Dionne, S. D. (2007). I am, I think I can, and I do: The role of personal identity, self-efficacy, and cross-application of experiences in creativity at work. *Creativity Research Journal*, *19*(2-3), 247–258. doi:10.1080/10400410701397339

Johnson, D., & Grayson, K. (2005). Cognitive and affective trust in service relationships. *Journal of Business Research*, *58*(4), 500–507. doi:10.1016/S0148-2963(03)00140-1

Karwowski, M., Lebuda, I., Wisniewska, E., & Gralewski, J. (2013). Big five personality traits as the predictors of creative self-efficacy and creative personal identity: Does gender matter? *The Journal of Creative Behavior*, *47*(3), 215–232. doi:10.1002/jocb.32

Kline, R. B. (2011). *Principles and practice of structural equation modeling (3. Baskı)*. Guilford.

Kouzes, J. M., & Posner, B. Z. (2006). *The leadership challenge* (Vol. 3). John Wiley & Sons.

Krejcie, R. V., & Morgan, D. W. (1970). Determining sample size for research activities. *Educational and Psychological Measurement*, *30*(3), 607–610. doi:10.1177/001316447003000308

Lancaster, G. (2005). *Research Methods in Management. A Concise Introduction to Research in Management and Business Consultancy, Jordan Hill*. Elsevier Butterworth-Heinemann Linacre House.

Lawler, E. J. (2001). An affect theory of social exchange. *American Journal of Sociology*, *107*(2), 321–352. doi:10.1086/324071

Lee, W. R., Choi, S. B., & Kang, S.-W. (2021). How Leaders' Positive Feedback Influences Employees' Innovative Behavior: The Mediating Role of Voice Behavior and Job Autonomy. *Sustainability*, *13*(4), 1901. doi:10.3390u13041901

Lemire, L., & Rouillard, C. (2005). An empirical exploration of psychological contract violation and individual behaviour. *Journal of Managerial Psychology*, *20*(2), 150–163. doi:10.1108/02683940510579786

Lester, S. W., Turnley, W. H., Bloodgood, J. M., & Bolino, M. C. (2002). Not seeing eye to eye: Differences in supervisor and subordinate perceptions of and attributions for psychological contract breach. *Journal of Organizational Behavior*, *23*(1), 39–56. doi:10.1002/job.126

Li, M., & Hsu, C. (2017). Customer participation in services and its effect on employee innovative behavior. *Journal of Hospitality Marketing & Management*, *26*(2), 164–185. doi:10.1080/19368623.2016.1215946

Li, M., & Hsu, C. H. (2016a). Linking customer-employee exchange and employee innovative behavior. *International Journal of Hospitality Management*, *56*, 87–97. doi:10.1016/j.ijhm.2016.04.015

Li, M., & Hsu, C. H. (2016b). A review of employee innovative behavior in services. *International Journal of Contemporary Hospitality Management, 28*(12), 2820–2841. doi:10.1108/IJCHM-04-2015-0214

Li, M., & Hsu, C. H. (2018). Customer participation in services and employee innovative behavior. *International Journal of Contemporary Hospitality Management, 30*(4), 2112–2131. doi:10.1108/IJCHM-08-2016-0465

Lin, C., Lin, P., Song, F. M., & Li, C. (2011). Managerial incentives, CEO characteristics and corporate innovation in China's private sector. *Journal of Comparative Economics, 39*(2), 176–190. doi:10.1016/j.jce.2009.12.001

Ma, E., & Qu, H. (2011). Social exchanges as motivators of hotel employees' organizational citizenship behavior: The proposition and application of a new three-dimensional framework. *International Journal of Hospitality Management, 30*(3), 680–688. doi:10.1016/j.ijhm.2010.12.003

Ma Prieto, I., & Pilar Perez-Santana, M. (2014). Managing innovative work behavior: The role of human resource practices. *Personnel Review, 43*(2), 184–208. doi:10.1108/PR-11-2012-0199

Micheli, P., Schoeman, M., Baxter, D., & Goffin, K. (2012). New business models for public-sector innovation: Successful technological innovation for government. *Research Technology Management, 55*(5), 51–57. doi:10.5437/08956308X5505067

Mohamed, E. S. A. (2020). The Role of Employee's Innovative Behavior in Strengthening the Impact of Customer Participation on Customer Engagement. *International Journal of Customer Relationship Marketing and Management, 11*(4), 1–19. doi:10.4018/IJCRMM.2020100101

Mu, R., & Wang, H. (2020). A systematic literature review of open innovation in the public sector: Comparing barriers and governance strategies of digital and non-digital open innovation. *Public Management Review*, 1–23. doi:10.1080/14719037.2020.1838787

Mulgan, G., & Albury, D. (2003). Innovation in the public sector. *Strategy Unit. Cabinet Office, 1*(1), 40.

Munton, A. G., & West, M. A. (1995). Innovations and personal change: Patterns of adjustment to relocation. *Journal of Organizational Behavior, 16*(4), 363–375. doi:10.1002/job.4030160407

NaseerD. R. (Producer). (2018, February 3rd). *Tribune*. Retrieved from https://tribune.com.pk/story/1625223/seven-minutes-rescue-1122-maintains-average-response-time

Nunkoo, R., & Ramkissoon, H. (2012). Power, trust, social exchange and community support. *Annals of Tourism Research, 39*(2), 997–1023. doi:10.1016/j.annals.2011.11.017

Preacher, K. J., & Hayes, A. F. (2008). Asymptotic and resampling strategies for assessing and comparing indirect effects in multiple mediator models. *Behavior Research Methods, 40*(3), 879–891. doi:10.3758/BRM.40.3.879 PMID:18697684

Ramayah, T., Lee, J., & In, J. (2011). Network collaboration and performance in the tourism sector. *Service Business, 5*(4), 411–428. doi:10.100711628-011-0120-z

Restubog, S. L. D., Bordia, P., & Tang, R. L. (2007). Behavioural outcomes of psychological contract breach in a non-western culture: The moderating role of equity sensitivity. *British Journal of Management, 18*(4), 376–386. doi:10.1111/j.1467-8551.2007.00531.x

Robinson, S. L., Kraatz, M. S., & Rousseau, D. M. (1994). Changing obligations and the psychological contract: A longitudinal study. *Academy of Management Journal, 37*(1), 137–152.

Schindler, P. L., & Thomas, C. C. (1993). The structure of interpersonal trust in the workplace. *Psychological Reports, 73*(2), 563–573. doi:10.2466/pr0.1993.73.2.563

Scott, S. G., & Bruce, R. A. (1994). Determinants of innovative behavior: A path model of individual innovation in the workplace. *Academy of Management Journal, 37*(3), 580–607.

Seo, H. M., Kim, M. C., Chang, K., & Kim, T. (2016). Influence of interpersonal trust on innovative behaviour of service workers: Mediating effects of knowledge sharing. *International Journal of Innovation Management, 20*(02), 1650026. doi:10.1142/S1363919616500262

Shalley, C. E., & Gilson, L. L. (2004). What leaders need to know: A review of social and contextual factors that can foster or hinder creativity. *The Leadership Quarterly, 15*(1), 33–53. doi:10.1016/j.leaqua.2003.12.004

Slåtten, T., & Mehmetoglu, M. (2011). What are the drivers for innovative behavior in frontline jobs? A study of the hospitality industry in Norway. *Journal of Human Resources in Hospitality & Tourism, 10*(3), 254–272. doi:10.1080/15332845.2011.555732

Sobel, M. E. (1982). Asymptotic confidence intervals for indirect effects in structural equation models. *Sociological Methodology, 13*, 290–312. doi:10.2307/270723

Song, W., Yu, H., Zhang, Y., & Jiang, W. (2015). Goal orientation and employee creativity: The mediating role of creative role identity. *Journal of Management & Organization, 21*(1), 82–97. doi:10.1017/jmo.2014.64

Tabachnick, B., & Fidell, L. (2013). Using Multivariate Statistics (6th ed.). Pearson Education Limited.

Thornhill, A., Saunders, M., & Lewis, P. (2009). *Research methods for business students*. Prentice Hall.

Uddin, M. A., Priyankara, H. R., & Mahmood, M. (2019). Does a creative identity encourage innovative behaviour? Evidence from knowledge-intensive IT service firms. *European Journal of Innovation Management, 23*(5), 877–894. doi:10.1108/EJIM-06-2019-0168

Vanderstoep, S. W., & Johnson, D. D. (2008). *Research methods for everyday life: Blending qualitative and quantitative approaches* (Vol. 32). John Wiley & Sons.

Verhoest, K., Verschuere, B., & Bouckaert, G. (2007). Pressure, legitimacy, and innovative behavior by public organizations. *Governance: An International Journal of Policy, Administration and Institutions, 20*(3), 469–497. doi:10.1111/j.1468-0491.2007.00367.x

Wang, A. C., & Cheng, B. S. (2010). When does benevolent leadership lead to creativity? The moderating role of creative role identity and job autonomy. *Journal of Organizational Behavior, 31*(1), 106–121. doi:10.1002/job.634

Wang, C.-J., Tsai, H.-T., & Tsai, M.-T. (2014). Linking transformational leadership and employee creativity in the hospitality industry: The influences of creative role identity, creative self-efficacy, and job complexity. *Tourism Management, 40*, 79–89. doi:10.1016/j.tourman.2013.05.008

Wang, L., Law, R., Hung, K., & Guillet, B. D. (2014). Consumer trust in tourism and hospitality: A review of the literature. *Journal of Hospitality and Tourism Management, 21*, 1–9. doi:10.1016/j.jhtm.2014.01.001

Wang, X. H., Fang, Y., Qureshi, I., & Janssen, O. (2015). Understanding employee innovative behavior: Integrating the social network and leader–member exchange perspectives. *Journal of Organizational Behavior, 36*(3), 403–420. doi:10.1002/job.1994

Woodman, R. W., Sawyer, J. E., & Griffin, R. W. (1993). Toward a theory of organizational creativity. *Academy of Management Review, 18*(2), 293–321. doi:10.5465/amr.1993.3997517

Xerri, M. (2013). Workplace relationships and the innovative behaviour of nursing employees: A social exchange perspective. *Asia Pacific Journal of Human Resources, 51*(1), 103–123. doi:10.1111/j.1744-7941.2012.00031.x

Xu, F. Z., & Wang, Y. (2020). Enhancing employee innovation through customer engagement: The role of customer interactivity, employee affect, and motivations. *Journal of Hospitality & Tourism Research (Washington, D.C.), 44*(2), 351–376. doi:10.1177/1096348019893043

Zhou, J. (1998). Feedback valence, feedback style, task autonomy, and achievement orientation: Interactive effects on creative performance. *The Journal of Applied Psychology, 83*(2), 261–276. doi:10.1037/0021-9010.83.2.261

Zhou, J., & George, J. M. (2003). Awakening employee creativity: The role of leader emotional intelligence. *The Leadership Quarterly, 14*(4-5), 545–568. doi:10.1016/S1048-9843(03)00051-1

Zhu, Y., Ritter, S. M., Müller, B. C., & Dijksterhuis, A. (2017). Creativity: Intuitive processing outperforms deliberative processing in creative idea selection. *Journal of Experimental Social Psychology, 73*, 180–188. doi:10.1016/j.jesp.2017.06.009

Chapter 9
Propensity to Purchase Organic Food:
An Integrative Model of Consumption Values in Malaysia

Khairul Nizam Mahmud
Universiti Utara Malaysia, Malaysia

Asmat-Nizam Abdul-Talib
https://orcid.org/0000-0001-6820-2918
Universiti Utara Malaysia, Malaysia

ABSTRACT

Organic food is becoming popular among today's millennial consumers because of increased awareness of healthy lifestyles. Scholars and practitioners attempt to understand what drives consumers to purchase organic foods toward developing market domination strategies and tactics. Since organic food tends to be more expensive than non-organic, this study aims to analyze the impact of consumer values on their tendency to buy organic food. Consumption values are an important factor that could drive consumer behavior and their preferences for goods or services. Consumption values are defined in terms of the required benefits from the purchase and consumption of the preferred products. Sheth, Newman, and Gross defined consumption values in terms of practical, social, emotional, epistemic, and conditional values.

INTRODUCTION

Organic food is the fastest-growing market in the food industry in many countries (Dettman & Dimitri, 2010). According to Business Wire, the global organic fresh food market is poised to grow by USD62.23 billion during 2019-2023, progressing at a Compound Annual Growth Rate (CAGR) of almost 15% during the forecast period. The market is driven by the growth of organic farming worldwide. In addition, sustainable organic fresh food production is anticipated to impact the growth of the organic fresh food market positively. Also, economic growth, urbanization, globalization, and trade liberalization have

DOI: 10.4018/978-1-7998-8678-5.ch009

significantly impacted consumers' food choices and preferences. The increasing consumers' demand for organic food products are mainly due to food safety concern (Hsu, Chang, & Lin, 2016; Wee, Ariff, Zakuan, & Tajuddin, 2014), health benefits (Mohamad, Rusdi, & Hashim, 2014), and environmental concern (Misra et al., 2020; Wang et al., 2020). Environmental degradation due to the use of chemicals in agriculture and individual consumption is a major public concern. Hence, green consumption is encouraged via the purchase of green food (Suki, 2016).

As social and political pressures increase, many firms have begun to adopt organic marketing strategies and promote their environmentally-friendly food as a source of strategic advantage. However, one of the biggest challenges companies face is influencing consumers to buy green food. Some consumers tend to equate organic food with a higher price. According to Bostan et al. (2019), the greatest challenges for organic food is to reduce the trade-off between productivity and long-term sustainability. Organic food can be defined as green food without any artificial fertilizers, pesticides, and additives in the process of production (Hansmann et al., 2020; Molinillo et al., 2020; Mohamad, Rushi, & Hashim, 2014). For food to be claimed organic, it has to be certified by an industrial body to ensure that the food is produced, stored, and processed without any artificial synthesized input and additives.

The United States is the highest producer of organic food (46%) while in Asia, China is the leading country (7%) (Saleki et al., 2019). However, in Malaysia, the organic concept and the development of organic food are still nascent (Saleki et al., 2019). Today, as consumers want to live a good life and a better quality of life, they start to consume organic food. As the number of consumers who are environmentally responsible is increasing, so is the number of organic food in the market. Facing imminent environmental degradation, the government of Malaysia is encouraging the public to go organic (Aziz et al., 2020). Consistently, the government has outlined strict environmental regulations and a regulatory framework for the conscious control of air quality and greenhouse gases in the country (i.e., Environmental Quality Act 1974) in an attempt to achieve sustainable development and improve the health of the population (Suki, 2016). Subsidies are also provided to promote the organic industry in Malaysia through the Malaysian organic certification program and the certification of farms according to the Malaysian standard MS1529:2001 (Tiraieyari, Hamzah, & Samah, 2014).

According to Somasundaram, Razali, and Santhirasegaram (2016), there has been an increase in the purchase of organic food in Malaysia. However, the value of local organic food is still low compared to imported organic food. More than 60 percent of organic food is imported, but it must bear a reliable 'certified organic' label from the source of the exporting countries. The demand for organic food in Malaysia is growing dramatically because of the changing healthy lifestyle that conventional food could not provide. Furthermore, currently, consumers are concerned with health and nutritious food and its effect on the environment, giving rise to a positive attitude and intention to consume organic food (Jeyakumar-Nathan et al., 2021; Katt & Meixner, 2020). According to Ghali and Hamdi (2015), the most common argument for consumers to purchase organic food is the concern for their health and preserving the environment. However, the propensity to purchase organic food in Malaysia still low. As such, this study is to investigate what could influence the Malaysian consumer's propensity to purchase organic food.

Most studies conducted in Malaysia on organic food considered the Theory of Planned Behavior (TPB) or Theory of Reasoned Action (TRA) in examining the purchasing behavior of consumers. However, studies that employed the Theory of Consumption Values (TCV) for green products are limited (Suki, 2016), especially for organic food. The use of TCV is relevant because an individual who appreciates and is concerned about something does not necessarily behave organically or purchase such a product. The gap between value and action is known as the 'value-action gap' (Zamani, Abdul-Talib & Ashari,

2016). Thus, the value-action gap is the gap that occurs when an individual's values or behavior do not correspond to his/her actions. According to Dickson (2001), the difference in value is a discrepancy between the high value consumers attribute in the environment and the relatively low level of action consumers take to address environmental problems. Value has been found to be an important predictor of the purchase intention of consumers (Thomé et al., 2020). In their study, Bradbury et al. (2014) found that the consumption of organic products was not linked to a reduction in cancer incidence. Because of this value-action gap, previous studies that used TPB or TRA could not translate value into action by consumers (Abdul-Talib & Abd-Latif, 2015; Teoh & Nor Azila, 2015), as only 40 per cent of behaviour can be explained by TPB or TRA (Werner, 2004). Nonetheless, previous studies (Wang et al., 2020) had adopted or adapted theory of consumption values, showing that the theory of consumption values could explain above 40 percent of behaviour. Therefore, this study speculates that functional value, social value, emotional value, epistemic value, and conditional value are likely to influence consumer choice of organic food. Hence, this study investigated the influence of consumption values on consumers' propensity to purchase organic food in Malaysia.

In the context of organic food purchasing, several authors have asserted that organic food retailers need to develop and implement effective green marketing practices to support consumers' decision-making process (Nguyen et al., 2019). Green marketing practices may include the production and distribution of environmentally-friendly food (e.g., organic food), marketing communications for green food (e.g., advertising, sales promotion, public relations, and publicity), eco-labeling and branding (Groening, Sarkis, & Zhu, 2018). These situational and environmental factors, unlike personal determinants, have been largely unexplored.

The finding of the present study has practical implications, especially for organic producers in Malaysia improve the development of organic food. Organic food is food that is harmless to consume, has very good quality, considers the welfare of animals, is healthy, and is produced according to the sustainable development principle (Lin et al., 2020; Liu, 2003). The recent progress of the organic food industry has compelled the Malaysian Agricultural Research and Development Institute to actively develop the organic farming sector by implementing various programs and activities. Organic food has been considered a new industry that contributes to economic growth. The production of organic food has become an innovative strategy for the Malaysian agricultural sector to sustain its competitive advantages. Hence, it is time for the Malaysian government to review its organic farming policy and change its paradigm to ensure that the local organic food industry becomes the engine of growth for the agricultural sector. The success of establishing this industry demands comprehensive strategies and collaboration from the government, producers, and marketers.

LITERATURE REVIEW

Theory of Consumption Value

The theory of consumption value essentially tries to explain why consumers choose products or services (Sharma, 2019; Sheth et al., 1991). The theory is concerned with how consumers make a judgment of whether to buy or not to buy a certain product based on different preference values of such a purchase. Drawing from various disciplines, such as social psychology, clinical psychology, sociology, economics, and experimental psychology (Zaidi et al., 2019; Tapachai & Waryszak, 2000), Sheth et al. (1991)

identified five consumption values. They are functional value, social value, emotional value, epistemic value, and conditional value. Sheth et al. (1991) developed a consumption value model to describe a consumer's preference processes of values and motive in a purchase. According to Sheth et al. (1991), three fundamental propositions are axiomatic to the theory of consumption value, as follows: (a) consumer choice is an act of several consumption values, (b) consumption values are independent, and (c) consumption values make deferential influences in any choice situation.

The theory has been employed and tested in more than 200 applications and has received empirical support (Amin & Tarun, 2020; Issock-Issock et al., 2019; Ramkissoon, Nunkoo, & Gursoy, 2009; Sheth et al., 1991). It has been applied to examine intention to purchase green products (Suki, 2016; Lin et al., 2010), hybrid cars (Teoh & Noor, 2015), green electrical products (Alesia, Stephan, & Geoffrey, 2014), mobile application use (Lim, Ahmad & Talib, 2019), adventure tourism (William & Soutar, 2009), and smartphones (Bodker, Gimpel, & Hedman, 2009). To date, the theory is yet to be applied to explain organic food consumption. Hence, the present study is an attempt to fill this gap.

The following discusses the role of each value in influencing consumer choice toward the development of the research hypotheses.

Research Model and Propositions

Functional Value and Purchase Propensity

Functional value relates to the functional usability of product attributes, which are physical and utilitarian benefits (Sheth et al., 1991). Sheth et al. (1991) defined functional values as "the perceived utility acquired from an alternative's capacity for functional, utilitarian, or physical performance. An alternative acquires functional value through the possession of salient functional, utilitarian, or physical attributes. Functional value is measured on a profile of choice attributes" (p. 160). That is, functional value refers to the benefit perceived or obtained from the functional, pragmatic, and physical performance of a situation (Amin & Tarun, 2020; Sheth et al., 1991). They argued that functional value is the main determinant of consumer choice in purchasing and consuming products or services. A product or service is said to have a functional value when it is perceived to have the following features: reliability, durability, and price (Abdul-Talib & Japari, 2020; William & Soutar, 2009). For example, when choosing a destination, tourists will consider exotic food, historical sites, and the quality of the facilities (Phau, Quintal, & Shanka, 2014). Consumers are easily affected by price and the quality of the product as a result of their experience and knowledge of the things they have purchased.

Past studies tended to show a positive relationship between functional value and consumer purchasing behavior (Woo & Kim, 2019; Kekec, 2015; Teoh & Noor, 2015) even though some studies did not find such a link (Amin & Tarun, 2020; Wong et al., 2019; Lin, Huang, & Wang, 2010; Williams & Soutar, 2009). Researchers have also found that consumers are generally positive about eco-friendly products and are willing to pay more for them to protect individual and social benefits (Liu, Pieniak & Verbeke, 2013; Tully & Winer, 2014). Suki (2016) reported that consumers appeared to be motivated by the functional benefits gained from product efficiency. Solaiman et al. (2017) found that functional value had a positive relationship with green purchase behavior. Therefore, this study proposes the following hypothesis:

Proposition 1: Functional value positively influences the propensity to purchase organic food.

Social Value and Purchase Propensity

Social value relates to the perceived product utility that is acquired from product's positive associations with consumer's personal geographic, demographic, socioeconomic, political and cultural dimensions, and from positive recognition of product attributes in social groups to which consumer belongs or intends to belong (Sheth et al., 1991). Sheth et al. (1991) defined social value as "the perceived utility acquired from an alternative's association with one or more specific social groups. An alternative acquires social value through association with positively or negatively stereotyped demographic, socioeconomic, and cultural-ethnic groups. Social value is measured on a profile of choice imagery" (p. 161). People's openness and hospitality, respectful treatment, genuine care for customers, and willingness to help are factors that can create social values (Danish et al., 2019; Phau, Quintal, & Shanka, 2014).

In today's competitive marketing environment, companies need to understand consumer behavior and develop relevant marketing strategies to offer products/services consumers want. Past research found that consumerism and the search for popularity were significant considerations young adult consumers make in their purchase decisions (Luomala et al., 2020; O'Cass & Siahtiri, 2013). O'Cass and Frost (2002) demonstrated that customers bought certain products for social recognition, such as reputation and prestige. Previous studies showed that consumers stayed in green hotels to be socially accepted (Tan et al., 2020; Ahn & Kwon, 2019; Teng, Wu, & Liu, 2015; Chen & Peng 2012; Lien et al., 2012). Social image was found to be the third biggest determinant of green buying behavior among young consumers in Hong Kong (Lee, 2008). Hung et al. (2011) conducted a study on consumer purchase of luxury brands in Taiwan and found out that social value was positively correlated with such purchase behavior. Therefore, this study proposes the following hypothesis:

Proposition 2: Social value positively influences the propensity to purchase organic food.

Emotional Value and Purchase Propensity

Sheth et al. (1991, p. 161) defined emotional value as "the perceived utility acquired from an alternative's capacity to arouse feelings or affective states. An alternatives acquires emotional value when associated with specific feelings or when precipitating or perpetuating those feeling Emotional value is measured on a profile of feeling associated with the alternative." Emotional value can also be described as any feelings and feelings resulting from the consumer's reaction when using the product (Abdul-Talib & Mohd Adnan, 2017) which can be positive, negative, or mixed. For example, when using cosmetic products that are free from synthetic and animal ingredients, consumers may feel more secure. Although any manufactured product may create emotional value for consumers, it is usually associated with the consumption of aesthetic and hedonic products, such as organic food. Hedonic products include multi-sensory features and imply experiential consumption, fun, and excitement, etc.

Ahmad and Juhdi (2008) showed that customers who were concerned about the environment had a healthy lifestyle and demonstrated more environmentally friendly behavior. Also, today's consumers are more aware of green purchase, which is associated with nature conservation and the promotion of a healthy lifestyle. When consumers have a strong feeling about the environment, they are likely to go for green products because they feel they are contributing toward protecting the environment and sustainable development (Yu & Lee, 2019; Suki, 2016). Therefore, this study proposes the following hypothesis:

Proposition 3: Emotional value positively influences the propensity to purchase organic food.

Epistemic Value

Epistemic value can be defined as "the perceived utility acquired from an alternative's capacity to arouse curiosity, provide novelty, and/or satisfy a desire for knowledge. An alternative acquires epistemic value by questionnaire items referring to curiosity, novelty, and knowledge" (Sheth et al., 1991, p. 162). Curiosity and creativity are innate in human nature (Shevlin, 2020; Candan &Yıldırım, 2013). Hence, consumers purchase a product due to familiarity with the current brand, high curiosity about a new product, or willingness to learn about the new product (Yeo, Mohamed, & Muda, 2016).

Knowledge is the main trait that affects consumers' decision-making process in identifying new product adoption (Wang et al., 2019; Wekeza & Sibanda, 2019). For example, consumers' actual recycling behavior was influenced by their knowledge of the recycling process (Samson & Voyer, 2014). According to Hessami and Yousefi (2013), product awareness plays an important part in product selection. Young consumers who are planning to purchase organic skincare products will seek additional information about the benefits, ingredients, and so on before they make the purchase. Solaiman et al. (2017) found that epistemic value had a positive relationship with green purchase behavior. However, Teoh and Noor Azila (2015) did not find such a link when investigating the purchase of hybrid cars among Malaysian consumers in Klang Valley.

Based on the above discussion, this study proposes the following hypothesis:

Proposition 4: Epistemic value positively influences the propensity to purchase organic food.

Conditional Valuc

Sheth et al. (1991) defined conditional value as "the perceived utility acquired by an alternative as the result of the specific situation or set of circumstances facing the choice maker. An alternative acquires conditional value in the presence of antecedent physical or social contingencies that enhance its functional or social value. Conditional value is measured on a profile of choice contingencies" (p. 162). Conditional value occurs when a product's utility depends on a particular situation or circumstance under which the product is purchased (Qasim et al., 2019; Zailani et al., 2019; Sheth et al., 1991). For example, the market today is highly focused on producing environmentally friendly based products that are less harmful to consumers. Another example reflecting conditional value is the greeting of cards for special events and ceremonies like birthdays or weddings. Another example is a wedding dress that would be valuable in case of an upcoming wedding or winter jacket in cold weather.

Conditional value addresses the situational nature of it, meaning that the perceived value of a product can vary from one purchase situation to another (William & Soutar, 2009). Even within a similar situation, the value might be perceived differently with time due to past experiences. Conditional value is an acquired utility derived from temporary functional or social values that appear under certain conditions (Kaur et al., 2021; Sheth et al., 1991). It is the least influential and the most ambiguous value dimension. Because conditional value appears under certain circumstances and conditions that a decision-maker faces, its existence as a distinctive value dimension becomes questionable (Woo & Kim, 2019; Williams & Soutar, 2009). Generally, consumers' conceptions of conditional value cannot be known until the condition that will change the behavior appear (Burcu & Seda, 2013).

Conditional value was found to be the most influential predictor of consumers' choice behavior (Qasim et al., 2019; Abdul-Talib, Abd-Razak & Abd-Latif, 2016; Lin & Huang, 2012). With regard to green products, Lin and Huang (2012) noted that conditional value could influence consumer choice as much as consumers consider environmental consequences when making purchasing decisions. Previous studies found that consumers bought certain products for specific circumstances and requirements (Bayer & Ke, 2013; Samson & Voyer, 2014). Solaiman et al. (2017) found out that conditional value had a positive relationship with green purchase behavior. Therefore, this study proposes the following hypothesis:

Proposition 5: Conditional value positively influences the propensity to purchase organic food.

Figure 1 illustrates the research model in this study.

Figure 1. Research model

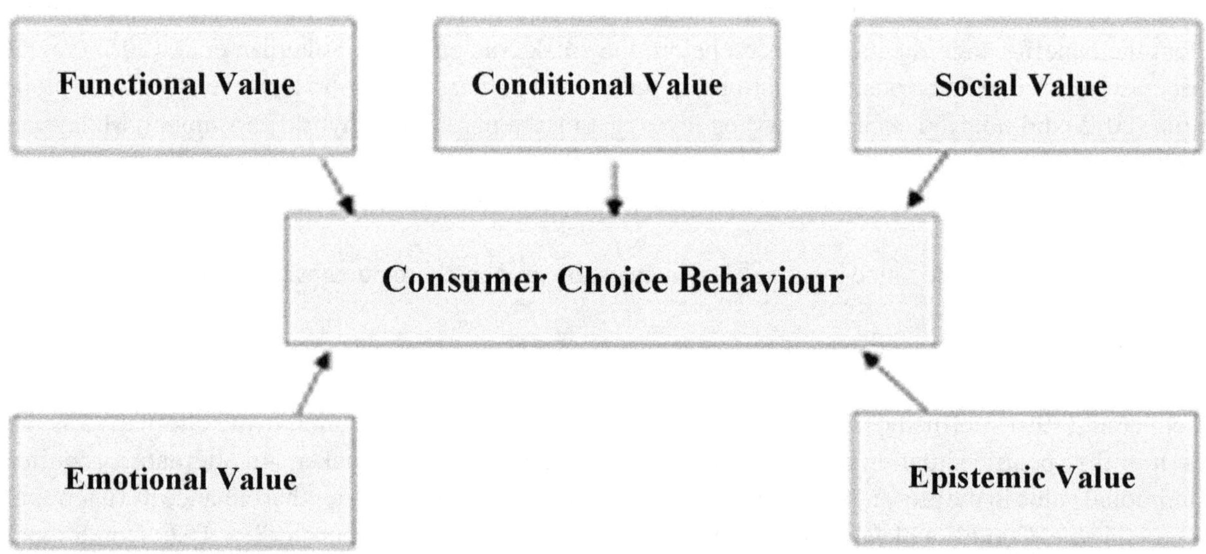

RESEARCH CONTRIBUTION

The present study contributes to both theory and practice, as discussed below.

Theoretical Contribution

The theoretical focus of this study is understanding how consumer consumption values affect the tendency to buy organic food among consumers in the Kuala Lumpur area in Malaysia. By examining the theoretical link between consumption values and propensity to purchase and consume organic food, the present study adds to the existing literature in organic markets in Malaysia.

The present research enhances our theoretical understanding of the application of the theory of consumption values in influencing consumer decision-making in buying and consuming organic food. To the awareness of the researcher, a few studies have applied the theory of consumption values to investigate purchasing behavior in the automobile, mobile phone, and tourism context. Based on the theory, past researchers investigated why consumers chose to buy a specific product, why they preferred one type of product over another, and why they chose one brand over another (Sheth et al., 1991). This study proposes that because of its functional, social, emotional, epistemic, and conditional values, consumers are likely to choose organic food.

Managerial Implications

This study also has several managerial implications. The findings will be useful to the managers in the organic food industry about improving their future marketing plans. The managers can use the findings to develop and implement plans that could motivate and persuade consumers to buy organic food. Producers or marketers should improve their marketing strategy because, when aligned with the overall corporate strategy, it could contribute toward organizational effectiveness and success. A good marketing strategy also involves the creation and development of good relationships with external stakeholders in the supply chains to deliver and sell the products in the market, a structured approach is needed where the plan should be an integral part of planning, creativity, vision and learning, processes of change, projects, and environmental analysis to meet the needs of the customers.

While many consumers in Malaysia support the environmental policies of the government, support is not always translated into behavior. The government has a vital role to play in this case in creating the right economic and social environment to motivate the public to behave accordingly. Environmental and social challenges in the global markets today require the government to be proactive in promoting their environmental responsibility, which can be fulfilled by collaborating in various environmental projects with corporate or third-sector organizations. The 'Organic Food for Nutrition' initiative, for example, exemplifies both the government and the private sector's constructive call for action. Additionally, employers in the government and the private sector could organize activities to raise awareness of the environment and promote environmentally-friendly working cultures or lifestyles, such as business to business marketing.

CONCLUSION AND FUTURE RESEARCH DIRECTIONS

The central objective of the propensity to buy organic food is to produce less harm to nature. A better understanding of consumer behavior will help producers, marketers, and policymakers promote less harmful consumer habits towards the environment. The findings of this study will help companies learn and understand the nature and expectations of consumers of organic food, and thus establish a suitable strategy to achieve long-term success. It is also hoped that the findings of this study will not only help the government and the industry of organic products around the world to understand consumer behavior in purchasing organic food but will also offer them some constructive suggestions about how to promote organic food consumption.

The study will also bring benefits to society in understanding the current and future trends in the organic food purchasing behavior of consumers. Since businesses play an important role in national economic development, they need to understand consumer preferences and the impact of their organic buying behavior on business success and societal change.

REFERENCES

Abdul-Latif, S.A. (2020). An examination of ethnic-based consumer ethnocentrism and consumer animosity. *Journal of Islamic Marketing*. ahead-of-print. doi:10.1108/JIMA-08-2019-0165

Abdul-Talib, A. N., Abd-Latif, S. A., & Abd-Razak, I. S. (2016). A study on the boycott motivations of Malaysian non-Muslims. *Journal of Islamic Marketing*, *7*(3), 264–287. doi:10.1108/JIMA-11-2014-0071

Abdul-Talib, A. N., & Abdul-Latif, S. A. (2015). Antecedents to willingness to Boycotts among Malaysian Muslims. In *Emerging Research on Islamic Marketing and Tourism in the Global Economy* (pp. 70–106). IGI Global. doi:10.4018/978-1-4666-6272-8.ch004

Abdul-Talib, A. N., & Japari, N. (2020). Brand Consciousness and Brand Loyalty: A Study on Foreign Brand Beauty and Skin Care Products. In Economic, Educational, and Touristic Development in Asia (pp. 121-134). IGI Global. doi:10.4018/978-1-7998-2239-4.ch006

Abdul-Talib, A. N., & Mohd Adnan, M. M. (2017). Determinants of consumer's willingness to boycott surrogate products. *Journal of Islamic Marketing*, *8*(3), 345–360. doi:10.1108/JIMA-08-2015-0065

Ahmad, S. N. B., & Juhdi, N. (2008). Consumer's perception and purchase intentions towards organic food products: Exploring the attitude among Malaysian consumers. *16th Annual Conference on Pacific Basin Finance, Economics, Accounting and Management*.

Ahn, J., & Kwon, J. (2019). Green hotel brands in Malaysia: Perceived value, cost, anticipated emotion, and revisit intention. *Current Issues in Tourism*, *23*(12), 1–16. doi:10.1080/13683500.2019.1646715

Alesia, S. G., Stephen, L. S., & Geoffrey, H. T. (2014). Consumption values, environmental concern, attitude and purchase intention in the context of organic products. In *2014 International Conference of the Association of Global Management Studies*. Said Business School, University of Oxford, UK.

Amin, S., & Tarun, M. T. (2020). Effect of consumption values on customers' green purchase intention: A mediating role of green trust. *Social Responsibility Journal*. doi:10.1108rj-05-2020-0191

Aziz, M. F. B. A., Mispan, M. S. B., & Doni, F. (2020). Organic Food Policy and Regulation in Malaysia: Development and Challenges. *Regulatory Issues in Organic Food Safety in the Asia Pacific*, 151–170. doi:10.1007/978-981-15-3580-2_10

Bayer, R. C., & Ke, C. (2013). Discounts and consumer search behavior: The role of framing. *Journal of Economic Psychology*, *39*, 215–224. doi:10.1016/j.joep.2013.08.003

Bødker, M., Gimpel, G., & Hedman, J. (2009). *The user experience of smart phones: A consumption values approach*. Paper presented at Global Mobility Roundtable, Cairo, Egypt.

Bostan, I., & Onofrei, M., Gavriluţă (Vatamanu), A. F., Toderaşcu, C., & Lazăr, C. M. (2019). An Integrated Approach to Current Trends in Organic Food in the EU. *Foods*, *8*(5), 144. doi:10.3390/foods8050144 PMID:31035453

Bradbury, K. E., Balkwill, A., Spencer, E. A., Roddam, A. W., Reeves, G. K., Green, J., Key, T. J., Beral, V., & Pirie, K. (2014). Organic food consumption and the incidence of cancer in a large prospective study of women in the United Kingdom. *British Journal of Cancer, 110*(9), 2321–2326. doi:10.1038/bjc.2014.148 PMID:24675385

Burcu, C., & Seda, Y. (2013). Investigating the relationship between consumption values and personal values of green product buyers. *International Journal of Economics and Management Sciences, 2*(12), 29–40.

Business Wire. (2020). *Global organic fresh food market 2019-2023: Evolving Opportunities*. Retrieved February 3, 2020, from https://www.businesswire.com/news/home/20200107005947/en/Global-Organic-Fresh-Food-Market-2019-2023-Evolving

Candan, B., & Yıldırım, S. (2013). Investigating the relationship between consumption values and personal values of green product buyers. *International Journal of Economics and Management Sciences, 2*(12), 29–40.

Chen, A., & Peng, N. (2012). Green hotel knowledge and tourists' staying behavior. *Annals of Tourism Research, 39*(4), 2211–2216. doi:10.1016/j.annals.2012.07.003

Danish, M., Ali, S., Ahmad, M. A., & Zahid, H. (2019). The influencing factors on choice behavior regarding green electronic products: Based on the green perceived value model. *Economies, 7*(4), 99. doi:10.3390/economies7040099

Dettmann, R. L., & Dimitri, C. (2010). Who's buying organic vegetables? Demographic characteristics of US consumers. *Journal of Food Products Marketing, 16*(1), 79–91. doi:10.1080/10454440903415709

Dickson, M. (2001). Utility of no sweat labels for apparel consumers: Profiling label users and predicting their purchases. *The Journal of Consumer Affairs, 35*(1), 96–119. doi:10.1111/j.1745-6606.2001.tb00104.x

Ghali, Z., & Hamdi, R. (2015). The purchase and consumption motivations of an organic product by the Tunisian consumer: An application on the prickly pear seed oil (PPS). *Journal of North African Research in Business, 11*, 211–233. doi:10.5171/2015.220428

Groening, C., Sarkis, J., & Zhu, Q. (2018). Green marketing consumer-level theory review: A compendium of applied theories and further research directions. *Journal of Cleaner Production, 172*, 1848–1866. doi:10.1016/j.jclepro.2017.12.002

Hansmann, R., Baur, I., & Binder, R. (2020). Increasing organic food consumption: An integrating model of drivers and barriers. *Journal of Cleaner Production, 275*, 123058. doi:10.1016/j.jclepro.2020.123058

Hessami, H. Z., & Yousefi, P. (2013). Investigation of major factors influencing green purchasing behavior: Interactive approach. *European Online Journal of Natural and Social Sciences, 2*(4), 584–596.

Hsu, S. Y., Chang, C. C., & Lin, T. T. (2016). An analysis of purchase intentions toward organic food on health consciousness and food safety with/under structural equation modeling. *British Food Journal, 118*(1), 200–216. doi:10.1108/BFJ-11-2014-0376

Hung, K.-P., Chen, A. H., Peng, N., Hackley, C., Tiwsakul, R. A., & Chou, C.-L. (2011). Antecedents of luxury brand purchase intention. *Journal of Product and Brand Management, 20*(6), 457–467. doi:10.1108/10610421111166603

Issock-Issock, P. B., Mpinganjira, M., & Roberts-Lombard, M. (2019). Modelling green customer loyalty and positive word of mouth. *International Journal of Emerging Markets, 15*(3), 405–426. doi:10.1108/IJOEM-09-2018-0489

Jeyakumar-Nathan, R., Soekmawati, Victor, V., Popp, J., Fekete-Farkas, M., & Oláh, J. (2021). Food Innovation Adoption and Organic Food Consumerism—A Cross National Study between Malaysia and Hungary. *Foods, 10*(2), 363. doi:10.3390/foods10020363 PMID:33562411

Katt, F., & Meixner, O. (2020). A systematic review of drivers influencing consumer willingness to pay for organic food. *Trends in Food Science & Technology, 100*, 374–388. doi:10.1016/j.tifs.2020.04.029

Kaur, P., Dhir, A., Talwar, S., & Ghuman, K. (2021). The value proposition of food delivery apps from the perspective of theory of consumption value. *International Journal of Contemporary Hospitality Management*. doi:10.1108/ijchm-05-2020-0477

Kekec, P., Thongpapanl, N., & Auh, S. (2015). Unveiling the Influence of the consumer wine appreciation dimension on purchasing behavior. In K. Kubacki (Ed.), *Ideas in marketing: Finding the new and polishing the old--developments in marketing science. Proceedings of the Academy of Marketing Science*. Springer. 10.1007/978-3-319-10951-0_242

Lee, K. (2008). Opportunities for green marketing: Young consumers. *Marketing Intelligence & Planning, 26*(6), 573–586. doi:10.1108/02634500810902839

Lien, C. Y., Huang, C. W., & Chang, H. J. (2012). The influence of green consumption cognition of consumers on behavioral intention: A case study of the restaurant service industry. *African Journal of Business Management, 6*(26), 7888.

Lim, F. W., Ahmad, F., & Abdul-Talib, A. N. (2019). Behavioural Intention towards Using Electronic Wallet: A Conceptual Framework in the Light of the Unified Theory of Acceptance and Use of Technology (UTAUT). *Imperial Journal of Interdisciplinary Research, 5*(1), 79–86.

Lin, J., Guo, J., Turel, O., & Liu, S. (2020). Purchasing organic food with social commerce: An integrated food-technology consumption values perspective. *International Journal of Information Management, 51*, 102033. doi:10.1016/j.ijinfomgt.2019.11.001

Lin, P., Huang, Y., & Wang, J. (2010). Applying the theory of consumption values to choice behavior toward green products. *Management of Innovation and Technology (ICMIT), 2010 IEEE International Conference on IEEE*, 348-353. 10.1109/ICMIT.2010.5492714

Lin, P. C., & Huang, Y. H. (2012). The influence factors on choice behavior regarding green products based on the theory of consumption values. *Journal of Cleaner Production, 22*(1), 11–18. doi:10.1016/j.jclepro.2011.10.002

Liu, R., Pieniak, Z., & Verbeke, W. (2013). Consumers' attitudes and behavior towards safe food in China: A review. *Food Control, 33*(1), 93–104. doi:10.1016/j.foodcont.2013.01.051

Luomala, H., Puska, P., Lähdesmäki, M., Siltaoja, M., & Kurki, S. (2020). Get some respect – buy organic foods! When everyday consumer choices serve as prosocial status signaling. *Appetite*, *145*, 104492. doi:10.1016/j.appet.2019.104492 PMID:31654656

Misra, R., Singh, S., & Mahajan, R. (2020). An analysis on consumer preference of ayurvedic products in Indian market. *International Journal of Asian Business and Information Management*, *11*(4), 1–15. doi:10.4018/IJABIM.2020100101

Mohamad, S. S., Rusdi, S. D., & Hashim, N. H. (2014). Organic food consumption among urban consumers: Preliminary results. *Procedia: Social and Behavioral Sciences*, *130*, 509–514. doi:10.1016/j.sbspro.2014.04.059

Molinillo, S., Vidal-Branco, M., & Japutra, A. (2020). Understanding the drivers of organic foods purchasing of millennials: Evidence from Brazil and Spain. *Journal of Retailing and Consumer Services*, *52*, 101926. doi:10.1016/j.jretconser.2019.101926

Nguyen, H. V., Nguyen, N., Nguyen, B. K., Lobo, A., & Vu, P. A. (2019). Organic food purchases in an emerging market: The influence of consumers' personal factors and green marketing practices of food stores. *International Journal of Environmental Research and Public Health*, *16*(6), 1037. Advance online publication. doi:10.3390/ijerph16061037 PMID:30909390

O'cass, A., & Frost, H. (2002). Status brands: Examining the effects of non-product-related brand associations on status and conspicuous consumption. *Journal of Product and Brand Management*, *11*(2), 67–88. doi:10.1108/10610420210423455

O'Cass, A., & Siahtiri, V. (2013). In search of status through brands from Western and Asian origins: Examining the changing face of fashion clothing consumption in Chinese young adults. *Journal of Retailing and Consumer Services*, *20*(6), 505–515. doi:10.1016/j.jretconser.2013.05.005

Phau, I., Quintal, V., & Shanka, T. (2014). Examining a consumption values theory approach of young tourists toward destination choice intentions. *International Journal of Culture, Tourism and Hospitality Research*, *8*(2), 125–139. doi:10.1108/IJCTHR-12-2012-0090

Qasim, H., Yan, L., Guo, R., Saeed, A., & Ashraf, B. (2019). The defining role of environmental self-identity among consumption values and behavioral intention to consume organic food. *International Journal of Environmental Research and Public Health*, *16*(7), 1106. doi:10.3390/ijerph16071106 PMID:30925666

Ramkissoon, H., Nunkoo, R., & Gursoy, D. (2009). How consumption values affect destination image formation. Perspectives on cross-cultural, ethnographic, brand image, storytelling, unconscious needs, and hospitality guest research. *Advances in Culture Tourism and Hospitality Research*, *3*, 143–168.

Saleki, R., Quoquab, F., & Mohammad, J. (2019). What drives Malaysian consumers' organic food purchase intention? The role of moral norm, self-identity, environmental concern and price consciousness. *Journal of Agribusiness in Developing and Emerging Economies*, *9*(5), 584–603. doi:10.1108/JADEE-02-2019-0018

Samson, A., & Voyer, B. G. (2014). Emergency purchasing situations: Implications for consumer decision-making. *Journal of Economic Psychology*, *44*, 21–33. doi:10.1016/j.joep.2014.05.004

Sharma, S. (2019). The role of perceived value and gender on customers' purchase intention of ride sharing services. *International Journal of Asian Business and Information Management, 10*(4), 31–46. doi:10.4018/IJABIM.2019100103

Sheth, J. N., Newman, B. I., & Gross, B. L. (1991). Why we buy what we buy: A theory of consumption values. *Journal of Business Research, 22*(2), 159–170. doi:10.1016/0148-2963(91)90050-8

Shevlin, H. (2020). Rethinking creative intelligence: Comparative psychology and the concept of creativity. *European Journal for Philosophy of Science, 11*(1), 16. Advance online publication. doi:10.100713194-020-00323-8

Solaiman, M., Halim, M. S. A., Manaf, A. H. A., & Nor Azila, M. N., Noor, & Raña, S. M. S. (2017). Consumption values and green purchase behavior: An empirical study. *International Business Management, 11*(6), 1223–1233.

Somasundram, C., Razali, Z., & Santhirasegaram, V. (2016). A review on organic food production in Malaysia. *Horticulturae, 2*(3), 12–18. doi:10.3390/horticulturae2030012

Suki, N. M. (2016). Consumer environmental concern and green product purchase in Malaysia: Structural effects of consumption values. *Journal of Cleaner Production, 132*, 204–214. doi:10.1016/j.jclepro.2015.09.087

Tan, L. L., Abd Aziz, N., & Ngah, A. H. (2020). Mediating effect of reasons on the relationship between altruism and green hotel patronage intention. *Journal of Marketing Analytics, 8*(1), 18–30. Advance online publication. doi:10.105741270-020-00067-7

Tapachai, N., & Waryszak, R. (2000). An examination of the role of beneficial image in tourist destination selection. *Journal of Travel Research, 39*(1), 37–44. doi:10.1177/004728750003900105

Teng, Y. M., Wu, K. S., & Liu, H. H. (2015). Integrating altruism and the theory of planned behavior to predict patronage intention of a green hotel. *Journal of Hospitality & Tourism Research (Washington, D.C.), 39*(3), 299–315. doi:10.1177/1096348012471383

Teoh, W. C., & Nor Azila, M. N. (2015). The importance of consumers' attitudes towards purchase intention of hybrid car in Malaysia. *Academic Research International, 6*(4), 111–122.

Thomé, K. M., Cappellesso, G., & Pinho, G. M. (2020). Food consumption values and the influence of physical activity. *British Food Journal, 123*(3), 943–957. doi:10.1108/BFJ-05-2020-0432

Tiraieyari, N., Hamzah, A., & Samah, B. A. (2014). Organic farming and sustainable agriculture in Malaysia: Organic farmers' challenges towards adoption. *Asian Social Science, 10*(4), 1–7. doi:10.5539/ass.v10n4p1

Tully, S. M., & Winer, R. S. (2014). The role of the beneficiary in willingness to pay for socially responsible products: A meta-analysis. *Journal of Retailing, 90*(2), 255–274. doi:10.1016/j.jretai.2014.03.004

Turel, O., Serenko, A., & Bontis, N. (2010). User acceptance of hedonic digital artifacts: A theory of consumption values perspective. *Information & Management, 47*(1), 53–59. doi:10.1016/j.im.2009.10.002

Wang, J., Pham, T. L., & Dang, V. T. (2020). Environmental consciousness and organic food purchase intention: A moderated mediation model of perceived food quality and price sensitivity. *International Journal of Environmental Research and Public Health, 17*(3), 850. doi:10.3390/ijerph17030850 PMID:32013260

Wang, L., Gao, Y., Yan, J., & Qin, J. (2020). From freemium to premium: the roles of consumption values and game affordance. *Information Technology & People*. doi:10.1108/itp-10-2019-0527

Wang, X., Pacho, F., Liu, J., & Kajungiro, R. (2019). Factors influencing organic food purchase intention in developing countries and the moderating role of knowledge. *Sustainability, 11*(1), 209. doi:10.3390u11010209

Wee, C. S., Ariff, M. S. B. M., Zakuan, N., Tajudin, M. N. M., Ismail, K., & Ishak, N. (2014). Consumer's perception, purchase intention and actual purchase behaviour of organic food products. *Review of Integrative Business and Economics Research, 3*(2), 378–397.

Wekeza, S., & Sibanda, M. (2019). Factors influencing consumer purchase intentions of organically grown products in shelly centre, Port Shepstone, South Africa. *International Journal of Environmental Research and Public Health, 16*(6), 956. doi:10.3390/ijerph16060956 PMID:30884921

Werner, P. (2004). Reasoned action and planned behaviour. In S. J. Peterson & T. S. Bredow (Eds.), *Middle range theories: Application to nursing research* (pp. 125–147). Lippincott, Williams & Wilkins.

Williams, P., & Soutar, G. N. (2009). Value, satisfaction and behavioral intentions in an adventure tourism context. *Annals of Tourism Research, 36*(3), 413–438. doi:10.1016/j.annals.2009.02.002

Wong, K. H., Chang, H. H., & Yeh, C. H. (2019). The effects of consumption values and relational benefits on smartphone brand switching behavior. *Information Technology & People, 32*(1), 217–243. doi:10.1108/ITP-02-2018-0064

Woo, E., & Kim, Y. G. (2019). Consumer attitudes and buying behavior for green food products. *British Food Journal, 121*(2), 320–332. doi:10.1108/BFJ-01-2018-0027

Yeo, B. L., Mohamed, R., Hj, N., & Muda, M. (2016). A study of Malaysian customers purchase motivation of halal cosmetics retail products: Examining theory of consumption value and customer satisfaction. *Procedia Economics and Finance, 37*, 176–182. doi:10.1016/S2212-5671(16)30110-1

Yu, S., & Lee, J. (2019). The Effects of Consumers' Perceived Values on Intention to Purchase Upcycled Products. *Sustainability, 11*(4), 1034. doi:10.3390u11041034

Zaidi, S. M. M. R., Lai, Y., Bhutto, M. Y., Ali, R., & Fahad, A. (2019). The influence of consumption values on green purchase intention: A moderated mediation of greenwash perceptions and green trust. *Pakistan Journal of Commerce and Social Sciences, 13*(4), 826–848.

Zailani, S., Iranmanesh, M., Sean Hyun, S., & Ali, M. (2019). Applying the theory of consumption values to explain drivers' willingness to pay for biofuels. *Sustainability, 11*(3), 668. doi:10.3390u11030668

Zakaria, N. (Ed.). (2016). *Handbook of research on impacts of international business and political affairs on the global economy*. IGI Global. doi:10.4018/978-1-4666-9806-2

Zakaria, N., & Amelinckx, A. (2020). *Transcending Cultural Frontiers*. Springer Singapore. doi:10.1007/978-981-15-4454-5

Zamani, S. N. M., Abdul-Talib, A. N., & Ashari, H. (2016). Strategic orientations and new product success: The mediating impact of innovation speed. International Information Institute Information, 19(7B), 2785-2790.

Chapter 10
Practicing Circular Economy in India:
Insights of Business Models on the Three Paradigms – Reduce, Reuse, and Recycle

Namita Kapoor
https://orcid.org/0000-0001-9661-1700
Amity University, Noida, India

Sangeeta Jauhari
Rabindranath Tagore University, India

Deepti Maheshwari
Rabindranath Tagore University, India

ABSTRACT

Circularity concept is not just recycling. It is basically a system that is restorative in the industrial processes that treat waste as a resource. It implies that once a product reaches the end of life, attempts should be made to utilize them by creating a value out of it. The present study is an exploratory study that aims at exploring the lessons of circular economy, which India can share with others through the analysis of business models of companies for the three paradigms: reduce, reuse, and recycle. For understanding the take-make-dispose model to take-make-reduce model, the analysis of business model of El Rhino has been carried out. For take-make-recycle model, business model of Saahas Zero Waste and Goonj as unique business models displaying an outstanding effect of share-reuse-prolong model has been studied.

INTRODUCTION

Indian society has always practiced circularity involving repair, reuse, and recycling products. With the rise in consumerism and increase in affordability there has been frequent replacement of assets which has increased the waste as well as retarded the adoption of circular economy. At every stage of value chain

DOI: 10.4018/978-1-7998-8678-5.ch010

there is requirement of the application of 5Rs: Reduce, Recycle, Reuse, Refurnish and Re- manufacture. The success of adoption of circular economy depends largely on consumer's awareness, mindset, and readiness to participate in it.

The tradition growth model of India was basically predicted through the "linear Model" economic model which is functioning against the limited resources of our planet. Also, this model generated massive waste in every stage of the product life cycle. For the growth of manufacturing sector, it is required that we should not only use the scarce resources diligently but also substitute the primary resources with secondary through the efficient management of secondary resource. Circular Economy can help in achieving this through operating in a closed loop to minimize the leakage or wastage of resources as less as possible through Sharing, Leasing, Repairing, Refurbishing and Recycling.

Circularity concept is not just recycling it is basically a system which is restorative in the industrial processes which treats the waste as a resource. It implies that once a product's life ends, attempts should be made to utilize them by creating a value out of it (Ellen Mc Arthur 2015). The transition from tradition to circular requires the changes in the functioning of organizations and reshaping of the supply chain process by infusing the mindset of sustainability in product designers. Circular Economy is a "economic model aimed at the efficient use of resources through waste minimization, long-term value retention, reduction of primary resources, and closed loops of products, product parts, and materials within the boundaries of environmental protection and socioeconomic benefits" Morseletto (2020). The Circular Business Model is the rationale of how an organization, creates, delivers, and captures value with and within the closed material loops. The present study is an exploratory study that aims at exploring the lessons of Circular Economy which India can share with others through the analysis of Business Models of companies for the three traditional paradigms of circular economy: Reduce, Reuse and Recycle. The circular Business model requires that products and or service should decrease environmental impact, increase social and economic benefits. The product or service must be more aligned to customer needs. In terms of value creation there should be significant changes in the value chain, product design such that repairability, durability, upgradation is possible. It requires the relationship strong among stake holders-retailers, suppliers, producers and even consumers. In terms of value capture, the new offering should also have new cost and new revenue models. For developing the case studies, we have used a traditional reduce, reuse and recycle principles of circular economy which specifies Reduce in the use/ consumption of non-renewable energy sources/resource and toxic resources, Reuse of products/service through innovations in design, processes, and business models and Recycle of waste into new resource for manufacturing or consumption.

UNDERSTANDING PROCESSES IN CIRCULAR ECONOMY: LITERATURE REVIEW

Recycling is "the re- introduction of residual materials into production processes so that they may be re formulated into the new products" UN 2003. This definition implies that recycling should not only emphases on recovering materials but also should focus on utilization of these materials to the new life cycle. The main requisite to achieve the introduction of recycled material is that the recycling should be of high quality. Recycling should also be done to reduce waste. Recycling can benefit business in terms of reduction in cost / minimization of cost for businesses that depend on primary materials. The price volatility of primary raw materials can be reduced through recycling (WEF et al 2014). Petrochemical substances can be recovered through recycling of plastic waste which can be used for manufacturing the plastics again or for manufacturing other chemicals (Hopewell et al. 2009). The development of plastic or chemical recycling involves the use and development of more viable innovations in technology (EMF,2016). Recycling can also be considered as a use of biological resource, which requires that the industries synchronizes across the supply chain and use the byproducts or wastages of production from other sectors (Jacobsen 2006; Velázquez2019). The decrease in the utilization and consumption of nonrenewable resources and energy by means of sharing or recycling happens only through the industrial symbiosis (Minunno,2020) There is a major difference between recycle and re use. Recycling requires the reprocessing of material or waste into new material, product or substance. The utilization of the treated water resource is also referred commonly as "Water recycling" and "water reuse" (Lazarova et al 2012).United Nations has defined recycling as the process of re-introduction of residual materials back into the production processes so that they are utilized to form new product. For many decades, this has been the most appropriate method of implementing circular economy principles by capturing the value of the existing products and materials and at the same time decreasing the use of primary materials. Recycling is defined as the "reprocessing of recovered material at the end of life returning them into supply chain" (Garcia, 2019)

Many studies have shown that consumers are the most essential actor and the main driving factor for the quality of the waste collection as well as the collection rate (Krook & Eklund, 2010; Ylä- Mella, 2015; Wagner & Lane 2013). Recycling has become a norm in many communities across the world. It is now seen as a common activity in which individuals and households carry out or promote recycling of particularly dry recyclables (i.e. paper, glass plastics and cans). The fact that some people prefer to recycle waste whereas some prefer against is still very much debatable as mentioned in a few papers. The conclusions drawn from these papers include a range of disciplinary perspectives, such as psychology, sociology and marketing. The knowledge of how to recycle as well as the access to recycling components and provision of services (e.g. recycling centers) plays a vital role in whether people recycle. Public education programs about recycling for younger adults and convenient recycling for older adults have been seen to have a positive impact on the willingness to recycle electronic waste (Saphores et al., 2012). The convenience of recycling is very important in order to maximize consumer participation to increase waste collection amounts. The term convenience is a subjective construct and therefore individuals have different recognitions of a convenient collection system (Wagner & Lane, 2013). Many researchers have stated that the willingness of consumers to recycle increases if the convenience to recycle is adequate.

Recycling behavior is based around the acceptance of normative behavior along with the perceived benefits of recycling as well knowledge of recycling services (Barr et al., 2001). The author concluded that recycling is not a value-based behavior. Waste minimization and reuse behaviors are undertaken by only a minority of the citizens. According to Tucker and Douglas (2007) concluded that there exists a strong link between waste prevention behavior and the acceptance of personal responsibility. If there are emotional aspects involved (such as embarrassment and guilt) rather than an individual's sense of duty, there is a higher chance for a waste prevention behavior. Consumers are willing to reduce waste generation only if certain emotional aspects are involved. Reduction in the extraction of primary resources through recycling can add towards multiple environmental benefits (EEA, 2016). It can also help reduce greenhouse gas emissions associated with material resource use. It is understood that there exists a direct relation between resource used and climate change. (Minunno,2020). The atmosphere is the largest dumping site for global waste as greenhouse gas emissions account for about 83 percent by weight of global material output (Taranis et al., 2016).

The definition provided by the United Nations (2003), for recycling should not be understood only as a process of mere recovery of materials, but also as a redirection towards the next lifecycle for the recovered materials. The issue of quality is very important and achieving high quality recycling is a prerequisite for effectively re-introducing materials in the process for production. Increased recycling can prove to be very cost-effective for industries. Those sectors that depend on primary materials could although find it a little difficult. Also, the use of secondary materials may decrease the need to purchase or extract primary materials. The use of recycled material could lead to reduction in price volatility associated with primary raw materials and the dependency on imports of materials (World Economic Forum et al., 2014).For example, the recycling of critical raw materials (CRMs) which are frequently imported from third world countries (European Commission, 2008). Chemical recycling of plastic waste is an interesting example related to the context of the previous information. This process involves the recovery of the petrochemical constituents of the polymer for it to be used for plastics re-manufacturing or that matter, production of other synthetic chemicals (Hopewell et al., 2009). It must be taken into consideration that further growth of chemical recycling would require the development of economically viable innovative technologies and addressing the presence of substances of concern in plastics (Ellen MacArthur Foundation, 2017; European Commission, 2015).

The **efficient use of resources** can result in the less usage of primary resources and using the resources carefully which are harmful, and their life is also short (Nilsson et al 2007, Unposed, 2006). The efficient use of resource is often considered to be a part of cleaner production which is basically conservation of raw materials, less use of raw materials, reducing the consumption of scarce resources- water and energy, avoiding the use of toxic materials in production and reducing waste and hazardous emissions leading to the decrease in effect -in the entire life chain (since extraction of primary resource to its final disposal (Hilson 2003). The reduction in effects are on environment, health and safety. (UNEP 2001). The "Eco-Design "has been linked with improving the efficient use of resource as it can cover all the aspects including- recycling, extending the product –life and remanufacturing. It also benefits the other aspect of de materialization (Almeida et al. 2010). The efficiency in usage of resources can also be achieved through reduction of waste in production (all stage including production, processing, packaging, transporting) as well as consumption, through this the environmental effects can also be minimized (Pimentel et. Al 2008, EMF2015)

The basic requirement for transiting to circular economy from linear is the maximum use of an energy source should be one which is **renewable**. The use of non – renewable energy source is huge, and it has multiple negative impacts on environmental hazards and most import is the dependence on imports (Rizos et al. 2017). There is availability of large number of renewable energy alternatives for replacing the traditional fossil fuels in different sectors. The use of these energy reduces the negative environmental, economic and social effects associated with traditional non- renewable energy sources, but it also has some challenges in terms of use of certain metals which may increase the dependence on imports. The alternate source of energy can also be generated through waste.

Recycling is very much limited in its ability to conserve the value of products at the material level. In many situations value could be preserved at the level of components or even in the case of complete products, thus reducing the amount of energy and labour that would have been wasted into making the products. Therefore, it can be said that recycling can only tackle a few of the issues related to resource scarcity and price volatility (Benton & Hazell, 2013). Hence, it is important to look towards the opportunity to preserve the value of products, such that not only the material value is recovered, but the labour, energy, investment and other types of inputs are recovered as well.

The most viable solution to that would be reuse of components within the circular economy. At its best, higher value preservation through reuse within a circular economy restores the products and components that have reached their end state back to their original state. Also, it restores them to their original state in a way that consumes the least amount of resources to deliver the same or improved function. This causes the preservation of value of the products at the highest level and reduces the level of risk that is associated with price volatility, resource scarcity, energy demand, and environmental impact (Circular,2015; Ikiz,2021). When looking at the preservation of this value at the end-of-use, the study It was found that for many of the products, reuse instead of recycling provided the highest value recovery to businesses and the greatest mitigation of risk (Benton & Hazell, 2013).

Reuse of products can lead to lesser quantity of waste generation which is a very important consideration for the future economy. The make-use-dispose method is not sustainable, and we cannot rely on it much longer. Recycling of products has gained momentum over the past decade or so and consumers consider recycling a better option than reuse in certain cases. A study suggested that the monetary value of raw materials derived from recycling a product is generally only about a fraction of the monetary value of the product if it is reused. So, the value created by the costs of labour, energy and capital goods during production disappears when products are recycled instead of reused (Bastien et. al., 2013). For example, in the case of smartphones, reusing the products provides a value of 290 British pounds (about half of the original product value), whereas the recycling value is only 72 pence. This indicates that the option of reuse could even prove to be more profitable for certain industries that recycling (Branca et al, 2020).

Reuse of products such as repairing or even remanufacturing proves to be more labour intensive than manufacturing. So, technically, greater reuse of a product will require significantly higher labour inputs and increase the need for creating more jobs in the economy (Deromedi, et al., 2014). Although reusing a product sounds an easy task to carry out, in application it is not all that easy. Furthermore, the increasing complexity of products makes it a challenge for effective and efficient recovery and reuse of products (European Commission, 2010).

Organizations must take the lead for a change to happen in the functioning of the economy. The processes and activities carried out by industries need to be streamlined in a manner that reusing products becomes easy for everyone. Fundamentally, it looks achievable, but companies are not yet convinced about the business case for high-value reuse activities. Organizations believe that the reuse of products could lead to the cannibalization of the new products that the company introduces into the market (Bastien et. al, 2013). Steps can be taken towards changing the view of companies and assuring them of their returns. It is extremely important for organizations to switch to reusing products, only then can a circular economy be successfully implemented.

The **next life to the used product** is the key to achieve circularity. This can be achieved through remanufacturing, re using or refurbishment. The material's value added is restored through the "core parts" through **remanufacturing** and **refurbishment**. Re manufacturing in an in-depth procedure to provide a discarded product as "new" product while refurbishment is just restoring a product's or its component's value (Weelden et. A. 2016). **Reuse** is just a re-selling or re usability of the product or its part (JRC, 2011b). All these processes generate the flow pf revenue for the business as they provide an opportunity to generate income by selling for many times (or at least a second time). Expensive parts are commonly used for **re-manufacturing** of goods like mobiles, cars, computers (EAF 2013a). This aspect is already being covered during the product designing phase and is related to the eco- friendly practices of the businesses (Bocken et al. 2015). Remanufacturing has both environmental as well as economic benefits (Pigosso et. al2010). The EMF (2013a) has projected that refurbishment can decrease the global iron –ore demand to around 4-6% by year 2025. Remanufacturing insists that corporates must retain their control over there produce and things and design proper buy back or take back procedures or process or system and the post-use stage of the good. This also requires the consumer's behavioral change to return their product to the manufacturer only (Prendiville et al 2015). Remanufacturing can also help in job creation in small firms as it is labor intensive which require the technician or the crafts men at the local level (EEA 2016). Job may further be created as remanufacturing requires the training and education to generate skillset for integrating design and remanufacturing to product life extension. (Gray et al 2006).

Providing a product life extension is much broader concept than designing **for reuse or remanufacturing**. Product life extension also addresses to the concept of providing long life- durability to the product. These products are designed for durability and concentrate on the customer services (Bocken et al 2016). There is no doubt regarding the environmental benefits from product life extension, but the major drawback is that it may affect the market for new technically upgraded products. (Novel et al. 2014). Reduction in the quantity of waste generated is at the heart of a circular economy. Waste management is a difficult task. Large quantities of waste are generated each day across the world. Most of it is dumped into lakes, rivers and oceans. Some of it is sent for waste disposal treatment whereas a certain quantity is recycled. For a circular economy to be successful, waste management must be effective, and the quantity of waste generated must be minimum. It takes up a lot of energy to dispose waste. There was a study conducted for the economy of the United Kingdom which suggested a potential of cost savings of up to £18 billion by reduction of waste for one year. The study also concluded that by reducing waste and improving material-resource efficiency the construction sector could potentially save up to £2,601 million for the year 2009 and lead to a reduction in greenhouse gas emissions (Hollins, 2011).

Preventing waste generation along the life-cycle stages of production and consumption can help avoid the loss of resources and minimize environmental impacts associated with waste management. In the food sector, significant quantities of food are wasted, new technologies such as precision farming, effective surplus management and educational measures can help prevent the generation of waste in the supply chain. Additionally, in agriculture there are several measures available to improve the efficiency of the use of phosphorus and reduce its inputs, such as optimization of land use, improvement of fertilizer application techniques and adjustment of livestock densities to available land (Schröder et al., 2011,). The food sector is one where more efficient processes could lead to a decrease in the consumption of energy resources (Stillitano,2021). Reduction in the waste generation in the US food system could lead to reduction in the fossil fuels used as input in the system (Pimentel et al., 2008).

Efficient use of resources can lead to the less use of primary resources. This process is aimed towards the concept of cleaner production that focuses on achieving material and energy resources efficiency in processes (UNEP &Sida, 2006). It also involves the careful use of resources and the replacement of resources that are hazardous or have a short life span (Nilsson et al., 2007). The term cleaner production refers to improvements in industrial production processes and products. Improvement in industrial production includes raw material conservation, reduced material inputs, reductions in consumption of energy and water, avoidance of toxic substances in processes and reduction of toxic emissions and waste. Cleaner production in the case of products includes reduction of impacts (environmental, health and safety) along the whole life chain (from raw material extraction to the final disposal) (Hinterberger & Schneider, 2001; Hilson, 2003; UNEP, 2001). A reduction in energy consumption and waste generation is very necessary going forward. The concept of circular clearly emphasizes the importance of preventing food wastage as a key step towards environmental sustainability. The European Commission has been actively involved in supporting several initiatives aimed at improving the sustainability of food waste management in Europe (Garcia et al., 2017).

The five Rs that fit into circular economy as described in Table 1 as follows:

Table 1. 5Rs circular economy process

Reduce	Reuse	Recycle	Re-manufacture	Repair / refurbish:
• Efficient utilization of primary resources • Use of renewable energy sources	• **reuse** the useful parts / components of a product, • to promote greater use of product-as-a-service through Sharing platforms.	• Creation of a closed loop system to utilize waste/ discarded material as a source of secondary resource, through extensive recycling	**Creating** new products by utilizing waste multi-sector industry co-operation and coordination.	Extension and preservation of product's life by innovative designs for the future. (ensuring it at the time of designing) Which in usage- - maximize the lifetime through repair, refurbish and upgrade and may extend a second life through take back strategy

Source: Author's Compilation

RESEARCH METHODOLOGY

The present study is an exploratory study that aims at understanding the concept of Circular Economy- the case studies of businesses using the three main Principles of Circular Economy- Reduce, Reuse and Recycle. The case study approach has been used to study the examples of Circularity framework of reduce, reuse, and recycle paradigms in India. "A business model describes the rationale of how an organization creates, delivers, and captures value" (Osterwalder, 2010). For analyzing the business models, the canvas proposed by Osterwalder and Pigneur (2010) is used. The details of the businesses used to understand the experience of Indian Business on the three paradigms of Circular Economy is expressed in Table2.

CIRCULAR BUSINESS MODELS IN INDIA

The Circular Business Model is the rationale of how an organization, creates, delivers, and captures value with and within the closed material loops. The circular Business model requires that products and or service should decrease environmental impact, increase social and economic benefits. The product or service must be more aligned to customer needs. In terms of value creation there should be significant changes in the value chain, product design such that repairability, durability, upgradation is possible. It requires the relationship strong among stake holders-retailers, suppliers, producers and even consumers. In terms of value capture, the new offering should also have new cost and new revenue models.

For developing the case studies, we have used a 3R closed loop system comprising REDUCE, RE-USE and RECYCLE

Table 2. Paradigms of circular economy

Company	Product involved	Circular Business Model	Input
Saahas Zero Waste	Waste Management	Recycle	WASTE
Goonj	Urban Disposed -clothes and other items	REUSE	Clothes, Stationary, Other Utility items
El Rhino	Paper Manufacturing	Reduce	Elephant and Rhino Dung

Source: Author's Compilation

- Reducing the use/consumption of non-renewable energy sources/resource and toxic resources.
- Reuse of products/service through innovations in design, processes, and business models
- Recycle of waste into new resource for manufacturing or consumption.

For understanding the business from Take-Make -Dispose to **Take-Make-Reduce** model, case study of El Rhino company is being developed. The company manufacture paper from animal dung and reduces the use of trees in paper making. Take-Make-Dispose model to **Share-Reuse-Prolong** model, Goonj is a unique business model that displays an outstanding effect of the reuse paradigm.The third principle involves adopting the recycle paradigm-**Take- Make- Recycle Model**. The benefits from recycling includes extraction of resources, job opportunities and enhancement of social economic status of individuals. Saahas Zero Waste is an example for this paradigm. Saahas Zero Waste has well defined process of collection, recycling, and distribution of recycled components from e waste and plastic waste.

Circular Business Model: Reduce Paradigm

El Rhino: Dung Paper

The company manages the entire dung paper production chain including collection, preparation, processing, and sale of finished dung paper goods (Value Capture). El rhino dung paper is made by the families who live around the forests of Assam. They share their home with rhinos, elephants and a variety of diverse flora and fauna. The Company engage these indigenous folks to roam the woods and collect rhino and elephant poo, as well as leaves, grass, bark, and other forest materials. By combining dung, natural fibers, and forest materials to make paper, the company help to reduce deforestation and save energy. The company take pride in using an assortment of grass, jute, water hyacinth, pineapple bark, local ahimsa silk, vegetable inks, ferns, flowers, betel nuts, turmeric, tea leaves and dead tree bark to embellish their products. The company manufacture paper from animal dung and reduces the use of trees in paper making. Take-Make- Dispose model to **Take-Make-Reduce Model**, case study of El Rhino is an exemplary example of creating value to the business . The awareness programs conducted by El rhino, the motivation and guidance to tribal for their contribution in production of paper from animal waste shows strong relationship among the stake holders. The companies need has identified and developed the different channels which includes online stores, exhibition, NGO, and companies' website for reaching out to its valuable customers.

The approach followed by El Rhino contributes to circular economy through conservation of nonrenewable natural resources and recycling of animal waste for production of eco-friendly and sustainable products. The company has unique business model as explained in Table3, for manufacturing sustainable products using animal waster as the input. The Company differentiated its product from manufactured papers through changing the input and the production process.

Table 3. Circular economy- Principle; REDUCE- El Rhino

<table>
<tr><td rowspan="2">Key Partners
Online Stores, Retailers, Exporters, Tribes</td><td>Key Activities
Create jobs for and build the skills of people primarily women</td><td rowspan="2">Value Propositions
Notebooks with Printed Covers Medium, Notebooks with Printed Covers Small, Notebooks with Saree Covers Medium, Playing Cards, Shine Gift Bags and Shine Table Lamp</td><td>Customer Relationship
Eco-friendly and green model guarantees trust and committed relationship around organic and premium offerings for all income segments.</td><td rowspan="2">Customer Segment
Individual Customers, Corporates from India and abroad</td></tr>
<tr><td>Key Resources
Leadership, Expertise in circular design, low cost setup, Business idea is exclusive and unique</td><td>Channels
Online Stores, Company's website, NGO, Exhibitions</td></tr>
<tr><td colspan="3">Cost Structure
Setup of infrastructure, Operational Cost includes salaries, delivery channels, procurement), cost of raw material</td><td colspan="2">Revenue Structure
Exports and domestic sales of paper and related products</td></tr>
</table>

Source: Author's Compilation

The company has contributed significantly by providing employment opportunity and creating sustainable livelihood to the tribal community in the rural area. The company has positioned themselves as a green enterprise involved in production of sustainable products and circular business model. The business model of EL Rhino is unique as they have worked with the tribal community, trained them for manufacturing paper, and conducted awareness programs for acceptance of the product. The company have their reach to the global market and have developed a wide range of sustainable products and developed new product streams including customized products.

Table 4 exhibits the company's positives which include spreading awareness about the sustainable products that can be produced from animal waste. EL Rhino has exemplary contributed in terms of augmenting the income of rural tribal, their full- time development including skill development. It is a real life example for reduce paradigms, it has helped in saving trees, oil, landfill space, energy and carbon equivalent, reduced inequalities, encourages responsible production, improved life on earth.

Circular Business Model: Recycle Paradigm

SAAHAS Zero Waste

Saahas Zero Waste is registered as a "small" company under the micro, small and medium enterprises regulations in India. They are committed to be the face of environmental and social change in the waste management sector. This change is enabled through their business model which includes revenues from waste and revenues from a service fee. Saahas Zero Waste is a socio-environmental enterprise with 20 years of experience in waste management & resource recovery. SZW ensure maximum recovery of resources from all streams of waste by diverting it away from landfills and sending it to the right destinations.

Table 4. Overview: El Rhino

Principle of Circular economy- REDUCE	
Company	El Rhino
Founded	2014
Founded By	Mahesh Bora, Nisha Bora
Reach	India and International
Circular Economy	Reduce, Eliminate use of trees & Plants for manufacturing paper
Positives	Spread awareness, Augmented income of rural tribal, full time development, skill development, saved trees, oil, landfill space, energy and carbon equivalent, reduced inequalities, encourages responsible production, improved life on earth
Challenges	Lack of social awareness and inferior per caption towards the use of animal waste-based products. Social taboo being associated with enterprises using animal manure

Source: Company's Website

Saahas Zero Waste is a registered, empanelled vendor with the government in Bengaluru, Noida & Chennai to manage waste. SZW, instituted a Materials Recovery Facility in 2017, which has the capacity to manage about 16 tonnes of waste per day.

Currently, they work with 80+ clients across Bangalore, Chennai, Hyderabad, Mumbai, and Goa – and manage 77 tonnes of waste a day. Through their initiatives, they are in line with UN's Sustainable Development Goals (SDGs) to facilitate economic progress, women empowerment, and action against climate change.

The transformation of waste to new products and recovering of components or materials, minimize material leakage and maximization of the economic value are part of the recycle paradigm. It helps in restoring the mismatch between the demand and supply of virgin resources (Kapoor et al 2021, Yong,2007, Tse 2015).In alignment with the principles of circular economy, the company has welled defined process of collection, recycling, and distribution of recycled components from e waste and plastic waste with global standard. They have focussed on every aspect of circular economy eco-friendly reuse, refurbishment, and recycling and they manage 122 tonnes of waste every day. Saahas Zero Waste has positioned themselves as a setup that has end to end sustainable reuse and recycling of e-waste. They have conducted extensive awareness programs which include social media campaigns, corporate events and collection drives, consulting services for effective waste management and guidance on extended producer responsibility regarding their integral solution for safe disposal and efficient recycling for environment protection. The value proposition includes recycling solutions, reverse logistic network, association with companies under corporate social responsibility, manufacturing from recycled materials: producing bags and backpacks, clothing, stationery, and sustainable construction material (Table 6).

The value delivery involves reverse logistic channel and online store for recycled products. The value capture is the difference in cost structures and revenue models. The analysis of cost structure and revenue flows clearly indicate the value capture from the circular activities.

The Third principle involves adopting the recycle paradigm-**Take- Make- Recycle Model** . The benefits from recycling includes extraction of resources, job opportunities and enhancement of social economic status of individuals. Saahas Zero Waste is an example for this paradigm. It has welled defined process of collection, recycling, and distribution of recycled components from e waste and plastic waste.

Table 5. Circular economy - Principle; RECYCLE- SAAHAS zero waste

<table>
<tr>
<td rowspan="2">Key Partners
Individuals, corporate, grassroot organizations, social activists, NGO, social activists, panchayats, Technology, and knowledge partners</td>
<td>Key Activities
Collect, reuse, redistribution of urban waste into rural resource, mass awareness, training, mobilizing people for rural development(roads/ wells/schools) launched schemes like-Cloth for work, not just piece of cloth, school to school, Rahat and Green Goonj</td>
<td rowspan="2">Value Propositions
Offering dignity, hygiene, skill development, income generation, building local infrastructure job opportunities for women.
Maximum use of Cloth and avoiding it reaching the landfill thus preventing environmental disaster.</td>
<td>Customer Relationship
Organizing awareness and collection camps, local rural meetings, and engagement schemes</td>
<td rowspan="2">Customer Segment
Rural population of India, for green Goonj-Customers in India</td>
</tr>
<tr>
<td>Key Resources
Leadership, Scalability, Global Recognition, Partner network for collection, building awareness and distribution, outreach and expertise</td>
<td>Channels
Collection centers, Distribution channels-Individuals, corporate, grassroot organizations, social activists, NGO, social activists, panchayats, Technology and knowledge partners</td>
</tr>
<tr>
<td colspan="2">Cost Structure
Operational costs (collection, training, salaries, delivery channels) Transportation and logistics, local awareness building</td>
<td colspan="3">Revenue Structure
Philanthropic funding, individual contributions, sponsorships, self-generated revenues from sale of old newspapers and products created from recycled material.</td>
</tr>
</table>

Source: Authors Compilation

Table6. Overview - SAAHAS

Principle of Circular economy- RECYCLE	
Company	SAAHAS ZERO WASTE
Founded	Journey Started in 2000
Founded By	Founder and CEO, Wilma Rodrigues
Reach	India
Circular Economy	Recycle, Waste Management
Positives	Providing dignified labour and livelihood: ensuring Ensuring legal minimum wages to all Safe and healthy working conditions Formalization of waste industry Government prescribed working hours and leaves Financial inclusion, upskilling and career advancement Provision of social security benefits No discrimination and harassment. 98 % Recovery of waste into resources.
Challenges	Humanity is the biggest challenge to achieve. The change in focus of utilization of resources from linear to circular is desired so that they can meet the targets both at the environmental as well as social front

Source: Authors Compilation

Circular Business Model: Reuse Paradigm

GOONJ

Goonj is a unique business model that displays an outstanding effect of a reuse paradigm. Take-make-dispose model to **Share-Reuse-Prolong** model (Tse et al., 2015)

The model Goonj has been implementing offers dignity, hygiene, skill development, income generation, opportunities for villagers especially women, as well as local infrastructure development opportunities for underserved villagers (Table 7). Goonj created an eco-system where in excess/ discarded material/ resources are transferred from urban to rural (disaster struck areas). Goonj) exhibits the value proposition that the companies should design the products in such a way that multiple social and environmental needs can be addressed, and the use of a product may be extended to its full until it reaches the land fill.

Table 7. Circular economy- Principle; reuse- GOONJ

<table>
<tr>
<td rowspan="2">Key Partners
Individuals, corporate, grassroot organizations, social activists, NGO, social activists, panchayats, Technology, and knowledge partners</td>
<td>Key Activities
Collect, reuse, redistribution of urban waste into rural resource, mass awareness, training, mobilizing people for rural development(roads/ wells/schools) launched schemes like-Cloth for work, not just piece of cloth, school to school, Rahat and Green Goonj</td>
<td rowspan="2">Value Propositions
Offering dignity, hygiene, skill development, income generation, building local infrastructure job opportunities for women.
Maximum use of Cloth and avoiding it reaching the landfill thus preventing environmental disaster.</td>
<td>Customer Relationship
Organizing awareness and collection camps, local rural meetings, and engagement schemes</td>
<td rowspan="2">Customer Segment
Rural population of India, for green Goonj-Customers in India</td>
</tr>
<tr>
<td>Key Resources
Leadership, Scalability, Global Recognition, Partner network for collection, building awareness and distribution, outreach and expertise</td>
<td>Channels
Collection centers, Distribution channels- Individuals, corporate, grassroot organizations, social activists, NGO, social activists, panchayats, Technology and knowledge partners</td>
</tr>
<tr>
<td colspan="2">Cost Structure
Operational costs (collection, training, salaries, delivery channels)
Transportation and logistics, local awareness building</td>
<td colspan="3">Revenue Structure
Philanthropic funding, individual contributions, sponsorships, self-generated revenues from sale of old newspapers and products created from recycled material.</td>
</tr>
</table>

Source: Author's Compilation

Goonj's business model is driven largely by the urban surplus. They have served the basic need of people in rural area with dignity and has been working in the socio-economic as wells as physical infrastrucural development of the rural areas (Value Proposition). Goonj has focused on prolonged use of products through transferring of urban waste/surplus to the rural area and entering the landfills thereby contributing positively to the environment. They have their own generated revenue stream from selling their green products as well as their philanthropy funding (Value Capture)

Table 8. Overview- GOONJ

Principle of Circular economy- REUSE	
Company	Goonj
Year of foundation	1998
Founded	Anshu Gupta and Meenakshi Gupta
Reach	Rural India
Contribution to circular economy	Promote circular economy by ensuring maximum use of each material.
Positives	Goonj has built a network of communities from urban to village India, channelizing material as a tool to address crucial gaps in rural infrastructure, water, environment, livelihood, education, health, disaster relief and rehabilitation. Its engagement with both the urban and rural population has galvanized a mass civic participation in addressing basic but neglected issues. Goonj's model of development implemented through its various Initiatives proposes a more inclusive alternative economy where everyone is an equal stakeholder in the process 1.Operations in 25 States and Union Territories. 2. Reached out to 4600+ villages. 3. Mobilized 6200+ development activities under Cloth for Work initiative. 4. Dealt with 5.5 million Kgs (5500 Tons) of material out of which approx.780 tons of textile waste used to create innovative up cycled handmade products, Sujni, Aasan, My-Pad etc. 5. Reached out 248,400+ carefully designed 'Family Kits' comprising essentials impacting more than 1.2 million people. Out of which 101,100+ families reached out through our disaster relief and rehabilitation work under the initiative 'Rahat'. 6. Reached out to 93,000+ people under the initiative 'Not Just a Piece of Cloth.' Reached 1,240,700+ cloth sanitary pads (My Pads) and 101,300+ undergarments to women and adolescent girls. 7. Reached out to 147,400+ students under the initiative 'School to School'. 8. 650+ collection drives as awareness camps, stalls & book fairs across major urban hubs
Challenges	Lack of openness in rural areas towards discussion on women specific issues Infrastructure cost and complexities Demand -supply mismatch Transportation and logistics Technology orientation- computerization of data and systems

Source: Author's Compilation

Goonj is an outstanding example for circular, sustainable, and social innovation which uses regenerative and restoration measures through reuse, remanufacture and recycle of clothing and other discarded products of the urban area. Goonj has built a network of communities from urban to village India, channelizing material as a tool to address crucial gaps in rural infrastructure, water, environment, livelihood, education, health, disaster relief and rehabilitation. Its engagement with both the urban and rural population has galvanized a mass civic participation in addressing basic but neglected issues. Goonj's model of development implemented through its various Initiatives proposes a more inclusive alternative economy where everyone is an equal stakeholder in the process. The major challenge that Goonj faces is the lack of openness in rural areas towards discussion on women specific issues, infrastructure cost and complexities, demand -supply mismatch. (Table 5B)

CONCLUSION

Circular Economy is a concept that brings management, resources, and residues together for the wellbeing of Economy, Livelihood and Environment. The evaluation of these models is based on their value propositions, value creation, value delivery and value capture..The shift to circular economy requires the businesses to revamp their supply chains for the development of reverse cycles (Bocken et.al, 2019; Frishamma et al.,2019). The way of doing business must have a radical shift to maximize the value of product and material under resource scarcity (Bocken et.al, 2018; S Goyal et.al, 2018). Experimentation is a way for companies to learn how value is created, diverted, and captured in this radical shift and provide the knowledge stream (Bockenet.al, 2020) towards circularity. Innovation and resource strategy are the two important dimensions of shift from linear to circular (Mentink et.al, 2014; Blocken et.al 2021). The examples from India demonstrate all three types of social innovation (Goonj), community innovation (EL Rhino) and Business model innovation (Saahas Zero Waste). The experiences from the cases of Indian company (Goonj) exhibit the value proposition that the companies should design the products in such a way that multiple social and environmental needs can be addressed, and the use of a product may be extended to its full until it reaches the land fill. For the value creation, there is need of an hour for setting up an integrated reverse logistics by the companies for collecting raw materials and utilizing it in product or service. (Saahas Zero Waste). The awareness programs conducted by El Rhino, the motivation and guidance to tribal for their contribution in production of paper from animal waste are exemplary examples of creating value to the business. The companies need to identify and develop the suitable channel for reaching out to its valuable customers (Value delivery). The companies must look for different sources of flow of revenue from their targeted clientele- Goonj's target customers are people from underprivileged sectors but still apart from philanthropy they are also coming up with their retail online store Green Goonj to support their projects.

REFERENCES

ADEME (French Environment and Energy Management Agency). (2014). *Economie Circulaire: Notions*. Version modifiéeoctobre 2014.

Ajzen, I., & Fishbein, M. (1980). *Understanding attitudes and predicting social behaviour*. Prentice Hall.

Almeida, C. M. V. B., Rodrigues, A. J. M., Bonilla, S. H., & Giannetti, B. F. (2010). Emergy as a tool for Ecodesign: Evaluating materials selection for beverage packages in Brazil. *Journal of Cleaner Production, 18*(1), 32–43. doi:10.1016/j.jclepro.2009.03.019

Barr, S., Gilg, A. W., & Ford, N. J. (2001). A conceptual framework for understanding and analyzing attitudes towards household-waste management. *Environment & Planning A, 33*(11), 2025–2048. doi:10.1068/a33225

Bastein, A. G. T. M., Roelofs, E., Rietveld, E., & Hoogendoorn, A. (2013). *Opportunities for a Circular Economy in the Netherlands*. TNO.

Benton, D., & Hazell, J. (2013). *Resource resilient UK: A report from the Circular Economy Task Force*. Green Alliance.

Beuren, F. H., Ferreira, M. G. G., & Miguel, P. A. C. (2013). Product-service systems: A literature review on integrated products and services. *Journal of Cleaner Production, 47*, 222–231. doi:10.1016/j.jclepro.2012.12.028

Bocken, N. M., de Pauw, I., Bakker, C., & van der Grinten, B. (2016). Product design and business model strategies for a circular economy. *Journal of Industrial and Production Engineering*, *33*(5), 308–320. doi:10.1080/21681015.2016.1172124

Bocken, N. M., Schuit, C. S., & Kraaijenhagen, C. (2018). Experimenting with a circular business model: Lessons from eight cases. *Environmental Innovation and Societal Transitions*, *28*, 79–95. doi:10.1016/j.eist.2018.02.001

Bonini, S., & Oppenheim, J. (2008). Cultivating the Green Consumer. *Stanford Social Innovation Review*, *6*(4), 56–61.

Branca, T. A., Colla, V., Algermissen, D., Granbom, H., Martini, U., Morillon, A., Pietruck, R., & Rosendahl, S. (2020). Reuse and recycling of by-products in the steel sector: Recent achievements paving the way to circular economy and industrial symbiosis in Europe. *Metals*, *10*(3), 345. doi:10.3390/met10030345

Braungart, M., McDonough, W., & Bollinger, A. (2007). Cradle-to-cradle design: Creating healthy emissions–a strategy for eco-effective product and system design. *Journal of Cleaner Production*, *15*(13-14), 1337–1348. doi:10.1016/j.jclepro.2006.08.003

Chan, R. Y. K., & Lau, L. B. Y. (2000). Antecedents of Green Purchases: A survey in China. *Journal of Consumer Marketing*, *17*(4), 338–357. doi:10.1108/07363760010335358

Circulair, N. (2015). *The Potential for High Value Reuse in a Circular Economy*. Academic Press.

Cordano, M., Welcomer, S., Scherer, R. F., Pradenas, L., & Parada, V. (2011). A cross-cultural assessment of three theories of pro-environmental behavior: A comparison between business students of Chile and the United States. *Environment and Behavior*, *43*(5), 634–657. doi:10.1177/0013916510378528

Cordell, D., Rosemarin, A., Schröder, J. J., & Smit, A. L. (2011). Towards global phosphorus security: A systems framework for phosphorus recovery and reuse options. *Chemosphere*, *84*(6), 747–758. doi:10.1016/j.chemosphere.2011.02.032 PMID:21414650

Demailly, D., & Novel, A. S. (2014). The sharing economy: make it sustainable. *Studies*, *3*(14.1).

Dervojeda, K., Verzijl, D., Rouwmaat, E., Probst, L., & Frideres, L. (2014). *Clean technologies circular supply chains*. EU report, 248-274.

EC. (2010). *European Commission – Joint Research Centre – Institute for Environment and Sustainability: International Reference Life Cycle Data System (ILCD) Handbook – General Guide for Life Cycle Assessment – Detailed Guidance, first edition*. March 2010. EUR 24708 EN. Luxembourg. Retrieved from https://publications.jrc.ec.europa.eu/repository/bitstream/JRC48157/ilcd_handbook-general_guide_for_lca-detailed_guidance_ 12march2010_isbn_fin.pdf

EC. (2015). *Communication from the commission to the parliament, the council and the European economic and social commitee and the commitee of the regions: Closing the loop – An EU action plan for the Circular Economy*. COM (2015) 614 final.

Economy, C. (2017). *Business Imperative for India*. Retrieved from https://www.teriin.org/sites/default/files/2018-03/TERI-YES_BANK_Circular_Economy_Report.pdf

EEA. (2016). *Developments in indicators: Total Material Requirement.* TMR.

Ellen MacArthur Foundation. (2017). *Priority Research Agenda.* Available at Error! Hyperlink reference not valid.

Frederiks, E. R., Stenner, K., & Hobman, E. V. (2015). Household energy use: Applying behavioural economics to understand consumer decision-making and behaviour. *Renewable & Sustainable Energy Reviews*, *41*, 1385–1394. doi:10.1016/j.rser.2014.09.026

Frishammar, J., & Parida, V. (2019). Circular business model transformation: A roadmap for incumbent firms. *California Management Review*, *61*(2), 5–29. doi:10.1177/0008125618811926

Garcia, G., Woolley, E., Rahimifard, S., Colwill, J., White, R., & Needham, L. (2017). A methodology for sustainable management of food waste. *Waste and Biomass Valorization*, *8*(6), 2209–2227. doi:10.100712649-016-9720-0 PMID:32010409

García-Barragán, J. F., Eyckmans, J., & Rousseau, S. (2019). Defining and measuring the circular economy: A mathematical approach. *Ecological Economics*, *157*, 369–372. doi:10.1016/j.ecolecon.2018.12.003

Gartner. (2016). *Market Share Analysis: Consulting Services, Worldwide, 2015.* Available at. https://www.gartner.com/doc/3317117/market-share-analysis-consulting- services.

Ghisellini, P., Cialani, C., & Ulgiati, S. (2016). A review on circular economy: The expected transition to a balanced interplay of environmental and economic systems. *Journal of Cleaner Production*, *114*, 11–32. doi:10.1016/j.jclepro.2015.09.007

Goyal, S., Esposito, M., & Kapoor, A. (2018). Circular economy business models in developing economies: lessons from India on reduce, recycle, and reuse paradigms. *Thunderbird International Business Review, 60*(5), 729-740.

Hilson, G. (2003). Defining "cleaner production" and "pollution prevention" in the mining context. *Minerals Engineering*, *16*(4), 305–321. doi:10.1016/S0892-6875(03)00012-8

Hollins, O. (2011). *Study into the feasibility of protecting and recovering critical raw materials through infrastructure development in the south east of England.* Oakdene Hollins Ltd.

Hopewell, J., Dvorak, R., & Kosior, E. (2009). Plastics recycling: Challenges and opportunities. *Philosophical Transactions of the Royal Society of London. Series B, Biological Sciences*, *364*(1526), 2115–2126. doi:10.1098/rstb.2008.0311 PMID:19528059

Ikiz Kaya, D., Pintossi, N., & Dane, G. (2021). An empirical analysis of driving factors and policy enablers of heritage adaptive reuse within the circular economy framework. *Sustainability*, *13*(5), 2479. doi:10.3390u13052479

JRC. (2011b). *Supporting Environmentally Sound Decisions for Waste Management - A technical guide to Life Cycle Thinking (LCT) and Life Cycle Assessment (LCA) for waste experts and LCA practitioners.* JRC Scientific and Technical Reports. https://tinyurl.com/zwen5p2

Kapoor, N., Jauhari, D. S., & Maheshwari, D. D. (2021). Understanding of Circular Processes and Its Impact on Indian Economy. *Journal of Contemporary Issues in Business and Government*, *27*(3), 2076–2084.

Kapoor, N., Jauhari, S., & Maheshwari, D. (2021). Policies for Promoting the Circular Economy in India. In Examining the Intersection of Circular Economy, Forestry, and International Trade (pp. 68-82). IGI Global.

Konietzko, J., Baldassarre, B., Brown, P., Bocken, N., & Hultink, E. J. (2020). Circular business model experimentation: Demystifying assumptions. *Journal of Cleaner Production*, *277*, 122596. doi:10.1016/j.jclepro.2020.122596

Krook, J., & Eklund, M. (2010). The strategic role of recycling centres for environmental performance of waste management systems. *Applied Ergonomics*, *41*(3), 362–367. doi:10.1016/j.apergo.2009.06.012 PMID:19691952

Lacy, P., Gupta, P., & Hayward, R. (2019). From incrementalism to transformation: Reflections on corporate sustainability from the UN global compact-Accenture CEO study. In *Managing sustainable business* (pp. 505–518). Springer. doi:10.1007/978-94-024-1144-7_23

Lane, G. W., & Wagner, T. P. (2013). Examining recycling container attributes and household recycling practices. *Resources, Conservation and Recycling*, *75*, 32–40. doi:10.1016/j.resconrec.2013.03.005

Lazarova, V., Sturny, V., & Sang, G. T. (2012). Relevance and Benefits of Urban Water Reuse in Tourist Areas. *Water (Basel)*, *4*(1), 107–122. doi:10.3390/w4010107

Li, Y., Beeton, R. J., Sigler, T., & Halog, A. (2016). Modelling the transition toward urban sustainability: A case study of the industrial city of Jinchang, China. *Journal of Cleaner Production*, *134*, 22–30. doi:10.1016/j.jclepro.2015.10.053

Lüdeke-Freund, F., Gold, S., & Bocken, N. M. (2019). A review and typology of circular economy business model patterns. *Journal of Industrial Ecology*, *23*(1), 36–61. doi:10.1111/jiec.12763

MacArthur, E. (2013). *Towards the circular economy, economic and business rationale for an accelerated transition*. Ellen MacArthur Foundation.

MacArthur, E. (2015). *Towards a circular economy: business rationale for an accelerated transition.* Academic Press.

Minunno, R., O'Grady, T., Morrison, G. M., & Gruner, R. L. (2020). Exploring environmental benefits of reuse and recycle practices: A circular economy case study of a modular building. *Resources, Conservation and Recycling*, *160*, 104855. doi:10.1016/j.resconrec.2020.104855

Murray, A., Skene, K., & Haynes, K. (2017). The Circular Economy: An interdisciplinary exploration of the concept and its application in a global context. *Journal of Business Ethics*, *140*(3), 369–380. doi:10.100710551-015-2693-2

Nilsson, L., Persson, P. O., Rydén, L., Darozhka, S., & Zaliauskiene, A. (2007). *Cleaner Production: Technologies and Tools for Resource Efficient Production*. Baltic University Press.

Osterwalder, A., & Pigneur, Y. (2010). *Business model canvas*. Self Published.

Pigosso, D. C., Zanette, E. T., Guelere Filho, A., Ometto, A. R., & Rozenfeld, H. (2010). Ecodesign methods focused on remanufacturing. *Journal of Cleaner Production, 18*(1), 21–31. doi:10.1016/j.jclepro.2009.09.005

Pimentel, D., Williamson, S., Alexander, C. E., Gonzalez-Pagan, O., Kontak, C., & Mulkey, S. E. (2008). Reducing energy inputs in the US food system. *Human Ecology, 36*(4), 459–471. doi:10.100710745-008-9184-3

Rizos, V., Tuokko, K., & Behrens, A. (2017). *The Circular Economy: A review of definitions, processes and impacts*. Academic Press.

Saphores, J. D. M., Ogunseitan, O. A., & Shapiro, A. A. (2012). Willingness to engage in a pro-environmental behavior: An analysis of e-waste recycling based on a national survey of US households. *Resources, Conservation and Recycling, 60*, 49–63. doi:10.1016/j.resconrec.2011.12.003

Stillitano, T., Spada, E., Iofrida, N., Falcone, G., & De Luca, A. I. (2021). Sustainable Agri-Food Processes and Circular Economy Pathways in a Life Cycle Perspective: State of the Art of Applicative Research. *Sustainability, 13*(5), 2472. doi:10.3390u13052472

Tse, T., Esposito, M., & Soufani, K. (2015, November). Why the circular economy matters. *European Business Review.*

Tucker, P., & Douglas, P. (2007). *WR0112: understanding household waste prevention behaviour*. Final Report & Technical Reports.

UNEP & Sida. (2006). Applying Cleaner Production to MEAs – Global Status Report. United Nations Environment Programme, Division of Technology, Industry and Economics.

Velázquez-Martínez, O., Valio, J., Santasalo-Aarnio, A., Reuter, M., & Serna-Guerrero, R. (2019). A critical review of lithium-ion battery recycling processes from a circular economy perspective. *Batteries, 5*(4), 68. doi:10.3390/batteries5040068

World Economic Forum. (2014). *Reorganize and streamline pure materials flows*. Author.

Ylä-Mella, J., Keiski, R. L., & Pongrácz, E. (2015). Electronic waste recovery in Finland: Consumers' perceptions towards recycling and re-use of mobile phones. *Waste Management (New York, N.Y.), 45*, 374–384. doi:10.1016/j.wasman.2015.02.031 PMID:25797074

Chapter 11
Reconfiguration of the Indian Film Industry During the COVID-19 Pandemic:
The Enablers and the Impeders

Selvalakshmi M
Thiagarajar School of Management, India

Kabila RM
Thiagarajar School of Management, India

ABSTRACT

The Indian film industry has consistently performed well across years and has emerged as the largest in the world in terms of the number of movies it produces annually. However, the year 2020 presented a crude shock to the prospects and promises of the industry. The catastrophic effect of the pandemic in the year 2020 led to the drop in the global box office by as much as 72% with a mere $12 billion collections across the world in the form of ticket sales. To understand the factors facilitating the Indian film industry to go beyond theatres during the pandemic and to explore the key challenges faced by the industry in light of its advancement, secondary data was collected from available publications, industry reports, and official websites of various bodies. The chapter aims at exploring the factors which contribute to the recent trends of the Indian film industry, attempts to identify the new and emerging challenges that plague its growth and how this transition can speed the recovery of Indian film industry as this would provide ample input to the various stakeholders of the industry.

INTRODUCTION

Entertainment Industry is a lucrative business market and the total annual spending across the globe on this industry is about one trillion dollars. (Vogel, H.L, 2020). The size of this multi-billion dollar economy overtakes the annual domestic gross product of several countries. In addition, its impact on the

DOI: 10.4018/978-1-7998-8678-5.ch011

society at large as a change agent by creating awareness and acceptance can never be denied. (Mehraj, H. K., etal, 2014)

Global movie box office revenue reached a record of 42.5 billion dollars in 2019 with theatrical, home, and mobile entertainment combined; it has topped 100 billion dollars. The total cinema screens surpassed 200,000 in 2019, due to the 12% increase in the Asia Pacific region.

The year 2020 presented a rude shock to the prospects and promises of the Industry. The Pandemic jolted the world and the business of cinema crumbled under pressure. The streaming services in theatres had to be closed for the first time in the history. Indian Film industry, the second largest in the World faced the brutal impacts of the pandemic as like any other industries but managed to balance it effectively taking the hard lessons. Digital media came handy as an alternative platform to reach the potential customers at a rapid pace with a wider audience.

The chapter aims at exploring the factors which contribute to the recent trends of Indian film Industry due to the Pandemic including the home and mobile entertainment to add to its revenue base, attempts to identify the new and emerging challenges which plague its growth and how this transition can speed the recovery of Indian film Industry as this would provide ample inputs to the various stakeholders of the industry.

BACKDROP OF THE INDIAN FILM INDUSTRY

The catastrophic effect of the Pandemic in the year 2020 lead to the drop in the global box office by as much as 72% with a mere 12$ billion collection across the world in the form of ticket sales (2020 Theme Report- Motion Picture Association)

Indian film Industry's origin dates back to nineteenth century with the first film being made in 1913 by Dadasaheb Phalke, acclaimed as the father of Indian cinema (Selvalakshmi etal, 2019) With the phenomenal growth of the industry since then, the industry evolved as a global enterprise with established markets in well over 90 countries and has been respected more for its business than Art. Indian film industry serves as the world's second movie capital next only to Hollywood with South Indian film industry comprising of Tamil, Telugu, Malayalam and Kannada accounting for more than 50% of the films produced (Murthy, 2013). Block buster movies such as Dangal and Bahubali II released in the year 2017 had successfully garnered a turnover of $15 billion, all across the world and running forward towards achieving record $20 billion. The Industry has been acknowledged for its diversity by reputed Hollywood directors (Murthy, 2015) and has gained the confidence across years in the world market that it can no longer be treated as marginal. (Raju, 2016)

The industry turnover crossed $1.2 billion in 2010, hovered around $2 billion in 2015 and is projected to grow steadily to $2.8 billion by 2020 (FICCI KPMG Report, 2017) While the revenue from the global movie box office was hovering around 42.5 billion dollars in 2019, Indian film Industry crossed its 10,000 crore (100 billion dollars) mark seeing a growth of 11.6% overtaking the previous year[1]. Due to the devastating effect of the pandemic, the year 2020, the industry turnover managed to close at $2.5 billion and has seen a turnover of $8.3 billion in 2021 (Statistica, 2021)

As a measure of coping up with the missed opportunities, the Industry went beyond theatres and included home and mobile entertainment to add to its revenue base. The Indian film industry benchmarks with Hollywood shows which have joined with Netflix and other OTT platforms transferring content via the internet for smooth and undeterred distribution of movies. The efforts are well received in the

FIGURE 1. 2020 top 15 global box office markets- all films (US$ Billions)

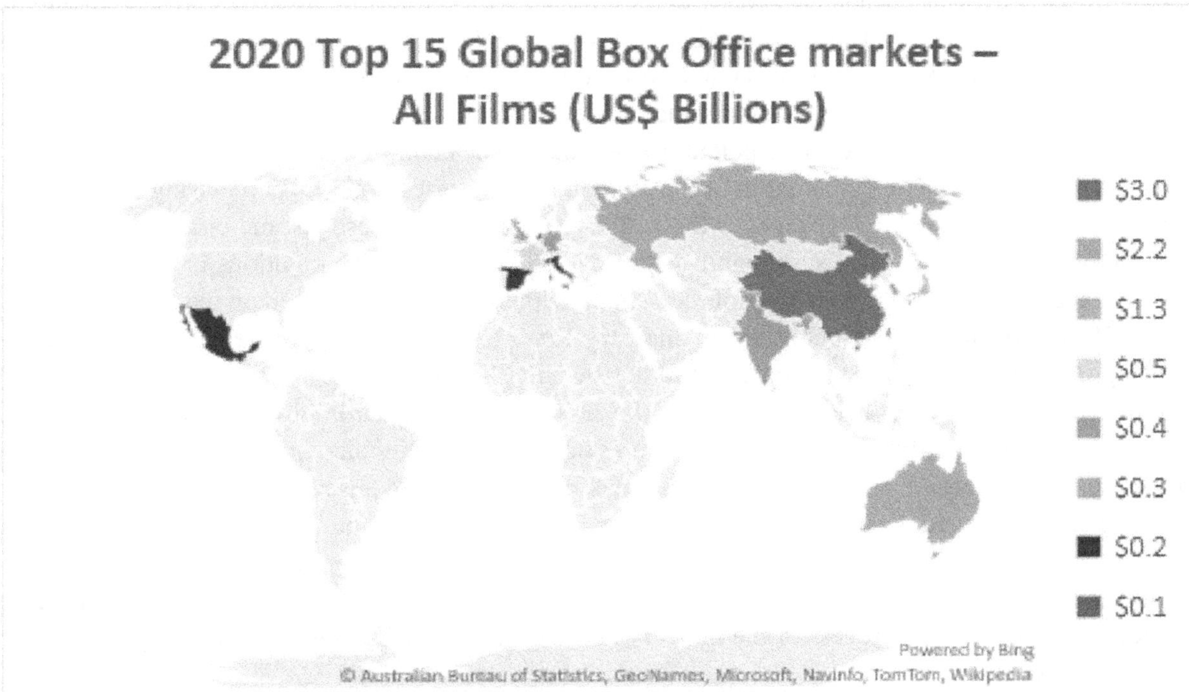

Source: Omdia, local sources; Data courtesy. MPA

overseas market as well. Zee5 TV, the largest Indian digital streaming service enjoyed a spike of its patronage even in countries abroad like Canada, Middle East and North Africa.

Though the revival is slow, today the Indian Media and Entertainment Industry projects a growth in the CAGR of 13.5% from 2019 to 2024 to reach US$43.93 billion in 2024. Despite the repeated attack of the waves of Corona and the eventual lockdowns, the promise of recovery, proves how the industry have transformed its resources to innate capabilities and aims at nurturing it to a unique competency.

PANDEMIC: THE CRITICAL MILESTONE

The Pandemic derailed the film industry from its progressive path by impacting on both the demand and supply side of business (Nhamo, G et al, 2020). While the need for film entertainment among people remained intact, the form, content and methods of the production and consumption were forced to undergo a sea change. Even after the vaccination drives, it is apparent that the scenario is to continue and evolve further in in the next few years. This clearly indicates the need for detailed research to understand the forces driving the industry in challenging times. He. P et al (2020) have identified Indian film industry as one among the few other selected industries such as public management and information technology which has not only showed its resilience, but also has portrayed a strong coping capacity and hence demanding extensive study.

Godwell Nhamo et al (2020) has also raised concerns about the lack of adequate research highlighting the impact of previous pandemics on the entertainment industry, despite its significant contribution to the country's economy. Xin and Mossig (2017) have highlighted the serious lag in research about the film industry at the global level and its actual evolution even before the pandemic.

The study is thus aimed at understanding the impacts of the pandemic on the World's second largest film industry which plays the role of a potential propeller of the country's economic growth.

The impacts of the factors arising out of the pandemic are overwhelming; yet a glaring point is that while some have served as an enabler for the active revival of the industry some other impacts have raised pertinent questions on the sustainability of the industry. Due to the limitations in the availability of empirical evidences after the eruption of the pandemic the study evolved based on the secondary data being collected from available publications, industry Reports and official websites of various bodies following the guidelines prescribed for case studies by Yin (2003).

Indian film industry has been emerging to the International standards through its conscious and sentient efforts in the form of Globalization, Professionalization, Digitalization, Integration and Corporatization (Selvalakshmi et al, 2020). The outbreak of the Pandemic posed a serious challenge to the execution of strategies in the planned pace and order. The impacts of the outbreak attacked the industry like a tsunami changing the flow of events. However, the results have surprisingly been both favorable and unfavorable to its emergence in the global markets. The enablers and impeders thus will form key milestones in the recovery process of the industry and also aid in facing new and emerging challenges which facilitates its growth.

ENABLERS FAVORING RECONFIGURATION

The creative and innovative approaches in handling the pressures due to the Pandemic has opened an air of freshness in the Indian Cinema. Kapoor & Kaufman (2020) in their recent study have remarked that during the pandemic, creative professionals engage in using their skills innovatively to prove their expertise in their field to achieve eminence. The Warriors of the Industry including directors, technicians and actors are thus actively redefining the boundaries of the craft

Firms have realized that it is time to get rid of the time old tools and techniques and look for new business strategies. The phenomenal amount of disruptions caused by the Pandemic has served as a catalyst in the evolution of service innovations with its main concern on spatial adaptability, social and health concerns and utilization of technology (Heinonen, K., & Strandvik, T, 2020)

1. The pandemic has induced a minimalistic approach in the Industry at the production level. Wedding scenes, crowded streets and natural backdrops have been largely avoided and shooting has gone back to the sets, wherein the Covid Protocols can be adhered easily.
2. Virtual production which utilizes 3D software and hardware including camera to interact with a virtual environment in a real- time basis has been on a steady rise in the film industry (Bennett, J., & Carter, C, 2014). The pandemic has brought out the dire need to explore new film making techniques and the producers and directors have understood the potentials of virtual production as a possible strategy. This method of production is inexpensive to film avoiding travel, reduces post-production works and even giving provision for the directors to make subtle and suitable changes

later in the films shot. Most importantly this method of production eliminates the need to have the artists being available in the production sets thereby enabling a Covid protected environment.

3. Perishability, the most challenging attribute of the services is being addressed righteously during the pandemic times by the industry. The release of movies in the OTT platforms helps in extending the lives of movies without losing its commercial value. The pandemic has induced the release of new Indian movies in the OTT platform for the first time giving it an opportunity to meet global audience on its release. Such as initiative demands tremendous efforts of networking and follow up in theatre release across countries.
4. Research has confirmed that release of movies in the online platforms like Netflix have eventually given a positive impact on ticket sales.(Parlow, A., & Wagner, S, 2018) .This has paved way for the new perception of the industry about the OTT services as complimenting and contributing to the revenues instead of acting as competitors to the theatres.
5. The Indian cinema has finally come in terms with avoiding extravaganza and larger than life portrayal of movies with unrealistic songs and fight scenes exorbitantly shot in exemplary foreign locations. The Malayalam movie 'C U soon' released on Amazon Prime Video in September 2020 has been a roaring success recognized widely for its unique and gripping storytelling technique (Sowmya Rajendran, 2020)
6. When the online platform offers multiple choices of movies in terms of language, genre, actors preference etc., still research indicates that there has been a striking similarity in the consumption of creative content by people around the world (Kapoor &Kaufman, 2020). This reinforces the need for social connect among people by expressing similarity in watching the creative content thereby creating a platform for deliberations. The quarantine period thus helped people across the world to develop social and emotional connect.

These factors have been the stimulus to support the growth and progress of Indian film Industry during the pandemic. Content supply seems to be resuming, although in small steps, thanks to these facilitators. Cinemas and events, on the other hand, remain closed mostly, with little hope of returning to box offices in the foreseeable future. Right from the creative content, online platforms to virtual production, these enablers have encouraged the industry keep going inspite of the various chokes that tried disrupting the industry. These facilitators aided the acceptance of the nourishing innovations among the consumers which was once thought as a big challenge. With this propulsion in the new technologies in Indian film industry and assuming the pandemic is under some form of control by the end of FY21, it, has projected the performance of digital and OTT industry as 33% rise in the FY22 and the most phenomenal part being the percentage increase of films in FY22 which is projected as 196%. (KPMG in India's Media and Entertainment Report, 2020) This pandemic has given a new impetus to cinema 2.0 – conceptualization of new projects and realignment of theatrical windows.

IMPEDERS DETERRING RECONFIGURATION

The avalanche effect of the pandemic raises pertinent doubts on the survival and sustainability of the Industry. It is therefore imperative to understand its role and relevance in setting the milestones for the revival of the industry,

1. The Indian Film industry is counting on its sustenance mainly based on its reliance on the OTT platform. But the economies of the VOD (Video on Demand)model which provides access of movies to the customers based on their demand and convenience without the need for a playback set up is never comparable to the theatres as in a normal scenario the box office revenues account for 60 -70 percent of the revenues from the movies. OTT platform may provide a reduced risk to movies which are in the small and medium budget due to the assured minimal revenue, but production houses which go in for heavy budget movies can never be able to cope up without massive theatre releases. The subscription rates for OTT platforms of users in India are quite nominal and also the practice of single subscription being used by multiple users is prevalent widely in India. This poses a serious challenge to the sustainability of the model as it cannot afford to invest in movies produced with exorbitant budgets readily at the time of release.
2. The current trend is that high budget movies released by major studios enjoy a positive relationship with revenues not only in India but also at the global level. The global reach and acclaim give way for sequels and also nominations of awards. The release of big budget movies in the OTT platform makes this trend highly improbable and hence was not promoted by the industry (Pangarker & vdM Smit, 2013).
3. While creativity is the only Mantra for the survival of the fittest, the dark side of spurious creativity during the time of crisis can never be underestimated (Cropley et al, 2010). Piracy is rampant in Indian film industry and there is a heavy demand for pirated Indian movies across the world. (Scaria, 2013) The online availability and accessibility of new movies in OTT platforms might therefore do more harm to the industry. Research indicates that pre-release piracy impacts the revenues negatively, while the post release piracy of a film content results in a 3% increase in the box office revenue. (Lu, S,et al, 2020) . Managing and controlling piracy is a perennial problem in the industry.
4. The increasing acceptance of animation and VFX movies in Indian film industry is encouraging and might serve to support the Covid protocols proclaimed by the Government. But the financial investment for establishing a sophisticated animation and VFX studio is exorbitant and needs continuous interface with suppliers from overseas for quality control. (Kumar &Vats, 2016). The industry is supported currently by many small production houses who predominantly rely on private financiers providing financial support on traditional modes (Lorenzen & Täube, 2008). The viability and growth of this model thus becomes questionable. The pandemic has a whole has imposed long term challenges on generation of funds for distribution, supporting the labour markets which thrive on the industry and connecting with international production houses about the readiness of the industry to accommodate foreign collaborations and investments. (Noonan, 2020)
5. According to an UNESCO report, there should well over be a lakh of theatres to entertain the huge Indian population. Due to the unprecedented rise in the cost of operations there has a declining trend in the number of cinema houses in India. (Rajadhyaksha, 2003). To enhance cost economies, the industry is resorting to multiplex theatres which is seeing a steady yet slow surge in its numbers unlike China which had boosted the investments and dramatically improved number of theatres to 60000 from a mere 9,000 screens.(Shankar& Ram, 2021)
6. According to the reports of the International Alliance of Theatrical Stage Employees(IATSE), the pandemic has resulted in the loss of around 120,000 below- the- line jobs in the entertainment Industry predominantly among those in the theatrical stage (Ozili, P. K., & Arun, T., 2020)

7. India has around 9600 theatrical screens including 2,950 multiplex screens as on 2019. The pandemic has resulted in a closure of these theatres for most part of the year 2020. When we calculate the labour involvement even with a rough estimation of 5 support staff per screen, it adds up to 48000 and the crisis has certainly devastated the livelihood of these people costing their lives dearly (Alam & Samikon, 2021) in their recent study on the film industry in Pakistan highlighted the lack of any kind of financial support or beneficial facilities from the Government unlike several other industries1

The coronavirus outbreak and its accompanying lockdowns have impacted the industry at multiple levels starting with the supply chains by hampering the production of content. and has disrupted the entire Media and Entertainment sector substantially. From the above discussed hindrances, it is evident that while OTT platform is seen as the only possible way out of the dependencies on theatres, they pose a major threat to the industry accompanied with piracy and decreased generation of funds. The stakeholders of the industry are in a crucial position to devise careful measures to diminish the gap between OTT and theatrical release. Understanding these impeders will encourage the concurrent growth of the industry which brings with it the amelioration of the box office bloom.

CONCLUSION

The pandemic brought all forms of outdoor entertainments to a standstill and had a direct adverse effect on the film Industry, resulting in a plethora of changes in the industry operations. Indian film Industry though plagued by the lack of a system driven approach and faced with challenges in the quality of the movies, gender disparity (Chatterjee, R., 2020), high degree of leveraging by family firms and actors (Taube, F.A., & Lorenzen, M, 2007), still is revered in the World Cinema for its unique characteristics (Yi-Yeh Lee etal, 2013). Despite these limitations, the Indian film industry has already started showing the impetus for revival and signs of recovery. In such as uncertain, complex and challenging times imposed by the pandemic, it is essential to understand, evaluate, analyze and project the implications of the changes to bring in stability, sustainability and progress in the Indian film Industry. This chapter highlighted the sum and substance of the key contributing variables – both enablers and impeders, the effective management of which becomes imperative in determining the industry prospects. Janosov, M. et al (2020) emphasizes on the role of luck as a crucial component to achieve the desired impact in any creative domain including the movie industry. The control of the pandemic thus may sure be the shower of good luck to the industry.

REFERENCES

Alam, A., & Samikon, S. A. (2021). Impact of the COVID-19 Pandemic on the Film Industry in Pakistan. *Journal of Insurance and Financial Management*, *4*(3).

Bennett, J., & Carter, C. (2014). Adopting virtual production for animated filmmaking. In *Proceedings of the 7th Annual International Conference on Computer Games, Multimedia and Allied Technology* (pp. 81-86). Global Science and Technology Forum (GSTF).

Bloomberg Businessweek. (2020, Aug. 3). Bollywood Gets a Covid Makeover. *Bloomberg Businessweek.*

Chatterjee, R. (2020). Confessions of Indian cinema's first woman superstar: Kanan Devi's memoirs, film history and digital archives. *Indian Film Stars: New Critical Perspectives*, 31.

Cropley, D. H., Cropley, A. J., Kaufman, J. C., & Runco, M. A. (Eds.). (2010). *The dark side of creativity*. Cambridge University Press. doi:10.1017/CBO9780511761225

He, P., Sun, Y., Zhang, Y., & Li, T. (2020). COVID–19's impact on stock prices across different sectors—An event study based on the Chinese stock market. *Emerging Markets Finance & Trade*, *56*(10), 2198–2212. doi:10.1080/1540496X.2020.1785865

Heinonen, K., & Strandvik, T. (2020). Reframing service innovation: COVID-19 as a catalyst for imposed service innovation. *Journal of Service Management.*

Janosov, M., Battiston, F., & Sinatra, R. (2020). Success and luck in creative careers. *EPJ Data Science*, *9*(1), 9. doi:10.1140/epjds13688-020-00227-w

Kapoor, H., & Kaufman, J. C. (2020). Meaning-making through creativity during COVID-19. *Frontiers in Psychology*, 11. PMID:33391115

Kohli-Khandekar. (2021, Apr. 26). The Covid effect: Pandemic has enhanced creative output Indian cinema. *Business Standard.*

Kumar, M. D., & Vats, A. (2016). Mapping animation and visual effects in Indian media and entertainment industry opportunities and threats. *International Journal of Humanities, Art and Social Studies, 1*(2).

Lee, Y. Y., Hsieh, M. J., & Fan, K. K. (2013). Study on Development of Indian Film Industry. *Applied Mechanics and Materials*, *311*, 544–549. doi:10.4028/www.scientific.net/AMM.311.544

Lorenzen, M., & Täube, F. A. (2008). Breakout from Bollywood? The roles of social networks and regulation in the evolution of Indian film industry. *Journal of International Management*, *14*(3), 286–299. doi:10.1016/j.intman.2008.01.004

Lu, S., Wang, X., & Bendle, N. (2020). Does Piracy Create Online Word of Mouth? An Empirical Analysis in the Movie Industry. *Management Science*, *66*(5), 2140–2162. doi:10.1287/mnsc.2019.3298

Mehraj, H. K., Bhat, A. N., & Mehraj, H. R. (2014). Impacts of media on society: A sociological perspective. *International Journal of Humanities and Social Science Invention*, *3*(6), 56–64.

Murthy, C. S. H. N. (2013). Film remakes as cross-cultural connections between North and South: A case study of the Telugu film industry's contribution to Indian filmmaking. *Journal of International Communication*, *19*(1), 19–42. doi:10.1080/13216597.2012.739573

Murthy, C. S. H. N. (2015). Rethinking what is special about Indian Cinema. *Media Asia*, *42*(1-2), 36–38. doi:10.1080/01296612.2015.1100377

Nandana. (2020, July 6). Do producers make less money on OTT compared to box office collections? *Business Line.*

Nhamo, G., Dube, K., & Chikodzi, D. (2020). Implications of COVID-19 on gaming, leisure and entertainment industry. In *Counting the Cost of COVID-19 on the Global Tourism Industry* (pp. 273–295). Springer. doi:10.1007/978-3-030-56231-1_12

Nhamo, G., Dube, K., & Chikodzi, D. (2020). *Counting the cost of COVID-19 on the global tourism industry*. Springer Nature. doi:10.1007/978-3-030-56231-1

Noonan, C. (2020). Public funding in a time of crisis: Film funds and the pandemic. *Baltic Screen Media Review*, (8), 10–17.

OziliP. K.ArunT. (2020). Spillover of COVID-19: impact on the Global Economy. Available at SSRN 3562570. doi:10.2139srn.3562570

Pangarker, N. A., & Smit, E. M. (2013). The determinants of box office performance in the film industry revisited. *South African Journal of Business Management*, *44*(3), 47–58. doi:10.4102ajbm.v44i3.162

Parlow, A., & Wagner, S. (2018). *Netflix and the Demand for Cinema Tickets-An Analysis for 19 European Countries*. Academic Press.

Rajadhyaksha, A. (2003). The 'Bollywoodization' of the Indian cinema: Cultural nationalism in a global arena. *Inter-Asia Cultural Studies*, *4*(1), 25–39. doi:10.1080/1464937032000060195

Rajendran. (2020, Sept. 2). 'C U Soon': Mahesh-Fahadh film is a reminder of what the Malayalam industry does best. *Mollywood Wednesday*.

Raju, K. K. (2016). Growth Driver of an Indian Economy-Make-in-India. *The Indian Journal of Commerce*, *68*(5).

Scaria, A. G. (2013). Online piracy of Indian movies: Is the film industry firing at the wrong target. *Mich. St. U. Coll. L. Int'l L. Rev.*, *21*, 647. doi:10.2139srn.2175621

Selvalakshmi, M., Verma, H., & Jain, N. (2020). Emergence of Indian Film Industry in the International Markets: Facilitators and Impeders. *International Journal of Asian Business and Information Management*, *11*(3), 32–44. doi:10.4018/IJABIM.2020070103

Shankar, K. S., & Ram, K. R. (2021). *Changing movie viewing patterns of moviegoers and the rise of multiplex theatres in India: Is it the end of the show for single-screen theatres*. Academic Press.

Taube, F.A., & Lorenzen, M. (n.d.). *Bollywood and the Banyan Tree Organization: Leveraging Family Interconnectedness in the Indian Film Industry*. Academic Press.

Vogel, H. L. (2020). *Entertainment industry economics: A guide for financial analysis*. Cambridge University Press.

Xiao, R. X., & Mossig, I. (2017). Co-evolution of institutions, culture and industrial organization in the film industry: The case of Shanghai in China. *European Planning Studies*, *25*(6), 923–940. doi:10.1080/09654313.2017.1300638

Yin, R. K. (2003). *Case Study Research: Design and Methods* (2nd ed.). Sage Publications.

ENDNOTE

[1] https://economictimes.indiatimes.com/industry/media/entertainment/indian-box-office-crosses-rs-10000-crore-mark-in2019/articleshow/74139131.cms?utm_

Chapter 12
New Business Development Strategy of Telecommunication Operators Based on a Smart Energy System:
Case of KT-MEG (Enhanced)

Junghwan Lee
Chungbuk National University, South Korea

Dongwook Kim
Korea Advanced Institute of Science and Technology, South Korea

ABSTRACT

This research studies the case of KT to see how a mobile operator expanded beyond its existing offerings to new smart energy business based on digital technology. Details were analysed specifically on how the business was developed, why the smart energy service was started, and what the success factors were. KT's smart energy business (KT-MEG: KT Micro Energy Grid) utilizes ICT to resolve energy issues such as global climate change and energy consumption growth. It also provides growth opportunities for KT with its KT-MEG platform. The authors analyze that KT was able to leverage sustainability as a new growth engine by developing new businesses to differentiate customer experience, create effective organization structure, and generate business impact in addition to application of latest ICT technologies such as artificial intelligence, IoT (internet of things), and big data. The results provide a good guideline for business transformation of ICT firms in the era of Industry 4.0.

INTRODUCTION

Telecommunications operators around the world are contemplating and competing intensely to secure new growth engine for future revenue (Y. Kang et al., 2010). As mobile markets become saturated, adding

DOI: 10.4018/978-1-7998-8678-5.ch012

subscribers into operators' networks is becoming much more difficult while regulatory pressure from the governments to drive the price down are limiting operators' profitability. Hence, the operators are endeavoring to expand beyond the traditional telecommunications business to new business opportunities via means such as M&A (Mergers and Acquisitions) and investment in new technologies (Jang, 2017). Examples include operators from a diverse range of markets. Verizon, a telecommunications operator in the United States of America, acquired online contents firm AOL (America Online) and internet business, Yahoo. AT&T, another telecommunications operator in the United States of America, acquired Direct TV and Time Warners. Softbank from Japan acquired a semiconductor chipset design company ARM. China is no exception where all three operators (China Mobile, China Unicom and China Telecom), invested in non-telecommunications firms such as Alibaba and in new technologies such as Internet of Things and Artificial intelligence. The industry is rapidly changing, which is especially highlighted in the mentions of a merger between T-Mobile and Sprint in the USA. The merger does not merely grow the scale of the companies but also enables the merged firms to acquire competence to prepare for the future (Deloitte_Consulting, 2018).

Korean operators (SK Telecom, KT, and LG Uplus) are no exception to this trend as they face saturation of revenue after explosive growth in the data traffic due to the adoption of smartphone. For example, the ARPU (Average Revenue per User) of the companies reduced from 2016 to 2020. SKT's ARPU fell from USD 31.33 to USD 26.82, LG Uplus' fell from USD 31.60 to USD 27.40, and KT's fell from USD 31.07 to USD 28.31 (Source: Investment Relations Presentations from respective companies).

Therefore, Korean operators are attempting to expand beyond its conventional mobile communications business to develop a new growth engine. Indeed, Korean operators have already acknowledged the importance of climate change (e.g., [1]risk of blackout in hot summer seasons, [2]Paris Agreement, policy support for renewable energy) and have been pushing the business of smart energy forward among many new business development candidates.

The smart energy business developed by Korean telecommunications operators is distinct from traditional energy demand businesses, where SI (Systems Integrator) firms replace large energy consuming equipment with highly efficient equipment, replace filament lamps with LED (Light Emitting Diode) lights and deploy energy management systems in venues such as offices and factories. This is because Korean telecommunications operators can leverage ICT (Information and Communications Technology) infrastructure, already owned by them, and exploit the full potential of ICT (Jeong et al., 2013). It is therefore remarkably interesting to investigate the cases of Korean operators where sustainability becomes a potential growth opportunity rather than a mandatory obligation to comply.

Therefore, this paper studies the case of KT, which is driving the most innovative energy service based on ICT in Korean market and exhibiting noteworthy performance, called KT-MEG (KT's Micro Energy Grid). We conducted in-depth with staffs in the product owner organization, R&D organization and management support organization that are affiliated with KT-MEG. This is to identify the unique characteristics, the performance, and the key success factors of KT-MEG. The three research questions below will be answered in this case study:

1. What differentiation of customer experience does KT-MEG provide?
2. How did KT operate its organization to develop KT-MEG?
3. Why did KT enter traditional energy demand market with its new ICT-based energy technology among many other possibilities?

The composition of the contents is as follows. The section 2 analyzes KT's energy business and strategy. Section 3 and 4 confirm and discuss the performance of KT's smart energy business. Section 5 analyzes success factors of the business and section 6 concludes with new strategies for telecommunications operators: energy-centric business transformation.

LITERATURE REVIEW

Customer Experience Differentiation

While service industry is taking a greater portion of the global economy, the competition within the industry is becoming fiercer. Therefore, firms are taking customer experience differentiation as the winning move, which leverages the individual needs of different customers (S. Lee, 2009).

"Differentiation" is defined as the uniqueness and the individuality that only one possesses, which is enabled by the mechanisms of human perception. It is known that a person tends to remember more of an experience that provides greater and a variety of stimuli. For example, only 10% of reading, 20% of listening, 30% of seeing, and 70% of peaking are committed to memory. This figure increases when a variety of stimuli are coupled: 50% of seeing while listening and 90% of speaking and acting are committed to memory. In other words, the human perception processes memory by receiving information and comparing it with previously acquired memory to determine which information to commit to memory. (Neumeier, 2005).

Traditional differentiation strategy leverages feature & benefit marketing to emphasize the benefits (e.g., design, price, and speed) that are relatively easier to be perceived by the customers. Such strategy requires a firm to engage in price wars and quick time-to-market. This indicates that perceptually simple differentiation is limited in effect and impact duration, but experience-based differentiation is different as experience provides the basis of memory that influences decision making. Therefore, differentiation of experience taps into the memory of customers to distinguish the subject from other product/service.

In the market today, it is very effective to respond to the competitive landscape by taking into account the following in service design: satisfy customer experience based on experience differentiation rather than merely fulfilling the features that are easily perceived by the customers (Shin et al., 2009). Customers tend to base their repurchase decisions or influence other's purchase decisions based on the image created by the differentiated experience.

Ambidextrous Organization

The paradox of innovation states that the efficiency of a firm is proportional to its scale, but innovation of the firm is inversely proportional to its scale, indicating the difficulty of a large firm to be innovative. Today's firms are pressured to enhance efficiency (e.g., cost reduction) and to innovate at the same time. That is, the firm must efficiently utilize its current competence while developing new competence for the future (Raisch et al., 2009).

Ambidextrous organization, a concept raised by Charles O'Reilly and Michael Tushman, is an organization that pursues stability based on its legacy businesses on one hand while pursuing new and innovative items (e.g., items that are likely to be pursued by venture firms) on the other hand. (H. Kang et al., 2014)

This is the type of organizational structure that a firm must adopt if it has large scale or has very lucrative and profitable legacy businesses (Simsek et al., 2009). This is because firms tend to settle for the status quo and become obtuse to changes in the world, and it is difficult for them to realize the future trends and potential crises whilst making profit currently. Therefore, this organizational structure attempts to encourage firms to try new items/approaches to enhance problem solving skills. Applying this in the field would mean that the firm needs to be divided into a team that oversees legacy business and another team that prepares for the future. These teams would require its own respective organizational structure, operational system, corporate culture, and office space, while the executives would need to invigorate and encourage the teams to persistently challenge for innovation. Therefore, ambidextrous organization is an effective structure for successful firms to not settle for what it has succeeded but to persistently innovate.

Disruptive Innovation

Innovation inherently implies that it completely transforms convention, institution, organization, and methodology into a new counterpart. In other words, it creates something different from the existing ones (Amabile, 1988).

Clayton Christensen described the superficially understood process of innovation and creation with the concept of disruptive innovation in his book 'Innovator's Dilemma'. He classified innovation into sustaining innovation and disruptive innovation (C. Christensen, 2013).

Sustaining innovation is what the public usually refers to as improvement (Yang et al., 2015). It enhances quality/performance based on existing good/service. For example, enhancing speed of a product or improving the process to reduce fault rates. The sustaining innovation provides better quality and performance to extend and continue the current industry structure. Therefore, the incumbents' competence is enhanced while new firms' entry into market would become more difficult.

On the other hand, disruptive innovation drives fundamental change. This is also understood as 'an innovation that changes the rule of the game' as it provides new performance attribute that existing good/service cannot provide. Unlike the connotation of disruptive, the disruptive innovation neither occurs only in the high-tech industries nor requires surprising/radical processes. In can be created in any good/service, where new good/service will survive in the market if it provides additional value on top of the existing value and, if not, will perish.

There are two types of disruptive innovation: low-end and new market. Low-end disruptive innovation occurs when new product based on low-cost technology is released in the market where mainstream products overachieve the needs of the customers. New-market, on the other hand, creates a new market based on rules of game that are different from that of the existing market (C. M. Christensen et al., 2015).

Disruptive innovation tends to be driven by new firms as it requires new value propositions that are not emphasized by incumbents. Innovation shakes the market formed by past innovations and creates a new market based on the new products. In this process, incumbents that are used to past value propositions are likely to encounter crisis if they do not adapt to the new change.

Therefore, in the perpetual innovation process, the firm that targets disruptive innovation must consider the reason existing products were not able to provide demanded value and provide clear resolution to the reason to create completely new value that supersedes existing products (H. Lee et al., 2016).

As any market leader can plummet and face crisis, firms must pursue innovation and creativeness to prepare for the rapidly changing industry landscape.

OVERVIEW OF KT'S SMART ENERGY BUSINESS

Background: South Korea's Energy Landscape and KT-MEG

South Korea has mainly relied on fossil fuels (65.7%) and nuclear energy (30.0%) to fuel its economy while the contribution of renewable energy has been marginal (4.3%). This was mostly due to the nature of Korea's energy market where government/public sector has tight control. For example, KEPCO (Korea Electric Power Corporation), Korea's public utility company, was the only firm that had responsibility to generate and supply Korea's energy until 2015 (GSMA, 2017).

However, the governments and energy suppliers started to recognize the advantages of renewable and smart energy systems. To stimulate the sector, the government introduced phased liberalization of the Korean energy market. Furthermore, government also sponsored R&D (Research and Development) project 'Korea Micro Energy Grid' that formed the basis of KT-MEG (KT-Micro Energy Grid: KT's smart grid solution) (GSMA, 2017).

KT runs in total of USD 20 billion businesses including mobile business, which has the second largest market share in Korean mobile communications market, and fixed businesses such as fixed internet and IPTV (Internet Protocol Television) (both with the top market share in the Korean market). In 2014, KT acknowledged the need for new growth engine and identified five new platform business opportunities in 2014: media, smart energy, enhancing public value of firms, finance and public safety.

The reason behind the selection of smart energy as one of the new business opportunities was that KT possessed a nationwide ICT infrastructure based on national network coverage, which leads to KT consuming 0.5% of Korea's overall energy consumption (2500GWh amounting to USD 300 million electricity fee in 2016). This is necessary to maintain the nationwide coverage of vast ICT infrastructure, and hence reduction of energy cost was a critical issue for KT to resolve. With these issues, KT was able to accumulate know-hows on optimizing the operation efficiency. Furthermore, KT adopted new innovations in energy demand technology based on big data analytics, artificial intelligence and cloud infrastructure (Greenstein et al., 2017).

This was a golden opportunity for KT, as it was able to apply much of its traditional strengths to the utilities sector. KT's competence in managing secure and reliable connected solutions, excellent billing platform, already established nationwide networks and significant investment in cutting-edge technologies such as artificial intelligence (AI) and Mobile IoT (Internet of Things) (Low Power Wide Area Network in licensed spectrum) were all relevant for the sustained development of Korean energy market (GSMA, 2017).

KT-MEG Business Scope and Evolution

In December 2015, KT commercialized KT-MEG after conducting government-sponsored R&D project 'Korea Micro Energy Grid'. KT-MEG is an integrated total control and management platform for energy that integrates energy experts and KT's core competence of 24/7 control and management.

KT MEG is, in essence, convergence of KT's ICT capability on energy industry and provides various services such as renewable energy (energy generation), energy efficiency (energy demand) and electric vehicle charging & energy demand operation (energy trade) to various venues including photovoltaic power plants, apartments, office buildings, hospitals, hotels, and factories.

KT MEG is available to both energy consumption and generation, where customers can connect to KT-MEG through LTE-M (Long Term Evolution for Machines), 3G (3rd Generation)/LTE (Long Term Evolution), RFID (Radio Frequency Identification), fixed-line communications, and NB-IoT (Narrowband IoT) that is to be supported by the end of 2018). As various types of connectivity are supported, KT-MEG has very few restrictions on the type of customers it can serve. With the commercial launch of Mobile IoT (licensed spectrum low power wide area technologies), the service will be able to further expand the reach. Energy use is relayed to the network control center in Gwacheon city, where experts monitor site usage and micro grid demand. These experts inform the customers on ways to ensure optimal grid balancing and power distribution. KT's cloud-based analytics platform, the 'e-Brain', enables this as it analyses usage trends and performs diagnostics in real time. KT's e-Brain is based on machine-learning and therefore is able to factor weather, usage patterns and profitability to generate its own prediction models that enable efficient management of energy generation, energy consumption and energy trading.

Figure 1. The comprehensive scope of KT's smart energy solution (Source: KT Sustainability Report)

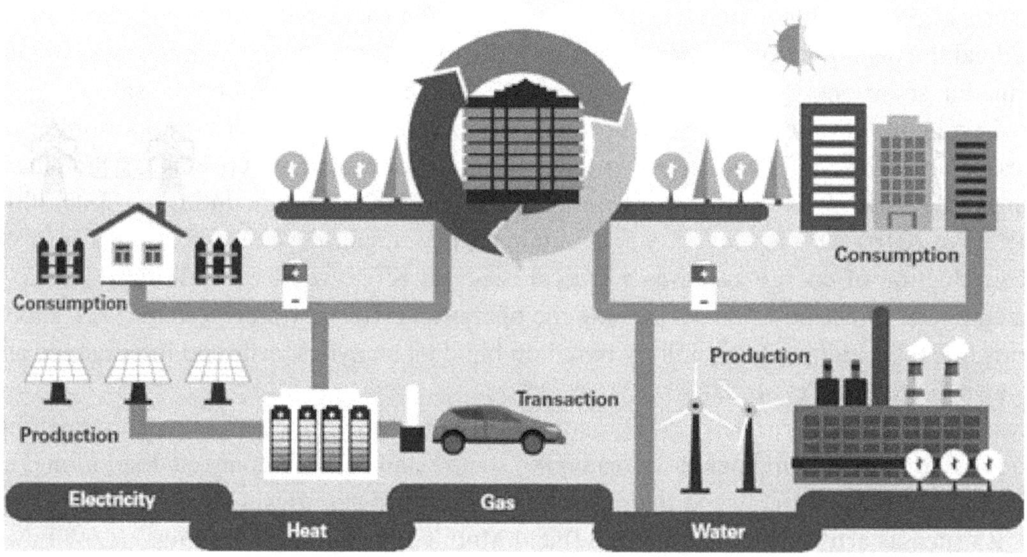

In energy generation, KT analyzes in real-time the factors that reduce efficiency of photovoltaic power plants (e.g., failures, overheating and dust) to maximize energy generation. KT also provides real-time remote failure response service for service recovery. KT's offerings are not limited to management of photovoltaic power plants but also in deployment of the power plants. In 2014, KT already deployed 7.5MW capacity photovoltaic power plant in Daecheok city with total of 13MW of deployment up to date (13MW is a capacity for 3,800 households to use electricity annually). KT-MEG monitors the status of power plants in real-time while providing reliable and economic management/operation of power plants with big data analytics based on various data (e.g., climate status and electricity generation status).

In energy consumption, KT aims to provide energy cost reduction and reliable operation by optimal management of energy facilities of venues such as buildings, factories, and hospitals. This is enabled by heat/electricity consumption demand forecast based on big data analytics and guidance on optimal operations & energy reduction. For example, KT helped hospital "P", with capacity of 500 infirmaries, to reduce its energy consumption by 30% with its ICT capability. A sports complex "B" in Gwangju also experienced a 75% reduction in its energy use by using KT-MEG.

For energy trading, KT additionally obtained license as an electricity grid service provider to provide re-selling of electricity and electric vehicle charging. KT's electricity vehicle offering, with mobile charging, expands the adoption of electricity vehicle by 50% while reducing the deployment cost of charging infrastructure by 83%. KT has applied the CTTS (Closed Transition Transfer Switch) technology to 60 sites of KT buildings in 2018 (Kim et al., 2019). This is accelerating the deployment of electricity vehicle charging infrastructure in Korea, where KT has deployed more than 6,000 electric car charging stations in 2019 (Kim et al., 2019).

There are also trials on energy demand resource operations, where mechanisms for forecasting situations requiring quick charging are in progress. This maximizes the energy reduction capability and consequently the stability of the electric grid.

The management and control of these services are centralized in KT-MEG Center (In Gyeonggi-do Gwacheon), where 35 energy specialists reside in the center for 24/7. The response becomes quicker when the center interconnects with KT's customer centers, which are spread throughout the nation.

Figure 2. Photo of KT-MEG center (Source: KT)

KT-MEG Business Scope and Evolution

KT-MEG has already been applied to buildings with high energy consumption such as Hospital and Sports Complex. The savings are realized by replacing some of the heat pumps with a new one and applying optimized control services. That is, KT-MEG continuously monitors the energy consumption of a building via measurements from sensors, building internal management system and IoT (Internet of Things). In the process, KT-MEG identifies various opportunities for savings and optimizes the equipment control to exploit those opportunities. KT-MEG specifically analyzes the effects of prominent variables (e.g., time of the day, day of the analysis, weather, and season) on energy consumption to not only identify reduction opportunities but also forecasts peak hours of energy consumption (see Figure 3). In Figure 3, KT-MEG provides the user information on the current weather, the status of energy production & consumption and the estimated revenue based on the operations. Furthermore, it also monitors how much has been charged and discharged by ESS (Energy Storage System) operations, the real-time status of operating different facilities monitored by the system, and finally the schedule of intelligent operation. This enables KT-MEG to preemptively identify measures to reduce energy consumption, resulting in innovative energy savings in addition to that of simply equipment replacement.

Figure 3. Information panel of KT-MEG system (Source: KT)

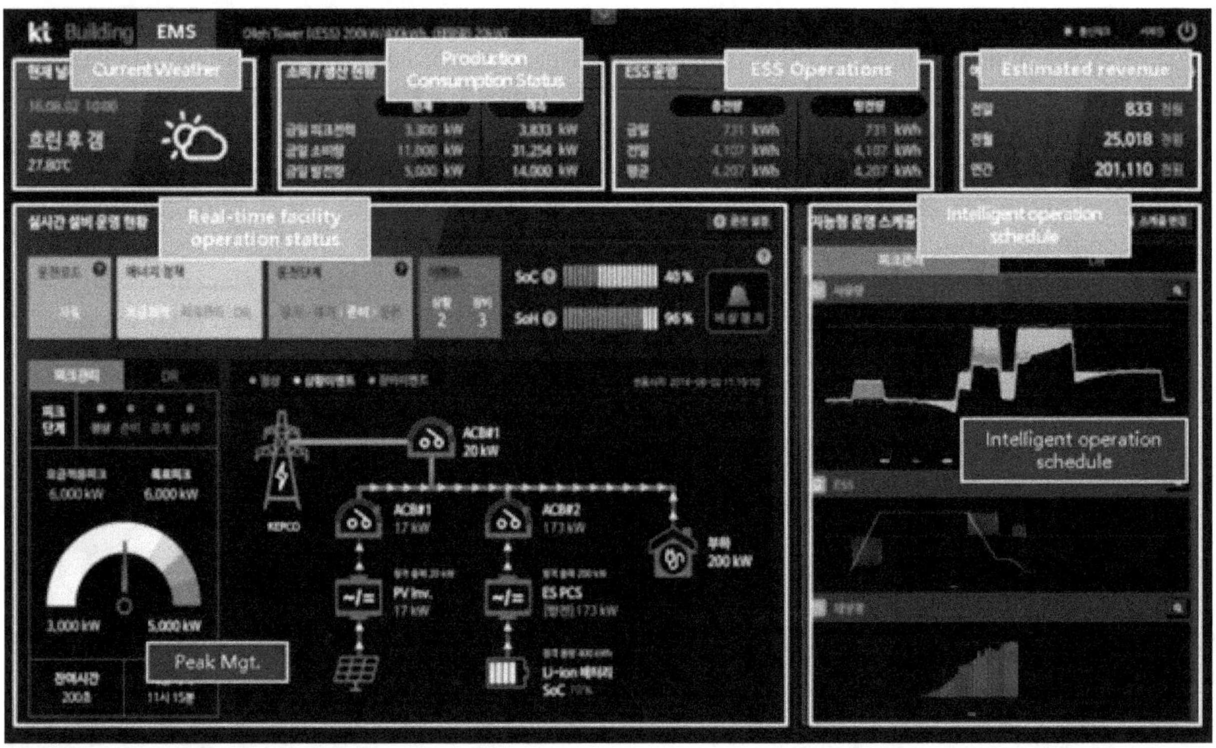

Hospital "P" that has 500 infirmaries experienced total of 71.8% energy reduction in January 2017 when it experimentally applied KT-MEG. Out of the 71.8%, 53.6% attributed to replacement of heat pump while additional 18.2% was attributed to ICT-based optimization capability of KT-MEG. The sports complex "H" also identified, with help of e-Brain big data analytics engine in KT-MEG, that the biggest opportunity for energy savings is 180tons of hot water disposed by Sauna facilities. With optimized plans of KT-MEG implemented, the sports complex was able to reduce its annual energy costs by 75% from KRW 280 million in 2016 to KRW 70M in 2017.

BUSINESS PERFORMANCE OF KT'S SMART ENERGY BUSINESS

Revenue Growth

The smart energy business leveraging KT's ICT capability is not only enhancing KT's brand image, but also enabling a new revenue stream. KT made less than KRW 20 billion in 2015, but in 2016 it monitored and controlled 851 sites through KT-MEG in 2016 leading to 100% growth in revenue (Park, 2017). In the first half of 2017, KT already made sales of KRW 100 billion with annual sales target of KRW 200 billion. Currently, KT-MEG Center is monitoring and controlling 3,300 sites (including energy efficiency consulting, demand resource operations and electric vehicle charging) currently (GSMA, 2017). In the future, it will integrate ESS (Energy Storage System) and AMI (Advanced Metering Infrastructure) to expand and advance KT-MEG system. Figure 5 concisely shows the growth of business performance of KT's smart energy business.

KT's performance has attracted attention of its competitors in Korea (SK Telecom and LGUplus) and they are also considering new energy services leveraging ICT capability as new business items. In addition, Korean regulators see KT's business as an opportunity to foster energy industry and adoption of environment-friendly energy sources.

Enhancing KT's Image and Status

Every year, world's largest exhibition of mobile and information communications technology is held in Barcelona, Spain. This exhibition is called Mobile World Congress (MWC) and KT's KT-MEG smart energy platform was awarded the best mobile award in the smart city in MWC Global Mobile Awards 2017 (Seoul_Newspaper, 2017). Global Mobile Awards is awarded by GSMA (GSM Association), which unites over 800 mobile operators and 300 companies in the broader mobile ecosystem and is considered as the "Oscar award" in the field of ICT. The smart city category awards services that contributed to changes and advances in smart cities by leveraging mobile technologies.

In addition to awards, KT deployed energy management systems in Las Vegas (Sahara Hotel) and Chicago (Montgomery), and deployed 3G-based AMI systems in Uzbekistan along with independent Photovoltaic power generation facilities (with Energy Storage System) in Rwanda. KT's performance is not limited to the Korean market, but KT is expanding globally with its technological excellence.

Transformation to Environment-Friendly Firm

KT has been selected as the best company for 4 consecutive years from 2013 by the Carbon Disclosure Project, a project that evaluates excellence in environmental management. It was also listed in the Carbon Management Honors Club for 4 consecutive years until 2017 (Chun, 2016).

As the selection illustrates, KT is considering developing its smart energy business beyond mere revenue creation to contributing to international environmental issues. KT already has been minimizing the energy consumption of networks by introducing energy efficient equipment and optimization of cooling systems. It has also been replacing lighting with higher efficiency LED lights to reduce building energy consumption. Recently, KT announced that it will replace a tenth (1,000) of its fleet of corporate vehicles (10,000) with electric vehicles and will be replacing all vehicles whose lifecycle ends with electric vehicles by 2020 (Lim, 2017). They currently have 30 electric vehicle charging sites within their offices but plans to extend it to all 400 offices to support its electric vehicles.

With its smart energy business, KT expects to reduce air pollution (e.g., fine dust and carbon monoxide) and operations & fuel cost for its corporate vehicles. This means that KT seeks not only business performance, but also remedies for international environmental issues.

KEY SUCCESS FACTORS

Customer Perspective: Differentiation of Customer Experience (Generation, Demand and Trade of Energy)

Traditional marketing emphasizes the features and the benefits of a product and considers consumer's processing of marketing stimulus as an important step. Bernd H. Schmitt from University of Columbia, however, emphasizes the role of experiential marketing, where customer experience in using the product is differentiated, in decision-making [21].

Rather than focusing on the results of new technologies, KT focused on creating a completely new customer experience in the energy business. This is because KT considered identification of unexplored markets/demands of the customer's lifestyle would be much more significant for the customer and the business than merely applying new technology to an existing market. In other words, KT prioritized systematically creating sustainable and novel customer experience based on technological insight. This was to ensure that KT established a firm brand in the new energy market as a new entrant.

As a result, KT did not focus on identifying the needs or the usage patterns of the customers, as this approach is useful for incremental innovation of existing products but not appropriate for developing completely new products that customers are not accustomed. Rather, KT integrated its network management and control capability based on KT-MEG Center to provide End-to-End management and control in energy market. This provides a completely new experience that no other traditional provider was able to support. This can be interpreted as an improvement of customer "experience" on existing energy markets with KT's ICT capability.

In this perspective, KT attempted to enhance the End-to-End customer experience that ranges from energy generation to energy demand and finally to energy trade. KT's major focus were as follows:

Table 1. KT's questions to achieve end-to-end experience (Source: KT)

Energy Generation	Energy Demand	Energy Trade
• How to enhance energy generation efficiency while maintaining the capacity of photovoltaic power plant and energy storage system?	• Is it possible to check the efficiency of energy consumption by comparing different neighbors/groups surrounding the user? • How to reduce the total energy cost?	• How to provide energy with less cost? • How to generate more profit from the generated energy in a stable manner?

Furthermore, while energy re-selling is not legally permitted, KT is aiming to expand its smart energy business to electricity trading. This is to prepare for the future growth and to exploit synergy with its current offerings of energy management & renewable energy businesses. Taking into the upcoming changes in the future energy paradigm, KT is considering becoming an energy prosumer where it will enable energy producers to sell energy directly to the consumers.

The key technology in this vision is intelligent analytics based on energy big data, which is an intelligent service that maximizes energy generation for energy producers, energy efficiency for energy consumers and optimizes transactions for energy market participants. KT is satisfying a diverse range of customer needs that arise from energy generation, energy demand and energy trade.

Organization Perspective: Ambidextrous Organization for New Energy Business

KT has been offering a portfolio of telecommunications services including internet and IPTV centered on the mobile communications proposition. However, new businesses often require risk-taking culture, long-term perspective and independent decision making, let alone overcome the inapplicability of knowledge and know-how from the existing businesses. This means that it is difficult to manage and develop both legacy business and new business in the same organization.

It is extremely difficult for a large established corporation like KT to create an independent organization focused on new business development. However, KT created Future Convergence Business Unit directly reporting to the CEO (Chief Executive Officer), which allows KT to be an ambidextrous organization that can maintain legacy businesses while taking risks to develop new businesses.

Figure 4. Organizational structure for KT (Source: Internal interview with KT's employee)

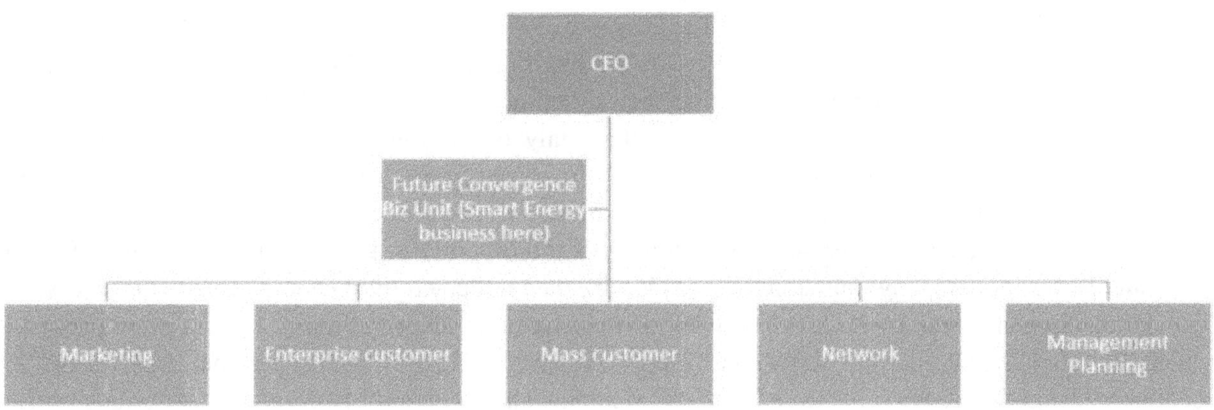

Ambidextrous organization is a concept proposed by Charles O'Reilly from Stanford University from his studies in the success and failures of various firms. For a large firm to sustain its market leadership and survive, ambidextrous organization is indispensable to maintain legacy business and experimental new business [22].

Ambidextrous organization enables a firm to acquire competence in both traditional markets and new markets. In other words, it can be defined as the coexistence of exploitation, which enhances the efficiency of the firm and reduces the risk, and exploration, which takes risks to exploit creativity. Simply put, ambidextrous organization is an organization that explores new opportunities while exploiting the core legacy competence. Such a firm innovates legacy products to gain competitive advantage and, at the same time, acquires new knowledge/capability to develop new innovative products to enter a new market.

KT recognized that dependence on only legacy businesses, no matter how profitable and effective the legacy business model is, cannot ensure sustainable revenue streams. Therefore, it was considering, even in the past, the means to proactively react to the changes and reallocate resources for legacy businesses towards new capability development.

The reason behind making an independent organization directly reporting to the CEO is because KT, with its immense size, is likely to be immersed in inertia when developing new businesses. This means that KT is likely to over-estimate the methods of legacy business such that it may avoid investing in new business models with some risk even if its legacy businesses are under threat.

The biggest issue in this process is striking a balance between legacy and new businesses. KT has sustained success with one telecommunications business, but it recognized the importance of new growth engines and transformed itself into an ambidextrous organization by making an independent organization focusing on new businesses that directly reports to the CEO.

Service Perspective: Disruptive Innovation with New Technology (Big Data and IoT)

When starting its smart energy business, KT noted that many enterprise customers (e.g., residential buildings, hotels, and smart factories) do not have good knowledge/information of their energy costs (e.g., plans, reduction opportunities and equipment lifecycle management). For small buildings, there were no energy specialists and therefore were less interested in reduction opportunities or had no capability to identify those opportunities even if they were interested.

Therefore, KT aimed at the low-end of the energy market and provided simple and affordable building energy reduction service called "Enereyes" to be distributed freely to building customers. This is in accordance with disruptive innovation as described by Innovator's Dilemma by Prof. Christensen. The Enereyes service is a mix of "energy" and "eyes" that analyzes building energy status and automatically provides cost reduction opportunities. KT debuted "Enereyes free" that can appeal to low-end target segment with affordable and attractive value proposition.

The unique feature of this service is that it utilizes the monthly usage data (iSmart) from KEPCO (Korean electricity company) and consolidates it with data collected by meters in 15-minute intervals. The data is then analyzed by KT's AI-based analytics engine to identify energy consumption patterns, which then suggests alternative energy consumption patterns optimized for the customer. Apartment "S" located in Daegu Korea was able to reduce 70% of annual shared electricity costs (i.e., cost not specific to households but are shared by all households in the apartment) by applying Enereyes service.

The big data analytics engine "ebrain" analyzes the variance of energy consumption patterns depending on different variables (e.g., time, day, and weather) and deduces relevant cost reduction opportunities. It also forecasts the energy consumption and predicts the peak demand time, which enables customers to reduce cost by managing energy demand and peak demand.

The Enereyes service is expected to be developed further and lite version will be offered soon. This version will monitor and predict energy consumption in real-time to provide professional consulting for energy reduction and a Premium version is also under development. This version will include real-time 24 hours monitoring and control of energy status of a building along with replacement of energy facilities.

Ultimately, KT aims to expand beyond enterprise buildings to consumer markets with the disruptive services. When KT brands itself as the new innovator in the energy services, we expect KT to be able to compete with direct supplier of electricity (KEPCO) in energy management market.

CONCLUSION

Implications of the Study

The 4th industrial revolution is expected to converge and add intelligence to traditional industries with latest technologies such as artificial intelligence, cloud, big data and IoT. As a result, boundaries distinguishing industries are blurring and business models are rapidly changing, where firms are faced with new opportunities for changes in all aspects ranging from technology, infrastructure, process, and platform. This case study analyzed the case of Korean mobile operator KT to see how a mobile operator expanded beyond its existing offerings of mobile, internet and media services to new businesses leveraging digital technology. The case study also analyzed in-depth how the business was developed, what the success factors were, and what the performance of the new business was.

KT's smart energy business utilizes ICT to resolve energy issues such as global climate change and energy consumption growth and provides growth opportunities for KT with its KT-MEG platform. KT-MEG platform analyzes, using ebrain engine, big data collected from energy generation, consumption, and trade to diagnose the energy issues along with forecast and alternatives. This provides new service experience for the customers and therefore makes KT-MEG an "integrated service platform business".

In this process, KT approached the issue in the perspective of innovation and applied aggressive measures to develop the energy businesses. For example, it did not pursue its traditional way (e.g., system, organization and means) of developing services but employed innovative approaches to foster competence and focusing intentionally on new businesses.

We expect that KT's case can be beneficial for other mobile operators in finding new growth opportunities in sustainability rather than perceiving it as a liability. We hope that other mobile operators and ICT companies will learn from this case and develop new businesses to differentiate customer experience, to create effective organization structure, and to generate business impact in addition to leveraging latest ICT technologies such as artificial intelligence, IoT and big data.

Limitations of this Research and Future Topics for Study

While this research was able to analyze the smart energy business of KT in the perspective of business transformation with details of business scope/strategy/organization, this research was not able to evaluate the business in the perspective of KT's employees and in the perspective of ICT industry. Therefore, future studies should, based on the results of this research, focus on the evaluation of the business from both in and out of the firm, the quantitative measurement of the impact of KT's smart energy business and comparative analysis with business transformation cases of non-Korean mobile operator. Such topics would provide more meaningful results that can benefit practice, academia, and the ecosystem overall.

REFERENCES

Amabile, T. M. (1988). A model of creativity and innovation in organizations. *Research in Organizational Behavior*, *10*(1), 123–167.

Christensen, C. (2013). *The innovator's dilemma: when new technologies cause great firms to fail*. Harvard Business Review Press.

Christensen, C. M., Raynor, M. E., & McDonald, R. (2015). What is disruptive innovation. *Harvard Business Review*, *93*(12), 44–53. PMID:17183796

Chun, G. (2016, October 31). KT added to carbon management honors club. *Energy Economy*. https://www.ekn.kr/news/article.html?no=246713

Deloitte. (2018). *Consulting*. Telecommunications Industry Outlook.

Greenstein, S., Zhu, F., & Herman, K. (2017). *Korea Telecom: Building a GiGAtopia (A) and (B)*. https://store.hbr.org/product/korea-telecom-building-a-gigatopia-a/617014?sku=617014-PDF-ENG

GSMA. (2017). *KT MEG: Korea's Smart Energy System*. GSMA.

Jang, S. (2017, February 6). "Difficult to grow with telecommunications only" Telcos reach out to new businesses. *Economy Chosun*. http://economychosun.com/special/special_view.php?boardName=C05&t_num=11200

Jeong, D., Kim, H., & Yoo, S. (2013). KT Smartgrid implementation. *Information and Communications Magazine*, *30*(2), 59–65.

Kang, H., Park, H., Yun, S., & Jung, H. (2014). Ambidextrous organization of COSMAX. *Korea Business Review*, *18*(1), 177–199.

Kang, Y., Ryu, M.-H., & Kim, S. (2010). Exploring sustainability management for telecommunications services: A case study of two Korean companies. *Journal of World Business*, *45*(4), 415–421.

Kim, Y.-M., Jung, D., Chang, Y., & Choi, D.-H. (2019). Intelligent micro energy grid in 5G era: Platforms, business cases, testbeds, and next generation applications. *Electronics (Basel)*, *8*(4), 468.

Lee, H., Kim, G., & Kim, M. (2016). Understanding disruptive innovation in the perspective of the market. *Korea Business Review*, *20*(1), 43–67.

Lee, S. (2009). Manage your customer's experience - CEM Marketing. *Marketing*, *43*(2), 73–76.

Lim, S. (2017, July 11). KT replaces its corporate vehicles with electric vehicles. *Maeil Economy*. http://news.mk.co.kr/newsRead.php?year=2017&no=465080

Neumeier, M. (2005). *The Brand Gap* (Revised Edition). Peachpit Press.

Park, J. (2017, March 31). KT Smart Energy business gets on track, targets 200B won revenue this year. *Financial News*. https://www.fnnews.com/news/201703311517431179

Raisch, S., Birkinshaw, J., Probst, G., & Tushman, M. L. (2009). Organizational ambidexterity: Balancing exploitation and exploration for sustained performance. *Organization Science*, *20*(4), 685–695.

Seoul Newspaper. (2017, March 1). KT Wins Glomo Awards. *Seoul Newspaper*. https://www.seoul.co.kr/news/newsView.php?id=20170302021023&wlog_tag3=naver

Shin, J., Choi, S., & Moon, T. (2009). Empirical study on the flow experience and intention to repurchase of mobile contents service. *Internet E-Commerce Research*, *9*(3), 115–132.

Simsek, Z., Heavey, C., Veiga, J. F., & Souder, D. (2009). A typology for aligning organizational ambidexterity's conceptualizations, antecedents, and outcomes. *Journal of Management Studies*, *46*(5), 864–894.

Yang, O., Park, J., & Lim, S. (2015). Xiaomi: Revolution of a rice grain. *Korea Business Review*, *19*(3), 83–118.

ENDNOTES

1. As risks and concerns over blackout persist due to instability of energy supply, there is a need for low-cost sustainable alternative energy.
2. Paris agreement now makes reduction of carbon emissions mandatory rather than optional. It has enabled attraction of global interest in reduction of energy consumption and greenhouse gas emissions.

Chapter 13
An Automated Geometric Appraisal Model:
A Computerized Performance-Based Incentive Policy Suitable for HEIs in India

Hari Govinda Rao Chukka
https://orcid.org/0000-0001-9821-9075
Vignan's Institute of Information Technology, India

Sampath Dakshina Murthy Achanta
https://orcid.org/0000-0002-9960-6373
Vignan's Institute of Information Technology, India

ABSTRACT

The idea of the circular economy is gaining steam in academia through the green economics of human resources policies in Asia. A high performance model delivers superior outcomes but does not deter praiseworthy professors from biased human interference. Using the computerized-based geometric performance base incentive model (CGPBI) is particularly beneficial in encouraging faculty who have achieved superior outcomes in all areas of science, academia, and other contributions. To fill this gap, the author proposed a geometric hybrid reward policy model that includes a number of fictitious variables such as topic tolerance, the effects of subject matter, and the average outcome across all subjects. This model uses Python to construct a standardized framework to gather data on the success of faculty. It provides a robust indication of comparative success and motivates workers to achieve more transparent performance outcomes. The author proposes the use of a multi-source assessment (MSA) to evaluate the faculty's annual results.

INTRODUCTION

The shift to a more lasting circular economy may be encouraged through digitisation. Digitization will also improve the efficiency and efficiency of company processes, assist in minimising waste, promote

DOI: 10.4018/978-1-7998-8678-5.ch013

product life and decrease transaction costs (Antikainen, M., 2018, p. 45). In order to facilitate and facilitate the circular economy, digitalisation will be the key tool (Larsson, A., and Lindfred, L., 2019, p.280). The digital database technologies that serve as new types of policy tools are being used for educational and governing institutions and activities. These digital policy tools are proof that digital database tools and infrastructures are the focus of education, knowledge, administration and management, both domestically and internationally (Williamson, B., 2016, p.123). Due to the digital revolution, e-HR has become the new method of HRM activity via new tools and apps on the web and computers. These apps have simplified HR professionals' jobs and enabled them to concentrate on their primary task, namely strategic human resources, rather than on departmental procedural labour (Meral, Y. (Ed.)., 2019, p. 382). Digital Human Resource Management is a digital transformation of HR processes and practices through the use of electronic, mobile, analysis and IT to enhance the efficiencies of HRM (Halid, H., 2019, p.96).

Green management of human resources (GHRM) is rapidly becoming a major topic in academic circles in organisational environmental management and its effect on green employee behaviour (Zhang, Y., 2019, p. 1). The Circular Economy is gaining traction in academia, industry, and policy making as an alternative model that minimises resource depletion, waste, and emissions. To implement the concept at the organisational level, business models are an important lever. (Geissdoerfer, M., et. al. 2020). The rapid advancement of technology has increased the number of digitalisations and continues to influence and change the way businesses operate (Halid, H., 2020, p.96).The use of long-term development methods to achieve a green economic transition is known as "green growth." Green economies put people's well-being ahead of increased efficiency in new technologies (Vargas-Hernández, J. G. 2021, p.1). The methods used to deal with digital solutions are critical components of digital technology that allow conducive, long-term work (Larsson, A., & Lindfred, L., 2019, p. 280). Digitization or digital transformation is something that all organizations have to do in order to be efficient and relevant in the future (Halid, H., 2020, p.96).

Moşteanu, N, (2020, p. 108) proposed that the business environment, strategy, and organisation, new technology, digitalization of everything, and the green economy will be approaching a change. The most often used words during the last decade, but especially in recent years, have been digitalisation, digital transformation, and the green economy. If a business wants to remain competitive in the market while still offering green products and services, it must change its management style (Moşteanu, N. R., et. al., 2020, p. 108). A sustainable green economy requires integrated, cooperative, and holistic institutions that span the whole economy horizontally as well as vertically. Effective policy instruments have become more widely available as a tool for addressing a wide range of environmental issues, from acid rain to climate change, since they are effective policies to address specific types of environmental issues through traditional regulatory and voluntary approaches (Rehberger, M., & Hiete, M., 2020, p. 4366).

With this background in mind, the research sought to digitalize incentive programmes by referring to the new digital technologies that are presently changing the academic sector. Incentives are quick incentives that have an immediate impact on performance (Rao, C. H. G et al., 2017, p.1). According to some studies, a faculty member is always paid depending on his or her productivity. Given the significance of output quality in driving productivity, many well-regarded academics may be driven to tolerate minor changes in status, since there is no instant way of recognising achievement and finding suitable incentives. As a consequence, a robust performance evaluation system helps an educational institution to create prospective forces; an examination of employee performance is needed to decide whether further training is required or if dismissal is warranted. The granting of an incentive is always preceded by an assessment of an employee at different levels. At the same time, it is essential to consider unique incentives for certain individual performances, which should be arranged in such a manner, that the employee is driven by acknowledgment of his or her work and self-esteem. According to psychometric research, motivation plays an essential part in the law of behaviour, and greater impetus results in preferred execution. As a result, a performance-based incentive approach is usually helpful in tying remuneration directly to particular organisational goals and management objectives (Johnson, S. M., and Papay, J. P., 2009, p.1; Liang, G., 2013, p. 324; Odden, A et. al, 2002, p.1).

PERFORMANCE INCENTIVE POLICY

In traditional policy, certain undesirable problems, such as politics, religion, caste, avarice, and friendship administration's binding, among others, have taken advantage of rewarding some inefficient individuals while neglecting brilliance (Rao, C. H. G et al., 2017, p.1). Later, in order to prevent wage inequalities between men and women on campus, teacher remuneration has long been focused exclusively on "personality development" factors such as "duration of service and degree of education achieved." This traditional pay method has recently been criticised because of the poor connection between a teacher's abilities, faculty growth, student performance, and faculty recognition. The PBI policy for professors would simply enhance an educational institution's good old boy's network. PBI pays competitively for competitive levels of performance and encourages workers to continuously learn new abilities. Even several of the academics agreed that most traditional performance-based reward schemes had difficulty promoting cooperation (Chamberlin, R. et. al., 2002, p. 31; Odden A, 2001, p.16). As a consequence, a large body of research argues that performance-based incentive schemes represent a change in pay scale proficiency (Mohrman Jr. et al., 1996, p.51).

LITERATURE REVIEW

Professors are traditionally paid on a regular salary basis, with only educational qualifications and years of experience determining their rank. The idea of a performance-based incentive has received a lot of attention in the literature during the last decade. Previously, the majority of programs focused on each employee's performance with a specific merit pay (Richardson, R., 1999, p.), but recent trends indicate that intellectual factors, such as knowledge and skills, are more likely to be evaluated (Chamberlin, R. et al., 2002, p.31; Odden et al., 2002, p.1).When it comes to creating performance-based compensation in the division, the idea of after-performance pay offers the most incentive to increase interesting results (Balch, R., and Springer, M. G., 2015, p.114). According to an administrative condensation study, teachers are the most essential component of learning and success (Darling-Hammond, L., 1997, 2, p.1). In a broader sense, the implementation of pay framework agreements is being pushed as an alternative to a single compensation plan with the aim of attracting and keeping competent individuals from different areas of employment. The compensation system is a critical component of any strategic management system designed to support the institution's strategic objectives (Bueno, C. and Sass, T. R., 2018, p.1). For teachers, classroom observations are the most often utilised evaluation method (Goe, L., et. al., 2008, p.1). Much research has been carried out to examine the strict structure of teacher compensation systems and their effect on student career development (Hanushek, E. A., et al., 2004, p.326; Lankford, H., et al., 2002, p.37). The bulk of teacher evaluation methods have emphasised instructor experience and credentials above performance (Odden A, 2001, p.16). Despite the fact that experience and advanced degrees are significant variables in teacher pay, they are not strongly linked to student performance or institutional results (Goldhaber, D., 2002, p.50; Rockoff, J. E., 2004, p.247).

Hoerr T (1998, p.326) proposed unmerited-driven system as unfairness for exceptional professors since they are not evaluated by effective criteria. Despite the fact that teachers' work is recognised, their pay does not always equal that of the private sector (Solmon, L. C., and Podgursky, M., 2000, p.1). Performance-based incentives are a particular policy of performance-based rewards (Chamberlin, R., et al., 2002, p.31). As a result, there is little evidence of the characteristics of a well-designed teacher incentive compensation scheme (Springer, M. G., and Taylor, L. L., 2016, 344). A popular education reform is "pay-for-performances." HEI faculty used to have integrated perks and salary, as well as the widest range of professorships and experience (Richardson, R., 1999, p.1). Many of the fundamental tasks of the existing higher education system may be fulfilled by managing performance. They are not linked to teacher performance or institutional outcomes, which are important drivers of teacher pay (Cekik, R., and Telceken, S., 2018, p.1881). Because of faulty politics, the increase in human inflow is unjust to outstanding instructors. Incentives based on performance Numerous studies on the performance evaluation of employees in institutions have been conducted using this technique. The following sections detail some of the assessment methods used.

Islam, R., and Bin Mohd Rasad, S., (2006, p.1) have applied the analytical hierarchy process (AHP) to reduce complexity in structural-hierarchical evaluation settings. The system's limitations include the need for expert decision software to generate weights and sub-criteria, as well as a large amount of time spent getting overall performance results.

Neogi, A., et al., (2011, p.595) proposed a 'Fuzzy Inference System' and a degradation approach (COG) employing the module Fuzzy Inference System, in addition to five FIS sub-modules (FIS). The major disadvantage is that an expert may easily change the system's inputs, including a variety of fluffy rules.

Ghosh, S., and Das, N. (2013, p.267) pioneered administrative monitoring and assessment of PMS Model performance in higher education institutions. The drawback of this approach was that it did not address hidden performance assessment features like mentoring and counselling.

Although it is restricted to the staff being assessed and can not access multi-users, Samuel et al. (2014, p.452) used fluid logic for the performance evaluation of human resources based on the idea of fluid set theory [30].

C. H. G. Rao et al. (2017, p.1) proposed a geometric model based on a mathematical premise that calls for performance-based rewards and therefore forms a comprehensive professional performance evaluation model. While the methodology and system-based process were fairly conventional, the method and system-based process were the most difficult.

Cekik, R., and Telceken, S. (2018, 1881) used the hypertext preprocessor (PHP) to create an efficient automated approach for reducing publication rating sentiment while analysing academic staff profiles. It was solely interested in assessing staff research and ignoring university performance. Macwan, N., and D. P. S. Sajja (2013, 324) utilised fluffy evaluation methods to speed up the assessment process and extract conclusive results from equivocal, unambiguous, or erroneous data. The assessment criteria utilised at the organisational level did not all matter equally. Instead of utilising conventional methods to categorise students based on exam results, Jamsandekar and Jamsandekar, S. S., & Mudholkar, R. R., (2013, p.158) used fuzzy inferences by fusing input data by developing the Fuzzy Inference System (FIS), a smart topic. However, because an intelligent, adaptive, and tutoring Internet-based system is required for student performance analysis, this approach necessitates the use of a human expert to uncover data correlations.Ojokoh, B., Akinsulire, V., and F. O. Isinkaye created "a crude model for the efficient assessment of academic staff from the promotional institution and a mathematical relationship approach" (2019, p.1). The model's main weakness is that it ignores comparison findings and peer evaluation. While considerable improvements in literature have been made in recent decades, there have been serious limitations in how knowledge is presented and used in higher education institutions. At this point, the study's goal is to examine the idea of PBI and its inadequacies in the application process for HEIs via all of these linked assessments.

STATEMENT OF THE PROBLEM

When compared to the history of the globe, PBI schemes in India are relatively new, and the majority of studies address the significance of PBI policy, difficulties, subtleties, and particular development methods in PBI policy (Rao, C. H. G et al., 2017, p.1). Many researches have been focused on the idea and its implementation process among school-level instructors. Despite the vast quantity of research, there is no specific study that provides a critical numerical model of usage at the institution level. There is little emphasis on the study of the mathematical model of PBI, particularly in the area of technical education in India. There is also a need to consider PBI policy problems in India, with a particular emphasis on technical institutions such as engineering schools, where performance evaluation is focused. In light of the above, current research examines the evaluation of the PBI Policy and conducted a study that reveals a mathematical notion for assessing performance appraisal in engineering schools. The consequences revealed by the analysis of the PBI structure will provide useful information to the strategy designers, personnel, and other partners of the institution. The evaluation would identify the areas that need to be evaluated and hone the understanding of the relationships between important components for staff assessment.

HYBRID MODEL PERFORMANCE BASED INCENTIVE (GHMPBI) POLICY

Educators are compensated based on their degrees and experience in various areas of the globe. However, a large number of experts have concluded that the benefits of experience are limited and that credentials have a small impact on understudies' performance (Rao, C. H. G et al., 2017, p.1). Educators' qualities will become more essential in the future. As a result of this distinction between educator remuneration and instructor execution, the possibility of budgetary motivating forces for instructors (commonly known as Performance Based Incentive or Merit Based Incentive) related to occasions of understudy execution has turned out to be increasingly acknowledged and well known. In this manner, a significant body of research has suggested that performance-based incentive frameworks with a mix of all factors included in setting goals constitute a change in pay scale productivity. Because of this pioneering approach based on the assumption that relative student performance has the potential for great effectiveness, but that approach has not yet been extensively explored, these techniques may function but have not been thoroughly tested (Neogi, A., Mondal, A. C., and Mandal, S. K., 2011, p. 595). With this purpose, this study developed a hybrid model that integrated all of the elements of faculty assessment.

Influence behind GHMPBI Policy

Classic PBI policies have been experimentally recognised as providing both objective and subjective assessments as GHMPBI policies (Rao, C. H. G et al., 2017, p.1). It promotes academic competitiveness in terms of outcomes, as well as research outputs that contribute to the Institute's goals. Higher achievers in our GHMPBI approach are continuously pushing for bigger incentives. As a result of the superior's ability to 'play' him rather than his basic principles, a series of absurd events ensue. While the GHMPBI policy is fully automated, it offers additional chances for individuals to demonstrate their competitiveness. A basic database system and simple software may be used to create a GHMPBI policy (Rao, C. H. G et al., 2017, p.1). Table 1 shows the specifications of the suggested model.

Table 1.

Criteria	Academic results	Student Feedback	Research & Development	Other Contribution
Maximum Credits Awarded	3	1	3	3
Scope of compensation	All faculty who can achieve maximum academic Results	All faculty who can achieve maximum student feedback score	All faculty who can progress through their research	All professors who can support the students, peers, and institute
Areas evaluated	Evaluated on the basis of demonstrated abilities and data that is thought to be related to improved employee performance. The academic results are published on a regular basis.	Assessed based on demonstrated abilities and learning that are connected to improved employee performance. Students often use the system.	Assessed on the basic of output connected to faculty research area. Often comes as quality distributions	Evaluated on the premise of workforce yield as additional commitments for advancement of understudy, self and establishment. Like, student counseling, discipline and Peers feedback often comes in the form of other credentials

Hypothesis and Methodology

Given the significance of the research and in light of the aforementioned characteristics, this study tries to evaluate the performance evaluation using a geometric model of experiments (Rao, C. H. G et al., 2017, p.1). The primary goal of this model is to provide a complete mathematical model that can be used by technical institutions to evaluate a faculty's yearly academic evaluation. These are the model's propositions:

The growth and development of any technical institution may be dependent on its overall student outcomes, student comments on faculty teaching style, institute research output, and other contributions (Rao, C. H. G et al., 2017, p.1). As a consequence, the author assumed that four fundamental criteria may affect the institute's development and growth: student academic performance, feedback, and faculty development via research and development. Subject-matter toughness is critical to achieving excellent outcomes. Since student results play an important part in PBI policy, several faculty members voiced their dissatisfaction, and it was also pointed out that student results are fortunately dependent on students' intellect and paper toughness. As a result, high-quality employees may be dissatisfied. As a consequence, this research analyses the comparison result scores within the same part as well as the results of the other sections.

The calibre of pupils may vary by class. As a result, the author believes that at an institution with several departments and instructors, a number of degrees play a significant role in teaching the same subject to various departments. Taking the aforementioned suggestions into account, the evaluation tries to investigate the following hypotheses:

H_1: It is hypothesized that there is a strong significant association between the result range within the same section and the result of the same subject in other section.
H_0: It is estimated that there is no relationship between individual subject result and other subject's results.

Building on the above premise, TEN-point scales are developed by GHMPBI to measure the performance of a professor at a technical institution. The GHMPBI policy mainly takes into consideration all the essential areas in which an employee's advancement is made, including academic results, research & development, academic feedback (ACF) and other contributions (OC). The weighted score specifications for the above criterion are as follows:

Weighted Academic Result Score (WARS) = 3 Marks
Weighted Academic Feedback Score (WAFS) = 1 Marks
Weighted Research & Development Score (WRDS) = 3 Marks
Weighted other contributions Score (Wocs) = 3 Marks

Mathematically it can be expressed as represented in the formula 1:

Assessment of "Academic Result Score (ARS)"

This criterion mainly focuses on the academic performance of an employee which covers the semester results of an employee in an academic year. The author proposes 3 marks in this criterion based on the following propositions:

a. It considers Individual Subject Result Analysis within the class/section when compared to other subjects of the same class.
b. It also considers the performance of individual subject result when compared to the result of the same subject in all sections of all the branches. Based upon above propositions, the author develops the following Geometric Hybrid Model for computation of Academic Performance Score (APS) can be calculated by using the formula 2.

Here åAPS.W_{AP} = Weighted average score of academic results performance

Table 2.

Branch	Subjects	Empl. Id	Result (Pass %)
IT	y_1 = CNS	**10432**	**95.12%**
	OSS	10093	90.24%
	x_1 = MC	**10088**	**100%**
	DP	10647	98%
	IRS	10646	97%
	DWDM	10094	90.24%

ARS_1 = Academic Result Score of a subject
x = Highest percentage of the subject result within the section
y = Percentage of the concerned subject of the individual faculty
z = Highest Percentage of the same subject result in the entire college within the semester
n = total number of papers taught by the individual faculty in stipulated period

Result Analysis and Interpretation

Case 1: Employee No: 10432 taught CNS subject for IT-IV-1and secured 95.12% result. The same subject (CNS) result of the other sections represented the Table 2, and Table 3. X_1 = 100% (Subject MC Result); y_1 = 95.12% (Subject CNS Result); z_1 = 100% (Subject CNS in section IV CSE – 1 Result =100%); i = subject number taught by a faculty; The calculation process of ARS_1 is completely explained with this example by using the formula 2.1.

Case 2: If the same Employee No: 10432 is also having OSS subject for IV CSE – 2 and he has secured 57% result. It is very low % when compared to other subject's result. The detailed result analysis the same section and other section are represented in the Table 4 and Table 5 where x_2 = *71% (Subject UMLDP result);* y_2 = *57% (OSS result;* Z_2 = *81% (Subject OSS result).* It is completely explained by using formula 2.2.

Case 3: Employee No: 11572 is having DWDM subject for IV CSE – 3 and secured 62% result. The same subject (DWDM) result represented in the Table 6 and Table 7 where x = *91%;* y = *62%;* z = *100%.* It is calculated by using formula 2.3.

Case 4: Employee No: 11573 is having SE subject for ECM and secured 68% result. The same subject (SE) result of the other sections represented in the Table 8 and Table 9 where x = *75%;* y = *68%;* z = *76%.* It is calculated by applying the formula 2.4.

Case Analysis and Interpretation

Case 1: In this case author attempted a stable result range between the results of same section and the result of the same subject when compared to other sections. That means the result range between CNS and other subjects of same section is 4.88%. Empl. Id: 10432 is positioned at second best in-terms of

Table 3.

Branch	Subject	Empl. ID	Result (Pass %)
IV CSE - 1	SPM	10441	100
	z_1= CNS	**10526**	**100**
	UMLDP	10540	100
	MC	10552	100
	DMDW	10572	100
	OSS	10009	100
IV CSE - 2	SPM	10420	100
	CNS	**10062**	**84**
	UMLDP	10539	98
	MC	10606	100
	DMDW	10467	100
	OSS	10072	89
IV CSE - 3	SPM	10441	80
	CNS	**10526**	**52**
	UMLDP	10540	91
	MC	10552	84

subject result of the same section. However, he also got a positive result through PBI system when it considers CNS result of other sections in the same semester. Therefore, PBI resulted with a positive score and awarded "2.978" score for given Empl.ID 10432.

Case 2: This paper also experimented with large result range in case 2. It is found that the result range between OSS and other subjects of same section is 14%. At the same time, it ranged with 24% when compared to other sections. Empl. Id. 11432 is positioned at last before in-terms of subject result of the

Table 4.

Branch	Subjects	Empl. Id	Result (Pass %)
IV CSE – 2	SPM	10441	60
	CNS	10526	52
	x_2 = UMLDP	**10540**	**71**
	MC	10552	64
	DMDW	10572	59
	y_2= OSS	**10432**	**57**

Table 5.

Branch	Subjects	Empl. Id	Result (Pass %)
IT Dept./ IV-1	CNS	10432	95.12%
	OSS	10093	80.24%
	MC	10088	100%
	DP	10647	100%
	IRS	10646	100%
	DWDM	10094	90.24%
IV CSE - 1	SPM	10441	100
	CNS	10526	100
	UMLDP	10540	100
	MC	10552	100
	DMDW	10572	100
	z_1= OSS	**10009**	**81**
IV CSE - 3	SPM	10420	100
	CNS	10062	84
	UMLDP	10539	98
	MC	10606	100
	DMDW	10467	100
	OSS	10072	79

same section. However, he got a positive result through PBI system when it considers OSS result of other sections in the same semester. Therefore, PBI resulted a positive score and awarded with "1.842".

Case 3: Empl. Id: 11572 had positioned at fourth among six subjects in-terms of subject result of the same section. However, he also got a negative result through PBI system when it considers DWDM result of other sections in the same semester. At this juncture, it can be noticed that the result range between DWDM and other subjects of same section is 29%. At the same time, it ranged with 33% when it

Table 6.

Branch	Subjects	Empl. Id	Result (Pass %)
IV CSE – 3	SPM	10441	80
	CNS	10526	52
	x_2 =UMLDP	10540	91
	MC	10552	84
	y_1= DWDM	10572	62
	OSS	10009	57

Table 7.

Branch	Subject	Empl. ID	Result (Pass %)
IT Dept./ IV-1	CNS	10432	95.12%
	OSS	10093	90.24%
	MC	10088	100%
	DP	10647	100%
	IRS	10646	100%
	DWDM	10094	90.24%
IV CSE - 1	SPM	10441	100
	CNS	10526	100
	UMLDP	10540	100
	MC	10552	100
	z_{1}= DWDM	10572	100
	OSS	10009	100
IV CSE - 2	SPM	10420	100
	CNS	10062	84
	UMLDP	10539	98
	MC	10606	100
	DWDM	10467	98
	OSS	10072	89

compared to other sections. Therefore, PBI resulted with a negative score and awarded "-0.6495" score and awarded with 0 score of PBI for given Empl.ID 11572.

Case 4: In this example, employee is having SE subject for ECM branch which is single section and at the same time, there is one competitive section for that i.e., IT is also single section. He positioned at third best among six subjects in-terms of subject result of the same section. However, he also got a positive result through PBI system when it considers SE result of other section in the same semester.

Table 8.

Branch	Subject	Empl. ID	Result (Pass %)
E.COM	y_{1}=CG	11001	75 %
	DAA	11002	60 %
	DICA	11003	52 %
	x_{2} = SE	11004	68 %
	MS	11005	70 %
	LICA	11006	50 %

Table 9.

Branch	Subject	Empl. ID	Result (Pass %)
IT	ADS	11007	65.12 %
	SE	11008	64.12 %
	CN	11009	72.68 %
	OS	11010	72.68 %
	WT	11012	57.56 %
	∑ 1= CG	11013	76.00 %

At this juncture, it can be noticed that the result range between SE and other subjects of same section is 7%. At the same time, it ranged with 8% when it compared to other sections. Therefore, PBI resulted with a positive score and awarded “2.8305” score for given employee.

1. If an employee secured x-y < 30 and z-x < 30 his/her PBI is always positive result
2. If an employee secured x-y > 30 and z-x < 30 his/her PBI is also positive result
3. If an employee secured x-y > 30 and z-x > 30 his/her PBI is negative result

From the analysis, it can be understood that the tendency of “academic result score” in different cases. The study identified a constant result of ARS with same result range between same section and other sections [case 1], At the same it also produces a low result of ARS where the result range Δzy is more than Δxy. It indicates that the top performer of the same section may not obtain good score if the range is high when compared to other sections [case 2, case 3]. The analysis also showed the impact of result range in [case 4]. At the outset, the faculties who have produced good result he/she will get good score even in the subject toughness situation. Therefore, the employees must secure a positive score of ARS to acquire good PBI score. Subsequently, he/she would be eligible for better increments.

Assessment of Academic Feedback Score (AFS)

This is the second criterion of the GHMPBI policy which proposed the following to assess the student’s feedback [25]. There are nine questions put forward to students, for that they will allot 0-10 marks for individual questions on individual subject. Finally, the study considers average score of subject feedback for individual subjects and consolidates total subjects feedback score and the details are presented in the Table 10. It can be calculated by using the formula 3.

Assessment of Research and Development Score (RDS)

The THIRD criterion of PBI is an Academic Research & Development and its main features are as given below:

Table 10.

Criterion	Question	S1	S2	S3	S4
Q1	Clarity in Presentation of Topics in the class & Subject knowledge of the faculty	SQ_{11}	SQ_{12}	SQ_{13}	SQ_{14}
Q2	Courteous and impartial to students	SQ_{21}	SQ_{22}	SQ_{23}	SQ_{24}
Q3	Coverage of the syllabus as per lecture plan	SQ_{31}	SQ_{32}	SQ_{33}	SQ_{34}
Q4	Discipline maintenance in the class	SQ_{41}	SQ_{42}	SQ_{43}	SQ_{44}
Q5	Doubt clearance	SQ_{51}	SQ_{52}	SQ_{53}	SQ_{54}
Q6	Faculty comes to class on time	SQ_{61}	SQ_{62}	SQ_{63}	SQ_{64}
Q7	Faculty speaks clearly and audibility	SQ_{71}	SQ_{72}	SQ_{73}	SQ_{74}
Q8	Faculty writes and draw legibly	SQ_{81}	SQ_{82}	SQ_{83}	SQ_{84}
Q9	Motivates the students to study	SQ_{91}	SQ_{92}	SQ_{93}	SQ_{94}
		AFS_1	**AFS_2**	**AFS_3**	**AFS_4**

1. This criterion mainly considers the faculty output in Research and development in an academic year
2. Here R&D includes Research article produced in the National and International Journals, Articles presented in the national and International Conferences, Conferences/ Workshops/ Symposium organized and participated.
3. It also considers the quality of research and ARDS score computed based on Global R&D quality indexes like, Citation, impact factor and H-index etc.

Statement of Evaluation Score of ARDS is shown as below.

Research and development is an integral part of innovation, the study considers that it is very essential for institutions and their staff to upgrade themselves and/or to upkeep the knowledge (Podgursky, M. J., and Springer, M. G., 2007, p. 909).Hence, it's considered to be very important for technical education. At this juncture, the author supposed that there are multiple corners of research & development criterion like, publications, participation in conferences, Workshops, Symposiums and FDP etc. It can be measured by using the formula 4.

Assessment of Other Activities Score:

The final criterion of GHMPBI is Performance Appraisal for Other Activities Score (OAS) done by an employee. The following are the main features of this criterion:

1. GHMPB OAS mainly examines the Institute's three core categories, which are faculty punctuality discipline, faculty engagement, and input from the relevant HOD and Principal department.

Table 11.

Category(c)	Paper with+(p)	Index/Citation value (i)	Weight (W_{pci})	Marks (M_{pci})	Total weighted score (TWS)
International Journal-Un Paid (with ISSN/ISBN)	H-Indexed	10 Above	1	3	3
		10-May	0.7		2.1
		0-5	0.4		1.2
	Impact factor	Above 3	1	2	2
		1.00 – 2.99	0.7		1.4
		0.01-0.99	0.4		0.8
	Other (Indexed)	Peer Reviewed/ Refereed	0.5	1.5	0.75
International Journal-Paid (JCR Indexed)	H-Indexed	10 Above	1	2	2
		10-May	0.7		1.4
		0-5	0.4		0.8
	Impact factor	Above 3	1	1.75	1.75
		1.00 – 2.99	0.7		1.225
		0.01-0.99	0.4		0.7
	Other(Indexed)	Peer Reviewed/ Refereed	0.5	1.5	0.75
National Journals-Unpaid	H-Indexed	10 Above	1	1.5	1.5
		10-May	0.7		1.05
		0-5	0.4		0.6
	Impact factor	Above 3	1	1.2	1.2
		1.00 – 2.99	0.7		0.84
		0.01-0.99	0.4		0.48
		Peer Reviewed/ Refereed	0.5	0.8	0.4
National Journals-Paid	H-Indexed	10 Above	1	1	1
		10-May	0.7		0.7
		0-5	0.4		0.4
	Impact factor	Above 3	1	0.8	0.8
		1.00 – 2.99	0.7		0.56
		0.01-0.99	0.4		0.32
		Peer Reviewed/ Refereed	0.5	0.6	0.3
International Conference Proceedings (Indexed)	With ISBN/ISSN	NA	1	0.5	0.5
	Without ISBN/ISSN	NA	0.8		0.4
National Conference Proceedings (Indexed)	With ISBN/ISSN	NA	1	0.5	0.5
	Without ISBN/ISSN	NA	0.8		0.4
Workshops/ Symposiums Organized	With Funding by other agencies	NA	1	1	1

2. This study also presumed that there are three additional qualities of faculty influences institutional growth. They are faculty discipline which includes punctuality, passion, innovation, integrity, patience etc.
3. This study also assumed that the role faculty plays a vital role in motivating or encouraging students through proper counseling. Hence, this also given importance for student counseling.

4. The strong PBI policy should respect Hierarchy and the feedback from peers.

From the view point of the above, the author allotted a thirty percentage of total score for this criterion. The Maximum score of this criterion is 3 Marks which includes:

Faculty Discipline - 1 Mark
Student Counseling - 1 Mark
HOD and Principal feedback - 1 Mark

PERFORMANCE-BASED INCENTIVES THROUGH MULTI-SOURCES ASSESSMENT APPROACH

PBI helps HEIs retain notable faculty on a regular basis and establishes objectives for both the faculty and the institutions. HEIs benefit from the PBI technique. PBI is a merit-based incentive approach that has an impact on the growth of all employees and even small HEIs. The performance of HEI employees may be evaluated by using appropriate benchmarks and objectives in reference to the organization's goals and commitments. The learning approach proposed to give the multi-source assessment proposal for faculty evaluation in HEIs is a CGPBI, and the quality of research work directly signifies the quality of teaching "(Computer-generated performance-based incentives). The proposed MSA approach (Multiple Sources Assessment) considers all independent CGP BI Policy elements such as "subject toughness," "subject outcomes," and "average results" for all subjects (Rao, C. H. G. et.al., 2021, p.185). This geometric methodology, notes Ravi Agrawal, "provides unambiguous indices for making appropriate judgements to categorise instructors based on performance while also constantly encouraging the potential to develop new abilities."

Importance of PBI Policy in New Arena of HFIs

In addition to the punctuality and discipline with which the students are present, the contemporary educational system places a major emphasis on OBE (output-based training). Each HEI must choose an appropriate administrative strategy in order to achieve its organisational goals. It benefits not just the instructor but also the students' performance and career opportunities. It also enables the faculty to use its capabilities while avoiding faculty accusations. This article focuses on the development of an acceptable model for performance evaluation and aims to find a remedy in performance evaluations for human intervention. It is a methodical, intermittent method of assessing an individual's quality in areas related to his or her present role. It gives employees the confidence to discuss their job obligations. It enables teachers to utilise their authority more effectively and improves student achievement. The article also provides a solution to the problem of human involvement in the evaluation of educational system performance.

Performance-Based Incentives through Multi-Sources Assessment Approach

Traditional PBI policy was primarily confined to outcomes and input from students. The CGPBI policy provides fair and accurate structural provisions for the collection of sufficient information. The GCPBI model employs an MSA (Multi-Source Evaluation) model that takes into account major features of cost management, optimum use of resources and time-saving methods (Rao, C. H. G. et.al., 2021, p.185). This methodology takes into account all components of performance assessment, such as academic performance, research contribution and feedback. The author's previous essay (Rao, C. H. G et al., 2017, p.1) included all the specifics of these criteria. The goal of the HEI was revised and the 'Research & Development Faculty' played an important part in HEI aims. 30% of the total performance of PBI measurement indicators is included in the criteria. Output: CGP BI may be deployed via an established site, and may be used for the assessment of the general performance of the faculty in private higher education institutions. This approach includes four criteria for assessing the performance of professors. The MSA model includes three main institute fields, such as "Discipline in punctuality at the Faculty, Student Counselling at the Faculty," and staff feedback. The entire performance of the PBI indexes is afterwards assessed for a weighted score of 3%.

Step-2: A geometric expression of measuring Research & Development Score (RDS)

$(\sum RDS.W_{RDS=}$ TWS. WRDS

where TWS = Total weighted score = $(W_{pci})_{.}(M_{pci})$;

W_{pci} = Wight of a paper category index; M_{pci} =Maximum marks of a paper in given category

Proposed Algorithm to Develop CGPBI Model

The CGPBI Model is an automated approached to produce performance appraisal scores without any human intrusion by using software (Rao, C. H. G. et.al., 2021, p.185).

Step 1: *Start*
Step 2: *Select a faculty f, who is teaching n subjects*
// Calculation of ARS - Academic Result Score
Step 3: *Consider a subject taught by faculty f which is not visited subiof section seci (If the faculty is teaching the same subject for more than one section consider them as different subjects) and mark that subject as visited*
Step 4: *Calculate the pass percentage yi of that subject in that section*
Step 5: *xi= max (Pass percentages of all subjects in section seci)*
Step 6: *zi = max (Pass percentages of subifrom all branches and sections)*
Step 7: *Calculate ARSi:*
ARSi = [[1 - (xi- yi)2 x 10]x3] + [[1 - (zi - yi)2 x 10] x 3] / 2
total = total + ARSi
Step 8: *Repeat steps 3,4,5,6,7 until all subjects taught by faculty f are visited.*
Step 9: *ARS = [total / n]*
//Calculation of AFS - Academic Feedback Score
Step 10: *For faculty f consider the feedback of each students Si*

Step 11:*For each student add the feedback SQifor each student*
AFSi=Σ SQi(1 <= i<= no. of questions)
Step 12: *Now calculate the total Academic Feedback Score:*
AFS = (AFS1+ AFS2+.... + AFSn) / n
//Calculation of RDS - Research and Development Score
Step 13*: Let P be the list of paper categories submitted by faculty f*
Step 14: *For each category:*
get h Index, impact Factor, other Index

Now we need to calculate wpci (Weight of paper category index) and mpci (Maximum marks for paper category index) for these three factors

```
wpci = { }
mpci = { }
(we use hashing)
if (category == "International Journal-Un Paid (with ISSN/ISBN)") {
        mpci ["hIndex"] = 3
        mpci ["impactFactory"] = 2
        mpci ["otherIndex"] = 1.5
        if (hIndex> 10){
                wpci["hIndex"] = 1
}
          else if(hIndex<= 10 and hIndex > 5){
                wpci["hIndex"] = 0.7
}
        else{
                wpci["hIndex"] = 0.4
        }
        if(impactFactor>= 3){
                wpci["impactFactor"] = 1
}
          else if(impactFactor< 3 and impactFactor >= 1){
                wpci["impactFactor"] = 0.7
}
        else{
                wpci["impactFactor"] = 0.4
        }
                wpci["otherIndex"] = 0.5
        }
```

Similarly, there are other categories based on which we need to calculate mpci and wpci as above

Step 15:

Now RDS = mpci[“hIndex”] x wpci[“hIndex”] + mpci[“impactFactor”] x wpci[“impactFactor”] + mpci[“otherIndex”] x wpci[“otherIndex”]

// Calculation of OAS - Other Activity Score
Step 16:
fs = Faculty Discipline Score
ss = Student Counselling Score
fds = HOD, Principle feedback Score
OAS =fs + ss + fds
//PBI
Step 17:
PBIScore = ARS + AFS + RDS + OAS

This research is implemented using a completely automated methodology for the creation of the performance-based evaluation system. For the calculation of PBI Score, a lot of parameters were studied. It may be possible to apply the Python programming used for the evaluation of PBI score to help complete current tasks.

CONCLUSION

Incentives are short incentives that have an instant influence on performance. Based incentives often create competitiveness among employees rather than collaboration among employees. The author developed a geometric hybrid model for performance evaluation that is ideal for technical institutions. The CGPBI model is an automated model that generates visible capabilities and delivers accurate and timely results. The model is totally automated, saves time, and provides analytical information to decision makers. The policy developed takes into consideration all variables, such as student results and comments, academic research results, and other inputs. This research could be useful in conducting teacher evaluations and raises. The examination finished with a sense of pleasure and completes compliance with the aforementioned advice. It will not be comprehensive, but it will meet the changing demands of the workers at specialised institutions.

AUTHORS’ NOTE AND DECLARATION OF CONFLICTING INTERESTS

Any mistakes remain the sole duty of the author. The perspectives communicated in this article don’t really mirror those of supporting organizations. The author proclaimed no potential irreconcilable situations as for the exploration, initiation, or potentially distribution of this article. Be that as it may, all credits, translations, deficiencies or blunders are our sole responsibility.

ACKNOWLEDGMENT

The author appreciate helpful comments and suggestions from management of VIGNAN'S institute of information technology and at the annual meetings of governing body. This work was supported by VIGNAN management. We would like to thank all the reviewers for their helpful comments and suggestions on earlier research. We are also thankful to our beloved chairman Dr. L. Rathaiah who encouraging in our research and also express my gratitude and heartfelt thanks to our beloved friend and colleague Professor Debnath Bhattacharyya who gave us a remarkable support to develop this chapter.

REFERENCES

Abulencia, A. S. (2018). Exploring the Education Agenda of the 16th Congress of the Philippines. *ATIKAN, 8*(1).

Antikainen, M., Uusitalo, T., & Kivikytö-Reponen, P. (2018). Digitalisation as an enabler of circular economy. *Procedia CIRP, 73*, 45–49. doi:10.1016/j.procir.2018.04.027

Balch, R., & Springer, M. G. (2015). Performance pay, test scores, and student learning objectives. *Economics of Education Review, 44*, 114–125. doi:10.1016/j.econedurev.2014.11.002

Bueno, C., & Sass, T. R. (2018). The effects of differential pay on teacher recruitment and retention. *Andrew Young School of Policy Studies Research Paper Series*, (18-07).

Camilleri, M. A., & Camilleri, A. (2018). The performance management and appraisal in higher education. In Driving Productivity in Uncertain and Challenging Times. British Academy of Management.

Cekik, R., & Telceken, S. (2018). A new classification method based on rough sets theory. *Soft Computing, 22*(6), 1881–1889. doi:10.100700500-016-2443-0

Chamberlin, R., Wragg, T., Haynes, G., & Wragg, C. (2002). Performance-related pay and the teaching profession: A review of the literature. *Research Papers in Education, 17*(1), 31–49. doi:10.1080/02671520110102534

Darling-Hammond, L. (1997). Doing what matters most: Investing in quality teaching. National Commission on Teaching & America's Future.

Geissdoerfer, M., Pieroni, M. P., Pigosso, D. C., & Soufani, K. (2020). Circular business models: A review. *Journal of Cleaner Production, 277*, 123741. doi:10.1016/j.jclepro.2020.123741

Ghosh, S., & Das, N. (2013). New model of performance management and measurement in higher education sector. *Management, 2*(8), 267–274.

Goe, L., Bell, C., & Little, O. (2008). *Approaches to evaluating teacher effectiveness: A research synthesis*. National Comprehensive Center for Teacher Quality.

Goldhaber, D. (2002). The mystery of good teaching. *Education Next, 2*(1), 50–55.

Halid, H., Yusoff, Y. M., & Somu, H. (2020, May). The Relationship Between Digital Human Resource Management and Organizational Performance. In *First ASEAN Business, Environment, and Technology Symposium (ABEATS 2019)* (p. 96-99). 10.2991/aebmr.k.200514.022

Hanushek, E. A., Kain, J. F., & Rivkin, S. G. (2004). Why public schools lose teachers. *The Journal of Human Resources*, *39*(2), 326–354. doi:10.2307/3559017

Hoerr, T. (1998). A case for merit pay. *Phi Delta Kappan*, *80*(4), 326–327.

Islam, R., & bin Mohd Rasad, S. (2006). Employee performance evaluation by the AHP: A case study. *Asia Pacific Management Review, 11*(3).

Jackson, C. K. (2012). Recruiting, retaining, and creating quality teachers. *Nordic Economic Policy Review*, *3*(1), 61–104.

Jamsandekar, S. S., & Mudholkar, R. R. (2013). Performance evaluation by fuzzy inference technique. *International Journal of Soft Computing and Engineering*, *3*(2), 158–164.

Johnson, S. M., & Papay, J. P. (2009). *Redesigning teacher pay: A system for the next generation of educators* (Vol. 2). Economic Policy Institute.

Lankford, H., Loeb, S., & Wyckoff, J. (2002). Teacher sorting and the plight of urban schools: A descriptive analysis. *Educational Evaluation and Policy Analysis*, *24*(1), 37–62. doi:10.3102/01623737024001037

Larsson, A., & Lindfred, L. (2019). Digitalization, circular economy and the future of labor: How circular economy and digital transformation can affect labor 1. In The Digital Transformation of Labor (p. 280-315). Academic Press.

Liang, G. (2013). Performance-related pay for teachers: An updated review. *Journal of Postdoctoral Research*, *1*(1), 99–117. doi:10.14304/SURYA.JPR.V1N1.10

Macwan, N., & Sajja, D. P. S. (2013). Performance appraisal using fuzzy evaluation methodology. *International Journal of Engineering and Innovative Technology*, *3*(3), 324–329.

Meral, Y. (Ed.). (2019). Tools and techniques for implementing international e-trading tactics for competitive advantage. Academic Press.

Mohrman, A. M. Jr, Mohrman, S. A., & Odden, A. R. (1996). Aligning teacher compensation with systemic school reform: Skill-based pay and group-based performance rewards. *Educational Evaluation and Policy Analysis*, *18*(1), 51–71. doi:10.3102/01623737018001051

Moşteanu, N. R., Faccia, A., & Cavaliere, L. P. L. (2020, August). Digitalization and green economy-changes of business perspectives. In *Proceedings of the 2020 4th International Conference on Cloud and Big Data Computing* (p. 108-112). 10.1145/3416921.3416929

Neogi, A., Mondal, A. C., & Mandal, S. K. (2011). A cascaded fuzzy inference system for university non-teaching staff performance appraisal. *Journal of Information Processing Systems*, *7*(4), 595–612. doi:10.3745/JIPS.2011.7.4.595

Odden, A. (2001). Defining Merit. *Education Matters*, *1*(1), 16–24.

Odden, A., Odden, A. R., & Kelley, C. (2002). *Paying teachers for what they know and do: New and smarter compensation strategies to improve schools*. Corwin Press.

Ojokoh, B., Akinsulire, V., & Isinkaye, F. O. (2019). An Automated Implementation of Academic Staff Performance Evaluation System based on Rough Sets Theory. *AJIS. Australasian Journal of Information Systems*, *23*, 23. doi:10.3127/ajis.v23i0.2033

Podgursky, M. J., & Springer, M. G. (2007). Teacher performance pay: A review. *Journal of Policy Analysis and Management*, *26*(4), 909–949. doi:10.1002/pam.20292

Rao, C. H. G., Doppala, B. P., Swathi, K., & Rao, N. T. (2021). Development of an Automated CGPBI Model Suitable for HEIs in India. In *Machine Intelligence and Soft Computing* (pp. 185–196). Springer.

Rao, C. H. G., Kosaraju, P. K., & Kim, H. J. (2017). Performance Based Incentives Policy: A Geometric Hybrid Model. *International Journal of Advanced Science and Technology*, *102*, 1–16. doi:10.14257/ijast.2017.102.01

Rehberger, M., & Hiete, M. (2020). Allocation of environmental impacts in circular and cascade use of resources—Incentive-driven allocation as a prerequisite for cascade persistence. *Sustainability*, *12*(11), 4366. doi:10.3390u12114366

Richardson, R. (1999). *Performance related pay in schools: An assessment of the green papers: A report prepared for the National Union of Teachers*. London School of Economics and Political Science.

Rockoff, J. E. (2004). The impact of individual teachers on student achievement: Evidence from panel data. *The American Economic Review*, *94*(2), 247–252. doi:10.1257/0002828041302244

Samuel, O. W., Omisore, M. O., & Atajeromavwo, E. J. (2014). Online fuzzy based decision support system for human resource performance appraisal. *Measurement*, *55*, 452–461. doi:10.1016/j.measurement.2014.05.024

Solmon, L. C., & Podgursky, M. (2000). *The Pros and Cons of Performance-Based Compensation*. Academic Press.

Springer, M. G., & Taylor, L. L. (2016). Designing incentives for public school teachers: Evidence from a Texas incentive pay program. *Journal of Education Finance*, *41*(3), 344–381. doi:10.1353/jef.2016.0001

Vargas-Hernández, J. G. (2021). Circular-Green Economy: Analysis Based on the Theory of Resources and Capabilities. In Examining the Intersection of Circular Economy, Forestry, and International Trade (pp. 1-17). Academic Press.

Williamson, B. (2016). Digital education governance: Data visualization, predictive analytics, and 'real-time'policy instruments. *Journal of Education Policy*, *31*(2), 123–141. doi:10.1080/02680939.2015.1035758

Zhang, Y., Luo, Y., Zhang, X., & Zhao, J. (2019). How green human resource management can promote green employee behavior in China: A technology acceptance model perspective. *Sustainability*, *11*(19), 5408. doi:10.3390u11195408

Chapter 14
Exploratory Study on User Satisfaction of E-HRM:
Evidence From Brunei Government Employee Management System (GEMS)

Fahmi Ibrahim
https://orcid.org/0000-0001-5016-7755
Universiti Teknologi Brunei, Brunei

Hazimah Suhip
Universiti Teknologi Brunei, Brunei

Kabiru Maitama Kura
https://orcid.org/0000-0001-7863-2604
Universiti Teknologi Brunei, Brunei

Liana H. M. Noor
Universiti Teknologi Brunei, Brunei

ABSTRACT

With the high demands to provide service quality, growing workforce, and globalization of economy, HR has transformed into an inevitable power of technology that transforms HRM into electronic human resource management (E-HRM) systems. Brunei Darussalam without exception is also practicing E-HRM in the government sector called government employee management system (GEMS). This chapter investigates the user satisfaction of E-HRM by examining the current status of GEMS in Brunei Darussalam. The user satisfaction was studied through seven elements: the implementation of E-HRM, training, user-friendliness, infrastructure, data security, technical support, and user support. Qualitative interview and descriptive quantitative method were conducted on HR officers from the public organization. Findings revealed that the GEMS are not able to provide satisfactory system. This chapter has developed a theoretical framework as a recommendation to integrate relevant elements, together with the influence of age, gender, and years of service that impact user satisfaction.

DOI: 10.4018/978-1-7998-8678-5.ch014

INTRODUCTION

The computer has undeniably affected every aspect of our lives, especially in the advent of information technology, together with communication technology (ICT). The necessity for efficiency, high responsiveness and prompt readiness among the workforce is sought after from ICT. According to Akinyede and Daramola (2013) the computer has remained one of the most powerful tools that has served as an aid to decision making in recent years, mostly because of its efficiency in terms of speed, accuracy, reliability, mass processing, cost and security, among others. It has inspired many advancements within today's workplace, in different sectors and fields; human resource management is no exception. Human resource management (HRM) activities were always carried out manually and paper intensive using the traditional method system. Presently, with the availability of ICT, human resource management has transformed to a sophisticated Electronic Human Resource Management (E-HRM) system.

HRM comprises all management practices and decisions, that affect the employees. In today's world, HRM are facing challenges which include competitive work environments, to allocate growing demands, provide service quality, growing workforce, globalization of economy and many more. To facilitate, HRM is moving to an inevitable power of technology that transforms HRM into E-HRM. E-HRM has a lot to offer and contains features representing the functions of a typical HRM department, that has claimed to be effective by saving time and effort to increase productivity. Brunei Darussalam without exception, has also been practicing E-HRM within the Government sector for over a decade, called the Government Employee Management System (GEMS). Effective management of employees, enhance well-being and satisfaction of employees, respond to employee conflict and management, keeping track of employee attendance, work-time and absenteeism are among the functions of HRM, in order to achieve an organisation's goals and strategies. The adoption of technology has simplified routine tasks, particularly with the continuous upgrades seen in its processing speed. Thus, introducing E-HRM may maximise HRM potential, content and positioning to positively impact the organisation's overall goals and strategies.

In the perspective of circular economy (CE), the utilization of E-HRM enables to transform the linear "take-make-use-dispose" model of production and consumption of IT into a circular model of resource management (Eposito et al., 2018). For Human Resource (HR) executives, trashing data, information and knowledge that could be repurposed and resold violates a basic tenet of efficiency: leave value at the 'dump' . A CE of E-HRM is designed to waste out unnecessary tasks, routines and tasks of the HR system and extending the useful life and restoring natural systems for user satisfaction. Additionally, there is also a rapidly evolving theoretical and critical literature on CE that suggests that, in order to achieve a true transformation away from the linear model and towards a circular management of resources, practices and strategies should go beyond the minimization of waste and towards a reframing of human and social behaviors such as consumption patterns with practices inspired by the sharing economy suggesting various forms of collaborative consumption (Hobson and Lynch, 2016; Moreu at al., 2017). Other practices are aiming at building awareness, at increasing knowledge and acquiring the appropriate skills through the training of managers and employees in organizations, strategies focused on the human and social dimensions of organizations influenced by the field of Green Human Resource Management (GHRM) (Chiapetta Jabbour, 2019).

The research on E-HRM is not new and has been applied frequently in the literature. However, this research will take the form of a new research, based on a different approach, by looking at user satisfaction on the Brunei Darussalam Government's own E-HRM system, which is called GEMS. The research was conducted the on four departments of Brunei government offices, as these departments were the ones that had more experience with the system. The users were considered the key elements in this research, as they were the ones who have been using the system on a daily basis. It was through the users that the researcher was able to gain information regarding their satisfaction towards the system. By looking into the users' satisfaction, the effectiveness of GEMS could be derived. This research highlights the importance of E-HRM, which aimed to investigate user satisfaction. This research also focuses on the current issues and analyses the improvements that needed to be made to enhance the performance of the system and to provide a better service for the users. The aim of this research is to investigate user satisfaction by examining the current status of GEMS in Brunei Darussalam from perceptions and views of all types of employees under the Government sector.

AN OUTLOOK OF HUMAN RESOURCE MANAGEMENT (HRM)

Human Resource Management (HRM) was previously known as "Personnel Management" (Mahapatro, 2010). The main function of HRM, regardless of whether it is in a public or private organisation, is to utilise human capital to achieve goals (Mahfod et al, 2017). Nayananjalee and Chamaru (2017) further supports this, by defining HRM as to identify, select, train and develop manpower to achieve organisational goals. According to O'Riordan (2017), HRM is primarily concerned with all aspects of how people are being managed within an organisation, and also the gathering and tracking of systems and policies. Paauwe and Boon (2009) further explained that HRM is responsible for managing payroll, employee attendance, employees' working hours, performance appraisal, and training and development to improve the KSA (Knowledge, Skills and Abilities) and more.

Nayananjalee and Chamaru (2017) claimed that HRM should be more strategic, cost efficient and flexible. Findikli and Bayarecelik (2015) believed that HRM should continuously update themselves and adapt to an evolving technology system, which will aid HRM processes. There is always a confusion between Human Resource Information System (HRIS) and Human Resource Management System (HRMS) (Poisat and Mey, 2017). HRIS is directed towards the HR department, specifically for HR staff. Meanwhile, HRMS is not only for the HR staff, but also extends to all employees. HRMS requires a broader technological support via the intranet or internet, which is known as the Electronic Human Resource System (E-HRM). Moving into the 21st century, HRM has been transitioning towards the E-HRM system; a web-based human resource management system (Strohmeier and Kabst, 2014).

THE ROLE OF INFORMATION AND COMMUNICATION TECHNOLOGY (ICT) IN HRM

Technological advancements have reshaped our way of life; the way we communicate and work. Technological advancements include improvements in computer hardware, software and databases. With the availability of computer hardware, software and databases, the emergence of web-based technology has continuously improved (Nayananjalee and Chamaru, 2017). Subsequently, ICT has been designed for faster and efficient work processes via the computer and internet/intranet. Analysing vast amounts of data can be simplified through ICT, as well as creating, organising, managing, and storing records and information better, as well as retrieving it with ease (Zhang and Wang 2006). Further improvements brought by ICT have reduced expenses on administration, increased productivity and improved decision-making processes (Rohila et al, 2017). In other words, ICT helps organisations lower their administration costs by improving employee communication and satisfaction, reducing processing time and providing real-time access to information (Saatcioglu, 2007). Thus, these technological advancements have efficiently affected the function of HRM. From the support and intervention of ICT, HRM has been innovated to E-HRM to transform HR functions paperless and become resource efficient (Davoudi and Fartash, 2012). ICT is believed to increase administrative and strategic functions of the HR department (Maheshwari and Vohra, 2015).

Drawing from the assumptions of Knowledge Management perspective, the role of ICT (both hardware and software) in HRM rests predominantly on the key assumptions of the *objectivist perspective* (Ibrahim et al., 2009; Ibrahim and Reid, 2010; Ibrahim and Ali, 2021). This refers as codification of KM strategy coined by Hansen et al. (1999). IT is a 'driver' of KM practices. Yet, ICT simply acts as a medium to search, codify, categorize, store and share explicit knowledge. Explicit knowledge – academic knowledge or ''know-what'' that is described in formal language, print or electronic media, often based on established work processes, use people-to-documents approach. Explicit knowledge is carefully codified, stored in a hierarchy of databases of E-HRM and is accessed with high quality, reliable, fast information retrieval systems. Once codified, explicit knowledge assets can be reused to solve many similar types of problems or connect people with valuable, reusable knowledge. Nevertheless, the utilization of ICT is criticized with warnings of 'dehumanizing the personnel department' (Bondarouk et al., 2017) which is in contrast of 'digital humanism' concept (Badarudin and Ibrahim, 2021) that is argued to suffer 'synoptic delusion'; the mistaken idea that it is possible to collect an organisation's knowledge in a single repository (Tsoukas, 2005:p.100).

ELECTRONIC HUMAN RESOURCE MANAGEMENT (E-HRM)

For more than four decades organizations have increasingly adopted E-HRM technology in the hope of achieving administrative and strategic benefits (Marler and Parry, 2015; Strohmeier, 2009) and talent acquisition (Johnson et al., 2021). E-HRM is defined as an umbrella term 'covering all possible integration mechanisms and contents between HRM and Information Technologies (IT), aiming at creating value within and across organizations for targeted employees and management' (Bondarouk and Ruël, 2009, p. 507). In the same line with process focus perspective, e-HRM has been defined as a set of 'configurations of computer hardware, software and electronic networking resources that enable intended or actual HRM activities (e.g. policies, practices and services) through coordinating and controlling individual and group-level data capture and information creation and communication within and across organizational boundaries' (Marler & Parry, 2015, p. 2). It was used to refer to the combination of ICT tools, and the processes and operations of HRM (Lengnick-Hall and Moritz 2003).

Wright and Dyer (2000) provided three types of E-HRM categories, specific to its functions. These three types are operational, relational and transformational. Firstly, operational refers to typical activities within a department, which are the recording of personal data, keeping records, departmental records and others (Marler, 2009). Secondly, relational comprises activities that are internal or external, in other words, the activities between the HR department and other departments, this function includes recruitment, learning, performance management and training. Thus, allowing employees to perform HR activities themselves, which will help HR to lessen administrative work and focus more on their priorities (Poisat

& Mey, 2017). Thirdly, transformational focuses more on strategic activities aimed towards achieving the mission and vision of the organisation (Snell et al., 2001).

The HRM function has been evolving and dramatically changing over time, E-HRM is seen to have the potential to transform all the traditional functions of HRM. However, Ruel et al., (2007) stated that E-HRM is still in its 'youth-phase', as E-HRM is a new managerial concept. Lee (2011) argued that despite being in its early stages, its popularity has been attracting both academic and organisations; its application is one of the most implemented and adopted in both public and private organisations (Strohmeier and Kabst, 2014). E-HRM is the devolution of HR functions and allows communication between the employees, management and managers, which is commonly accessed via intranet using web-based technologies (Ruel et al., 2007). It can transmit digitised information from one computer to another computer, which includes text, sound and visual images (Shilpa and Gopal, 2011). With the availability of E-HRM, HR functions have been transformed paperless, become resource efficient and more flexible (Mago, 2016). However, the importance of the E-HRM is crucial for security, as it uses a restricted or private communication network that can only be accessed internally within the organisation, which is restricted from public use or access (Espinosa et al, 2010). Information that is stored in E-HRM is highly sensitive; stores office data and volumes of employees' personal information thus, internal security is very critical and should be secured with passwords.

Even with the optimistic outlook of the potential benefits of E-HRM reported in literature, organisations need to be conscious on the probable consequences. Gardner, Lepak and Bartol (2003) argued that the adoption of E-HRM was merely transitioning the administrative tasks to technology-based. Therefore, it did not necessarily support strategic decision-making nor improve HR services but simply to support routine administrative tasks. To establish an evidence-based correlation of E-HRM and strategic HRM, a study by Marler and Fisher (2013) conclude that 'very little systematic evidence concerning whether E-HRM was related to strategic outcomes, but there was considerable evidence advocating the moderating role of contextual factors in these relationships' (Bondarouk et al, 2016). Perhaps the significant need for understanding of the factors affecting E-HRM adoption and consequences of E-HRM brings a more valuable and compelling proposition. It is important to note that the factors affecting adoption can be divided into three categories: technology, organisational and people factors, also known as the TOP framework (Bondarouk et al.,2016) where the people factors were distinguished as the pivotal factor as user acceptance to the new technology and the mindsets of the employees on the value of E-HRM have an impact to E-HRM adoption.

BACKGROUND OF CASE STUDY OF GEMS

GEMS is an E-HRM system, implemented by the Brunei Darussalam Government in order to have a 21st century information system which is modern, interactive, excellent and integrated civil service (Brunei Prime Minister's Office, 2009). This system has been driven by the Infotech Division under the Public Service Department of the Prime Minister's office. Referring to the GEMS booklet (Brunei Prime Minister's Office, 2009), GEMS processes daily HRM functions which are attendance, leave application, exit leave application, benefits entitlement, car and house loan application, allowances, performance appraisals, training and promotions which are all managed on one system, via the One Government Network (OGN). OGN is a secure intranet connection that can only be accessed within the Government offices (E-Government National Centre, 2019).

Benefits of GEMS

Based on the Government owned newspaper (Public Service Department, 2015), the benefits of GEMS are as follows:

- The head of department/division/unit will be able to monitor the officers' and staff members' information records easily and quickly, because all the information is kept in one database.
- To prevent any false attendance time, as GEMS is using the Global Server Time; to have accurate attendance which is not from the time of the computer nor personal watch.
- Employees are able to use their own office computer to use the system.
- To reduce the usage of paper.

User Satisfaction

There are a large number of researches based on ICT that represent various measures and settings. According to Ibrahim and Yusoff (2013), there are a variety of factors that have been recognised to have influence on the end-user satisfaction, in fact user satisfaction has been tested to be a dependent variable and the mediator to other variables. Many studies on the adoption of technology proved that user satisfaction is a vital driver of ICT success (Mahmood et al., 2000; Ma and Ye, 2015). Additionally, users contribute to the impact of the success of the implementation of ICT. Based on users' experience, the technical support, infrastructure, data security and user- friendliness have a significant relationship with user satisfaction (Qteishat and Alshibly, 2014).

Figure 1. Satisfaction model (Qteishat and Alshibly, 2014)

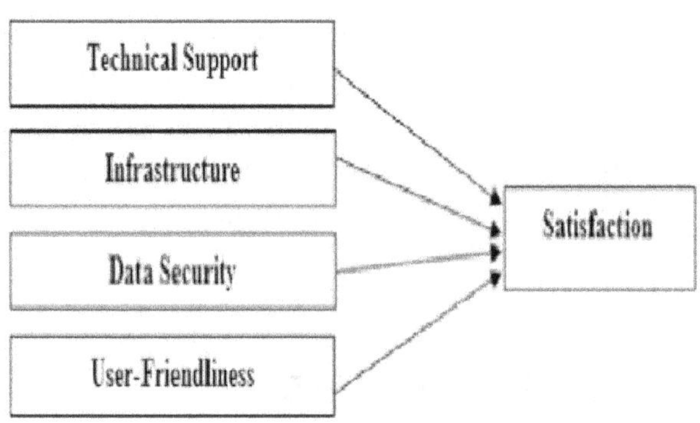

Technical Support

When implementing technology in a working environment, it is important have technical support to provide assistance when there is a problem with the system or to have any enquiries (Ghavifekr and Rosdy, 2015). The ability to provide satisfactory technical support by assisting users with the help needed will lead to user satisfaction (Bondarouk et al., 2017). Moreover, technical support will provide users to operate E-HRM successfully in an organisation (Ma and Ye, 2015).

Infrastructure

According to Kaur and Kaur (2015) one of the objectives of E-HRM is to allow quicker response to users related services. E-HRM infrastructure would allow the system to run faster, which consists of hardware, software and internet for it to function (Office of Government Commerce, 2002). Focusing on the infrastructure is necessary, as there is a positive connection between infrastructure and user satisfaction; if there is a breakdown or slow infrastructure it can disrupt the system from user being able to use it (Poisat and Mey, 2017).

Data Security

E-HRM stores large amount of private data, that can be sensitive for outside sources from entering or gaining the data, one of the problems would be identity theft (Kaur, 2013). Kaur and Kaur (2015) believe that the objective of E-HRM is to offer personal data security and privacy. Therefore, it is critical to have a strong security protection when implementing E- HRM to guard employees' information (Torres and Arias, 2009). Any security breaches will directly affect the users, which cause users to distrust and have limit interaction with the system (Lippert and Swierez, 2005).

User-Friendliness

One of the main reasons why E-HRM is introduced to provide an adequate and simple method to process HRM. User-friendliness is closely connected to greater adoption success and user satisfaction (Bandarouk, 2016). A non-friendly system would increase the amount of HR task than reducing it (Parry and Tyson, 2011). Furthermore, a non-user-friendly system not only increase the amount of HR work, but also it would be challenging and time-consuming for the users to familiarise to the system.

RESEARCH METHODS

Both quantitative descriptive study and qualitative research methods were used in this paper. The initial total number of surveys that were distributed were 200 surveys. However, the total number that the researcher received back were 140 surveys. These surveys were in close-ended questions manner. sections. The first section focused on the demographic structure of GEMS users. The second section of the survey design was adapted from Qteishat and Alshibly's (2014) satisfaction model where the 'variables' consist of technical support, infrastructure, data security, user-friendliness and user satisfaction, by extracting information from the participants using the Likert scale to rate the participants' satisfaction level towards GEMS. A quantitative method would be the appropriate method as it has been perceived to be able to reflect the opinions of a wider population.

Qualitative research has been was utilised to complement the quantitative method with the aim developing an extensive understanding of how people perceive their experience. Therefore, the qualitative method was conducted on a small sample, such as open-ended interviews, to gain in-depth answers in order to better understand GEMS, as well as understanding their behaviour towards GEMS. In addition, interviewing respective officials was also employed to gain information on their projected recommendations, background of GEMS usage and issues that they have faced throughout the implementation of

GEMS. According to Qu and Dumay (2011), interviews in research aimed to cover factual and meaning level, which would allow people to convey to others a situation from their own perspective and in their own words. Although many researchers have claimed that interviews were time consuming, however for this research, the interview method was suitable for the purpose of high degree of validity as the researcher only required four interviews with the HR Department Division at the four Government departments that have used GEMS for since first was implemented and also one representative from the Infotech Division. Thematic analysis was used to analyse the data that was gathered from the interviews.

RESULTS AND FINDINGS

Survey Results

This section will explore the data extracted from the survey; which was adapted from Qteishat & Alshibly's (2014) satisfaction model where the variables consist of technical support, infrastructure, data security, user-friendliness and user satisfaction. Descriptive statistics was utilised to analyse the data.

Figure 2. Frequently E-HRM function

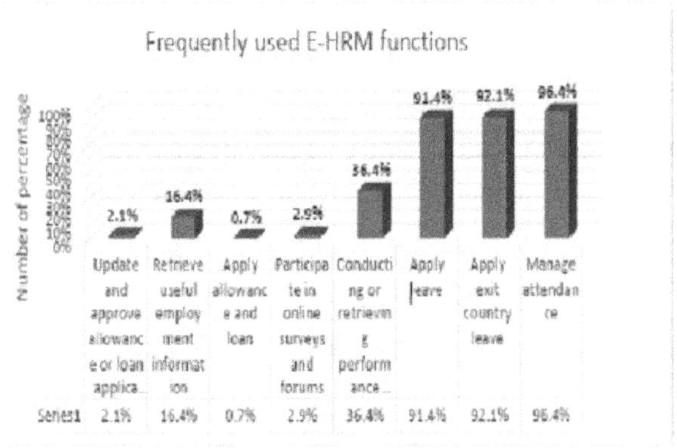

There are three types of E-HRM with specific functions (Swaroop, 2012). The three functions are operational (emphasis on employee service records, recording employees' biodata), relational (focuses on the internal or external activities such as recruitment, training, performance appraisal) and transformational (concerns with strategic areas such as knowledge management, strategic reorientation which is more towards achieving the mission and vision of the organization). According to a statement by the Prime Minister's Office (2008), GEMS is an E-HRM system where employees should be able to update and approve allowance applications, access comprehensive employment information, manage recruitment activities, analyse employees' records, apply allowances and loans, retrieve information and participate in online surveys, hence, providing all of the E-HRM functions. However, looking at the chart above (Figure 2), it can be seen that only certain functions were being frequently used by the employees. The most utilised functions were, manage attendance (96.4%), apply exit country leave (92.1%), and apply leave (91.4%). Only 36.4% conduct or retrieve performance appraisal. While updating and approving of allowances or loan applications, retrieving useful employment information, applying of allowance and participating in online surveys were below 20%. Based on the results, it is claimed that GEMS has not been fully utilised and among the three types of E-HRM, and it clearly shows that GEMS only functions as operational.

1. Technical Support

Technical support is examined into three matters: GEMS technical support is easy to find through the website, GEMS helpline is easily available and when there is a problem with GEMS, the technician will be ready to help quickly and efficiently. Respondents were asked to rate strongly agree, agree, disagree and strongly disagree to the statements provided.

a. GEMS technical support is easy to find through the website
Majority of the respondents had agreed (57.1%) that GEMS technical support was easy to find through the website. While 21.4% disagreed and 10.7% strongly agreed and strongly disagreed. The researcher believes that, the respondents mainly agreed to this because GEMS had been implemented for 10 years; therefore, respondents have familiarised themselves to the website.

b. GEMS helpline is easily available
56.8% respondents agreed that the GEMS helpline is easily available, 20.9% disagreed, 14.4% strongly agreed and 7.9% strongly disagreed that the GEMS helpline is easily available. The reason why the 56.8% agreed that the GEMS helpline is easily available, was because the telephone was not the only method that has been available to contact technical support, the other methods were via email and through the mobile application *WhatsApp*.

c. When there is a problem with GEMS the technician will be ready to help quickly and efficiently
According to the findings, 56.4% agreed to the statement, 25% disagreed, 10.6% strongly agreed and 7.9% strongly disagreed. The researcher identified that the reason to why 56.4% agreed to the statement was because these respondents share the same building as the technicians are located, hence it is easy for them to reach. While the 25% who disagreed and 7.9% who strongly disagreed belonged to the departments that were located quite far from the building where the technicians is situated.

From what can be seen in all of the three matters the results showed that the highest rating was above 50% which inclined towards agree. When comparing the left and right quadrants, it indicated that the ratings inclined towards a favourable rating than bad rating in terms of technical support. Thus, respondents were satisfied with the GEMS technical support.

2. Infrastructure

This section will look into the findings of the users' satisfaction towards the GEMS infrastructure, focusing on internet connectivity.

a. Unstable internet connection makes it hard to access GEMS

62.1% strongly agreed that unstable internet connection makes it hard to access GEMS, 28.6% agreed, 7.1% disagreed and 2.1% strongly disagreed. Internet connection is essential for E-HRM to function. However, from the findings, the users strongly agreed that the internet connection was unstable which made it difficult for them to access GEMS. This could be because, the department has been using OGN. With OGN, when there are many users using the internet at the same time, the internet connection would overload with over usage, thus causing it to lag.

3. Data Security

This section focuses on the findings of the users' satisfaction on GEMS data security; which focuses on two statements: 'GEMS is secure from virus/hacking and safe from identity theft' and 'GEMS should have identity checks to avoid other people from accessing'.

a. GEMS is secured from virus/hacking and safe from identity theft
According to the findings, 59% agreed, 19% strongly agreed, 16% disagreed and 6% strongly disagreed. This shows that the respondents felt confident and safe that their personal information has been kept in GEMS.

b. GEMS should have identity checks to avoid other people from accessing
Majority of the respondents had agreed (47.5%) and strongly disagreed (43.2%) that GEMS should have identity checks to avoid other people from accessing the respondents' accounts on GEMS. Although most of the respondents felt that keeping their information on GEMS was safe, however majority of the respondents still had uncertainties on its safety and should have identity checks to avoid other people from accessing. Therefore, it would be beneficial that during the training, trainers could explain the safety features of the system.

4. User Friendliness

This section will look into the findings of the users' satisfaction towards GEMS user friendliness, which looked into three statements: 'I find it easy to use GEMS', 'It was easy and quick to use GEMS at the beginning', 'It is easy to access information on GEMS' and 'Changing and entering my personal information is easy to do'.

a. It was easy and quick to use GEMS at the beginning
According to the respondents 42% disagreed that it was easy and quick to use GEMS at the, 35% agreed, 15% strongly disagreed and 8% strongly agreed.

b. I find GEMS user interface to be complicated and hard to use
It was indicated that the satisfactory level of the respondents' experience with the GEMS user interface were mixed responses, whereby 35% strongly agreed and 35% disagreed. However, despite both 'strongly agree' and 'disagree' having the same percentages at 35%, when comparing it to the 28% of responses who agreed, which was more than the 2% who strongly agreed, it can be concluded that the users were not satisfied with the user interface.

5. Overall User Satisfaction

This section looks into the overall user satisfaction. Similar to previous sections, respondents were provided with a statement and were asked to rate. The statement 'Overall, I am satisfied with GEMS because of its quality that is effective and it facilitates users than traditional system'. Based on findings, it can be seen that majority of the respondents disagreed to the statement (44.3%), 39.3% agreed, 10% disagreed and 6.4% strongly agreed.

Preliminary Survey Analyses and Data Screening

Prior to conducting the main analyses of survey, the data collected were subjected to preliminary analyses in terms of statistical outliers, normality, and multicollinearity. This was to ensure that the statistical assumptions necessary for multivariate analysis were satisfied. Results pertaining to each of the key assumptions are reported in Table 1.

Table 1. Cook's distance

			Range	
Mean	**Median**	**SD**	**Min**	**Max**
0.0120	0.00234	0.0587	3.77e-8	0.685

For this study, multivariate outliers were assessed by using Cook's distance with a great influence on the regression results. As shown in Table 1, there was no values above the limit of Cook's distance > 0.50 (Pardoe, 2012) and no further cases were excluded.

Robustness Check

To confirm whether the assumption of multicollinearity had been satisfied, tolerance and variance inflation factor (VIF) values were evaluated. According to (Hair et al., 2010), tolerance values above .10 and VIF values less than 10 indicate no multicollinearity among the independent variables. Table 2 summarises the results of multicollinearity test among independent variables. It shows that the tolerance values ranged from 0.631 to 0.870, and VIF values ranged from 1.15 to 1.22, thereby suggesting that multicollinearity was not a major concern in the study.

Furthermore, to confirm that the normality assumption has not been violated, first, the skewness and kurtosis statistics were checked. According to (Kline, 2011), the assumption of multivariate normal distribution becomes a major concern when the skewness and kurtosis statistics are greater than ± 3 and ± 10, respectively. Table 3 summarizes the descriptive statistics of the normality test that demonstrate the result is normal.

Table 2. Collinearity

	VIF	Tolerance
Technical Supports	1.20	0.831
Infrastructure	1.22	0.818
Data security	1.15	0.870
User friendliness	1.59	0.631

Table 3. Descriptive of the study variables

				Skewness		Kurtosis	
	N	Mean	SD	Skewness	SE	Kurtosis	SE
Gender	140						
Year of Service	140						
Technical Supports	140	2.28	0.674	0.488	0.205	0.321	0.407
Infrastructure	140	1.77	0.636	0.313	0.205	-0.340	0.407
Data security	140	1.89	0.542	0.472	0.205	1.444	0.407
User friendliness	140	2.49	0.693	0.337	0.205	-0.254	0.407
User satisfaction	140	2.46	0.712	0.208	0.205	-0.255	0.407

The descriptive statistics of the study variables, which were based on gender, year of service, technical supports, infrastructure, data security, user friendliness, and user satisfaction. As shown in frequencies gender Table 4, the largest percentage of the participants in this study was female. The female constituted 92, representing 65.7 % of the participants, while the remaining 48 (34.3%) were their male counterparts.

In terms year of service of the participants as shown in Table 5, 26 (18.6 %) had less than 5 years in service, then 38 (27.1 %) who had 6-9 years. Then, 30 (21.4 %) had less than 10-19 years in service and finally, of the participants, 46 (32.9 %) spent more than 20 years in service.

Table 4. Frequencies of gender

Levels	Counts	% of Total	Cumulative %
Male	48	34.3 %	34.3 %
Female	92	65.7 %	100.0 %

Table 5. Years of service

Levels	Counts	% of Total	Cumulative %
Less than 5 years	26	18.6 %	18.6 %
6-9 years	38	27.1 %	45.7 %
10-19 years	30	21.4 %	67.1 %
More than 20 years	46	32.9 %	100.0 %

Linear Regression

Results of the multiple linear regression indicated in Table 6, there was a collective significant effect among the technical supports, infrastructure, data security, user friendliness and user satisfaction, ($F(47.6) = 135$, $p < .001$, $R^2 = .32$). The individual predictors were examined further and indicated that technical supports ($t = 0.1242$, $p = 0.901$), and infrastructure ($t = -0.0607$, $p = 0.952$) were found to be not significant predictors in the model. However, regression results indicated that there was a significant association between data security and user friendliness ($t = 3.2551$, $p = 0.001$) and ($t = 9.6438$, $p < .001$), respectively.

To ascertain whether this goal had been achieved, the R^2 values for the endogenous latent construct was calculated and evaluated. The result in Table 7 demonstrated that the regression model explained 0.585 of the total variance in user satisfaction. This suggests that the four exogenous latent variables, namely, technical supports, infrastructure, data security, user friendliness collectively explained 58.5% of the variance in user satisfaction. Hence, following Falk and Miler (1992), it can be concluded that an acceptable amount of variance was explained in the baseline Partial Least Square (PLS) path model for this study.

Table 6. Model coefficients

Predictor	Estimate	SE	95% Confidence Interval		t	p
			Lower	Upper		
Intercept	0.24374	0.2576	-0.2657	0.753	0.9463	0.346
Technical Supports	0.00798	0.0643	-0.1192	0.135	0.1242	0.901
Infrastructure	-0.00417	0.0687	-0.1400	0.132	-0.0607	0.952
Data security	0.25412	0.0781	0.0997	0.409	3.2551	0.001
User friendliness	0.69204	0.0718	0.5501	0.834	9.6438	< .001

Table 7. Model fit measures

Model	R	R^2	Overall Model Test			
			F	df1	df2	p
1	0.765	0.585	47.6	4	135	< .001

Interview Findings

This section provides a narrative of themes emerged from the analysis of data. The themes were grouped into three main section: current status, issues and improvement. The sub- themes are functions, internet connection, traditional method, layout, user and training described as follows;

Current Status Diagnosis

Current status refers to the status of GEMS when it was diagnosed during the case study . The two current statuses that were repetitively mentioned were functions and internet connection. This is beneficial for the researcher as exploring the current status of GEMS was the aim and one of the objectives of this research.

Figure 3.Thematic analysis of interview findings

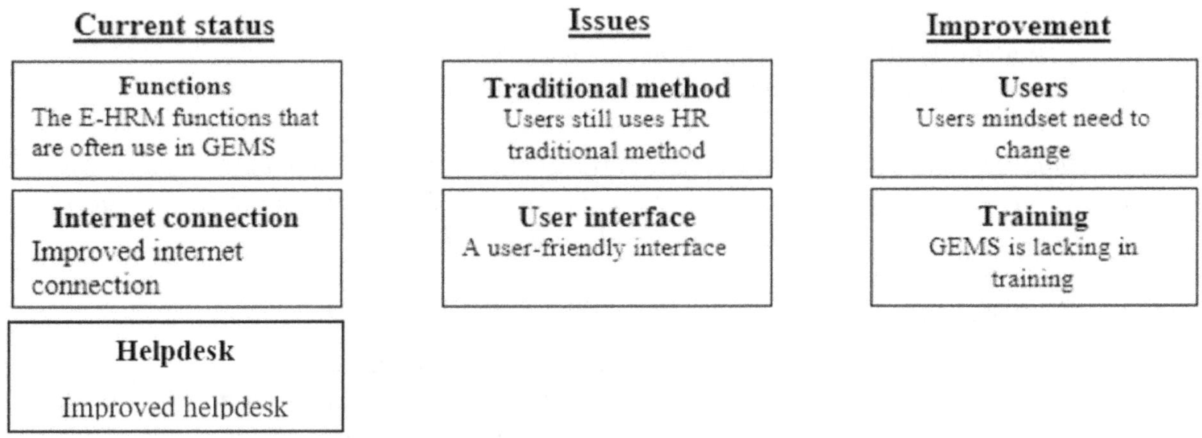

1. Functions

E-HRM is categorised into three types, which are operational, relational and transformational (Wright and Dyer, 2000). These types of E-HRM comes with specific functions; operational focuses on basic activities such as employee service, keeping records, recording employees' biodata; relational emphasis on HR and the internal or external activities such as recruitment, training, performance appraisal; and transformational focuses on achieving the mission and vison of the organisation (Snell et al., 2001). For E-HRM to function effectively, it is important to fully utilise the functions of E-HRM that contribute towards user effectiveness.

According to the interviews, four HR officers shared similar statements.

It is good that GEMS is in one user interface which consists of attendance, applying leave and your record of training, your personal records. (HR 1)

GEMS is definitely useful, for leave, attendance. Where users record the information themselves, receiving a reward, medal, certificate of courses they had attended. (HR 2)

GEMS offer a lot of features, to speed up work processes, especially entering record data of staff, updating the up to date address, biodata, qualifications. (HR 3)

It is an online system that is used by all Government officers and staff members for applications of leave, exit country leave, appraisal and attendance. (HR 4)

However, when asked what functions were often used on GEMS by the officers and staff members, four of the interviewees had similar answers. These were attendance, applying exit country leave and leave, despite being aware that there were other functions available to make use of.

Well as a whole, employees and staff, they use GEMS primarily for attendance, exit country leave and applying for leave. (HR 1)

Just attendance, apply leave and apply exit country leave. (HR 2)

Normally to key in attendance, employee portfolio too but seldom, extracting information of attendance, leave also seldom because of paper application. Basically, just attendance. (HR 3)

Usually, certain sections in this department uses certain features, for HR is updating record service, on application leave, extend leave, for finance division they need GEMS for increment. Other officers and employee mainly attendance, exit country leave and leave. (HR 4)

2. Internet Connection

Internet is the main enabler of E-HRM implementation. Without internet connectivity, work processes will not function,thus, E-HRM is highly dependent on this technology. In the case of GEMS HR officers, they mentioned that at the beginning of the implementation of GEMS, one of the main problems encountered was that they could not access the system due to slow internet connectivity or unstable connection. However, today it has improved as the hardware and software has been upgraded.

With GEMS you need a system, you need electricity, internet connectivity. So, when this system is down it is not fully reliable, but now internet connection is stable. However, if there's a problem with it, in the end we still need to use the traditional method. (HR 1)

Previously the problem, it was the internet connection, but now it is stable already. But people still have the mindset that the network is still lagging. (HR 2)

From time to time, internet connectivity is slow and affecting GEMS, thus GEMS cannot be accessed, no connectivity thus no data recorded, but starting 2016 the connectivity is better. But when there's a problem we mainly use biometric or log book. (HR 3)

Just network, because it can slowdown the process, applications will be slow. But now it is stable already. (HR 4)

From these statements it was demonstrated that the Infotech division seems to actively resolve and improve connectivity issues to guarantee consistent internet connectivity. However, from the statements above, two of the HR personnel mentioned that if there was a problem with the connectivity, they will resort to the traditional HR method, which is paper. Following this, the researcher managed to ask the four HR officers, whether they still used the traditional method which can be seen as an issue for user satisfaction, as the main purpose of E-HRM is to innovate HR into one system and to be resource efficient

3. Helpdesk

The purpose of GEMS helpdesk is to provide centralised information and support management service to handle internal or external queries. Previously, GEMS helpdesk can only be reached through telephone line, which were hard to reached. Currently, the Infotech division had applied other methods via email or *WhatsApp* mobile messenger, as an improvement for the GEMS helpdesk service.

Before if there is a problem, we have to call usually hard to reach, but now if there is a problem we just need to email or WhatsApp massage we can send a picture of the problem and we will have an instant reply, so the technical corporation is now good. (HR 2)

4. Data Security

Data security is the practice of protecting digital information from unauthorized access, corruption, or theft throughout its entire lifecycle. It's a concept that encompasses every aspect of information security from the physical security of hardware and storage devices to administrative and access controls, as well as the logical security of software applications (Joshi et al., 2002). It also includes organizational policies and procedures as been practiced by Brunei government;

All the data are being kept by EGNC (E-Government National Center) and as well at Ministry of Finance so there's two backup system. So EGNC are the one monitoring the security measurements. If there is a problem they will inform us immediately (HR 2)

Encountered Issues

The issues refer to the problems where the HR personnel believe may be causing dissatisfaction amongst GEMS users. Two matters raised by the HR personnel were the active use of the traditional method and the non-friendly user interface. This section revealed the one of the research focus that examined current issues and analyses the improvements that needed to be made to enhance the performance of the system and to provide a better service for the users.

1. Traditional Method

E-HRM is an innovative method to resolve HR processes to manage employees, replacing various types of manual systems; mainly from using manpower to a simplified one integrated system. Based on the interview below, all the departments were still using both GEMS and the traditional method. Thus, causing it to be a two-way process instead of one simplified process. HR 1 mentioned that;

Our department currently uses both, both in a sense that when we are applying for leave, we have to fill in the form and approval needs to be first obtained from the designated head of division and from there, they will give it to the administration side for me to sign and give approval. So, it's a two-way process but at the same time we need to key in into GEMS as well, so it's a two-way process and it's a hassle. (HR 1)

The reason why the departments were still insisting on using both methods was because, from time to time they have been unable to access GEMS and feared that data might be missing from the system due to instability. Therefore, they needed two types of storing data as a backup plan. Another reason why they required this traditional method was because all of the Ministries in Brunei Darussalam are under the Government's control where personnel from one Ministry do not have access granted to the data from another Ministry. Therefore, the only way to access the data is to print out, which according to HR 2 "it is thick, it cannot be back-to-back". With the traditional method, they would be able to show specific requested physical data without having to print all the data stored in GEMS.

At times we are unable to access GEMS, so if there is a need for emergency or more detailed information, we will refer to the record service. So, it's like a backup plan, if there is a problem and we fear information suddenly goes missing, we need to have a backup. Since our department is under the Prime Minister's office, we do not need to print it out, it's already in the system, but if other departments need it, we have to print it and it is thick, it cannot be back-to-back. That's the reason why we still use both. (HR 2)

E-HRM is a one integrated system. However, as seen above, the traditional method was still actively used, for example, the traditional HR method was still being used for attendance through the use of log-books, papers and the biometric (fingerprint) system.

There are some departments that use GEMS but they also use the finger print and manual system. Well... they do not need a lot of systems just for attendance, I think they need to simplify GEMS, just to use one system... but you know, with GEMS you need a system, you need electricity, internet connectivity... so when this system is down it's not that fully reliable (HR 1)

Some other departments they use three systems: biometric, GEMS and log-book just for attendance. (HR 3)

Due to this, HR 3 further explained that in their departments, some users did not want to use the GEMS attendance application "they want to use what they already have, here we have two: biometric and another is logbook".

2. User Interface

A user-friendly layout E-HRM affects the way users' function with the system and affects the outcome of user satisfaction. A complicated layout can cause users to be dissatisfied. Based on the interviews, both HR 1 and HR 4 stated that GEMS is not user-friendly.

GEMS is not really attractive, in terms that.... sorry to say it's not that user friendly and it has a lot of buttons and icons that you need to fill in... they need to improve the interface to simplify, and to attract people to use gems. (HR 1)

If for myself it's fine, but for those who are new they are most likely computer literate so it's convenient, those who are senior they need more guidance because for a computer illiterate, in addition to the difficult layout, I can say that it's not user friendly, so it should be made convenient for all ages. (HR 4)

Improvements Initiative

Improvements focus on the enhancements mentioned by the HR officers. The two improvements which need to be implemented were concerned with the users themselves and the training of the users. This section will answer the second research question, which asked the issues that GEMS users and HR faced when using GEMS and what improvements needed to be made in GEMS.

1. User

The focus of this research is the users, because without users, E-HRM would not have existed. According to HR 4, GEMS is important as it *"Brings more advantage, because it speeds up process, application is instantaneous and it's paperless"*. However, despite the importance of GEMS, during the interview, the researcher observed that one of the improvements that should be made to achieve user satisfaction was from the users themselves, which was to change their mindset. Below are the interviews statements stating that the user's mindset needed to change.

Usually the problem is our staff members, they tend to forget and always last minute. Our struggle is to cultivate and maintain frequent usage of GEMS. When GEMS was first introduced, just to key in attendance can take more than 10 minutes, but now it is less than 10 seconds, but the people here still have that mindset of the problems that occurred before. Previously, the problem was the network, but now it is the people's mindset. (HR 2)

If there is no support from the employees themselves, the system is not useful, because the data is being updated by HR so they need to work together with the employees. If the data is not updated and when the data is needed, but it's not accurate so eventually the system is useless. (HR 3)

Some of our staff members previously seldom used the computer, suddenly they have to use it, so they are hesitant and lazy to use it. (HR 4)

2. Training

After reading and re-reading the interviews, the researcher concluded that the users lacked exposure and training on GEMS. Referring to the interviews, it is important for the Infotech division to give training, re-training and improve on their marketing strategy (exposure). HR 4 stated that, the Infotech division needed to expose all employees rather than giving one main focal person the task to expose GEMS to all employees. At the same time, the HR officer further stated that all of the change management team, application team, technical team should be there when giving training to all the users, to explain the updates, to elaborate the problems associated with GEMS and what issues had been resolved.

One is the change management team, they should expose the advantages to all of the users, not one main focal point, they need to explain the importance of the functions of GEMS, the application team and the technical team should be there during the training to explain what causes certain problems and what they have already fixed. (HR 3)

HR 3 further explain that, if all the users were to be involved in the training, the users would be able to voice out their opinions, because depending on one representative from their department to spread the knowledge would not be beneficial. All users should understand what the benefits of GEMS were towards the users.

Employees can voice out their opinions, because we cannot depend on one focal person to spread the knowledge of GEMS in the department. The Infotech Unit will need to explain this to all by themselves. So, the mindset of the people needs to change, what advantage GEMS brings for them. For example, when it is stated in the GEMS employee portfolio that their highest qualification is O'level, however, their highest qualification is a degree and when they apply for a promotion they will definitely get rejected. Furthermore, HR has many things to do, not just to take care of one employee, so each employee will need to update themselves and inform the HR on any updates they had made. (HR 3)

Meanwhile, HR 1 compared GEMS to another Information System used within the Ministries in Brunei Darussalam, called Tafis. The HR officer mentioned that GEMS was not as widely utilised as Tafis. However, Tafis has been constantly evolving because training has been done on a yearly basis and all the users would be informed whenever there were new updates and improvements being made, where they prove support and offer guidance to all employees. Therefore, training and exposure is important to attain user satisfaction.

In terms of GEMS exposure to the users, GEMS is not strong enough and it's a bit of a hassle because if you were to compare GEMS to Tafis. Tafis is constantly evolving... and they provide training usually on a yearly basis. When they want to introduce a different, new and improved system within the Tafis, they would be very proactive in informing the government service officers and employees on how to use it and how to use it on a daily basis and then they provide user support guidance. Clear support guides... in comparison to GEMS, GEMS is not very thorough, thus GEMS is not very impressive and attractive for employees to use. (HR 1)

EXTENDED E- HRM THEORETICAL FRAMEWORK DEVELOPMENT

This section discusses the findings with reference initial framework used for the research which is based on based on the Qtesihat and Alshibly's (2014) satisfaction model and new extended theoretical framework. It was identified in the literature that a number of key issues were addressed in order to successfully implement E-HRM to achieve user satisfaction. However, from the findings with the literature's insights, it showed that there were gaps within the Qteishat & Alshibly's (2014) satisfaction model. The model focused on only four factors to achieve satisfaction, which were technical support, infrastructure, data-security and user-friendliness. However, it is suggested that there were other elements that needed to be included in the new extended conceptual framework discussed as below.

Qteishat and Alshibly's (2014) satisfaction model as discussed in previous section was mainly focused on the satisfaction towards ICT technology in general. However, after analysing the findings, three areas extended from initial framework were uncovered that is suitable and could contribute as recommendation to a better understanding, specifically for E-HRM user satisfaction of GEMS. The three areas are the implementation of E-HRM, training and user support.

The Implementation of E-HRM

Implementation is the transition period, in the case of E-HRM, it is the transition of HRM. Klein and Sorra (1996) stated that, the usage of the targeted use of innovative technology should be increasingly consistent, skilful and committed. These targeted users were those expected to support, use and adapt to the new HRM settings (Bondarouk et al., 2009). Therefore, to successfully reach the users to adapt to

Figure 4. Extended Theoretical Framework of E-HRM

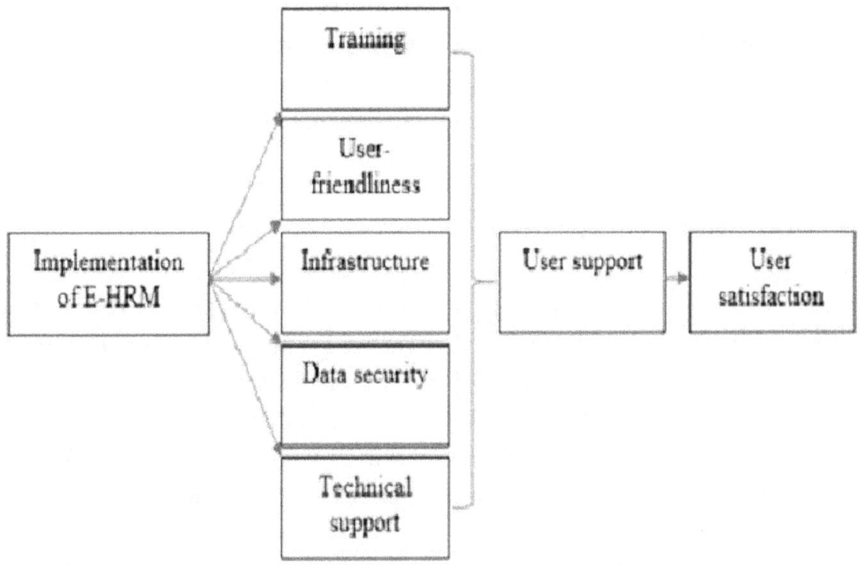

the system, it was important to gain information on the importance of E-HRM, specifically on GEMS for this research.

To successfully implement E-HRM, knowledge of the different types of E-HRM functions is vital, as it offers the HR departments guidance on which type should be implemented, based on the benefits that will be gained from the outcome linked to the type of E-HRM function implemented (Snell et al., 2001). Despite GEMS having extensive features, users have not made use of the other features. E-HRM is most effective when all the functions of the E-HRM are fully utilised. However, GEMS users only mainly utilised GEMS for three purposes: attendance, apply leave and apply exit country leave.

Training

GEMS trainings were argued to be insufficient. This could be the danger as shortages of qualified staff able to adapt to the increasingly technology driven workplace will slow down HR's transformation (Baesens et al, 2017). Training is one of the most important components in the implementation of E-HRM. Providing sufficient training for users would provide a positive influence towards achieving favourable outcomes of user satisfaction. According to Parry and Tyson (2011), "Organisations that fail to do so, report that systems do not provide the desired efficiency savings as users frequently have to contact HR to obtain support". In other words, users have no awareness of the features of E-HRM and face difficulties operating the system, therefore, users would not take advantage of the full functionality and would depend on HR.

User-Friendly

User-friendly was reported to greatly influence user satisfaction (Bondarouk, 2016). According to Priya and Munivenkatappa (2017), user-friendliness was closely linked because without a user-friendly interface system it would be challenging and time-consuming for the users to adapt to the new system during or after training is provided. Additionally, Parry and Tyson (2011) stated that a non-user-friendly E-HRM would increase the amount of HR tasks, rather than reducing it. From the findings it demonstrates GEMS is complicated and difficult to use. This is further claimed through survey data shows how significant user friendliness towards user satisfaction. The results shows that the users were dissatisfied and provides assertion that GEMS was not user-friendly.

Infrastructure – Internet Connection

Technological infrastructure is a necessary function of E-HRM (Nivlouei, 2014). Infrastructure refers to hardware, software, internet and website interface necessary for ICT to function (Office of Government Commerce, 2002). Venkatesh et al. (2003) stated that E-HRM infrastructure existed to support the system, and supported both the HR and IT departments, in order to provide assistance to the users with a highly responsive and available system. According to Poisat and Mey (2017), there is a positive relationship between infrastructure and user satisfaction. Looking back at the findings, GEMS' unstable internet connection made it difficult to access the system. However, it was argued that the internet connection has been improved, as the hardware and software had been upgraded. In fact, it was specified that the internet connection was no longer a problem, as it was the 'mindset' of the users that needed to be changed. This may imply the survey results have shown infrastructure is insignificant towards user satisfaction.

Data Security

It is critical to maintain high levels of security to protect user information with any E-HRM implementation (Torres & Arias, 2009). Any security breaches affect users significantly, as it can erode the users' trust and limit interactions with the E-HRM system. (Lippert & Swierez, 2005). From the findings has shown that appropriate measures were taken by the government agency – EGNC and Ministry of Finance to store and secure all data. Further, survey data confirms that data security is significant to user satisfaction.

When properly implemented, robust data security strategies will protect an organization's information assets against cybercriminal activities, but they also guard against insider threats and human error, which remains among the leading causes of data breaches these days. The findings highlighted the importance of the E-HRM security as indicated in literature where GEMS uses a restricted or private communication network that can only be accessed internally within the organisation, which is restricted from public use or access (Espinosa et al, 2010). Information that is stored in E-HRM is highly sensitive; stores office data and volumes of employees' personal information thus, internal security is very critical and should be secured with passwords accessed by EGNC only.

Technical Support

Technical support refers to a service which offer technology users help, through the incorporation of technology in the working environment (Ghavifekr and Rosdy, 2015). Ma and Ye (2015) claimed that technical support was critical for E-HRM, as it provided users the capability to operate E-HRM successfully within the organisation. A good technical support will assist users with the help required, and the ability to achieve this will lead to user satisfaction with E-HRM (Bondarouk et al., 2017). Refer to the findings, previously the technical support was a problem as support could only be obtained through the telephone. However, this was rectified through the introduction of other methods such as through e-mail and the mobile messaging application called *WhatsApp*. Thus, this contributes towards the employees' satisfaction towards the GEMS technical support. This is consistent with the survey findings where technical support discovered not significant towards the user satisfaction.

User Support

User support has been considered a great influence towards determining whether E-HRM is a success or not (Poisat and Mey, 2017). When users engage with an E-HRM system, users will be able to observe their satisfaction of the system; the support of the users positively influenced their satisfaction (Bondarouk, 2017). Based on the interview findings it can be seen that is GEMS becomes impractical. It was mentioned that the reason why user support was not strong enough, was because they still had the mindset that the internet connection was still a problem. As a matter of fact, the internet connection was no longer the problem as the hardware and software had been upgraded. Furthermore, a number of users hardly or never used the computer, however, due to the implementation of GEMS they were obligated to use the computer without skills. On the other hand, GEMS was not thoroughly implemented simultaneously across in all government agencies and not all civil servants (of all job positions) are required to use GEMS. This perhaps the contributing factor for the reluctance of usage - inconsistency of implementation and 'non-complusory' adoption.

It was discovered that the reason why this become an issue because the users were still actively using the traditional method. The main purpose why E-HRM was formed was to fasten workflow through one integrated system rather than using many types of traditional manual systems (Snell et al., 1995). The respondents claimed that the reason why they had to use both GEMS and the traditional method was because, the traditional method acted as their back-up system and would act as a support if there were any problems with GEMS. This shows that, the respondents were satisfied with GEMS but still had doubts on the stability of the system. Some respondents were using more than one HRM system. Refer back to what had been mentioned by Snell et al. (1995), the main purpose to why E-HRM was formed was to fasten workflow through one integrated system, rather than using many types of traditional manual systems. However, the respodents were not only using GEMS but also used two other methods which were the logbook and biometric systems. Therefore, to achieve user satisfaction, the departments would need to opt for one HRM system.

Furthermore, it was also claimed that without user support, GEMS would not be useful due to low usage and inaccurate data. The government had spent 10 million just to implement GEMS at the beginning, however, it was such a waste as user support seemed to be lacking due to the users' preference towards traditional practices. Perry and Tyson (2011) pointed out that many previous studies mentioned that managers had difficulties in encouraging users to make use of E-HRM, because traditional methods were still actively used. Therefore, it is important to gain user support through motivation and changing their mindsets, with regards to adopting GEMS and less usage of the traditional system.

User Satisfaction

Referring to the previous sections based on the conceptual framework, utilisation of the implemented E-HRM functions, sufficient training, creation of a user-friendly interface, strong infrastructure system, secure data security, good support from the technical support and attain user support, were the key elements to determine user satisfaction.

From the discussions above, it can be seen that the users were only satisfied with the data security and technical support. Other than that, users were not satisfied with the GEMS functions, due to the lack of training, non-friendly interface and user support. As for the GEMS infrastructure system, users claimed that it was weak. However, based on the interview, the infrastructure was mentioned to have been improved and it was the users' mindset that needed to be motivated, which led to a lack in user support.

This is related to the argument indicated the people factors were distinguished as the pivotal factor as user acceptance to the new technology and the mindsets of the employees on the value of E-HRM have an impact to E-HRM adoption (Bondarouk et al.,2016).

CONCLUSION

From the results of the findings and discussion in previous section, in conclusion, the employees are not fully satisfied with the system although with their ten years of experience. In order to successfully implement E-HRM and achieve user satisfaction, it was identified that there are few numbers of key elements that needed to address based on the Qtesihat and Alshibly (2014) satisfaction model which are technical support, infrastructure, data security and user-friendliness. However, it was found that there are gaps within the framework. Therefore, an extended conceptual framework is developed to include training and user support to address user satisfaction of E-HRM that fits into CE concept as they provide the tools that are able to lower costs, automate tasks, and even create economic value. This is in line with the argument that CE should go beyond the minimization of waste and towards a reframing of human and social behaviors such as aiming at building awareness, at increasing knowledge and acquiring the appropriate skills through the training of managers and employees in organizations, strategies focused on the human and social dimensions of organizations influenced by the field of Green Human Resource Management (GHRM) (Chiapetta Jabbour, 2019).

The extended framework developed in this study has the potential to provide a guideline for GEMS practitioners. Accordingly, the proposed framework is intended to be neither normative — as it describes how organisations ought to function and not necessarily how they actually do function — nor a rigid set of prescriptive rules that guarantees GEMS success. However, the framework can serve as a useful guideline for drawing attention to the theoretical underpinnings of the concept of user satisfaction of E-HRM, government information systems and the characteristics of E-HRM. Traditional HR methods are still being use actively, together with GEMS. Resulted from insufficient training and non-user-friendly interface, it causes traditional methods to be much more favourable. Therefore, to improve GEMS usage, it would be wise to discourage the traditional methods from being use in the departments. Furthermore, with lack of training which causes, the system to be non-user friendly for the employees, correspondingly, causes employees to have negative mindset towards GEMS.

REFERENCES

Akinyede, R. O., & Daramola, O. A. (2013). Neutral network web-based human resource management system model. *International Journal of Computer Networks and Communication Security*, *1*(3), 75–87.

Badarudin, P. A., & Ibrahim, F. (2021). Knowledge-Based Practices in Disaster Management: Development Towards Digital Humanism. In W. S. H. Suhaili, N. Z. Siau, S. Omar, & S. Phon-Amuaisuk (Eds.), *Computational Intelligence in Information Systems* (pp. 13–25). Springer. doi:10.1007/978-3-030-68133-3_2

Baesens, B., De Winne, S., & Sels, L. (2017, Winter). Is Your Company Ready for HR Analytics? *MIT Sloan Management Review.*

Bondarouk, T., & Brewster, C. (2016). Conceptualising the future of HRM and technology research. *International Journal of Human Resource Management*, *27*(21), 2652–2671. doi:10.1080/09585192.2016.1232296

Bondarouk, T., Parry, E., & Furtmueller, E. (2017). Electronic HRM: Four decades of research on adoption and consequences. *International Journal of Human Resource Management*, *28*(1), 98–131. doi:10.1080/09585192.2016.1245672

Bondarouk, T., & Ruël, H. J. M. (2009). Electronic human resource management: Challenges in the digital era. *International Journal of Human Resource Management*, *20*(3), 505–514. doi:10.1080/09585190802707235

Bondarouk, T., Ruël, H. J. M., & van der Heijden, B. (2009). E-HRM Effectiveness in a Public Sector Organization: A Multi-Stakeholder Perspective. *International Journal of Human Resource Management*, *20*(3), 578–590. doi:10.1080/09585190802707359

Brunei Prime Minister's Office. (2009). *Line manager self-service booklet*. Retrieved August 11, 2018, from http://www.gems.gov.bn/gemshelpcentre/Resource/GEMS BD_TR_Line%20Man ager%20Booklet%20Content_v0.15.pdf

Chiappetta Jabbour, C. J., Sarkis, J., Lopes de Sousa Jabbour, A. B., Scott Renwick, D. W., Singh, S. K., Grebinevych, O., Kruglianskas, I., & Filho, M. G. (2019). Who is in charge? A review and a research agenda on the 'human side' of the circular economy. *Journal of Cleaner Production*, *222*, 793–801. doi:10.1016/j.jclepro.2019.03.038

Davoudi, S. M. M., & Fartash, K. (2012). Electronic human resource management: New avenues which leads to organizational success. *Journal of Multidisciplinary Research*, *1*(2), 75–87.

E-Government national centre. (2019). *One government network.* Retrieved 27 June, 2019, from http://www.egnc.gov.bn/SitePages/OGN.aspx

Espinosa, D. J., & Lujan, S. M. (2010). *Putting e-HR into practice: The case of the University of Alicante*. Retrieved 27 April, 2019, from http://www.egnc.gov.bn /SitePages/OGN.aspx.http://ceur-ws.org/Vol-570/paper020.pdf

Esposito, M., Tse, T., & Soufani, K. (2018). Introducing a Circular Economy: New Thinking with New Managerial and Policy Implications. *California Management Review*, *60*(3), 5–19. doi:10.1177/0008125618764691

Falk, R. F., & Miller, N. B. (1992). *A Primer for Soft Modeling*. University of Akron Press.

Findikli, M. A., & Bayarcelik, E. B. (2015). Exploring the outcomes of Electronic Human Resource Management (E-HRM). *Procedia: Social and Behavioral Sciences*, *207*, 424–431. doi:10.1016/j.sbspro.2015.10.112

Gardner, S. D., Lepak, D. P., & Bartol, K. M. (2003). Virtual HR: The impact of information technology on the human resource professional. *Journal of Vocational Behavior*, *63*(2), 159–179. doi:10.1016/S0001-8791(03)00039-3

Ghavifekr, S., & Rosdy, W. A. W. (2015). Teaching and learning with technology: Effectiveness of ICT integration in schools. *International Journal of Research in Education and Science*, *1*(2), 175–191. doi:10.21890/ijres.23596

Hair, J. F., Black, W. C., Babin, B. J., & Anderson, R. E. (2010). *Multivariate data analysis* (7th ed.). Pearson.

Hobson, K., & Lynch, N. (2016). Diversifying and de-growing the circular economy: Radical social transformation in a resource-scarce world. *Futures*, *82*, 15–25. doi:10.1016/j.futures.2016.05.012

Ibrahim, F., & Ali, D. N. (2021). Evaluating Knowledge Management Practices in Higher Education Institutions (HEIs): Towards KMPro Framework Guidelines. In S. Zyngier (Ed.), *Handbook of Research on Knowledge Management Tools in Higher Education* (pp. 221–245). IGI Global.

Ibrahim, F., Edgar, D., & Reid, V. (2009). Assessing the role of knowledge management in adding value: Moving towards a comprehensive framework. *Journal of Information & Knowledge Management*, *8*(4), 275–286. doi:10.1142/S0219649209002397

Ibrahim, F., & Reid, V. (2010). Integrated Use of Information Technology and People Involvement for Knowledge Management. *International Journal of Technology, Knowledge and Society*, *6*(2), 163–180. doi:10.18848/1832-3669/CGP/v06i02/56086

Ibrahim, H., & Yusoff, Y. (2013). *Satisfaction towards E-HRM in government organisations of Malaysia: A proposed model based on field theory*. Retrieved August 11, 2018, from https://pdfs.semanticscholar.org/779d/152a79c2763072028c022416f49a3d5c0954.Pdf?_ga=2.174827874.1187198535.1561975056-741735385.1561975056

Johnson, R. D., Stone, D. L., & Lukaszewski, K. M. (2021). The benefits of eHRM and AI for talent acquisition. *Journal of Tourism Futures*, *7*(1), 40–52. doi:10.1108/JTF-02-2020-0013

Joshi, J. B. D., Ghafoor, A., Aref, W. G., & Spafford, E. H. (2002). Security and Privacy Challenges of a Digital Government. In W. J. McIver & A. K. Elmagarmid (Eds.), *Advances in Digital Government. Advances in Database Systems* (Vol. 26). Springer. doi:10.1007/0-306-47374-7_7

Kaur, A., & Kaur, R. (2015). Electronic human resource management. *International Journal of Business and Management*, *2*(2), 1118–1125.

Kaur, P. (2013). E-HRM: A Boon or Bane? *Journal of Management*, *1*(1), 35–38.

Klein, K. J., & Sorra, J. S. (1996). The Challenge of Innovation Implementation. *Academy of Management Review*, *21*(4), 1055–1080. doi:10.5465/amr.1996.9704071863

Kline, R. B. (2011). *Principles and practice of structural equation modeling*. Guilford Press.

Lee, I. (2011). Modeling the benefit of e-recruiting process integration. *Decision Support Systems*, *51*(1), 230–239. doi:10.1016/j.dss.2010.12.011

Lengnick-Hall, M. L., & Moritz, S. (2003). The impact of e-HR on the human resource management function. *Journal of Labor Research*, *24*(3), 365–379. doi:10.100712122-003-1001-6

Lippert, S. K., & Swierez, P. M. (2005). Human resource information system and technology trust. *Journal of Information Science*, *31*(5), 340–353. doi:10.1177/0165551505055399

Ma, L., & Ye, M. (2015). The Role of Electronic Human Resource Management in Contemporary Human Resource Management. *Open Journal of Social Sciences*, *3*(04), 71–78. doi:10.4236/jss.2015.34009

Mago, R. (2016). E-HRM Electronic human resource management. *International Journal of Business and Scientific Research*, *23*, 41–47.

Mahapatro, B. B. (2010). New age human resource management. New Delhi: New Age International (P) Ltd.

Maheshwari, S., & Vohra, V. (2015). Identifying critical HR practices impacting employee perception and commitment during organizational change. *Journal of Organizational Change Management*, *28*(5), 872–889. doi:10.1108/JOCM-03-2014-0066

Mahfod, J., Noof, Y., Khalifa, Y., & Faisal, A. M. (2017). Electronic Human Resource Management (E-HRM) System. *International Journal of Economic Research*, *14*(15), 563–575.

Mahmood, M. A., Burn, J. M., Gemoets, L. A., & Jacquez, C. (2000). Variables Affecting Information Technology End-User Satisfaction: A Meta-Analysis of the Empirical Literature. *International Journal of Human-Computer Studies*, *52*(4), 751–771. doi:10.1006/ijhc.1999.0353

Marler, J. (2009). Making human resources strategic by going to the Net: Reality or myth? *International Journal of Human Resource Management*, *20*(3), 515–527. doi:10.1080/09585190802707276

Marler, J. H., & Parry, E. (2015). Human resource management, strategic involvement and e-HRM technology. *International Journal of Human Resource Management*, 1–21. doi:10.1080/09585192.2015.1091980

Moreau, V., Sahakian, M., van Griethuysen, P., & Vuille, F. (2017). Coming Full Circle: Why Social and Institutional Dimensions Matter for the Circular Economy. *Journal of Industrial Ecology*, *21*(3), 497–506. doi:10.1111/jiec.12598

Nayananjalee, W. T., & De Alwis, A. (2017). *HR Professionals Perception towards Electronic Human Resource Management*. Retrieved from https://www.researchgate.net/publication/320163215_HR_Professionals_Perception_towards_Electronic_ Human_ Resource_Management

Nivlouei, F. B. (2014). Electronic Human Resource Management System: The Main Element in Capacitating Globalization Paradigm. *International Journal of Business and Social Science*, *5*(2), 147–159.

O'Riordan, J. (2017). *The practice of human resource management*. State of public service research paper. Retrieved August 11, 2018 from https://www.ipa.ie/_ fileUpload/Documents /the_practice _of_hrm.pdf

Office of Government Commerce. (2002). *ICT infrastructure management*. The Stationary Office.

Paauwe, J., & Boon, C. (2009). Strategic HRM: A critical review. In D. F. Collings & T. W. Geoffrey (Eds.), *Human resource management: A critical approach* (pp. 38–54). Routledge.

Pardoe, I. (2012). *Applied regression modeling* (2nd ed.). Wiley. doi:10.1002/9781118345054

Parry, E., & Tyson, S. (2011). Desired goals and actual outcomes of e-HRM. *Human Resource Management Journal*, *21*(3), 335–354. doi:10.1111/j.1748-8583.2010.00149.x

Poisat, P., & Mey, M. R. (2017). Electronic human resource management: Enhancing or entrancing? *Journal of Human Resource Management*, *15*, 1–9.

Prime Minister's Office. (2008). *What you need to know about GEMS*. Retrieved August 11, 2018, from http://www.gems.gov.bn/gemshelpcentre/Resource/GEMS%20Awareness %20 Pamphlet%20v0.6.pdf

Priya, S. & Munivenkatappa. (2017). A study on the satisfaction level of employees towards e-hrm systems. *International Journal of Applied Research*, *3*(9), 467–471.

Public Service Department. (2015, Oct. 14). GEMS aplikasi rekod kedatangan. *Pelita Brunei,* p. 13.

Qteishat, M., Alshibly, H. H., & Al-ma'aitah, M. A. (2014). The impact of e-ticketing technique on customer satisfaction: An empirical analysis. *Journal of Information Systems and Technology Management*, *11*(3), 519–532. doi:10.4301/S1807-17752014000300001

Qu, Q. S., & Dumay, J. (2011). The qualitative research interviews. *Qualitative Research in Accounting & Management*, *8*(3), 238–264. doi:10.1108/11766091111162070

Rohila, A., Yadav, K., & Ghanghas, B. (2017). Role of Information and communication technology (ICT) in agriculture and extension. *Journal of Applied and Natural Science*, *9*(2), 1097–1100. doi:10.31018/jans.v9i2.1328

Ruel, H. J. M., Bondarouk, T., & van der Velde, M. (2007). The contribution of e-HRM to HRM effectiveness. Results from a quantitative study in a Dutch Ministry. *Employee Relations*, *29*(3), 280–291. doi:10.1108/01425450710741757

Saatcioglu, O. Y. (2007). *What determines user satisfaction in erp projects: benefits, barriers or risks*. Retrieved August 12, 2018, from https://pdfs.semanticscholar.org/02e0/ fd1caef0c5c47c9488dfb952d3f360c0f5d3.pdf

Shilpa, V., & Gopal, R. (2011). The implications of implementing electronic- human resource management (E-HRM) systems in companies. *Journal of Information Systems and Communication*, *2*(1), 10–29.

Snell, S. A., Stueber, D., & Lepak, D. P. (2001). Virtual HR departments: Getting out of the middle. *Cornell University*. Retrieved August 12, 2018, from https://digitalcommons. Ilr.cornell.edu/cgi/viewcontent.cgi?referer=https://www.google.com/&httpsredir=1&article=1070&context=cahrswp

Strohmeier, S. (2009). Concepts of e-HRM consequences: A categorisation, review and suggestion. *International Journal of Human Resource Management*, *20*(3), 528–543. doi:10.1080/09585190802707292

Strohmeier, S., & Kabst, R. (2014). Configurations of E-HRM an Empirical Exploration. *Employee Relations*, *36*(4), 333–353. doi:10.1108/ER-07-2013-0082

Torres, T. O., & Arias, M. O. (2009). *Human resources information systems: Challenges in e-hrm*. IGI Global.

Tsoukas, H. (2005). *Complex Knowledge: Studies in Organizational Epistemology*. Oxford Press.

Venkatesh, V., Morris, M. G., Davis, G. B., & Davis, F. D. (2003). User acceptance of information technology: Toward a unified view. *Management Information Systems Quarterly*, *27*(3), 425–478. doi:10.2307/30036540

Wright, P. M., & Dyer, L. (2000). *People in the E-Business: New challenges, new solutions*. Ithaca: Cornell university, school of industrial and labor *relations*.

Zhang, L., & Wang, H. (2006). Intelligent information processing in human resource management: An implementation case in China. *Expert Systems: International Journal of Knowledge Engineering and Neural Networks*, *23*(5), 356–369. doi:10.1111/j.1468-0394.2006.00416.x

Chapter 15
Green Consumerism in Brunei Darussalam:
Exploratory Study on Purchasing Behaviour

Fahmi Ibrahim
https://orcid.org/0000-0001-5016-7755
Universiti Teknologi Brunei, Brunei

Siti Wardah Abd Rahman
https://orcid.org/0000-0002-7837-0998
Universiti Teknologi Brunei, Brunei

Nurul Hafizah Jefri
Universiti Teknologi Brunei, Brunei

ABSTRACT

The aim of this chapter is to analyze the relationship of the demographic and socio-psychological determinants on consumers' green purchase behaviours in Brunei Darussalam, with the application framework of the affect-behaviour-cognition (ABC) model. A total of 119 consumers from different backgrounds participated in this study, whereby 113 respondents participated in the online questionnaire, and the other six respondents were interviewed. It is discovered that consumers who are more environmentally conscious are not necessarily likely to purchase green products, but are actually involved in green behaviours. However, in the environmental aspects of awareness, concern, and knowledge, the other factors, monthly income and educational level, did not possess major significance. The product attributes such as price and availability of the green products played a significant role in consumer buying decisions which will lead to the value-action gap phenomenon. Moreover, this study discovered the government is needed to promote and encourage green purchase behaviours in Brunei Darussalam.

DOI: 10.4018/978-1-7998-8678-5.ch015

INTRODUCTION

Protecting and conserving the environment is not a one man's job, however one man can make a difference. Globalization and the Fourth Industrial Revolution (IR4) have led to the impacts on the environment either positively or negatively. Over the past few decades, environmental degradation has become a crucial matter that has captured global attention - from the rising sea level, global warming, climate change, scarcer natural resources, pollution from various sources to biodiversity loss which were mostly inflicted by humans. As a result, these concerning impacts are not only burdening the Earth, but the living things in it as well. Moreover, as the detrimental effects continue to occur, consumers are becoming attentive to the topic of green consumerism. People have become more environmentally aware after recognizing how serious ecological problems actually are (Han et al., 2009). As the result consumers' sensitivity towards the environment has escalated because of the damaging outcome of human behavior on the environment, and the urgency to end it (Leonidou et al., 2010). This is supported by Wahid et al. (2011) where it was mentioned that consumers are fully aware of the huge effect that their buying behaviour has on the environment. Hence, green consumerism behaviors occupy an increasingly important role in advocating environmental awareness. From a report by the UN Intergovernmental Panel on Climate Change implies that changing lifestyle, diet and reducing energy consumption can have a considerable impact in lessening the destructive environmental degradation (Sachdeva et al., 2015).). In addition, there are increasing number of studies that found consumers' environmental ethics, moral obligation, and green attitude to be significant factors of green consumption (Akhtar et al., 2021; Testa et al., 2020; Yue et al., 2020).

The conservation and protection of the environment continued as an essential factor of Brunei Darussalam's development process with the aim of sustainable development and, this is corresponding with Brunei Vision 2035. It is also observed that, the nation's consumers are becoming more aware and knowledgeable on the importance of protecting the environment, from efforts by different bodies. For example, the Government have implemented formulated policies and strategies on the environment to move towards this goal (Ahmad et al., 2015). Some of the initiatives, including organizing environmental awareness activities and programmes such as (i) 'No Plastic Bag Weekend', which the government aims to slowly get rid of plastic bag use by 2019 (Abu Bakar, 2018) - this effort had been elevated to 'No Plastic Bag Everyday' which effectively command on 31st December 2018 (Brudirect, 2018), (ii) participation in Earth Hour event, car-free day every Sunday during 'Bandarku Ceria', (iii) reduction in the use of Styrofoam; along with (iv) the creation of local environmental clubs such as Green Brunei and Beach Bunch. Small Medium Enterprises (SMEs) are also joining in this "movement" by selling environmentally friendly products such as metal straws as a replacement for plastic straws, recyclable clothes, sustainable toothbrushes, kitchen utensils and make-up brushes and the initiative of the #zerowastebrunei campaign by local businesses, along with the advocative support of Non-Governmental Organizations (NGOs) in the nation. The aim of this study is to analyze the relationship of environmental knowledge, the demographic and socio-psychological determinants and consumers' green purchase behaviours in Brunei Darussalam, with the application framework of the Affect-Behaviour-Cognition (ABC).

RELEVANT FRAMEWORK – ABC MODEL

This study applied the modified model called Affect-Behaviour-Cognition (ABC) model, introduced by Guagnano et al. (1995) which is then further explored by Stern (2000), aims to better understand human behaviour. This model suggests that, consumer green behaviour is not only determined by attitude, but also by contextual factors. The core approach to Stern's theory is the assumption that behaviour is responsible for the organism and its environment. In the language of ABC, behavior (B) is 'an interactive product of personal sphere attitudinal variables (A) and contextual factors (C)' (Stern, 2000). Attitudinal factors considered in such theory might comprise a heterogeneity of norms, values, and personal beliefs as well as the tendency to act in certain ways. Furthermore, attitude can be defined as "evaluations of people, objects and ideas" (Fishbein & Ajzen, 1975). Attitudes are structured by personality, motivation, perception and emotion, and the building of attitudes can be contributed from different factors. It can be concluded that attitude comprises of three key elements: Affective, Behavioural and Context or Cognitive, also known as the ABC model. Affect comprises to the emotional reaction of an individual consumer and how they feel about an object, whilst Behavioural relates to the consumer's intention to respond and act in a manner toward an object and Cognitive states the consumers' beliefs about an object (Hawkins & Mothersbaugh, 2010).

Figure 1. Attitude components and manifestations
Adapted from Hawkins and Mothersbaugh (2010).

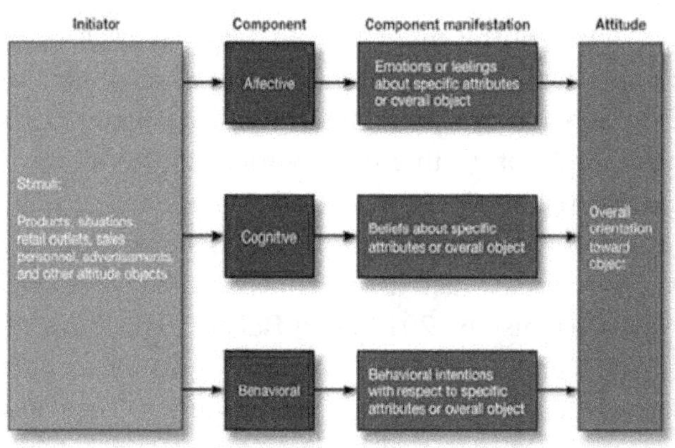

As shown in Figure 1 the structure of the ABC model are between the determinant of attitudes (i.e. internal factors) and contextual determinants. Specifically, the theory asserts that, the attitude-behaviour connection is solid when contextual determinants are weak or even non-existent; and that means that there is no link between attitudes and behaviours when contextual determinants are "either strongly negative or strongly positive" (Stern, 2000). Stern (2000) then further gave an example of recycling, where he mentioned when there is an access of recycling facilities (either very easy or very hard), it is significant because this will determine whether or not people will apply the pro-recycling attitudes. There are two cases in that will happen in this situation, whereby firstly no one recycles; and secondly, most people recycle. In another situation, nonetheless, in which it is practicable, but not certainly easy and convenient to recycle. Thus, it can be said that the relationship between "green" attitude and recycling behaviour is the strongest. To summarize, under supportive conditions, even an individual with weak environmental attitudes behave in an environmentally friendly way, whereas in restrictive conditions, an individual with highly positive environmental attitudes also may be discouraged to show environmentally friendly behaviour (Joshi & Rahman, 2015).

CONSUMER BEHAVIOR AND GREEN CONSUMERISM

Economically, consumer refers to a person who has a budget, which can be used to spend on available goods and services on the market for their usage. The behaviour is defined as the actions taken in order to satisfy desires and needs, which is often related to the consumer's environment (Beauprez, 2010). Consumer behaviour examines how individuals or groups decide how to spend their available resources such as time, money and effort on products (Liebenberg, 2015). To some extent, purchases are influenced by consumer behaviour by being the primary activators in consumers' purchasing activities. Moreover, consumers use a decision-making approach when buying products or services to satisfy needs. It is claimed that a consumer's perception of a product is also affected by the behavior (Agyeman, 2014). Correspondingly, in order for any firm seeking to succeed in a competitive environment, consumers are considered to be a vital player (Beauprez, 2010). Thus, it is crucial to adapt and to understand how the consumers' decision making process takes place, along with their behavioural patterns. Ultimately, consumers are rationally and psychologically different from each other - with subjective decisions' making. Consumers often make careful and rational choices by trying to choose what they believe to be the best and better choice, in turn to maximize their advantages and minimizing disadvantages (Ding, 2015). Likewise, if an individual often follow a particular pattern of purchasing, they are assumed to raise particular questions during each of the different stages; from identification of need, seeking different options, exploring options available, purchase selection and after purchase appraisal, in order to change their personal perceptions towards green marketing into action (Kataria et al., 2013). Further, as an example; during the identification stage, individuals will first decide for themselves, whether the products they want to buy is a need or a want; other choices that satisfy the environmental worries need to be explored during the information phase; then in the consideration phase, they will have to assess the socio-environmental factors; next, they will question themselves at the transaction stage whether they can hold the purchase of goods; and after purchasing, the individuals will be investigating the possibility of using the old products (Kataria et al., 2013).

Additionally, Ding (2015) stated that consumers entrust more on the internal information which is the first-hand experience, but also contrast it with external information which often obtained from family, friends and other references. When internal information is limited, consumers trust those who have a close personal relationship with them, in comparison to media and advertisements, other information sources and channels (Gershoff and Johar, 2006). In contrast, Lee and Cho (2019) find that in American context, media exposure and attention to corporate sustainability communication positively influences consumers' environmental protection behavior intention and green purchasing behavior intention. Their findings are consistent with previous studies' results regarding how media exposure and the attention given to news about environmental issues positively affect audiences' pro-environmental behaviors (Huang, 2016; Liao et al., 2016).

On the other hand, environmental consciousness can affect consumer behaviour (Follows & Jobber, 2000). Evidence has shown that consumers have become more likely to express their environmental worries by purchasing environmentally friendly goods and services (Fisher et al., 2012). A green consumer can be defined as a consumer who is specifically distressed with the environment in their behavioral purchasing, consumption practices, and inspect the consequences of their behaviour on the natural environment around them (Liebenberg, 2015). Green consumers are differentiated as purchasing green products when the chance presents itself. This type of consumers usually avoids harmful products that may be damaging to living things, which during usage or manufacturing has an environmentally damaging outcome, which uses significant amounts of non-renewable energy or involves unethical testing on human or animal subjects. Predominantly, every consumer who shows environmentally friendly behaviour tendencies is categorized as a green consumer (Sarumathi, 2014). It is also discovered that green consumers are more likely to pay more for green products. For example, Chen and Chang (2012) find that in Taiwan's context, that green perceived value would positively affect green trust and green purchase intentions. This can be viewed to be beneficial to governments and businesses considering making changes in eco-friendly policy (Agyeman, 2014). However, green perceived risk would negatively influence both green trust and green purchase intentions. An opposite results are found by Issock (2019) who find that in South African context, environmental knowledge only marginally moderates the relationship between consumption values (such as functional value, economic value, emotional value, social value, and environmental value) and green customer satisfaction. Environmental knowledge also only marginally moderates the relationship between green customer satisfaction and green customer trust and loyalty. In fact, consumption values partially influence green customer satisfaction, which, in turn, affect green customer trust and loyalty, and positive word-of-mouth.

Green consumerism is a complex approach that includes environmental preservation in reducing pollution, and sustainable use of non-renewable resources (McEachern & McClean, 2002). Green consumerism is defined as the production, promotion, and preferential consumption of goods and services on the basis of their pro-environment claims (Akenji, 2014). Some of the examples of green products are fair trade coffee, a petrol-electricity hybrid car, and energy efficient electrical appliances. Green consumerism essentially aims to not change the system, but to alter the production processes and the products that are being consumed. Furthermore, green consumerism is related with green products and green consumers. While green products are products that are striving to protect or to enhance the natural environment by conserving energy and/or resources and minimizing or eliminating the use of pollutants, toxic agents, and waste (Ritter et al., (2015), green consumer behaviour can be classified into two common categorizes (Shabani et al., 2013). Firstly, minimizing the consumption of energy resources, viz reducing behaviours such as carpooling and reducing electricity usage and secondly, green purchasing behaviour. Common examples of green purchase behaviours are purchasing green products such as energy-saver light bulbs, metal straws and using eco-friendly vehicles. Much of the curtailment doings are from an everyday mundane activity, and in turn, they may have a significant impact on the environment. These types of behaviours also cost-effective, but often involve frequent efforts. Jansson et al. (2010) argues these types of behaviours replace capital for energy, which means that consumers spend and invest in more efficient technologies or products with the aim to minimize the detrimental impact on the environment. Some examples of these behaviours include buying a more fuel-efficient, less polluting vehicle and changing to energy efficient light bulbs. Shabani et al. (2013) further added that, reduction behaviours do not usually cost a lot of money, but rather changes in individuals' personal habits are needed. Individuals' personal habits are different from the green purchase behaviours whereby there will be an additional one time expenses with a potential for future savings. This is further supported

Figure 2. Conceptual framework

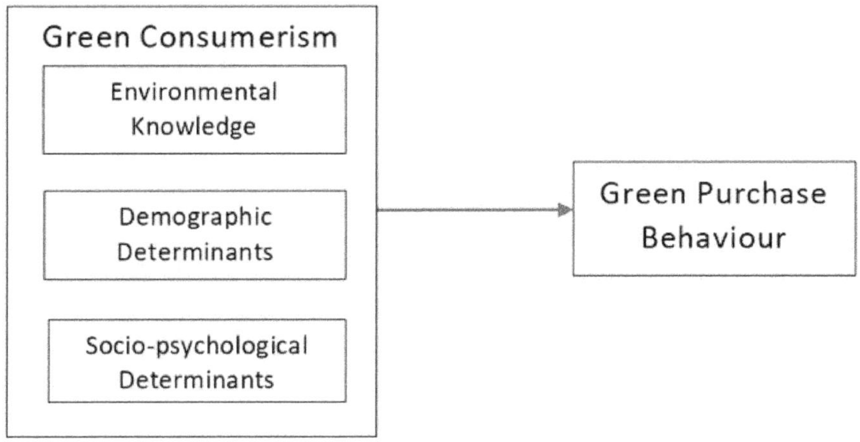

by Styvén and Mariani (2020) who find that in UK, perceived sustainability and economic motivations influence positive attitude toward buying secondhand.

METHODOLOGY

This research will be adopting the exploratory approach as there is still little or no known research available regarding green consumerism in Brunei Darussalam. Exploratory study is mostly used in situations where limited information is available, and it is when the researcher seeks to have the ability to be flexible for future explore areas of research (Cooper & Schindler, 2006). The main aim of an exploratory study is to gain a better understanding of an issue or matter, and being able to seek new insights on new phenomena and to assess the phenomena in a new perspective. Thus, exploratory approach is appropriate for this study.

A total of 113 online responses were recorded for the questionnaire via Google Form. Reed *et al.* (1971) suggested a minimum sample size of 120 to be used for 90% confidence interval, 146 for 95% confidence interval, and 210 for 99% confidence interval. It is important to note that the sample size is close to 120. Given that the design of the questionnaire is one of the important stages in the survey research methodology process that will affect the response rate of data collection, the questionnaire was designed simple and understandable and non-ambiguous words used (Zikmund, 2003). In other words, clear and straightforward. The questionnaire only include relevant questions in order to collect relevant data for the study. This study used both English and Malay language questionnaire in order to have high validity and consistency from respondents. The questionnaire was adapted from Sinnappan and Rahman (2011), Ooi et al. (2012), and more specifically from Tang (2014) with slight changes being made in order to apply to the Brunei Darussalam's context. The questionnaire were distributed via various online platforms especially through social media and communication tools such as WhatsApp and Instagram. The online questionnaire divided into 4 sections; Section A (Demographics Profile), Section B (General Knowledge about Green Consumerism), Section C (Determinants Influencing Green Purchase Behav-

Figure 3. Respondents' gender

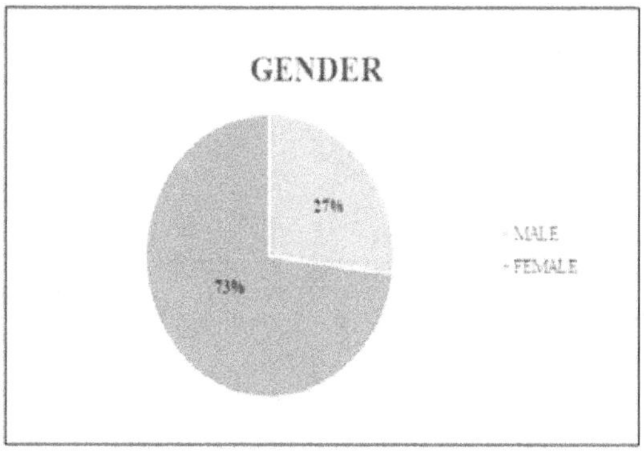

iours) and Section D (Green Purchase Behaviours). The questionnaire was constructed in accordance to the theoretical model (see Figure 2) which developed from literature analysis embedded in ABC model.

For this study, in order to gain a more primary understanding of consumers knowledge and awareness on their purchase behaviour on green products, semi-structured interviews was applied. Semi-structured interviews was conducted as a guided conversation, and pre-set questions were prepared to guide the interview. Additional spontaneous questions also occurred depending on the flow of the interview, hence making this method apt to provide valid and rich data that are not available when working with large samples (Gorra, 2007) by using survey questionnaire. Six respondents were selected for the interview among respondents based on their availability and interest to participate in further research as indicated in the questionnaire survey. Five interviews were face to face interviews, and one interview was conducted via WhatsApp messenger application. The pre-set questions being asked in the semi-structured interview was extracted from the questionnaire, as a guidance for the interview, and spontaneous questions were also asked, in response to the respondents unique answers. The set up of the interviews were informal, conversation-like, and in dual language (Malay and English) according to the respondent's preferences.

FINDINGS AND DISCUSSIONS

In this section, the demographic profile of the respondents will be presented first, followed by general knowledge on green consumerism, the determinants that influence green purchase behaviour, descriptive statistics and correlation matrix, and the challenges faced by consumers in regards to green purchase behaviour. The section will be wrapped up with summary of findings.

Respondents' Demographics Profile

A total of 73% of female (83 respondents) and 27% (30 respondents) answered the questionnaire in Figure 3, with the majority of the respondents were from the 25 - 40 years old age group (49%) - a total of 55 respondents, the second biggest group was from 19 - 24 years old (33% ; 37 respondents), followed by 15% ; 17 respondents) of 40 years old and above age group and the smallest percentage came from the 18 years and below age group (4%) with only 4 respondents.

Figure 4. Respondents' age group

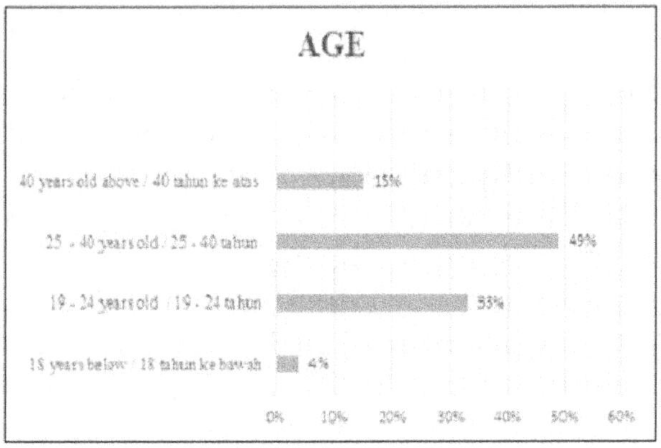

Demographics factors emerged to be one of the dominant determinants in green behaviour as studied by Kollmuss and Agyman (2002). The study found that gender, age, educational background, income level, and profession are considered to be the demographic determinants that remarkably influence the consumers (Kauffman et al., 2012).

The findings from this study shows that there is a notable contrast between male and female respondents from both methodologies towards green purchase behaviour. This study confirmed the result of Tan and Lau (2010) as they inaugurated that, there is a significant dissimilarity between gender in green purchasing behaviour. This meant that, all of the respondents, regardless of their gender are concerned about environmental issues but from the study's questionnaire, the percentage of female respondents buying green products are higher than the male respondents, this is supported by the three interviewed female respondents whereby three of them had purchased green products, which agreed with a study conducted by Rezai et al. (2011) stated that females are more likely to purchase green products such as organic food and other sustainable green products than males.

From the findings shown in Figure 4, 49 percent of respondents are from the 25 - 40 years old group. From this group, most of the respondents are more knowledgeable and aware about the environmental issues, and are most likely to purchase green products such as using metal straws and recyclable bags.

Figure 5. Respondents' education level

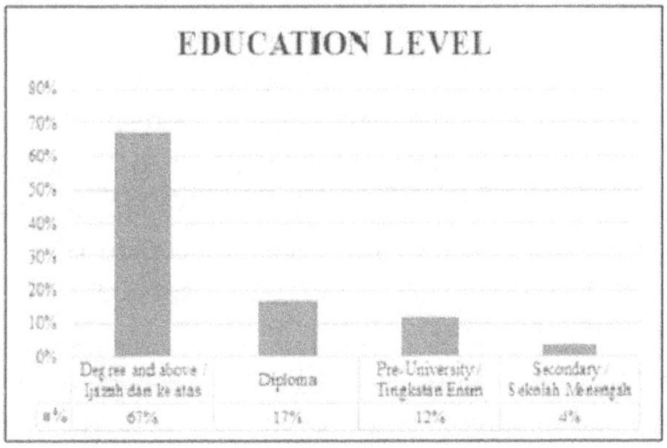

This is in contrast with a study conducted by Sinnappan and Rahman (2011) whereby they stated that, the age group of 20 years and below played a more significant role in comparison to other age groups in purchasing green products in Malaysia's context.

In Figure 5, 76 respondents (67%) attained degree and above qualifications, 17% of 19 respondents had diploma qualifications, 12% (13 respondents) with pre-university qualification and 5 respondents (4%) with secondary-level educational qualification.

Educational background also acts as a determinant to their purchasing behaviors. This could possibly because of the environmental related topics are either being exposed, discussed, and shared during their academic life - as this can be seen from the respondents' answers. This claim is supported by a research conducted in Pakistan by Ali et al. (2011) revealed the consumers who are more highly educated have a positive attitude and towards green products, and more willing to buy green products as compared to the less educated consumers. However, this determinant could not be the main factor in the demographics determinants, as respondents such Respondent D who possesses "O" level qualification has more environmental knowledge and environmental awareness than Respondent A who acquired Diploma qualification. And, both of the respondents are male. This meant that, all of the respondents, regardless of their educational background are concerned about environmental issues. Both male and female respondents have full understanding on their responsibility towards environmental protection, and most of them are compliant to behave in a green manner.

Figure 6. Respondents' monthly income

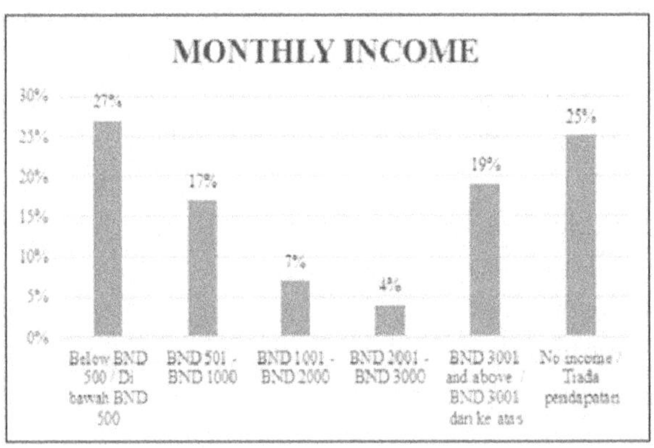

In the monthly income section (Figure 6), the highest contributor of respondents came from respondents with income below BND 500 or USD 377 (27% ; 31 respondents), the second group with a significant 25% came from those with no monthly income with a total of 28 respondents. The third group was from the highest monthly income group (BND 3001 or USD 2261 and above) with 19% ; 22 respondents, the next group was those with monthly income of BND 501 - BND 1000 or USD 378 – USD 754 (17% ; 19 respondents). Followed by 7% which was 8 respondents earned BND 1001 - BND 2000 or USD 755 – USD 1507, and lastly the lowest percentage of 4% (5 respondents) with BND 2001 - BND 3000 or USD 1508 – USD 2261 monthly income.

Based on the findings, there is no considerable difference between monthly income and the green purchase behaviours. This is contradicting to what Awad (2011) stated whereby income was positively

Figure 7. Level of respondents' knowledge on green consumerism

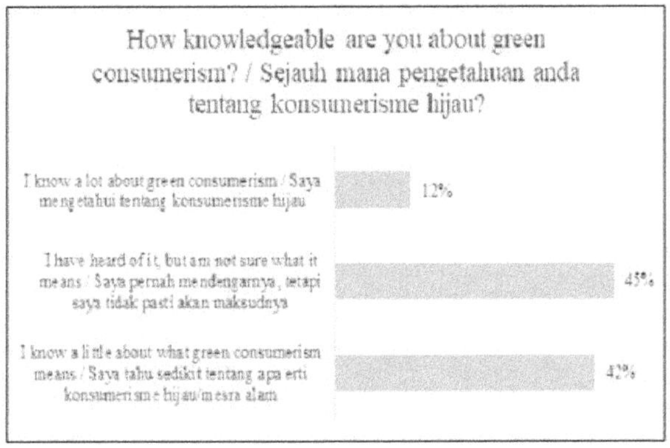

correlated to green purchase behaviours, due to the fact that most green products are more expensive than the conventional products. The findings from the questionnaire stated that 64 per cent of respondents have had purchased green products before, but this is uncorrelated with the responses from the monthly income sections, where it showed 27 percent of respondents have income below BND $500, and 25 percent of respondents do not earn monthly. The same result yielded from the interviews' responses whereby similarities in green purchase behaviours were found between Respondent B who is earning BND $450 a month Respondent F with an income of BND $1,000 per month.

Hawkins and Mothersbaugh (2010) mentioned in their book that income allows purchases, but does not normally explain or cause them. They gave an example of a university professor that may have similar income as a plumber. Yet, it is possible that their consumption processes and behaviours for products will differ. They further added that occupation and education are two factors that directly affects preferences for products, activities and media; but income is the one factor that provide the means to acquire them. Lastly, income is used as an indicator for demographic determinant.

General Knowledge on Green Consumerism

From Figure 7 below, the highest percentage was 45% which means that the respondents have "*heard about green consumerism but are not sure what it means*", whereas 42% of respondents answered *"I know a little about what green consumerism means"* and lastly, only 12% (total of 14 respondents) know *"a lot about green consumerism"*. From in the interview findings shown reasonable awareness towards green consumerism.

Respondents E: *"Very much aware because its one of my interest due to transnational corporation which their operations causing in environmental degradation"*
Respondent B: *"Awareness occurs because of people and natural environment"*
Respondent F: *"I know via environmental issues"*

As shown in Figure 8, a big portion of the answers (46%) stated that they were not sure what is green consumerism. 27% of the respondents answered yes, while 13% stated that they did not know about green consumerism. For this question, it was through interview which means that respondents

Figure 8. Respondents' understanding of green consumerism

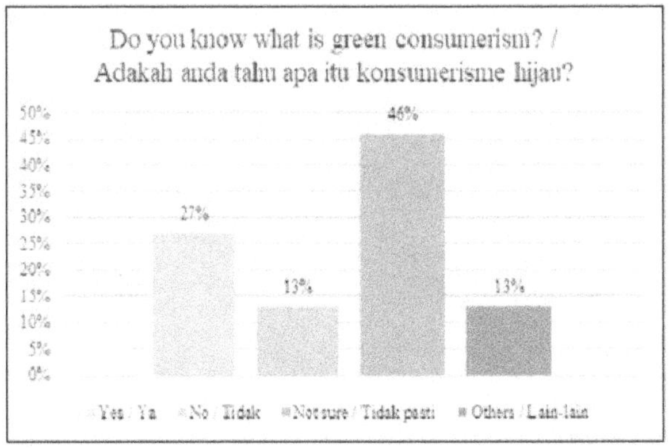

can express their own definition of green consumerism. Few respondents had provided their definition and understanding of green consumerism.

Respondent A: *"Green consumerism basically related to global warming and land pollution"*
Respondent C: *"I have mixed viewpoint as I define it the purchase we make to protect the environment'*

Figure 9 above shows the percentage of respondents practicing green consumerism. A total of 51% of respondents were not sure about their green behaviour, 18% were actively practicing green consumerism, and 15% were not practicing green purchase behaviours. The responses from an open-ended question which allowed the respondents to give examples on their green consumerism practice which indicated behaviours such as using metal straws and using recycle bags. Nevertheless, low percentages 'unsure' due to the level of knowledge of the green consumerism as explained in the interviews;

Respondent E: *"I am sorry I know about the surface of green consumerism"*
Respondent C: *"Quite know about it but there is still a lot to know"*
Respondent D; *"I am not really self aware"*

Figure 9. Respondents' practice of green consumerism

Figure 10. Respondents' purchase of green products

The responses further explained where awareness is inadequate to put into practice.

Respondent E: *"It is worrying but not doing much towards it"*
Respondents C: *"I am not really worry that's why leading me taking things for granted'*
Respondents D: *"Peer pressure plays a role as well, I have high awareness because of others but not really practice it"*

A total of 64% respondents answered they purchased green products shown in Figure 10, whereas 25% were not sure if they ever purchased green products, and 11% of respondents did not (or had not) purchased any green products. The results further explained by the interviewees;

Respondent A: *"I buy green thing as much I aware of not using plastic bags and using recycled bags"*
Respondent B: *"I am influenced by social media spread of issues and initiatives of healthy foods and diet"*

Respondents' perception of green products was also asked. It can be seen from Figure 11 that 82% of respondents answered that, green products are *"good and sustainable for the environment"*. 66% answered green products are *"something natural"*, 25% had the perception that green products are "expensive", 14% answered green products are *"durable"*, 32% stated that green products are *"energy efficient"* and lastly about 36% answered green products are *"for the future"*.

Respondent D: *"Very much worrying because I am thinking of future generations"*
Respondent F: *"It is all about development and mentality of people"*

Determinants Influencing Green Purchase Behaviours

Affective

In the Environmental Concern, the first statement was Brunei Darussalam's environment is my major concern. 3 percent of respondents strongly disagreed with the statement; 5 percent of respondents dis-

Figure 11. Respondents' perception of green products

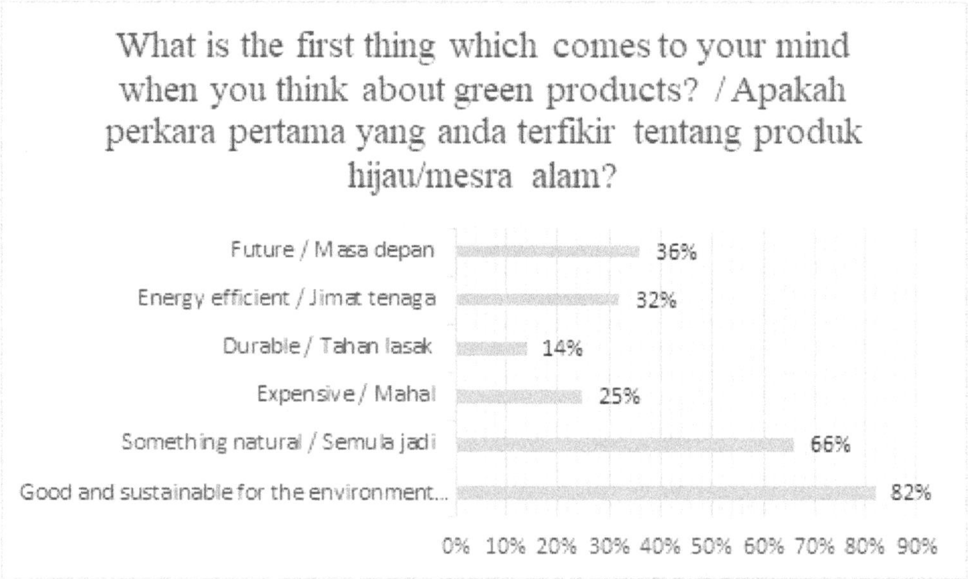

agree with the statement; 29 percent of respondents had a neutral viewpoint; 25 percent respondents agreed; and 38 percent of respondents strongly agreed with the statement. The interviews findings were quite consistent on this matter;

Respondent D: *"Everyone in this world plays a part"*
Respondent B: *"I am not spending a lot of green stuff, I try my best to use those products"*

Social media and media has significant role in raising environmental concern among respondents

Respondent B: *"Social media spread of issues and initiatives"*
Respondent D: *"From many Instagram posts, it's quite promoting about green consumerism like using recycle bags with plastic bag ban. I think it is the way forward"*
Respondent E: *"Education and mass media plays an important role"*

However, small percentage not concern about the environment;

Respondent C: *"Environmental issues not affecting one's life"*

The second statement was ***'I am involved in environmental protection problem in Brunei Darussalam'***. As can be seen from Figure 13, 6 percent of respondents strongly disagreed with the statement; 24 percent of respondents disagree with the statement; 46 percent of respondents had a neutral viewpoint; 19 percent of respondents agreed; and 5 percent of respondents strongly agreed with the statement. The findings showed majority neither agree nor disagree perhaps unsure how to get involved in the environmental protection measures. This further explained by respondents in the interview;

Figure 12. Environmental concern: Brunei Darussalam's environment is my major concern

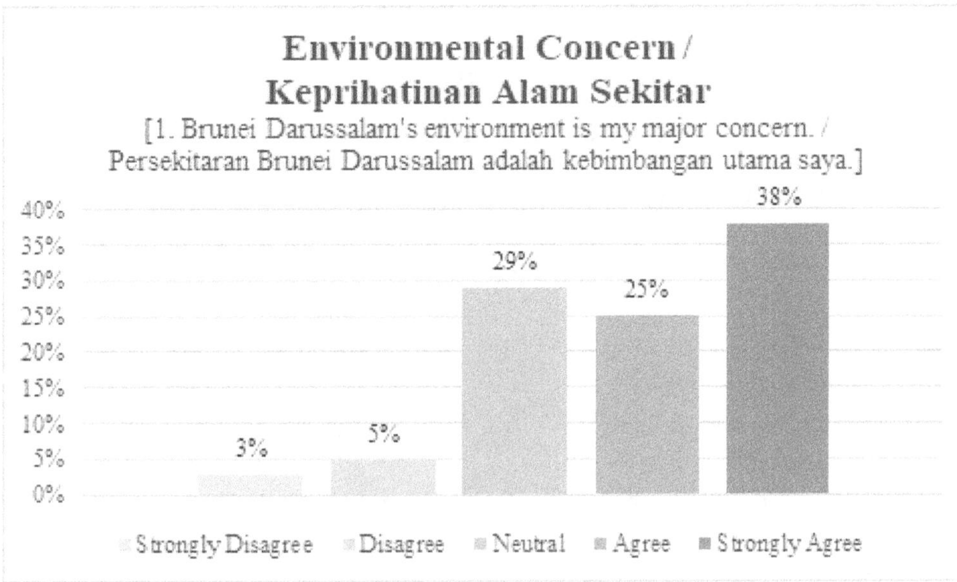

Respondent D: *"People and government are responsible and need to work together"*
Respondent E: *"Not everyone cares about the environment"*
Respondent F: *"Actually we have to fulfill and satisfy the need and perhaps people would be motivated and join as well"*

Figure 13. Environmental concern: I am involved in environmental protection problem in Brunei

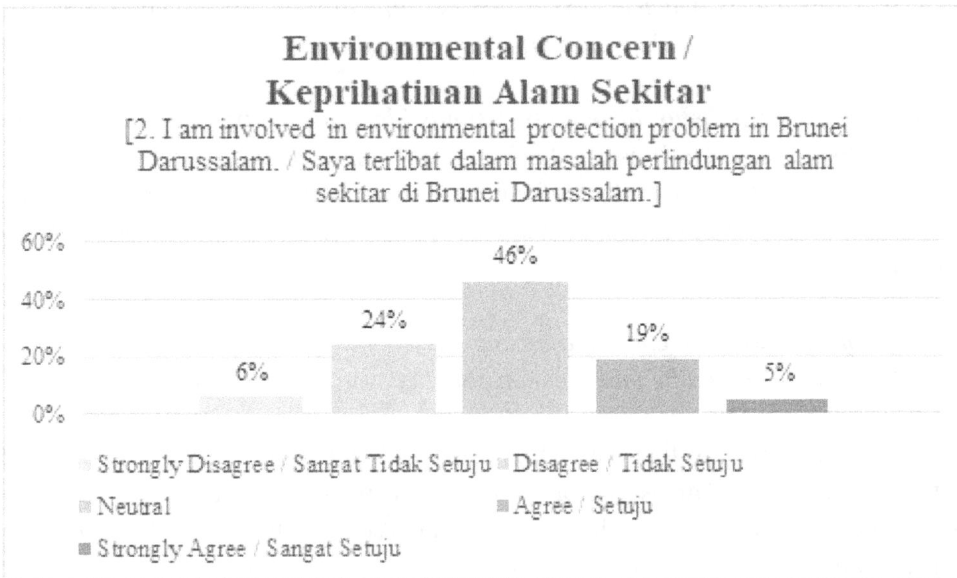

Figure 14: Environmental Concern: I often think about how environmental quality in Brunei can be improved

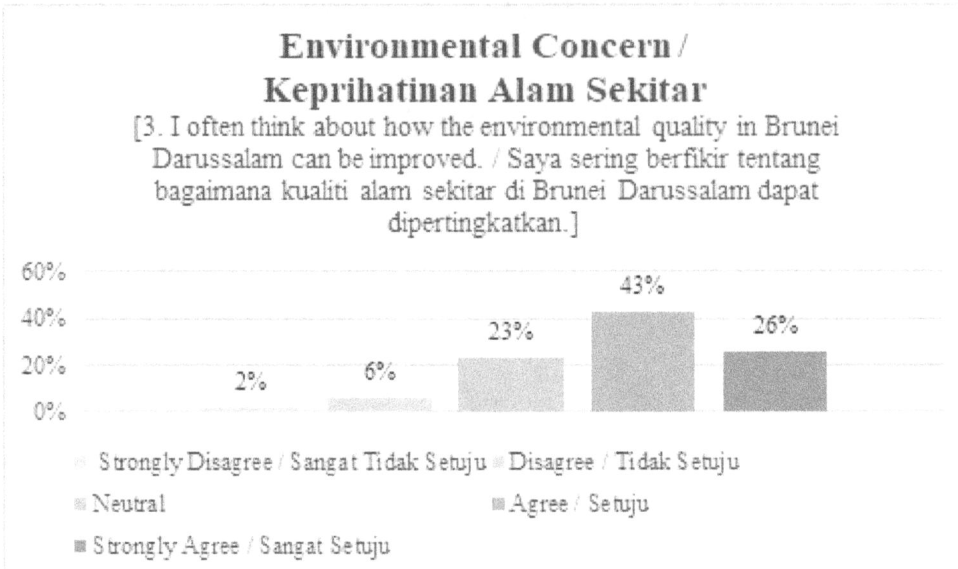

The third statement was ***I often think about how the environmental quality in Brunei can be improved*** shown in Figure 14. 2 percent of respondents strongly disagreed with the statement; 6 percent of respondents disagree with the statement; 23 percent of respondents had a neutral viewpoint; 43 percent of respondents agreed; and 26 percent of respondents strongly agreed with the statement. The findings from interviews as below;

Respondent C: *"We have high hopes on Brunei and maybe by baby steps, people can engage a little more"*
Respondent E: *"The emphasis because environment is affecting life. The temperature is rising and ozone layer on top becoming thin which affected by the global warming"*

The fourth statement ***I think I should be more responsible in protecting the environment in Brunei Darussalam***. From this statement as illustrated in Figure 15, 2 percent of respondents strongly disagreed with the statement; 2 percent of respondents disagree with the statement; 13 percent respondents had a neutral viewpoint; 37 percent of respondents agreed; and 46 percent of respondents strongly agreed with the statement.

Respondent E: *"Brunei's environment could be improved"*
Respondent F: *"I think we should be more responsible because it affects us indirectly"*

All in all, it can be summarized that there is a positive relationship between environmental concern and green purchase behaviours. This is supported by a study in Hong Kong by Lee (2008) which found that environmental concern was a strong factor of green purchase behaviour. Also, consumers that are more concern and concern to the environmental issues are more willing to pay extra and purchase green

Figure 15. Environmental concern: I think I should be more responsible in protecting the environment in Brunei Darussalam

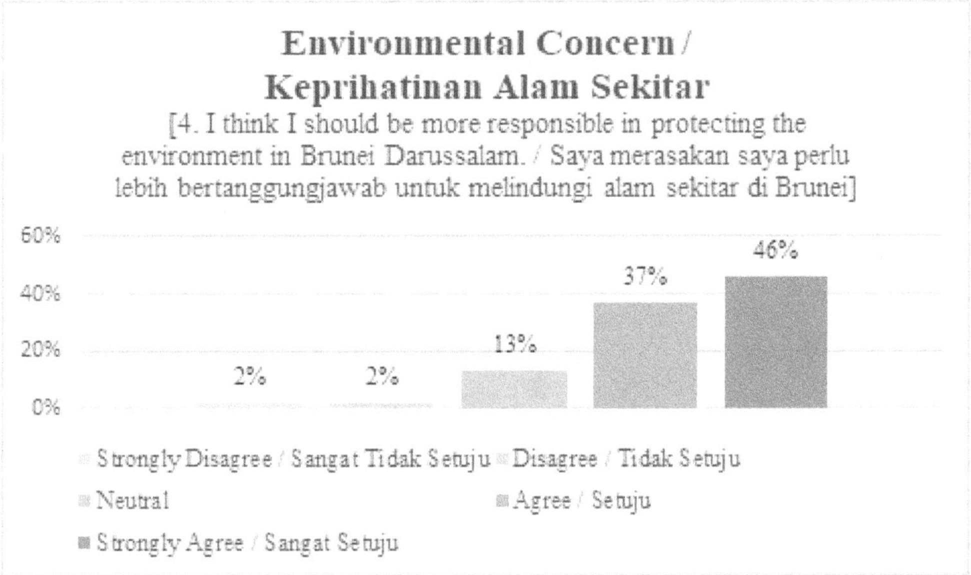

products (Kim & Choi, 2005). This is apparent from the questionnaire's responses, whereby 38 percent strongly agreed that Brunei Darussalam's environment is their concern and, 43 percent agreed that, they often think about how the environmental quality in the country can be improved, although the respondents are in the neutral zone with 46 percent in involvement in environmental protection but, 46 percent of respondents strongly agreed with the statement that, they should be more responsible in protecting the environment in Brunei Darussalam. Hence, the level of one's environmental concern is linked with their desire and interest to purchase green products (Biswas et al., 2000). And, environmental concern would and could be a crucial determinants, especially for marketers as this will allow them to target the pro-environmentalist consumers (Mostafa, 2007).

In Perceived Environmental Responsibility, the first statement was ***Environmental protection starts with me.*** The responses are compared in Figure 16 where 3 percent of respondents strongly disagreed with the statement; 3 percent respondents disagree with the statement; 13 percent respondents had a neutral viewpoint; 38 percent of respondents agreed; and 43 percent of respondents strongly agreed with the statement.

The second statement was ***I think I should have so much responsibility in protecting the environment in Brunei Darussalam***. It can be seen from Figure 17 that 1 percent of the respondents strongly disagreed with the statement; 5 percent of respondents disagree with the statement; whereas 24 percent of respondents had a neutral viewpoint; 38 percent of respondents agreed; and 32 percent of respondents strongly agreed with the statement.

The third statement was ***I am willing to take up responsibility to protect the environment in Brunei Darussalam***. Figure 18 shows that none of the 113 respondents strongly disagreed with the statement; 5 percent of respondents disagree with the statement; 33 percent of respondents had a neutral viewpoint; 38 percent of respondents agreed; and 24 percent of respondents strongly agreed with the statement.

Figure 16. Perceived Environmental Responsibility: Environmental protection starts with me

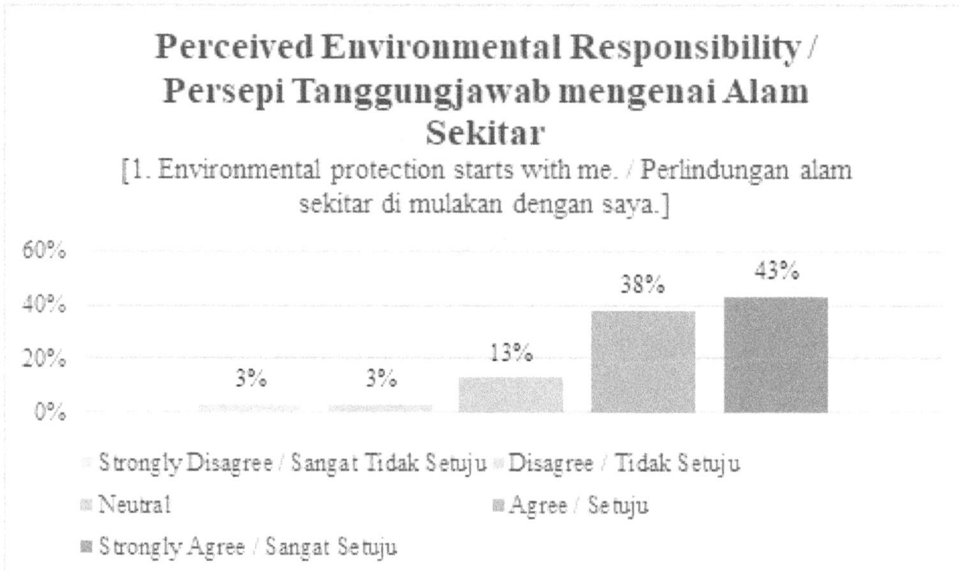

The fourth statement was ***Environmental protection is the responsibility of the environmental organization, not me.*** As shown in Figure 19, 18 percent of respondents strongly disagreed with the statement; 28 percent of respondents disagree with the statement; 21 percent of respondents had a neutral viewpoint; 15 percent of respondents agreed; and 18 percent of respondents strongly agreed with the statement. The findings showed mixed responses from respondents as one interviewee stated;

Figure 17. Perceived Environmental Responsibility: I think I should have so much responsibility in protecting the environment in Brunei Darussalam

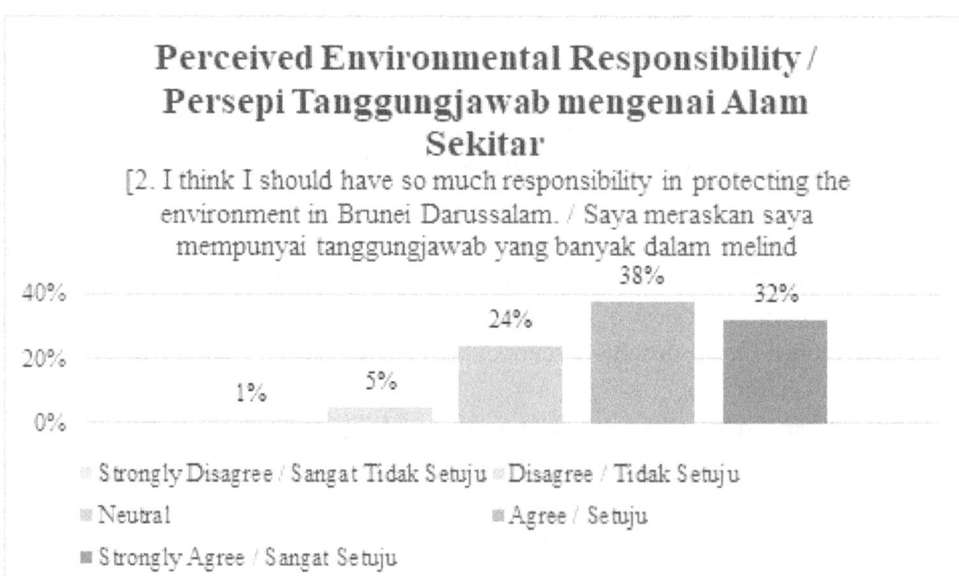

Figure 18. Perceived environmental responsibility: I am willing to take up responsibility to protect the environment in Brunei

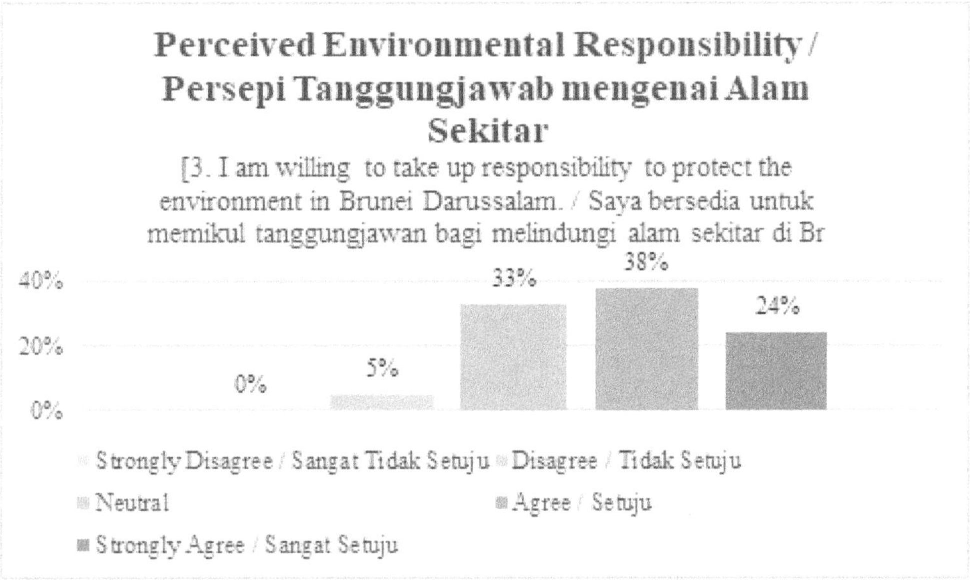

Respondent D: *"Bruneians need to be 'pushed' to certain extent"*
Respondent E: *"I am not aware of environmental health"*

Figure 19. Perceived environmental responsibility: Environmental protection is the responsibility of the environmental organization, not me.

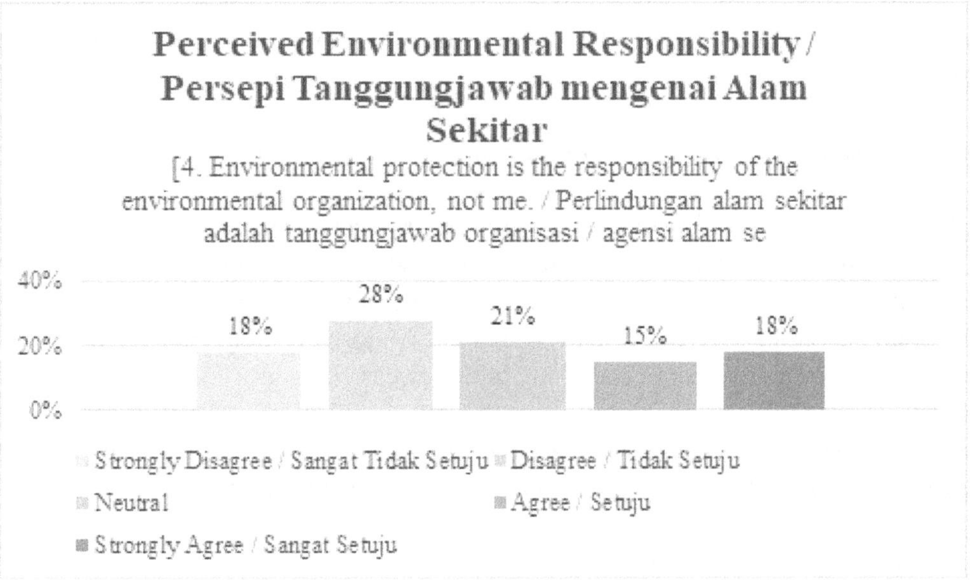

Figure 20. Perceived environmental responsibility: Green products do not perform as well as non-green products

The fifth statement was ***Green products do not perform well as non-green products***. Figure 20 displays that 7 percent of respondents strongly disagreed with the statement; 19 percent of respondents disagree with the statement; 50 percent of respondents had a neutral viewpoint; 17 percent of respondents agreed; and 8 percent respondents strongly agreed with the statement. Some percentages of interview responses quite critical on this matter:

Respondent C: *"Green products are expensive"*
Respondent F: *"I am not willing to purchase green products or change products"*

High percentages of neutral viewpoint because of lacks of report/research on comparison of green and non green products.

Respondent D: *"I can't be sure because I don't really see many statistics in Brunei"*

The sixth statement was ***I feel proud when I buy or use green products.*** As shown in Figure 21, 1 percent of respondents strongly disagreed with the statement; 5 percent of respondents disagree with the statement; 32 percent of respondents had a neutral viewpoint; 33 percent respondents agreed; and 29 percent of respondents strongly agreed with the statement. Majority respondents have positive behaviour towards buy and use green products as stated my interviewees;

Respondent E: *"I feel proud because it makes you empathic on the world and future children"*
Respondent F: *"Green products is very, very important for sustainability"*

Figure 21. Perceived environmental responsibility: I feel proud when I buy or use green products

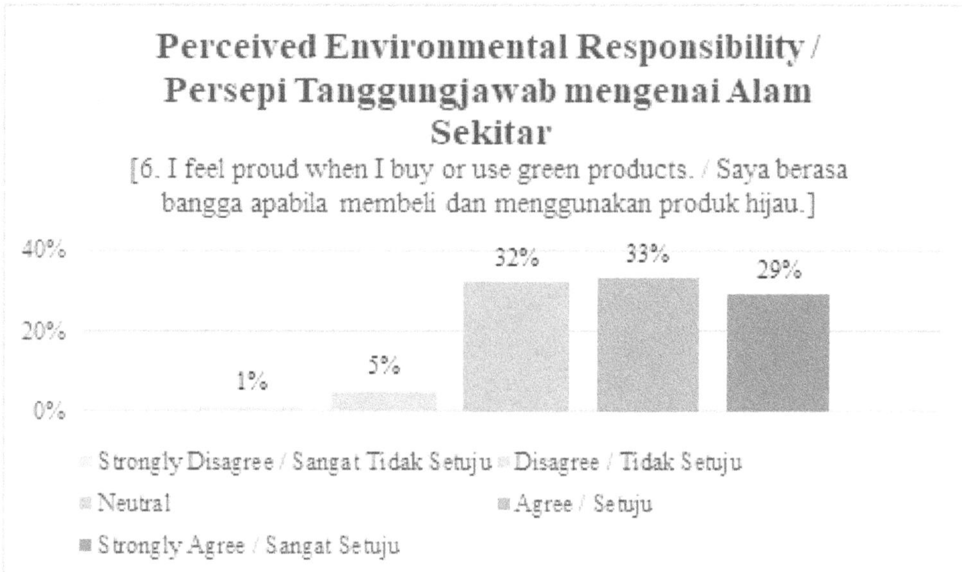

The perceived environmental responsibility is showing a linkage with green purchase behaviours. According to Tang (2014), in order to possess the green purchase behaviours, environmental responsibility needed to be embedded to one's self. Thus, with well educated, and informed individuals, they are more willing to bear the responsibility to protect, save and preserve the environment. From both findings, it is evident that, the majority of the respondents believed that, they themselves are responsible for the impacts on the environment. 43 percent strongly agreed that, environmental protection starts with themselves, 38 percent agreed that, they should have been more responsible and willing to be involved in environment protection activities. Respondent C added:

"Everyone is guilty including myself. I don't want to be like ignorant person but I think I am contributing to this massive problem as well."

Though, some people still thinks that, environmental protection is solely the responsibility of the government or other parties such as the huge corporations, therefore resulting in reluctance to commit and sacrifice with the government's policy (Lai, 2000).

25 percent of respondents have the perceptions that green products do not perform as well as non-green products. This could be due to the fact that they have not purchased any green products, whilst 50 percent of the questionniare's respondents were in the neutral zone. 62 percent of respondents agreed that they felt proud when they bought or used green products. The possible reason behind this is because after buying green products, the respondents or consumers feel good about their green purchase, as they are contributing to the betterment of the environment.

Figure 22. Environmental attitude: It is essential to promote green living in Brunei

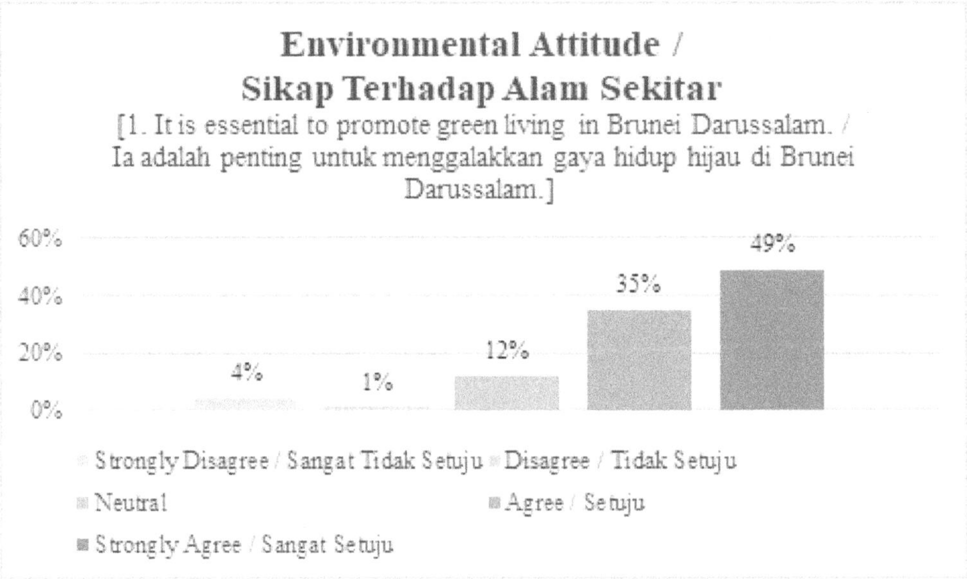

Behaviour

In this section, there are three sub-headings; Environmental Attitude, Perceived Effectiveness of Environmental Behaviour and Government Initiative. All of the questions being asked were in the form of statements.

Environmental Attitude

In the Environmental Attitude, the first statement was ***It is essential to promote green living in Brunei Darussalam.*** Figure 22 shows that 4 percent respondents strongly disagreed with the statement; 1 percent of respondents disagree with the statement; 12 percent of respondents had a neutral viewpoint; 35 percent of respondents agreed; and 49 percent of respondents strongly agreed with the statement.

The second statement was I strongly agree that more environmental protection is needed in Brunei Darussalam. Figure 23 illustrates that 4 percent of respondents strongly disagreed with the statement; none of the respondents disagreed with the statement; 14 percent of respondents had a neutral viewpoint; 25 percent of respondents agreed; and 58 percent of respondents strongly agreed with the statement.

Respondent F: *"I think word of mouth is quite effective to promote green living in here"*

The third statement was ***It is very important to raise environmental awareness***. It can be seen from Figure 24 that 4 percent of respondents strongly disagreed with the statement; 1 percent of respondents disagree with the statement; 9 percent of respondents had a neutral viewpoint; 23 percent of respondents agreed; and 64 respondents strongly agreed with the statement.

The fourth statement was ***Environmental protection issues are none of my concern.*** As can be seen from Figure 25, 42 percent of respondents strongly disagreed with the statement; 25 percent of

Figure 23. Environmental attitude: I strongly agree that more environmental protection works are needed in Brunei Darussalam

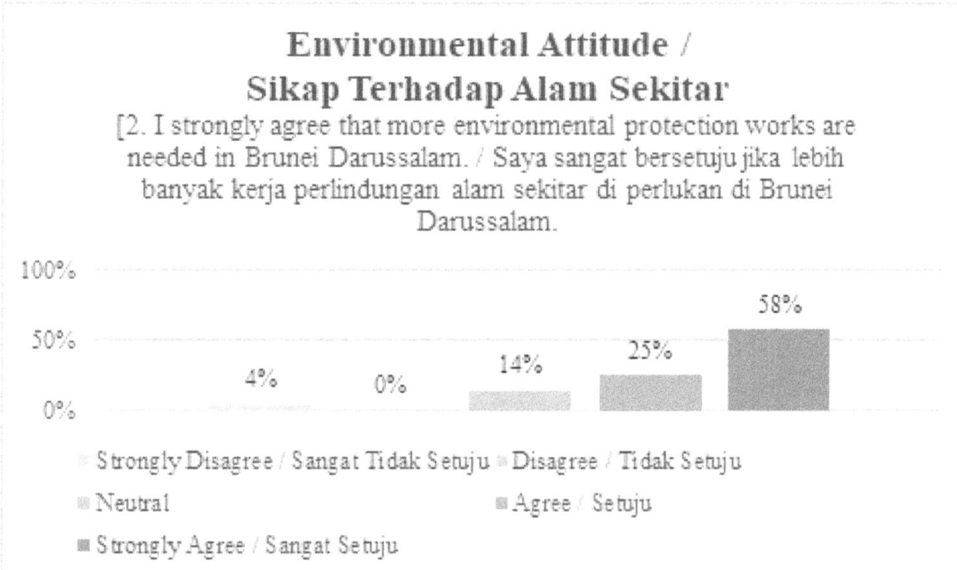

respondents disagree with the statement; 16 percent of respondents had a neutral viewpoint; 9 percent of respondents agreed; and lastly 9 percent of respondents strongly agreed with the statement. It shows big majority respondents are environmentally concerned.

The findings from this study shows that environmental attitude has a positive relationship with consumers' green purchase. This is evident from the questionnaire, as most respondents chose strongly

Figure 24. Environmental attitude: It is very important to raise environmental awareness among Bruneian

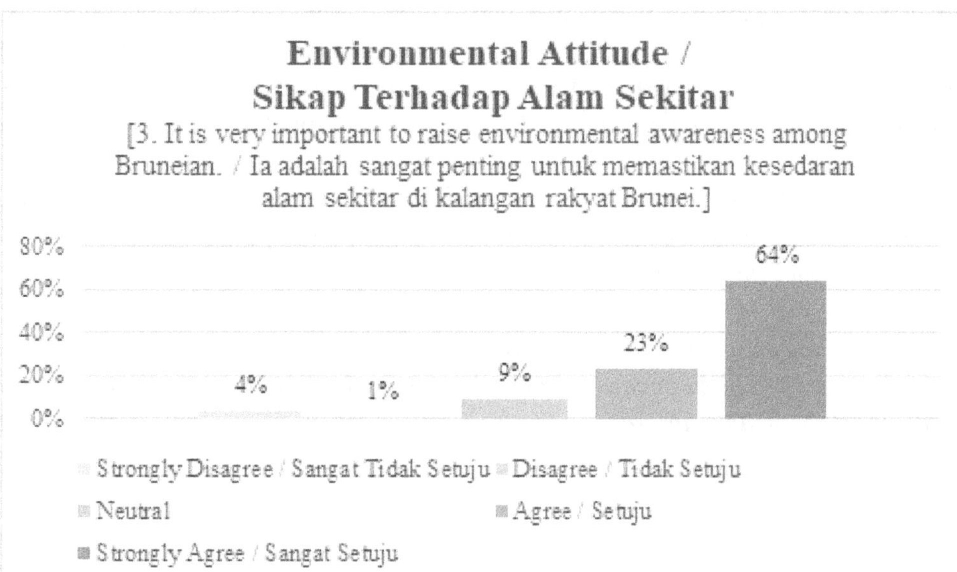

Figure 25. Environmental attitude; Environmental protection issues are none of my concern

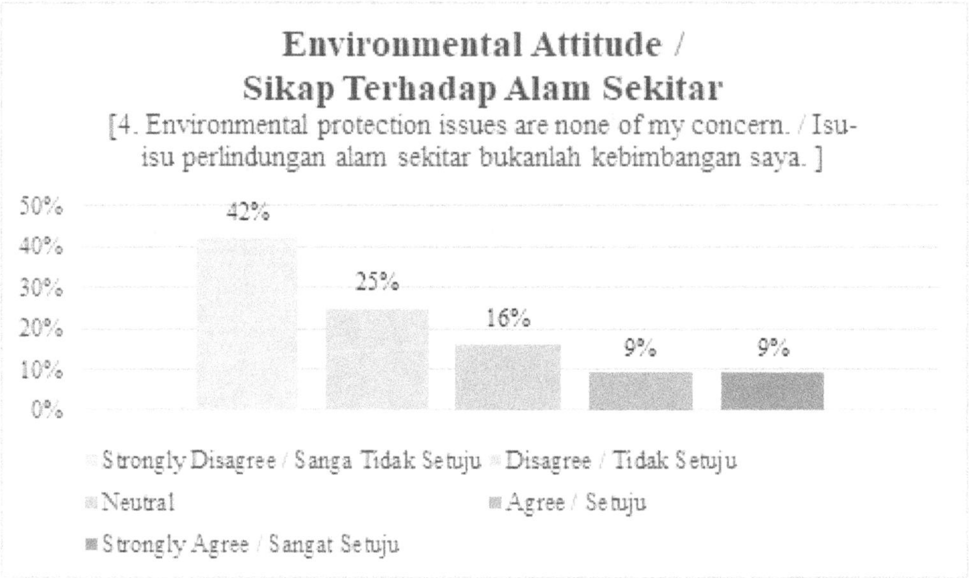

agreed with all four statements. Firstly, 49 percent strongly agreed with promoting green living in the country; secondly, 58 percent strongly agreed that more environmental protection works are needed in Brunei Darussalam; thirdly, raising environmental awareness were strongly agreed by 64 percent of respondents and lastly, 42 percent respondents strongly disagreed that environmental protection issues are none of their concern.

Furthermore, Paco et al., (2009) added that attitude is not necessarily used as a foundation for consumers in their purchasing behaviours and decision, yet, Mostafa (2007) had a different view whereby environmental attitude of consumers can actually affect their green purchasing behaviours. This statement is further second by Beckford et al. (2010) who suggested that environmental attitude has a positively significant impact on green purchase behaviours. This could link up with the ABC model as it claimed that, under supportive conditions, even an individual with weak environmental attitudes behave in an environmentally friendly way, whereas in restrictive conditions, an individual with highly positive environmental attitudes also may be discouraged to show environmentally friendly behaviour (Joshi & Rahman, 2015).

When asked "Do you think by doing and participating in the green behaviours such as recycling, reusing materials or using reusable bags, metal straw, will have an impact on you and the environment as a whole?", Respondent E answered:

"The attitudes need to has a big impact on ourselves because after we learn something, we will try to do or behave in a certain manner, and once we realized that behaviour is good for us and the environment, we will want to repeat the behaviours repeatedly, and there is always lessons in everything we do....."

Figure 26. Perceived effectiveness of environmental behaviour: I think if I carry out some pro-environmental behaviour in my life, I would, contribute a lot to our environment

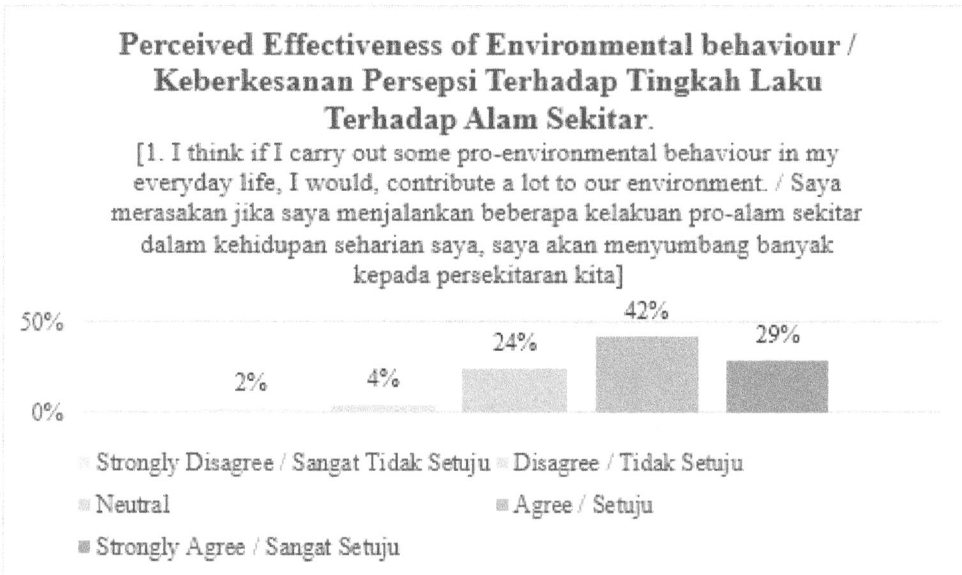

Perceived Effectiveness

In the Perceived Effectiveness of Environmental Behaviour, the first statement was ***I think if I carry out some pro-environmental behaviour in my everyday life, I would contribute a lot in my everyday life.*** 2 percent of respondents strongly disagreed with the statement; 4 percent of respondents disagree with

Figure 27. Perceived effectiveness of environmental behaviour: I think my participation in environmental protection would influence others to participate

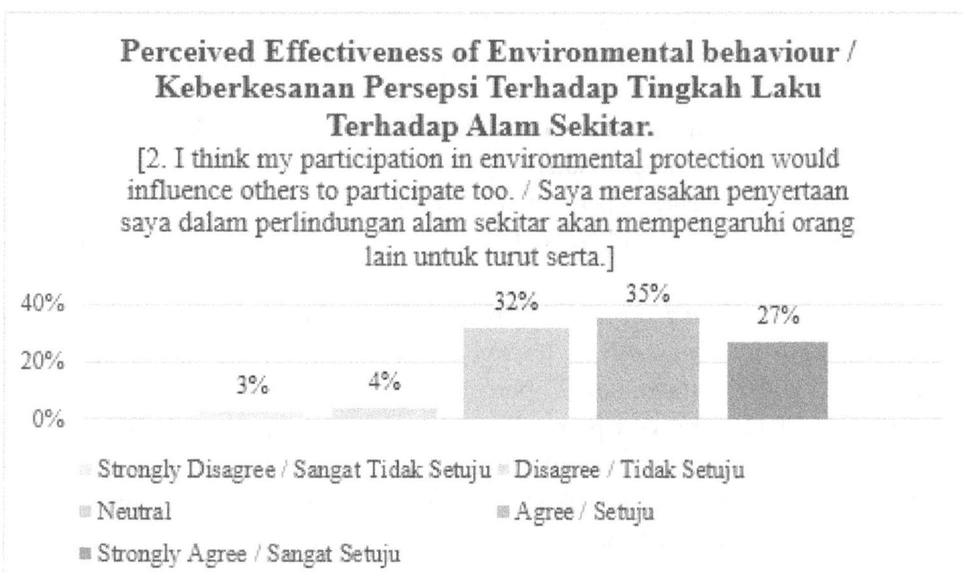

Figure 28. Perceived effectiveness of environmental behaviour: The environmental quality of Brunei Darussalam will stay the same even if I engage in some pro-environmental behaviour

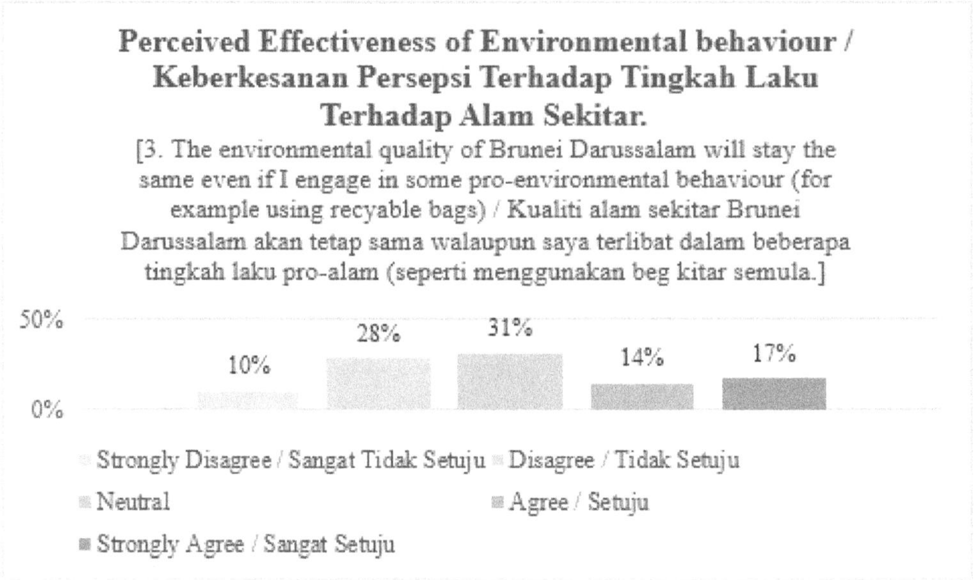

the statement; 24 percent of respondents had a neutral viewpoint; 42 percent of respondents agreed; and 29 percent respondents strongly agreed with the statement.

The second statement was **I think my participation in environmental protection will influence others to participate**. As shown in Figure 27, 3 percent of respondents strongly disagreed with the statement; 4 percent of respondents disagree with the statement; 32 percent of respondents had a neutral viewpoint; 35 percent of respondents agreed; and 27 percent respondents strongly agreed with the statement.

Respondent F: *"I do not really practice green consumerism because my surroundings also not doing it, why should I?"*

The third statement was **The environmental quality of Brunei Darussalam will stay the same if I engage in some pro-environmental behaviour**. Figure 28 below shows that 10 percent of respondents strongly disagreed with the statement; 28 percent of respondents disagree with the statement; 31 percent of respondents had a neutral viewpoint; 14 percent of respondents agreed; and 17 percent of respondents strongly agreed with the statement.

The fourth statement was ***Even I recycle and reuse things, the environmental quality of Brunei Darussalam will remain as it is currently is.*** It can be seen from Figure 29 that 15 percent of respondents strongly disagreed with the statement; 27 percent of respondents disagree with the statement; 27 percent of respondents had a neutral viewpoint; 25 percent respondents agreed; and lastly 7 percent of respondents strongly agreed with the statement.

From the fourth statements in this subsection, it is clear that the respondents understand and know that, if they carry out pro-environmental behaviours, it will contribute to the reduction of environmental issues with 42 percent agreed and 29 percent agreeing strongly, and it would also encourage others to

Figure 29. Perceived effectiveness of environmental behaviour: Even if I recycle and reuse things, the environmental quality of Brunei Darussalam will remain as it currently is

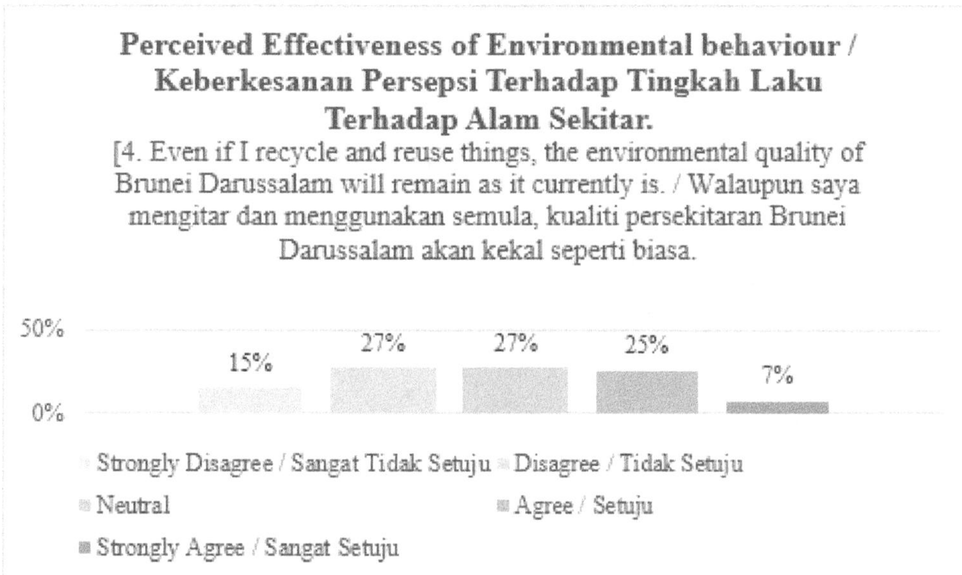

participate too - 35 percent agreed and 27 percent strongly agreed. These findings evidently shows a positive correlation between green purchase behaviours and perceived effectiveness of environmental behaviour. Additionally, in various studies, perceived effectiveness of environmental behaviour is a key determinant in environmental awareness and green behaviours which leads to more green contribution to the environment. Undoubtedly, Kim and Choi (2005) stated that the level of effectiveness recognized consumers differs from one individual to another, and according to them, this was conditioned by direct and indirect environmental knowledge and experiences. These findings and literatures verified what Respondent C was saying whereby:

"Yes, for sure but those things that you just mentioned is just the minimal effort that a person can do. It's not that hard to use bags but maybe to some people it's not hard to use containers instead of plastic or anything like that..."

Government Initiative

In Government Initiative, the first statement was ***Environmental protection is the responsibility of the government, not me.*** Figure 30 shows that 19 percent of respondents strongly disagreed with the statement; 32 percent of respondents disagree with the statement; 27 percent of respondents had a neutral viewpoint; 12 percent of respondents agreed; and 10 percent of respondents strongly agreed with the statement.

Respondent E: *"With government initiative such 'no plastic bag' we are more aware of situations"*

Figure 30. Government initiative: Environmental protection is the responsibility of the government, not me

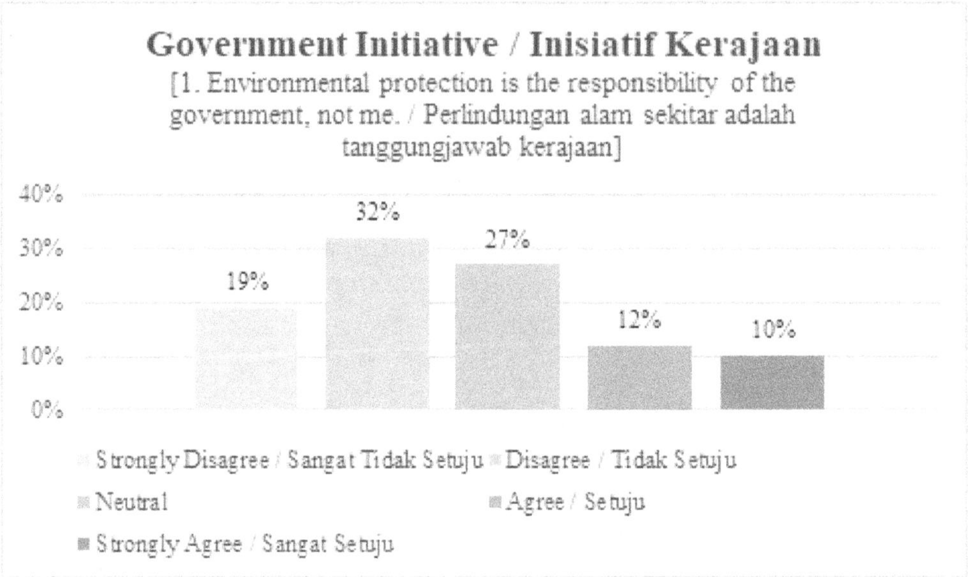

The second statement was ***With the enforcement of no plastic bag everyday, it has helped me to be more environmentally aware***. As shown in Figure 31, 5 percent of respondents strongly disagreed with the statement; 6 percent of the respondents disagreed with the statement; 16 percent of the respondents had a neutral viewpoint; 32 percent of respondents agreed; and 41 percent of respondents strongly agreed with the statement.

Figure 31. Government Initiative: With the enforcement of no plastic day everyday, it has helped me to be more environmentally aware

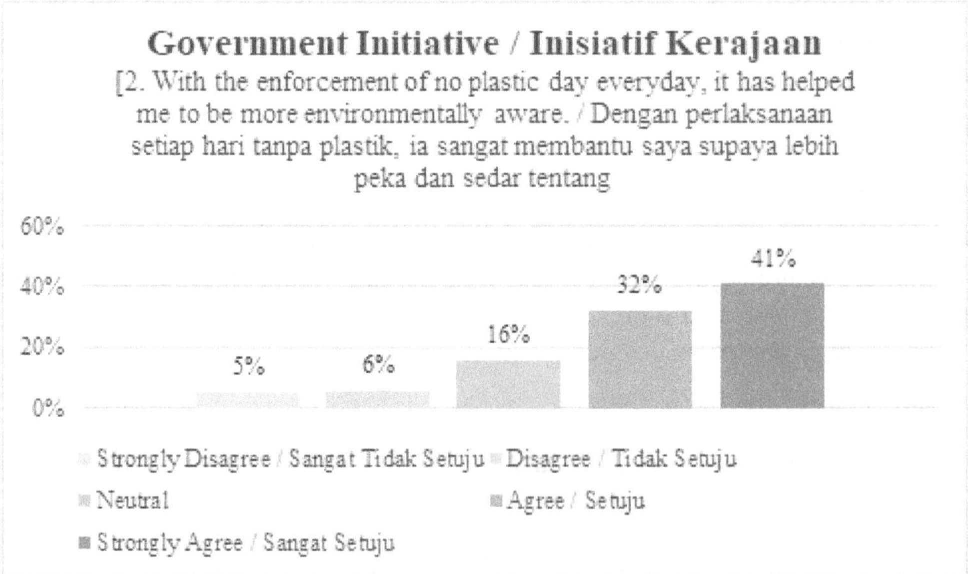

Figure 32. Government initiative: Schools and higher institutions should require all students to take a course dealing with environment and conservation problems

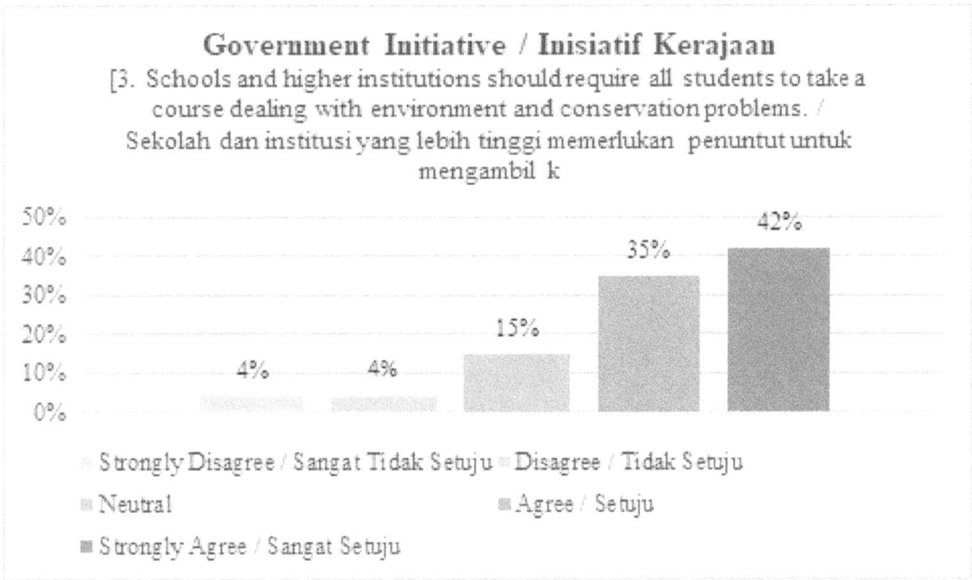

Respondent F: *"The more we do it, the more we think about it"*

The third statement was ***School and higher institutions should require all students to take a course dealing with environment and conservation problems***. Figure 32 illustrates that 4 percent of respondents strongly disagreed with the statement; 4 percent of respondents disagree with the statement; 15 percent of respondents had a neutral viewpoint; 35 percent of respondents agreed; and 42 percent of respondents strongly agreed with the statement.

The fourth statement was ***The government should subsidize research on technology for environmental protection (for example recycling waste products).*** As can be seen in Figure 33, 3 percent of respondents strongly disagreed with the statement; 4 percent of respondents disagree with the statement; 12 percent of respondents had a neutral viewpoint; 35 percent of respondents agreed; and lastly 45 percent of respondents strongly agreed with the statement.

Respondent F: *"There are efforts but minimal"*
Respondent E: *"NGO's are not really doing much"*

The last statement was ***Government should enforce more environmental rules and regulations.*** Figure 34 shows that 4 percent of respondents strongly disagreed with the statement; 2 percent of respondents disagree with the statement; 12 percent of respondents had a neutral viewpoint; 28 percent respondents agreed; and 53 percent respondents strongly agreed with the statement.

Respondent D: *"Implementing stricter rules and regulations may be good idea"*
Respondent D: *"Needs drastic change where no plastic bag also must be applied to small businesses"*

Figure 33. Government initiative: The government should subsidize research on technology for environmental protection

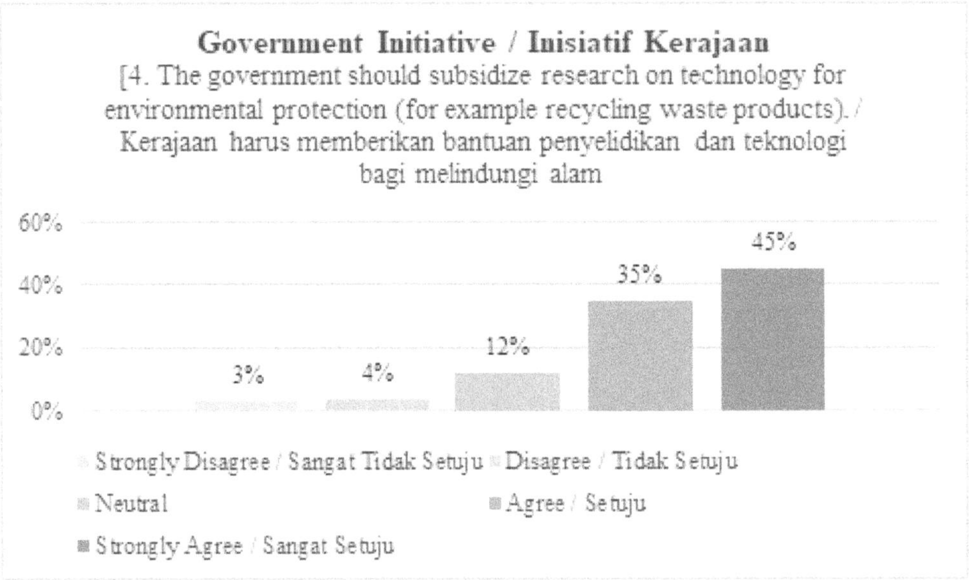

For this study, it is evident that government initiative have a significantly important position and relationship with consumers' green purchase behaviours. This result is aligned with what Tsen et al. (2006) and Sinnappan and Rahman (2011) research whereby the government holds a central position in green behaviour. At this day and age, environmental advocates are not limited to government agencies but have extended to other agencies such as Non-Governmental Organizations (NGOs) and companies

Figure 34. Government initiative: Government should enforce more environmental rules and regulations

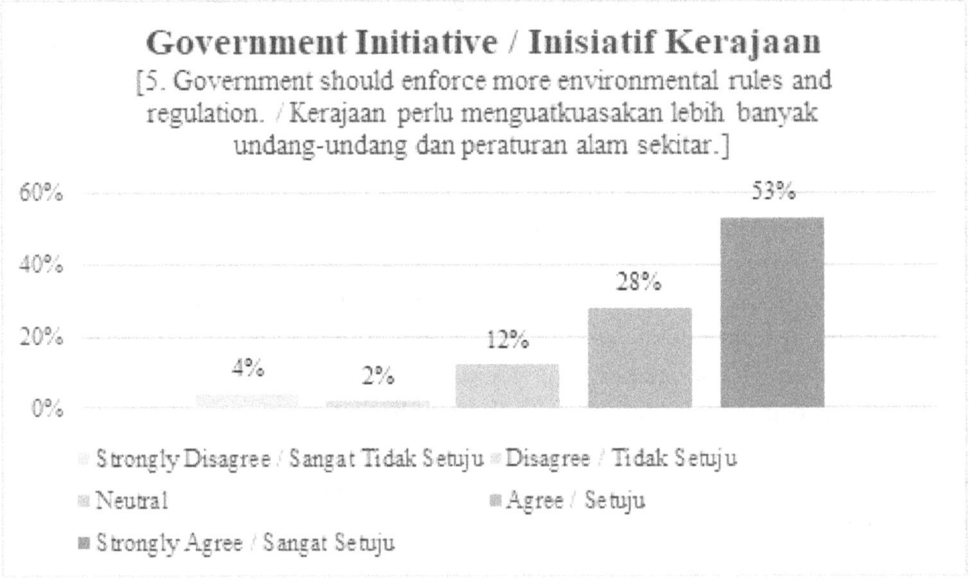

as well. The findings from the questionnaire indicates that the respondents are very much aware that, the government is not the only one that is responsible for the deteriorating impacts of the environment. With the implementation of No Plastic Day Everyday by the Brunei Government, 41 percent of respondents agreed strongly that this initiative has helped them to be more environmentally conscious. Other than that, the other two statements under this subsection are giving further initiatives that could be done by the government which are requirements for students to attend a course in order to deal with environment and conservation problems with 42 per cent strongly agreed, and only 4 percent strongly disagreed.

Also, subsidizing research and development on technology that could lead to effective environmental protection with 45 percent strongly agreeing and only 3 percent strongly disagreeing. One good example of this is from the research and development efforts of 12 Canadian engineering students of the University of Sherbrooke in Quebec who built Hoola One, a tiny microplastics vacuum without separating any of the sand from the beach. Hoola One has been tested at Hawaii's Kamilo Beach. The mechanisms of Hoola One is by using a handheld hose which will then sucks up plastics and sand and dumps it all into a huge water tank. Thus, since rocks and sand have a heavier capacity than plastic, they will sink to the bottom of the tank which can be dumped back onto the beach whilst plastic being the lighter material will floats to the top of the water tank (Corbley, 2019).

All interviewed respondents agreed the government played a massive role in implementing and directing the future of environmental protection in the country.

Respondent A: *"I think the people and the government itself played an important role....'*
Respondent B: *"I am aware of the no plastic day every day and I can say that I try my best to practice this..."*

Moreover, one respondent suggested an example done by other countries in minimizing the environmental effects. Respondent C stated that:

"If you see Bali or other countries like Cambodia, Vietnam, they're not using plastic to wrap up their fruits anymore. They're using banana leaves."

This initiative is apparent in supermarkets around Asia, which was pioneered by street vendors in Thailand for years, but now supermarkets are using this green idea to replace regular plastic packaging or wrappers to banana leaves. With Thailand's supermarket adopting this method, Vietnam is also joining the green footsteps. Other than wrapping perishable goods with banana leaves, supermarkets such as Lotte Mart is planning to use banana leaves for fresh meat products. And, some supermarket in Vietnam is offering biodegradable bags made with corn powder in its stores for consumers (General, 2019).

Hence, governments and organizations need to work together in order to realize sustainability for the future. So, all initiatives that involve government goals and agendas in realizing sustainability needs commitment from all aspects and parties as to care for and improve the well being of the society. Mat Said et al. (2003) further emphasized that the initiatives need to include education and public environmental awareness to ensure that sustainable green consumption practices to be a success.

Figure 35. Environmental knowledge: Global environmental problems are worsening

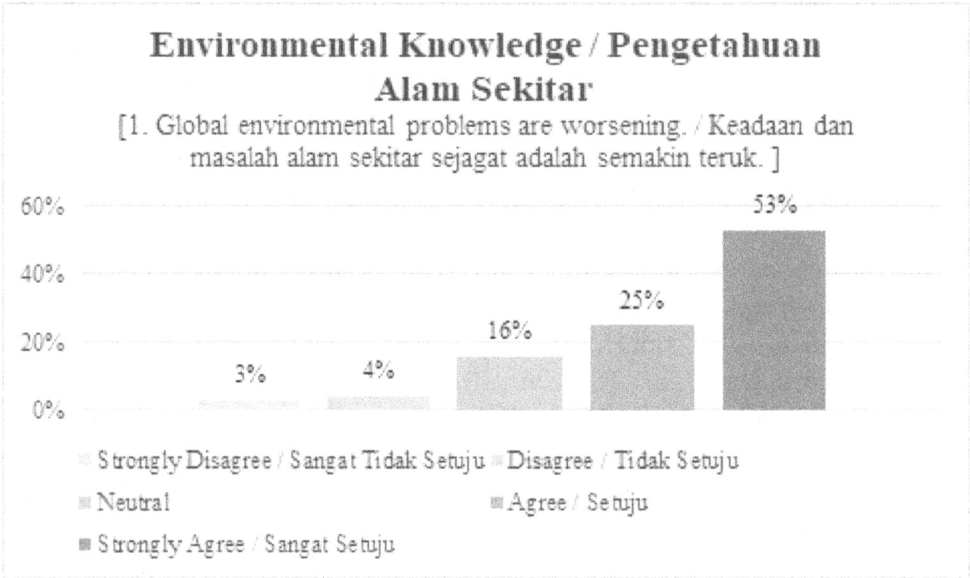

Cognition

In Cognition sub-section, it involved the Environmental Knowledge of respondents. Under this section, there was 11 statements were asked to the respondents.

Figure 36. Environmental knowledge: I think Brunei Darussalam's environmental problems are worsening

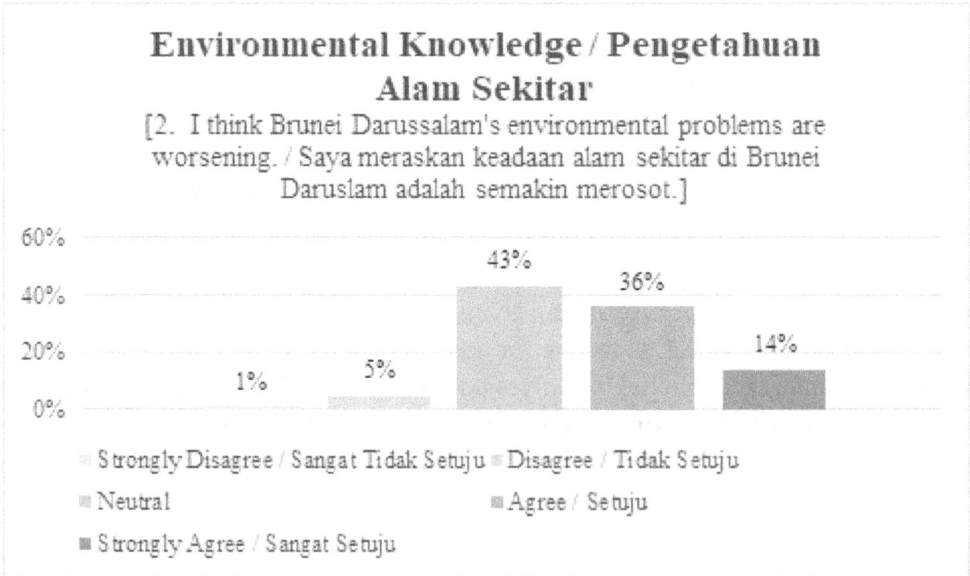

Figure 37. Environmental knowledge: Brunei Darussalam's environmental problems are threatening our health

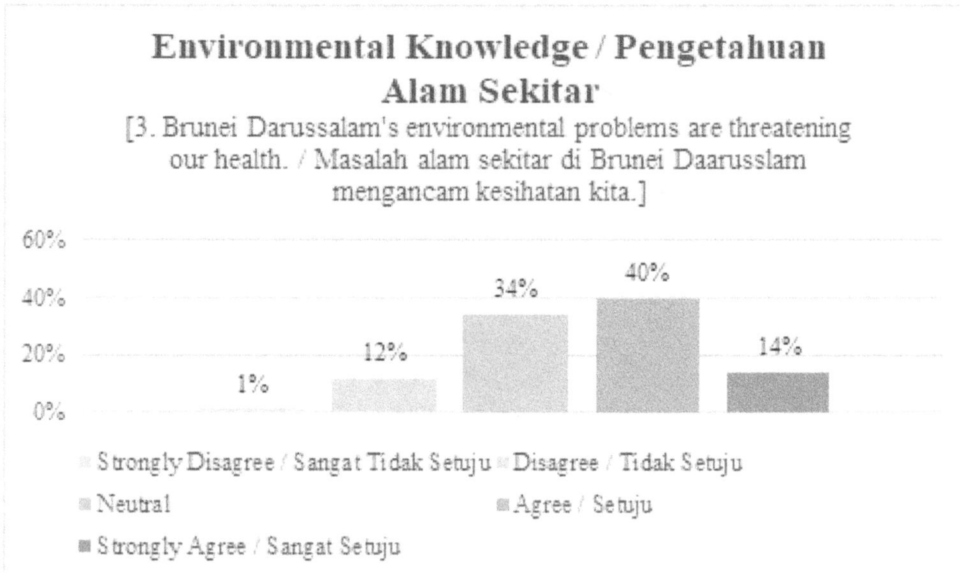

Environmental Knowledge

The first statement was ***Global environmental problems are worsening.*** Figure 35 shows that 3 percent of respondents strongly disagreed with the statement; 4 percent of respondents disagree with the state-

Figure 38. Environmental knowledge: I think Brunei Darussalam's environmental problems need to be dealt urgently

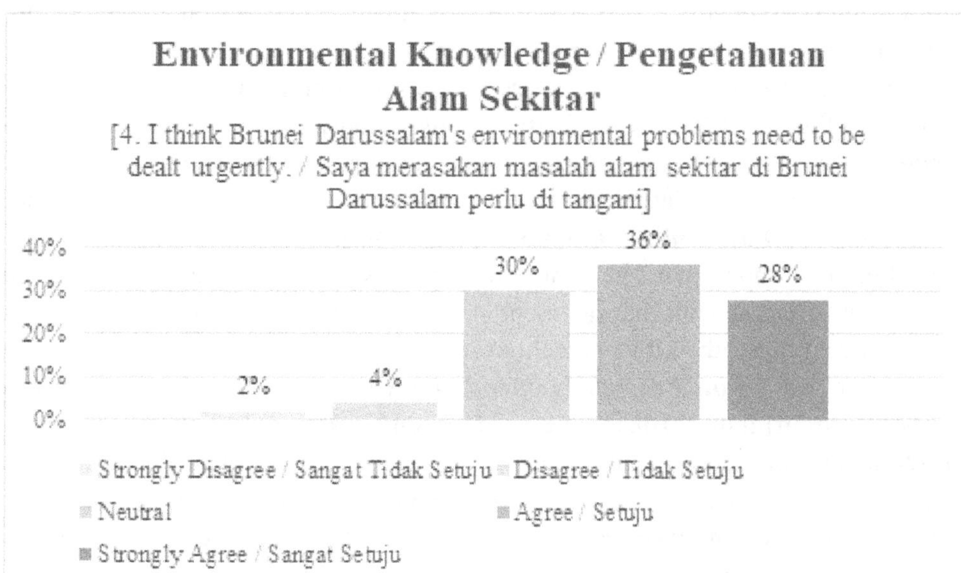

Figure 39. Environmental knowledge: I am willing to make sacrifices to protect the environment by using organic products

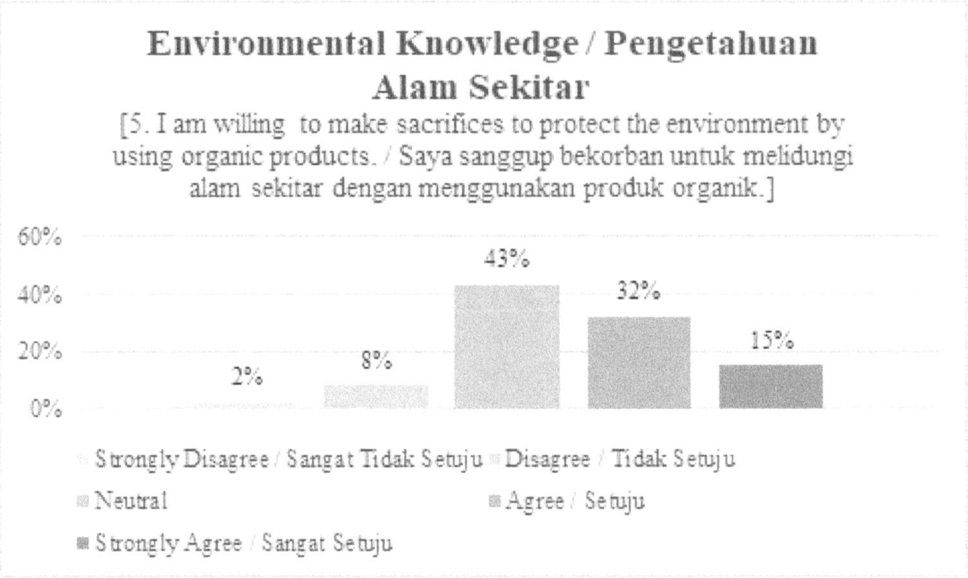

ment; 16 percent of respondents had a neutral viewpoint; 25 percent respondents agreed; and 53 percent of respondents strongly agreed with the statement.

The second statement was **I think Brunei Darussalam's environmental problems are worsening**. As can be seen in Figure 36, 1 percent of respondents strongly disagreed with the statement; 5 percent of the respondents disagreed with the statement; 43 percent respondents had a neutral viewpoint; 36 percent respondents agreed; and 14 percent of respondents strongly agreed with the statement.

The third statement was ***Brunei Darussalam's environmental problems are threatening our health***. Figure 37 shows that 1 percent of respondents strongly disagreed with the statement; 12 percent of respondents disagree with the statement; 34 percent of respondents had a neutral viewpoint; 40 percent of respondents agreed; and 14 percent of respondents strongly agreed with the statement.

The fourth statement was I think Brunei Darussalam's environmental problems need to be dealt urgently. As shown in Figure 38, 2 percent of respondents strongly disagreed with the statement; 4 percent of respondents disagree with the statement; 30 percent of respondents had a neutral viewpoint; 36 percent of respondents agreed; and lastly 28 percent of respondents strongly agreed with the statement.

The fifth statement was **I am willing to make sacrifices to protect the environment by using organic products**. Figure 39 shows that 2 percent of respondents strongly disagreed with the statement; 8 percent of respondents disagree with the statement; 43 percent of respondents had a neutral viewpoint; 32 percent of respondents agreed; and 15 percent of respondents strongly agreed with the statement.

The sixth statement was ***I would definitely intend to buy those products that are environmentally friendly.*** It can be seen from Figure 40 that 4 percent of respondents strongly disagreed with the statement; 5 percent of respondents disagree with the statement; 37 percent of respondents had a neutral viewpoint; 32 percent of respondents agreed; and 22 percent respondents strongly agreed with the statement.

The seventh statement was ***I actively seek out information about organic or green products.*** Figure 41 shows that 3 percent of respondents strongly disagreed with the statement; 19 percent respondents

Figure 40. Environmental knowledge: I would definitely intend to buy those products that are organic

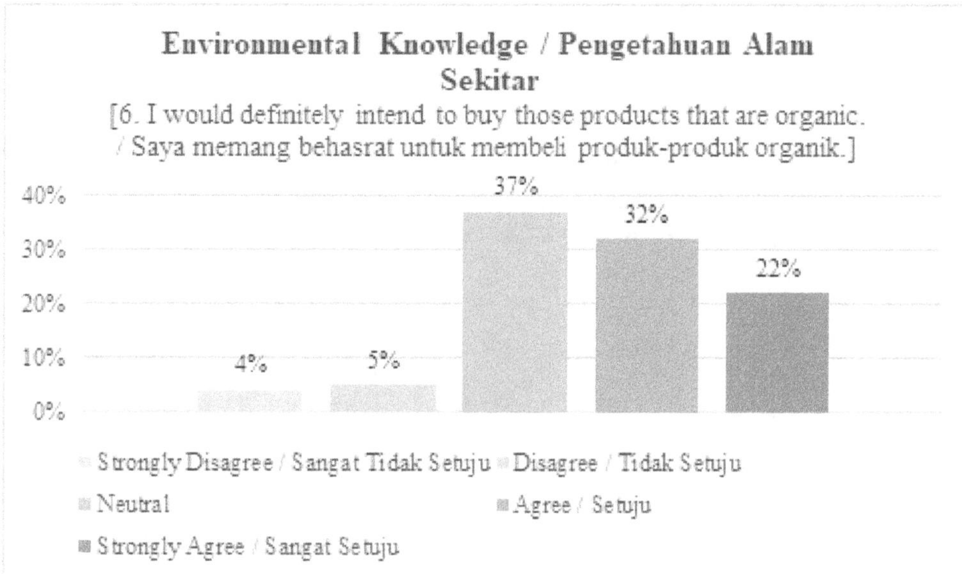

disagree with the statement; 38 percent respondents had a neutral viewpoint; 26 percent of respondents agreed; and 15 percent respondents strongly agreed with the statement.

The eighth statement was I would switch from my usual brands and buy environmentally safe products. As shown in Figure 42, 1 percent of respondents strongly disagreed with the statement; 9 percent of respondents disagree with the statement; 43 percent of respondents had a neutral viewpoint; 28 percent of respondents agreed; and 19 percent of respondents strongly agreed with the statement.

Figure 41. Environmental knowledge: I actively seek out information about organic or green products

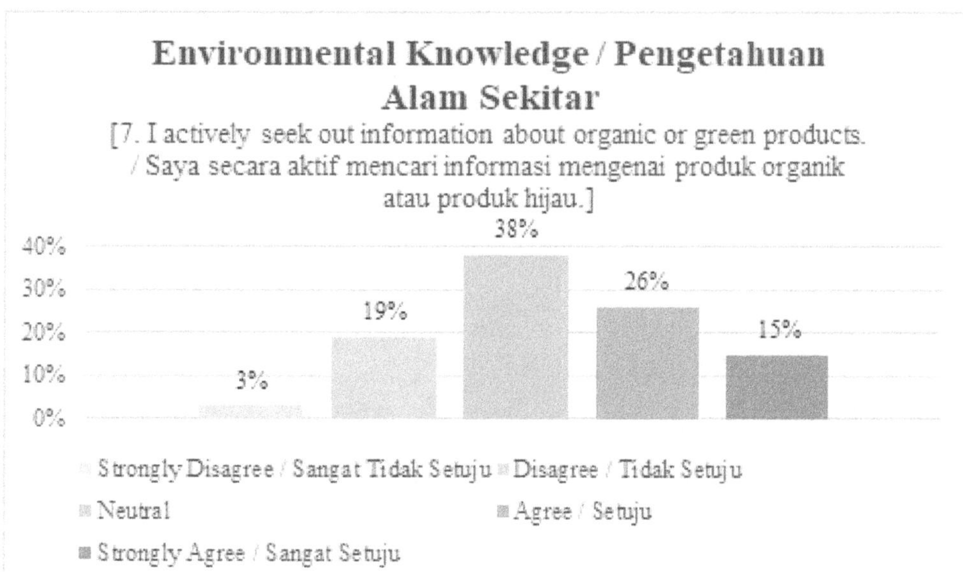

Figure 42. Environmental knowledge: I would switch from my usual brands and buy environmentally safe products.

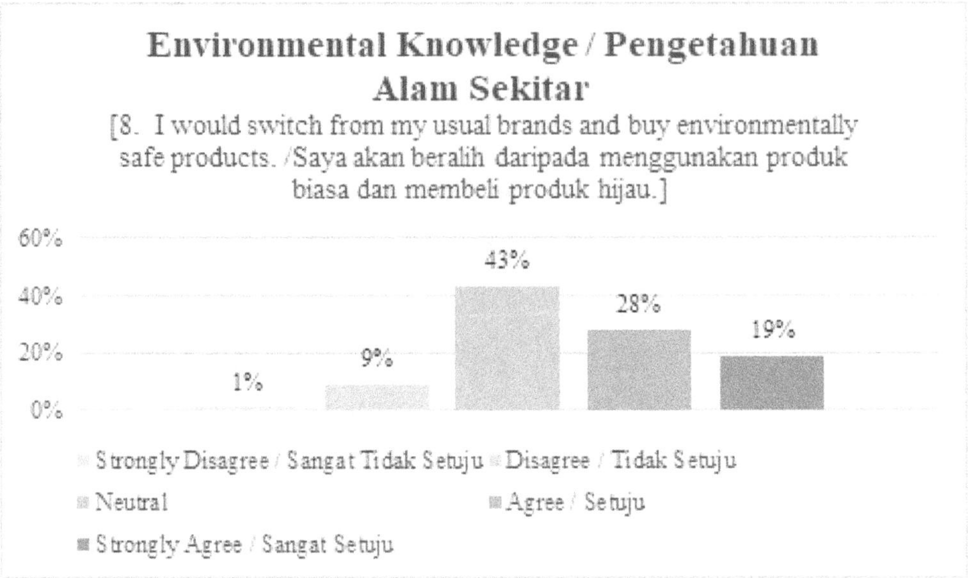

Next, the ninth statement stated ***I consider my knowledge to be high regarding green issues***. Figure 43 shows that 9 percent of respondents strongly disagreed with the statement; 24 percent of respondents disagree with the statement; 40 percent of respondents had a neutral viewpoint; 17 percent respondents agreed; and 11 percent of respondents strongly agreed with the statement.

Figure 43. Environmental knowledge: I consider my knowledge to be high regarding green issues

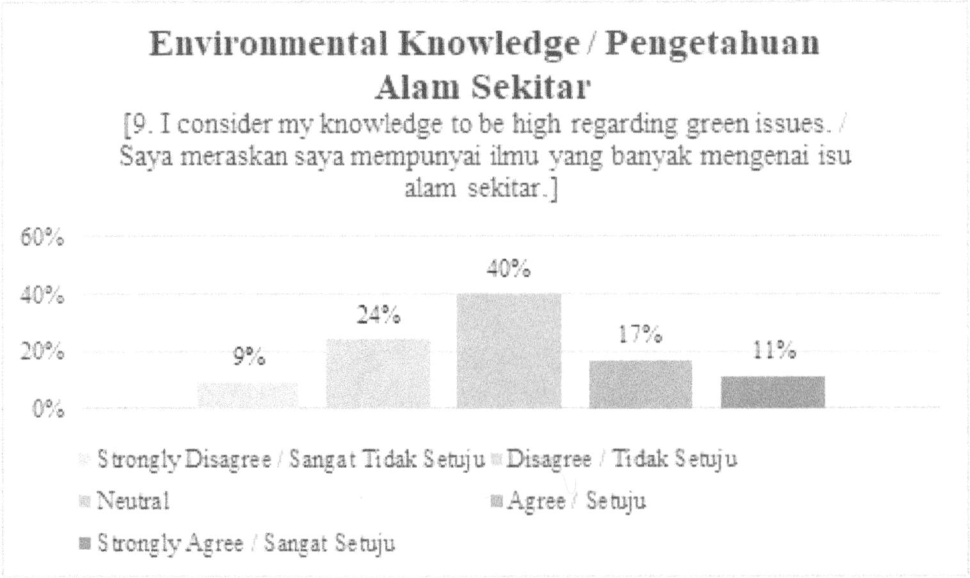

Figure 44. Environmental knowledge: The concept of buying green products depends on individual knowledge towards green issues

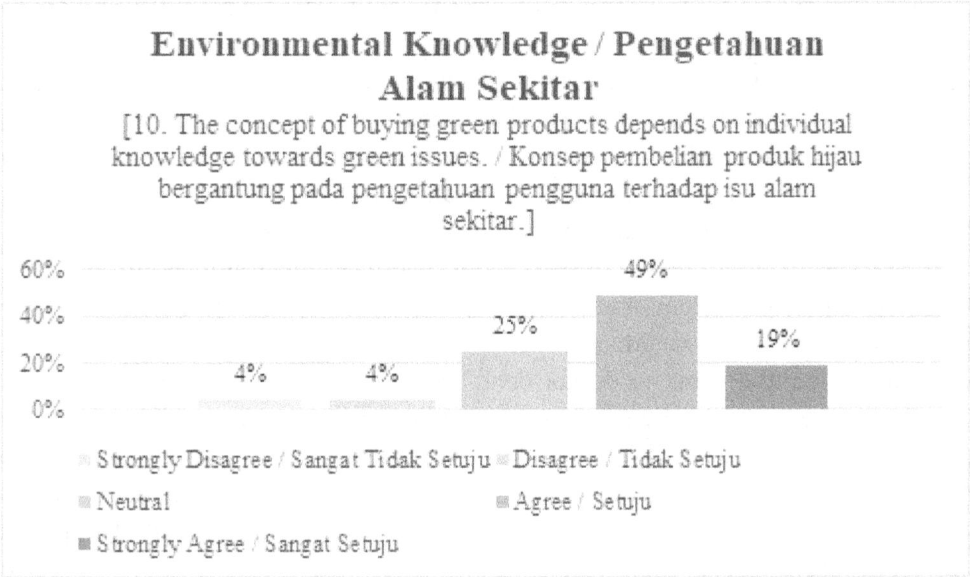

The tenth statement was the concept of buying green products depends on individual knowledge towards green issues. As can be seen in Figure 44, 4 percent of respondents strongly disagreed with the statement; 4 percent of respondents disagree with the statement; 25 percent of respondents had a neutral viewpoint; 49 percent of respondents agreed; and 19 percent of respondents strongly agreed with the statement.

Figure 45. Environmental knowledge: Green product will ensure a long and healthy life for me

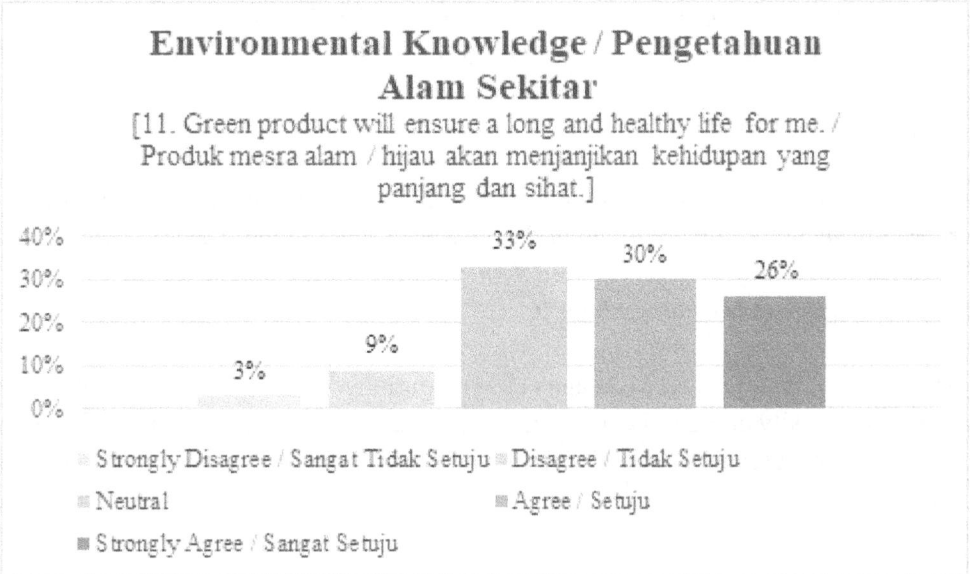

Lastly, the eleventh statement was '**Green products will ensure a long and healthy life**'. Figure 45 shows that 3 percent of respondents strongly disagreed with the statement; 9 percent of respondents disagree with the statement; 33 percent of respondents had a neutral viewpoint; 30 percent of respondents agreed; and 26 percent of respondents strongly agreed with the statement.

The findings from both questionnaire and semi-structured interviews shows a noteworthy association between environmental knowledge and green purchase behaviours. Sinnappan and Rahman (2011) stated that consumers would be more willing to take actions due to the fact that environmental problems will directly or indirectly affect one's quality of life, especially their health.

From the findings of the questionnaire, 53 percent of respondents strongly agreed that the global environmental problems are worsening but only 43 percent had a neutral view of thinking the Brunei Darussalam's environmental problems are worsening, but 40 percent Brunei Darussalam's environmental problems are threatening one's health, with the majority of the respondents (43 percent) agreed that the nation's environmental problems need to be dealt urgently. Thus, in order to do that, respondents or consumers need to make sacrifices by purchasing green or organic products. When asked about their intention to purchase green products, 37 percent had a neutral viewpoint, and this somehow shows their hesitancy due to some restrictive factors. Furthermore, only 19 percent of respondents strongly agreed that they actively seek out information about green products, and only 19 percent of respondents would switch from their products from the conventional products to green products. Most of the respondents (40 percent) are in the neutral position in valuing their environmental knowledge, and only 11 percent strongly agreed that their environmental knowledge is high.

With that being said, 49 percent agreed and believed that, the concept of buying green products depends on individual knowledge towards green issues, and 33 percent of respondents had a neutral view whilst 26 percent had a strongly agreed regarding the statement that green products will ensure a long and healthy life.

This is further emphasized by the all six respondents from the semi-structured interviews whereby all of them agreed that green purchase behaviours depend on individual's knowledge on green issues. Respondent B stated:

"I do agree that buying green products depends on individual knowledge because after knowing what happened on environmental degradation and it makes you empathetic on the world and future children..."

Whilst, Respondent C responded:

I think I can take both sides on that - one 'a' and 'b'. For 'a', maybe that person is knowledgeable enough about the green consumerism and willing to make a change. The second type 'b', they are aware about the changes that are happening in the world and then they know what contributes to the changes but still they wouldn't even want to do anything about it.

This is evident from Banerjee and Mckeage (1994) mentioned that the perception of an individual to the seriousness and intensity could affect one's green purchase behaviours. To put differently, individuals that do not behave in a green manner believe that environmental problems will unfold by themselves and vice versa.

Figure 46. Green Purchase Behaviour: When I want to buy a product, I look at the ingredients label to see if it contains ingredients that are environmentally damaging

Green Purchase Behaviours in Brunei Consumers

Section D was intended to investigate the green purchase behaviour among consumers in Brunei Darussalam. It was also in the form of statements The first statement was ***When I want to buy a product,***

Figure 47. Green Purchase Behaviour: I prefer green products over non-green products when the products qualities are similar

Figure 48. Green Purchase Behaviour: I choose to buy products that are environmentally friendly

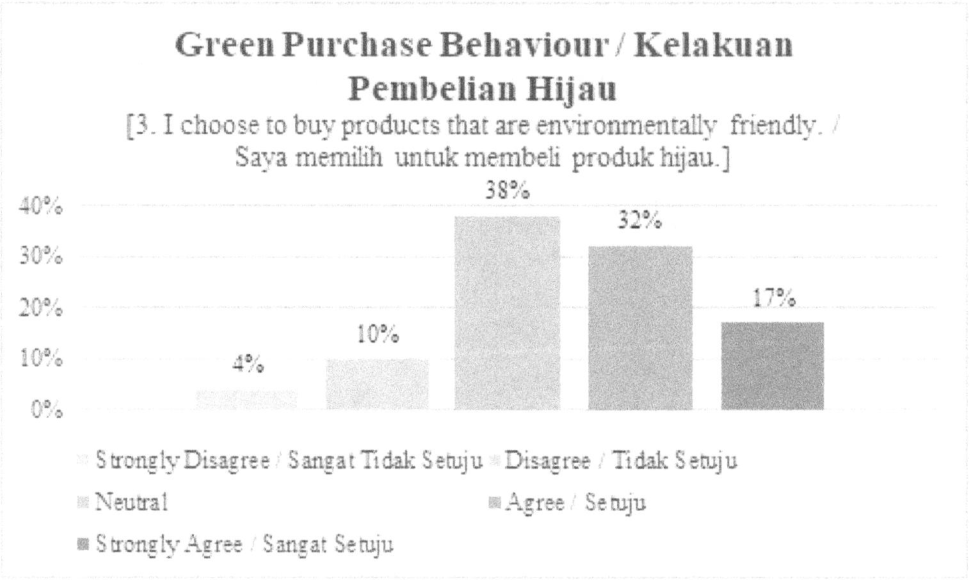

I look at the ingredients label to see if it contains ingredients that are environmentally damaging. Figure 46 shows that 10 percent of respondents strongly disagreed with the statement; 28 percent of respondents disagree with the statement; 35 percent of respondents had a neutral viewpoint; 18 percent of respondents agreed; and 10 percent respondents strongly agreed with the statement.

The second statement was ***I prefer green products over non green products when the products qualities are similar.*** As shown in Figure 47, 5 percent of respondents strongly disagreed with the statement; 8 percent of the respondents disagreed with the statement; 42 percent of respondents had a neutral viewpoint; 27 percent of respondents agreed; and 18 percent of respondents strongly agreed with the statement.

The third statement was ***I choose to buy products that are environmentally friendly***. Figure 48 shows that 4 percent of respondents strongly disagreed with the statement; 10 percent of respondents disagree with the statement; 38 percent respondents had a neutral viewpoint; 32 percent respondents agreed; and 17 percent respondents strongly agreed with the statement.

Respondent D: *"I buy although green product is limited"*

The fourth statement was **I buy green products even if they are more expensive than the non green ones.** As can be seen in Figure 49, 10 percent of respondents strongly disagreed with the statement; 19 percent of respondents disagree with the statement; 49 percent of respondents had a neutral viewpoint; 17 percent of respondents agreed; and lastly 5 percent respondents strongly agreed with the statement.

Respondent F: *"I believe people who have knowledge and awareness will buy green products if they can afford it"*

Figure 49. Green Purchase Behaviour: I buy green products even if they are more expensive than the non-green ones

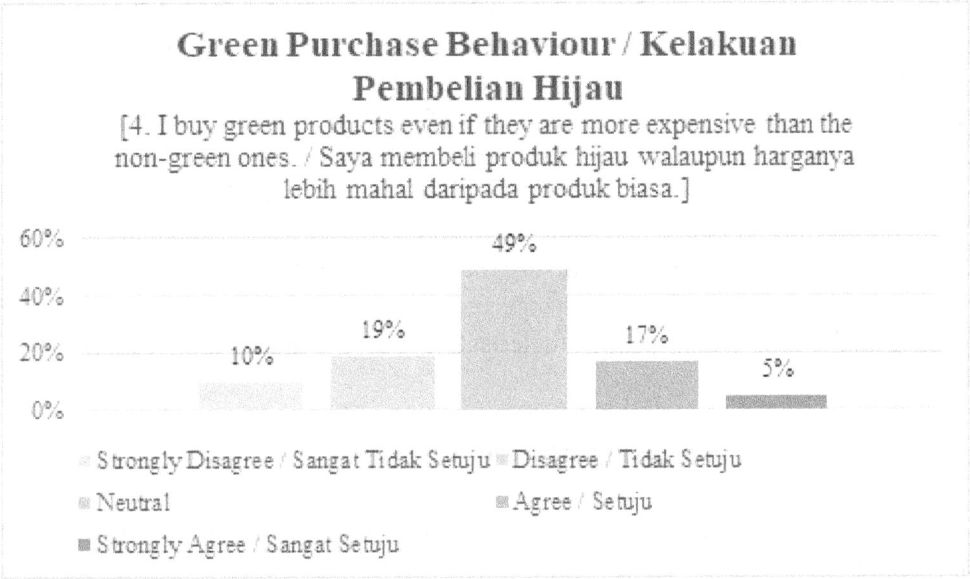

The last and fifth statement was **I buy green products because they are considered to be a symbol of social status**. Figure 50 shows that 22 percent of respondents strongly disagreed with the statement; 23 percent of respondents disagree with the statement; 33 percent of respondents had a neutral viewpoint; 8 percent of respondents agreed; and 9 percent of respondents strongly agreed with the statement.

Figure 50. Green Purchase Behaviour: I buy green products because they are considered to be a symbol of social status

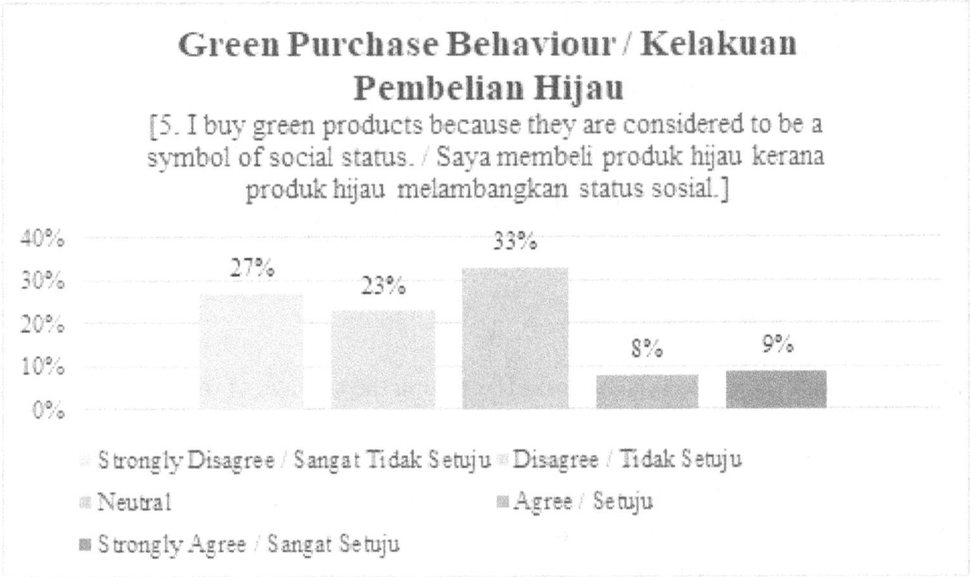

From this study, it is difficult to determine whether or not the respondents are practicing green consumerism behaviours. This is evident from the 51 percent of respondents from the respondents that answered *Not Sure / Tidak Pasti* to the Do you practice Green Consumerism? Question with 11 percent of respondents answered that they never purchase green products but 64 percent of respondents answered *Yes / Ya* to ever purchasing green products. When asked in an open-ended section of the questionnaire, a few (12 percent) of respondents gave some examples of their green practice. Some of the answers that they gave was metal straws, recyclable bags, reusable facial pads, utensils, not using plastic excessively, and looking for fair trade products along with purchasing for products that come with biodegradable packages. Similar to the questionnaire's responses, the interviewed responses are actively participating in the green behaviour especially with minimizing the usage of plastic bags, and using recyclable bags. Although, a portion of the respondents from the questionnaire not actively practicing greenly, 90 percent of the respondents are willing to switch from their usual products and brands and purchase environmentally friendly and safe products.

Descriptive Statistics and Correlation Matrix

Descriptive Statistics and Correlation Matrix are calculated by Jamovi software as shown in Table 1 below where green purchase behaviour, environmental knowledge, and socio-psychological determinants (independent variable) are measured. However, the demographic determinants are not measured in this study, thus are not included because the responses to the questions of demographic determinants use nominal scales which are inconsistent measurements. How they are calculated are explained in the following.

Green Purchase Behaviour

Green purchase behaviour is measured by taking the average of responses to these questions;

- When I want to buy a product, I look at the ingredients label to see if it contains ingredients that are environmentally damaging.
- I prefer green products over non-green products when the products qualities are similar.
- I choose to buy products that are environmentally friendly.
- I buy green products even if they are more expensive than the non-green ones.
- I buy green products because they are considered to be a symbol of social status.

The responses to these questions are in ordinal scale ranging from 1 to 5, i.e. "from strongly disagree to strongly agree".

Environmental Knowledge

Environmental knowledge (cognition) is measured by taking the average of responses to these questions;

- I think Brunei Darussalam's environmental problems need to be dealt urgently.
- I am willing to make sacrifices to protect the environment by using organic products.
- I would definitely intend to buy those products that are organic.
- I actively seek out information about organic or green products.

- I would switch from my usual brands and buy environmentally safe products.
- I consider my knowledge to be high regarding green issues.
- The concept of buying green products depends on individual knowledge towards green issues.
- Green product will ensure a long and healthy life for me.
- Global environmental problems are worsening.
- I think Brunei Darussalam's environmental problems are worsening.
- Brunei Darussalam's environmental problems are threatening our health.

The responses to these questions are in ordinal scale ranging from 1 to 5, i.e. "from strongly disagree to strongly agree".

Socio-Psychological Determinants

Socio-psychological determinants (both affect and behaviour) are measured by taking the average of responses to the questions of environmental concern, perceived environmental responsibility, environmental attitude, perceived effectiveness of environmental behaviour and government initiative as follows

Environmental Concern (Affective);

- Brunei Darussalam's environment is my major concern.
- I am involved in environmental protection problem in Brunei Darussalam.
- I often think about how the environmental quality in Brunei Darussalam can be improved.
- I think I should be more responsible in protecting the environment in Brunei Darussalam.

Perceived environmental responsibility (Affective);

- Environmental protection starts with me.
- I think I should have so much responsibility in protecting the environment in Brunei Darussalam.
- I am willing to take up responsibility to protect the environment in Brunei Darussalam.
- Environmental protection is the responsibility of the environmental organization, not me. (inverse)
- Green products do not perform as well as non-green products. (inverse)
- I feel proud when I buy or use green products.

Environmental attitude (Behaviour);

- It is essential to promote green living in Brunei Darussalam.
- I strongly agree that more environmental protection works are needed in Brunei Darussalam.
- It is very important to raise environmental awareness among Bruneian.
- Environmental protection issues are none of my concern. (inverse)

Perceived effectiveness of environmental behaviour (Behaviour);

- I think if I carry out some pro-environmental behaviour in my everyday life, I would, contribute a lot to our environment.
- I think my participation in environmental protection would influence others to participate too.
- The environmental quality of Brunei Darussalam will stay the same even if I engage in some pro-environmental behaviour. (inverse)

- Even if I recycle and reuse things, the environmental quality of Brunei Darussalam will remain as it currently is. (inverse)

Government initiative (Behaviour);

- Environmental protection is the responsibility of the government, not me. (inverse)
- With the enforcement of no plastic day everyday, it has helped me to be more environmentally aware.
- Schools and higher institutions should require all students to take a course dealing with environment and conservation problems.
- The government should subsidize research on technology for environmental protection (for example recycling waste products).
- Government should enforce more environmental rules and regulation.

The responses to these questions are in ordinal scale ranging from 1 to 5, i.e. "from strongly disagree to strongly agree" except the questions that are labelled as inverse. Pro-green behaviours are reflected in the responses to the questions when they are inversed in ordinal scale ranging from 1 to 5, i.e. "from strongly agree to strongly disagree".

Table 1. Descriptive statistics and correlation matrix

	Variable	Mean	Standard Deviation	1	2	3
1	Green Purchase Behaviour	3.04	0.808	1		
2	Environmental Knowledge	3.60	0.666	0.556	1	
3	Socio-Psychological Determinants	3.80	0.540	0.229	0.653	1

Table 1 shows that on average, socio-psychological determinants are the highest (mean = 3.80, standard deviation = 0.540) on ordinal scale ranging from 1 to 5 that means "from strongly disagree to strongly agree", compared to environmental knowledge (mean = 3.60, standard deviation = 0.666) and green purchase behaviour (mean = 3.04, standard deviation = 0.808).

The results of Pearson correlation among socio-psychological determinants, environmental knowledge and green purchase behaviour are also shown in Table 1. The results revealed that environmental knowledge is positively correlated to green purchase behaviour at medium level (correlation = 0.556). It indicates that environmental knowledge may contribute to green purchase behaviour. Socio-psychological determinants are also positively correlated to green purchase behaviour but at weak level (correlation = 0.229). Likewise, the correlation of independent variables; environmental knowledge and socio-psychological determinants are positive but at higher level (correlation = 0.653). It indicates stronger correlation, i.e. environmental knowledge may contribute to socio-psychological determinants.

Challenges Faced by Consumers' Green Purchase Behaviours

Price of Green Product

In the questionnaire, respondents were asked to pick answers that describe green products. 25 percent of respondents selected the "Expensive / Mahal" answer's option. Similar to the interviewed respondents, all of them expressed their opinions by stating that green products are on the higher price point. Respondent F mentioned:

"I would but only if I earn more. right now, I can contribute to not use plastics... well to be honest, my main priorities are needs and price of course"

According to Sharma (2011), price is ought to be one of the dominant determinants in the green marketing mix. It is studied that, consumers show their readiness to pay more if they believed that the products provide extra value that can come from a better taste and improved function etc. Sharaf and Perumal (2018) explained in their research that an overpriced green product often results to a higher environmental cost. The price is a crucial factor and this could affect consumers deterring from buying green products in a positive manner (Peattie, 2001; Boztepe, 2012). Additionally, consumers who paid more for green products purchase products that are classified in the lower cost category such as recycle paper bags, and often paid less environmental characteristics attention to more expensive items such as cars and electrical appliances as the consumers have to pay premium prices (Pedro & Lemke, 2013).

Availability of Green Products

This is another point raised by respondents particularly during the interview sessions. When asked, most of them were only aware of certain green products, or it could due to the fact that they are 'unconsciously' aware if a product is actually a green product, for example, a hybrid car. The availability of green products in Brunei is still not as widely accessible as hoped, but Brunei is getting more exposed to the green movement. Thus, the unavailability of the green products acts as a barrier for consumers' green purchase behaviours.De-Pelsmacker et al. (2003) stated that, green products are often limited and are sometimes not sold in a proper shops, which agreed with Robinson and Smith's (2002) study that 52 percent of respondents were said to not go green due to the fact that the products were scarce, along with poor marketing of the green products said Mainieri et al. (1997). Repondent A expressed his view by saying:

"It is very hard to find green products here ..., and I don't know where to find them. So I guess, I can not be considered as a green consumer?"

Therefore, it can be said that, green purchase behaviours depends on how time-saving products are to consumers, and the availability of the green products (Blackwell et al., 2006).

Exposure of Green Products

From the 6 interviews being conducted, all of the respondents mentioned social media as their main source of environmental information. With the availability and accessibility of social media networks such as Instagram and Facebook - the people, especially the respondents are becoming more aware about the environmental issues.

For instance, Respondent B:

"I followed some NGOs and online sellers on Instagram and I've seen they're active in promoting environmental problem ways of tackling this is quite helpful and I tend to share it with people".

This is supported by a Moser and Uzzell's (2003) study which stated that mass media represent an important role in educating consumers to understand the seriousness of environmental issues. For instance, marketers or sellers deliver the message in regard on how their products are green and how consumers can contribute in decreasing the detrimental impacts of the environment.

Lack of Stricter Rules and Regulations

Lacked of stricter rules and regulations is one of the commonalities discovered from the interview findings. All of them said that they agreed that government played a crucial role towards green purchasing behaviours, and shared that stricter rules and implementations are needed to be implemented. The responses from the interviewed respondents are parallel with the questionnaire's responses whereby 53 percent of respondents strongly agreed that government should enforce more environmental rules and regulations. This is consistent with a study by Tsen et al. (2006). Some of the respondents said that government had not done enough, as mentioned by Respondent C:

"... we need a step-up because it's only so little the government or the people here doing so little like when it comes to eating habits... I just think that the government or the people here they are doing the minimal when we should be doing something drastic, we are aware that the world is dying but we still doing the minimal."

Moreover, the government has the main role to protect social interest through appropriate rules and regulation. With stricter regulations along with the increased environmental awareness, this will allow more environmental strategies to allow changes in behaviour. Thus, Dummett (2006) believed that the laws and regulations implemented by the government need to be more active and this will eventually lead to more green behaviours. One of the ways that could be implemented by the Bruneian's government is by imposing environmental penalties and taxes on consumers. Not just blindly implementing policies, but the policies and regulations need to be proactive and effective in order to realize the sustainable development plans especially in the environmental field.

Summary of Findings

Table 2 below presents the summary of findings for green purchasing behaviour and the determinants that affect green purchasing behaviour. It presents three determinants that affect green purchasing behaviour;

affective, behaviour and cognition. For affective determinant, in terms of environmental concern, majority of the respondents strongly agree that Brunei's environment is their major concern and they should be more responsible in protecting the environment, although majority of them are neutral when they are asked if they are involved in environmental protection. Their responses for environmental concern are consistent with their responses for perceived environmental responsibility, which is another affective determinant. Majority of the respondents strongly agree that environmental protection starts with themselves. Also, majority of them agree that they should have responsibility in protecting the environment, they are willing to take up responsibility to protect the environment and they feel proud when they buy or use green product. Consistent with their previous responses, majority of them disagree that environmental protection is not their responsibility but the environmental organization. However, majority of them are neutral with the statement saying 'Green products do not perform as well as non-green products'.

The next determinant is concerned with behaviour. Behavioural determinants consist of environmental attitude, perceived effectiveness of environmental behaviour and government initiative. In terms of environmental attitude, majority of the respondents strongly agree that it is essential to promote green living in Brunei, more environmental protection works are needed in Brunei, and it is very important to raise environmental awareness among Bruneians. Consistent with their previous responses, majority of them strongly disagree that environmental protection issues are none of their concern. On the other hand, in terms of for perceived effectiveness of environmental behaviour, majority of them agree that they think if they carry out some pro-environmental behaviour, they would contribute a lot to the environment and think their participation in environmental protection would influence others to participate. However, majority of them are neutral with that statement saying 'The environmental quality of Brunei Darussalam will stay the same even if I engage in some pro-environmental behaviour'. On the other hand, there are two majority groups with equal proportion of respondents (27%) who are neutral and disagree with the statement saying 'Even if I recycle and reuse things, the environmental quality of Brunei Darussalam will remain as it currently is'. Comparing their responses for perceived effectiveness of environmental behaviour and environmental attitude, their responses for one of the statements for perceived effectiveness of environmental behaviour are not consistent with their responses for the other statements for perceived effectiveness of environmental behaviour, and environmental attitude. In terms of government initiative, majority of them strongly agree with the following statements; 'With the enforcement of no plastic day everyday, it has helped me to be more environmentally aware', 'Schools and higher institutions should require all students to take a course dealing with environment and conservation problems', 'The government should subsidize research on technology for environmental protection', and 'Government should enforce more environmental rules and regulations'. Consistent with their previous responses, majority of them disagree that environmental protection is the responsibility of the government, not themselves.

The final determinant is concerned with cognition. In terms of environmental knowledge, majority of them strongly disagree that global environmental problems are worsening. Also majority of them agree with the statements saying 'Brunei Darussalam's environmental problems are threatening our health', 'I think Brunei Darussalam's environmental problems need to be dealt urgently', and 'The concept of buying green products depends on individual knowledge towards green issues'. However, majority of them are neutral with the following statements saying 'I think Brunei Darussalam's environmental problems are worsening', 'I am willing to make sacrifices to protect the environment by using organic products', 'I would definitely intend to buy those products that are organic', 'I actively seek out information about organic or green products', 'I would switch from my usual brands and buy environmentally safe products', and 'Green product will ensure a long and healthy life for me'.

Table 2. Summary of findings for green purchasing behaviour and determinants that affect green purchasing behaviour

Figure	Statement	Proportion of respondents with the following view				
		Strongly Disagree	Disagree	Neutral	Agree	Strongly Agree
	AFFECTIVE					
	1) Environmental Concern					
12	Brunei Darussalam's environment is my major concern.	3%	5%	29%	25%	38%
13	I am involved in environmental protection problem in Brunei.	6%	24%	46%	19%	5%
14	I often think about how environmental quality in Brunei can be improved.	2%	6%	23%	43%	26%
15	I think I should be more responsible in protecting the environment in Brunei Darussalam.	2%	2%	13%	37%	46%
	2) Perceived Environmental Responsibility					
16	Environmental protection starts with me.	3%	3%	13%	38%	43%
17	I think I should have so much responsibility in protecting the environment in Brunei Darussalam.	1%	5%	24%	38%	32%
18	I am willing to take up responsibility to protect the environment in Brunei.	0%	5%	33%	38%	24%
19	Environmental protection is the responsibility of the environmental organization, not me.	18%	28%	21%	15%	18%
20	Green products do not perform as well as non-green products.	7%	19%	50%	17%	8%
21	I feel proud when I buy or use green products.	1%	5%	32%	33%	29%

Figure	Statement	Proportion of respondents with the following view				
		Strongly Disagree	Disagree	Neutral	Agree	Strongly Agree
	BEHAVIOUR					
	1) Environmental Attitude					
22	It is essential to promote green living in Brunei.	4%	1%	12%	35%	49%
23	I strongly agree that more environmental protection works are needed in Brunei Darussalam.	4%	0%	14%	25%	58%
24	It is very important to raise environmental awareness among Bruneian.	4%	1%	9%	23%	64%
25	Environmental protection issues are none of my concern.	42%	25%	16%	9%	9%
	2) Perceived Effectiveness of Environmental Behaviour					
26	I think if I carry out some pro-environmental behaviour in my life, I would contribute a lot to our environment.	2%	4%	24%	42%	29%
27	I think my participation in environmental protection would influence others to participate.	3%	4%	32%	35%	27%
28	The environmental quality of Brunei Darussalam will stay the same even if I engage in some pro-environmental behaviour.	10%	28%	31%	14%	17%
29	Even if I recycle and reuse things, the environmental quality of Brunei Darussalam will remain as it currently is.	15%	27%	27%	25%	7%

Figure	Statement	Proportion of respondents with the following view				
		Strongly Disagree	Disagree	Neutral	Agree	Strongly Agree
	3) Government Initiative					
30	Environmental protection is the responsibility of the government, not me.	19%	32%	27%	12%	10%
31	With the enforcement of no plastic day everyday, it has helped me to be more environmentally aware.	5%	6%	16%	32%	41%
32	Schools and higher institutions should require all students to take a course dealing with environment and conservation problems.	4%	4%	15%	35%	42%
33	The government should subsidize research on technology for environmental protection.	3%	4%	12%	35%	45%
34	Government should enforce more environmental rules and regulations.	4%	2%	12%	28%	53%
	COGNITION					
	1) Environmental Knowledge					
35	Global environmental problems are worsening.	3%	4%	16%	25%	53%
36	I think Brunei Darussalam's environmental problems are worsening.	1%	5%	43%	36%	14%
37	Brunei Darussalam's environmental problems are threatening our health.	1%	12%	34%	40%	14%
38	I think Brunei Darussalam's environmental problems need to be dealt urgently.	2%	4%	30%	36%	28%
39	I am willing to make sacrifices to protect the environment by using organic products.	2%	8%	43%	32%	15%

Figure	Statement	Proportion of respondents with the following view				
		Strongly Disagree	Disagree	Neutral	Agree	Strongly Agree
40	I would definitely intend to buy those products that are organic.	4%	5%	37%	32%	22%
41	I actively seek out information about organic or green products.	3%	19%	38%	26%	15%
42	I would switch from my usual brands and buy environmentally safe products.	1%	9%	43%	28%	19%
43	I consider my knowledge to be high regarding green issues.	9%	24%	40%	17%	11%
44	The concept of buying green products depends on individual knowledge towards green issues.	4%	4%	25%	49%	19%
45	Green product will ensure a long and healthy life for me.	3%	9%	33%	30%	26%
	GREEN PURCHASE BEHAVIOUR					
46	When I want to buy a product, I look at the ingredients label to see if it contains ingredients that are environmentally damaging.	10%	28%	35%	18%	10%
47	I prefer green products over non-green products when the products qualities are similar.	5%	8%	42%	27%	18%
48	I choose to buy products that are environmentally friendly.	4%	10%	38%	32%	17%
49	I buy green products even if they are more expensive than the non-green ones.	10%	19%	49%	17%	5%
50	I buy green products because they are considered to be a symbol of social status.	27%	23%	33%	8%	9%

In the final part of the survey, the respondents were asked about their green purchase behaviour. Majority of them are neutral with all statements for this section saying 'When I want to buy a product, I look at the ingredients label to see if it contains ingredients that are environmentally damaging', 'I prefer green products over non-green products when the products qualities are similar', 'I choose to buy products that are environmentally friendly', 'I buy green products even if they are more expensive than the non-green ones', and 'I buy green products because they are considered to be a symbol of social status'. Even so, bigger proportions of respondents agree and strongly agree with the following statements saying 'I prefer green products over non-green products when the products qualities are similar', and 'I choose to buy products that are environmentally friendly'. On the other hand, bigger proportions of respondents disagree and strongly disagree with the following statements saying 'When I want to buy a product, I look at the ingredients label to see if it contains ingredients that are environmentally damaging', and 'I buy green products even if they are more expensive than the non-green ones'. These latter responses are not consistent with their responses for environmental concern (affective) and environmental attitude (behaviour).

The findings in Table 2 seem to be consistent with the findings in table 1, in which environmental knowledge is positively correlated to green purchase behaviour at medium level (correlation = 0.556). It indicates that environmental knowledge may contribute to green purchase behaviour. Socio-psychological determinants are also positively correlated to green purchase behaviour but at weak level (correlation = 0.229).

CONCLUSION AND RECOMMENDATION

In conclusion, consumers who are more environmentally conscious are not necessarily likely to purchase green products, however, they have characteristics in green behaviours. This study further reveals that in green purchasing behaviours under the demographic determinants; gender and age of the respondents have less significance compared to the educational levels and monthly income of the respondents. However, in the environmental awareness, concern and environmental knowledge, the two factors; monthly income and educational level do not possess major significance. Other than the two initial determinants (demographic and socio-psychological), other factors have stood out from the findings of the study. The product attributes such as price and characteristics of green products are playing a role in consumer's buying decisions which will lead to the value-action gap phenomenon. Lastly, this study demonstrate that the government needs to take a more active measure in promoting the green purchase behaviour in Brunei Darussalam. The study is not without limitations due to the sample size of the study was limited to 113 respondents but this is close representative of the population of Brunei Darussalam as suggested by Reed et al. (1971). Nevertheless, this study provides the opportunity for further research in larger scale.

REFERENCES

Abu Bakar, R. H. (2018, April 16). Brunei aims to phase out plastic bags in supermarkets by 2019: Thursday to Sunday now designated "No Plastic Bag" days. *The Scoop*. https://thescoop.co/2018/04/16/brunei-aims-phase-out-plastic-bags-2019/

Agyeman, C. (2014). Consumers' Buying Behavior Towards Green Products: An Exploratory Study. *International Journal of Management Research and Business Strategy*, *3*, 188–197.

Ahmad, N. A., Kamis, N. Q., Mahdini, & Adilah, S. S. (2015). *Brunei Moving Forward: Brunei's sustainable measures for a successful environmental development*. https://asianjournaloflegalstudies.wordpress.com/2016/08/31/brunei-moving-forward-bruneis-sustainable-measures-for-a-successful-environmental-development/

Akenji, L. (2014). Consumer scapegoatism and limits to green consumerism. *Journal of Cleaner Production*, *63*, 13–23. doi:10.1016/j.jclepro.2013.05.022

Akhtar, R., Sultana, S., Masud, M. M., Jafrin, N., & Al-Mamun, A. (2021). Consumers' environmental ethics, willingness, and green consumerism between lower and higher income groups. *Resources, Conservation and Recycling*, *168*, 105–274. doi:10.1016/j.resconrec.2020.105274

Ali, A., Khan, A. A., Ahmed, I., & Shahzad, W. (2011). Determinants of Pakistani consumers' green purchase behaviour: Some insights from a developing country. *International Journal of Business and Social Science*, *2*(3), 217–226.

Awad, T. A. (2011). Environmental segmentation alternatives: Buyers' profiles and implications. *Journal of Islamic Marketing*, *2*(1), 55–73. doi:10.1108/17590831111115240

Banerjee, B., & McKeage, K. (1994). How green is my value: Exploring the relationship between environmentalism and materialism. *Advances in Consumer Research. Association for Consumer Research (U. S.)*, *21*, 147–152.

Beauprez, C. (2010). *Consumer behavior and buying profile in the Wooden Housing Industry in France* [Unpublished bachelor's thesis]. Turku University of Applied Sciences.

Beckford, C. L., Jacobs, C., Williams, N., & Nahdee, R. (2010). Aboriginal environmental wisdom, stewardship, and sustainability: Lessons from the Walpole island first nations, Ontario, Canada. *The Journal of Environmental Education*, *41*(4), 239–248. doi:10.1080/00958961003676314

Biswas, A., Licata, J. W., McKee, D., Pulling, C., & Daughtridge, C. (2000). The recycling cycle: An empirical examination of consumer waste recycling and recycling shopping behaviors. *Advertisement and Environmental Issues, 19*(1), 93-115.

Blackwell, R. D., Miniard, P. W., & Engel, J. F. (2006). *Consumer Behavior* (10th ed.). Thomson Higher Education.

Boztepe, A. (2012). Green marketing and its impact on consumer buying behavior. *European Journal of Economic and Political Studies*, *5*(1), 5–21.

Brudirect. (2018, December 31). *The No Plastic Bag Everyday Initiative Begins On 31 December 2018*. Retrieved from https://www.brudirect.com/news.php?id=60531

Chen, Y. S., & Chang, C. H. (2012). Enhance green purchase intentions: The roles of green perceived value, green perceived risk, and green trust. *Management Decision*, *50*(3), 502–520. doi:10.1108/00251741211216250

Cooper, D. R., & Schindler, P. S. (2006). *Business Research Methods* (9th ed.). McGraw-Hill Irwin.

Corbley, M. (2019, June 27). Students Design Beach Vacuum That Can Suck Up Microplastics While Leaving All the Sand. *Good News Network.* https://www.goodnewsnetwork.org/students-design-beach-vacuum-cleaner-for-plastic/

De-Pelsmacker, P., Driesen, L., & Rayp, G. (2003). Are fair trade labels good business? Ethics and coffee buying intentions. *The Journal of Consumer Affairs*, *2*, 39.

Ding, C. G., & Tseng, T. H. (2015). On the relationships among brand experience, hedonic emotions, and brand equity. *European Journal of Marketing*, *49*(7/8), 994–1015. doi:10.1108/EJM-04-2013-0200

Dummett, K. (2006). Drivers for corporate environmental responsibility. *Environment, Development and Sustainability*, *8*(3), 375–389. doi:10.100710668-005-7900-3

Fisher, C., Bashyal, S., & Bachman, B. (2012). Demographic impacts on environmentally friendly purchase behaviors. *Journal of Targeting. Measurement and Analysis for Marketing*, *20*(3), 172–184. doi:10.1057/jt.2012.13

Follows, S. B., & Jobber, D. (2000). Environmentally responsible purchase behaviour: A test of a consumer model. *European Journal of Marketing*, *34*(5/6), 723–746. doi:10.1108/03090560010322009

General, R. (2019). Supermarkets in Asia are Now Using Banana Leaves Instead of Plastic Packaging. *Nextshark*. https://nextshark.com/banana-leaves-asia-plastic-packaging/

Gershoff, A. D., & Johar, G. V. (2006). Do You Know Me? Consumer Calibration of Friends' Knowledge. *The Journal of Consumer Research*, *32*(4), 496–503. doi:10.1086/500479

Gorra, A. (2007). *An analysis of the relationship between individuals' perceptions of privacy and mobile phone location data - a grounded theory study* [PhD thesis, Leeds Metropolitan University]. https://www.academia.edu/6331343/Chapter_3_-Methodology_PhD_thesis_Andrea_Gorra_Chapter_3_Research_Methodology

Guagnano, G. A., Stern, P. C., & Dietz, T. (1995). Influences on Attitude-Behavior Relationships: A Natural Experiment with Curbside Recycling. *Environment and Behavior*, *27*(5), 699–718. doi:10.1177/0013916595275005

Han, H., Hsu, L. T. J., & Lee, J. S. (2009). Empirical investigation of the roles of attitudes toward green behaviors, overall image, gender, and age in hotel customers' eco-friendly decision-making process. *International Journal of Hospitality Management*, *28*(4), 519–528. doi:10.1016/j.ijhm.2009.02.004

Hawkins, D., & Mothersbaugh, D. (2010). *Consumer Behavior: Building Marketing Strategy* (11th ed.). McGraw-Hill Irwin.

Huang, H. (2016). Media use, environmental beliefs, self-efficacy, and pro-environmental behavior. *Journal of Business Research, 69*(6), 2206–2212. doi:.031 doi:10.1016/j.jbusres.2015.12

Issock, P. B. I., Mpinganjira, M., & Roberts-Lombard, M. (2019). Modelling green customer loyalty and positive word of mouth: Can environmental knowledge make the difference in an emerging market? *International Journal of Emerging Markets*, *15*(3), 405–426. doi:10.1108/IJOEM-09-2018-0489

Jansson, J., Marell, A., & Nordlund, A. (2010). Green consumer behavior: Determinants of curtailment and eco-innovation adoption. *Journal of Consumer Marketing*, *27*(4), 358–370. doi:10.1108/07363761011052396

Joshi, Y., & Rahman, Z. (2015). Factors Affecting Green Purchase Behaviour and Future Research Directions. *International Strategic Management Review*, *3*(1), 128–143. doi:10.1016/j.ism.2015.04.001

Joshi, Y., & Rahman, Z. (2015). Factors Affecting Green Purchase Behaviour and Future Research Directions. *International Strategic Management Review, 3*(1), 128–143.

Kataria, A., Aakanksha, K., & Ruchi, G. (2013). Factors Affecting Green Buying Behavior: An In-Depth Study of Indian Consumers. *Journal of Management Research*, *1*(2), 3–17.

Kaufmann, H. R., Pann, İ. M., Khan, F. A., & Orphanıdou, Y. (2012). Factors Affecting Consumers' Green Purchasing Behavior: An Integrated Conceptual Framework. *Amfiteatru Economic*, *15*(31), 50–56.

Kim, Y., & Choi, S. M. (2005). Antecedents of green purchase behavior: An examination of collectivism, environmental concern, and PCE. *Advances in Consumer Research. Association for Consumer Research (U. S.)*, *32*, 592.

Kollmuss, A., & Agyeman, J. (2002). Mind the gap: Why do people act environmentally and what are the barriers to pro-environmental behavior? *Environmental Education Research*, *8*(3), 239–260. doi:10.1080/13504620220145401

Lai, O. K. (2000). *Greening of Hong Kong: Forms of manifestation of environmental movements. In the dynamics of social movement in Hong Kong*. City University Press.

Lee, J., & Cho, M. (2019). The Effects of Consumers' Media Exposure, Attention, and Credibility on Pro-environmental Behaviors. *Journal of Promotion Management*. Advance online publication. doi:10.1080/10496491.2019.1699629

Lee, K. (2008). Opportunities for green marketing: Young consumers. *Marketing Intelligence & Planning*, *26*(6), 573–586. doi:10.1108/02634500810902839

Leonidou, L. C., Leonidou, C. N., & Kvasova, O. (2010). Antecedents and outcomes of consumer environmentally friendly attitudes and behaviour. *Journal of Marketing Management*, *26*(13-14), 1319–1344. doi:10.1080/0267257X.2010.523710

Liao, Y., Ho, S. S., & Yang, X. (2016). Motivators of pro-environmental behavior: Examining the underlying processes in the influence of presumed media influence model. *Science Communication*, *38*(1), 51–73. doi:10.1177/1075547015616256

Liebenberg, P. (2015). *Identifying Factors that Influence Green Purchasing Behaviour in South Africa*. North-West University.

Mainieri, T., Barnett, E., Valdero, T., Unipan, J., & Oskamp, S. (1997). Green buying: The influence of environmental concern on consumer behavior. *The Journal of Social Psychology*, *137*(2), 189–204. doi:10.1080/00224549709595430

Mat Said, A., Ahmadun, F. R., Hj Paim, L., & Masud, J. (2003). Environmental Concerns, Knowledge and Practices Gap Among Malaysian Teachers. *International Journal of Sustainability in Higher Education*, *4*(4), 305–313. doi:10.1108/14676370310497534

McEachern, M., & McClean, P. (2002). Organic purchasing motivations and attitudes: Are they ethical? *International Journal of Consumer Studies*, *26*(2), 85–92. doi:10.1046/j.1470-6431.2002.00199.x

Moser, G., & Uzzell, D. L. (2003). Environmental Psychology. In T. Millon & M. J. Lerner (Eds.), *Comprehensive Handbook of Psychology: Personality and Social Psychology* (Vol. 5, pp. 419–445). John Wiley & Sons. doi:10.1002/0471264385.wei0517

Mostafa, M. M. (2007). Gender differences in Egyptian consumers green purchase behavior: The effects of environmental knowledge, concern and attitude. *International Journal of Consumer Studies*, *31*, 220–229.

Ooi, J. M., Kwek, C. L., & Keoy, K. H. (2012). The Antecedents of Green Purchase Intention among Malaysian Consumers. *Asian Social Science Archives*, *8*(13), 248–263. doi:10.5539/ass.v8n13p248

Paco, A. D., & Raposo, M. (2009). "Green" segmentation: An application to the Portuguese consumer market. *Marketing Intelligence & Planning*, *27*(3), 364–379. doi:10.1108/02634500910955245

Peattie, K. (2001). Golden goose or wild goose? The hunt for the green consumer. *Business Strategy and the Environment*, *10*(4), 187–189. doi:10.1002/bse.292

Pedro, P. L. J., & Lemke, F. (2013). Exploring green consumers' product demands and consumption processes: The case of Portuguese green consumers. *European Business Review*, *25*(3), 281–300. doi:10.1108/09555341311314825

Reed, A. H., Henry, R. J., & Mason, W. B. (1971). Influence of Statistical Method Used on the Resulting Estimate of Normal Range. *Clinical Chemistry*, *17*(4), 275–284. doi:10.1093/clinchem/17.4.275 PMID:5552364

Rezai, G., Mohamed, Z., & Shamsudin, M. N. (2011). *Malaysian Consumer's Perceptive Towards Purchasing Organically Produce Vegetable (2nd International Conference on Business and Economic Research (2nd ICBER 2011) Proceeding, Issues 2011–310).* Conference Master Resources. https://econpapers.repec.org/RePEc:cms:2icb11:2011-310

Ritter, M., Borchardt, M., Vaccaro, G. L. R., Pereira, G. M., & Almeida, F. (2015). Motivations for Promoting The Consumption Of Green Products In An Emerging Country: Exploring Attitudes Of Brazilian Consumers. *Journal of Cleaner Production*, *106*, 507–520. doi:10.1016/j.jclepro.2014.11.066

Robinson, R., & Smith, C. C. (2002). Psychosocial and Demographic Variables Associated with Consumer Intention to Purchase Sustainable Produced Foods as Defined by the Midwest Food Alliance. *Journal of Nutrition Education and Behavior*, *34*(6), 316–325.

Sachdeva, S., Jordan, J., & Mazar, N. (2015). Green consumerism: Moral motivations to a sustainable future. *Current Opinion in Psychology*, *6*, 60–65. doi:10.1016/j.copsyc.2015.03.029

Sarumathi, S. (2014). Green Purchase Behavior–A Conceptual Framework of Socially Conscious Consumer Behavior. *Global Journal of Finance and Management*, *6*(8), 777–782.

Shabani, N., Mahboobeh, A., Mohammad, T., Hamed, B., & Marjan, N. F. (2013). The Study of Green Consumers' Characteristics and Available Green Sectors in the Market. *International Research Journal of Applied and Basic Sciences*, *4*(7), 1880–1883.

Sharaf, M. A., & Perumal, S. (2018). How Does Green Products' Price and Availability Impact Malaysians' Green Purchasing Behavior? *The Journal of Social Sciences Research*, *4*(3), 28–34.

Sharma, Y. (2011). Changing consumer behaviour with respect to green marketing–a case study of consumer durables and retailing. *International Journal of Multidisciplinary Research*, *1*(4), 152–162.

Sinnappan, P., & Abd Rahman, A. (2011). Antecedents of green purchasing behaviour among Malaysian consumers. *International Business Management*, *5*(3), 129–139. doi:10.3923/ibm.2011.129.139

Stern. (2000). *Stern's Attitude-Behaviour-Context Model*. Retrieved 2019, June 19th, from http://www.cres.gr/behave/pdf/Stern_ABC_model.pdf

Styvén, M. E., & Mariani, M. M. (2020). Understanding the intention to buy secondhand clothing on sharing economy platforms: The influence of sustainability, distance from the consumption system, and economic motivations. *Psychology and Marketing*, *37*(5), 1–16. doi:10.1002/mar.21334

Tan, B. C., & Lau, T. C. (2010). Attitude towards the environment and green products: Consumers' perspective. *Journal of Management Science and Engineering*, *4*(2), 27–39.

Tang, S. M. (2014). *Factors That Influence Green Purchase Behaviour of Malaysian Consumers* [Masters Thesis]. Universiti Tunku Abdul Rahman.

Tang. (2014). *Factors That Influence Green Purchase Behaviour of Malaysian Consumers* [Masters Thesis]. Universiti Tunku Abdul Rahman. Retrieved 2019, June 19th from http://eprints.utar.edu.my/1299/1/Final_Research_Project_(MBA).pdf

Testa, F., Pretner, G., Iovino, R., Bianchi, G., Tessitore, S., & Iraldo, F. (2020). Drivers to green consumption: A systematic review. *Environment, Development and Sustainability*. Advance online publication. doi:10.100710668-020-00844-5

Tsen, C. H., Phang, G., Hasan, H., & Buncha, M. A. (2006). Going green: A study of consumers' willingness to pay for green products in Kota Kinabalu. *International Journal of Business and Society*, *7*(2), 40–54.

Vermeir, I., & Verbeke, W. (2006). Sustainable food consumption: Exploring the consumer "attitude – behavioral intention" gap. *Journal of Agricultural & Environmental Ethics*, *19*, 169–194. Retrieved June 11th, 2019, from https://www.eur.nl/sites/corporate/files/Vermeir_and_Verbeke__JAEE__2006.pdf

Wahid, N. A., Rahbar, E., & Shyan, T. S. (2011). Factors influencing the green purchase behavior of Penang environmental volunteers. *International Business Management*, *5*(1), 38–49. doi:10.3923/ibm.2011.38.49

Yue, B., Sheng, G., She, S., & Xu, J. (2020). Impact of Consumer Environmental Responsibility on Green Consumption Behavior in China: The Role of Environmental Concern and Price Sensitivity. *Sustainability*, *12*(5), 1–16. doi:10.3390u12052074

Zikmund, W. G. (2003). *Business research methods* (7th ed.). South-Western Publishing.

Chapter 16
Prospect of Promoting Sikkim as a Smart Tourism Destination:
A Descriptive Analysis

Supriya Dam
Netaji Subhash Mahavidyalaya, Udaipur, India

ABSTRACT

Since 2006, Sikkim progressively switching to a full-fledged tourism-centred state having declared it a predominant industry as an engine for its economic growth. The state accounted for the highest influx of foreign tourists amongst the eight north eastern states of India during the last 20 years or so. The smart city mission was commissioned by government of India as a centrally sponsored scheme destined to provide financial support for the allotted cities to the extent of INR. 100 Crore per city per year spanning over five years. Studies suggest that induction of smart city concept will act as precursor for growth of smart tourism destinations (STDs) across the country. The STD as a concept revolves around "6A's," an essential ingredient for promoting smart tourism in destinations. Incidentally, two cities in Sikkim have been enlisted amongst the top 100 cities in India for promoting smart city, instrumental in promoting STD in tourism-driven states. The chapter delves into the concept of smart city as an antecedent for promoting STD along with conditions with respect to Sikkim.

I. INTRODUCTION

Of late, increased use of information and communication technology (ICT) tools has been common phenomenon across all sphere of life especially to gain competitive advantage over the competitors, tourism is no exception. One way to address such impending societal challenges is the use of cutting-edge technologies (Townsend, 2013) in economic spheres to promote sustainable development. Especially within tourism, technologically driven innovations have had a large impact on the development of the industry (Hjalager, 2010). Robust ICT developments, initiating smartness and smart places have been recognised to cause a paradigm shift within the tourism industry (Buhalis, 2015) in recent times.

DOI: 10.4018/978-1-7998-8678-5.ch016

The notion of smartness finds its origin in the 90s, although it proliferated significantly after 2008 (Hollands, 2008, 2015). Initially, the concept was coined as a complex technological infrastructure, embedded within urban areas to foster economic, social and environmental prosperity (IBM, 2014; Meijer and Bolívar, 2015). More specifically, it posited the integration of ICT to improve processes and interconnect sub-systems (Townsend, 2013), to ultimately tackle the economic, social and environmental challenges imposed by urbanism (Caragliu et al., 2011). This implication of cutting-edge technology triggered concepts such as the smart planet (IBM, 2015), smart city (Hollands, 2008) and more recently, the smart tourism destination (Buhalis and Amaranggana, 2014). In fact, smart city concept has been seen as a precursor for promoting STDs in recent times.

At the international level, a ranking of Smart Cities Report in 2020-21 suggests Singapore, Seoul, London, Barcelona, Helsinki, New York City, Montreal, Shanghai, Vienna, Amsterdam are the top ten smart cities in the world. During 2019, city of London was considered the world`s "smartest" city, New York takes the second spot, followed by Amsterdam, Paris, Reykjavic, Tokyo, Singapore, Copenhagen, Berlin down the order, while Vienna ranked 10th (SCG: 2021) in that list showed its better performance during 2020-21. It goes to show intense competition prevailing amongst the top smart cities based on chosen parameters and benchmarking level increases in each criterion in every successive year's. Unfortunately, none of the Indian cities featured in the ranking of 50 smart cities across the world for 2019 and 2020-21, indicative of the cities selected under the Smart City Mission sponsored by Government of India are yet achieve the required level of performance and competitiveness as shown by the leading smart cities in the world.

Lavasa, a planned hill station in Maharashtra, is the first STD in India overseen by Hindustan Construction Company (HCC) of India acted as special purpose vehicle (SPV) for the project. The destination is suiatbly placed amidst seven hills and 60 kilometres away from lakefront spread over 25,000 acres land. This place is known for hospitality, health and wellness, education sector for setting up tourism institutions among others'. (Rvo, 2015). In the list of top 50 Indian Cities, Bengaluru, Pune, Ahmedabad, Chennai, Surat were the top smart cities in descending order for the year 2020 whereas Guwahati (ranked 46) was the lone smart city amongst the eight North Eastern States (NESs) in India during the period (MHUA: 2020).

The concept of Smart City (SC) represents an environment where technology is embedded with socio-economic activities of the city. In fact, technology synergise with city's social components in order to improve citizens quality of life while boosting destination's service efficiency, such as optimising the use of energy and better traffic monitoring (Vicini et al. 2012). "Smart cities are essentially urban clusters with smooth transportation, e-governance, and better social infrastructure, including health care and education. Smart is not just about technology-enabled, but also about power, water, transportation and solid waste management" (Kandpal, 2016). In fact, the dimensions of smart city take the following shape.

Figure 1 illustrates six overriding dimensions of smart city includes smart economy, smart mobility, smart living, smart environment, smart people and smart governance. Each of these narratives is associated with each segment in urban setting in an ICT linked environment literally act as facilitator for transition to smart tourism development in destinations.

In fact, each sub-components of smart city features critical to local decision makers emphasising on the use of smart technologies for enhancing tourism experiences (Boes et al, 2016). It embraces use of innovative technologies in management decision making processes to enhance effectiveness and better quality of life for the stakeholders in the one hand while enhancing smart tourism experience for the

Figure 1. Components of smart city.
Source: *Rudolf, G., Fertner, C., Kramar, H., Kalasek, R., Pichler-Milanovic, N., & Meijers, E. (2007).*

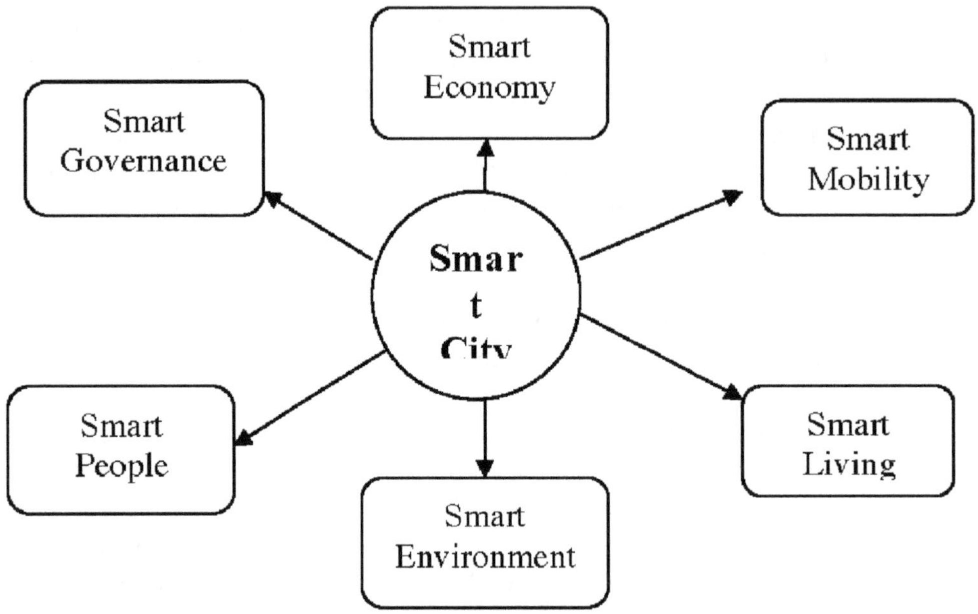

visitors (Gretzel et al., 2015). In fact, introduction of smart city concept in tourism domain aimed at addressing specific travel related needs (Sahoo et al, 2019) considered essential in post Covid 19 scenario.

The Smart Cities Mission (SCM) of Government of India (GOI, 2015) was introduced to promote core infrastructure for the cities to provide a decent quality of life to its citizens, a clean and sustainable environment and application of 'smart' solutions; emphasising the importance of ICT as the key driver for development. As a part of the scheme, 100 cities were chosen for Smart City Mission to begin with and 20 cities were shortlisted for up-gradation. In the next lot another 27 cities enlisted for SCM, Namchi and Gangtok, the twin cities in Sikkim, featured in the scheme for the SCM. The Scheme was primarily introduced as a Centrally Sponsored Scheme (CSS) and the Indian Government destined to provide financial support to the SCM to the extent of Rs. 48,000 crores over a period of five years i.e. on an average Rs. 100 crore earmarked for per city per year. The core infrastructure parameter for Smart City Projects commissioned by Government of India includes:

- Adequate water supply,
- Assured electricity supply,
- Sanitation, including solid waste management,
- Efficient urban mobility and public transport,
- Affordable housing, especially for the poor,
- Robust IT connectivity and digitalization,
- Good governance, especially e-Governance and citizen participation,
- Sustainable environment,
- Safety and security of citizens, particularly women, children and the elderly, and
- Health and education.

In fact, the defining characters' of SCM were indicative of smart application in tourism destinations primarily to reap advantage of using cutting edge technologies along with making arrangement for employment opportunities for locals on the other. The abovementioned infrastructure parameters' commissioned by Government of India for smart cities are not limited to ten parameters' alone; leaving scope for further additions/deletions depending on the ecological balance of destinations'. Present study examines the status of STDs in two prominent cities in Sikkim on the basis of published reports and spot visits to respective sites in an attempt to assess the paradigm shift from traditional tourism offerings in the tiny Eastern Himalayan State.

OBJECTIVES AND METHODOLOGY

The basic objective of this descriptive study is to assess the prospect of promoting STD in the twin cities in Sikkim, namely Namchi and Gangtok. The objectives are to:

- throw light upon conditions considered essential for STD;
- make an overview of STD progress in twin cities in accordance with national infrastructure parameters framed; and
- make a descriptive assessment of the prospect of STD in Sikkim.

Present study will purely be based on secondary data compiled from books, journals, published reports and internet publications available for citation. Consultation with officials from the Department of Tourism, Government of Sikkim will be supplemented by the national level studies carried out by Ministry of Tourism, Government of India along with other relevant bodies like Gangtok Smart City Development Ltd (GSCDL), Namchi Smart City Ltd. (NSCL), India Smart City Mission (ISCM) engaged as special purpose vehicle (SPV) in this field of study. Viewpoints of hoteliers and tour operators are considered critical for accomplishment of this study, due weightage will be given to them during the course of this study. Collected data would be processed and analyzed by using suitable statistical tools as per need of the study. As the study purely based on secondary information, limitations of using the same would apply.

The study comprised of seven sections. Section I introduces the smart city concept and its inter-linkages with smart tourism destinations. Section II encompasses the objectives and methodology adopted for the study. Section III dealt with review of available literature followed by the conditions necessary for promoting STD (Section IV). Section V and VI highlights the budgetary support and foreign tourist influx along with theoretical assessment for STD respectively. Lastly, section VII concludes the chapter with priority areas for action.

REVIEW OF LITERATURE

Smart City concept got impetus not only for the benefits accruing to the city concerned but also act as precursor to smart tourist destination by enhancing smart tourism experiences. In fact, use of smart technologies facilitates tourism progress in host destinations thereby allowing destination managers to play a key role in its promotion. In such an arrangement, people are linked to technology (Latour, 2005; Meijer and Boliver, 2015) collaborately enhancing economic, social and environmental well being, i.e.

sustainable development for all (Vargo and Lusch, 2004). The interaction between digital ecosystem of cutting age technologies with an ecosystem of heterogeneous human actors promotes socio-technical synergy for common good (Meijer and Boliver, 2015).

In other words, "smart tourist city is the result of interconnectedness between tourist city and the smart city" (Habeeb & Weli: 2020: 199) in a destination in which concerned government plays a critical role for its sustenance. Choudhury and Dixit (2018) argued that tourists' and stakeholders' smartness needs to accord due attention rather than destination level smartness as reported by number of studies. Gunarekha and Binoy (2018) stressed the need for comprehensive digital marketing approach with a view to meet challenges and opportunities posed by technology adoption for promoting smart tourism in destinations. Linking innovation to tourism practices, Tuzunkan (2017) observed that induction of smart technologies in tourism can transform new ideas and inventions into marketable ones considered essential for tourism growth in destinations (Tukunkan: 2017). Sahoo et al (2019) argued that, in spite of potential, the transition to smart from conventional tourism destinations takes its usual time especially due to change in role played by the stakeholders in embracing digital technology. Vasavada and Padhiyar (2016) voiced concern for inadequacy of literature concerning smart tourism presumptions, doubts along with its societal and experimental impacts.

Liberato et al (2018) outlined the importance of connectivity at the destination level and availability of technologies (like internet, smart phones and other mobile devices and applications) are considered essential in providing smart tourism experience. Studies opined that mobile device can intervene the behavioural and psychological dimension of tourism experience pave the way for feasible search of information, its processing and sharing of the same to both present and prospective travellers (Tussyadiah and Fesenmaier, 2009; Wang et al., 2010).

STD thus involves integration of technologies, systems, services, capabilities into an organised network which essentially open access and provides for flexible future development in smart destinations (Albino et al, 2015). In other words, it's a process of integrating destination with multiple community stakeholders through dynamic platforms that ensures flows of knowledge intensive communication and decision support systems (Buhalis & Amaranggana, 2014).

Jeong and Shin's (2019) opined that attributes like informativeness, interactivity and personalisation are key to enhance tourism experiences, satisfaction and revisit intentions of tourists' visiting smart tourism destinations. Pai et al (2020) also observed that smart tourism technology experience (STTE) revolves around informativeness, accessibility, interactivity, personalisation and security. In fact, STTE ranges between accessibility and personalisation with satisfaction plays a key role in revisit intentions of travellers'.

Sigala (2020) stressed the need for technology enabled tourism for reopening it post Covid 19 through mobility tracing apps, robotised-AI touch less service delivery, digital health passports, identity controls, social distancing, crowding controls and provision for safety and security among others; directly endorsing smart tourism applications as a way forward. Van et al (2020) postulate that use of socially interactive gadgets in tourism encompasses tourism organisation's commitment to future technologies, and also enriching value and service quality expectations of frightened visitors to tourism sites. Again, endorsing tour bubble framework along with new service innovations via human-machine interaction is prerequisites in post Covid 19 scenario.

Present study takes into account the plight of STD in twin cities in Sikkim for the first time since 2016-17 when the Smart City Mission (SCM) was launched in the tiny Eastern Himalayan State.

CONDITIONS FOR SMART TOURISM DESTINATIONS (STDS)

Smart tourism destination can be defined as "a platform, which is implementing ICTs such as Cloud Computing and Internet of Things and End User Internet Service System to offer the tourist personalized information and enhanced services established by mobile end-user devices" (Boes, 2015). In order to make a tourism destination smart, the dynamic connection of stakeholders through technological platforms is a key factor. The main objective of these platforms is to create a quick information exchange regarding all tourism related activities (Buhalis & Amaranggana, 2014).

Figure 2. Interface of components of smart tourism destination.
Adapted from Sahoo et al 2019 & Buhalis & Amaranggana, 2014

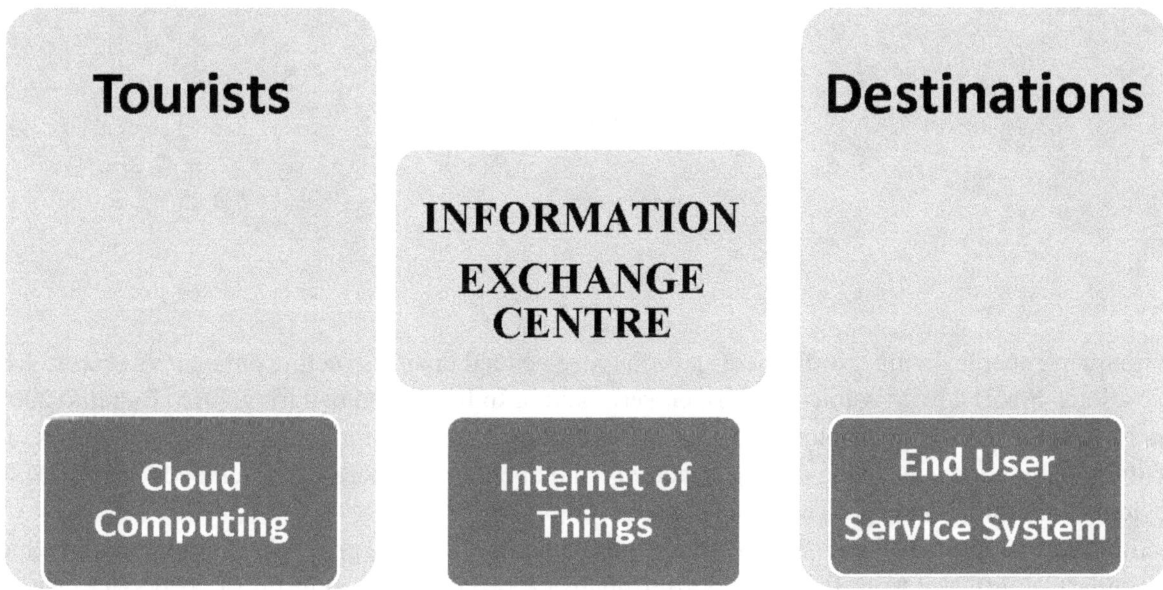

Figure 2 depicts the interface amongst the key components of STDs directly regulated through information exchange centres or central networking system engaged for the same. The information exchange centres usually act as neural network by making use of cloud computing and internet of things in destination management as well as end user service system and applications as desired by tourists.

For fixed cost reduction and information sharing, cloud computing takes an active role in facilitating STDs. "It streamlines the overall delivery of services and resources, helps keeping costs under control and provides for easy access to productive, efficient and competitive web platform for promoting tourism" (Nadda et al, 2020). Internet of Things (IoT) promotes real time connectivity between digital and physical world. It is defined as "network that connects anything in anytime and at any place in order to identify, locate, manage or monitor smart objects" (Mingjun et al, 2012). In the words of Buhalis & Amaranggana (2014), IoT supports "providing information and analysis as well as automation and control while the End-User Internet Service System refers to different applications at numerous levels".

Figure 3 enlists the common elements of smart city and smart tourism destination for facilitating smart tourism experiences to the visitors. The concurred elements of smart city include smart mobility,

Figure 3. Transformation of smart city to smart tourism experience
Source: Buhalis, D., & Amaranggana, A. (2014) pp. 377-389.

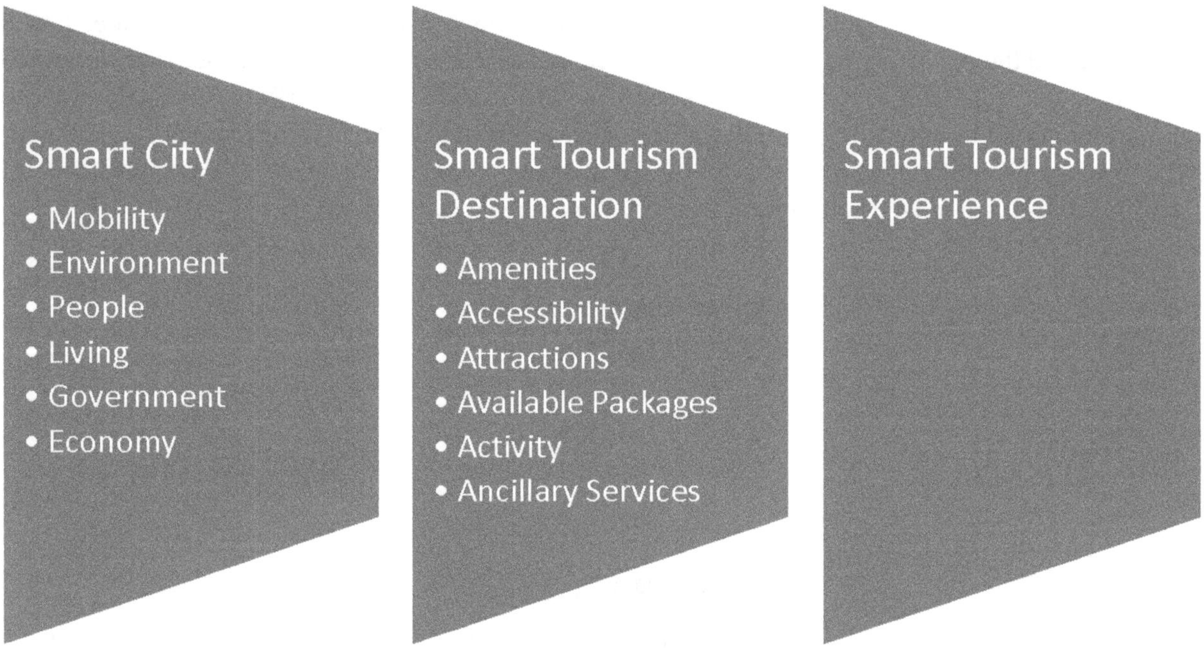

environment, people, living, government and economy, echoed in infrastructure parameters proposed by the National Smart City Mission (NSCM), Government of India drafted in during 2015. Buhalis (2000) widely acclaimed '6 A' principles, as mentioned in figure 3, for smart tourism includes amenities, accessibility, attractions, available packages, activity and ancillary services firmly embedded in STD for providing smart tourism experience to the visitors.

Similarly, Cohen (2012) also unleashed a number of smart tourism principles for application which are similar yet different from Buhalis (2000). Buhalis (2000) termed it in terms of "6 A's" i.e. Attractiveness, Accessibility, Amenities, Available Packages, Activities as well as Ancillary Services. While Cohen (2012) coined it as smart activities of people, mobility, environment as well as smart living. A comparative analysis of both the parameters of smart tourism applications are listed below.

Table 1 establishes a chord between the theories coined by Buhalis (2014) and Cohen (2012) with respect to smart tourism applications in destination level components. It indicates different nomenclature associated with the same tourism applications and similar utility functions as depicted in the table. Robust IT connectivity associated with virtual and augmented reality help promote digital environment in urban cities. Buhalis termed it as attraction whereas Cohen relates it to smart people and smart mobility. Vehicle tracking and monitoring for getting real time information considered essential in today's world and an integral part of planning mechanism of stakeholders'. It obviously deals with accessibility/smart mobility as prescribed by Buhalis and Cohen respectively in destination area. Efficiency in energy consumption and pollution control relates to sustainability aspect of STD fittingly termed as amenities and smart environment by Buhalis and Cohen correspondingly. Tourism applications for available packages, translation of language and guiding functions obviously speaks about smart people and mobility. Access to information 'any time any where' from smart devices linked to web marketing aspect of STD

Table 1. Comparative parameters of tourism applications in smart tourism destinations

Parameters of Tourism Applications	Utility function	Destination components (Buhalis 2000)	Smart tourism destinations (Cohen 2012)
Virtual reality (VR) and Augmented reality (AR) helps to experience digital environment of tourism sites.	Interpretation	Attractions	Smart people, smart mobility
Vehicle tracking and monitoring system for getting real-time information and location of vehicles.	Planning	Accessibility	Smart living, smart mobility
Energy efficient green hotels for reducing consumption of electricity and pollution.	Sustainability	Amenities	Smart environment
Applications for showing available tour packages, translation of languages and providing guidance to the tourists on the visit.	Guiding	Available packages	Smart people, smart mobility
Access to information about nearby attractions to visit, visiting hours through mobile devices.	Marketing	Activities	Smart mobility
Generating direct and quick feedback from tourists through ICTs regarding service quality and required demands.	Generating Feedback	Ancillary Services	Smart living

Source: Buhalis, D., & Amaranggana, A. (2014) Smart tourism destinations. In Z. Xiang & I. Tussyadiah (Eds.), Information and communication technologies in tourism 2014 (pp. 553–564). Dublin:Springer.

Cohen, B. (2012). Smart cities hub., from http://smartcitieshub.com/2012/11/11/smart-cities-ranking-methodology/

epitomises as activities and smart mobility by the Buhalis and Cohen respectively. Generating direct online feedback from tourists' about service quality and requisite demands are integral part of ancillary services facilitates smart living.

BUDGETARY ALLOCATION AND TOURIST INFLUX

Nestled in the Eastern Himalayan Zone, Sikkim a tiny mountainous North Eastern State (NES) blessed with picturesque sites, spectacular terrain, snowy mountains, breath-taking forests with exotic flora and fauna, sacred lakes, pristine glaciers, cascading waterfalls, holy caves, medicinal hot springs, roaring rivers and gentle streams dotted the State. Native population of around 6.19 lakh persons directly endorse tourism as the prime money spinner for the economy in comparison to other economic activities. Its serene environment with hosting attitude of locals made the state an ultimate tourism destination in the North Eastern Region (NER). This tourism oriented state had declared tourism sector as an industry in 2006 and entire economic activity has been centred on tourism.

As the seven out of ten citizens engaged either directly or indirectly in tourism, Government of Sikkim unleashed a series of policy measures to keep the sector vibrant over the years prior to onset of Covid 19. Comparative budgetary support for the state as a percentage of Gross State Domestic Product (GSDP) evinced from the following figure 4 given below:

The tiny hill state, along with Goa, accounts for highest percentage of state budgetary allocation towards tourism during the year 2018-19. This should not be seen in isolation as each and every developmental effort inside the state has been directed at promoting tourism inside the territory. Again, Master plans, Perspective Plans, Plans for Trekking, two tourism policies suggests State's eagerness to view tourism as one of the vibrant sector of the economy; irrespective of the state winning "UN's Oscar for Best

Figure 4. Tourism expenditure percentage of states' budgetary allocation across India during 2018-19
Source: The Economic Times online edition dated 13th Dec, 2019

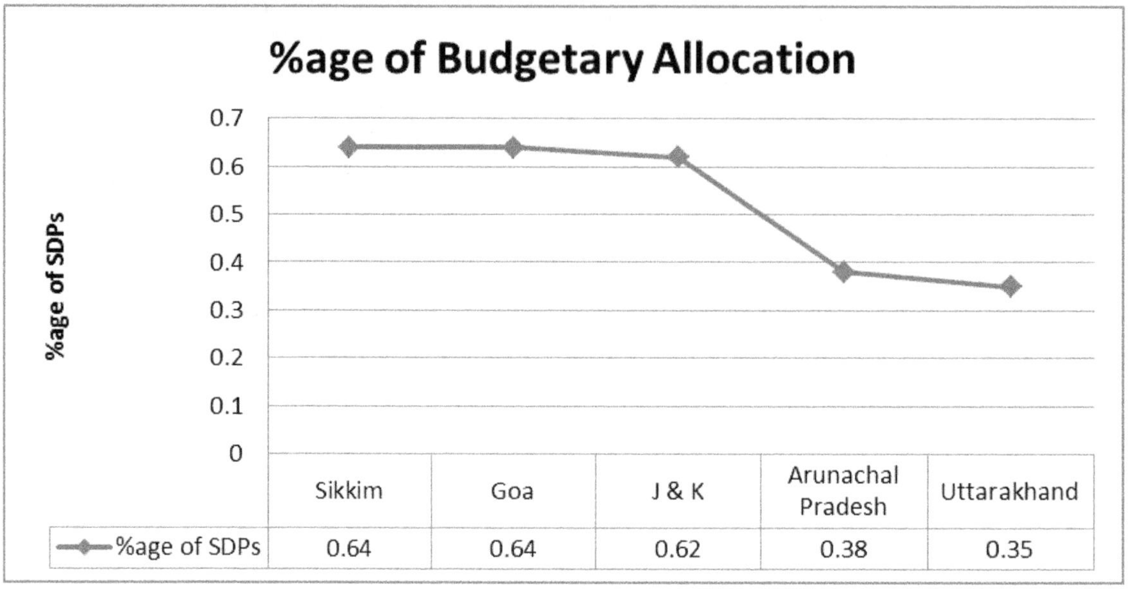

Policies to Become World's First Organic State" in its primary sector by the UN Food and Agriculture Organization (FAO) in recent times.

Table 2. Foreign Tourists Arrivals in North East India during 2010-2017

States/Year	2010	2011	2012	2013	2014	2015	2016	2017
Arunachal Pradesh	3395	4753	5135	10846	5204	5705	6598	7147
Assam	15157	16400	17543	17638	21537	24720	19456	21760
Manipur	389	578	749	1708	2769	3660	3064	3497
Meghalaya	4177	4803	5313	6773	8664	8027	8476	12051
Mizoram	731	658	744	800	921	798	942	1155
Nagaland	1132	2080	2489	3304	2585	2769	3260	4166
Sikkim	20757	23602	26489	31698	49175	38479	66012	49111
Tripura	5212	6046	7840	11853	26688	34866	36780	69894

Source: India Tourism Statistics 2010-17, Ministry of Tourism, Govt. of India

Table 3 depicts foreign tourist arrivals (FTAs) in the eight NESs during the period of 2010-17. It shows the tiny hilly state is experiencing highest FTAs during the period of eight years' with the exception of 2017. On an average, the state draws 38,165 foreign tourist per year was highest amongst the NESs during the period.

In the last decade, tourism sector in Sikkim registered impressive growth rates of 10-12 per cent per annum. The sectors contribution to Gross State Domestic Product for 2016-17 stands at INR. 1,44,735

Lakhs and total contribution pegged at 7.68 per cent which is expected to go up given the influx of tourists in subsequent periods (DoT: 2019). Out of 1,33,388 foreign tourists visiting the state during 2019-20, 60,542 and 56,781 tourists' came from Bangladesh and Nepal respectively during the period. Lifting of restrictions for Bangladeshi citizens to visit Sikkim had worked in favor of the State as scores of citizens from neighboring country travelled to Sikkim during the period. However, domestic tourism remains the mainstay of Sikkim as it accounts for little over 91 per cent of the total visitors travelled to the state during the last decade or so.

Sources from Department of Tourism, Government of Sikkim reveal that the State possesses around 30,000 rooms to generate a lodging business of around INR 6 Crore a day with over 90% accommodation occupancy rate during peak season March-May as well as September-November each year. Amongst the accommodation units, home-stays need a special mention primarily because of involvement of locals and source of providing wholesome tourism experience for the visitors. The state has hundreds of registered tour operators divided to five specified categories ranging from grade A to general. Similarly, there are around 25, 000 registered taxis plying in the destination and also sizeable number of tourist guides and porters catering to the services as per requirements. However, ten months of lock down in two phases virtually crippled the economy literally robbed off INR 600 Crore (PTI:2020) from tourism alone.

STATUS OF STD IN SIKKIM

Being an organic state with increased emphasis on maintaining ecological balance, in-built system of solid waste management, power as well as mobile and transport connectivity via West Bengal makes a strong case for promoting STDs in Sikkim. Tourism orientation distinguishes the state from the other North Eastern States (NESs) of India justifies its selection for the smart city mission. Let us look at the cities undergoing NSCM programmes amongst NESs as of now.

Table 3. Shortlisted cities in NER for smart city mission

Sl No	Name of City Shortlisted	Name of States	Population (Numbers)*
1	Guwahati	Assam	962334
2	Imphal	Manipur	268243
3	Shillong	Meghalaya	354325
4	Aizawl	Mizoram	291000
5	Kohima	Nagaland	107000
6	Namchi	Sikkim	12190
7	Gangtok	Sikkim	100000
8	Pasighat	Arunachal Pradesh	24656
9	Agartala	Tripura	400004

Source: Compiled from Mission document
As per 2011 Census.

Table 3 exhibits a list of nine cities shortlisted for smart city mission during 2015 and project work for the same have been undergoing in full swing in those States'. It can be observed that city population of Guwahati (Assam) was highest while Namchi (Sikkim) having least population from among the North Eastern Cities chosen for the NSCM. Again, Sikkim is the only State in the NER in which two prominent cities, namely Gangtok (East District) and Namchi (South District), chosen for NSCM program.

Table 4. District-wise geographical area and population in Sikkim

Districts	Head Quarters	Population*	Literacy Rate*	Area Sq Km	DOP (sq km)#
East Sikkim	Gangtok	283583	83.85%	954	257
North Sikkim	Mangan	43709	78.01%	4226	10
South Sikkim	Namchi	146850	81.42%	750	175
West Sikkim	Geysing	136435	77.39%	1166	106

*As per Census 2011
Density of Population per square kilo meter
Source: Directorate of Economics, Statistics, Monitoring and Evaluation (DESME), Sikkim.

Table 4 highlights district-wise population, its density, area and literacy rate of Sikkim as per 2011 census. It can be noticed that district-wise density of population (DOP) per square area ranges from 10 sq km (in North District) to 257 sq km (in East District) depending on geographical scenario of the State. Incidentally, East District (head quarter Gangtok) and South District (head quarter Namchi) commands highest density of population and literacy rate in consonance with inhabitable area in comparison to other two districts indicative of increased rate of urbanization in East and North Districts' in particular.

Gangtok, the State Capital of Sikkim located at 27.3325°N 88.6140°E at an elevation of 1,650 m (5,410 ft) from sea level. The town's population of 100,000 as per 2011 census are largest in the State along with different ethnicities such as Bhutia, Lepcha and Indian Gorkhas dotted the area. The Smart City Vision document for Gangtok strives for "promoting an innovative new age economy along with expanding tourism base by offering an enviable quality of life in an ecologically responsible manner" (MUD:2016). The Gangtok Smart City Project was formally launched in June, 2018 with 14 projects to begin with (GoS: 2019a). The Integrated Command and Control (ICC), considered as heart of smart cities, were allotted to Bharat Electronics Ltd (BEL) for the city.

The Gangtok Smart City Development Limited (GSCDL) has been entrusted as special purpose vehicle (SPV) for implementation of Smart City Project (SCP) inside the territory with active cooperation of Gangtok Municipal Corporation (GMC) and Urban Development Housing Department (UDHD), Government of Sikkim. Consultation with GSCDL officials, tour operators, hoteliers as well as taxi operators in the city has given us the following impressions:

- GSCDL seeks to achieve 80 per cent technical efficiency in projects concerning SCM in the city;
- As the city boasts of top ten cleanest city in India (2015) scaled up to top eight cleanest city during 2016, the induction of SCM seeks to carry forward the solid waste management program under the active participation of UDHD; also ensuring proper collection, disposal and treatment of sewage generated;

Figure 5. Map of Gangtok

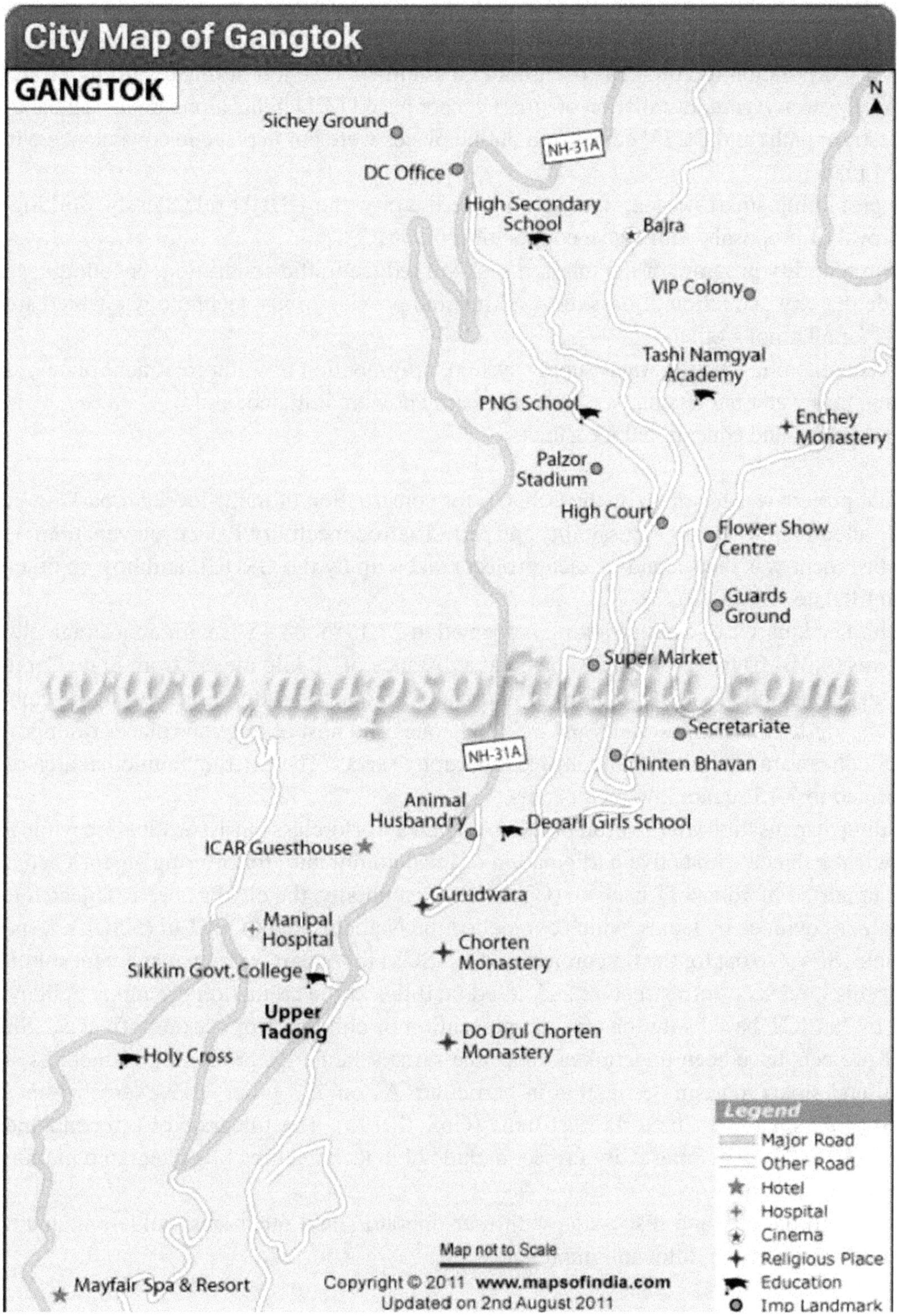

- For improving safety and security measures, 24 X 7 wireless communication centre overseen by State Police Department put in place to look into the matter;
- For energy availability and reduction of outages, Teesta V project of National Hydroelectric Power Corporation (NHPC) has been doing a commendable job in this regard by producing 510 MW of power. Again, installation of smart censor based LED lights along the along the staircases, pedestrian paths and CCTV cameras in public places were put in place in consonance with overall SCM plans;
- For promoting smart housing facilities inside the city, the UDHD relentlessly working for easy approval of proposals with active cooperation of GMC;
- Urban mobility program of the mission seeks to reduce traffic congestion, encourage walkability inside the city, reduction of on-street parking and provide robust technology enabled smart solutions for all among others;
- For smoothening existing water supply system, up-gradation of water treatment plants, smart metering, rain water harvesting, waste water treatment were initiated; and
- Smart health and educational measures.

The first project was taken up by the GSDCL for construction of multi-level car parking-cum-commercial development with easy accessibility and pedestrian connectivity. Palace rejuvenation, retrofitting and refurbishment was the second of such projects taken up by the GSDCL and host of others' which continued till date (GT:2019).

Namchi, headquarter of South Sikkim, is located at 27.17°N 88.35°E with an average elevation of 1,315 metres (4,314 ft) from sea level situated at a distance of 78 kilo meters from State Capital Gangtok. The city house one football stadium of national repute along with numerous sight-seeing points, monasteries, gardens, hills, waterfalls and trekking zones and host of religious places of importance for Hindus (Siddheswara Dham) and Buddhist (Samdruptse) sects. The existing municipal area of Namchi town confined to 7.15 square kilo meters only.

The ruling dispensation wish to promote Namchi into a world-class tourist destination while maintaining ecological balance with active participation of local community for offering an enriched quality of life well supported by robust IT back up (GT:2019). Perennially, the city has been subjected to potable water crises, as evinced by locals, which compelled the Namchi Smart City Ltd (NSCL), a special purpose vehicle (SPV), to opt for the first project under NSCM for 'smart water management solutions'. The second of this kind was 'infrastructure and allied facilities at the cremation ground at Aahley Gumpa' followed by 'an ICT based solutions for the prevention of children from sexual offences'. Since then, a number projects have been undertaken under the same scheme for promoting Namchi as smart city in general and smart tourism destination in particular. As on 25th June, 2019, Namchi was the highest ranked (36th) smart city in North East India (GoS: 2019b). The Integrated Command and Control Centre (ICCC) of Namchi Smart City Project include high tech features like integrated platform, smart governance among others.

Spot visits to the city and discussion with tour operators and other stakeholders including NSCL officials have given us the following impressions:

- For improving the quality of life, facilities like better transport condition in the city, water availability and reduction of water wastages, solid waste management, safety/security conditions and improving the status of housing were given due weightage. Other aspects got due attention were

Figure 6. Map of Namchi

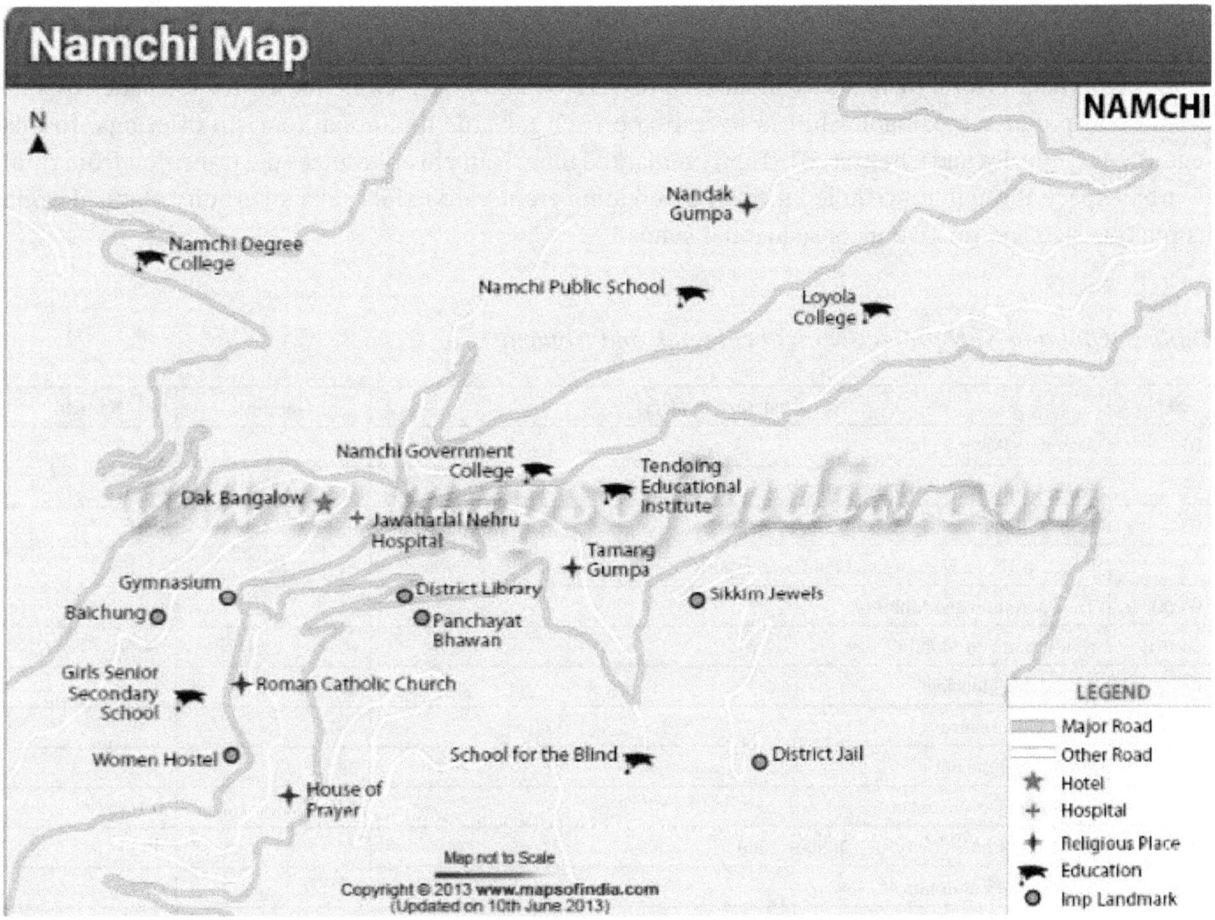

economic regeneration and transformation, effective and efficient governance and service delivery, marketing, branding and promotion, sound and sustainable practices, modularity and mobility, accessibility and ambience, reform and regeneration, transformation and technology among others'.

- For promotion of area based approach, stress on walkability across the city were given due attention in consonance with sustainable lifestyle of the State. Such an approach aimed at connecting activity centers like shopping areas, handicraft marts, tea gardens, organic farms, handicraft workshops, stadiums etc. among others'. Again, an effort like this is also used to control vehicular pollution in the one hand while ensuring energy efficiency on the other. Similarly, empowering citizens through enhanced participation via socially interactive mechanism applicable to both citizens and tourists'.
- Other multi-purpose tasks include assured electricity supply with smart metering, metered water supply, provisions for sanitation and solid waste management, smart roads and community bins, multipurpose tech booths (e-government kiosk), mobile and apps for taxi operators, smart parking, energy efficient street lighting, modern police kiosks etc.; and

- City provides adequate and high quality education facilities within reachable distance in ten minutes.

Development efforts of this sort in an area of 7.15 square kilo meters known for touristic reasons destined to produce a palpable shift in overall approach towards traditional tourism offerings. In this regard, McDulle-Ra and Chettri (2019) aptly remarked that "Namchi epitomizes the transition from rural to urban space through tourism led growth by creating front yard exhibit aka smart city status despite its relative size and relative inconsequential status".

Table 5. Ongoing STD project-work in Gangtok and Namchi

Sl No	Infrastructure Projects	Gangtok	Namchi
01	Adequate Water Supply	02	01
02	Assured Electricity Supply (Energy)	02	03
03	Sanitization including Solid Waste Management	05	05
04	Efficient Urban Mobility and Public Transport:		
04 (a)	Transportation and Mobility	11	01
04 (b)	Non-motorized Mobility	07	04
05	Affordable Housing	01	01
06	Good Governance:		
06 (a)	Area Development	09	06
06 (b)	Economic Development	05	01
07	Robust IT Connectivity and Digitalization	02	02
08	Sustainable Environment	01	01
09	Safety and Security	01	04
	Total	46	29

Source: MHUA (2021) & NSCL (2020)

Table 5 shed light on ongoing STD project work in both Gangtok and Namchi as a part of NSCM. Altogether, 46 and 29 projects Gangtok and Namchi respectively are either in verge of completion or will be completed in near future as divulged by the GSCDL and NSCL in accordance with existing plans and policies. For Gangtok, present thrust is given on transportation and mobility (11 projects) followed by area development (9 projects), non-motorised mobility (7 projects), sanitization and solid waste management and economic development (5 projects apiece), adequate water supply, assured electric supply and robust IT connectivity and digitalization (two projects apiece), and safety and security, sustainable development, affordable housing (one project apiece) in descending order.

For Namchi, NSCL is now overseeing implementation of 29 projects of which area development (6 projects) precedes over others, followed by sanitization and solid waste management (5 projects), safety and security and non-motorised transport (4 projects apiece), assured electric supply (3 projects), robust IT connectivity and digitalisation (two projects) and one apiece in sustainable development, transportation and mobility and adequate water supply.

CONCLUSION

The Smart City Projects in Sikkim is far from completion but the two chosen cities of the State have made steady progress in implementation of this Centrally Sponsored Scheme (CSS) since the launch of the program. Among the two smart cities in Sikkim, Namchi made good strides in implementation of the schemes primarily because of its small size and population along with active role played by implementation authorities over the years'. The project for the city has entered Stage II and the city already ranked 36 amongst top 50 smart cities in India during 2018-19. In new normal situation, smart tracking of tourists through ICCC connected via mobile device can work in favour of the destination in the long run. Again, implementation of adequate water supply would address long standing potable water scarcity of the destination along with stakeholders' participation in decision making process. Similarly, transformation from traditional tourism offerings to STD will present better income earning opportunities for the locals as evinced by taxi and tour operators'.

Walkability, pedestrian pathways, non-motorised mobility inside the extended Namchi city can profitably be implemented due to its small urban areas and associated sustainability considerations. In the non-motorised mobility segment, additional ropeways connecting Samdruptse and Siddheswara Dham, situated 5 kilo meters distance of Namchi market, can provide convenient travelling mode for both locals and tourists'. At present, 2.74 kilo meter long ropeways are operational connecting PWD Rest House to Rock Garden and Rock Garden to Samdruptse, can easily be extended to connect Samdruptse and Siddheswara Dham depending on feasibility study. Again, for promoting the city as smart tourist destination, major construction works have been carried out all across its geographical space raising questions about ecological sustainability of the destination.

Gangtok Smart City Mission, on the other, implemented on relatively bigger scale due to its coverage of geographical space of about 19.2 sq km having population of over 100000 as per 2011 census. Gangtok enjoys better economic space as well, in comparison to Namchi, due to its State capital status and also as a major commercial hub in Sikkim. Due to this, the city attracts a number of tourists as well as vehicles to reach the slated destination inside the city and also as transit route for others. In doing so, vehicular movements are quite pronounced during peak season exerting pressure on land masses. UDHD report (2019) suggests daily plying of high proportion of shared taxis are indicative of substantial public transit demand for work trips inside the Gangtok city. Again, uniform rise in employment across municipal wards of city set to multiply deluge of people in the coming days due to application of Smart City Projects thereby creating insurmountable pressure on the landscape to sustain. Although, promotion of non-motorable mobility along with multi-story smart car parking facility, pedestrian friendly walkways can reduce the quantum of vehicular pollution to some extent especially for non-regular commuters like tourists'; however, transit demand for work trips and to other destinations will remain as usual in week days.

One way to deal with the volume of both human and vehicular traffic is through extension of existing ropeways connecting strategical points inside the city. At present, Gangtok ropeways starting from Deorali en route to Tashiding Secretariat via Sikkim Legislative Assembly covering a distance of 935 meters. Such a service can easily be extended to strategic points depending on positive feasibility report. For redressing regular commuters, stage career buses at specific time frame can be an option to ponder over. Lastly, development of alternate roads is already in place to divert transit traffic from the strategic points inside the city.

Selection of two cities from an ecologically fragile destination could benefit the State in three counts. Firstly, Namchi could draw sizeable tourists who otherwise preferred to conduct Gangtok centred tours as followed by visitors during the last two decades or so. Similarly, cascading impact of being smart city, a portion of economic activity will be shifted to Namchi as well along with adjoining vehicular movement can act as deterrent against deteriorating carrying capacity of the State. The devastation occurred during 2011 earth quakes necessitate adoption of environmentally responsible tourism practices in place of volume growth advocacy as followed by destinations of similar kind (Gossling et al: 2020). The Smart City Mission has reached the second stage in Sikkim and when completed, it will address all the pending issues including fragility and narrow connectivity especially during rainy season.

REFERENCES

Albino, V., Berardi, U., & Dangelico, M. R. (2015). Smart Cities: Definitions, Dimentions and Initiatives. *Journal of Urban Technology*, *22*(1), 3–21. doi:10.1080/10630732.2014.942092

Boes, K., Buhalis, D., & Inversini, A. (2016). Smart Tourism Destinations: Ecosystems for Tourism Destination Competitiveness. *International Journal of Tourism Cities*, *2*(2), 108–124. doi:10.1108/IJTC-12-2015-0032

Buhalis, D. (2000). Marketing the competitive destination of the future. *Tourism Management*, *21*(1), 97–116. doi:10.1016/S0261-5177(99)00095-3

Buhalis, D. (2015). *Working definitions of smartness and smart tourism destination*. Available at: http://buhalis.blogspot.co.uk/2014/12/working-definitions-of-smartness-and.html

Buhalis, D., & Amaranggana, A. (2014). Smart tourism destinations. In Z. Xiang & L. Tussyadiah (Eds.), *Information and Communication Technologies in Tourism 2014* (pp. 553–564). Springer.

Caragliu, A., Del Bo, C., & Nijkamp, P. (2011). Smart cities in Europe. *Journal of Urban Technology*, *18*(2), 65–82. doi:10.1080/10630732.2011.601117

Choudhury, R. R., & Dixit, S. K. (2018). Prospect and Challenges in Smart Tourism in India: Case Study of Smart City Bhubaneswar. *International Journal of Creative Research Thoughts*, *6*(I), 242–248.

Cohen, B. (2012). *What exactly is a Smart City?* Retrieved from: https://www.fastcoexist.com/1680538/what-exactly-is-a-smart-city

Gossling, S., Scott, D., & Hall, C. M. (2020). Pandemics, tourism and global change: A rapid assessment of COVID 19. *Journal of Sustainable Tourism*, *29*(1), 1–21. doi:10.1080/09669582.2020.1758708

Government of Sikkim (GoS). (2019a). *4th Anniversary of Smart City Project*. Retrieved from: https://www.sikkim.gov.in/media/press-release/press-info?name=Video+conference+organised+to+mark+4th+anniversary+of+Smart+City+Project

Government of Sikkim (GoS). (2019b). *Namchi Smart City Mission*. Retrieved from: https://www.sikkim.gov.in/media/press-release/press-info?name=Press+Conference+at+the+office+of+Namchi+Smart+City+Mission

Grant Thornton (GT). (2019). *Smart Cities Mission- A Story of Unique Interventions*. Retrieved from: https://www.grantthornton.in/globalassets/1.-member-firms/india/assets/pdfs/smart_cities_compendium_final.pdf

Gretzel, U., Werthner, H., Koo, C., & Lamsfus, C. (2015). Conceptual Foundations for Understanding Smart Tourism Ecosystems. *Computers in Human Behavior*, *50*, 558–563. doi:10.1016/j.chb.2015.03.043

Gunarekha, B. S., & Binly, T. A. (2018). Digital marketing Transformation for the Smart Tourism Ecosystem: A Study. *Journal of Emerging Technologies and Innovative Research*, *5*(2), 216–222.

Habeeb, N. J., & Weli, S. T. (2020). Relationship of Smart Cities and Smart Tourism: An Overview. *Hightech Innovation Journal*, *1*(4), 194–202. doi:10.28991/HIJ-2020-01-04-07

Hjalager, A.-M. (2010). Progress in Tourism Management: A Review of Innovation Research in Tourism. *Tourism Management*, *31*(1), 1–12. doi:10.1016/j.tourman.2009.08.012

Hollands, R. G. (2008). Will the real smart city please stand up? Intelligent, progressive or entrepreneurial? *City*, *12*(3), 303–320. doi:10.1080/13604810802479126

Hollands, R. G. (2015). Critical Interventions into the Corporate Smart City. *Cambridge Journal of Regions, Economy and Society*, *8*(1), 61–77. doi:10.1093/cjres/rsu011

IBM. (2014). *Smartercities*. Retrieved from: www.ibm.com/smarterplanet/us/en/smarter_cities/overview/?lnk1/4fkt-scit?lnk1/4fkt-smci-uken

IBM. (2015). *A smarter planet*. Retrieved from: www.ibm.com/smarterplanet/uk/en/overview/ideas/indcx.html

Indian Government. (2014). *Smart City Guidelines*. Retrieved on 7 Dec - 2019, http://smartcities.gov.in / writereaddata/SmartCityGuidelines.pdf

Jasrotia, A., & Gangotia, A. (2018). Smart Cities to Smart Tourism Destination: A Review Paper. *Journal of Tourism Intelligence and Smartness*, *1*(1), 47–56.

Jeong, M., & Shin, H. H. (2019). Tourists' Experiences with Smart Tourism Technology at Smart Destinations and Their Behaviour Intentions. *Journal of Travel Research*, *59*(8), Pp1464–Pp1477. doi:10.1177/0047287519883034

Kandpal, V. (2016, April 7). *Challenges In Financing Smart City Projects In India*. Retrieved November 18, 2019, from http://swarajyamag.Com/smart-cities/chall-enges-in-financing-smart-city-projects-in-india

Latour, B. (2005). *Reassessing the Social: An Introduction to Actor-Network Theory*. Oxford University Press.

Liberato, P., Alen, E., & Liberato, D. (2018). Smart Tourism Destinations Triggers Consumers Experiences Case of Porto. *European Journal of Management and Business Economics*, *27*(1), 6–25. doi:10.1108/EJMBE-11-2017-0051

Liberato, P., Alen, E., & Liberato, D. (2018). Smart Tourism Destinations Triggers Consumers Experiences Case of Porto. *European Journal of Management and Business Economics*, *27*(1), 6–25.

Lusch, R. F., & Vargo, S. L. (2014). *Service Dominant Logic: Premises, Perspectives, Possibilities*. Cambridge University Press. doi:10.4324/9781315699035

McDule-Ra, D., & Chettri, M. (2019). Himalayan Boom Boom: Rural urban transition in Namchi, Sikkim. *Development and Change*, *49*(6), Pp1471–Pp1494. doi:10.1111/dech.12450

Meijer, A., & Bolívar, M. P. R. (2015). Governing the Smart City: A Review of the Literature on Smart Urban Governance. *International Review of Administrative Sciences*, *82*(2), 392–408. doi:10.1177/0020852314564308

Mingjun, W., Zhen, Y., Wei, Z., Xishang, D., Xiaofei, Y., & Chenggang, S. (2012). A Research on Experimental System for Internet of Things Major and Application Project. In *System Science, Engineering Design and Manufacturing Informatization*. 10.1109/ICSSEM.2012.6340722

Ministry of Housing and Urban Affairs (MHUA). (2020). *City Ranking 2020*. Retrieved from: https://eol.smartcities.gov.in/dashboard

Ministry of Housing and Urban Affairs (MHUA). (2021). *Smart City: Gangtok*. Retrieved from: https://smartcities.gov.in/node/191

Ministry of Urban Development (MUD). (2016). *India Smart City Mission- Gangtok*. Retrieved from: https://smartcitygangtok.com/images/SCP%20Gangtok.pdf

Nadda, V., Chaudhary, H. S., & Arnott, I. (2020). *Cloud Computing in Tourism*. doi:10.4018/978-1-5225-9783-4.ch007

Namchi Smart City Ltd. (2020). *Project List: Namchi Smart City Ltd*. Retrieved from: https://namchismartcity.co.in/wp-content/uploads/2020/03/Project-List-NSCL.pdf

Pai, C. K., Liu, Y., Kang, S., & Dai, A. (2020). The Role of Perceived Smart Tourism Technology Experience for Tourist Satisfaction, Happiness and Revisit Intentions. *Sustainability*, *12*(16), 6592. doi:10.3390u12166592

Press Trust of India (PTI). (2020). *Sikkim Suffers Rs. 600 Crore Blow as Covid Cripples Tourism Industry*. Retrieved from: https://www.business-standard.com/article/current-affairs/2020-sikkim-suffers-rs-600-crore-blow-as-covid-cripples-tourism-industry-120122700409_1.html

Rudolf, G., Fertner, C., Kramar, H., Kalasek, R., Pichler-Milanovic, N., & Meijers, E. (2007). *Smart Cities-Ranking of European Medium-Sized Cities*. Rapport technique, Vienna Centre of Regional Science. Retrieved from: http://curis.ku.dk/ws/files/37640170/smart_cities_final_report.pdf

Rvo. (2015). *Smart Cities in India*. Retrieved from www.rvo.nl/sites/smart/cities/india: http://www. rvo.nl/ sites/default/files/Smart%20Cities%20India.pdf

Sahoo, S. S., Mukunda, B. G., & Kanungo, D. (2019). Smart City and Tourism: An Analysis of Development of Bhubaneswar as a Smart City. *International Journal of Research and Analytical Review*, *6*(1), 246–256.

Sigala, M. (2020). Tourism and Covid 19: Impacts and Implications for Advancing and Resetting Industry and Research. *Journal of Business Research*, *17*, 312–321. doi:10.1016/j.jbusres.2020.06.015 PMID:32546875

Smart City Governments (SCG). (2021). *Top 50 Smart City Governments: Introduction*. Retrieved from: https://www.smartcitygovt.com/introduction

Tussyadiah, L. P., & Fesenmaier, D. R. (2009). Mediating Tourist Experience Access to Places Via Shared Video. *Annals of Journal Research*, *36*(1), 24–40.

Tuzunkan, D. (2017). The Relationship between Innovation and Tourism: The Case of Smart Tourism. *International Journal of Applied Engineering Research*, *12*(23), 13861–13867.

Urban Development and Housing Department (UDHD). (2019). *Techno-Economic Feasibility Report of Cable Car as Public Transport for Gangtok*. Final Report. Urban Mass Transport Company.

Van, N.T.T., Vrana, V., Duy, N.T., Minh, D.X.H., Dzung, P.T., Mondol, S.R. & Das, S. (2020). The Role of Human-Machine Interactive Devices for Post Covid 19 Innovative Sustainable Tourism in Ho Chi Minh City, Vietnam. *Sustaiability*, *12*(9523), 1-30.

Vargo, S. L., & Lusch, R. F. (2004). Evolving a Dominant Logic for Marketing. *Journal of Marketing*, *68*(1), 1–17. doi:10.1509/jmkg.68.1.1.24036

Vasavada, M., & Padhiyar, Y. J. (2016). Smart Tourism: Growth for Tomorrow. *Journal for Research*, *1*(12), 55–61.

Wang, D., Park, S., & Fesenmaier, D. R. (2010). An examination of information services and smartphone applications. *Proceedings of 16th Annual Graduate Student Research Conference in Hospitality and Tourism.*

Chapter 17
An Explanatory Study of User Satisfaction:
Evidence From Brunei Health Information and Management System (Bru-HIMS)

Fahmi Ibrahim
https://orcid.org/0000-0001-5016-7755
Universiti Teknologi Brunei, Brunei

Nurhidayatul Aqilah Gulihana
Universiti Teknologi Brunei, Brunei

Heru Susanto
Universiti Teknologi Brunei, Brunei

ABSTRACT

In achieving one of Brunei Vision 2035, which is to be among the top 10 in the world for quality of life, Ministry of Health (MOH) Brunei Darussalam has responded by implementing Brunei Healthcare Information and Management System (Bru-HIMS) that is equivalent to international best practices. Bru-HIMS has been implemented for about eight years since it first launched on 11 September 2012 where the outcome to user experience is unknown. Hence, this chapter investigates user satisfaction on Bru-HIMS specifically at RIPAS hospital and studies improvement towards providing quality healthcare in Brunei. DeLone and McLean Information System framework is applied to evaluate Bru-HIMS user satisfaction based on the six variables: information quality, system quality, service quality, intention to use and usage, perceived net benefits, and user satisfaction. Questionnaire survey was conducted to obtain primary data from Bru-HIMS. The findings demonstrate positive relationships between the six variables, which indicates Bru-HIMS has positively influenced Bru-HIMS users.

DOI: 10.4018/978-1-7998-8678-5.ch017

INTRODUCTION

In a circular economy (CE), waste generation is minimized through the careful design of new products and an industrial process in which materials constantly circulate in a "closed-loop system" (Fisher and Pascucci, 2017). Waste has become extremely present across the whole planet, and raw materials are in demand more than ever. Applying the CE concept encourages environmental protection and social prosperity (Jawahir and Bradley, 2016), sustainability of public organizations (Klein et al., 2020) while enabling economic growth in line with sustainable development. A circular economy can reduce environmental devastation in the whole system, as well as increase the generation of new added value. The current linear 'production' method uses energy in all production phases; it is based on the "extract-produce-use-dump" model and represents an unsustainable production model. A circular economy enables an economic system in which raw materials circulate and are transformed from one form into another, resulting in no or minimal waste generation. The idea behind the circular economy concept has been developing as a consequence of realizing the negative environmental impact of the linear production method. Previous research indicated that indicating that the limited research on CE practices and strategies in public organizations which focused so far on the areas of public internal operations, internal operations and processes, and public service delivery. In this book chapter, we determine the application of the CE concept that may apply in the context of effectiveness of Bru-HIMS implementation.

One of Brunei Vision 2035 objective is to be among the top 10 in the world for quality of life (Brunei Vision 2035, 2018). The aim is to provide Bruneians with political stability and high standard of living at the same time ensuring appropriate care and support for member of the society as well as the environment. Realizing the needs to enhance the efficiency and effectiveness of patient care, services, work processes and patient safety, Ministry of Health (MOH) Brunei Darussalam has responded by implementing an e-Health initiative that is equivalent to international best practices called Bru-HIMS (Brunei Darussalam Healthcare Information and Management system). The action made by MOH was also to respond to His Majesty the Sultan and Yang Di-Pertuan of Brunei Darussalam's Titah in 2000 regarding his view on the establishment of e-Brunei that aim to minimise the use of paper and going towards global information technology (Brunei Resources, 2005). This in line with sustainability issue that concerns organizations and policy makers. Information technology has significant importance for managing and containing carbon emissions. According to a study by McKinsey (Boccaletti et al. 2008), IT related production and consumption accounted for only about 2% of overall carbon emissions in 2007. However, the share of IT's footprint is likely to go up to about 3% by 2020, an increase of about 80% from the current levels. Much of this anticipated increase is because of the high growth rate of computing needs in developed world and large scale adoption of PC, mobile phones and proliferation of data centers in developing economies such Brunei. The realization that information technology has significant importance for managing and containing carbon emissions, and therefore is vital for sustainable development, has resulted in a movement to promote deployment of environmentally conscious practices in managing IT under the concept of green information systems (IS) or green IT. Melville (2010) defines green information systems or information system for environmental sustainability as "IS enabled organizational practices and processes that improve environmental and economic performance".

Figure 1 above shows Bru-HIMS implementation plan in Brunei Darussalam. Bru-HIMS supports in managing and storing endless flow of patient's information through an Electronic Patient Record (EPR) System (Ministry of Health Brunei Darussalam, n.d.). Function of the system includes appointment system, outpatient management system, in patient management system, clinical care system, laboratory

Figure 1. Bru-HIMS implementation phase

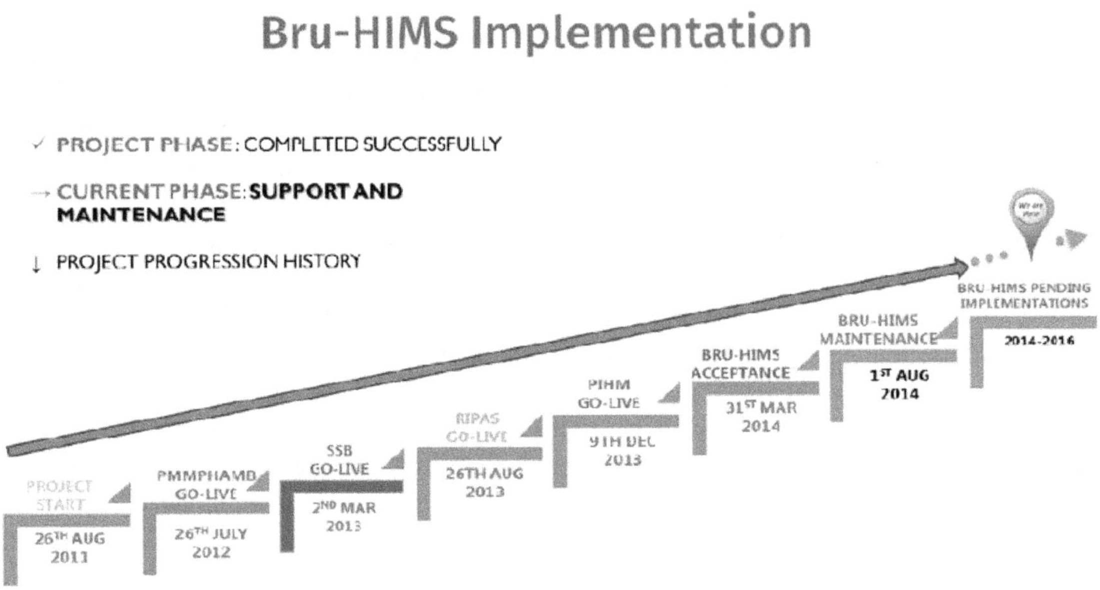

system, pharmaceutical system, radiology system, accident and emergency system, nursing system, operation theater system and asset system. The concept adopts by Bru-HIMS system called 'One Patient One Record'. It replaces the traditional manual system by which patient's record can be retrieved from all government hospitals by an individual's unique BN number. Bru-HIMS aim to enhance in providing best medical care through efficient and effective hospital and healthcare centres management by improving patient-handling process where real-time health patient record can be access by health professionals, reduce patient waiting time, reduce paper work time for nurses and efficiently manage inventory and resources (Ishajaya, 2012).

What remains for Vision 2035 in terms of high quality of life to be realised is the effectiveness of the implementation as well as the continuous improvements and developments. The realisation depends on the support from Bru-HIMS users. Therefore, the main focus of this study in Brunei Darussalam is to investigate satisfaction level of Bru-HIMS users specifically at RIPAS hospital by understanding the impacts of the implementation on user's satisfaction referring to DeLone and McLean's Information system (IS) evaluation framework. With under the backdrop of CE and sustainability of green IS/IT, the practical contribution of the study would help Ministry of Health Brunei Darussalam enhance the quality of care, revise practices and deliver better services with one aim which is to improve healthcare quality in Brunei.

LITERATURE REVIEW

Electronic Health Record (EHR)

Sidek and Martins (2017) claim that storing health information digitally help facilitating healthcare professionals in accessing information electronically by the use of Electronic Health Records (EHR).

According to Bowman (2013), the implementation of EHR will transform the current healthcare system and result in consistent, safer and efficient high-quality care. It is difficult to express the classification and exact meaning of EHR. However, Nguyen, Bellucci and Nguyen (2014) describes that the implementation of EHR can be classified into various type which includes Electronic Patient Record (EPR). One of the widely recognized benefits of EPR is that it grants real-time access to patient data that helps in preventing medical error (O'Malley, Grossman, Cohen, Kemper, & Pham, 2009). When EPR implementation has reached its maturity stage, it will produce positive impact on healthcare quality where some of the functions include knowledge and decision support, clinical activity support, diagnosis and treatment support and specialty specific support (Van den Branden, Wiratunga, Burton, & Craw, 2011).

According to Handayani, Hidayanto and Budi (2017), in ensuring the implementation of EHR flows as plan, management should create IT plans and roadmap and deliver it to users on the benefits that can be achieved so that high quality EHR will be created with the involvement of users in every phase of EHR development. Also, evaluation of the outcome should be periodically conducted to ensure the implementation of EHR run in accordance with the development of the organization, technology and plans. In placing more emphasis, Chen and Hsiao (2012) claims that it is crucial to provide sufficient support from the top management, proper selection of qualified project team member should be made and staff's need should be properly address by delivering high system quality. This claim is supported by similar research done by Nur Izzatty Ismail, Nor Hazana Abdullah and Alina Shamsuddin (2015) in Malaysian Public Hospital that successful adoption of EHR are highly dependent on human skills, experience, information quality and satisfaction.

DeLone and McLean's Information System Evaluation Framework

In comparison from all other theories, DeLone and McLean Information system evaluation framework has been selected to be used in this research as it is the most common evaluation framework and is applicable in Brunei context as Bru-HIMS is not newly implemented in Brunei. According to Ojo (2017), an updated DeLone and McLean's model construct an information system success measures based on six interrelated elements by which quality is the focal point of this model; information quality, system quality and service quality. These elements subsequently affect information system use and user satisfaction. This model also proposes some benefits derived from the implementation of the information system. Pai and Huang (2011) points out that the previous DeLone and McLean information system success model did not measure service quality. However, in the past, many scholars agree on adding dimension of service quality into the original version model as service quality have great impact on information system use and user satisfaction.

Information Quality

Nguyen, Bellucci and Nguyen (2014) identifies some of the important characteristics of improving information quality that includes the ability to deal with issues regarding data overload, data availability, completeness of information, timely and better access, accuracy and up-to-date patient information. Gunningberg, Fogelberg-Dahm and Ehrenberg (2009) point out that there is a positive perception in terms of gathering complete information.

Shortly after EHR being implemented at regional hospital in Denmark, Bossen, Jensen and Udsen (2013) found out that nurses find it easy to find and document information in the EHR. This claim is

Figure 2. Research model - DeLone and McLean's information system evaluation framework

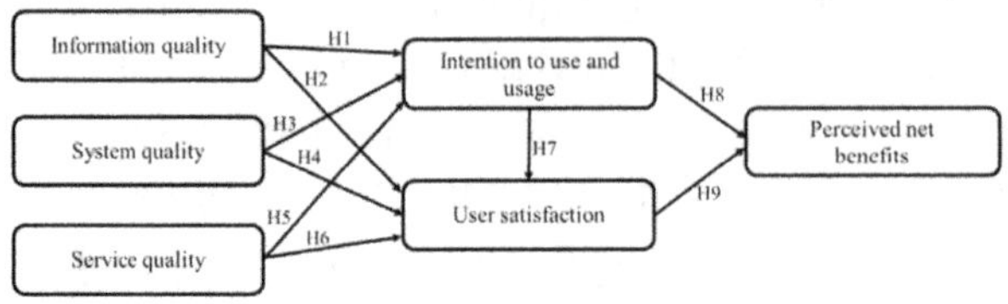

supported by similar research done by Bowman (2013) that the goal of implementing EHR is to reduce medical errors and reports new types of errors to ensure the safety of patient and quality of care. However, physicians claim that they are dissatisfied with the new transcription structuring as diagnoses and prescriptions logically should not be separated for easy reference. Moreover, medical secretaries also agree that new structure model is confusing. Hence, it is important to understand and identify user's acceptance prior to the implementation of EHR.

According to Yarborough and Smith (as cited in Handayani, Hidayanto, & Budi, 2017), some of the significant barriers to staff's technology acceptance are personal characteristics, organizational issues and technology. Therefore, in order to increase user acceptance, better implementation planning of EHR should be conducted by the management (Handayani, Hidayanto, & Budi, 2017). Studies on Malaysian public hospital reveals that there is low satisfaction level amongst medical staffs as sometimes it is hard to document information or make adjustment because the system does not work well (Lizawati Salahuddin, et al., 2018). In terms of accuracy, according to Seymour (2012), complete information usually found in EHR. Silow-Carrol, Edwards and Rodin (2012) supports that detailed patient information can be store and retrieved in the EHR system. However, Chao, Hu and Ung (2013) claims that crucial patient care information could not be retrieved by nurses. This could be due to problem with system interface that lead to system downtime, data loss, delays, errors and poor decisions (Bowman, 2013). In fact, Weiskopf, Hripcsak, Swaminathan, & Weng (2013) claims that different user has different needs that determine the completeness level of information recorded in the system that is relevant to them.

Based on the research by Sidek and Martins (2017) in Brunei dental department, as long as staff logged-in in a clinic, they can access and retrieve full up-to-date patient's information as compared to the traditional method by which patient will be ask about their medical history or new diagnosed illness. However, another study at a regional hospital in Denmark found out that physiotherapists and physicians have different view on how up to date data in the EHR are. Physiotherapists have no problem with updated data as they entered data directly to the EHR. However, physicians relied on medical secretaries to record their transcription. Hence, due to medical secretaries' slow performance, there was a delay in recording physician transcription into the EHR (Bossen, Jensen, & Udsen, 2013).

In terms of data availability, doctors have better access to patient's information with the implementation of EHR (Walji, Taylor, Langabeer, & Valenza, 2009). However, Salahuddin, et al. (2018) claims that information such as blood test, x-rays result and medication cannot be viewed in the EHR during system downtime that disrupt doctor's work. EHR system was found to be excessive with the amount of digital information (Whittaker, Aufdenkamp, & Tinley, 2009). This leads to issues in organizing and retrieving the information in the EHR system (Saleem, et al., 2009). This claim is supported by Bossen, Jensen and Udsen (2013) that reports too much information lead to dissatisfaction with EHR amongst physicians as it led to issues in dealing with data and information retrieval.

System Quality

Looking from clinician's perspective, system quality main focus is on the usability, usefulness and portability of the EHR (Nguyen, Bellucci, & Nguyen, 2014). Mc Quaid, et al (2010) agrees that towards continuous improvement and future development of EHR, usefulness and usability were the most crucial element of EHR implementation. According to Ojo and Popoola (2015), technical factors is the most important factor that lead to the success of Electronic Health Information and Management System which consists of the compatibility of both hardware and software, system implementation are supported by proper infrastructure, user friendly software, sufficient hardware components, system's provider provide sufficient technical support and adequate expertise for the operating the system.

Al-Azmi, Al-Enezi and Chowdhury (2009) supports that it is easy to use and learn the EHR system. According to Hadji and Degoulet (2016), nurses use EHR to plan their schedule and interact with flowcharts. Whereas, EHR are being used by physician to review investigation results. As for medical secretarial, EHR help them to produce patient medical reports that will add on information such as appointment schedule automatically into the EHR. However, Walji, Taylor, Langabeer and Valenza (2009) found out that clinicians suggested improvement in terms of the usability of EHR system. In placing more emphasis on usability, Bowman (2013) points out that lack of user-friendly functionality, system complexity and workflow incompatibility are some of the reason of usability errors. Salahuddin, et al. (2018) supports that in Malaysian public hospital, information such as blood investigation, patient notes, medication and other related information cannot be open concurrently as there is only limited number of windows that can be open at one time. The claim is also supported by an interview-based study by Bossen, Jensen and Udsen (2013) that found out medical secretaries are not satisfied with EHR system that required many mouse clicks. In recent studies of Bru-HIMS in Brunei dental department, Sidek and Martins (2017) has confirmed that Bossen, Jensen and Udsen are indeed true by which some the negative feedback of Bru-HIMS related to the usability of the system are excessive clicking that create extra burden to staffs and is time consuming.

Bossen, Jensen and Udsen (2013) identify that various function of EHR such as patient data, medication information, test results, and notes created by physiotherapist, physicians and nurses are beneficial. In ensuring the usefulness of the information, Bowman (2013) suggest that both system providers and users should develop guidelines to ensure quality, complete and accurate documentation. According to Maya Abdullah Maamuon, Muhammad Haikal Satria, Eko Supriyanto and Jasmy Yunus (2015), improvement in quality of work in terms of saving time, making job easier and fulfilling the user's needs and requirement are some of the outcome expected by users. This claim is supported by Hadji and Degoulet (2016) by which there is a positive correlation between perceived usefulness and work performance. People will decide whether to use the system to the extent where they believe the system will help them in performing their jobs better. The implementation of EHR is to improve health care quality for patient. However, the usefulness of the system for patient was limited as it was not well designed (Hess, et al., 2007). Poor ease of use and limited functionality are the main reason patient did not use EHR system in the United Kingdom (Greenhalgh, Hinder, K., Bratan, & Russell, 2010).

According to Bossen, Jesen and Udsen (2013), staffs finds login response time and EHR response time is satisfactory and seldom crash occurs which indicates the system is stable. However, physicians who makes plan and decision on patient medication sometimes find system performance are poor and cannot tolerate with the unavailability of the system that could affect patient's conditions. These studies are supported by Salahuddin, et al. (2018) that speak patient-care is highly dependent on EHR because patient information is stored in the system and frequently viewed by doctors and other medical staffs. However, due to frequent system crash, majority of the staff claims that the system is not reliable. Moreover, other studies have found out that some of the problems related to EHR are slow response of the system, nurses spent more time in documenting and retrieving patient's information that decrease their time spent with patient and less clinician-patient interaction (Kossman, 2006). In terms of EHR portability, limited attention has been given to support mobile healthcare (Yau, Williams, & Brown, 2011).

Service Quality

According to Ojo (2017), service quality refers to the quality of support delivered by information system department and outsource provider. Research found out that ongoing technical support and staff training are closely related in supporting the use and adoption of EHR system (Nguyen, Bellucci, & Nguyen, 2014). Moreover, Ojo and Popoola (2015) found out that there is a positive correlation between technical factors and the success of Electronic Health Information Management System (EHIMS). These studies have found similar results where availability of infrastructure, functional integration of system components, employee's capability in using the system, compatibility of the system and communication network are some of the technical factors considered towards the success of information system in Malaysia (Hussein, Selamat, & Abdul Karim, 2005). Besides, other factors that affect users' acceptance of EHR implementation are management motivation, involvement of champion, communication and participation of end users in the design of EHR implementation (Handayani, Hidayanto, & Budi, 2017).

Figlietti (2016) agrees that successful adoption and use of EHR system can be done through quality training that improve clinician's proficiency in using the system. In placing more emphasis, Bossen, Jensen and Udsen (2013) claims that staff should be guided with brief training during the introduction implementation period rather than extensive and complicated hands-on training. Effective and adequate training can result in better time management, increase user satisfaction and more accurate records (Boyer, Samuelian, Fieschi, & Lancon, 2010). However, in the case of Brunei, Yusof Sidek and Martins (2017) found out that due to lack of information, lack of training and lack of support results in different staff have different unprescribed steps to use the system. In recent studies, Hertin and Al-Sanjary (2018) reports that lack of computer and basic IT skills and knowledge is a big challenge to the implementation of EHR system. This study is supported by Nguyen, Bellucci and Nguyen (2014) which reminds that lack of efficiency, failure to reach the potential use of EHR and poor utilisation of EHR are the results of ineffective and inadequate training.

As mentioned previously, ongoing technical support is one of the important success factors of EHR. This is supported by Lizawati Salahuddin, et al. (2018) that agrees flow of healthcare process is affected by users with lack of EHR knowledge and experience that will cause errors. Hence, to fully utilize EHR, step-by-step process on how to use EHR should be properly explain to enable appropriate completion of task and avoid risk to patients and delay in patient care. Salahuddin, et al. (2018) also reports that during EHR system is down, medical staffs are not able to transcribe manual notes into the system as there is no relevant policy and procedures to follow. These studies are supported by Larsen, Fong, Wernz, &

Rarwani (2017) that reports downtime procedures in some hospital did not exist and even if it does, it was not properly followed.

Bossen, Jensen and Udsen (2013) states that high responsiveness and extra efforts from the IT departments helps to resolve EHR performance problem. Moreover, in order to enhance user's satisfaction, it is important for IT department to cooperate with the system providers in providing up-to-date information on EHR. However, a study in Brunei dental department found out that system developer neglect suggestion for changes and feedback from the end-users (Yusof Sidek & Martins, 2017). Also, the main source of problem was due to the goal agreed for project were not properly examined and investigated by the stakeholders.

Regarding information system infrastructure services, Hertin and Al-Sanjary (2018) claims that Malaysian Public Hospital experience lack of facilities issues of inadequate computer and laptop to access EHR system. Studies by Salahuddin, et al. (2018) in three Malaysian public hospital also found similar result where task cannot be done on time due to delay in data entry as a result of limited and poor maintenance computers to the extent that they have to share or compete to use available computers.

Intention to Use and Usage

According to Bossen, Jensen and Udsen (2013), staff agrees that EHR supports their work procedures, facilitate the accessibility of information for their work and no new work-related task are required. Moreover, patient's records are available on EHR that makes physicians highly dependent as it eases retrieval of patient daily measurement data such as temperature, blood pressure and pulse. Also, medical secretaries do not have to keep track of records that moves from one department to another that could also take time in locating the records when needed.

However, these claims are contended by Sidek and Martins (2017) based on study in Brunei dental department, who found out that some staffs are reluctance to use Bru-HIMS as they preferred the traditional way of documentation. Similar studies by Hertin and Al-Sanjary (2018) in Malaysian public hospital reports that acceptance level is low mainly amongst staffs who has work longer and wish to maintain the traditional system. Furthermore, staff's lack of trust in the system that force them to write written record in case of system error or failure also affect their intention to use Bru-HIMS (Sidek & Martins, 2017). In addition, studies by Hertin and Al-Sanjary in Malaysian public hospital (2018) reveal that due to limited knowledge about the systems, there is low acceptance level amongst those staffs that have worked for more than 20 years as they still prefer to use the traditional paper base method.

Keller, Kelling, Cornelius, Oni, & Bright (2015) claims that EHR improve communication efficiency and collaboration amongst medical staffs as it improves workflow efficiencies that result in improvements of patient care. According to Sidek and Martins (2017), during the Bru-HIMS adoption period, training in terms of duration and content was insufficient, non-essential aspect of the system was covered in the training, materials given are not in line with the training conducted, poor schedule and inconsistent system session duration as some of the training are done years before the actual system is implemented. Moreover, due to poor public relation management, public complaints and confusion are not sufficiently addressed. Furthermore, EHR implementation was not properly communicated to the end-users and the implementation phase was done too quickly.

Perceived Net Benefits

DeLone and McLean (2016) defines net impact as the result to which organisation achieve success from the degree of contribution to information system. According to Hadji and Degoulet (2016), it is important to ensure EHR system meet the user's need because net benefits are closely related to user's intention to use and satisfaction. Moreover, it is crucial for the users to understand and perceive the benefits of EHR to avoid reluctance in using the system (Handayani, Hidayanto, & Budi, 2017). When users understand the benefits gained from using EHR, their productivity and motivation will increase which lead them in performing their job effectively and increase performance (Hadji & Degoulet, 2016). Nguyen, Bellucci and Nguyen (2014) provide evidence that some outcomes of EHR are changes in workloads, improved in clinical documentation, increase productivity and improve workflow.

In regards to clinical documentation practice and quality, according to Salahuddin, et al. (2018), EHR has replaced paper records but during system downtime, doctors have to rely on memory to enter information into the system as they did not write down notes as backup. According to Hertin and Al-Sanjary (2018), their studies in Malaysian public hospital, discover that EHR reduce paper work time by which it reduces double work, minimize duplication of data and helps medical staffs in archiving information related to patients and administration. However, these claims are opposed by Salahuddin, et al. (2018) that claims due to limited computers, doctors might have to write down update patient-care plan and information on paper and enter the information later. This might result in delay in data entry into the system, delay in medicine ordering and delay in delivery of patient-care. In addition, Steininger, Stiglbauer, Baumgartner and Engleder (2014) reports that additional workload, poor usability of medical record system and loss of privacy as third parties might find access to gain information from the EHR are factors that fear doctors in using EHR.

METHODOLOGY

Experimental research design was used for this study. 115 responds were managed to be collected from the Bru-HIMS users at RIPAS hospital. Primary data was collected through a self-administered questionnaire in both Malay and English. Questionnaire survey is used because one of the most effective way to gather large amount of data. DeLone and McLean's Information system evaluation framework were used as a guide in designing the questionnaire. Mainly, Likert scale type of questions was designed to indicate respondent's degree of agreement. The questionnaire also comprises of open-ended questions to better understand respondent's opinion and suggestions. For descriptive statistical analysis, Microsoft Excel was used to store and processed data that has been collected. In order to improve the validity and reliability, before distributing questionnaires to the respondents, pilot test has been done to get valuable insights, improve research design and resolving potential issues and problems. Moreover, the survey questionnaires target the right respondents which in this study are Bru-HIMS users specifically at the RIPAS hospital.

DISCUSSION OF FINDINGS AND HYPOTHESIS TESTING

The objective of this study was to investigate investigate Bru-HIMS user's satisfaction on Bru-HIMS by using the DeLone and McLean's Information system evaluation framework and to explore area for improvements to enhance the effectiveness of Bru-HIMS. Pearson's correlation statistical analysis was undertaken to test the relationship of the variables and thematic analysis was used to relate the result with problems and recommendation from respondents.

Information Quality

Referring to Figure 3, mean indicates that the most common difficulties experienced by Bru-HIMS users is finding information in Bru-HIMS as mentioned by the respondents where past record is hard to find especially when patient has many appointments at various clinics. Research done by Bowmen mentioned in the literature review stated that information in electronic health record should be easy to find to enable professionals make immediate action and ensure quality of care.

Figure 3. Information quality

Questions	Mean
It is easy to find information in Bru-HIMS	3.10
Information in Bru-HIMS is always up-to-date	3.30
Bru-HIMS generate complete report	3.31
I am satisfied with the accuracy of Bru-HIMS	3.42
Information in Bru-HIMS appears orderly and easy to read	3.53
Bru-HIMS provide sufficient information	3.58
With Bru-HIMS, I am able to access the information I need in time	3.60
Bru-HIMS make it easy to document information	3.70
Bru-HIMS provide me with the information I need for my work	3.77

Moreover, the second lowest mean shows that some respondents claim to experience receiving information in Bru-HIMS that is not up-to-date by which both patient and relatives contact details is wrong due to patient changing phone number. Hence, it is difficult to send SMS appointment reminder as well as for contacting patient relatives during emergency. Bossen, Jensen and Udsen found similar findings where there is delay in updating patient information due to medical secretaries' slow performance in entering data into EHR.

Furthermore, findings indicate majority of the respondents experienced Bru-HIMS generating complete record. However, the mean shows that some of the respondents stating the opposite and point out that patient photo is not in the system. With that being said, anyone can use other people Bru-HIMS provided that person know the person identity card number and date of birth. Also, patient details are not complete for example missing identity card number causing patient having two Bru-HIMS number. To add on, one respondent state that some clinical diagnoses are not included in Bru-HIMS. This finding is supported by Chao, Hu and Ung (2012) in the literature review where crucial patient care information could not be retrieved by nurses. Some of the reason of insufficient information gain from Bru-HIMS stated by the respondents are due to note lost when system lagging, notes are not recorded as per signed off when many tabs are open while typing patient and clinical notes and there is no billing information included in Bru-HIMS.

Next, the mean shows that respondents are satisfied with the accuracy of Bru-HIMS. This statement is supported by Seymour (2012) where accurate information usually found in the EHR. Also, respondents agreed that information in Bru-HIMS appears orderly and easy to read. However, some respondents mentioned that clinical notes are not in order of dates which makes it difficult to review. Bowman (2013) supports the findings stated in the literature review by which physicians are dissatisfied with the transcription structure that makes it not easy for reference.

Most of the respondents also agreed that with Bru-HIMS information are easily documented and mostly needed for their work. Also, they can access information needed in time. Lorenzi, Kouroubali, Detmer, & Bloomrosen, 2009 (2009) report that EHR provide information especially for physician to access patient information in order to provide appropriate patient care. However, some respondents point out that several windows in Bru-HIMS cannot be opened simultaneously and some data cannot be inserted in Bru-HIMS for example dental charts.

System Quality

In terms of interoperability of Bru-HIMS, as shown by the mean in Figure 4, respondents often experience seldom crashes with Bru-HIMS. Kossman (2006) in the literature review supports that frequent system crashes makes staff claim the system as not reliable. Respondents claims that the crashes occur without giving warning and there is no back up data to refer which makes it difficult to retrieve patient's details and history.

Figure 4. System quality

Questions	Mean
Seldom crashes occur with Bru-HIMS	2.73
Bru-HIMS is user friendly	3.08
The response time of Bru-HIMS is acceptable	3.19
It has been easy for me to learn how to use Bru-HIMS	3.25
Bru-HIMS response time for login is satisfactory	3.32
I can get related information while using Bru-HIMS	3.70
Bru-HIMS SMS appointment reminder for patient is very useful	3.90

Second lowest mean indicates that some respondents have difficulties in using Bru-HIMS and action should be taken for users to fully utilise Bru-HIMS. Some of the difficulties of using Bru-HIMS mentioned by the respondents are due to too many password to fill in when opening sub-page, so many unnecessary clicking for most task for example in printing blood result, multiple Bru-HIMS account cannot be open at the same time on one computer, extra steps need to be done to search for patient who

Figure 5. Service quality

Questions	Mean
I received sufficient training on how to use Bru-HIMS	2.83
RIPAS hospital has adequate computer to access Bru-HIMS	2.87
The reported bugs on Bru-HIMS got fixed in acceptable time frame	2.94
I am satisfied with the available user guide	2.97
I am satisfied with the help I received when facing difficulty with Bru-HIMS	3.15
Bru-HIMS downtime is acceptable	3.18
I am satisfied with the support I received in the use of Bru-HIMS	3.20
I received good respond from the technical support team	3.29
When Bru-HIMS system is down, we have policies and procedures to follow	3.29

does not have yellow identity card, some work process cannot be done if multiple windows are opened and wrong data cannot be corrected. Al-Azmi, Al-Enezi and Chowdhury (2009) argued with the findings as they believe that EHR system is easy to use and learn as stated in the literature review. However, there are certain factor that should be taken into consideration stated by Bowman (2013) in the literature review by which some reason of usability error is due to system complexity and workflow incompatibility.

Furthermore, findings point out that improvements need to be made for Bru-HIMS to have a better response time even though most of the respondents agreed that Bru-HIMS response time for login is satisfactory and overall response time is acceptable. Some respondents mention that system lagging occurs most of the time. For instance, lagging issues occurs between pages and clicks, when retrieving data for example surgical operation notes and internet lagging. As a result, user cannot retrieve patient's record that cause delay treatment and increase patient waiting time as well as delay in documenting information. Similar finding stated by Kossman (2006) in the literature review by which slow response of the system is a common problem.

In addition, referring to the findings, majority of the respondents are able to get related information in Bru-HIMS and finds appointment reminder for patient very useful. Although, some respondents disagreed and claims that patient did not receive SMS for appointments and SMS notification can be faulty such that wrong SMS notification (for example wrong date and time) was sent to patient. Because of this, nurses have to contact patients to change the appointment date which creates more task for nurses and time consuming.

Service Quality

As shown in Figure 5, service quality is mainly affected due to lack of training given to Bru-HIMS users on how to use Bru-HIMS. Respondents claim that there are still lots of features in Bru-HIMS never been learn and use. One respondent also said that he or she have not attended any training on how to use Bru-HIMS. A research in Brunei by Sidek and Martin (2017) supports the findings that different staff have different steps on using Bru-HIMS due to lack of training as stated in the literature review.

Figure 6. Intention to use and usage

Questions	Mean
I have sufficient knowledge about Bru-HIMS	2.75
I received adequate training on how to use Bru-HIMS	2.90
The Bru-HIMS implementation plan was adequately communicated to us	3.10
My questions about the use of Bru-HIMS were sufficently answered	3.12
Bru-HIMS improve communication efficiency (e.g. between departments)	3.43
Bru-HIMS improve collaboration (e.g. among doctors)	3.43
Generally, Bru-HIMS supports my work procedures	3.74
I am highly dependent on Bru-HIMS for my task	3.83

In the literature review, Hertin and Al-Sanjary (2018) claims that inadequate computer and laptop to access EHR system cause difficulties and delay in documentation and treatment. Similar to this study, findings show that RIPAS hospital do not have adequate computer to access Bru-HIMS. Moreover, findings indicate that in order to improve user's productivity, reported bugs should be fixed in acceptable time frame. Some respondents point out that reported bugs fixed delayed and lagging issues takes long time to fix that subsequently affect treatment especially during urgent situation. However, most respondents agreed that Bru-HIMS downtime is acceptable.

Furthermore, findings of this research found that most respondents are satisfied with the available user guide and only few respondents were not satisfied. One respondent mentions that they are unsure on how to change practitioner's name when patient was wrongly registered under a different practitioner. Hence, it shows that user guide should be reviewed to update on the common problems experienced by users and provide ways to tackle the problems immediately.

Referring to Figure 5, mean imply that some users still not receive adequate assistance when having difficulty by which they have to make complaints via Bru-HIMS Helpdesk which operators are in Malaysia. This result in slow action taken in resolving the complains compared to when it was handled by Ishajaya (2012) previously where they act instantly on the day of complaint.

Furthermore, finding indicates that users have a proper policies and procedure when experiencing system down. This finding is in contrast with research done by Salahuddin et al. (2018) stated in the literature review where medical staff claim that there is no relevant policy and procedure to follow when problem occurs with the EHR. Hence, findings of this research indicate that action has been taken to maintain the usability of Bru-HIMS in providing quality patient care. Besides, findings also state that support received are satisfying as technical support team are doing great in responding to user's difficulties.

Intention to Use and Usage

Findings illustrated in Figure 6 shows that user's intention to use Bru-HIMS is affected due to having insufficient knowledge about the system. Hertin and Al-Sanjary (2018) states similar findings in the literature review which result in low acceptance level and preference issues where user prefer the traditional paper-based method. This is because the functionality of Bru-HIMS is quite extensive but user only

Figure 7. Perceived net benefits

Questions	Mean
Bru-HIMS reduce medication error	3.17
Bru-HIMS improve interactions with patient	3.35
Bru-HIMS is more secure than paper records	3.49
I enjoyed the practices after the implementation of Bru-HIMS	3.53
Bru-HIMS improves my productivity	3.61
Bru-HIMS make the hospital service better	3.64
Bru-HIMS reduce paper work time	3.67
Generally, Bru-HIMS has made my work easier	3.69
Bru-HIMS has positive impact on quality of my task	3.69

aware of the general functions mainly for recording patient's data. Hence, it affects user's willingness to use the system as they feel traditional method is more beneficial and convenient.

Abdul Azim Kassim (2015) reports that in filing electronic record, training on coding is given to more than 100 healthcare professionals in order to make it easier for healthcare professionals to store, retrieve data and facilitate in analysing comparison of data. However, findings found out that due to lack of training to some user's or lack of assessment on how to use Bru-HIMS during the adoption period cause some users have insufficient knowledge about Bru-HIMS and negatively affect their intention to use and usage. Research done by Sidek and Martins (2017) in Brunei context also mentioned similar findings stated the literature review.

As mentioned in the literature review, research done by Sidek and Martin (2017) found out that EHR implementation was not properly communicated to the end-users as implementation phase was done too quickly. However, findings of this study found out that Bru-HIMS implementation plan was adequately communicated to the users and user inquiries about the use of Bru-HIMS were sufficiently answered. This indicates that there is an improvement done by Ministry of Health (MOH) in communicating the implementation plan to the end-users and respond to their inquiries to ensure Bru-HIMS implementation achieve the aim and objectives.

In addition, findings point out that Bru-HIMS improve communication efficiency (e.g. between department) and collaboration (e.g. among doctors). Keller, Kelling, Cornelius, Oni and Bright (2015) agree that EHR improve both communication efficiency and collaboration directing to improvement in workflow efficiencies and patient care. Apart from that, findings show that Bru-HIMS support user work procedure which makes them highly dependent on Bru-HIMS in doing their task. However, some respondents mentioned few difficulties experienced with Bru-HIMS that affect their intention to use and usage. Two common problem mentioned is difficulty in printing laboratory such as blood result and histology result and sometimes delay was encountered between sites for same patient due to data replication issues.

Perceived Net Benefits

Figure 7 present positive result of Bru-HIMS implementation. Based on the finding, it implies that Bru-HIMS does reduce medication error. ONC (The Office of the National Coordinator for Health Information Technology) (2012) supports that with EHR, clinicians are being provided with best practice guidance and specific patient medication information which guide the process of decision making. Moreover, finding indicates most respondents agreed that Bru-HIMS improve interaction with patients and is more secure than paper record. Street, et al. (2014) supports that with EHR, clinicians can maintain the flow of conversation with patient in ensuring effective communication.

Furthermore, the findings show that respondents enjoyed the practices after the implementation of Bru-HIMS that led to improvement in user's productivity. Moreover, Bru-HIMS make the hospital service better, reduce paper work time, made work easier for users and overall has positive impact on quality of task. These findings are supported by Hertin and Al-Sanjary (2018) stated in the literature review that EHR reduce double work, minimise duplication of data and patient information is more accessible that make work easier.

User Satisfaction

Clearly, finding indicates that Bru-HIMS users are satisfied with the implementation of Bru-HIMS. This shows that Bru-HIMS implementation has given a positive impact to quality of work as well as in achieving Brunei Wawasan 2035 which is to be among the top ten in the world for quality of life.

In answering to the forth research question of this study, some of the suggestions mentioned by Bru-HIMS users to enhance the effectiveness of Bru-HIMS in terms of improving information quality are to delete duplicated file in order to avoid confusion, implement Bru-HIMS offline that plays an important role during system crashes where all offline patient data will automatically updated in the system when the network has been fixed, user have the ability to amendments the wrong information documented in the system and to update all information in Bru-HMS especially past records.

Under system quality, the respondents suggest to make Bru-HIMS more user friendly by reducing umber of clicks for each service to save time and minimise human error for example in registering and admitting patient, the link should be directed on assigning the bed for the patient. Hence, user can just do it by a single click. Moreover, Bru-HIMS should be user friendly in terms of making it simpler to use, make information more understandable for easy reference, minimise password entered, less unnecessary window and remove unused icon in the system.

Under usefulness of Bru-HIMS, respondents suggested to improve SMS system by providing features for SMS appointment cancellation and change appointment as well as making it possible for patients to do appointment online booking or changing appointment via online. In improving the response time of Bru-HIMS, it is important to anticipate future Bru-HIMS problems and increase speed of Bru-HIMS services. Moreover, in order to reduce system crashes, there should be a backup system as an alternative when server down or system breakdown.

Furthermore, respondents also give suggestion on improving service quality. First, respondents suggested Bru-HIMS to have a systematic approach to management of the system and information should be communicated and shared with the end users. By doing so, user guide should be implemented and continuously revised whenever feedback or common complaints are received from Bru-HIMS users. Apart from that, respondents also suggest that end user should have an ongoing training either yearly or every two years to update on Bru-HIMS. Also, all nurses must attend Bru-HIMS monthly training for security and updates. Pursuing this further, there are also respondents suggesting that ongoing training should be given to users on regular term for better usage as there are lots of features in Bru-HIMS that are not being used due to lack of training. Important to consider, training for new staff should be given especially for doctors which not only limited to crash course.

In terms of technical support, respondents suggested to make it easier for staff to request for access on Bru-HIMS at certain wards within their scope of work according to their department or unit. Another suggestion to improve service quality in terms of the support received in the use of Bru-HIMS, Bru-HIMS technicians should have frequent meetings with the end users to get feedback in order to improve and tackled issues and problems brought up from all section immediately. When facing difficulties with Bru-HIMS, respondents proposed a focal person to be assigned on call or on shift to make them more accessible, faster response in resolving the issues when needed and avoid issues on Bru-HIMS users deciding which issue is whose responsibility as well as waiting for another party to solve the problem. Also, a focal person needs to be assigned every month to go around all the wards just to make sure that all computers including barcode printer are working. Moreover, a helpline should be developed that can directly understand all features in specific modules without the end users spending much time in explaining the details especially when there are issues during system down and lagging. Additionally, the respondents also request to increase number of computers to access Bru-HIMS.

In increasing Bru-HIMS users intention to use and usage, Bru-HIMS should support end users work procedure by making it easier to print blood result, having search button and filter option for looking at keywords in clinical note to help expedite finding the correct info or documents, dental software should be included, have separate window dedicated for quick viewing and access of x-ray result, having a direct link to view clinical radiological image online and straight forward process in requesting laboratory request, have panel of laboratory investigation to ease clinician by just tick on the test that wish to be done, allow creation of individual patient list, implement smart card for login, notes should be auto-save similar like Microsoft Word to avoid notes lost when system crash, allocate specific icon which direct to patients past medical history and doctor's notes and increase ability to tend dataset with graph for a more extended duration.

In addition to increasing Bru-HMS user's intention to use and usage, respondents suggested for Bru-HIMS to have panel on the from page that highlight updated patient allergies and all forms of risk, add button for drug information as feature present in Bru-HIM around 2014 and easier to require research data. Moreover, frequent technical updates for doctors should be made for those who are not fully acquaintance with the system, allow utility of tagging or labeling patients as 'infection precaution required' or whether patient have contagious disease to facilitate pre-eruptive appropriate placement (isolation ward) and alerting extra care during blood dressing or taking blood sample. Also, the system should always update patient contact information to improve SMS appointment reminder. Pharmacist suggests that duplication of prescription should not be allowed and active patient prescription should be cancelled before prescribing new ones for pharmacy to immediately supply patient's medicines and to prevent misuse of medication.

Importantly, to improve communication efficiency, respondents suggested that updated patient information from different departments should be centralized and automatically recorded in nurse notes to enable nurses brainstorm on what should be done to the patient in term of nursing care process. Next, thorough handover between parties should be made because not all end user has knowledge on specific modules especially the EIS.

Table 1. Inter-correlations among information quality, system quality, service quality, intention to use and usage, user satisfaction and perceived net benefits

	Variables	Mean	1	2	3	4	5	6
1	Information Quality	3.48	-					
2	System Quality	3.31	0.35	-				
3	Service Quality	3.08	0.29	0.47	-			
4	Intention to Use and Usage	3.29	0.29	0.20	0.22	-		
5	User Satisfaction	4.69	**0.59**	0.44	0.41	0.37	-	
6	Perceived Net Benefits	3.54	0.34	0.26	0.29	0.29	0.37	-

In general, Bru-HIMS has helped improve the quality of clinical documentation practices, workflows and productivity. However, there are some factors often overlooked. Hence, respondents suggest that confidentiality on patient's chart in Bru-HIMS should be strongly maintain and improved. Moreover, doctor medication request should not be auto print to avoid misuse. Next, by having a more user-friendly system, it will help to reduce error. Further, attention need to be giving in revising and considering access request to facilities on few responsibilities for nurses. For Bru-HIMS to have positive impact on user's quality of task, end users must be active in solving the issues and are well aware of the module they are in charge of. Also, in order to make the hospital service better, respondents suggested that Bru-HIMS should increase patient information confidentiality, information technology security and accessibility should be improved and doctors need to have typing skills in order to properly utilise the system.

Table 2. Hypotheses result

Hypothesis	p-value	Result
H1: Information quality will positively affect intention to use and usage	0.29	Very weak positive correlation
H2: Information quality will positively affect user satisfaction	0.59	Moderate positive correlation
H3: System quality will positively affect intention to use and usage	0.20	Very weak positive correlation
H4: System quality will positively affect user satisfaction	0.44	Weak positive correlation
H5: Service quality will positively affect intention to use and usage	0.22	Very weak positive correlation
H6: Service quality will positively affect user satisfaction	0.41	Weak positive correlation
H7: Intention to use and usage will positively affect user satisfaction	0.37	Weak positive correlation
H8: Intention to use and usage will positively affect perceived net benefit	0.29	Very weak positive correlation
H9: User satisfaction will positively affect perceived net benefits	0.37	Weak positive correlation

Research Hypotheses

As illustrated in Table 1, there are positive correlation among all the variables summarised in Table 2 below. Findings for both qualitative and quantitative confirm and support the hypothesis.

Variables vs. Intention to Use and Usage

H1: Information quality will positively affect intention to use and usage
H3: System quality will positively affect intention to use and usage
H5: Service quality will positively affect intention to use and usage

According to Table 2, information quality, system quality and service quality has a very weak positive correlation with intention to use and usage. This significantly confirms that the three variables positively affect Bru-HIMS users' intention to use and usage. The correlation between system quality and intention to use and usage is the weakest among the three variables. This is supported by the lowest mean of the question under system quality indicating frequent crashes occur with Bru-HIMS. Ten respondents mention that frequent system crashes are one of the difficulties encountered with Bru-HIMS. Apart from that, twenty-five Bru-HIMS user's complaint that Bru-HIMS response time is not acceptable because system lagging occurs most of the time. As for service quality, due to insufficient training, Bru-HIMS users are not familiar on how to use Bru-HIMS and respondents also claim that information is hard to find in Bru-HIMS and suggesting for filter and search button to be included in Bru-HIMS. For these reasons, this might cause Bru-HIMS users to have less intention to use Bru-HIMS hence result in the weak positive correlation.

Variables vs. User Satisfaction

H2: Information quality will positively affect user satisfaction
H4: System quality will positively affect user satisfaction
H6: Service quality will positively affect user satisfaction
H7: Intention to use and usage will positively affect user satisfaction

From all the hypotheses, only information quality and user satisfaction have a moderate positive correlation. This is because all questions under information quality have mean more than 3 indicating that most of the respondents agreed to the statements. For example, most of the respondents agreed that Bru-HIMS provide information needed for their work, Bru-HIMS makes it easy to document information, Bru-HIMS makes information is accessible in time, Bru-HIMS makes sufficient information and information appears orderly and easy to read. With this in mind, it clearly shows that information quality has positive influence over satisfaction. In relation to user satisfaction, system quality, service quality and intention to use and usage have a weak positive correlation. For example, under intention to use and usage, due to most respondents are not receiving adequate training on how to use Bru-HIMS during the adopting period, this reduce their intention to use the system and subsequently reduce satisfaction level. Moreover, under service quality, most of the respondents claims that RIPAS does not have adequate computer to access Bru-HIMS. This affect user's satisfaction in using the system as limited computer cause delay in doing task. Furthermore, an example for system quality, most respondents disagreed that Bru-HIMS is user friendly mainly due to so many unnecessary clicks. Hence, this affect Bru-HIMS user's satisfaction.

Variables vs. Perceived Net Benefit

H8: Intention to use and usage will positively affect perceived net benefit
H9: User satisfaction will positively affect perceived net benefits

Referring to Table 2, finding illustrates that intention to use and usage and perceived net benefits has a very weak positive correlation. An example to relate intention to use and usage and perceived net benefit is since Bru-HIMS users have less intention to use the system because they are only aware of the general functions of Bru-HIMS which mainly for recording patient's data. Hence, Bru-HIMS has less positive impact on quality of task because functionality of Bru-HIMS actually is quite extensive. Therefore, this proves that intention to use and usage has a very weak positive correlation with perceived net benefits because users did not fully utilize the system. Meanwhile user satisfaction and perceived net benefits has a weak positive correlation due to some respondents are not satisfied with the implementation of Bru-HIMS. For example, respondents are dissatisfied with the information quality due to data replication issue that cause confusion and error that is not supporting user's work and procedure. Therefore, this result in user satisfaction having weak positive correlation with perceived net benefits.

CONCLUSION

Based on the findings, statistical analysis confirms that information quality, system quality and service quality positively influence intention to use and usage. However, the correlation among the three variables are very weak. Moreover, findings indicate that user system quality, service quality and intention to use and usage have a weak positive correlation with user satisfaction. Only information quality has a moderate positive correlation indicating that information quality has achieved the average user's satisfaction level. Furthermore, this study shows that Bru-HIMS users have less intention to use the system which affect the benefits that should be gained from using Bru-HIMS. Also, due to some users that are not satisfied with the implementation, this also affect the perceived net benefit. Against the backdrop of CE and Green IT/S, which have the potential to be substantial, by using IS - Bru-HIMS to support initiatives EHR . This is because while improving the information quality, system quality, service quality and intention to use of Bru-HIMS that perhaps lead to high degree user satisfaction, it will be reducing their negative environmental impacts related to energy consumption and waste associated with the use of hardware and software, tends to have a direct and positive impact.

REFERENCES

Al-Azmi, S. F., Al-Enezi, N., & Chowdhury, R. I. (2009). Users' attitudes to an electronic medical record system and its correlates: a multivariate analysis. *The HIM Journal*. Retrieved November 5, 2018 from https://www.researchgate.net/profile/Rafiqul_Chowdhury3/publication/26311041_Users%27_attitudes_to_an_electronic_medical_record_system_and_its_correlates_A_multivariate_analysis/links/00b49527af853611f3000000/Users-attitudes-to-an-electronic-medical-recor

Boccaletti, G., Loffler, M., & Oppenheim, J. M. (2008). How IT Can Cut Carbon Emissions. *The McKinsey Quarterly*, (October), 1–5.

Bossen, C., Jensen, L. G., & Udsen, F. W. (2013). Evaluation of a comprehensive EHR based on the DeLone and McLean model for IS success: Approach, results, and success factors. *International Journal of Medical Informatics*, *82*(10), 940–953. doi:10.1016/j.ijmedinf.2013.05.010 PMID:23827768

Bowman, S. (2013). *Impact of Electronic Health Record Systems on Information Integrity: Quality and Safety Implications*. Perspectives in Health Information Management. Retrieved February 13, 2019, from https://www.ncbi.nlm.nih.gov/pmc/articles/PMC3797550/pdf/phim0010-0001c.pdf

Boyer, L., Samuelian, J. C., Fieschi, M., & Lancon, C. (2010). Implementing electronic medical records in a psychiatric hospital: A qualitative study. *International Journal of Psychiatry in Clinical Practice*, *14*(3), 223–227. doi:10.3109/13651501003717243 PMID:24917324

Brunei Vision 2035. (2018). Retrieved October 17, 2018 from Embassy of Brunei Darussalam to the United States of America: https://www.gov.bn/SitePages/Wawasan%20Brunei%202035.aspx

Chao, W. C., Hu, H., & Ung, C. O. (2013). Benefits and Challenges of Electronic Health Record System on Stakeholders: A Qualitative Study of Outpatient Physicians. *Journal of Medical Systems*. Retrieved November 5, 2018 from https://www.researchgate.net/profile/Hao_Hu11/publication/249321144_Benefits_and_Challenges_of_Electronic_Health_Record_System_on_Stakeholders_A_Qualitative_Study_of_Outpatient_Physicians/links/00b4952dc8dd7b02ee000000/Benefits-and-Challenges-of-Electroni

Chen, R., & Hsiao, J. (2012). An investigation on physicians' acceptance of hospital information system: A case study. *International Journal of Medical Informatics*, *81*(12), 810–820. doi:10.1016/j.ijmedinf.2012.05.003 PMID:22652011

DeLone, W. H., & McLean, E. R. (2016). *Foundations and Trends in Information System*. Retrieved February 10, 2019 from https://www.nowpublishers.com/article/DownloadSummary/ISY-005

Figlietti, C. D. (2016). *Developing an Electronic Health Record Training Program for New Employees*. Retrieved November 5, 2018 from Doctor of Nursing Practice (DNP) Projects: https://repository.usfca.edu/cgi/viewcontent.cgi?article=1105&context=dnp

Fischer, A., & Pascucci, S. (2017). Institutional incentives in circular economy transition: The case of material use in the Dutch textile industry. *Journal of Cleaner Production*, *155*, 17–32. doi:10.1016/j.jclepro.2016.12.038

Greenhalgh, T., Hinder, S. K. S., Bratan, T., & Russell, J. (2010). Adoption, non-adoption, and abandonment of a personal electronic health record: case study of HealthSpace. *BMJ*. Retrieved November 5, 2018 from http://sci-hub.tw/https://doi.org/10.1136/bmj.c5814

Gunningberg, L., Fogelberg-Dahm, M., & Ehrenberg, A. (2009). Improved quality and comprehensiveness in nursing documentation documentation of pressure ulcers after implementing an electronic health record in hospital care. *Journal of Clinical Nursing*, *18*(11), 1557–1564. doi:10.1111/j.1365-2702.2008.02647.x PMID:19220607

Hadji, B., & Degoulet, P. (2016). Information system end-user satisfaction and continuance intention: A unified modeling approach. *Journal of Biomedical Informatics*, *61*, 185–193. doi:10.1016/j.jbi.2016.03.021 PMID:27033175

Handayani, P. W., Hidayanto, A. N., & Budi, I. (2017). User acceptance factors of hospital information systems and related technologies: Systematic review. *Informatics for Health & Social Care*. Retrieved February 6, 2019, from sci-hub.tw/10.1080/17538157.2017.1353999 PMID:28829650

Hertin, R. D., & Al-Sanjary, O. (2018). Performance of Hospital Information System in Malaysian Public Hospital: A Review. *IACSIT International Journal of Engineering and Technology*, *7*(4), 24–28. doi:10.14419/ijet.v7i4.11.20682

Hess, R., Bryce, C. L., Paone, S., Fischer, G., McTigue, K. M., Olshansky, E., & Siminerio, L. (2007). Exploring Challenges and Potentials of Personal Health Records in Diabetes Self-Management: Implementation and Initial Assessment. *Telemedicine Journal and e-Health*, *13*(5), 509–517. doi:10.1089/tmj.2006.0089 PMID:17999613

Hussein, R., Selamat, H., & Abdul Karim, N. S. (2005). The impact of technological factors on information systems success in the electronic government context. *The Second International Conference on Innovations in Information Technology*, 6-7. Retrieved February 6, 2019 from https://pdfs.semanticscholar.org/3051/fe1d66792683073bc0f6eafe63e4a95de48f.pdf

Ishajaya. (2012). *Bru-HIMS will bring better efficiency to Brunei Healthcare*. Retrieved June 23, 2019, from http://www.ishajaya.com/index.php?option=com_content&view=article&id=70:06-june-2012-bru-hims-will-bring-better-efficiency-to-brunei-healthcare&catid=8&Itemid=115

Ismail, N. I., Abdullah, N. H., & Shamsuddin, A. (2015). Adoption of Hospital Information System (HIS) in Malaysian Public Hospitals. *Procedia: Social and Behavioral Sciences*, *172*, 336–343. doi:10.1016/j.sbspro.2015.01.373

Jawahir, I. S., & Bradley, R. (2016). Technological Elements of Circular Economy and the Principles of 6R-Based Closed-Loop Material Flow in Sustainable Manufacturing. *Procedia CIRP*, *40*, 103–108. doi:10.1016/j.procir.2016.01.067

Kassim. (2015). *MoH staff trained to file health data*. Retrieved Jun 4, 2019, from The BT Archive: https://btarchive.org/news/national/2015/08/08/moh-staff-trained-file-health-data

Keller, M. E., Kelling, S. E., Cornelius, D. C., Oni, H. A., & Bright, D. R. (2015). *Enhancing Practice Efficiency and Patient Care by Sharing*. Perspective in Health Information Management. Retrieved February 20, 2019 from https://www.ncbi.nlm.nih.gov/pmc/articles/PMC4632871/

Kossman, S. P. (2006). Perceptions of Impact of Electronic Health Records on Nurses' Work. *Consumer-Centered Computer-Supported Care for Healthy People*, 337-341. Retrieved November 5, 2018 from https://ebooks.iospress.nl/publication/9218

Larsen, E., Fong, A., Wernz, C., & Rarwani, R. (2017). Implications of Electronic Health Record Downtime: An Analysis of Patient Safety Event Reports. *Journal of the American Medical Informatics Association: JAMIA*, 1–5. Retrieved February 20, 2019, from https://www.researchgate.net/publication/317335260_Implications_of_electronic_health_record_downtime_An_analysis_of_patient_safety_event_reports PMID:28575417

Lorenzi, N. M., Kouroubali, A., Detmer, D. E., & Bloomrosen, M. (2009). How to successfully select and implement electronic health records (EHR) in small ambulatory practice settings. *BMC Medical Informatics and Decision Making*, *9*(15), 1–13. doi:10.1186/1472-6947-9-15 PMID:19236705

Maamuon, M. A., Satria, M. H., Supriyanto, E., & Yunus, J. (2015). *Exploring Factors Influencing 'Perceived Usefulness' and Its Relationship on Hospital Information System End User Satisfaction.* Retrieved February 14, 2019 from https://pdfs.semanticscholar.org/196f/57f014c06b2bd1db61bfcd37aaee4c9a128a.pdf

Mc Quaid, L., Breen, P., Grimson, J., Normand, C., Dunne, M., Delanty, N., & Fitzsimons, M. (2010). Socio-technical considerations in epilepsy electronic patient record implementation. *International Journal of Medical Informatics*, *79*(5), 349–360. doi:10.1016/j.ijmedinf.2010.01.013 PMID:20181511

Melville, N. (2010). Information Systems Innovation for Environmental Sustainability. *Management Information Systems Quarterly*, *34*(1), 1–21. doi:10.2307/20721412

Ministry of Health Brunei Darussalam. (n.d.). *Introduction Bru-HIMS*. Retrieved October 30, 2018 from http://www.moh.gov.bn/SitePages/Bru-HIMS%20Introduction.aspx

Nguyen, L., Bellucci, E., & Nguyen, L. T. (2014). Electronic health records implementation: An evaluation of information system impact and contingency factors. *International Journal of Medical Informatics*, *83*(11), 779–796. doi:10.1016/j.ijmedinf.2014.06.011 PMID:25085286

O'Malley, A. S., Grossman, J. M., Cohen, G. R., Kemper, N. M., & Pham, H. H. (2009). Are Electronic Medical Records Helpful for Care Coordination? Experiences of Physician Practices. *Journal of General Internal Medicine*, *25*(3), 177–185. doi:10.100711606-009-1195-2 PMID:20033621

Ojo, A. I. (2017). Validation of the DeLone and McLean Information System Success Model. *Health Informatics Research, 23*(1), 60-66. Retrieved November 5, 2018 from https://www.ncbi.nlm.nih.gov/pmc/articles/PMC5334133/pdf/hir-23-60.pdf

Ojo, A. I., & Popoola, S. O. (2015). Some Correlates of Electronic Health Information Management System Success in Nigerian Teaching Hospitals. *Biomedical Informatics Insights*, *7*, 1–9. doi:10.4137/BII.S20229 PMID:25983557

ONC (The Office of the National Coordinator for Health Information Technology). (2012). *Health Information Technology Patient Safety Action & Surveillance Plan for Public Comment.* Retrieved June 4, 2019, from https://www.healthit.gov/sites/default/files/safetyplanhhspubliccomment.pdf

Pai, F. Y., & Huang, K. I. (2011). Applying the Technology Acceptance Model to the introduction of healthcare information systems. *Technological Forecasting and Social Change*, *78*(4), 650–660. doi:10.1016/j.techfore.2010.11.007

Resources, B. (2005). *The Thrusts and Strategies of the Brunei Darussalam's E-Government Programme*. Retrieved June 23, 2019, from http://www.bruneiresources.com/speeches/pehinhazair_strategiesegovernment.html

Salahuddin, L., Ismail, Z., Hashim, U. R., Ikram, R., & Ismail, N. H., & Naim, M. H. (2018). Sociotechnical factors influencing unsafe use of hospital information systems: A qualitative study in Malaysian government hospitals. *Health Informatics Journal*. Retrieved February 8, 2019, from sci-hub.tw/10.1177/1460458218759698 PMID:29521162

Saleem, J. J., Russ, A. L., Justice, C. F., Hagg, H., Ebright, P. R., Woodbridge, P. A., & Doebbeling, B. N. (2009). Exploring the persistence of paper with the electronic health record. *International Journal of Medical Informatics*, *78*(9), 618–628. doi:10.1016/j.ijmedinf.2009.04.001 PMID:19464231

Seymour, T. J., Frantsvog, D., & Graeber, T. (2012). Electronic Health Records (EHR). *American Journal of Health Sciences*, *3*(3), 201–210. doi:10.19030/ajhs.v3i3.7139

Sidek, Y. H., & Martins, J. T. (2017). Perceived critical success factors of electronic health record system implementation in a dental clinic context: An organisational management perspective. *International Journal of Medical Informatics*, *107*, 88–100. doi:10.1016/j.ijmedinf.2017.08.007 PMID:29029696

Silow-Carrol, S., Edwards, J. N., & Rodin, D. (2012). *Using Electronic Health Records to Improve Quality and Efficiency: The Experience of Leading Hospitals.* Retrieved November 5, 2018 from The Commonwealth Fund: https://pdfs.semanticscholar.org/0e75/8272eab4ba74933ed4fdf860362f2365f3d3.pdf

Steininger, K., Stiglbauer, B., Baumgartner, B., & Engleder, B. (2014). Factors Explaining Physicians' Acceptance of Electronic Health Records. In *47th Hawaii International Conference on System Science* (pp. 2768-2777). Retrieved February 10, 2019 from https://ieeexplore.ieee.org/stamp/stamp.jsp?tp=&arnumber=6758948

Street, R. Jr, Liu, L., Farber, N. J., Chen, Y., Calvitti, A., Zuest, D., Gabuzda, M. T., Bell, K., Gray, B., Rick, S., Ashfaq, S., & Agha, Z. (2014). Provider interaction with the electronic health record: The effects on patient-centered communication in medical encounters. *Patient Education and Counseling*, *96*(3), 315–319. doi:10.1016/j.pec.2014.05.004 PMID:24882086

Van den Branden, M., Wiratunga, N., Burton, D., & Craw, S. (2011). Integrating case-based reasoning with an electronic patient record system. *Artificial Intelligence in Medicine*, *51*(2), 117–123. doi:10.1016/j.artmed.2010.12.004 PMID:21232927

Walji, M. F., Taylor, D., Langabeer, J. R. II, & Valenza, J. A. (2009). Factors Influencing Implementation and Outcomes of a Dental Electronic Patient Record System. *Journal of Dental Education*, *73*(5), 589–600. doi:10.1002/j.0022-0337.2009.73.5.tb04734.x PMID:19433534

Weiskopf, N., Hripcsak, G., Swaminathan, S., & Weng, C. (2013). Defining and measuring completeness of electronic health records for secondary use. *Journal of Biomedical Informatics*, *46*(5), 830–836. doi:10.1016/j.jbi.2013.06.010 PMID:23820016

Whittaker, A. A., Aufdenkamp, M., & Tinley, S. (2009). Barriers and Facilitators to Electronic Documentation in a Rural Hospital. *Journal of Nursing Scholarship, 41*(3), 293-300. Retrieved November 5 5, 2018 from http://sci-hub.tw/https://doi.org/10.1111/j.1547-5069.2009.01278.x

Yau, G. L., Williams, A. S., & Brown, J. B. (2011). Family physicians' perspectives on personal health records: Qualitative study. *Canadian Family Physician Medecin de Famille Canadien*, *57*(5). Retrieved November 5, 2018, from https://www.ncbi.nlm.nih.gov/pmc/articles/PMC3093606/pdf/0570e178.pdf PMID:21642732

Chapter 18
Employee Motivation for Training and Development: A Study of a Pharmaceutical Company in Sikkim

Sangita Saha
https://orcid.org/0000-0002-4676-5370
Sikkim Manipal Institute of Technology, Sikkim Manipal University, India

Saibal Kumar Saha
https://orcid.org/0000-0002-7842-698X
Sikkim Manipal Institute of Technology, Sikkim Manipal University, India

Jaya Rani Pandey
Sikkim Manipal Institute of Technology, Sikkim Manipal University, India

Ajeya Jha
https://orcid.org/0000-0003-0491-5008
Sikkim Manipal Institute of Technology, Sikkim Manipal University, India

ABSTRACT

Training and development is an important function of human resource management. Employees need to regularly undergo training and development programmes to update themselves with the latest technologies and skills, which help to increase the efficiency of the organization. Motivating employees to undergo a training programme is often a challenge faced by employees. This study aims to find the motivating factors for employees to undertake a training and development programme. With a sample size of 172 employees from a leading pharmaceutical company in Sikkim, India, responses were collected and analysed. It was found that interest for updating oneself with the latest technology, better chance of career exploration, commitment to train from the company's end, and encouragement provided from subordinates play significant roles in motivating employees in undertaking a training and development programmes.

DOI: 10.4018/978-1-7998-8678-5.ch018

INTRODUCTION

With the speed by which innovation and disruption are happening in the business processes and technologies, it is essential for organizations to upskill their employees and be ready for meeting the challenges of the dynamic business requirements. To attain high performances in an organization, an effective training and development system is indispensable (Hossain, 2014). A study conducted with HR professionals revealed that 92.6% of the HRs believe organizations need to focus on knowledge management practices and should regularly conduct training and development programmes for their employees (Maity, 2019). Various factors have been attributed to workers for their productivity. Studies reveal that motivation (Kazaz et al., 2008) is the most important factor that influences worker productivity. Others being self-confidence (Marín & Roelofs, 2017), attitude (Tam & Fung, 2012), and problem-solving skills (Małachowski & Korytkowski, 2016). According to Olanipekun (2018), motivation is the competency that drives the workers to accomplish their goals. Several studies across the world have highlighted the importance of training and development in organizations and its positive correlation with productivity (Al Amin Khan et al., 2021; Al Karim, 2019; Johari & Jha, 2020; Karam, 2019). In India too, with industrialization and introduction of service sectors, the need for training and development for upskilling its employees has become a dire necessity (. & Rani, 2019; Bhattacharyya & Nair, 2019; Gronseth et al., 2019; Gupta et al., 2021; Kulkarni et al., 2019; Punjani, 2019; S. et al., 2020; Sekhon & Kathuria, 2019).

Nestled in the lap of the Himalayas, Sikkim is a small state in India. The state is in its infancy stage in terms of industrial culture. The prevalent culture of private jobs differs from the rest of India. Because of hard living conditions and the rough Himalayan terrain, facilities of transport, communication, access to industries and jobs are poor (Sharma et al., 2020). There is a lack of literature regarding training and development activities and efforts of human resource management towards improving the performance of organizations in Sikkim. Hence, this study tries to throw some light on the motivational factors towards training programmes in the state of Sikkim. The study is based on a survey conducted in a pharmaceutical company in Sikkim.

LITERATURE REVIEW

Training and development are recurring HR activities of an organization and are required to aid the employees to adapt to new technologies, environments and enable them to enhance their decision making and problem-solving skills. Motivation is the encouragement needed for an employee to work efficiently in an organization. Employees are required to be motivated for their self-development and for increasing the organizational productivity (Al Karim, 2019). Organizations frequently conduct training sessions for their employees and try to have a competitive edge over their competitors (Schuler & MacMillan, 1984). Training may have a direct or indirect effect on organizational commitment and employee motivation (Meyer & Allen, 1991). It also helps in employee retention and reduction in turnover rates (Abba, 2018). For keeping pace with technology, companies regularly engage in training their employees to enhance their skills and optimize the potential of their workforce (Delery & Doty, 1996).

Companies recruit employees from various backgrounds. It is important to map the right motivation strategy with the right employee, which may encourage the employee to undertake a training programme. Some employees are motivated by monetary factors, while others may find better career opportunities to be attractive. Others may be motivated by encouragement from supervisors or peers (Bibi et al., 2018). There are many factors which may be used by HRs to motivate their employees for training.

Motivation is a study concerning "why people behave in a certain way". Mitchell (1982) defined motivation as 'the degree to which an individual wants and engages in certain specified behaviours'. Mitchell (1982) identified four characteristics of motivation:

1. it is an individual phenomenon in which every individual is considered being exclusive
2. motivational theories persist in demonstrating the uniqueness of individuals in some form
3. it is intentional in which it is assumed that workers' control motivation, which affects the behaviour of individuals
4. it is multi-layered

There are three attributes of motivation: "intrinsic", "extrinsic" and "amotivation". Motivation to accomplish a job because it is enjoyable, interesting, pleasurable is called "intrinsic" motivation (Ryan & Deci, 2000; Wen Lim et al., 2018). The motivation that drives a person to perform a task that helps to earn awards or praise or evade retribution is called "extrinsic" motivation (Waugh, 2002). The state of absence of any motivation to perform any task is called "amotivation" (Gagné et al., 2015). Motivation for work and rewards that workers derive from work are the foundations of the relationship between an organization and its members. A manager needs to know how to get cooperation from their staff to achieve the set goals and objectives of an organisation (Rodriguez & Walters, 2017). Motivation based purely on reward and punishment is difficult to sustain over time (Ben-Hur & Kinley, 2016). Most of the organizations pay insufficient attention to the potential power of intrinsic motivators.

Motivation research hails from history, which considers employee's needs (Van Iddekinge et al., 2018). Farren (2000) identified twelve human needs: well-being, work/career, family, health and social relationships, spirituality, community, leisure, economic, learning, home/shelter, mobility, and environment/safety. Extrinsic motivation is interrelated to 'tangible' rewards like security, promotion, contract of service, salary and fringe benefits, the work environment and conditions of work (Turner, 2017). Intrinsic motivation is related to 'psychological' rewards like carrier growth opportunity, achievement and challenges, positive recognition, receiving appreciation, and being treated in a caring and attentive way (DeVaro et al., 2017). Psychological rewards are characterised by the actions and behaviour of individual managers. Kets de Vries (2001) recommends that there are many motivational needs, like physiological needs, enjoyment and sensual needs, and attachment/affiliation needs.

F. W. Taylor believed in the economic needs of motivation and is motivated by high wages. For such employees, Weaver (1988) recommended a 'Theory M' programme of motivation, which was based on direct cash rewards for high average performance. Many employees are progressively motivated by broader concerns such as their life/work balance, flexible working opportunity, personal development and growth and career advancement and a sense of identification with the values of the organisation (Buil et al., 2019). The changes in work environment and concepts of 'psychological contract' are helping to influence the motivational factors related to work (Balven et al., 2018).

METHODOLOGY

To accomplish the objective of the study, a questionnaire was developed using a five-point Likert scale. The face validity of the questionnaire was checked by showing the questionnaire to five experts. The reliability of the questionnaire was checked using Cronbach's alpha. Since the direction of some variables: "Task hindrance", "Salary", "Promotion", "Work requirement", "Productivity" and "Not important" (as shown in table 1) were negative, the responses were reverse coded for ensuring data sanctity for calculating Cronbach's alpha. The value of Cronbach's alpha got was 0.703. A sample size of 172 was used through the quota sampling method to get the responses from each department of a major pharmaceutical company in Sikkim, India. The size of the population was 447 at the time of the study. Permission to conduct the survey was taken from the HR head of the company. The self-developed questionnaire comprised two sections: Section 1 contained questions related to the demographic characteristics of the respondents and section 2 comprised 20 questions to measure the motivational factors for training and development of the employees. The survey was conducted by a face-to-face interview with the participants. The researcher visited different departments of the pharmaceutical company in Sikkim: HR, Finance, Production, Packing, and Quality Control. The data got through the survey were coded and analysed using SPSS version 26 and MS Excel 2016.

RESULTS AND DISCUSSION

Sample Characteristics

The survey comprised 29% female and 71% male respondents. 69% of them were married while the rest 31% were unmarried. 21% of the respondents had education up to masters' level, 36% bachelor, 5% diploma, and 38% up to school level.

Employees not only act in line with the economic motives but are also guided by many needs (Ozkeser, 2019). Table 1 gives a brief description of the variables that were identified and used for the research. Each variable has also been associated with a need, based on Maslow's need hierarchy theory.

Percentage Analysis

Table 2 gives the percentage of response that was got for each of the variables. On analysing the responses, it is found that 84% of the employees agreed that the training provided by their company was good. 87% also agreed that training programmes were important. 78% felt that training helped them to get incentives. Most of the employees, i.e. 94%, felt that training was important to get insights for career exploration. 84% considered training important for their career planning and that their organization showed commitment to conduct training for their employees regularly. The same percentage of employees also feel that their subordinates supported them to undertake training programmes. Support received from colleagues was reported to be 93%. Only 30% of the respondents believed that their day-to-day tasks did not allow them to go for training. 85% reported that their supervisors encouraged them for training while 80% confirmed receiving support from top management. 76% reported that they received support from family members as well. Only 55% reported that attending the training was because of peer influence and increment in salary. Only 18% opined that if they do not do the training, they may not get promoted.

Table 1. Description of variables

Sl. No.	Statements	Variable	Need
1	I want to do training because the training provided by my company is very good.	Good	Security
2	In order to keep myself up to date with the latest technologies training is important.	Technology	Security
3	Trainings help me to get incentives.	Incentive	Recognition
4	Trainings are important to get insights for career exploration.	Exploration	Self-actualization
5	Training is important for career planning.	Planning	Self-actualization
6	My organization is committed to train its employees regularly.	Commitment	Social
7	Whenever I go for training, my subordinates support me.	Subordinate support	Social
8	My colleagues support and encourage me to undergo training.	Subordinates encouragement	Social
9	My day-to-day task does not allow me to go for training.	Task hindrance	security
10	My supervisor encouraged me to go for training.	Supervisor encouragement	Social
11	I got support from top management to go for training.	Management support	Social
12	My family members support me to go for training.	Family support	Social
13	I want to go for training because my colleagues are also doing the training.	Colleagues	Social
14	If I do not do the training, my salary will not increase.	Salary	Security
15	If I do not do the training, my promotion will not happen.	Promotion	Recognition
16	If I do not do the training, I will not be able to do my work properly.	Work requirement	Self-actualization
17	Going for training means loss of work and productivity.	Productivity	Self-actualization
18	Going for training means fun and opportunity to learn new thing.	Learn	Self-actualization
19	Going for training means time out from my work.	Time out	Social
20	Training is not important.	Not important	Recognition

50% of the employees showed concern that training is important for doing their work properly. Only 12% agreed with the statement that spending time for training meant loss of work and productivity. 71% of the respondents believed that training was fun, a means for learning new things and a time out from their daily work. Only 22% of the respondents felt that training was not important.

Task Hindrance

From figure 1, it is seen that 30% of the respondents felt that their day-to-day tasks did not allow them to go for training. However, only 49% disagreed with the statement. The statement was disagreed by a majority of the female (25%) respondents. The responses of males were nearly equal (28% agreed and 23% disagreed).

Table 2. Motivation for training responses

Sl. No.	Variables	SD (%)	D (%)	NAND (%)	A (%)	SA (%)
1	Good	0	6	10	48	36
2	Technology	0	0	3	57	40
3	Incentive	1	5	16	48	30
4	Exploration	0	0	6	57	37
5	Planning	0	3	13	33	51
6	Commitment	0	2	7	55	36
7	Subordinate support	0	0	16	63	21
8	Subordinates encouragement	0	2	5	58	35
9	Task hindrance	26	23	21	23	7
10	Supervisor encouragement	2	2	10	58	27
11	Management support	0	5	15	60	20
12	Family support	1	3	19	60	16
13	Colleagues	8	17	19	31	24
14	Salary	8	17	19	31	24
15	Promotion	21	43	19	12	6
16	Work requirement	7	26	17	35	15
17	Productivity	33	37	19	6	6
18	Learn	12	13	5	41	30
19	Time out	12	13	5	41	30
20	Not important	34	34	10	17	5

SD=Strongly Disagree, D=Disagree, NAND=Neither Agree Nor Disagree, A=Agree, SA=Strongly Agree

Figure 1. Day to day task does not allow

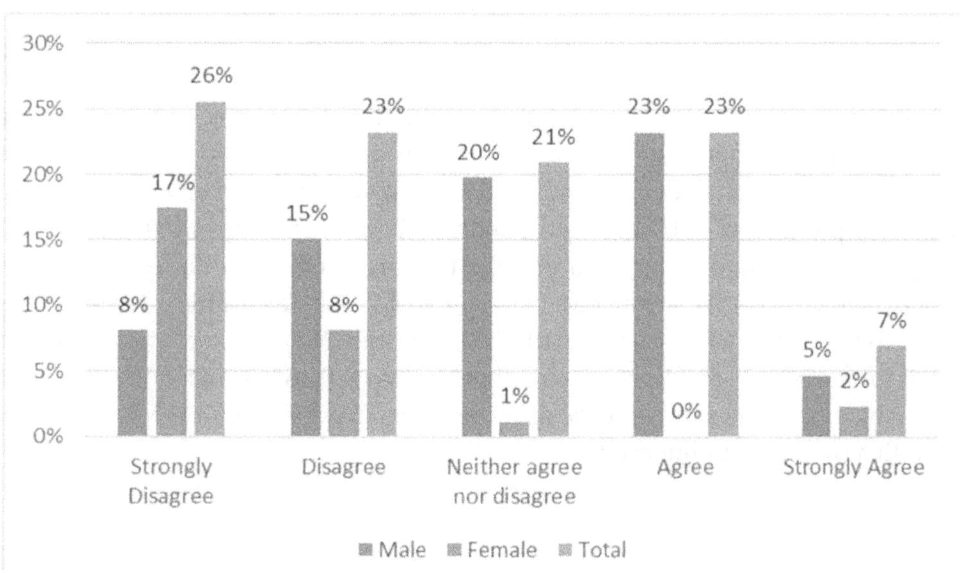

Colleagues

From figure 2, it is observed that following peers for doing a training programme act as motivation among 55% of the respondents. However, only 25% disagreed with the statement. The study of Basford and Offerman (2012) also suggests that co-workers exert a substantial impact on their fellow employees and work environment. Employee motivation is important for successfully running a business. This area is often overlooked by employers. The connection between external and internal environments a significant impact on workplace motivation. Employers should also consider the significance of worker satisfaction and happiness.

Figure 2. Training by colleagues

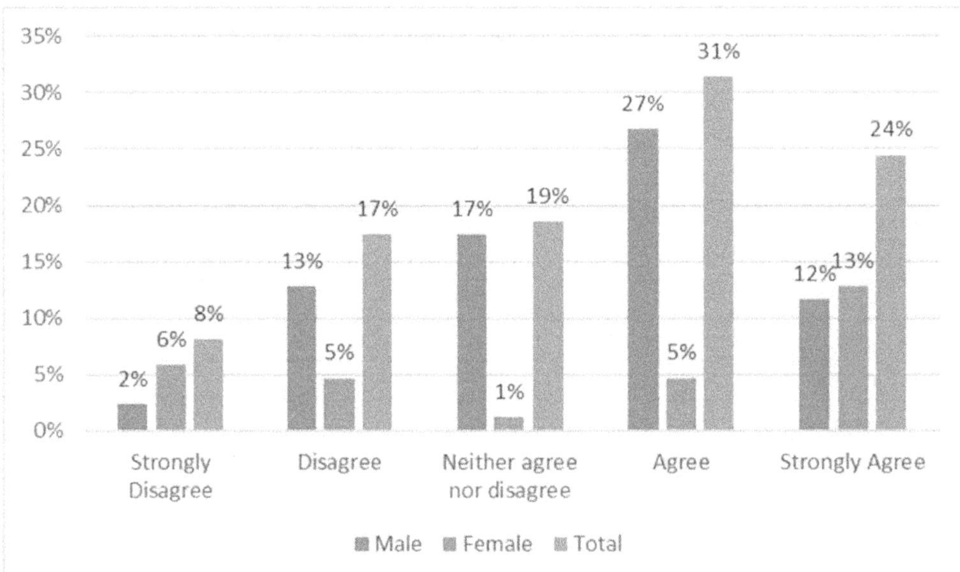

Salary

From figure 3, salary is an important component in the employer-employee relationship. It is interesting to note that 18% of the respondents felt that training has a direct and proportional relationship with salary. However, 64% of the respondents do not consider any relationship between training and salary.

For the variable "promotion" 50% of the respondents felt that training is important for promotion. 12% of the respondents felt that if they don't do the training, they could not do their work properly. However, 70% disagreed with the statement. 71% felt that going for training would cause a loss of work and productivity. Only 25% disagreed with the statement. 71% of the respondents felt that training is a platform for having fun and learning new things. Only 22% of the respondents felt that training programmes provided time out of work. 68% of respondents disagreed with the statement. 88% of the respondents felt that training was important.

Figure 3. Salary will not increase

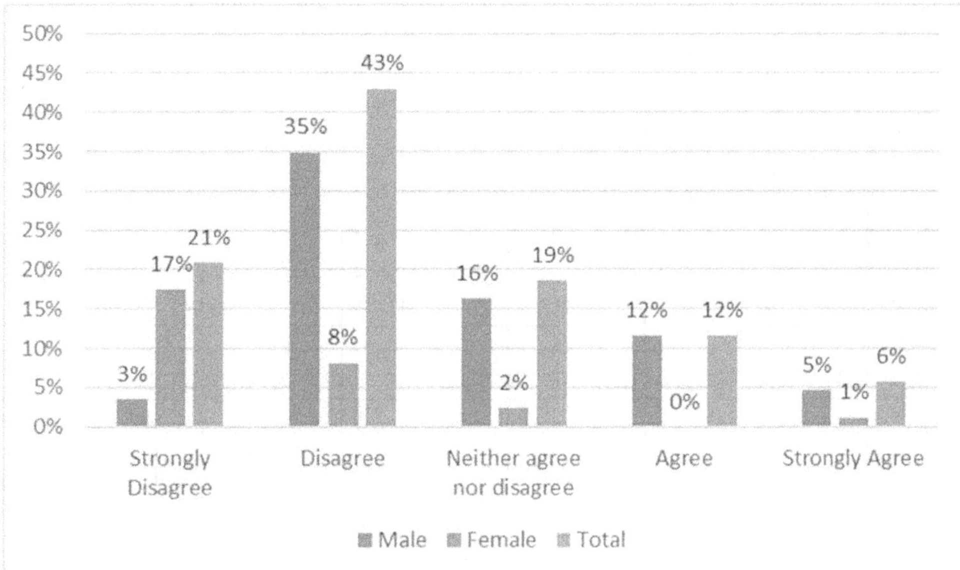

Correlation Analysis

Summary of the correlation table 3 is:

- Training provided by the company is good has a positive moderate correlation with the perception that training is important for career planning (0.47), company's commitment to training its employees regularly (0.52), support (0.46) and encouragement of subordinates (0.41), support from top management (0.50) and support from family members (0.44).
- Training helps to get incentives has a positive moderate correlation with the perception that training is important for career planning (0.45).
- Training is important to get insights for career exploration has a positive moderate correlation with the perception that training is important for career planning (0.45).
- Training is important for career planning has a positive moderate correlation with the company's commitment to training its employees regularly (0.41) and support from family members (0.57).
- The company's commitment to training its employees regularly has a positive moderate correlation with encouragement from subordinates (0.51), support from top management (0.44) and support from family members (0.44). However, it has a negative moderate correlation with the perception that training is not important (-0.41).
- Support of subordinates has a positive moderate correlation with encouragement from subordinates (0.51) and support from top management (0.60).
- The perception that day-to-day task does not allow one to undertake training programme has a positive moderate correlation with the perception that if one does not do the training their salary will not increase (0.53), their promotion will get halted (0.40), their productivity will decrease (0.46) and the perception that going for training means time out from work (0.56).

Table 3. Correlation between different motivation factors for training

Sl. No.		*Good*	*Technology*	*Incentive*	*Exploration*	*Planing*	*Commitment*	*Subordinate support*	*Subordinates encouragement*	*Task hinderence*	*Supervisor encouragement*	*Management support*	*Family support*	*Colleagues*	*Salary*	*Promotion*	*Work requiremen*	*Productivity*	*Learn*	*Time out*	*Not important*
1	Good	1.00																			
2	Technology	0.17	1.00																		
3	Incentive	0.32	0.06	1.00																	
4	Exploration	0.26	0.32	0.13	1.00																
5	Planing	0.47	0.27	0.45	0.45	1.00															
6	Commitment	0.52	-0.02	0.19	0.17	0.41	1.00														
7	Subordinate support	0.46	0.08	0.11	0.32	0.15	0.37	1.00													
8	Subordinates encouragement	0.41	-0.03	0.34	0.20	0.38	0.51	0.47	1.00												
9	Task hinderence	-0.23	-0.07	-0.12	0.16	-0.27	-0.20	0.07	-0.37	1.00											
10	Supervisor encouragement	0.21	-0.01	0.08	0.12	0.19	0.21	0.26	0.39	-0.01	1.00										
11	Management support	0.50	-0.03	-0.04	0.17	0.08	0.44	0.60	0.39	0.07	0.40	1.00									
12	Family support	0.44	0.22	0.18	0.33	0.57	0.44	0.22	0.28	-0.05	0.29	0.37	1.00								
13	Colleagues	0.29	-0.04	0.32	0.03	0.19	0.19	0.24	0.29	0.00	0.05	0.10	-0.01	1.00							
14	Salary	-0.07	0.11	0.12	0.31	0.01	-0.22	0.23	-0.11	0.53	-0.05	0.10	0.10	0.19	1.00						
15	Promotion	0.04	0.01	0.18	0.15	0.01	0.00	0.25	0.02	0.40	0.26	0.19	0.09	0.27	0.68	1.00					
16	Work requirement	-0.06	0.32	0.09	0.31	-0.04	-0.21	0.24	-0.03	0.34	0.11	0.25	0.06	0.22	0.63	0.59	1.00				
17	Productivity	-0.14	-0.12	0.09	-0.01	-0.05	-0.31	-0.17	-0.29	0.46	-0.02	-0.01	0.01	-0.09	0.40	0.33	0.18	1.00			
18	Learn	-0.11	0.21	-0.30	0.34	-0.10	-0.24	0.22	-0.15	0.32	0.17	0.29	0.02	-0.02	0.35	0.21	0.52	-0.01	1.00		
19	Time out	-0.04	-0.16	-0.10	0.12	-0.15	-0.24	0.03	-0.12	0.56	0.14	0.20	0.02	0.09	0.37	0.25	0.34	0.43	0.45	1.00	
20	Not important	-0.18	-0.38	0.02	-0.20	-0.18	-0.41	-0.13	-0.20	0.33	-0.02	0.03	-0.08	0.09	0.46	0.39	0.26	0.59	0.10	0.55	1.00

- The perception that if one does not do the training their salary will not increase has a strong positive correlation with the perception, that if one does not do the training their promotion will get halted (0.68) and cannot do the work properly (0.63). It is also positively correlated with the perception that training is not important (0.46).
- The perception that if one does not do the training their promotion will get halted has a positive moderate correlation with the perception that in the absence of training one cannot do the work properly (0.59).
- The perception that in the absence of training one cannot do the work properly has a positive moderate correlation with the perception that training provides an opportunity to learn new things and have fun (0.52).
- The perception that spending time on training leads to loss of work and productivity has a positive moderate correlation with perception that going for training means time out from work (0.43) and the perception that training is not important (0.59).
- The perception that training provides an opportunity to learn new things and have fun has a positive moderate correlation with the perception that going for training means time out from work (0.45).

- The perception that going for training means time out from work has a positive moderate correlation with the perception that training is not important (0.55).

T-Test

A t-test was conducted to check whether the responses got for the 20 variables associated with motivation for training were significant or not. Since the direction of some variables: "Task hindrance", "Salary", "Promotion", "Work requirement", "Productivity" and "Not important" (as shown in table 1) were negative, the responses were reverse coded for conducting the t-test. One sample t-test was conducted with test value = 4 (as the value of 4 and above signified acceptance of the variable). Significance was checked at a 95% confidence level, p-values less than 0.05 signified that the variables were significant. Hence, in table 4, the highlighted cells show the significant variables. Similar results were got in a study conducted in Bangladesh with teachers and was found that training and development, participation in decision making, recognition, and workplace flexibility, and work environment had a statistically significant relationship with motivation (Anjum et al., 2021).

Table 4. Summary of t-test

Sl. No.	Parameters	p-value of t-test	Significance
1	Good	0.122	Not significant
2	Technology	0.000	Significant
3	Incentive	0.902	Not significant
4	Exploration	0.000	Significant
5	Planning	0.001	Significant
6	Commitment	0.001	Significant
7	Subordinate support	0.483	Not significant
8	Subordinates encouragement	0.000	Significant
9	Task hindrance	0.000	Significant
10	Supervisor encouragement	0.602	Not significant
11	Management support	0.558	Not significant
12	Family support	0.124	Not significant
13	Colleagues	0.000	Significant
14	Salary	0.002	Significant
15	Promotion	0.000	Significant
16	Work requirement	0.000	Significant
17	Productivity	0.215	Not significant
18	Learn	0.018	Significant
19	Time out	0.000	Significant
20	Not important	0.004	Significant

Factor Analysis

Factor analysis for the 20 variables was done using the Maximum Likelihood method with Promax (Kappa 4) rotation. The KMO and Bartlett's test was significant (0.000) with sampling adequacy of 0.692. The total variance explained as shown in table 5 is 56.56%.

Table 5. Total variance explained.

Factor	Initial Eigenvalues			Extraction Sums of Squared Loadings			Rotation Sums of Squared Loadings
	Total	% of Variance	Cumulative %	Total	% of Variance	Cumulative %	Total
1	4.347	21.734	21.734	3.540	17.701	17.701	3.294
2	4.063	20.315	42.049	3.685	18.426	36.127	3.353
3	1.889	9.443	51.492	1.687	8.434	44.561	2.670
4	1.726	8.631	60.124	1.450	7.249	51.810	2.489
5	1.384	6.918	67.042	0.950	4.751	56.561	2.242

Figure 4. Scree plot

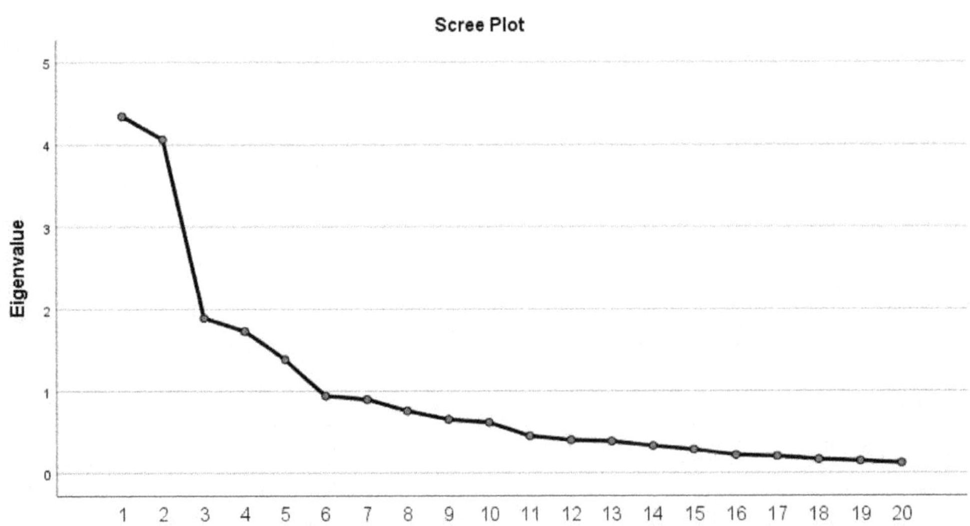

As per the scree plot (shown in figure 4), five factors can be extracted. The pattern matrix with variables for each of the factors is displayed in table 6. The variables "Good", "Commitment", "Subordinate support", "Subordinates encouragement", "Supervisor encouragement" and "Management support" are components of factor 1. As these variables revolve around support and encouragement received from the company and its people, the factor has been named "Company Support". Modern motivational factors have become progressively globalized. The work of Khan and Wajidi (2019) states that companies are giving importance to effective management and team building to survive and prosper.

The variables "Task hindrance", "Salary", "Promotion" and "Work requirement" are components of factor 2. Since these variables are directly related to the benefits of employees, the factor has been termed as "Rewards". Brooks and Fenner (2018) state that materialistic behaviour can be extrinsically motivated by monetary goals which boost happiness, status and identity of an employee, which further affects employee performance and organizational outcomes. Many people confirm that there is a direct correlation between salary and employee productivity. However, Rynes, Gerhart, & Minette (2004) stated that money is not the only motivator nor it is the primary motivator for everyone. Internal promotions are rewards given to employees for their efforts (Chan, 1996). It is important for both employers and employees and can affect employee and organizational performance (Bossler & Grunau, 2020). It increases an employee's organizational and external social status and enhances the job satisfaction level.

The variables "Technology", "Productivity", "Time out" and "Not important" are components of factor 3. As these variables are related to the internal factors of an organization, the factor has been termed as "Internal". A healthy and friendly work environment is an important factor that motivates employees to work properly. A comfortable workplace is a basic requirement for an employee. Fair procedures are important for "quality of work-life" and essential to build a cordial employer-employee

Table 6. Pattern matrix

Sl. No.	Parameters	1	2	3	4	5
1	Good	0.583				
2	Commitment	0.596				
3	Subordinate support	0.655				
4	Subordinates encouragement	0.545				
5	Supervisor encouragement	0.453				
6	Management support	0.938				
7	Task hindrance		0.409			
8	Salary		0.851			
9	Promotion		0.841			
10	Work requirement		0.773			
11	Technology			-0.476		
12	Productivity			0.64		
13	Time out			0.599		
14	Not important			0.822		
15	Family support				0.506	
16	Exploration				0.578	
17	Planning				0.895	
18	Incentive					0.611
19	Colleagues					0.356
20	Learn					-0.743

relationship (Schappe & Doran, 1997). Motivated employees enjoy their job within their workplace and give outstanding performance, as compared to less motivated employees (Khan & Wajidi, 2019).

The variables "Family support", "Exploration" and "Planning" are components of factor 4. These factors are related to the career of an employee and affect his family. Hence, the factor is named "Career". Employees constantly lookout for better career opportunities and self-advancement. They are also interested to climb the ladder within an organization. Internal promotions can encourage proper behaviours and increase employee production rates. Career advancement influences the workers' behaviours and attitudes, such as motivation and organizational commitment, mainly with stable employment (Takahashi, 2006).

The variables of the fifth factor are "Incentive", "Colleagues" and "Learn". These factors revolve around the interest of the employee in training. Hence, this factor is termed "Interest". By creating a culture that demands and generates motivation, employers can use existing norms to train and promote the desired levels of motivation amongst employees. To motivate employees for undertaking training and development programmes, it needs to satisfy an employee's job-related needs, career-related needs, and personal-related needs (Aziz & Ahmad, 2011).

CONCLUSION

The objective of the study was to find the motivating factors for employees to undertake a training programme. From the study conducted, it is evident that motivation is important for persuading employees to undertake training and development programmes in an organization. As training is an essential part of an organization, it needs to be carried out regularly for the employees. From the findings of the survey, it is clear that employees are motivated to keep themselves up-to-date with the latest technologies, to have better career options and planning. An organization's commitment to training the employees and encouragement received from subordinates also play a significant role in motivating the employees to undertake training and development programmes. Hence, in order to motivate the employees for future training programmes, organizations may highlight career, technology and future prospects. Studies also show that the effectiveness with which training is transferred depends on the motivation to transfer (Arefin & Islam, 2019). A study conducted on 1705 Australians found that training motivation did not mediate the effects of the work environment on participation. However, it moderated the prediction of employer support (Tharenou, 2001). Another study conducted with 343 trainees from different service organizations in Norway found that intrinsic motivation moderated the relationship between perceived training opportunities and organizational citizenship behaviours (Dysvik & Kuvaas, 2008). A study conducted with employees of a Dutch government office found that a combination of company practices with individual supporting conditions, such as employees' motivation, is a novel approach to understand the personal development plans of employees (Eisele et al., 2013).

The study is limited to a survey conducted in a pharmaceutical company in the state of Sikkim, India. The study can be repeated for a larger geographical area and with different industries. It would also be interesting to find out the differences in the motivating factors across various industry types. With larger sample sizes, conclusive research may be carried out using advanced techniques like confirmatory factor analysis and structural equation models.

REFERENCES

Abba, M. T. (2018). Effects of training and development on employee retention in Bauchi State Metropolis Banks. *Operations Research*, *4*(1), 24–39.

Al Amin Khan, M., Kumar Tarofder, A., & Ferdous Azam, S. M. (2021). Critical factors affecting employees' motivation and productivity in Bangladeshi satellite television channels. *European Journal of Social Sciences Studies*, *5*(6). Advance online publication. doi:10.46827/ejsss.v5i6.985

Al Karim, R. (2019). Impact of Different Training and Development Programs on Employee Performance in Bangladesh Perspective. *International Journal of Entrepreneurial Research*, *1*(2), 8–14. doi:10.31580/ijer.v1i2.497

Anjum, N., Islam, M. A., Choudhury, M. I., & Saha, J. (2021). Do Intrinsic Rewards Matter on Motivation? *SEISENSE Journal of Management*, *4*(1), 47–58. doi:10.33215jom.v4i1.534

Arefin, M. S., & Islam, N. (2019). A Study on the Motivation to Transfer Training in the Banking Industry of Bangladesh. *SA Journal of Human Resource Management*, *6*(1), 45–72. doi:10.1177/2322093718803210

Aziz, S. F. A., & Ahmad, S. (2011). Stimulating training motivation using the right training characteristic. *Industrial and Commercial Training*.

Balven, R., Fenters, V., Siegel, D. S., & Waldman, D. (2018). Academic entrepreneurship: The roles of identity, motivation, championing, education, work-life balance, and organizational justice. *The Academy of Management Perspectives*, *32*(1), 21–42. doi:10.5465/amp.2016.0127

Basford, T. E., & Offermann, L. R. (2012). Beyond leadership: The impact of coworker relationships on employee motivation and intent to stay. *Journal of Management & Organization*, *18*(6), 807–817. doi:10.5172/jmo.2012.18.6.807

Ben-Hur, S., & Kinley, N. (2016). Intrinsic motivation: The missing piece in changing employee behavior. *Perspectives for Managers*, *192*, 1.

Bhattacharyya, S. S., & Nair, S. (2019). Explicating the future of work: Perspectives from India. *Journal of Management Development*, *38*(3), 175–194. doi:10.1108/JMD-01-2019-0032

Bibi, P., Ahmad, A., & Majid, A. H. A. (2018). The impact of training and development and supervisor support on employees retention in academic institutions: The moderating role of work environment. *Gadjah Mada International Journal of Business*, *20*(1), 113. doi:10.22146/gamaijb.24020

Bossler, M., & Grunau, P. (2020). Asymmetric information in external versus internal promotions. *Empirical Economics*, *59*(6), 2977–2998. doi:10.100700181-019-01749-7

Brooks, L. M., & Fenner, C. (2018). The Effect of Materialistic Behavior on the Workplace Motivation in Business Managers. *Academy of Business Research Journal*, *4*, 26–41.

Buil, I., Catalán, S., & Martínez, E. (2019). Encouraging intrinsic motivation in management training: The use of business simulation games. *International Journal of Management Education*, *17*(2), 162–171. doi:10.1016/j.ijme.2019.02.002

Chan, W. (1996). External recruitment versus internal promotion. *Journal of Labor Economics*, *14*(4), 555–570. doi:10.1086/209822 de Vries, M. F. R. K. (2001). Creating authentizotic organizations: Well-functioning individuals in vibrant companies. *Human Relations*, *54*(1), 101–111. doi:10.1177/0018726701541013

Delery, J. E., & Doty, D. H. (1996). Modes of theorizing in strategic human resource management: Tests of universalistic, contingency, and configurational performance predictions. *Academy of Management Journal*, *39*(4), 802–835. doi:10.5465/256713

DeVaro, J., Maxwell, N., & Morita, H. (2017). Training and intrinsic motivation in nonprofit and for-profit organizations. *Journal of Economic Behavior & Organization, 139*, 196–213.

Dysvik, A., & Kuvaas, B. (2008). The relationship between perceived training opportunities, work motivation and employee outcomes. *International Journal of Training and Development*, *12*(3), 138–157. doi:10.1111/j.1468-2419.2008.00301.x

Eisele, L., Grohnert, T., Beausaert, S., & Segers, M. (2013). Employee motivation for personal development plan effectiveness. *European Journal of Training and Development*, *37*(6), 527–543. doi:10.1108/EJTD-02-2013-0015

Farren, C. (2000). Mastery: The critical advantage. Management C, 21, 95–105.

Gagné, M., Forest, J., Vansteenkiste, M., Crevier-Braud, L., van den Broeck, A., Aspeli, A. K., Bellerose, J., Benabou, C., Chemolli, E., Güntert, S. T., Halvari, H., Indiyastuti, D. L., Johnson, P. A., Molstad, M. H., Naudin, M., Ndao, A., Olafsen, A. H., Roussel, P., Wang, Z., & Westbye, C. (2015). The Multidimensional Work Motivation Scale: Validation evidence in seven languages and nine countries. *European Journal of Work and Organizational Psychology*, *24*(2), 178–196. doi:10.1080/1359432X.2013.877892

Gronseth, S., Gronseth, S., Dalton, E., Alvarez, B., Iglesias, I., Vergara, P., Ingle, J. C., Pacheco-Guffrey, H., Bauder, D., Cooper, K., Anderson, C., Anderson, K., Intatano, V., Semingson, P., Pole, K., Armstrong, K., Boreham, B., Mack, T., Harris, L., . . . Yearta, L. (2019). Using UDL-related methods in education, teacher training, and job-development. *Society for Information Technology & Teacher Education International Conference, 2019*(1), 245–249.

Gupta, A., Saha, S. K., Sharma, N. D., & Jha, A. (2021). Perceptual Differences Across Various Stakeholder Groups: A Study of Challenges for Skill Development in Sikkim, India. *International Journal of Asian Business and Information Management*, *12*(3), 43–66. doi:10.4018/IJABIM.20210701.oa4

Hossain, A. (2014). An overview on effective employee training systems of private sector commercial banks in Bangladesh. *International Journal of Ethics in Social Sciences*, *2*(1), 33–44.

Johari, S., & Jha, K. N. (2020). Impact of Work Motivation on Construction Labor Productivity. *Journal of Management Engineering*, *36*(5), 04020052. doi:10.1061/(ASCE)ME.1943-5479.0000824

Karam, A. A. (2019). The Impact of Training and Development on Different Cultural Employees Performance through Interaction Employees Motivation in Erbil Public and Private Banks. *Mediterranean Journal of Social Sciences*, *10*(1), 193–206. doi:10.2478/mjss-2019-0017

Kazaz, A., Manisali, E., & Ulubeyli, S. (2008). Effect of basic motivational factors on construction workforce productivity in Turkey. *Journal of Civil Engineering and Management*, *14*(2), 95–106. doi:10.3846/1392-3730.2008.14.4

Khan, M. R., & Wajidi, A. (2019). Role of leadership and team building in employee motivation at workplace. *GMJACS*, *9*(1), 11.

Kulkarni, R., Chauhan, S., Patil, A., Shivkumar, P., Tayade, S., Dohate, N., Patil, A., Deshpande, A., & Karnataki, M. (2019). Impact of Training on Awareness and Knowledge of Service Providers About Maternal Near-Miss Events in Maharashtra, India. *Journal of Obstetrics and Gynaecology of India*, *69*(6), 529–534. doi:10.100713224-019-01259-7 PMID:31844368

Maity, S. (2019). Identifying opportunities for artificial intelligence in the evolution of training and development practices. *Journal of Management Development*, *38*(8), 651–663. doi:10.1108/JMD-03-2019-0069

Małachowski, B., & Korytkowski, P. (2016). Competence-based performance model of multi-skilled workers. *Computers & Industrial Engineering*, *91*, 165–177. doi:10.1016/j.cie.2015.11.018

Marín, L. S., & Roelofs, C. (2017). Promoting Construction Supervisors' Safety-Efficacy to Improve Safety Climate: Training Intervention Trial. *Journal of Construction Engineering and Management*, *143*(8), 04017037. doi:10.1061/(ASCE)CO.1943-7862.0001330

Meyer, J. P., & Allen, N. J. (1991). A three-component conceptualization of organizational commitment. *Human Resource Management Review*, *1*(1), 61–89. doi:10.1016/1053-4822(91)90011-Z

Mitchell, T. R. (1982). Motivation: New directions for theory, research, and practice. *Academy of Management Review*, *7*(1), 80–88. doi:10.5465/amr.1982.4285467

N., & Rani, S. (2019). Effectiveness of Training on Food Processing among Women in Haryana, India. *Current Journal of Applied Science and Technology, 33*(6), 1–6. doi:10.9734/cjast/2019/v33i630103

Olanipekun, A. O., Xia, B., Hon, C., & Darko, A. (2018). Effect of Motivation and Owner Commitment on the Delivery Performance of Green Building Projects. *Journal of Management Engineering*, *34*(1), 04017039. doi:10.1061/(ASCE)ME.1943-5479.0000559

Ozkeser, B. (2019). Impact of training on employee motivation in human resources management. *Procedia Computer Science*, *158*, 802–810. doi:10.1016/j.procs.2019.09.117

Punjani, K. (2019). Objectives of the Study Chart 1 (Source: Planning Commission India-11th five year plan) " " Skill Development : The Key to Economic Prosperity A Study On The Requirement Of Skills Development For The Success Of "Make In India" Project. *Tactful Management Research Journal*. www.makeinindia.com

Rodriguez, J., & Walters, K. (2017). The importance of training and development in employee performance and evaluation. *World Wide Journal of Multidisciplinary Research and Development*, *3*(10), 206–212.

Ryan, R. M., & Deci, E. L. (2000). Intrinsic and Extrinsic Motivations: Classic Definitions and New Directions. *Contemporary Educational Psychology*, *25*(1), 54–67. doi:10.1006/ceps.1999.1020 PMID:10620381

Rynes, S. L., Gerhart, B., & Minette, K. A. (2004). The importance of pay in employee motivation: Discrepancies between what people say and what they do. *Human Resource Management*, *43*(4), 381–394.

S., C., V., J., S, K. N., G., R., & V., R. D. (2020). A Study on the Effectiveness of Human Resource Information System (HRIs) on Bureau Veritas Consumer Product Services (India) Pvt. Ltd. *NOLEGEIN-Journal of Human Resource Management & Development*, 1–9. http://mbajournals.in/index.php/JoHRMD/article/view/624

Schappe, S. P., & Doran, A. C. (1997). How does fair treatment affect employee commitment to an organization? A field study of financial holding company employees. *The Mid-Atlantic Journal of Business*, *33*(3), 191.

Schuler, R. S., & MacMillan, I. C. (1984). Gaining competitive advantage through human resource management practices. *Human Resource Management*, *23*(3), 241–255. doi:10.1002/hrm.3930230304

Sekhon, A. K., & Kathuria, L. M. (2019). Corporate Social Responsibility: A Case Study of Vardhman Textiles Limited in India. *MANTHAN: Journal of Commerce and Management*, *6*(2), 105. doi:10.17492/manthan.v6i2.187351

Sharma, B., Saha, S. K., & Jha, A. (2020). Understanding Inter-Relational Dynamics of Different Factors Impacting the Cymbidium Orchids-Based Economy in Sikkim, India Using DEMATAL. In *Handbook of Research on Managerial Practices and Disruptive Innovation in Asia* (pp. 282–299). IGI Global. doi:10.4018/978-1-7998-0357-7.ch016

Takahashi, K. (2006). Effects of wage and promotion incentives on the motivation levels of Japanese employees. *Career Development International*, *11*(3), 193–203. doi:10.1108/13620430610661722

Tam, V. W. Y., & Fung, I. W. H. (2012). Behavior, attitude, and perception toward safety culture from mandatory safety training course. *Journal of Professional Issues in Engineering Education and Practice*, *138*(3), 207–213. doi:10.1061/(ASCE)EI.1943-5541.0000104

Tharenou, P. (2001). The relationship of training motivation to participation in training and development. *Journal of Occupational and Organizational Psychology*, *74*(5), 599–621. doi:10.1348/096317901167541

Turner, A. (2017). How does intrinsic and extrinsic motivation drive performance culture in organizations? *Cogent Education*, *4*(1), 1337543. doi:10.1080/2331186X.2017.1337543

Van Iddekinge, C. H., Aguinis, H., Mackey, J. D., & DeOrtentiis, P. S. (2018). A meta-analysis of the interactive, additive, and relative effects of cognitive ability and motivation on performance. *Journal of Management*, *44*(1), 249–279. doi:10.1177/0149206317702220

Waugh, R. F. (2002). Creating a scale to measure motivation to achieve academically: Linking attitudes and behaviours using Rasch measurement. *The British Journal of Educational Psychology*, *72*(1), 65–86. doi:10.1348/000709902158775 PMID:11916465

Weaver, T. (1988). Theory M: Motivating with money. *The Cornell Hotel and Restaurant Administration Quarterly*, *29*(3), 40–45. doi:10.1177/001088048802900314

Wen Lim, H., Li, N., Fang, D., & Wu, C. (2018). Impact of Safety Climate on Types of Safety Motivation and Performance: Multigroup Invariance Analysis. *Journal of Management Engineering*, *34*(3), 04018002. doi:10.1061/(ASCE)ME.1943-5479.0000595

Chapter 19
Employee Performance in the Fast Food Industry: A Mediating Role of Happiness

Muhammad Imran
https://orcid.org/0000-0001-7126-2831
Universiti Utara Malaysia, Malaysia

Hammad Wajid
https://orcid.org/0000-0002-0616-1054
The Islamia University of Bahawalpur, Pakistan

ABSTRACT

The main purpose of this research is to find the relationship of role overload (RO), love of money (LOM), empowerment (EMP), and work engagement (WE) on employee performance (EP) in the fast food industry and also to find the mediating effect of happiness (HAP) between RO, LOM, EMP, and WE on employee performance and moderating role of the spirit of work (SOW) on happiness and employee performance (EP). The data was gathered using the online survey method through questionnaires from the employees of fast food restaurants of South Punjab, Pakistan. The sample size was 297. The smartPLS 3 was used to analyze the data. The result findings show that LOM, WE, and HAP have an influence on EP while RO and EMP have no influence on EP. There was a mediating effect of HAP between EMP and EP whereas there was no mediating influence of HAP between RO, LOM, WE, and EP. No moderating role of SOW between HAP and EP was found. This study findings are very useful for manager/owner of the restaurant the increase their employee performance, which leads to firm high performance.

INTRODUCTION

Over the few years it has been observed that restaurant industry has flourished to a great extent in Pakistan. Fast food restaurant sector is the second biggest industry in Pakistan. It reports for 16% of total employment in service sector (Awan & Nawaz, 2015). Pakistan possesses world's eighth largest market

DOI: 10.4018/978-1-7998-8678-5.ch019

with regards to fast food business. There are more than 1000 wide ranging food preparing endeavors in Pakistan. Due to increasing fast food business a large number of employments is being carried in this industry. Most of the population now comes to fast food restaurant. The employees had a great challenge in handling large number of orders daily and dealing with the customers (Awan & Nawaz, 2015).

The significant element that has been firmly connected with this industry is the fierce competition. While the GDP of the Pakistan is giving indications of slow economic growth and development, the inexpensive food industry is by all accounts encountering higher measures of growth. Industry projections propose it to be a $1 billion per year market that worldwide and residential cooking styles and cafés appear to do very well (Riaz, Ahmed, & Akhtar, 2019).

However, in most of the firms the departmental heads put extra stress and pressure on the employees to accomplish organizational goals and desired performance. It is a frequent scenario in restaurant business where front line employees frequently need to manage stringent and troublesome customers which affects their job performance. Concerning the activity outlook itself, the workers of restaurants are regularly connected with elongated working hours, shifts, repeated projections, strain and clash and incompetent administration. It has also been observed that workers were paid low salaries and provided poor working conditions; resultantly there is a possibility of employee turnover and low job performance (Amran, Ghazali, & Siti Fatimah, 2018).

Moreover, this research study has extensive significance and importance. Previous Studies have been done in the developed economies. Very seldom has any research like this been organized on this topic in Pakistan. This research study is also significant because it will enhance knowledge of managers about role overload, love of money, empowerment and work engagement in the work life of an employee. Mediating and moderating variables have been used with independent and dependent variables to make this research a unique one. With this knowledge the managers will be able to implicate effective Human Resource Management strategies to motivate employees to achieve organizational goals and also to make their job more satisfying (Aydin, 2018).

LITERATURE REVIEW

Employee Performance

Measurement of worker performance is a movement that is exceptionally essential since it is very well may be utilized as a proportion of achievement in supporting the success of the firm worker (Gunawan & Amalia, 2015). Employee performance can by and large be characterized as all the conduct workers participate in while at work. It might likewise indicate to the profession like activity of a worker and how well those exercises were accomplished. Job performance ascribes to the quality and amount that are accomplished by worker or group of workers in the wake of finishing a given responsibility (Fonkeng, 2018).

Role Overload and Employee Performance

Role Overload that specifies when the workers role expectations surpass the resources or time accessible to satisfy allotted duties (Karimi et al., 2017). Somebody who encounters role over-load will for the most part have emotions that go astray from his typical capacity. This condition triggers stress in the working environment because of hurdles or claim that emerge refers to role overload (Garaika, 2019).

Role overburden is a basic precedent of work strain, as it scatters belongings (Kim, Lee, & Shin, 2019). Shultz, Wang and Olson (2010) expressed that workers under job role overburden had the most elevated stage of refutation wellbeing. Karimi et al., (2017) expressed that job over-burden prompted word related stress. Also, a few past investigations revealed that job over-burden negatively affected mindset and approach of workers (Malik, et al., 2013). The over-burden representatives shows poor productivity and low performance however the outcome uncovered that the performance of an individual boosts up to a small degree with addition in role overload as a specific stage of strain is useful for execution yet it develops disappointment (Mittal & Bhakkar, 2018). This research study incurs following hypothesis:

H1a: Role Overload has significant relationship with on Employee Performance.
H1b: Role Overload has significant relationship with on Employee Performance under mediating role of Happiness.

Love of Money and Employee Performance

Cash is a significant part of everyday life; it significantly affects motivation and working conduct. In USA, achievement is estimated by wealth and salary. Even though cash is utilized all around, the value and significance of money is not universally accepted. Tang, Shin-Hsiung Tang, and Arocas (2005) stated that the mind set towards money are found out through the socialization procedure built up in adolescence and kept up through grown-up life. In all businesses, supervisors use cash to pull in, contain, and galvanize workers. Its absence brings about high turnover, low responsibility, and counterproductive conduct. Granting workers with money related bonuses is a significant help to workers and way to enhance the workers performance (Keller & Price, 2014). Cash is an outward factor than internal factors, well-kept up characteristic inborn factors that really affect work execution (Wildiani et al., 2019). This research study incurs following hypothesis:

H2a: Love of Money has significant relationship with on Employee Performance.
H2b: Love of Money has significant relationship with on Employee Performance under mediating role of Happiness.

Empowerment and Employee Performance

Empowering is a show of making and extending potential by executing with others, which is designated "instinctive empowerment" and can impact their very own conduct, Call "self-empowerment". (Barroso Castro et al., 2008). Employees so unequivocally want control in the work environment that they will persistently endeavor to build their degree of apperceive impact - in any event, when the association places hindrances in their way. Endorsement is relied upon to greatly affect work perspectives than on real execution. The investigation of this research tends to be reasoned that worker's empowerment can positively impact employee performance inside a firm. Greater the worker's endorsement quality higher will be firm's execution (Nadeem et al., 2018). As per Rob and Margret Brown (2017), 'empowerment' isn't simply a question of assigning work power to the activity holders. It implies that 'everybody can make a move to upgrade their work, either in close to home or organizational terms. This research study incurs following hypothesis between the relationship of empowerment and employee performance:

H3a: Empowerment has significant relationship with on Employee Performance.
H3b: Empowerment has significant relationship with on Employee Performance under mediating role of Happiness.

Work Engagement and Employee Performance

Work commitment is comprehended as a positive mind-set comprising of life, devotion, and ingestion in work. Dynamism is portrayed by elevated levels of vitality and mental obstruction, want, and readiness to contribute exertion and diligence in that exertion when confronted with challenges. Commitment shows as eagerness, motivation, and pride in the work. Ingestion happens when solid dosages of satisfaction and focus are seen while playing out the work. Engaged workers have raised degrees of vitality, commitment and are generally looked for due to the significant effect on personalized, group and organizational stages. In same situation, a committed worker is viewed as a cornerstone of continuing focused edge (A.Gruman & Saksb, 2011). This research study incurs following hypothesis:

H4a: Work Engagement has significant relationship with on Employee Performance.
H4b: Work Engagement has significant relationship with on Employee Performance under mediating role of Happiness.

Happiness and Employee Performance

Happiness is a case of being bliss. Happy workers are the individuals who experience energetic feelings, for example, bliss, intrigue and pride and inconsistent negative feelings, for example, bitterness, uneasiness and outrage. Happiness is constantly connected with positive life and work results, for example, life fulfillment, great wellbeing conditions, high work execution and responsibility (Abarar et al., 2019). Happiness has certain effects on the performance of workers with increased outcome. In an examination, utilizing an exploratory plan, happiness of workers is demonstrated to be more beneficial than their less happy partners. Happiness leads to enhanced performance (Othman et al, 2018). Happiness is playing a mediating role between RO, LOM, EMP, WE and employee performance. This research study incurs following hypothesis between the of happiness and employee execution:

H5: There is positive relationship between happiness and employee performance.

Spirit of Work and Employee Performance

The spirit of work clarifies the ability and excitement of somebody to serve and do their obligations as well as could be expected. Work confidence is the disposition of an individual (Abrar, Shabbir, Hussain, & Sana-ud-Din, 2019) and gathering towards his workplace and on his deliberate collaboration to be ready to give his capacities completely as per the primary needs of the organization. All organizations that need to accomplish high efficiency guarantee that there is spirit of work and collaboration among workers. Specifically, numerous specialists contend that collaboration is exceptionally powerful in organizations where the prerequisite for spread of data is extremely high. In this way, an association is seen between data the executives and cooperation.

Spirit of work moderates the role between Happiness and employee performance in this research as it can be seen observed that spirit of work will make the relationship between happiness and employee performance stronger. A high spirit at work combined with happiness will boast the performance of the worker (Danish, et al., 2019). This research study incurs following hypothesis between the relation of happiness and employee performance and spirit of work as moderator:

H6: Spirit of work moderates the relationship between happiness and employee performance.

Research Framework

Herzberg's Two Factor Theory of Motivation represents the connections among workers job satisfaction and job dissatisfaction in the surroundings where the worker carries out the work. Herzberg et al. (1959) gathered information from interviews with 200 designers and bookkeepers to comprehend motivating factors that identified with workers fulfillment or disappointment with their business. Motivation factors are those that can influence workers' activity perspectives to be increasingly positive since representatives' self-completion needs are fulfilled. Example of motivating factors incorporate accomplishment, acknowledgment, positive input, more responsibilities, headway, and advancement, just as the work itself (Herzberg et al., 1959). The outcomes showed that job aspects are accurately determined with employment satisfaction, while others make job dissatisfaction. As mentioned by Herzberg, motivating aspects (likewise called work satisfiers) are basically natural work aspects that leads to contentment. Hygiene factors (likewise called job dissatisfiers) are outside aspects of the enterprise. Hygiene aspects include firm policy, supervision, enterprise conditions, interpersonal connections, salary benefits and job guarantee. As per the Price and Mueller (1981) model, monotonous effort decreases contentment. Nonetheless, laborers are bound to be happy with their work when they are taking part in work related choices, getting business related data, shaping dear fellowships with others busy working, acquiring sensible and reasonable remuneration, and appreciating open doors for advancement the satisfaction leads to happiness in workers. According to Herzberg theory (1966) the motivating factors which include responsibilities is used as role overload where an employee performs different tasks at the same time and similarly motivating factors also explains the employee empowerment where he can manage relations with his coworkers and can work freely.

The Hygiene factors which include working conditions which explains that better environment provides higher work engagement in the employees, they are more committed and eager to fulfill their duties. Salary benefits are part of hygiene factors according to Herzberg which explains that love of money increases the satisfaction in the employees and hence improved their performance (Holston-Okae & Mushi, 2018).

Conceptual Framework

Figure 1.

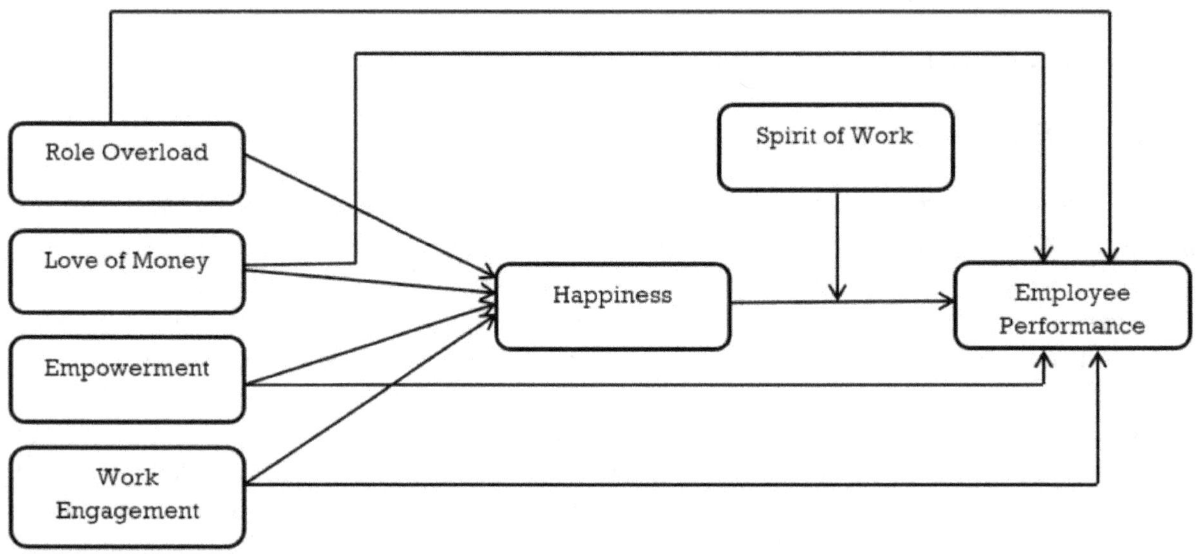

Methodology

This nature of this research study is quantitative, and it is a descriptive research. Descriptive research is a resolute procedure of gathering data regarding current circumstances, procedures, patterns and after that making sufficient and precise understanding about such information with the benefit of statistical tool (Jalagat, 2017). The data was collected using the primary source. Survey methods have two kinds which are Interviews and Questionnaires. For this research online questionnaires were used collect to gather data

Population Sample Size and Sampling Technique

The population of this research is the employees of Fast food restaurants from south Punjab such as Bahawalpur, Lodhran and Multan. It is commonly acknowledged that larger sample size are better (Comrey & Lee, 1992). Comrey and Lee (1992) said that a sample size of 50 is very poor, 100 is poor, 200 is fair, 300 is good, 500 is very good and 1000 is excellent. The data collected for this research is from 297 respondents from employees of restaurants of Bahawalpur, Lodhran and Multan. The sample size for this research is n = 297.

This research used non-probability sampling technique because population was unknown and sampling frame was not available. Due to the ongoing Corona Virus situation and implementing safety precautions data was collected using snowball sampling.

Measurement Scale

Different scales will be used for measuring variables in this research. The role overload was measured using the scale taken from (Jalagat, 2017). The love of money was measured using the Love of Money Scale (Arocas & Li Ping Tang, 2004). The empowerment was measured using the Empowerment Scale (Niehoff et al, 2001). The work engagement was measured using the Work and Well-being Survey (UWES) (Schaufeli et al, 2006). The Happiness was measured using Employee Happiness scale (Othman et al., 2018). The Spirit of Work was measured using Spirit of Work Scale (Kinjerski & Skrypnek, 2006). The Employee Performance was measured using Employee Performance scale (Rodwell et al., 1998). The online questionnaire uses five-point Likert scale.

Data Analysis

The data was analyzed using Smart PLS 3. Structural Equation Modelling (PLS- SEM) was used for analysis of collected data.

FINDINGS AND DISCUSSION

In this research the Measurement Model (Outer Model) and Structural Model (Inner Model) was discussed using Smart PLS 3.

Measurement Model (Reflective Measurement Model)

The measurement model investigates the connection between indicators and constructs (linkage between observed and latent variables). It was also called as Confirmatory Factor analysis (CFA) (Hair et al., 2014). In this research the reflective measurement model was discussed which was also called as outer model. In reflective measurement model the arrow points from construct to indicators. The relationship between construct and indicator in reflective measurement model was also called as loadings (Hair et al., 2014).

Construct Reliability and Validity

The table 1 shows the internal consistency reliability which was analyzed using Smart PLS 3. The measurement model was checked using construct reliability and validity. All the individual items reliability was investigated, and it was found out above the loading value of 0.7. The above table shows that the construct reliability was investigated through Cronbach's Alpha, Composite Reliability (CR) and Average Variance Extracted (AVE). All the constructs were having Cronbach's Alpha greater than 0.7 except construct (role overload and spirit of work). A general acknowledged principle is that Cronbach's Alpha value of 0.6-0.7 shows an adequate acceptable level of reliability, a Cronbach Alpha value of 0.8 or higher is very good. Anyhow, values of construct reliability higher than 0.95 are not acceptable, because there may be a sign of redundancy (Hulin, Netemeyer, & Cudeck, 2001).

Table 1.

Variables	Cronbach's Alpha	Composite Reliability (CR)	Average Variance Extracted (AVE)
RO	0.622	0.792	0.561
LOM	0.765	0.842	0.516
EMP	0.740	0.837	0.562
WE	0.760	0.839	0.513
HAP	0.809	0.863	0.513
SOW	0.603	0.790	0.557
EP	0.800	0.862	0.555

RO = Role Overload; LOM = Love of Money; EMP = Empowerment; WE = Work Engagement; HAP = Happiness; SOW = Spirit of Work; EP = Employee Performance

The Composite Reliability values of all constructs were higher than 0.7 and the Average Variance Extracted (AVE) values for all constructs were also higher than 0.5 which shows that all constructs CR and AVE were greater than the minimum acceptable level (Hair et al., 2014).

Discriminant Validity

The table 2 shows that the Discriminant Validity was checked to confirm outside consistency of model using Heterotrait – Monotrait (HTMT) Ratio introduced by (Henseler, Ringle & Sarstedt, 2015). Wherever if the HTMT ratio is less than one, discriminant validity can be viewed as set up (Henseler, Ringle & Sarstedt, 2015). The above table shows that all the values of HTMT ratios of all constructs were under one, so discriminant validity was established.

Table 2.

	EP	EMP	HAP	LOM	RO	SOW	WE
EP							
EMP	0.730						
HAP	0.812	0.947					
LOM	0.711	0.777	0.777				
RO	0.630	0.677	0.660	0.717			
SOW	0.383	0.157	0.224	0.195	0.165		
WE	0.950	0.824	0.875	0.752	0.643	0.374	

RO = Role Overload; LOM = Love of Money; EMP = Empowerment; WE = Work Engagement; HAP = Happiness; SOW = Spirit of Work; EP = Employee Performance

Structural Model (Inner Model)

The structural model investigated the connection between independent variable and dependent variable also known as latent variables. The relationship between IV and DV was also called as path coefficients (Hair et al., 2014). Structural Model was also called as Inner Model.

Path Coefficients (Total Effects)

Path coefficients shows the relationship between independent variables and dependent variable. Path coefficients were examined using bootstrapping technique keeping subsample at 5000 to find out beta values, T values and p values. Anyhow in this research five direct relationship were evaluated and found out by five direct relationship hypotheses.

Table 3.

Hypothesis	Beta	Std. Deviation	T value	P value
RO → EP	0.096	0.050	1.898	0.058
LOM → EP	0.150	0.060	2.499	0.012
EMP → EP	0.143	0.075	1.898	0.058
WE → EP	0.493	0.079	6.228	0.000
HAP → EP	0.199	0.095	2.104	0.035

The table 3 shows that the hypothesis is tested keeping p value at 0.05 (two-tailed). All that hypothesis whose T value are above 1.96 and p value less than 0.05 were accepted. The table shows that hypotheses 1a: Role Overload has significant response on employee performance has T value of 1.898 and P value 0.058, so the hypotheses test shows that H1a is not accepted which means role overload has no effect on employee performance. The hypotheses 2a: Love of Money has significant response on employee performance has T value 2.499 and P value 0.012, so the hypotheses test shows that H2a is accepted which means that love of money has significant effect on employee performance. The value of beta is 0.150 which also shows that Love of money has positive influence on employee performance. The hypotheses 3a: Empowerment has significant response on employee performance has T value 1.898 and P value 0.058, so the hypotheses test shows that H3a is not accepted which means that empowerment has no effect on employee performance. The hypothesis 4a: Work Engagement has significant response

Table 4.

Hypothesis	Beta	Std. Deviation	T value	P value
RO → HAP → EP	0.014	0.012	1.215	0.224
LOM → HAP → EP	0.032	0.019	1.649	0.099
EMP → HAP → EP	0.084	0.041	2.044	0.041
WE → HAP → EP	0.060	0.043	1.393	0.164

Table 5.

Hypotheses	Beta	Std. Deviation	T value	P value
SOW ↓ HAP → EP	0.032	0.047	0.682	0.495

on employee performance has T value 6.228 and P value 0.000, so the hypotheses test shows that H4a is accepted which means that work engagement has significant effect on employee performance. The value of beta is 0.493 which also means that Work Engagement has positive influence on employee performance. The hypotheses 5: Happiness has positive response on employee performance has T value 2.104 and P value 0.035, so the hypotheses test shows that H5 is accepted which means that Happiness has significant effect on employee performance. The value of beta is 0.199 which also proves that Happiness has positive influence on employee performance.

Specific Indirect Results (Mediation Model)

Specific Indirect Results were investigated using bootstrapping technique keeping subsamples at 5000 to find out the beta values, T values and P values. Anyhow in this research four indirect relationship (mediation) were evaluated and found out by four indirect relationship (mediation) hypothesis.

The table no. 4 shows the mediation effect between independent variable and dependent variable. All the hypothesis was tested keeping p value at 0.05 (two-tailed). All those hypotheses whose T value were above 1.96 and p value less than 0.05 are accepted. The table shows that the hypotheses 1b: Role Overload has significant response on Employee Performance under mediating role of Happiness has T value 1.215 and P value 0.224, so the hypotheses test shows that H1b is not accepted which means that there is no mediation effect of happiness between the relationship of role overload and employee performance. The hypotheses 2b: Love of money has significant response on Employee Performance under mediating role of Happiness has T value 1.649 and P value 0.099, so the hypotheses test shows that H2b is not accepted which means that there is no mediation effect of happiness between the relationship of love of money and employee performance. The hypotheses 3b: Empowerment has significant response on Employee Performance under mediating role of Happiness has T value 2.044 and P value 0.041, so the hypotheses test shows that H3b is accepted which means that there is mediation effect of happiness between the relationship of empowerment and employee performance. The hypotheses 4b: Work Engagement has significant response on Employee Performance under mediating role of Happiness has T value 1.393 and P value 0.164, so the hypotheses test shows that H4b is not accepted which means that there is no mediation effect of happiness between the relationship of work engagement and employee performance.

Moderation Model

Moderation model was investigated using bootstrapping technique keeping subsamples at 5000 to find out the beta values, T values and P values. Anyhow in this research one indirect relationship (moderation) was evaluated and found out by one indirect relationship (moderation) hypothesis.

The table no. 5 shows that the hypotheses 6: Spirit of work moderates the relationship between happiness and employee performance has T value 0.682 and P value 0.495, so the hypotheses test shows that H6 is not accepted which means that there is no moderation effect between the relationship of happiness and employee performance.

CONCLUSION OF THE STUDY

The present research study found out that LOM, WE and HAP has influence on Employee Performance which is also explained from past studies (Keller & Price, 2014; Kim, Han & Park, 2019; (Othman et al, 2018) while there was no influence of RO and EMP on employee performance. This is due to fact that the ongoing situation of corona virus has affected complete country. The patterns of work performance of workers have changed due to which RO and EMP has no influence on EP. In this research study there was found a mediation effect of happiness on relationship of empowerment and employee performance. This result has made contribution to the existing theory that empowered workers are happier and have enhanced performance to accomplish tasks. There was no mediation effect of happiness between RO and EP, LOM and EP, WE and EP. This is also due to the reason that the ongoing situation of corona virus has affected complete country. The patterns of work performance of workers have changed. This research also found out no moderation effect of spirit of work between the relationship of happiness and employee performance this is also due the reason that the ongoing situation of corona virus has affected complete country. The patterns of work performance of workers has changed and they have no influence of spirit of work. It is also since this research was conducted in South Punjab, Pakistan that's why results vary.

This research was cross sectional study, future studies should base on longitudinal studies. The large sample size could not be gathered due to the ongoing situation of corona virus in Pakistan and data was gathered through online survey questionnaire. Future studies should include large data size. This research has many insignificant results. Future studies should include new variables to test the results.

REFERENCES

Abrar, M., Shabbir, R., & Hussain, I., & Sana-ud-Din. (2019). Impact of Customer Animosity and Attitude on Purchase Intention in Fast-Food Industry of Pakistan. *Pakistan Journal of Social Sciences, 39*(3), 959–969.

Amran, F. W., Ghazali, H., & Siti Fatimah, M. (2018). Perceived Level Of Stress Among Casual Dining Restaurant Employees In Klang Valley, Malaysia. *International Journal of Modern Trends in Social Sciences, 1*(2), 9-14.

Arocas, R. L., & Li Ping Tang, T. (2004). The Love of Money, Satisfaction, and the Protestant Work Ethic: Money Profiles Among University professors in the USA and Spain. *Journal of Business Ethics, 50*(4), 329–354. doi:10.1023/B:BUSI.0000025081.51622.2f

Awaan, P. D., & Nawaz, M. (2015). Socio - Economic Determinants of Fast Food Industry Growth in Pakistan. *Food Science and Quality Management, 43*, 2224–2237.

Aydin, O. T. (2018). Impact of Demographic Variables on Job Stress Factors: A Study on Turkish Employees. *Journal of Business research Turk*, 803-826.

Barroso Castro, C., Villegas, M. P., & Casillas, C. B. (2008). Transformational leadership and followers' attitudes: The mediating role of psychological empowerment. *International Journal of Human Resource Management, 19*(10), 1842–1863. doi:10.1080/09585190802324601

Comrey, A. L., & Lee, H. (1992). *A first course in factor analysis*. Lawrence Erlbaum Associates, Inc.

Danish, R. Q., Ali, N., Ali, H., Afzal Humayon, A., Bilal Ahmed, M., & Gohar, A. (2019). Spirit and Innovation at Work in Software Houses of Pakistan: How Does Job Satisfaction Intervene the Relationship? *European Online Journal of Natural and Social Sciences, 8*(1), 66–78.

Fonkeng, C. (2018). *Effects of job-stress on employee performance in an enterprise. A microfinance institution in Cameroon*. Centria University of Applied Sciences.

Garaika, G. (2019). The Effects Of Fatigue, Role Overload And Stress On Farmer'S Work Safety. *Journal of Management, 36*(6), 1699–1724.

Gruman, A., & Saks, A. M. (2011). Performance management and employee engagement. *Human Resource Management Review, 21*(2), 123–136. doi:10.1016/j.hrmr.2010.09.004

Gunawan, H., & Amalia, R. (2015). Wages and employees performance: The quality of work life as moderato. *Journal of Economics and Financial Issues*, 234-248.

Hair, J. F., Black, W., Babin, B., & Anderson, R. (2010). *Multivariate Data Analysis* (7th ed.). Pearson.

Hair, J. F., Hult, G., Ringle, C., & Sarstedt, M. (2014). *A Primer on Partial Least Square Structural Equation Modeling (PLS - SEM)*. SAGE.

Henseler, J., Ringle, C., & Sarstedt, M. (2015). A new criterion for assessing discriminant validity in variance-based structural equation modeling. *Journal of the Academy of Marketing Science, 43*(1), 115–135. doi:10.100711747-014-0403-8

Herzberg, F. (1966). *Work and the nature of*. World Publishing.

Herzberg, F., Mausner, B., & Snydermann, B. (1959). *The motivation to work*. Wiley.

Hulin, C., Netemeyer, R., & Cudeck, R. (2001). Can a Reliability Coefficient Be Too High? *Journal of Consumer Psychology, 10*(1), 55–58. doi:10.1207/S15327663JCP1001&2_05

Jalagat, R. (2017). Determinants of Job Stress and Its Relationship on Employee Job Performance. *American Journal of Management Science and Engineering, 2*(1), 1–10. doi:10.11648/j.ajmse.20170201.11

Karimi, R., Omar, Z., Alipour, F., & Karimi, Z. (2014). The influence of role overload, role conflict, and role ambiguity on occupational stress among nurses in selected Iranian hospitals. *International Journal of Asian Social Scienece, 4*, 34–40.

Kim, C. Y., Lee, J. H., & Shin, S. Y. (2019). Why Are Your Employees Leaving the Organization? The Interaction Effect of Role Overload, Perceived Organizational Support, and Equity Sensitivity. *Sustainability, 11*(3), 657. doi:10.3390u11030657

Kim, W., Han, S., & Park, J. (2019). Is the Role of Work Engagement Essential to Employee Performance or 'Nice to Have'? *Sustainability, 11*(4), 1050–1067. doi:10.3390u11041050 PMID:30809384

Kinjerski, V., & Skrypnek, B. (2006). Measuring The Intangible: Development Of The Spirit At Work Scale. *Academy of Management Best Conference Paper*, A1-A6.

Malik, M., Sajjad, M., Hyder, S., Ahmad, M., Ahmed, J., & Hussain, S. (2013). Role overload: A cause of diminishing employee retention and productivity. *Middle East Journal of Scientific Research, 18*, 1573–1577.

Mittal, M., & Bhakkar, D. (2018). Examining the Impact of Role Overload on Job Stress, Job Satisfaction and Job Performance-A study among Married Working Women in Banking Sector. *International Journal of Management Studies, 5*(2), 7–19. doi:10.18843/ijms/v5i2(7)/01

Nadeem, M. T., Zia-uD-din, M., Riaz, W., Shafique, M. Z., & Sattar, A. (2018). The Effects of Employees Empowerment on Organizational Performance: A Case of Hotel Industry in Pakistan. *International Journal of African and Asian Studies, 47*.

Niehoff, B. P., Moorman, R., Blakely, G., & Fuller, J. (2001). The Influence of Empowerment and Job Enrichment on Employee Loyalty in a Downsizing Environment. *Group & Organization Management, 26*(1), 93–113. doi:10.1177/1059601101261006

Othman, A. K., Mahmud, Z., Noranee, S., & Noordin, F. (2018). Measuring Employee Happiness: Analyzing the Dimensionality of Employee Engagement. *Proceedings of the 7th International Conference on Kansei Engineering and Emotion Research*, 19-22. 10.1007/978-981-10-8612-0_90

Robbins, S. J. (2013). *Organizational Behavior* (15th ed.). Pearson.

Robbins, S. P., & Coulter, M. (2002). *Management* (7th ed.). Prentice Hall.

Rodwell, J. J., Kienzle, R., & Shadur, M. (1998). The Relationships Among Work-Related Perceptions, Employee Attitudes, And Employee Performance: The Integral Role Of Communication. *Human Resource Management, 37*(3 & 4), 277–293. doi:10.1002/(SICI)1099-050X(199823/24)37:3/4<277::AID-HRM9>3.0.CO;2-E

S., K., & Price, C. (2014). *Beyond Performance: How Great Organizations Build Ultimate Competitive Advantage*. New York: Wiley.

Schaufeli, W. B., Bakker, A., & Salanova, M. (2006). The Measurement of Work Engagement With a Short Questionnaire: A Cross-National Study. *Educational and Psychological Measurement, 66*(4), 701–716. doi:10.1177/0013164405282471

Schaufeli, W. B., Martínez, I., Marques Pinto, A., Salanova, M., & Bakker, A. (2002). Burnout and Engagement in University Students: A Cross-National Study. *Journal of Cross-Cultural Psychology, 33*(5), 464–481. doi:10.1177/0022022102033005003

Tang, T. L., & Chiu, R. K. (2003). Income, money ethic, pay satisfaction, commitment, and unethical behavior: Is the love of money the root of evil for Hong Kong employees? *Journal of Business Ethics, 46*(1), 13–30. doi:10.1023/A:1024731611490

Tang, T. L., Shin-Hsiung, D., & Arocas, R. (2005). Money Profiles: The Love of Money, Attitudes, and Needs. *Personnel Review*, *34*(5), 603–618. doi:10.1108/00483480510612549

Widiani, N. P., Putri, I., Sari, M. R., & Wirajaya, I. (2019). The Effect of Love of Money and Emotional Intelligence on Employee Performance with Organizational Citizenship Behavior as Mediating Variable. *International Research Journal of Engineering, IT & Scientific Research*, *5*(1), 39–49.

Chapter 20
The Influence of Training, Performance Appraisal, and Organizational Support on Employee Service Behavior With Compensation as a Mediator

Muhammad Imran
https://orcid.org/0000-0001-7126-2831
The Islamia University of Bahawalpur, Pakistan

Tehmina Ambreen
The Islamia University of Bahawalpur, Pakistan

ABSTRACT

The training, performance appraisal, organizational support, and compensation are playing a very important role in enhancing employee service behavior in the police department. The main objective of this study is to examine the impact of training, performance appraisal, and organizational support on employee service behavior, with the mediating role of compensation. Data was collected from the employees of Punjab police through the questionnaire. The partial least square structural equation modeling (PLS-SEM) has been employed for data analysis. The results of the study found a positive and significant relationship between training, performance appraisal, organizational support, and employee service behavior. Furthermore, compensation plays the mediating role between training, performance appraisal, organizational support, and employee behavior in Punjab police, Pakistan. As per the findings of the study, employee behavior can be improved with the help of training, performance appraisal, organizational support, and compensation.

DOI: 10.4018/978-1-7998-8678-5.ch020

INTRODUCTION

The situation regarding effective implementation of law & order in Pakistan is suffering from the last few decades. The numbers of criminal incidents are increasing day by day in Punjab, Pakistan. At this time, internal and external security threats are become main issues of Pakistan. In this regard, the Police department is the main stakeholder to assure the effective implementation of law & order in country (Raza & Mehmood, 2014).

On the other hand, police are the department where people come to solve their issues but in result employees of police department are misbehaved with them (Lersch & Mieczkowski, 2005). In our society, Police is playing the crucial role to fulfill the requirement of the clients but in real the role of police in society is conflicted one. However, the coordination between police and citizens is abhorrent. In other words the citizens are trying to solve their problems themselves without taking help of police due to their rude behavior (Akhtar, Rafiq, Asif, Saeed, & Kashif, 2012).

However, there are many studies have investigated the factors such as monitoring, motivation, management, trust, legitimacy and public cooperation, which can influence behaviour of employees in Police department (Dick & Metcalfe, 2001; Guzy & Hirtenlehner, 2015; Nagin, Rebitzer, Sanders, & Taylor, 2002). Moreover, most of past research have investigated the police and public interactions, some of studies have investigated the officer characteristics, organizational variables, and community characteristics in context of police behavior. In respect of organizational variables such as training, performance appraisal, organizational support and compensation are considered potential antecedents for better police behavior.

Furthermore, the police department is playing important role in the society of any country, it is also responsible to provide safety & security and implement the rules and regulations which provide protection to society. In other words, Police department in Punjab, Pakistan is not fulfilling their responsibilities, even though they are misbehaving with public. This misbehavior of employee is affecting reputation of Police department. Moreover, this misbehavior of employees is showing the incompetence of higher management and Government. According to past studies, it is suggested that the higher management and Government should introduce the different practices to improve the performance of Police department, which is very important for the Police department as well as whole community of Pakistan. On the other hand, the success of any organization depends on co-friendly behavior environment because it can improves the performance of organization (Kim, Kim, Choi, & Phetvaroon, 2019).

The behavior of employee plays a significant role in any organization to achieve their goals. Along with, training, performance appraisal, organizational support and compensation can improve the behavior of employees, more specifically, in Police department of Punjab, Pakistan (Muster & Schrader, 2011). The training of all employees in every department plays an important role because the trained employees could face every problem and can handle every situation that they face in the working environment. Besides, in the police department, the training can play the important role to enhances the skills and abilities of the employees (Lancaster, Di Milia, & Cameron, 2013). In Addition, the performance of employees' is evaluated through performance appraisals practice, whether the employees are working according to the set standards or not. As well as performance appraisal practice has shown the positive impact on employee service behavior. Although, performance appraisal is considered very important for any organization (Mandip, 2012).

Perceived organizational support is significantly effective in terms of supporting employees performance. Organizational support is equally important for employee's behavior. Hence, organizational support can be the source of good employee service behavior in Police department of Punjab, Pakistan.

Furthermore, the compensation practice is also very important to improve the employee service behavior. The employees are compensating in terms of overtime, bonuses, share, and gifts that have monetary and non-monetary values. In other words, organization are facilitating the employees in term of house rent and facility of free transport etc. Additionally, compensation can play the mediating role between training, performance appraisal, organizational support, and employee service behavior due to its nature. However, based on past literature, there are very few studies have been conducted to investigate the impact of training, performance appraisal, organizational support with mediating role of compensation on employee service behavior. This research will answer the following questions:

1. Is there relationship between training, performance appraisal, organizational support, and employee service behavior of Punjab police?
2. Is there compensation playing mediatory role between training, performance appraisal, organizational support, and employee service behavior of Punjab police?

LITERATURE REVIEW

Employee Service Behavior

Employee service behaves refers to behaviour during service to get respect, appreciation from boss, customers and as well as maintain friendly environment at workplace. Remember that office is not a place where you can only shout, criticize with your management and customers. Employees at service need to feel important to develop a positive attitude and sense of loyalty toward organization. The respect is highly important at service to avoid the discrimination (Mishra, Pareek, & Chakrabarti, 2020).

Furthermore, relationship between training, performance appraisal, organizational support and employee service behavior at service is increasing day by day. A few studies are published on training, performance appraisal, organizational support, and employee service behavior link. The training, performance appraisal, organizational support influences the employee service behavior at service The current study suggested toward the gap literature by discovering the results of training, performance appraisal, organizational support on the employee service behavior at place of work (Dumont, Shen, & Deng, 2017).

Employee Training and Employee Service Behavior

Training is important for the growth of any organization especially, for public organizations which directly deals with the public. Henceforward, training is increasing the knowledge, skill, and talent of a police officer. Even though, it helps us to inspire the police officer to accept a great responsibility and to increase the working capacity (Singh, 2017).

Furthermore, for every organization trained and experienced person are required to perform the daily work tasks. Even so, if the current employees are doing potential job and they can meet their requirements, still training is the main element for any organization to sustain the employees as well as organization performance. Whereas, learning processes is a sequence of programmed behavior in which knowledge is given to the employees and trial will guide their behavior.

According to, Diamantidis and Chatzoglou (2014) that trainees were targeted on the acquired knowledge, skills and behavior. Whereas, the training refers the trainee's information, skills, and behavior.

When the training is in completion, trainees need to deliver the acquired information and their skills to daily job and to enhance their job performance progressively (Ramasamy, 2017).

However, human resource practices such as training & development improves the working ability of employees at service and also to tackle the various problems (Liebowitz, 2010). In most recent study revealed that training is a potential contributor into employee service behaviour significantly (Amrutha & Geetha, 2021). So, on the basis of literature discussion, the current study proposes the following hypothesis;

H1: There is positive relationship between the training and the employee service behavior.

Performance Appraisal and Employee Service Behavior

Performance appraisal is an essential for organization which is enhancing the performance of employee (Rudman, 2020). Although, this is obligation of any organization to evaluate the employee's performance and describe their job responsibilities. However, organizations are introducing the performance evaluation standard to increase the employee performance as well as their good behavior.

Additionally, performance appraisal practice is giving direction to employee to increase their inspiration, long-run individual performance and career development

In past research stated that the performance appraisal practice shows the positive relationship with employee service behavior. Although, performance appraisal is very important for every organization, some of studies noticed that performance appraisal of staff have positive relation with employees behavior and productivity of the organization (Ali & Jadoon, 2012). On the basis of past literature, few studies shown the positive impact of performance appraisal on good employee service behavior (Armstrong-Stassen & Lee, 2009). However, this study believes performance appraisal can be the influential practice to improve the employee's behavior in Punjab Police, Pakistan.

H2: There is positive relationship between performance appraisal and employee service behavior.

Perceived Organization Support and Employee Service Behavior

Perceived Organizational support provides values to consumers and stakeholders whereas, organizational support evaluates the organizational success for their employees (Antony & Bhattacharyya, 2010). Even though, some of researchers stated that employee service behavior based on organization support. The organizational support is making positive change into employee's behavior. Hence, employee's feels that organization give them highly support.

The past studies findings found the positive and direct effect of organizational support on employee service behavior, organizational citizenship behavior and turnover. Hence, on the past researches sated that organizational support has positive impact on employee good behavior (Alfes, Shantz, Truss, & Soane, 2013). The study proposes the following hypothesis;

H3: There is positive relationship between perceived organizational support and employee service behavior.

Compensation as a Mediator

Compensation refers to providing financial benefits to employees in regard of their good performance or act (Armstrong & Brown, 2005). Hence, this strategy encourages the employee to give their ultimate performance. In Addition, Compensation is managing the people, and it supports the success of business. Even though, compensation is a positive relationship in which emotional bond was adopted and people can be adjusted easily (Patnaik & Padhi, 2012).

Furthermore, compensation package is the gift for the employees those work for the achievement of organization and its motivated employee to work more for the success of organization. Hence, compensation from the organization is entranced the employee's behavior.

In Addition, this study analyzes compensation as mediator between training, performance appraisal, organizational support, and employee service behavior. Hence, training improves employee skills and by offering compensation employee take parts in different training to work better in organization (Vui-Yee, 2018). Even though, the compensation system in associate organization ought to be adopted as a technique to influence and modify employee service behavior that best much the atmosphere (Khurshid & Darzi, 2016). Whereas the financial incentives are utilized in most cases to inspire workers on inexperience practices and such compensation is applied basically to the employees' behavior and it is modifying through incentives towards maintained environment friendly compensation structure.

Furthermore, compensation is important factor effecting how and why employees work in organization refers to remuneration for employees who come from the completion of their work and influencing employees to work in an organization. Eisenberger, Huntington, Hutchison, and Sowa (1986) explained that employees who have perception that organization providing support and care for their welfare then they will show strive towards the achievement of organization goals. According to, employee considers that organization in receipt of support is high then the employee will unite the membership as a member of the organization and then develop a positive perception of the organization (Niehoff & Moorman, 1993).

H4: There is mediating role of compensation between training and employee service behavior.
H5: There is mediating role of compensation between performance appraisal and employee service behavior.
H6: There is mediating role of compensation between organizational support and employee service behavior.

Research Framework

Social exchange theory shows relation involving within social exchange between employee and organization (Emerson, 1976). Hence, social exchange involves norms and term to the organization, so that benefits are provided to employees, managers, and partners. If supervisor does not provide good feedback to the employee, then employee does not give positive feedback and contract was not held. Even though, social relationship between employee and supervisor or manager is very important for the behavior of an employee in the department. According to social exchange theory, training change the employee service behavior and guide the employee accordingly, the service and employee perform well in the department with different people. Whereas compensation and performance appraisal also supported social exchange theory because employee get satisfied through given incentives and rewards and they try to work better in the department.

According to, this study perceived organizational support is taken as independent variable based on this theory organizational support has direct influence on employee service behavior. Whereas, perceived organizational support increase employee attachment to the organization and more effort from the employee toward organization is provided because if organization support employee they work hard for the department if the employee feel that organization is not supporting then their effort toward the department reduced (Eisenberger et al., 1986).

Hence, social exchange theory explores the relation of compensation as a mediator between the training, performance appraisal, organizational support, and employee service behavior. According to social exchange theory, employee training, compensation and performance appraisal and organizational support is important for the department success and mostly employee service behavior change when they get organizational support (Alfes et al., 2013).

Figure 1. Research framework

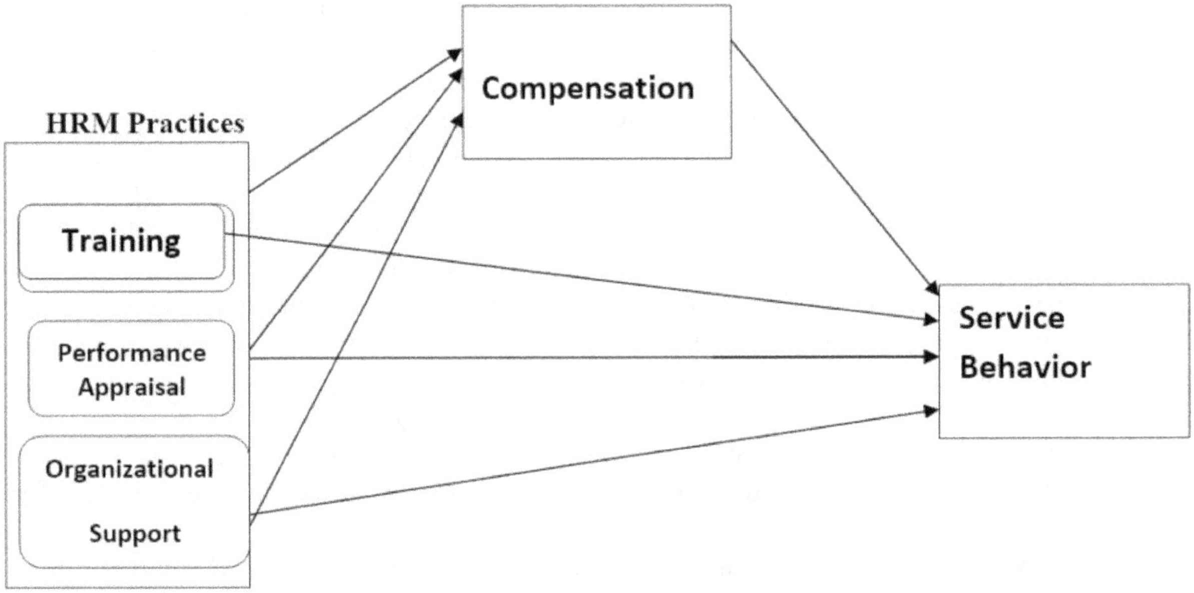

METHODOLOGY

This study is taken the responses from the Punjab Police of Pakistan. The total number of employees that are working in Punjab police are 1, 80,000 (Raza & Mehmood, 2014). Krejcie and Morgan (1970) sample size table was taken to find the 377-sample size for this study. This study used the random sampling technique to distribute the questionnaires among the respondents. Furthermore, Excel (Rand) has used to select the participants.

The 7-point Likert scale has been used in this current study. The questionnaire of training with 3 items, performance appraisal with 5 items, compensation with 5 items, employee service behavior through 8 items and organizational support with 7 items were taken from the study of Rensis (1932). This is more relevant with current context of the study. Moreover, the face and context validity were confirmed through the involvement of professor and police department experts. At the final stage, the pilot study was conducted to verify the reliability and validity of the scale as well.

ANALYSIS AND FINDINGS

The main objective of this chapter is to provide research results which is calculated through SPSS and Smart PLS. In respect of Smart PLS-SEM, two step approach has used such as measurement model and structural model. In measurement model, run the algorithm to test the data reliability and validity and the structural model run the bootstrapping to accept and reject the hypothesis.

Measurement Model

The measurement model consisting of the reliability, validity tests, there explanation and results are discussed below.

Reliability Test

The Cronbach alpha, composite reliability, average variance extracted criteria used to test the current study data reliability. The threshold values of Cronbach alpha, composite reliability are 0.70 and AVE value is about 0.05 (Nunnally & Bernstein, 1994). However, all values of present study construct found more than threshold values, the results can be seen in table 4.1 and figure 2.

Table 1. Reliability results

Constructs	Cronbach's Alpha	rho_A	Composite Reliability	Average Variance Extracted (AVE)
Compensation(C)	0.777	0.786	0.848	0.529
Employee service behavior (EB)	0.750	0.751	0.834	0.501
Organizational support	0.757	0.758	0.837	0.508
Performance Appraisal(PA)	0.788	0.796	0.855	0.541
Training(T)	0.719	0.719	0.842	0.640

Discriminant Validity

According to J. F. Hair, Ringle, and Sarstedt (2013), for assessment of discriminant validity the Fornell-Larker criterion should be use. The Fornell-Larker criteria assess the shared variance between the constructs of the research model. However, the Fornell-Larker criteria assessed by comparing AVE for each construct with correlation present in the matrix of correlation (Henseler, 2009). The table 4.2 shows Fornell-Larcker Criterion result with square root, the AVE is greater than the other construct, so discriminate validity of constructs is achieved.

Figure 2. Measurement model PLS algorithm

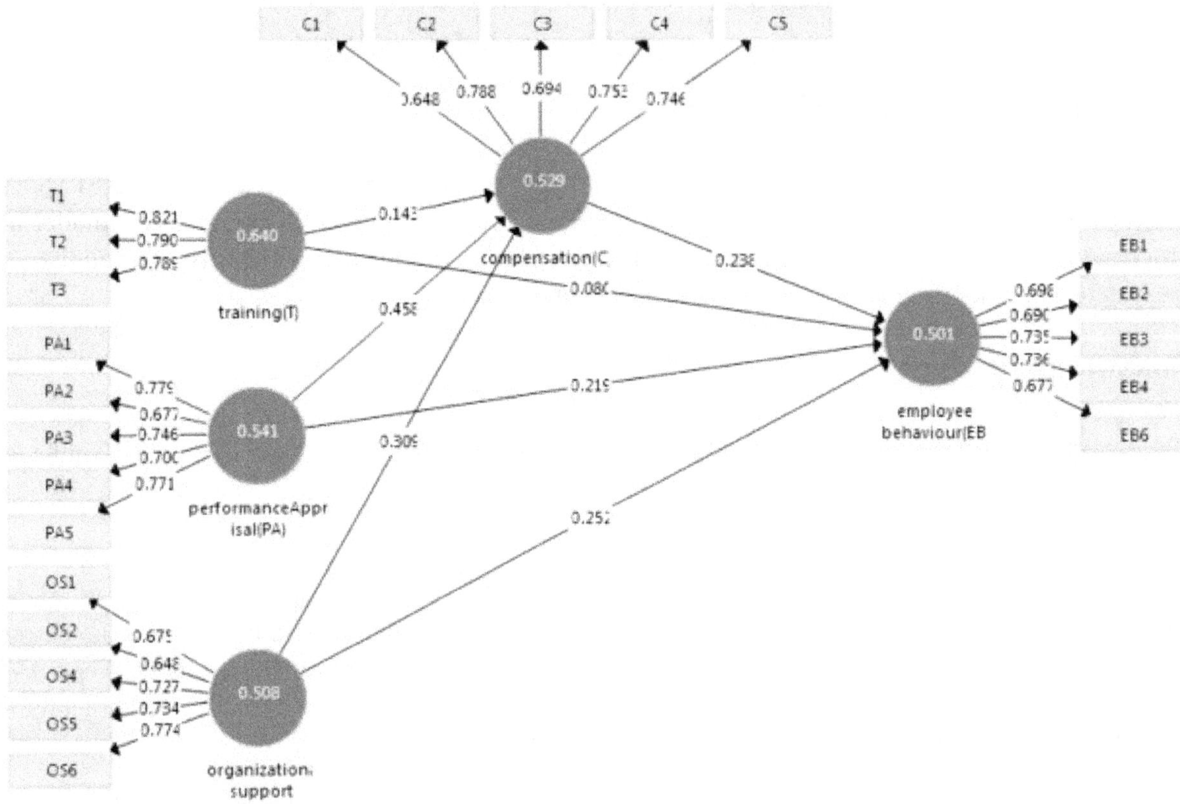

Table 2. Discriminant validity

Constructs	Compensation (C)	employee service behavior (EB)	organizational support	Performance Appraisal (PA)	Training (T)
Compensation (C)	0.727				
Employee service behavior(EB)	0.619	0.708			
Organizational support	0.673	0.594	0.713		
Performance Appraisal(PA)	0.737	0.598	0.607	0.736	
Training(T)	0.619	0.518	0.6	0.634	0.8

The Structural Model

After the successful assessment of measurement model, the structural model has run to draw the results of the study. The bootstrapping has run at 5000 interactions term to validate the hypothesis (J. Hair, 2014). The results of direct relationship between dependent and independent variables can be seen in table 4.3.

Figure 3. PLS algorithm direct relationship

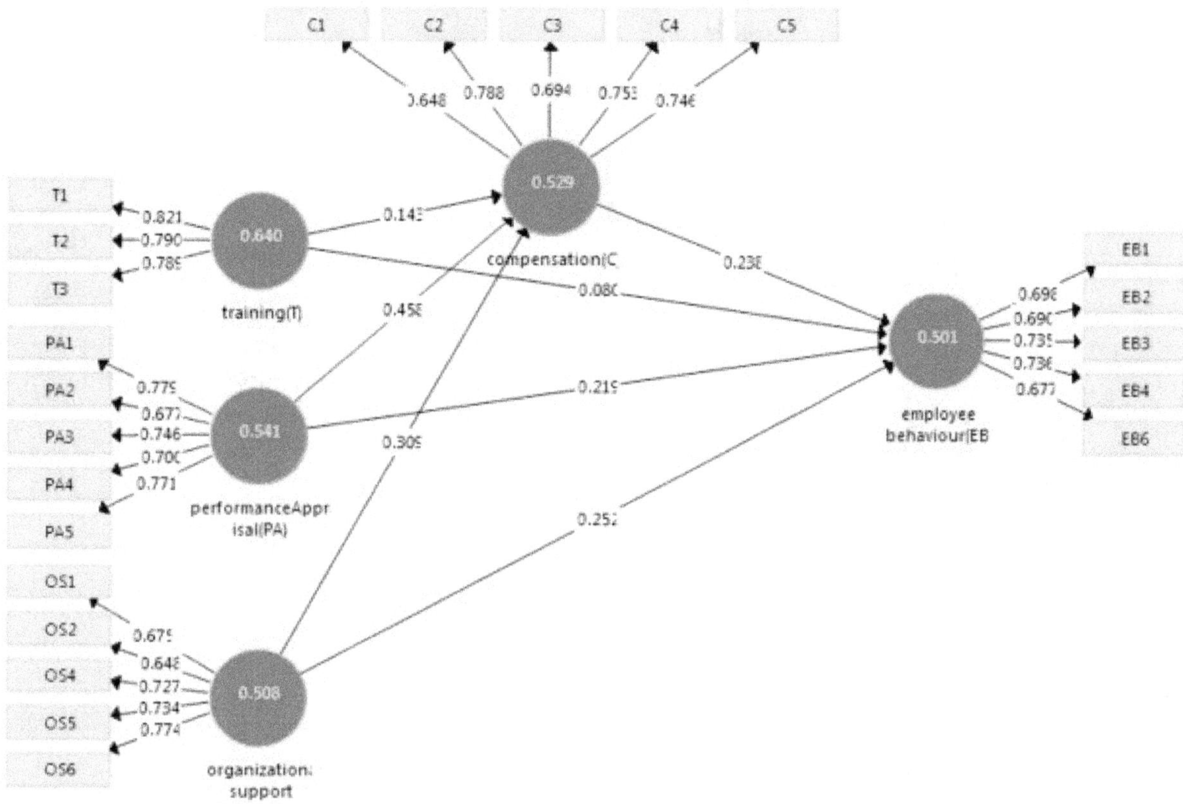

Table 3. PLS algorithm direct relationship

Hypothesis	Sample Mean (M)	Standard Deviation (STDEV)	T Statistics (|O/ STDEV|)	P Values
H1: Training(T) -> Employee service behavior(EB)	0.112	0.049	2.313	0.021
H2: Performance Appraisal(PA) -> Employee service behavior (EB)	0.329	0.046	7.177	0.000
H3: Organizational support -> Employee service behavior(EB)	0.329	0.05	6.562	0.000

Mediation Test

The Preacher and Hayes (2008) mediation approach has used to draw the mediation results, the results of mediation analysis can be seen in table 4.4.

Figure 4. PLS SEM bootstrapping (indirect relationship)

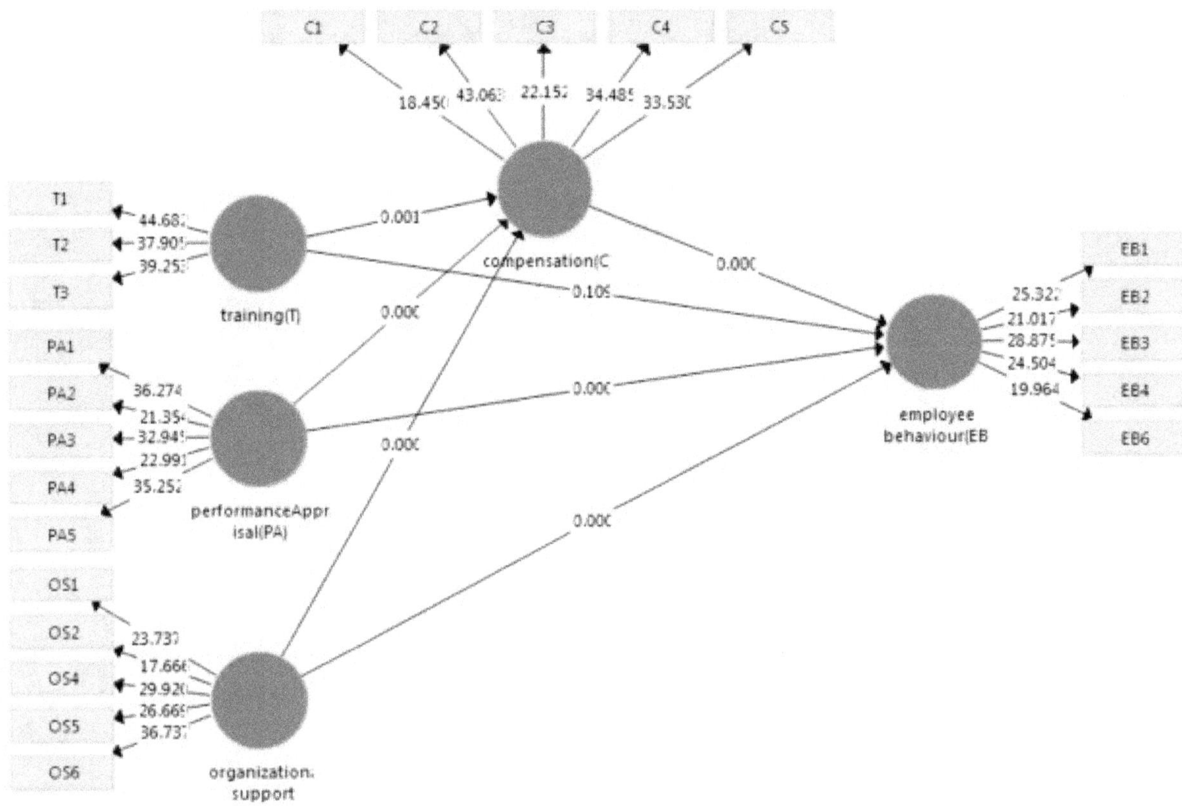

Table 4. Results of mediation test

Hypothesis	Sample Mean (M)	Standard Deviation (STDEV)	T Statistics (lO/ STDEVl)	P Values
H4: Training(T) -> Compensation (C) -> Employee service behavior (EB)	0.034	0.013	2.556	0.011
H5: Performance Appraisal(PA) -> Compensation(C) -> Employee service behavior (EB)	0.109	0.028	3.922	0.000
H6: Organizational support -> compensation(C) -> Employee service behavior (EB)	0.074	0.021	3.557	0.000

DISCUSSION, CONCLUSION AND RECOMMENDATION

Discussion and Conclusion

The result shows that there is a positive impact of training on employee service behavior (t=2.313; p<0.01, SO H1 is accepted. A significant positive influence of performance appraisal on Employee service behavior found (t=7.117; p<.05); so H2 is also supported. Furthermore, the relationship between organizational support and EB found significant as (t=6.56; p<.01), hence H3 accepted.

Moreover, compensation has found mediating role between training and employee service behavior (t=2.556 ;p<0.05), performance appraisal and employee service behavior (t=3.922;p<0.05), and organizational support and employee service behavior(t=3.557 ;p<0.05), hence the H4, H5 and H6 are accepted.

Therefore, first objective of this study is to identify the relationship between Training, performance appraisal, organizational support and employee service behavior of Punjab police. The finding shows that training has significant and positive effect on employee service behavior. Secondly results stated the positive relationship between performance appraisal and employee service behavior. Moreover, this study shows the positive relationship between employee service behavior and performance as well. These findings are align with study of Yamoah (2013). The second objective of the study to examine compensation the mediating role between training, performance appraisal, organizational support, and employee service behavior. However, the current study revealed the mediating role of compensation between training, performance appraisal, organizational support, and employee service behavior.

Implications

The employee service behavior can be changed through more effective implementation of tanning, performance appraisal, organizational support. In this study primary data were collected to conclude the study. Previous researchers were used SPSS and AMOS, MPlus software to get results but here the current study employed the PLS-SEM and SPSS both to gain positive result. Indifferent searches 5-point Likert scale was used, this study taken the 7-point Likert scale to collect the data.

Limitations and Future Recommendations

This study is taken the cross-sectional approach to collect the data; the future studies could take the longitudinal approached to collect the data for more precision results. The current study only collected the data from Punjab police, which can be violate the justification of total population or generalization of results. Therefore, the future studies should involve the other provinces police of Pakistan to generalize the findings.

REFERENCES

Akhtar, A., Rafiq, S., Asif, A., Saeed, A., & Kashif, M. (2012). Public perceptions of police service quality: Empirical evidence from Pakistan. *International Journal of Police Science & Management*, *14*(2), 97–106. doi:10.1350/ijps.2012.14.2.266

Alfes, K., Shantz, A. D., Truss, C., & Soane, E. C. (2013). The link between perceived human resource management practices, engagement and employee behaviour: A moderated mediation model. *International Journal of Human Resource Management*, *24*(2), 330–351. doi:10.1080/09585192.2012.679950

Ali, Q., & Jadoon, M. Z. I. (2012). Towards an indigenous perspective on HRM: A study of textile industry of Pakistan. *Studies*, *1*(2), 1–10.

Amrutha, V., & Geetha, S. (2021). Linking organizational green training and voluntary workplace green behavior: Mediating role of green supporting climate and employees' green satisfaction. *Journal of Cleaner Production*, *290*, 125876. doi:10.1016/j.jclepro.2021.125876

Antony, J. P., & Bhattacharyya, S. (2010). Measuring organizational performance and organizational excellence of SMEs–Part 2: an empirical study on SMEs in India. *Measuring Business Excellence*.

Armstrong, M., & Brown, D. (2005). Reward strategies and trends in the United Kingdom: The land of diverse and pragmatic dreams. *Compensation and Benefits Review*, *37*(4), 41–53. doi:10.1177/0886368705277659

Armstrong-Stassen, M., & Lee, S. H. (2009). The effect of relational age on older Canadian employees' perceptions of human resource practices and sense of worth to their organization. *International Journal of Human Resource Management*, *20*(8), 1753–1769. doi:10.1080/09585190903087156

Diamantidis, A. D., & Chatzoglou, P. D. (2014). Employee post-training behaviour and performance: Evaluating the results of the training process. *International Journal of Training and Development*, *18*(3), 149–170. doi:10.1111/ijtd.12034

Dick, G., & Metcalfe, B. (2001). Managerial factors and organisational commitment-A comparative study of police officers and civilian staff. *International Journal of Public Sector Management*, *14*(2), 111–128. doi:10.1108/09513550110387336

Dumont, J., Shen, J., & Deng, X. (2017). Effects of green HRM practices on employee workplace green behavior: The role of psychological green climate and employee green values. *Human Resource Management*, *56*(4), 613–627. doi:10.1002/hrm.21792

Eisenberger, R., Huntington, R., Hutchison, S., & Sowa, D. (1986). Perceived organizational support. *The Journal of Applied Psychology*, *71*(3), 500–507. doi:10.1037/0021-9010.71.3.500

Emerson, R. M. (1976). Social exchange theory. *Annual Review of Sociology*, *2*(1), 335–362. doi:10.1146/annurev.so.02.080176.002003

Guzy, N., & Hirtenlehner, H. (2015). *Trust in the German police: determinants and consequences for reporting behavior. In Trust and legitimacy in criminal justice*. Springer.

Hair, J. (2014). Partial Least Squares Structural Equation Modeling (PLS-SEM): An Emerging Tool for Business Research. *ResearchGate*, 106-121.

Hair, J. F. Jr, Ringle, C. M., & Sarstedt, M. (2013). Partial least squares structural equation modeling: Rigorous applications, better results and higher acceptance. *Long Range Planning*, *46*(1-2), 1–12. doi:10.1016/j.lrp.2013.01.001

Henseler, J. (2009). *The Use of Partial Least Squares Path Modeling in International Marketing*. JAI Press.

Khurshid, R., & Darzi, M. A. (2016). Go green with green human resource management practices. *Clear International Journal of Research in Commerce & Management, 7*(1).

Kim, Y. J., Kim, W. G., Choi, H.-M., & Phetvaroon, K. (2019). The effect of green human resource management on hotel employees' eco-friendly behavior and environmental performance. *International Journal of Hospitality Management*, *76*, 83–93. doi:10.1016/j.ijhm.2018.04.007

Krejcie, R. V., & Morgan, D. W. (1970). Determining sample size for research activities. *Educational and Psychological Measurement*, *30*(3), 607–610. doi:10.1177/001316447003000308

Lancaster, S., Di Milia, L., & Cameron, R. (2013). Supervisor behaviours that facilitate training transfer. *Journal of Workplace Learning*, *25*(1), 6–22. doi:10.1108/13665621311288458

Lersch, K. M., & Mieczkowski, T. (2005). Violent police behavior: Past, present, and future research directions. *Aggression and Violent Behavior*, *10*(5), 552–568. doi:10.1016/j.avb.2004.10.002

Liebowitz, J. (2010). The role of HR in achieving a sustainability culture. *Journal of Sustainable Development*, *3*(4), 50–57. doi:10.5539/jsd.v3n4p50

Mandip, G. (2012). Green HRM: People management commitment to environmental sustainability. *Research Journal of Recent Sciences*, 244–252.

Mishra, R., Pareek, G., & Chakrabarti, T. (2020). Green HRM Practices Effectiveness on the Psychological Contract: The Changing Nature of Employee-Employer. *International Journal of Recent Advances in Multidisciplinary Topics*, *1*(1), 37–39.

Muster, V., & Schrader, U. (2011). Green work-life balance: A new perspective for green HRM. *German Journal of Human Resource Management*, *25*(2), 140–156. doi:10.1177/239700221102500205

Nagin, D. S., Rebitzer, J. B., Sanders, S., & Taylor, L. J. (2002). Monitoring, motivation, and management: The determinants of opportunistic behavior in a field experiment. *The American Economic Review*, *92*(4), 850–873. doi:10.1257/00028280260344498

Niehoff, B. P., & Moorman, R. H. (1993). Justice as a mediator of the relationship between methods of monitoring and organizational citizenship behavior. *Academy of Management Journal*, *36*(3), 527–556.

Nunnally, j. c., & Bernstein, I. H. (1994). The Capability Approach and Evaluation of the Well-Being in Senegal: An Operationalization with the Structural Equations Models. *The Assessment of Reliability. Psychometric Theory,* 248-292.

Patnaik, B., & Padhi, P. C. (2012). Compensation management: A theoretical preview. *TRANS Asian Journal of Marketing & Management Research*, *1*(1), 39–48.

Preacher, K. J., & Hayes, A. F. (2008). Asymptotic and resampling strategies for assessing and comparing indirect effects in multiple mediator models. *Behavior Research Methods*, *40*(3), 879–891. doi:10.3758/BRM.40.3.879 PMID:18697684

Ramasamy, A. (2017). *A study on implications of implementing green HRM in the corporate bodies with special reference to developing nations*. Academic Press.

Raza, S. H., & Mehmood, D. B. (2014). Efficiency differences among law enforcing units in Punjab, Pakistan: Application of Data Envelopment Analysis. *Pakistan Journal of Applied Economics*, 17–37.

Rensis, L. (1932). Technique for the Measurement of Attitudes. *Archives of Psychology*.

Rudman, R. (2020). *Performance planning and review: Making employee appraisals work*. Routledge. doi:10.4324/9781003116684

Singh, D. (2017). Police Training in Punjab: An Evaluating Study towards training facilities at PPA, Phillaur. *International Research Journal of Commerce Arts and Science, 8*(9).

Vui-Yee, K. (2018). Linking training and development to employee turnover intention: are performance management and compensation sequential mediators? *Journal for Global Business Advancement,* 564 - 586.

Yamoah, E. E. (2013). Relationship between compensation and employee productivity. *Singaporean Journal of Business, Economics and Management Studies, 51*(1115), 1–5.

Chapter 21
Technology Gap:
Information and Communication Technology Trade and Sustainability Issues in India

Ritu Rana
https://orcid.org/0000-0002-2241-0807
National Institute of Technology Hamirpur, India

Manoj Sharma
National Institute of Technology Hamirpur, India

Ajay Singh
Indian Institute of Technology Jammu, India

ABSTRACT

This chapter extends the authors' previous research work in which an examination of causality was conducted between foreign direct investment (FDI), economic growth (GDP), and the environment (CO2 emissions and energy consumption [EC]) in the Indian context. Two more important variables (i.e., trade openness and technology gap) were also added. The chapter further examines the effects of information and communication technology (ICT) trade on both GDP and the environment of India. The results of previous model show that FDI is neither causing GDP nor is it bridging the technology gap. The results also indicate the existence of pollution haven hypothesis (PHH) in India as FDI is causing both CO2 and EC. Also, FDI is, though not causing the GDP directly, doing so indirectly through CO2 validating the existence of PHH. FDI is causing trade openness in India, but that openness is again causing more FDI, which is doing no good for India. The results of ICT trade model indicate that both GDP and ICT exports cause CO2 in India. Also, both the GDP and ICT exports are consuming energy in India.

DOI: 10.4018/978-1-7998-8678-5.ch021

INTRODUCTION

Globalisation of businesses has made economic activities cross all the boundaries. Economic activities are routed to achieve extreme economic growth. India is one among the developing countries that are framing policies to help achieve economic growth by encouraging and promoting a huge amount of business activities. At the same time, these activities become the cause of what is known as the green house gas (GHG) emissions. Reducing these GHG emissions from the highly polluting emerging economies without limiting the pace of their economic development is one of the most popular debates that have attracted global attention.

Four basic factors are involved in the process of economic development i.e., human and natural resources and building up of capital and technology (Hitam and Borhan, 2012). The developing countries rely mostly on the foreign capital and technology for their economic development. Over the last two decades, FDI flows have considerably increased all around the world (Seker et al., 2015). As per Bokpin (2017), it is largely considered that FDIs influence the economic prospects of recipient nation positively. Vu et al. (2006) also found that FDI has statistically significant positive effects on economic growth operating directly and through labor productivity.

It is also considered that technology transfer provided by developed countries contributes to the productivity growth in developing countries (Xu, 2000). In the words of Borensztein et al. (1998), FDI is an important vehicle for the transfer of technology, contributing relatively more to growth than domestic investment. Although FDI is expected to increase long-run growth in the host country via technological upgrading and knowledge spillovers, the extent to which FDI is growth-enhancing depends on the degree of complementarity and substitution between FDI and domestic investment (De Mello, 1999).

Several relaxations in taxes, environmental standards and regulations are being provided to foreign investors to increase the level of economic activities which, ultimately, are expected to bring economic growth. Markets are thus made open to the global investors through trade liberalisation for the sake of economic growth.

Hence, the idea of promoting and encouraging huge amounts of investments in business activities is considered good for any developing country like India, but there exist negative effects of such activities on the natural environment of the host country as several manufacturing processes make misuse of the natural resources. Investors from developed countries exploit the resources of developing countries as these countries have free trade policies and relaxed environmental laws. Shao (2018) found that dirty foreign investments flow to low-income countries. The reason for this he found is that in the absence of FDI-attracting factors such as infrastructure and skilled labor, low-income countries use lax environmental regulations and these low-income countries emerge as innocent pollution havens because they cannot afford the costs of implementing and monitoring environmental regulations. As per Elliot and Shimamoto (2008), there are concerns that less developed countries could competitively undercut each other's environmental regulations to attract FDI. This may result in these countries becoming "pollution havens", where multinational corporations (MNCs) locate operations in order to save on environmental related costs (Blanco et al., 2011). In this scenario, the MNCs that have more to gain from relocating are those in the most pollution-intensive industries e.g. in Iron and Steel, Non-Ferrous Metals, Industrial Chemicals, Pulp and Paper, and Non- Metallic Mineral Products.

India is one among those countries that strive for increase in their economic growth. For this purpose, Indian government continues to emphasize on creating favourable operating environments for both domestic and foreign investors through tax reductions/ exemptions, relaxed labour laws and natural environmental regulations, etc. But, several economic activities involve highly polluting and ecologically inefficient manufacturing processes, technologies and facilities that led to environmental degradation in several forms like pollution of water bodies, toxic substances emissions, deforestation, loss of biodiversity, etc. Bokpin (2017) explained the negative effects of higher environmental degradation on the labour hours also as a result of health problems; and their consequences reduce the productive capacity. Increased economic activity is to blame for such patterns of environmental destruction.

India is the fourth largest total GHG emitter in the world although it is one of the lowest per capita emitter countries (Alam et al., 2011). But still, developing countries, including India, commonly held a view that reduction in GHG emissions may constraint economic growth. Hence, investigation of causality relationships among FDI, economic growth and the natural environment becomes crucial in order to formulate strategies to cope up with the global warming and climatic instability.

Technology has helped the mankind since the outset of human history. It has helped ease the burden of humans at work as well as at home. It has also helped in improving the quality of lives of human beings. One of the greatest benefits that technology has provided to the people using it is shortening the distance between people around the world with the help of better communication devices. Almost everyone in this world today uses smart devices to communicate with each other and, thus, makes his work easier and faster.

The information and communication technology (ICT) trade has increased all over the world in the past few decades. Thus, ICT trade becomes one of the reasons for the economic growth of a country. In India, investments in information and communication technology have tremendously increased in the past few decades. ICT has now become an important component of the economy. In the current scenario, ICT directly or indirectly operates and controls most of the economy.

Researchers in the area of economics have predicted that a distinction between developed, developing and under-developed countries can be made with the help of information on their share of spending in gross domestic product (GDP). The countries with economies that are either moving towards being developed or developing countries are imperatively dependent on ICT. Thus, information technology is a crucial factor in economic growth of India.

In the words of Balakrishnan (2007), "ICT forms a growing percentage of GDP of developed economies, a slightly lower percentage of GDP in emerging economies such as India, China, and Korea, and only a negligible portion of GDP in less-developed nations". Thus, it is evident that economy of India is becoming increasingly dominated by ICT growth. It is evident from Table 1 that since the year 2000, ICT trade (i.e., exports and imports) in India has witnessed an enormous increase in past few years, and consequently the GDP of India has improved.

But everything in this world comes with a cost. The heightened use of ICT has put the environment at risk because it consumes a lot of energy. Thus, due to ICT trade, sustainability has become one of the major concerns globally. The sustainability concerns differ among countries.

This chapter extends the authors' previous research work published in Rana and Sharma (2020) in which an attempt was made to study the causal relationships between FDI, economic growth and the natural environment with a multivariate dynamic approach in Indian context. The work now extends in this chapter to examine the causal relationships between the ICT trade, economic growth and environment of India while taking into account the level of energy consumption as an important factor in the relationship and applying the Granger (-non) causality testing technique.

Table 1. ICT trade in India since 2000

Year	ICT Exports (% of total goods exports)	ICT Imports (% of total goods imports)
2000	1.685471626	5.450758254
2001	1.956287673	5.936395516
2002	1.559692076	7.039299194
2003	1.611938214	8.41673495
2004	1.425727608	8.307327436
2005	1.108673226	7.636875634
2006	1.108662997	7.649593873
2007	1.074197444	7.378689099
2008	0.973301949	4.08829509
2009	3.450177114	7.788600699
2010	1.998035608	6.30845334
2011	2.182670486	5.973562352
2012	1.980050891	5.311031088
2013	1.591772775	5.775121902
2014	0.973665883	6.311804078

Source: (World Development Indicators for India, World Bank)

Background

Several studies have been conducted so far to investigate the relationship between Foreign Direct Investment (FDI) and the relative improvements in the Economic Growth (EG) of the host country. The number of researchers and academicians who support the fact that FDI is the major driver of EG, especially in developing countries, is considerably higher than those who argue it to be untrue. It is evident in a literature review conducted by Almfraji and Almsafir (2014). They concluded that previous studies largely prove that FDI brings positive effects on host country's EG and only in a few cases brings negative or null effects. They reviewed several factors of host country that may influence FDI-EG relationship and found that: adequate levels of human capital, well-developed financial markets and open trade regimes positively affect FDI-EG relation; dependency on foreign investments and technical gap contributes negatively; effect from income level is conflicting; and attention should be paid to the quality of political environment. To further elaborate their finding that FDI has positive effects on EG but a dependency on foreign investments may have some negative effects, it is needful here to quote the findings of Jorgenson et al. (2007). In their study of 39 less developed countries, including India, they found that less developed countries that largely depend on FDI in the manufacturing sector for their growth as compared to domestic investment, are more prone to higher per capita levels of various noxious gas emissions as compared to less dependent economies. They concluded that foreign capital has inherent motive to ignore environmental consequences for maximum profits. Thus there arises a moderating role of good governance and quality institutions on the FDI-environment relationship as suggested by Bokpin (2017) in the African context. As per him, FDI promotion must be done in a restricted manner while keeping the environmental sustainability in consideration; and governance and institutions must be strengthened to regulate the firms' activities as the presence of quality institutions can assure the effects of FDI less harmful to the environment. Shahbaz et al. (2015) while investigating for high, middle and low-income countries also supported enforcing stringent environmental laws and providing more incentives to polluting firms for abiding legal emissions standards in low-income countries, though they included India in the middle-income panel and suggested command and control test with economic incentives for environmental regulations. Mehta (2002), in his study on the Indian mining sector, proposed Indian government to include codes of conduct that regulate and control the behaviour of large companies entering India to prevent indiscriminate exploitation of natural resources. He also advised preventing the trend of lowering the environmental standards to attract FDI. Acharyya (2009) examined the impacts of FDI on the GDP growth and CO_2 emissions and found that FDI does have a positive long-run impact on GDP growth but at the same time, it also has a quite large positive impact on CO_2 emissions too. It clearly signifies that as FDI increases, the EG increases and at the same time risk for natural environment increases. Baek and Koo (2008), in their study on the relationship between FDI and environment in case of China and India, also found that FDI-GDP has a positive long run relationship; and FDI- SO_2 emissions too have positive long-run relationship which is mainly due to the FDI inflow of pollution-intensive industries due to the un-strict environmental regulations.

To have a look at the current state of FDI, economic growth and CO_2 emissions in India, it is important to mention here that India Brand Equity Foundation (IBEF, 2018) is of the opinion that Indian government has taken many initiatives in recent years such as relaxing FDI norms across sectors such as defence, PSU oil refineries, telecom, power exchanges, and stock exchanges, among others to achieve technical know-how and generate employment. As far as the effects of FDI on economic growth is concerned, India is the second highest ranked emerging market in the top 10 in *The 2018 A.T. Kearney Foreign Direct Investment Confidence Index* (Kearney, 2018). If a look is taken on the effects of FDI on the environment of India, India's CO_2 emissions grew by an estimated 4.6% in 2017, despite a turbulent year for its economy; and given India's early stage of economic development, low per-capita emissions and its large population, there is significant scope for its emissions to increase (Andrew, 2018).

Various theories and hypothesis have been formulated in FDI-EG-Environment debate like; Environmental Kuznets Curve (EKC) supporting the promotion of FDI for EG as growth will further contribute to solution for environmental problems (Grossman and Krueger, 1991; Shafik and Bandyopadhyay, 1992; Kuznets, 1995); Porter Hypothesis supporting FDI and stricter environmental regulations to form the basis for innovation resulting in the increased competitiveness of the firm; Pollution Haven Hypothesis (PHH) stating that FDI promotes the flow of polluting industries from developed countries to less developed and pollution haven countries as explained by Johnson and Turner (2010). These theories have got several supports and criticisms by academicians depending on the scope of their studies in different countries' contexts (Cole, 2004; Hitam and Borhan, 2012; Avazalipour et al., 2013; Rana and Sharma, 2019).

The finance literature consists of a well debated rationale for the need of foreign investment in less developed countries due to several benefits it provides to the host country e.g. bridging the internal resource and savings gap, increasing managerial abilities, reducing foreign exchange shortage and improving balance of payment (Aliyu, 2005). One of the major benefits that FDI is considered to bring to the host country is the technology transfer (e.g. Li and Liu, 2005; Xu, 2000; and Schembri and Petit, 2009). Several studies have linked FDI with the environmental pollution on the basis of pollution haven hypothesis and have tried to find out the causal relationships among them (e.g. Seker et al., 2015; Shahbaz et al., 2015; Jorgenson et al., 2007; and Bokpin, 2017). Openness to trade i.e., trade liberalisation has also been used as a variable to examine such relationships (e.g. Choi et al., 2010). Energy consumption is considered a variable of utmost importance in the studies of causal relationships among environmental pollution and economic growth. Several studies have used energy consumption as an endogenous variable to examine such relationships (e.g. Alam et al., 2011; Choi et al., 2010; and Seker et al., 2015).

Although it has been recognised that relationships among environmental pollution, foreign capital accumulation and economic growth indicators are of great importance in development theory (Xepapadeas, 2005) yet, there is no solidarity regarding the dynamic causal relationship between them in the same framework, especially for India with a dynamic multivariate approach. While FDI's effects on EG and CO_2 emissions have been tested several times (using various causality testing techniques), there are only a few studies which evaluates the dynamic causality relationship between them along with a few other important variables like energy consumption, trade liberalisation and technology gap for India in particular. Alam et al. (2011) is one among such studies that tries to examine dynamic causal relationships between income growth, CO_2 emissions and energy consumption specifically for India. The main focus of their study was, however, on examining the causal relationship between only three variables, as mentioned earlier i.e., income growth, CO_2 emissions and energy consumption. Linh and Lin (2015) also tried to examine the dynamic causality relationships among CO_2 emissions, energy consumption, economic growth and FDI in 12 most populous Asian countries including India, but their study did not apply the Toda Yamamoto (TY) approach proposed in the year 1995 and was focused on and limited to a few variables. In this chapter, the authors have tried to study a wider aspect of the causal relationship between FDI, EG, CO_2 emissions and energy consumption while taking the level of trade openness and technology gap as important variables in such relationship. Authors have also tried to focus on the information and communication technology trade as it is considered as the main reason for bring in the technology revolution globally and thus affected the environment we live in.

The study is important for at least four reasons. First, knowledge on the effects of FDI on EG and at the same time on natural environment (symbolised by CO_2 emissions and energy consumption) of India. Second, knowledge on the role of trade openness in FDI-EG-natural environment relationship (though Choi et al., 2010 used trade openness as an important variable in this relationship, still a dynamic causality testing technique was not used and it was not concerned with India specifically). Third, knowledge on the importance of technology gap in FDI-EG-natural environment relationship. Fourth, knowledge on the effects of ICT trade on both the economic growth and the environment of India. This is the unique and important part of the study because the variable 'ICT', to the best of authors' knowledge, has never ever been used in examining the EG-natural environment relationship with a dynamic multi-variate approach.

THE MODEL AND THE METHODS

The study is conducted in a phased manner. In the first phase, the study used the previously published linear regression model to examine the relationship between FDI, economic growth and environmental degradation in India during 1980-2014. In the previous model, CO_2 emissions were taken as the representative of environmental degradation as CO_2 emission is considered the main cause for global warming and climatic instability (IPCC, 1996) and is considered the major global pollutant. The initial model was:

$$CO_2 = f(GDP, FDI, OPEN, EC, TG) \quad (1)$$

and the equation of the model was:

$$lnCO_{2_t} = {}^{2}{}_{0} + {}^{2}{}_{1}(lnGDP)_t + {}^{2}{}_{2}(lnFDI)_t + {}^{2}{}_{3}(OPEN)_t + {}^{2}{}_{4}(lnEC)_t + {}^{2}{}_{5}(TG)_t + u_t \quad (2)$$

where, CO_{2_t} was carbon dioxide emissions per capita (metric tons); GDP_t was gross domestic product per capita (current US$); FDI_t was net inflows of foreign direct investment (BoP, current US$); $OPEN_t$ was a measure of trade liberalisation; EC_t was energy consumption or energy use per capita (kg of oil equivalent); TG_t was a measure of technology gap; and u_t was the error term or the stochastic random variable; all at time *t*.

Following Choi et al. (2010), trade liberalisation at time *t* i.e., $OPEN_t$ was measured as the sum of imports and exports as a percent of total GDP in a given year as follows:

$$OPEN_t = IMP_t + EXP_t \quad (3)$$

where, IMP_t was imports of goods and services (% of GDP) and EXP_t was exports of goods and services (% of GDP) at time *t* and Consistent with Li and Liu (2005), technology gap was measured as follows:

$$TG_t = \frac{GDP_{max_t} - GDP_t}{GDP_t} \quad (4)$$

where, GDP_{max_t} was the GDP per capita (current US $) of the United States of America (USA) at time *t*.

GDP of USA was used as GDP_{max} i.e., the highest GDP in the world because the economy of USA ranks 1st in the world in terms of GDP as per GDP Ranking Table (World Bank Group, 2016). In that same table, the economy of India ranks 7th. Thus, there is a huge gap in the GDP of both the economies. This gap in GDP, or in final goods and services produced, was attributed to the gap in technology used in both the economies because the production and economic growth largely depends on the quality of technology involved. This measure, thus, indicates that the GDP gap in both the economies was because of the new and advanced technology used by USA which India lacks. A relative measure of technology gap was used in the model. This gap not only affects the production outcome but also affects the environment due to several ecologically inefficient processes involved in production. Also, in the words of Gandolfo (1998), technology gap is the advantage enjoyed by the country that introduces new goods as a consequence of research activity and entrepreneurship, new goods are produced and the innovating country enjoys a monopoly until the other countries learn to produce these goods: in the meantime they have to import them.

The data on all the variables used for this model (for the period 1980-2014) was sourced from one of the globally reliable sources i.e., World Development Indicators (WDI) of World Bank Group (2016) Data Reports for India.

The main econometrics methodology used in this model was the Modified Wald (MWALD) test proposed by Toda and Yamamoto (1995). Though there are several methodologies in the literature for testing causality such as Granger (non-) causality (Engle and Granger, 1987), Sims causality (1972) and causality in Johansen and Juselius (1990) Error Correction Mechanism (ECM), TY multivariate approach for testing the causality has its advantages over the other tests. It can be used even when the variables are integrated of different orders. It requires the estimation of an augmented Vector Auto-Regression (VAR) irrespective of whether the time series is integrated or cointegrated (Ahmed, 2015). If the system has a unit root, the conventional OLS (Ordinary Least Square) of VAR in level-based Wald statistics have non-standard asymptotic distribution that may involve annoying parameters (Toda and Phillips, 1993). TY procedure put restrictions on the parameters of VAR (*l*) from an augmented VAR ($l+i_{max}$) model, where *l* is the optimal lag length and i_{max} is the maximum order of integration of variables (Alam et al., 2011). The VAR ($l+i_{max}$) model in TY approach is written as:

$$y_t = \pm + {}^{2}{}_{1} y_{t-1} + \ldots + {}^{2}{}_{l+i_{max}} y_{t-(l+i_{max})} + \mu_t \tag{5}$$

where y_t consists of *K* endogenous variables, α is a vector of intercept terms, β are coefficient matrices and ε_t are white noise residuals. The null hypothesis in TY causality is based on zero restriction on first *l* parameters (H_0: $\beta_1 = \ldots = \beta_l = 0$) of the *kth* element of y_t. Until $l\,^3\, i_{max}$, the model is valid (Kuzozumi and Yamamoto, 2000).

In the previous model, at first, the maximum order of integration (i_{max}) of the variables was obtained with the help of unit root tests. All unit root tests with an optimal lag length were performed with deterministic elements i.e. a time trend and a constant. The unit root tests performed in the study included Augmented Dickey Fuller (ADF) unit root test and Phillips-Perron (PP) unit root test for obtaining robust results. The appropriate maximum lag length (*l*) for the variables was chosen the next. A VAR (*l*) in levels of the data was then set up including an intercept in each equation. The residuals were then examined to see whether the VAR in levels is well specified. AR Roots Table and AR Roots Graph were used to examine the stability of the VAR model so formed, White Heteroskedasticity (No Cross Terms) test was used to examine homoskedasticity among the residuals and normality among residuals was examined with the help of J-B (Jarque-Bera) statistic through square root of correlation (Doornik-Hansen) method. Serial Correlation Lagrange's Multiplier (LM) test was used for examining serial independence among the residuals. Next, Autoregressive-Distributed Lag (ARDL) Bounds test, a cointegration technique was used to determine any cointegrating equations among the variables so that an Error Correction Term (ECT) can be introduced. Finally, a levels VAR model was re-estimated with i_{max} additional lags (i.e., $l+i_{max}$ lags in total) of each of the variables into each of the equations to examine the causality among variables.

In the second phase, another model has been introduced. The second model uses a linear regression model to examine the relationship between ICT exports, economic growth and environmental degradation in India during 2000-2014. The second model is:

$$\boldsymbol{CO_2 = f(GDP, EC, ICT\_exp)} \tag{6}$$

and the equation of the model is:

$$\boldsymbol{lnCO_{2_t}} = {}^{2}{}_{0} + {}^{2}{}_{1}(\boldsymbol{lnGDP})_t + {}^{2}{}_{2}(\boldsymbol{lnEC})_t + {}^{2}{}_{3}(\boldsymbol{lnICT\_exp})_t + \boldsymbol{u_t} \tag{7}$$

where, $\boldsymbol{CO_{2_t}}$ is carbon dioxide emissions per capita (metric tons); GDP_t is gross domestic product per capita (current US$); EC_t is energy consumption or energy use per capita (kg of oil equivalent); $\boldsymbol{ICT\_exp_t}$

is ICT goods exports (% of total goods exports); and u_t is the error term or the stochastic random variable; all at time t.

The data on all the variables used for this model (for the period 2000-2014) is also sourced from WDI of World Bank Group 2019 Data Reports for India. Data is collected up to the year 2014 because of the availability limitations.

In the second model also, at first, the stationarity is tested of all the variables under study with the help of unit root tests. All unit root tests with an optimal lag length are performed with deterministic elements i.e. a time trend and a constant. The unit root tests performed in this model also include ADF and PP unit root test for obtaining robust results. Next, the appropriate maximum lag length (l) for the variables has been chosen for the study. A VAR (l) in levels of the data is then set up including an intercept in each equation. The residuals were then examined to see whether the VAR in levels is well specified. AR Roots Table and AR Roots Graph are used to examine the stability of the VAR model so formed, White Heteroskedasticity (No Cross Terms) test is used to examine homoskedasticity among the residuals and normality among residuals is examined with the help of J-B statistic through Cholesky of Covariance (Lutkepohl) method. Serial Correlation LM test is used for examining serial independence among the residuals. Next, ARDL Bounds test is used to determine any cointegrating equations among the variables. Finally, pair-wise Granger (-non) causality testing techniques is applied to examine the causal relationships among all the variables.

RESULTS AND DISCUSSIONS

Testing of Stationarity

Dickey and Fuller (1979, 1981) devised a procedure to test for non-stationarity known as the Dickey-Fuller (DF) unit root test and then an Augmented Dickey Fuller (ADF) unit root test that was used in the previous work to obtain maximum order of integration (i_{max}) of the variables, before estimating the TY model, along with the PP unit root test as Phillips and Perron (1988) states that ADF unit root test under rejects when the data series are subject to both: a deterministic trend and an exogenous shock that causes structural break. The null hypothesis under ADF and PP unit root test is "the variable has a unit root" i.e., the variable is non-stationary. Deterministic elements i.e. a time trend and a constant were included in the unit root tests. Table 2 displays the p-values of ADF and PP unit root tests results for the data series of all the variables in the first model at levels and at first differences.

The ADF unit root test results indicate that $lnCO_2$, $lnGDP$, $OPEN$, $lnEC$ and TG are non-stationary at level but are integrated of first-order i.e. I(1) at 1% significance level whereas, $lnFDI$ is stationary i.e. I(0), at 10% significance level and virtually at 5% significance level too. So, maximum order of integration as per ADF unit root test was 1.

The PP unit root test results indicate that $lnCO_2$, $lnGDP$, $OPEN$, $lnEC$ and TG are non-stationary at level but are integrated of first-order i.e. I(1) at 1% significance level whereas, $lnFDI$ is stationary i.e. I(0), at 10% significance level. So, maximum order of integration as per PP unit root test was 1.

Concluding both the unit root tests performed on the variables, i_{max} was determined as 1 i.e., i_{max}=1 in the first model.

Table 3 displays the p-values of ADF and PP unit root tests results for the data series of all the variables in the second model at levels and at first differences.

Table 2. ADF and PP unit root tests results for first model

Variable	ADF		Order of Integration	PP		Order of Integration
	At Level	At First Difference		At Level	At First Difference	
$\ln CO_2$	0.7989	0.0004***	I(1)	0.7048	0.0004***	I(1)
lnGDP	0.9108	0.0003***	I(1)	0.9108	0.0003***	I(1)
lnFDI	0.0515**	-	I(0)	0.0582*	-	I(0)
OPEN	0.4058	0.0002***	I(1)	0.4058	0.0002***	I(1)
lnEC	0.9948	0.0011***	I(1)	0.9883	0.0009***	I(1)
TG	0.8956	0.0002***	I(1)	0.8956	0.0002***	I(1)

Note: ***, ** and * indicate significance level at 1%, 5% and 10%, respectively

Table 3. ADF and PP unit root tests results for second model

Variable	ADF		Order of Integration	PP		Order of Integration
	At Level	At First Difference		At Level	At First Difference	
$\ln CO_2$	0.1785	0.0785*	I(1)	0.0080***	-	I(0)
lnGDP	0.8313	0.0567**	I(1)	0.7687	0.0037***	I(1)
lnEC	0.1866	0.1054*	I(1)	0.1866	0.1054*	I(1)
lnICT_exp	0.4491	0.0213**	I(1)	0.4542	0.0213**	I(1)

Note: ***, ** and * indicate significance level at 1%, 5% and 10%, respectively

The ADF unit root test results indicate that $lnCO_2$, *lnGDP*, *lnEC* and *lnICT_exp, i.e.* all the variables under second model are non-stationary at level but are integrated of first-order i.e. I(1) at 5% and 10% significance levels. *lnEC* is virtually I(1) at 10% significance level. The PP unit root test results indicate that *lnGDP*, *lnEC* and *lnICT_exp* are non-stationary at level but are integrated of first-order i.e. I(1) at 1%, 10% and 5% significance levels respectively whereas, $lnCO_2$ is stationary i.e. I(0), at 1% significance level. So, it is concluded from both the unit root tests that the second model has a combination of both I(0) and I(1) variables.

Optimal Lag Selection

To select the optimum lag for both the models, four different lag selection criterion were examined, namely, Final Prediction Error (FPE), Akaike information Criterion (AIC), Schwarz Criterion (SC) and Hannan-Quinn (HQ) Criterion.The various information criteria suggest that a maximum lag length of 2 for each variable should be used in the first model (Table 4), i.e. $l=2$ and 1 for each variable should be used in the second model (Table 5).

Table 4. Optimal lag selection for first model

Lag	FPE	AIC	SC	HQ
0	8.55e-05	7.659868	7.931960	7.751419
1	2.88e-09	-2.678745	-0.774099*	-2.037890
2	1.71e-09*	-3.429492*	0.107708	-2.239332*

Note: * indicates lag order selected by the criterion

Table 5. Optimal lag selection for second model

Lag	FPE	AIC	SC	HQ
0	1.97e-08	-6.393825	-6.211237	-6.410726
1	9.13e-11*	-11.89707*	-10.98413*	-11.98158*

Note: * indicates lag order selected by the criterion

Residual Diagnostics of VAR (*l*) at Level

For the first model, a VAR (2) model in the levels of the data, including an intercept in each equation is set up, as l=2 here. The residuals were then examined to make sure that the VAR is well specified. Results of the various tests performed on the residuals are shown in Table 6 and Fig. 1. The estimated model is dynamically stable as shown by the AR Roots Graph (in Fig. 1) below and the information provided by the AR Roots table (in Table 6). The null hypothesis under White Heteroskedasticity (No Cross Terms) is "no heteroskedasticity" which cannot be rejected in the results. The null hypothesis under J-B statistics of Square root of correlation (Doornik-Hansen) test is "residuals are multivariate normal" that too cannot be rejected in the results. Null hypothesis under Serial correlation LM test is "no serial correlation exists" that again, cannot be rejected. Thus, the residuals are found to be homoskedastic, normally distributed and free from serial correlation and the first model is found to be stable with 2 lags. Thus, optimum lag is selected to be 2 i.e., l=2 in the first model.

Table 6. Diagnostic test results of VAR (1) in levels for first model

Diagnostic Test	Test Statistic	p-value
VAR Stability (AR Roots Table)	No root lies outside the unit circle	-
White Heteroskedasticity (No Cross Terms)	513.0124	0.3809
J-B test (Doornik-Hansen)	7.198507	0.8442
Serial Correlation LM (with l=2)	45.37129	0.1361

For the second model, a VAR (1) model in the levels of the data, including an intercept in each equation is set up, as l=1 here. The residuals were then examined to make sure that the VAR is well specified. Results of the various tests performed on the residuals are shown in Table 7. The estimated model is found to be dynamically stable as checked by the AR Roots Graph and the information provided by

Figure 1. AR roots graph for first model

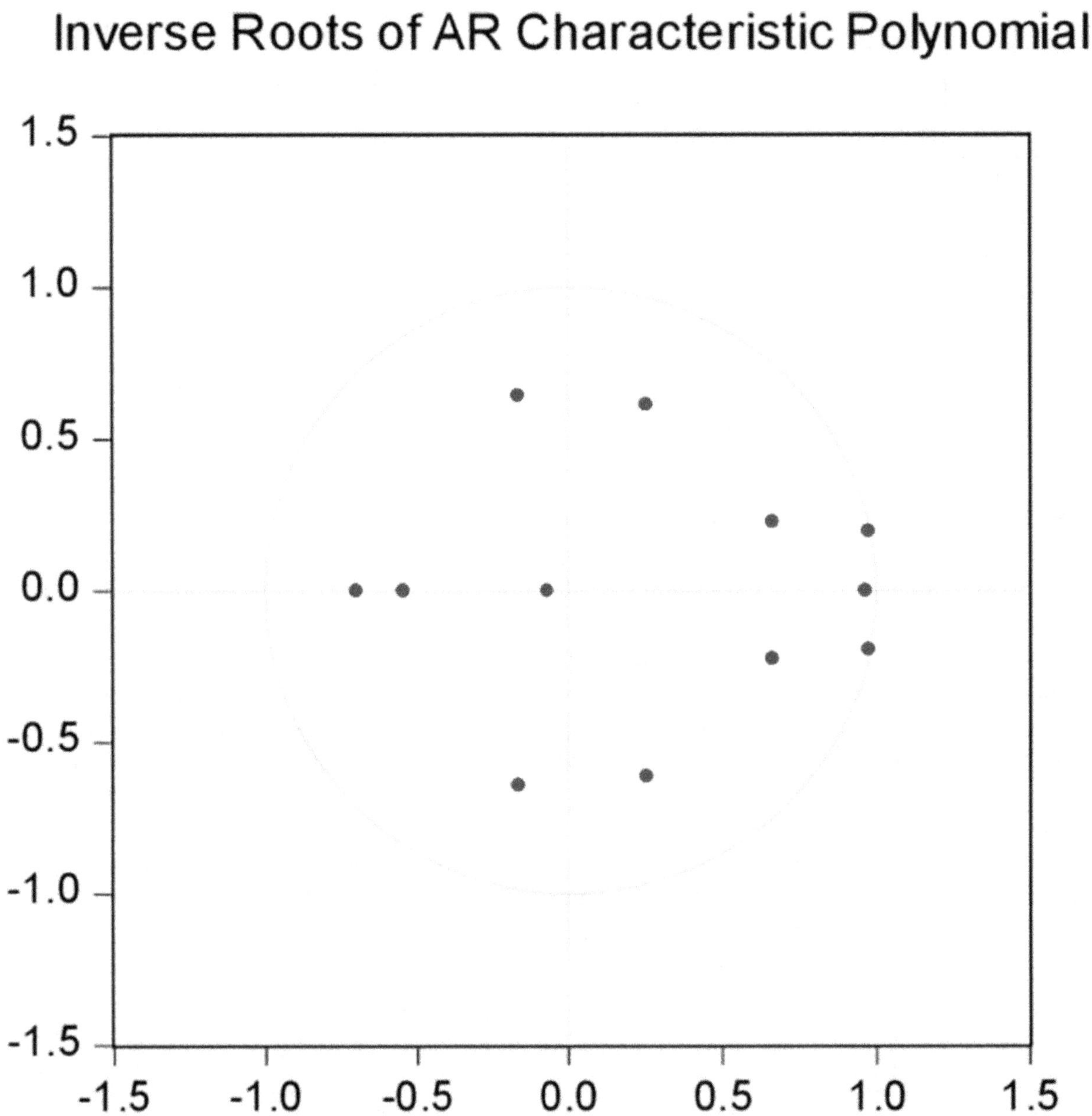

the AR Roots Table (mentioned in Table 7). The null hypothesis of "no heteroskedasticity" in White Heteroskedasticity (No Cross Terms) test cannot be rejected in the results of second model. Similarly, the null hypothesis under J-B Statistics of Cholesky of Covariance (Lutkepohl) test i.e., "residuals are multivariate normal" too cannot be rejected in the results of second model. The null hypothesis under Serial correlation LM test i.e., "no serial correlation exists" cannot again be rejected in the second model. Hence, it is evident from the results that there was no serial correlation found among the residuals of the

VAR (1) equations; and the residuals were found to be homoskedastic and normally distributed for the second model. Also, the VAR (1) in levels model is dynamically stable for the second model.

Table 7. Diagnostic test results of VAR (1) in levels for second model

Diagnostic Test	Test Statistic	p-value
VAR Stability (AR Roots Table and Graph)	No root lies outside the unit circle	-
White Heteroskedasticity (No Cross Terms)	79.68867 (Chi-Sq.)	0.4888
Cholesky of Covariance (Lutkepohl)	2.498807 (J-B Stat)	0.9618
Serial Correlation LM (with l=1)	0.654410 (Rao F-stat)	0.7714

ARDL Bounds Test

From the results of ADF and PP unit root tests performed above, it is concluded that all the variables are integrated of first order i.e., I(1) in the first model except *lnFDI* which is stationary i.e., I(0) but none is found to be integrated of second order i.e., I(2). In this condition, ARDL bounds testing methodology of Pesaran and Shin (1999) and Pesaran et al. (2001) is preferred to test for any cointegrating equation among variables. This technique is preferred above Johansen (1988) cointegration technique because Johansen cointegration technique can be applied only when all the variables are integrated of same order i.e., I(1) but ARDL bounds testing technique can be used with a mixture of I(0) and I(1) data. A general ARDL model is written as follows:

$$\Delta Y_t = \beta_0 + \sum_{i=1}^{k} \beta_i \Delta y_{t-i} + \sum_{i=0}^{k} \delta_i x_{t-i} + \varphi_1 y_{t-1} + \varphi_2 x_{t-1} + \mu_t \quad (8)$$

where, β_i and δ_i are short-run coefficients; φ_1 and φ_2 are ARDL long-run coefficients; μ_t is the disturbance term and k is the number of lags.

An ARDL model of lag 1 was set up for the first model which was found to be dynamically stable (Fig. 2 based on Recursive Estimates, CUSUM test) and free from autocorrelation (Serial Correlation LM test's *p-value* = 0.1791) but the Wald test for coefficient restrictions showed the F-statistic of 2.202614 which is lesser than the lower bound value of Pesaran's Table at 5% critical value. Hence, the null hypothesis of "no cointegration" cannot be rejected. Thus, there was no cointegration found among the variables in the first model (and hence, no ECT will be introduced), but as per Giles (2011), cointegration result does not affect the final results of the causality analysis under TY multivariate approach.

For the second model, an ARDL model with 1 lag was set up which was also found to be dynamically stable (based on Recursive Estimates, CUSUM test). Also, the residuals of the model were found to be normally distributed, homoskedastic and free from autocorrelation (Table 8).

In Pesaran's Table with unrestricted intercept and unrestricted trend, the upper bound value at 5% significance level is 4.57 with $k = 4$, or the number of explanatory variables as 4. In this second model, the Wald test for coefficient restrictions showed the F-statistic of 3.593357 with a p-value of 0.1216. The value F-statistic obtained is lower than the upper bound value of Pesaran's Table. Hence, the null

Figure 2. CUSUM test for ARDL model stability for first model

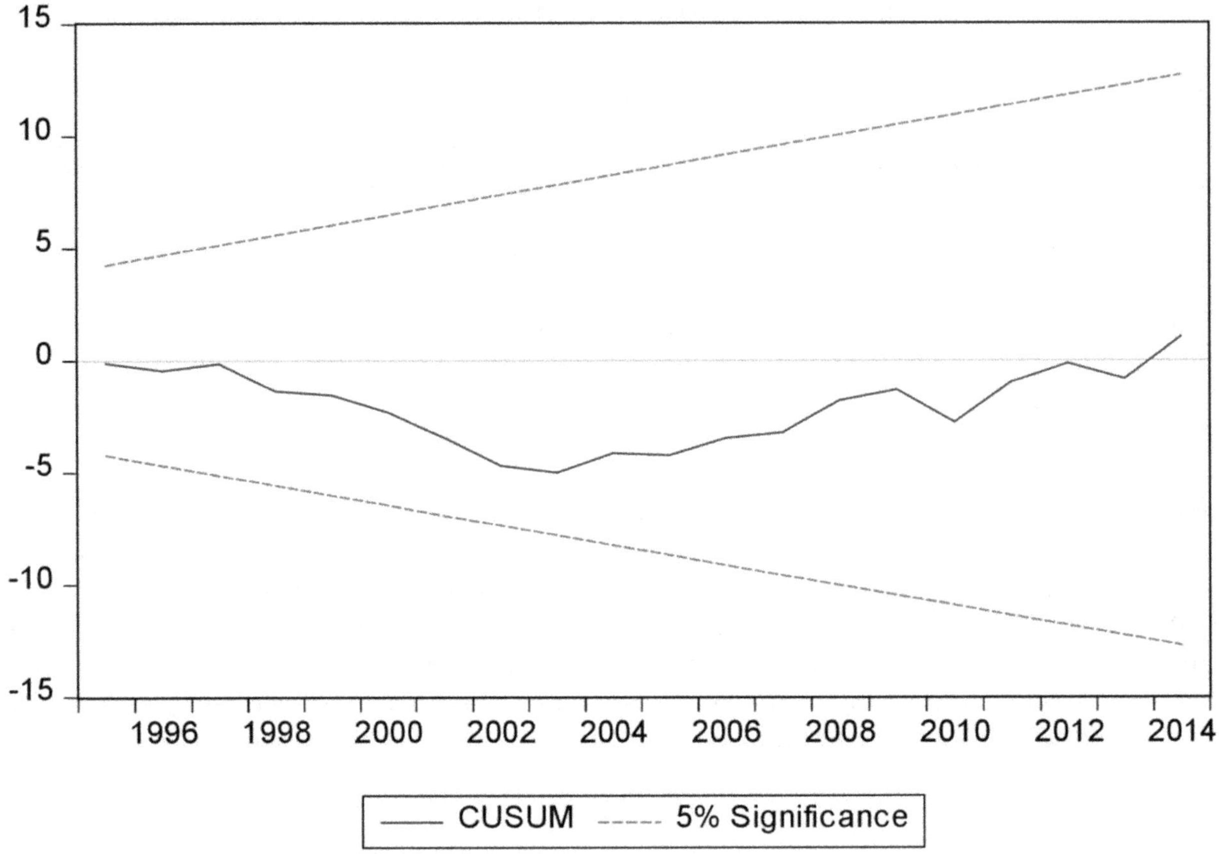

hypothesis of "no cointegration" cannot be rejected. It is thus concluded that all the variables in the second model are not cointegrated and do not exhibit long-run relationship among them.

Granger (-Non) Causality Results

Finally, a VAR model in levels is then set up again for the first model but with 1 additional lag (i.e., $l+i_{max}=2+1=3$ lags) of each of the variables into each of the equations this time as i_{max} is 1. The lag interval for the endogenous variables is left to be at 1 to 2, and the extra (3rd) lag of each variable is declared to be an exogenous variable. The model in Eq. (5) can be written in six different equations i.e. for all the six variables under consideration e.g. for the variable $lnCO_2$, the equation can be written as follows:

Table 8. Diagnostic test results of residuals of ARDL model with 1 lag for second model

Diagnostic Test	Test Statistic	p-value
Breusch-Pagan-Godfrey Heteroskedasticity	0. 833322 (F-stat.)	0.6185
Normality Test (Jarque-Bera)	1.522728	0.467029
Serial Correlation LM (with l=1)	0.070845 (F-stat.)	0.8074

$$lnCO_{2_t} = \alpha_1 + \sum_{i=1}^{l} \beta_{1i} lnCO_{2_t} + \sum_{j=l+1}^{i_{max}} \beta_{2i} lnCO_{2_{t-j}} + \sum_{i=1}^{l} \gamma_{1i} lnGDP_t + \sum_{j=l+1}^{i_{max}} \gamma_{2i} lnGDP_{t-j}$$

$$+ \sum_{i=1}^{l} \delta_{1i} lnFDI_t + \sum_{j=l+1}^{i_{max}} \delta_{2i} lnFDI_{t-j} + \sum_{i=1}^{l} \varphi_{1i} OPEN_t + \sum_{j=l+1}^{i_{max}} \varphi_{2i} OPEN_{t-j} \quad (9)$$

$$+ \sum_{i=1}^{l} \vartheta_{1i} lnEC_t + \sum_{j=l+1}^{i_{max}} \vartheta_{2i} lnEC_{t-j} + \sum_{i=1}^{l} \rho_{1i} TG_t + \sum_{j=l+1}^{i_{max}} \rho_{2i} TG_{t-j} + \epsilon_t$$

Similarly, the other five different equations can be written for all the five remaining variables under first model. In the words of Giles (2011), the coefficients of extra lags will not be included when the subsequent Wald tests are conducted. If the lag interval would have been specified to be from 1 to 3, then the coefficients of all three lags would have been included in the Wald tests, and this would have been incorrect as the Wald test statistic would not have had its usual asymptotic chi-square null distribution. Granger (non-) causality is then tested for the first model using a standard Wald test with the hypothesis that the coefficients of (only) the first l lagged values of variables are zero in the equations of the other variables. It is important to note that the Wald test statistics will be asymptotically chi-square distributed with 2 degrees of freedom under the null and the extra lag that was introduced by adding i_{max} to l, is not included in the test results. Rejection of the null implies a rejection of Granger (non-) causality i.e., a rejection supports the presence of Granger causality.

The results of the Granger (non-) causality test for the first model are shown in Table 9 and Fig. (s) 3 and 4. Table 9 provides the chi-square stats information with their corresponding p-values in parentheses. To help understand clearly the results of causality relationships found among all the variables of first model, a diagram in circular form is drawn as shown in Fig. 3. Similarly, Fig. 4 represents the diagram of various inter-relationships found among different variables in the first model. Although the main aim of the study is to examine the effects of FDI on economic growth and natural environment of India and examine the causality relationships between these three important variables only i.e., FDI, economic growth and CO_2 emissions, but the study would be incomplete, or we can say, the results will not be accurate if one will not take into account other important variables that largely affect these three variables under study and not monitor the causality relationships among all of these variables. Thus, the reason behind establishing these inter-relationships among all the variables is to get an accurate and detailed causality.

The pair-wise Granger (-non) causality tests results of the second model are given in Table 10 below. Rejection of the null implies a rejection of Granger (non-) causality i.e., a rejection supports the presence of Granger causality.

Findings

Results of the first model in Table 9 and Fig. (s) 3 and 4 show that variables are forming several inter-linked inter-relationships with other variables. The inter-relationships shown in i, ii and iii (in Fig. 4) are almost similar and inter-linked. Similarly, inter-relationships shown in iv, v and vi are also similar and inter-linked. The explanations of these relationships are as follows:

Table 9. Pair-wise granger (-non) causality results for first model

Dependent Variable	MWALD Test						Causality Inference
	$lnCO_2$	lnGDP	lnFDI	OPEN	lnEC	TG	
$lnCO_2$	-	2.935485 (0.2304)	5.100266 (0.0781)*	0.176559 (0.9155)	3.418096 (0.1810)	4.003435 (0.1351)	CO_2¬FDI
lnGDP	5.169558 (0.0754)*	-	3.399969 (0.1827)	1.602100 (0.4489)	0.992909 (0.6087)	1.781919 (0.4103)	GDP¬CO_2
lnFDI	4.213923 (0.1216)	7.838256 (0.0199)**	-	6.829382 (0.0329)**	0.132292 (0.9360)	3.953737 (0.1385)	FDI¬GDP FDI¬OPEN
OPEN	5.316818 (0.0701)*	5.908679 (0.0521)**	5.176256 (0.0752)*	-	1.592658 (0.4510)	2.079663 (0.3535)	OPEN¬CO_2 OPEN¬GDP OPEN¬FDI
lnEC	9.333615 (0.0094)***	11.67809 (0.0029)***	14.12163 (0.0009)***	1.767089 (0.4133)	-	17.89066 (0.0001)***	EC¬CO_2 EC¬GDP EC¬FDI EC¬TG
TG	6.114471 (0.0470)**	1.831321 (0.4003)	3.470185 (0.1764)	1.137118 (0.5663)	0.785265 (0.6753)	-	TG¬CO_2

Note: ***, ** and * indicate significance level at 1%, 5% and 10%, respectively; p-values are in parentheses; and ¬ denotes a uni-directional causality

- **CO_2-GDP-FDI:** There is uni-directional causality from CO_2 to GDP, which is a clear indication that the level of economic growth in India is largely caused by the degradation in the natural environment. Uni-directional causality from GDP to FDI signifies that the level of economic growth is one of the main causes of attracting foreign capital inflows in India. Finally, uni-directional causality from FDI to CO_2 represents FDI as one of the causes of environmental degradation. Also, FDI is not causing GDP directly but indirectly through CO_2 emissions.
- **CO_2-OPEN-FDI:** There is uni-directional causality from CO_2 to OPEN, which indicates that the trade liberalisation in India is largely caused by the degradation in the natural environment i.e., due to the concern about the environment India has made its markets open for free trade in the hope of receiving any new cleaner technologies. Bi-directional causality between OPEN and FDI signifies that open markets (like economic growth) are one of the main causes of attracting foreign capital inflows in India and FDI brings more trade openness in Indian markets. But again, FDI is causing environmental degradation.
- **CO_2-GDP-OPEN:** Uni-directional causalities from CO_2 to GDP and OPEN; and uni-directional causality from GDP to OPEN indicate that environmental degradation is driving the economic growth in India and also this economic growth is bringing openness in Indian markets.
- **CO_2-GDP-TG-EC:** Inter-linked uni-directional causality from CO_2 to GDP and TG and ultimately from GDP and TG to EC shows that environmental degradation drives the economic growth as well as the technology gap in India (could be negatively or positively) and this level of economic growth and the gap in technology ultimately become the cause of energy consumption. CO_2 is not just directly causing energy consumption but also through technology gap and income growth that it drives. This relationship can be made clear by dividing it into two parts and discussing them separately; and this is what follows next.

Figure 3. Causality relationships in first model

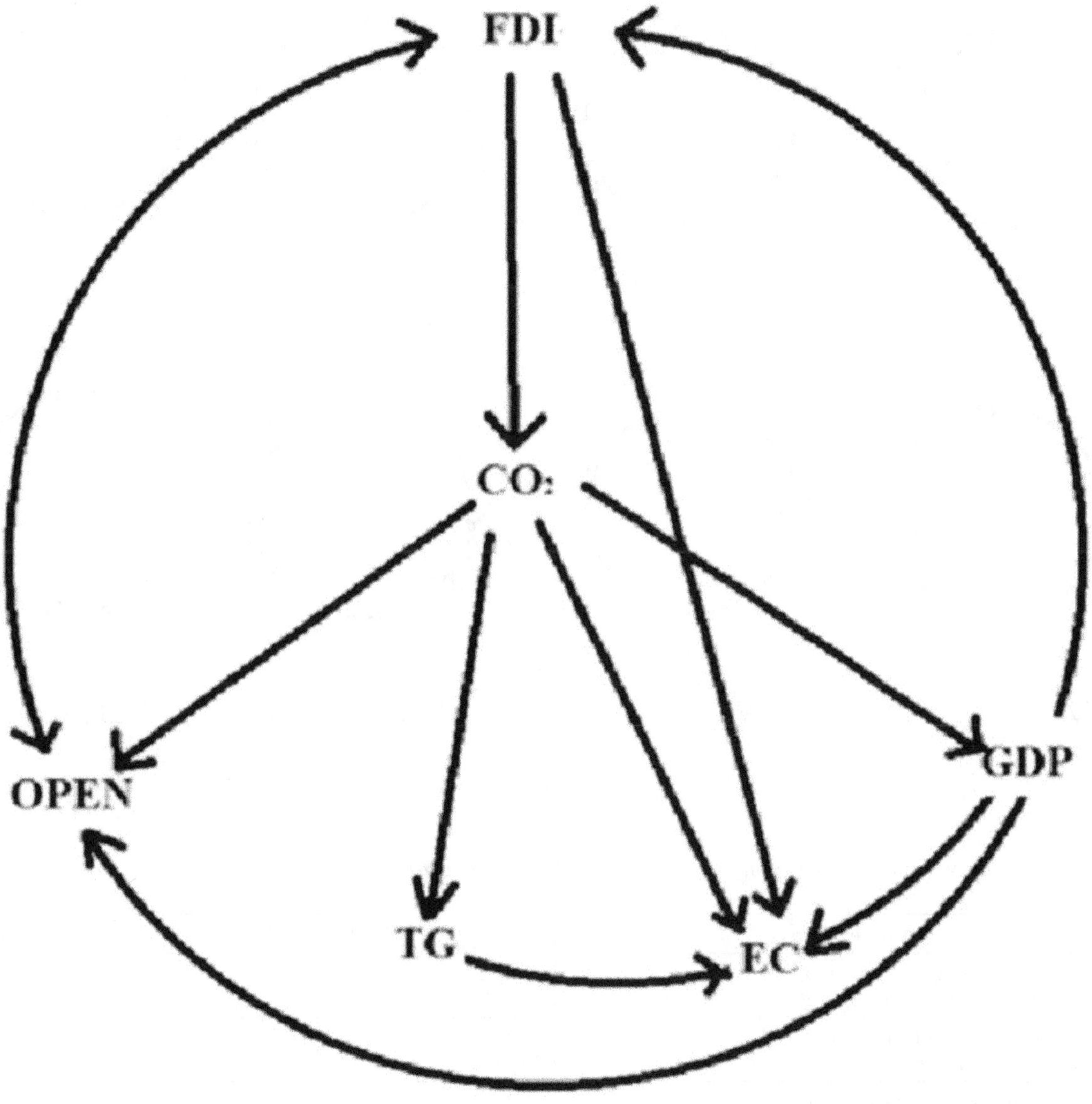

- **CO_2-GDP-EC:** Environmental degradation in India is driving the level of economic growth and ultimately this economic growth becomes the cause of energy consumption, though energy consumption is not causing CO_2 emissions.
- **CO_2-TG-EC:** Environmental destruction makes India to look for and adopt advanced cleaner technologies in economic activities that ultimately affects the consumption of energy. This result can be seen in a sense that if technology gap is widened, it may cause more energy consumption; on the contrary, if this technology gap is shortened by newer and cleaner technological processes and techniques, there will be lesser energy consumption.

Figure 4. Inter-relationships among variables in first model

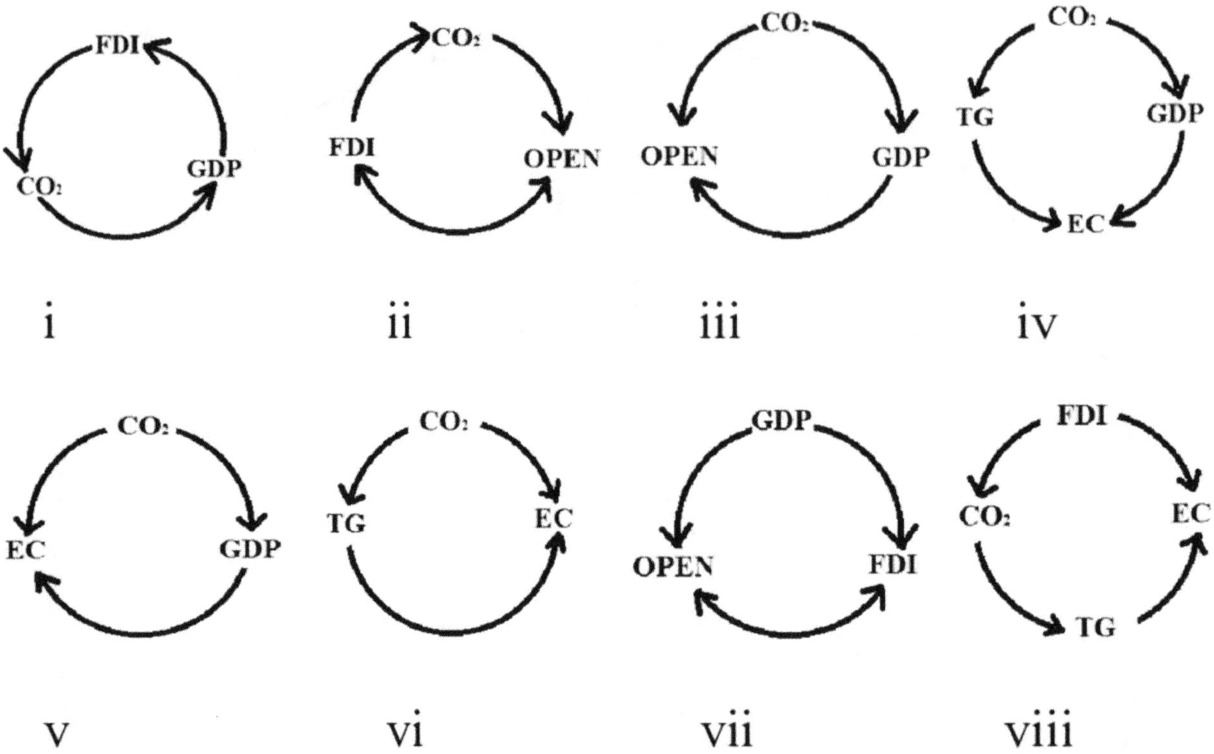

Table 10. Pair-wise granger (-non) causality results for second model

Null Hypothesis	F-stat.	p-value
lnGDP does not Granger Cause $lnCO_2$ $lnCO_2$ does not Granger Cause lnGDP	11.5115 0.01376	0.0060 0.9087
lnEC does not Granger Cause $lnCO_2$ $lnCO_2$ does not Granger Cause lnEC	0.49134 2.45740	0.4979 0.1453
lnICT_exp does not Granger Cause $lnCO_2$ $lnCO_2$ does not Granger Cause lnICT_exp	18.3340 0.12118	0.0013 0.7343
lnEC does not Granger Cause lnGDP lnGDP does not Granger Cause lnEC	0.06505 5.00407	0.8034 0.0469
lnICT_exp does not Granger Cause lnGDP lnGDP does not Granger Cause lnICT_exp	0.00987 0.01828	0.9226 0.8949
lnICT_exp does not Granger Cause lnEC lnEC does not Granger Cause lnICT_exp	6.55283 0.02549	0.0265 0.8760

- **GDP-FDI-OPEN:** Uni-directional causality from GDP to FDI and a bi-directional causality between trade openness and FDI signify that it is the level of economic growth and the open markets in India that is attracting more of FDI inflows. Also, the presence of FDI and the level of economic growth are causing trade openness in Indian markets.

- **FDI-CO_2-TG-EC:** It is evident from the results that there is uni-directional causality from FDI to CO_2 and EC. This result indicates that FDI is one of the causes of CO_2 emissions and energy consumption in India. And, as discussed earlier, CO_2 emissions are forcing Indian government to minimise the technology gap because it is causing more of energy consumption.

Based on the Granger (-non) causality test results in Table 10 for the second model of ICT Trade, following are the main findings of the second model:

- **GDP causes CO_2:** Results indicate that the economic growth is becoming the cause for environmental degradation in India. There is a unidirectional causality found from GDP to CO_2 confirming that the level of economic growth in India is achieved after degrading the environmental performance.
- **ICT_exp causes CO_2:** The manufacturing and exporting of ICT goods and services also cause environmental degradation in India. The results indicate a unidirectional causality from ICT exports to CO_2 emissions showing that the ICT products that are produced in India for the purpose of exporting in the international markets become the cause for an increase in the CO_2 emissions in the country.
- **GDP causes EC:** The results also show that to achieve a certain level of economic growth, a lot of energy is consumed in India. Unidirectional causality found from GDP to EC indicates that economic growth of India becomes one of the causes for the consumption of energy.
- **ICT_exp causes EC:** A unidirectional causality is also found from ICT exports to EC. This result indicates that the manufacturing of ICT goods and services for the purpose of exporting them in the international markets becomes one of the causes for consumption of more energy in India. This energy consumption is ultimately considered to be the cause of environmental degradation. Thus ICT exports consume a lot of energy.

CONCLUSION AND RECOMMENDATIONS

This chapter is an extended version of the investigations done by the authors in their previous research work examining the dynamic Granger (non-) causality relationship mainly among FDI, economic growth and the natural environment of India while taking trade openness, energy consumption and technology gap into consideration, using a multivariate and dynamic TY approach, for the period 1980-2014. It further examines the dynamic Granger (non-) causality relationship among ICT exports, economic growth, energy consumption and CO_2 emissions in India for the period 2000-2014.

Compared to the previous study of Alam et al. (2011) for India, in which the same dynamic multivariate TY approach has been used but for the period 1971-2006 (36 years), this study provides much wider view of the relationship among FDI-EG-natural environment by taking into account two more important variables that affect economic growth and natural environment i.e., trade openness and technology gap. Alam et al. (2011) found a bi-directional causality among CO_2 emissions and energy consumption, whereas, this study shows a uni-directional causality from CO_2 emissions to energy consumption. There is no causality found from energy consumption to CO_2 emissions.

The results from the TY Model conclude mainly that Pollution Haven Hypothesis (PHH) does exist in case of India. The results of first model show that India is making its markets open for free trade and

FDI with the hope of increasing economic growth and reducing technology gap which ultimately will reduce the environmental degradation. But, FDI is not causing economic growth in terms of GDP directly, though it is causing GDP indirectly through CO_2 emissions, validating the existence of Pollution Haven Hypothesis in India. FDI is even not bridging the technology gap, or maybe it is bridging but not in that proportion in which inflows of FDI are coming to India. FDI is also not reducing environmental degradation rather it is acting as one of the causes of CO_2 emissions in India that supports the existence of Pollution Haven Hypothesis in India.

Apart from being one of the causes of CO_2 emissions, FDI is also causing energy consumption. Though FDI is making Indian markets open for free trade but that openness is again bringing more FDI to India and hence, this vicious circle continues to move further. Also, more openness to Indian markets may be misused by domestic dirty investors that lack advanced and cleaner technologies causing CO_2 emissions; and involve themselves in dirty trade (i.e. import and export dirty goods) though increasing the level of GDP.

Hence, it is recommended that regular checks and visits may be done to the sites of high polluting industries. Emission limits must be defined for the polluting industries and every effort should be made to make them comply with the rules. India should also limit its openness regarding export to and import from other countries. Import of dirty goods may be banned, if possible, or may be reduced to a certain limit. Similarly, 'exports' means excess production in the country, which in turn will use several renewable and non-renewable resources and even wastage of them causing environmental pollution.

Thus, strict measures are recommended for Indian government to make a check on the foreign investment inflows because India is expecting cleaner technologies from foreign investments but is getting environmental destruction in return even after opening its markets for free trade and not even getting that level of economic growth as is expected from the foreign capital inflows.

The results from the Granger (-non) causality for the second model conclude mainly that both the economic growth and ICT trade cause environmental degradation and energy consumption in India.

Unidirectional causalities have been found from GDP and ICT exports to both CO_2 and energy consumption. These results indicate that ICT trade in India is becoming one of the main causes for energy consumption and ultimately for environmental degradation (in terms of CO_2 emissions) in India.

Although it is not clear from the results whether these ICT exports are helping in growing the Indian economy but this is for sure that they are degrading the environment and consume more of energy. It is therefore recommended to the Indian government that an environmental check should be made on the ICT companies that produce ICT goods to be exported in foreign markets. Also, stricter environmental laws and regulations are required to be framed and implemented.

Economic growth of the country should also be based on cleaner and environmentally-sound manufacturing processes. Limits should be defined for the quantity of ICT goods to be exported out of the country. A check is also required on the quantity of energy consumed by the ICT industry so that this energy consumption does not ultimately become the reason for more of environmental degradation. All these steps will then make the ICT trade in India both economically and environmentally sound.

ACKNOWLEDGMENT

This research received no specific grant from any funding agency in the public, commercial, or not-for-profit sectors.

REFERENCES

Acharyya, J. (2009). FDI, Growth and the Environment: Evidence from India on CO_2 Emission during the Last Two Decades. *Journal of Economic Development, 34*(1), 43–58. doi:10.35866/caujed.2009.34.1.003

Ahmed, S. F. (2015). Investigating the causal relationship between FDI and economic growth using Toda-Yamamoto Approach: Evidence from Bangladesh. *ELK Asia Pacific Journal of Finance and Risk Mangement, 6*(3), 35–49.

Alam, M. J., Begum, I. A., Buysse, J., Rahman, S., & Huylenbroeck, G. V. (2011). Dynamic Modeling of Causal Relationship between Energy Consumption, CO_2 Emissions and Economic Growth in India. *Renewable & Sustainable Energy Reviews, 15*(6), 3243–3251. doi:10.1016/j.rser.2011.04.029

Aliyu, M. A. (2005). Foreign Direct Investment and the Environment: Pollution Haven Hypothesis Revisited. *8th Annual Conference on Global Economic Analysis.*

Almfraji, M. A., & Almsafir, M. K. (2014). Foreign Direct Investment and Economic Growth: Literature Review from 1994 to 2012. *Procedia: Social and Behavioral Sciences, 129*, 206–213. doi:10.1016/j.sbspro.2014.03.668

Andrew, R. (2018). *Guest Post: Why India's CO_2 Emissions Grew Strongly in 2017.* Retrieved from www.carbonbrief.org

Avazalipour, M. S., Zandi, F., Saberi, R., Hakimipour, N., & Damankeshideh, M. (2013). The Impact of FDI on Environmental Resources in Selected Countries (NON-OECD). *International Journal of Research and Reviews in Applied Sciences, 17*(1), 111–115.

Baek, J., & Won, W. K. (2008). A dynamic approach to the FDI-environment nexus: the case of China and India. *No 6508, 2008 Annual Meeting, American Agricultural Economics Association (New Name 2008: Agricultural and Applied Economics Association).*

Balakrishnan, N. (2007). Information technology and communications security in India. *Science and Technology to Counter Terrorism: Proceedings of an Indo-U.S. Workshop*, 31-42.

Blanco, L., Gonzalez, F., & Ruiz, I. (2011). *The Impact of FDI on CO2 Emissions in Latin America.* Pepperdine University, School of Public Policy Working Papers. Paper 28.

Bokpin, G. A. (2017). Foreign direct investment and environmental sustainability in Africa: The role of institutions and governance. *Research in International Business and Finance, 39*, 239–247. doi:10.1016/j.ribaf.2016.07.038

Borensztein, E., De Gregorio, J., & Lee, J. W. (1998). How Does Foreign Direct Investment Affect Economic Growth? *Journal of International Economics, 45*(1), 115–135. doi:10.1016/S0022-1996(97)00033-0

Choi, E., Heshmati, A., & Cho, Y. (2010). An Empirical Study of the Relationships between CO_2 Emissions, Economic Growth and Openness. *IZA Discussion Papers*, (5304), 1–27.

Cole, M. A. (2004). Trade, the pollution haven hypothesis and the environmental Kuznets curve: Examining the linkages. *Ecological Economics, 48*(1), 71–81. doi:10.1016/j.ecolecon.2003.09.007

De Mello, L. (1999). Foreign Direct Investment-Led Growth: Evidence from Time Series and Panel Data. *Oxford Economic Papers*, *51*(1), 133–151. doi:10.1093/oep/51.1.133

Dickey, D. A., & Fuller, W. A. (1979). Distribution of the Estimators for Autoregressive Time Series with a Unit Root. *Journal of the American Statistical Association*, *74*(366), 427–431. doi:10.2307/2286348

Dickey, D. A., & Fuller, W. A. (1981). Likelihood Ratio Statistics for Autoregressive Time Series with a Unit Root. *Econometrica*, *49*(4), 1063. doi:10.2307/1912517

Elliott, R., & Shimamoto, K. (2008). Are ASEAN Countries Havens for Japanese Pollution-Intensive Industry? *World Economy*, *31*(2), 236–254. doi:10.1111/j.1467-9701.2007.01088.x

Engle, R., & Granger, C. W. J. (1987). Cointegration and Error Correction: Representation, Estimation and Testing. *Econometrica*, *55*(2), 251–276. doi:10.2307/1913236

Gandolfo, G. (1998). *International Trade Theory and Policy: With 12 Tables*. Springer. doi:10.1007/978-3-642-61680-8

Giles, D. (2011, April 29). *Testing for Granger Causality*. Retrieved from http://davegiles.blogspot.in/2011/04/testing-for-granger-causality.html

Grossman, G. M., & Krueger, A. B. (1991). *Environmental Impacts of a North American Free Trade Agreement. NBER Working Paper Series,* 3914.

Hitam, M. B., & Borhan, H. B. (2012). FDI, Growth and the Environment: Impact on Quality of Life in Malaysia. *Procedia: Social and Behavioral Sciences*, *50*, 333–342.

IBEF. (2018). *Foreign Direct Investment (FDI).* Retrieved from www.ibef.org

IPCC. (1996). Second Assessment on Climate Change. International Panel on Climate Change. Cambridge, UK: Cambridge University Press.

Johansen, S. (1988). Statistical Analysis of Cointegration Vectors. *Journal of Economic Dynamics & Control*, *12*(2), 231–254.

Johansen, S., & Juselius, K. (1990). Maximum likelihood estimation and inference on cointegration- with applications to the demand for money. *Oxford Bulletin of Economics and Statistics*, *52*(2), 169–210.

Johnson, D., & Turner, C. (2010). *International Business: Themes and Issues in the Modern Global Economy* (2nd ed.). Routledge, Taylor & Francis Group.

Jorgenson, A. K., Dick, C., & Mahutga, M. C. (2007). Foreign Investment Dependence and the Environment: An Ecostructural Approach. Society for the Study of Social Problems, Oxford University Press.

Kearny, A. T. (2018). *The 2018 A.T. Kearney Foreign Direct Investment Confidence Index.* Retrieved from www.atkearney.com

Kuznets, S. (1995). Economic Growth and Income Inequality. *The American Economic Review*, *45*, 1–28.

Kuzozumi, E., & Yamamoto, T. (2000). Modified lag augmented autoregressions. *Econometric Reviews*, *19*, 207–231.

Li, X., & Liu, X. (2005). Foreign Direct Investment and Economic Growth: An Increasingly Endogenous Relationship. *World Development*, *33*(3), 393–407.

Linh, D. H., & Lin, S. M. (2015). Dynamic Causal Relationships Among CO_2 Emissions, Energy Consumption, Economic Growth and FDI in the Most Populous Asian Countries. *Advances in Management and Applied Economics*, *5*(1), 69–88.

Mehta, P. S. (2002). The Indian Mining Sector: Effects on the Environment & FDI Inflows. *CCNM Global Forum on International Investment, Conference on Foreign Direct investment and the Environment*.

Pesaran, M. H., & Shin, Y. (1999). An autoregressive distributed lag modelling approach to cointegration analysis. In S. Strom (Ed.), *Econometrics and Economic Theory in the 20th Century: The Ragnar Frisch Centennial Symposium*. Cambridge University Press.

Pesaran, M. H., Shin, Y., & Smith, R. J. (2001). Bounds testing approaches to the analysis of level relationships. *Journal of Applied Econometrics*, *16*, 289–326.

Phillips, P. C. B., & Perron, P. (1988). Testing for unit root in time series regression. *Biometrika*, *75*, 335–346.

Rana, R., & Sharma, M. (2019). Dynamic causality testing for EKC hypothesis, pollution haven hypothesis and international trade in India. *The Journal of International Trade & Economic Development*, *28*(3), 348–364.

Rana, R., & Sharma, M. (2020). Dynamic causality among FDI, economic growth and CO_2 emissions in India: With open markets and technology gap. *International Journal of Asian Business and Information Management*, *11*(3), 15–31.

Schembri, P., & Petit, O. (2009). Clean technology transfers and North-South technological gap: An important issue for environmental policies. *Inter Economics*, *120*, 109–130.

Seker, F., Ertugrul, H. M., & Cetin, M. (2015). The Impact of Foreign Direct Investment on Environmental Quality: A Bounds Testing and Causality Analysis for Turkey. *Renewable & Sustainable Energy Reviews*, *52*, 347–356.

Shafik, N., & Bandyopadhyay, S. (1992). Economic growth and environmental quality: time-series and cross-country evidence. World Bank Publications.

Shahbaz, M., Nasreen, S., Abbas, F., & Anis, O. (2015). Does Foreign Direct Investment Impede Environmental Quality in High, Middle and Low-income Countries? *Energy Economics*, *51*, 275–287.

Shao, Y. (2018). Does FDI affect carbon intensity? New evidence from dynamic panel analysis. *International Journal of Climate Change Strategies and Management*, *10*(1), 27–42. https://doi.org/10.1108/IJCCSM-03-2017-0062

Sims, C. A. (1972). Money, income and causality. *The American Economic Review*, *62*, 540–552.

Toda, H. Y., & Phillips, P. C. B. (1993). Vector autoregressions and causality. *Econometrica*, *61*, 1367–1393.

Toda, H. Y., & Yamamoto, T. (1995). Statistical inferences in vector autoregressions with possibly integrated processes. *Journal of Econometrics*, *66*, 225–250.

Vu, T. B., Gangnes, B., & Noy, I. (2006). *Is Foreign Direct Investment Good for Growth?: Evidence from Sectoral Analysis of China and Vietnam.* Working Papers 200801, University of Hawaii at Manoa, Department of Economics.

World Bank Group. (2016a). *World Development Indicators 2016*. Retrieved from http://databank.worldbank.org/data/reports.aspx?source=2&country=IND#

World Bank Group. (2016b). *Gross Domestic Product 2016*. Retrieved from https://databank.worldbank.org/data/download/GDP.pdf

World Bank Group. (2019). *World Development Indicators 2019*. Retrieved from http://databank.worldbank.org/data/reports.aspx?source=2&country=IND#

Xepapadeas, A. (2005). Economic Growth and the Environment. Handbook of Environmental Economics, 1(2), 1219-1271.

Xu, B. (2000). Multinational enterprises, technology diffusion, and host country productivity growth. *Journal of Development Economics*, *62*, 477–493.

Compilation of References

Abba, M. T. (2018). Effects of training and development on employee retention in Bauchi State Metropolis Banks. *Operations Research*, *4*(1), 24–39.

Abdullah, N. A. H. N., & Zain, S. N. M. (2011). The Internationalization Theory and Malaysian Small Medium Enterprises (SMEs). *International Journal of Trade. Economics and Finance*, *2*(4), 318–322.

Abdul-Latif, S.A. (2020). An examination of ethnic-based consumer ethnocentrism and consumer animosity. *Journal of Islamic Marketing*. ahead-of-print. doi:10.1108/JIMA-08-2019-0165

Abdul-Talib, A. N., & Japari, N. (2020). Brand Consciousness and Brand Loyalty: A Study on Foreign Brand Beauty and Skin Care Products. In Economic, Educational, and Touristic Development in Asia (pp. 121-134). IGI Global. doi:10.4018/978-1-7998-2239-4.ch006

Abdul-Talib, A. N., Abd-Latif, S. A., & Abd-Razak, I. S. (2016). A study on the boycott motivations of Malaysian non-Muslims. *Journal of Islamic Marketing*, *7*(3), 264–287. doi:10.1108/JIMA-11-2014-0071

Abdul-Talib, A. N., & Abdul-Latif, S. A. (2015). Antecedents to willingness to Boycotts among Malaysian Muslims. In *Emerging Research on Islamic Marketing and Tourism in the Global Economy* (pp. 70–106). IGI Global. doi:10.4018/978-1-4666-6272-8.ch004

Abdul-Talib, A. N., & Mohd Adnan, M. M. (2017). Determinants of consumer's willingness to boycott surrogate products. *Journal of Islamic Marketing*, *8*(3), 345–360. doi:10.1108/JIMA-08-2015-0065

Abebe, M. (2014). Electronic commerce adoption, entrepreneurial orientation and small- and medium-sized enterprise (SME) performance. *Journal of Small Business and Enterprise Development*, *21*(1), 100–116. doi:10.1108/JSBED-10-2013-0145

Abrar, M., Shabbir, R., & Hussain, I., & Sana-ud-Din. (2019). Impact of Customer Animosity and Attitude on Purchase Intention in Fast-Food Industry of Pakistan. *Pakistan Journal of Social Sciences*, *39*(3), 959–969.

Abrate, G., Fraquelli, G., & Viglia, G. (2012). Dynamic pricing strategies: Evidence from European hotels. *International Journal of Hospitality Management*, *31*(1), 160–168. doi:10.1016/j.ijhm.2011.06.003

Abu Bakar, R. H. (2018, April 16). Brunei aims to phase out plastic bags in supermarkets by 2019: Thursday to Sunday now designated "No Plastic Bag" days. *The Scoop*. https://thescoop.co/2018/04/16/brunei-aims-phase-out-plastic-bags-2019/

Abubakar, R. A., Kura, K. M., & Ringim, K. J. (2018). Total quality management, firm performance and the moderating role of competitive intensity. *Journal of International Business. Economics and Entrepreneurship*, *3*(1), 10–20.

Abulencia, A. S. (2018). Exploring the Education Agenda of the 16th Congress of the Philippines. *ATIKAN, 8*(1).

Acharyya, J. (2009). FDI, Growth and the Environment: Evidence from India on CO_2 Emission during the Last Two Decades. *Journal of Economic Development*, *34*(1), 43–58. doi:10.35866/caujed.2009.34.1.003

Adam, C. S., & Bevan, D. L. (2005). Fiscal deficits and growth in developing countries. *Journal of Public Economics, 4*(1), 571–597. doi:10.1016/j.jpubeco.2004.02.006

ADEME (French Environment and Energy Management Agency). (2014). *Economie Circulaire: Notions.* Version modifiéeoctobre 2014.

Adler, N. J. (2008). Global leadership: giving oneself for things far greater than oneself. In International Dimensions of Organizational Behavior (5th ed.). Thomson.

Aftab, M., & Rehman, I. U. (2017). Exchange rate risk and the bilateral trade between Malaysia and Singapore. *Studies in Economics and Finance, 34*(3), 407–426. doi:10.1108/SEF-08-2015-0188

Aghion, P., Dewatripont, M., & Stein, J. C. (2008). Academic freedom, private-sector focus, and the process of innovation. *The RAND Journal of Economics, 39*(3), 617–635. doi:10.1111/j.1756-2171.2008.00031.x

Aguilo, E., Riera, A., & Rossello, J. (2005). The Short-Term Price Effect of a Tourist Tax through a Dynamic Demand Model: The Case of the Balearic Islands. *Tourism Management, 26*(3), 359–365. doi:10.1016/j.tourman.2003.07.005

Agyeman, C. (2014). Consumers' Buying Behavior Towards Green Products: An Exploratory Study. *International Journal of Management Research and Business Strategy, 3*, 188–197.

Ahmad, N. A., Kamis, N. Q., Mahdini, & Adilah, S. S. (2015). *Brunei Moving Forward: Brunei's sustainable measures for a successful environmental development.* https://asianjournaloflegalstudies.wordpress.com/2016/08/31/brunei-moving-forward-bruneis-sustainable-measures-for-a-successful-environmental-development/

Ahmad, S. N. B., & Juhdi, N. (2008). Consumer's perception and purchase intentions towards organic food products: Exploring the attitude among Malaysian consumers. *16th Annual Conference on Pacific Basin Finance, Economics, Accounting and Management.*

Ahmedov, I. (2020, July). The Impact of Digital Economy on International Trade. *European Journal of Business and Management Research, 5*(4), 1–7. doi:10.24018/ejbmr.2020.5.4.389

Ahmed, S. F. (2015). Investigating the causal relationship between FDI and economic growth using Toda-Yamamoto Approach: Evidence from Bangladesh. *ELK Asia Pacific Journal of Finance and Risk Mangement, 6*(3), 35–49.

Ahn, J., & Kwon, J. (2019). Green hotel brands in Malaysia: Perceived value, cost, anticipated emotion, and revisit intention. *Current Issues in Tourism, 23*(12), 1–16. doi:10.1080/13683500.2019.1646715

Ajzen, I., & Fishbein, M. (1980). *Understanding attitudes and predicting social behaviour.* Prentice Hall.

Akbar, F., & Haitham Obaid, A. A. (2014). Explaining the relationship between creativity, Explaining the relationship between creativity, Innovation and entrepreneurship. *International Journal of Economy. Management and Social Sciences, 3*(12), 1–4.

Akenji, L., Bengtsson, M., Kato, M., Hengesbaugh, M., Hotta, Y., Aoki-Suzuki, C., Gamaralalage, P. J. D., & Liu, C. (2019). Circular economy and plastics: A gap-analysis in ASEAN member states. Brussels: European Commission Directorate General for Environment and Directorate General for International Cooperation and Development, Jakarta: Association of Southeast Asian Nations (ASEAN).

Akenji, L. (2014). Consumer scapegoatism and limits to green consumerism. *Journal of Cleaner Production, 63*, 13–23. doi:10.1016/j.jclepro.2013.05.022

Akhtar, A., Rafiq, S., Asif, A., Saeed, A., & Kashif, M. (2012). Public perceptions of police service quality: Empirical evidence from Pakistan. *International Journal of Police Science & Management*, *14*(2), 97–106. doi:10.1350/ijps.2012.14.2.266

Akhtar, R., Sultana, S., Masud, M. M., Jafrin, N., & Al-Mamun, A. (2021). Consumers' environmental ethics, willingness, and green consumerism between lower and higher income groups. *Resources, Conservation and Recycling*, *168*, 105–274. doi:10.1016/j.resconrec.2020.105274

Akinyede, R. O., & Daramola, O. A. (2013). Neutral network web-based human resource management system model. *International Journal of Computer Networks and Communication Security*, *1*(3), 75–87.

Al Amin Khan, M., Kumar Tarofder, A., & Ferdous Azam, S. M. (2021). Critical factors affecting employees' motivation and productivity in Bangladeshi satellite television channels. *European Journal of Social Sciences Studies*, *5*(6). Advance online publication. doi:10.46827/ejsss.v5i6.985

Al Karim, R. (2019). Impact of Different Training and Development Programs on Employee Performance in Bangladesh Perspective. *International Journal of Entrepreneurial Research*, *1*(2), 8–14. doi:10.31580/ijer.v1i2.497

Alagaraja, M., Rose, K., Shuck, B., & Bergman, M. (2015). Unpacking organizational alignment: The view from theory and practice. *Journal of Organizational Learning and Leadership.*, *13*(1), 18–31.

Alam, A., & Samikon, S. A. (2021). Impact of the COVID-19 Pandemic on the Film Industry in Pakistan. *Journal of Insurance and Financial Management*, *4*(3).

Alam, M. J., Begum, I. A., Buysse, J., Rahman, S., & Huylenbroeck, G. V. (2011). Dynamic Modeling of Causal Relationship between Energy Consumption, CO_2 Emissions and Economic Growth in India. *Renewable & Sustainable Energy Reviews*, *15*(6), 3243–3251. doi:10.1016/j.rser.2011.04.029

Ala-Mutka, K. (2011). *Mapping digital competence: Towards a conceptual understanding*. Academic Press.

Alarcón, D., Sánchez, J. A., & De Olavide, U. (2015). *Assessing convergent and discriminant validity in the ADHD-R IV rating scale: User-written commands for Average Variance Extracted (AVE), Composite Reliability (CR), and Heterotrait-Monotrait ratio of correlations (HTMT).* Paper presented at the Spanish STATA Meeting.

Al-Ayed, S. I. (2019). The impact of strategic human resource management on organizational resilience: An empirical study on hospitals. *Business: Theory and Practice*, *20*(1), 179–186. doi:10.3846/btp.2019.17

Al-Azmi, S. F., Al-Enezi, N., & Chowdhury, R. I. (2009). Users' attitudes to an electronic medical record system and its correlates: a multivariate analysis. *The HIM Journal*. Retrieved November 5, 2018 from https://www.researchgate.net/profile/Rafiqul_Chowdhury3/publication/26311041_Users%27_attitudes_to_an_electronic_medical_record_system_and_its_correlates_A_multivariate_analysis/links/00b49527af853611f3000000/Users-attitudes-to-an-electronic-medical-recor

Albino, V., Berardi, U., & Dangelico, M. R. (2015). Smart Cities: Definitions, Dimentions and Initiatives. *Journal of Urban Technology*, *22*(1), 3–21. doi:10.1080/10630732.2014.942092

Alesia, S. G., Stephen, L. S., & Geoffrey, H. T. (2014). Consumption values, environmental concern, attitude and purchase intention in the context of organic products. In *2014 International Conference of the Association of Global Management Studies*. Said Business School, University of Oxford, UK.

Alesina, A., de Broeck, M., Prati, A., & Tabellini, G. (1992, Oct.). Default risk on government debt in OECD Countries. *Economic Policy: A European Forum*, 427-463.

Alfes, K., Shantz, A. D., Truss, C., & Soane, E. C. (2013). The link between perceived human resource management practices, engagement and employee behaviour: A moderated mediation model. *International Journal of Human Resource Management*, *24*(2), 330–351. doi:10.1080/09585192.2012.679950

Alhnity, H., Mohamad, A., & Ishak, A. K. (2016). Impact of Entrepreneurial Orientation on Small Business Performance: Moderating Role of Government Intervention. *International Review of Management and Marketing*, *6*(S7), 95–100.

Al-Hyari, K., Al-Nasour, M., Alnsour, M., Al-Weshah, G., & Abutayeh, B. (2011). Exporting Performance and Manufacturing Activities in Jordanian SMEs: External Barriers and Relationships. *International Journal of Global Business*, *4*(1), 44–72.

Ali, M. K., & Iftikhar, I. (n.d.). *An Empirical Study of the Effectiveness of Public Relation Campaigns of Rescue 1122*. Academic Press.

Ali, A., Khan, A. A., Ahmed, I., & Shahzad, W. (2011). Determinants of Pakistani consumers' green purchase behaviour: Some insights from a developing country. *International Journal of Business and Social Science*, *2*(3), 217–226.

Ali, Q., & Jadoon, M. Z. I. (2012). Towards an indigenous perspective on HRM: A study of textile industry of Pakistan. *Studies*, *1*(2), 1–10.

Aliyu, M. A. (2005). Foreign Direct Investment and the Environment: Pollution Haven Hypothesis Revisited. *8th Annual Conference on Global Economic Analysis*.

Aliyu, M. S., Rogo, H. B., & Mahmood, R. (2015). Knowledge management, entrepreneurial orientation and firm performance: The role of organizational culture. *Asian Social Science*, *11*(23), 140–152.

Alm, E., Colliander, N., Deforche, F., Lind, F., Stohne, V., & Sundstrom, O. (2016). *Digitizing Europe: Why Northern European Frontrunners Must Drive Digitalization of the EU Economy*. The Boston Consulting Group (BSG).

Almeida, C. M. V. B., Rodrigues, A. J. M., Bonilla, S. H., & Giannetti, B. F. (2010). Emergy as a tool for Ecodesign: Evaluating materials selection for beverage packages in Brazil. *Journal of Cleaner Production*, *18*(1), 32–43. doi:10.1016/j.jclepro.2009.03.019

Almfraji, M. A., & Almsafir, M. K. (2014). Foreign Direct Investment and Economic Growth: Literature Review from 1994 to 2012. *Procedia: Social and Behavioral Sciences*, *129*, 206–213. doi:10.1016/j.sbspro.2014.03.668

Altinay, L., Madanoglu, M., De Vita, G., Arasli, H., & Ekinci, Y. (2015). The interface between organizational learning capability, entrepreneurial orientation, and SME growth. *Journal of Small Business Management*, *54*(3), 871–891. doi:10.1111/jsbm.12219

Altıntas¸, M. H., Tokol, T., & Harcar, T. (2007). The effects of export barriers on perceived export performance: An empirical research on SMEs in Turkey. *EuroMed Journal of Business*, *2*(1), 36–56. doi:10.1108/14502190710749947

Altnaa, U., Vasa, L., & Neszmelyi, G. I. (2021). The Role of Network Ties on SMEs Internationalization Process in the Developing Countries/Emerging Markets: A Comparison between Mongolia, China, and Malaysia. *International Journal of Economics and Business Administration*, *9*(1), 274–291. doi:10.35808/ijeba/672

Amabile, T. M. (1988). A model of creativity and innovation in organizations. *Research in Organizational Behavior*, *10*(1), 123–167.

Amabile, T. M., & Pratt, M. G. (2016). The dynamic componential model of creativity and innovation in organizations: Making progress, making meaning. *Research in Organizational Behavior*, *36*, 157–183. doi:10.1016/j.riob.2016.10.001

Amin, M. (2018). Effects of job stress on employee engagement and organizational commitment: a study on employees of emergency rescue service rescue 1122 district Peshawar. *City University Research Journal, 8*(2).

Amin, S., & Tarun, M. T. (2020). Effect of consumption values on customers' green purchase intention: A mediating role of green trust. *Social Responsibility Journal*. doi:10.1108rj-05-2020-0191

Aminu, I. M. (2015). *Mediating role of access to finance and moderating role of business environment on the relationship between strategic orientation attributes and performance of small and medium enterprises in Nigeria*. Universiti Utara Malaysia.

Amran, F. W., Ghazali, H., & Siti Fatimah, M. (2018). Perceived Level Of Stress Among Casual Dining Restaurant Employees In Klang Valley, Malaysia. *International Journal of Modern Trends in Social Sciences, 1*(2), 9-14.

Amrutha, V., & Geetha, S. (2021). Linking organizational green training and voluntary workplace green behavior: Mediating role of green supporting climate and employees' green satisfaction. *Journal of Cleaner Production*, *290*, 125876. doi:10.1016/j.jclepro.2021.125876

Anbumozhi, V. (2019, September 11*). Circular economy for plastics: What is at stake for Asean?* Retrieved from https://www.nationthailand.com/opinion/30376083

Anbumozhi, V., & Kim, J. (Eds.). (2016). Towards a circular economy: Corporate management and policy pathways. Jakarta: Economic Research Institute for ASEAN and East Asia (ERIA).

Anbumozhi, V., & Kimura, F. (Eds.). (2018). Industry 4.0: Empowering ASEAN for the circular economy. Jakarta: Economic Research Institute for ASEAN and East Asia (ERIA).

Anderson, K. J. (2001). Internet use among college students: An exploratory study. *Journal of American College Health*, *50*(1), 21–26. doi:10.1080/07448480109595707 PMID:11534747

Andervin, M., & Jansson, J. (2016). Att leda digital transformation. California Management Review, 61, 15–42.

Andrade, M. S. O., & Göksel, A. (2017). Organizational alignment case study of Ministry of Justice of Cape Verde. *International Journal of Business and Management Invention*, *6*(4), 25–35.

Andrew, R. (2018). *Guest Post: Why India's CO_2 Emissions Grew Strongly in 2017*. Retrieved from www.carbonbrief.org

Angeli, C., & Valanides, N. (2012). Epistemological beliefs and ill-structured problem-solving in solo and paired contents. *Journal of Educational Technology & Society*, *15*(1), 2–14.

Anjum, N., Islam, M. A., Choudhury, M. I., & Saha, J. (2021). Do Intrinsic Rewards Matter on Motivation? *SEISENSE Journal of Management*, *4*(1), 47–58. doi:10.33215jom.v4i1.534

Anthopoulos, L., Siozos, P., & Tsoukalas, I. (2007). Applying participatory design and collaboration in digital public services for discovering and re-designing e-government services. *Government Information Quarterly*, *24*(2), 353–376. doi:10.1016/j.giq.2006.07.018

Antikainen, M., Uusitalo, T., & Kivikytö-Reponen, P. (2018). Digitalisation as an enabler of circular economy. *Procedia CIRP*, *73*, 45–49. doi:10.1016/j.procir.2018.04.027

Antony, J. P., & Bhattacharyya, S. (2010). Measuring organizational performance and organizational excellence of SMEs–Part 2: an empirical study on SMEs in India. *Measuring Business Excellence*.

Anwar, J., & Hasnu, S. (2017a). Strategic patterns and firm performance: Comparing consistent, flexible and reactor strategies. *Journal of Organizational Change Management*, *30*(7), 1015–1029. doi:10.1108/JOCM-03-2016-0053

Arbache, J. (2018) Seizing the Benefits of the Digital Economy for Development. *International Centre of Trade and Sustainable Development.* https://www.ictsd.org/opinion/seizing-the-benefits-of-the-digital-economy-for-development

Arefin, M. S., & Islam, N. (2019). A Study on the Motivation to Transfer Training in the Banking Industry of Bangladesh. *SA Journal of Human Resource Management*, *6*(1), 45–72. doi:10.1177/2322093718803210

Arkin, C. (2019, November 4). Waste exports: The rubbish dump is closed. *Heinrich Böll Foundation.* Retrieved from https://www.boell.de/en/2019/11/04/waste-exports-rubbish-dump-closed

Armstrong, M., & Brown, D. (2005). Reward strategies and trends in the United Kingdom: The land of diverse and pragmatic dreams. *Compensation and Benefits Review*, *37*(4), 41–53. doi:10.1177/0886368705277659

Armstrong-Stassen, M., & Lee, S. H. (2009). The effect of relational age on older Canadian employees' perceptions of human resource practices and sense of worth to their organization. *International Journal of Human Resource Management*, *20*(8), 1753–1769. doi:10.1080/09585190903087156

Arocas, R. L., & Li Ping Tang, T. (2004). The Love of Money, Satisfaction, and the Protestant Work Ethic: Money Profiles Among University professors in the USA and Spain. *Journal of Business Ethics*, *50*(4), 329–354. doi:10.1023/B:BUSI.0000025081.51622.2f

ASEAN Secretariat, . (2015). *The ASEAN ICT masterplan 2020.* ASEAN Secretariat.

ASEAN Secretariat, . (2016). *Master plan on ASEAN connectivity 2025.* ASEAN Secretariat.

ASEAN Secretariat, . (2020a). *ASEAN Sustainable Development Goals Indicators Baseline Report 2020.* ASEAN Secretariat.

ASEAN Secretariat, . (2020b). *ASEAN Statistical Yearbook 2020.* ASEAN Secretariat.

ASEAN Secretariat, . (2021, January). *ASEAN Digital Masterplan 2025.* ASEAN.

Asemi, A. (2005). Information searching habits of Internet users: A case study on the Medical Sciences University of Isfahan, Iran. *Webology*, *2*(1), 10.

Asgary, A., Ozdemir, A. I., & Özyürek, H. (2020). Small and Medium Enterprises and Global Risks: Evidence from Manufacturing SMEs in Turkey. *Int J Disaster Risk Sci*, *11*(1), 59–73. doi:10.100713753-020-00247-0

Asia Society. (2018). *Disruptive Asia 2018.* Asia Society Australia.

Assael, H. (1998). *Consumer Behavior and Marketing Action* (6th ed.). South Western College Publishing.

Avazalipour, M. S., Zandi, F., Saberi, R., Hakimipour, N., & Damankeshideh, M. (2013). The Impact of FDI on Environmental Resources in Selected Countries (NON-OECD). *International Journal of Research and Reviews in Applied Sciences*, *17*(1), 111–115.

Avolio, Sosik, Kahai, & Baker. (2014). *E-leadership: Re-examining transformations.* Academic Press.

Awaan, P. D., & Nawaz, M. (2015). Socio - Economic Determinants of Fast Food Industry Growth in Pakistan. *Food Science and Quality Management*, *43*, 2224–2237.

Awad, T. A. (2011). Environmental segmentation alternatives: Buyers' profiles and implications. *Journal of Islamic Marketing*, *2*(1), 55–73. doi:10.1108/17590831111115240

Aydin, O. T. (2018). Impact of Demographic Variables on Job Stress Factors: A Study on Turkish Employees. *Journal of Business research Turk*, 803-826.

Aziz, M. F. B. A., Mispan, M. S. B., & Doni, F. (2020). Organic Food Policy and Regulation in Malaysia: Development and Challenges. *Regulatory Issues in Organic Food Safety in the Asia Pacific*, 151–170. doi:10.1007/978-981-15-3580-2_10

Aziz, S. F. A., & Ahmad, S. (2011). Stimulating training motivation using the right training characteristic. *Industrial and Commercial Training*.

Bacik, R, & Turakova, A. (2018). The analysis of culture differences defined in Lewis's model and impact on corporate culture. *Journal of Global Science,* 1-6.

Badarudin, P. A., & Ibrahim, F. (2021). Knowledge-Based Practices in Disaster Management: Development Towards Digital Humanism. In W. S. H. Suhaili, N. Z. Siau, S. Omar, & S. Phon-Amuaisuk (Eds.), *Computational Intelligence in Information Systems* (pp. 13–25). Springer. doi:10.1007/978-3-030-68133-3_2

Baek, J., & Won, W. K. (2008). A dynamic approach to the FDI-environment nexus: the case of China and India. *No 6508, 2008 Annual Meeting, American Agricultural Economics Association (New Name 2008: Agricultural and Applied Economics Association).*

Baesens, B., De Winne, S., & Sels, L. (2017, Winter). Is Your Company Ready for HR Analytics? *MIT Sloan Management Review.*

Bagozzi, R. P., & Yi, Y. (1988). On the evaluation of structural equation models. *Journal of the Academy of Marketing Science*, *16*(1), 74–94. doi:10.1007/BF02723327

Bak, H. (2020). Supervisor feedback and innovative work behavior: The mediating roles of trust in supervisor and affective commitment. *Frontiers in Psychology*, *11*, 11. doi:10.3389/fpsyg.2020.559160 PMID:33041923

Balakrishnan, N. (2007). Information technology and communications security in India. *Science and Technology to Counter Terrorism: Proceedings of an Indo-U.S. Workshop*, 31-42.

Balch, R., & Springer, M. G. (2015). Performance pay, test scores, and student learning objectives. *Economics of Education Review*, *44*, 114–125. doi:10.1016/j.econedurev.2014.11.002

Balven, R., Fenters, V., Siegel, D. S., & Waldman, D. (2018). Academic entrepreneurship: The roles of identity, motivation, championing, education, work-life balance, and organizational justice. *The Academy of Management Perspectives*, *32*(1), 21–42. doi:10.5465/amp.2016.0127

Banerjee, B., & McKeage, K. (1994). How green is my value: Exploring the relationship between environmentalism and materialism. *Advances in Consumer Research. Association for Consumer Research (U. S.)*, *21*, 147–152.

Bani-melhem, S., Abukhait, R., Shamsudin, F. M., & Al-hawari, M. A. (2021). How and when does job challenge promote the innovative behaviour of public sector employees? *International Journal of Innovation Management*, 2150069. doi:10.1142/S1363919621500699

Bani-Melhem, S., Zeffane, R., & Albaity, M. (2018). Determinants of employees' innovative behavior. *International Journal of Contemporary Hospitality Management*, *30*(3), 1601–1620. doi:10.1108/IJCHM-02-2017-0079

Barney, J. B. (1997). *Gaining and sustaining competitive advantage*. Addison-Wesley.

Barroso Castro, C., Villegas, M. P., & Casillas, C. B. (2008). Transformational leadership and followers' attitudes: The mediating role of psychological empowerment. *International Journal of Human Resource Management*, *19*(10), 1842–1863. doi:10.1080/09585190802324601

Barr, S., Gilg, A. W., & Ford, N. J. (2001). A conceptual framework for understanding and analyzing attitudes towards household-waste management. *Environment & Planning A*, *33*(11), 2025–2048. doi:10.1068/a33225

Basford, T. E., & Offermann, L. R. (2012). Beyond leadership: The impact of coworker relationships on employee motivation and intent to stay. *Journal of Management & Organization*, *18*(6), 807–817. doi:10.5172/jmo.2012.18.6.807

Bastein, A. G. T. M., Roelofs, E., Rietveld, E., & Hoogendoorn, A. (2013). *Opportunities for a Circular Economy in the Netherlands*. TNO.

Bauer, W., Hammerle, M., Schlund, S., & Vocke, C. (2015). Transforming to a hyper-connected society and economy– towards an "Industry 4.0". *Procedia Manufacturing*, *3*, 417–424. doi:10.1016/j.promfg.2015.07.200

Bavakutty, M., & TK, M. S. (1999). *Internet services in Calicut University*. Academic Press.

Bawany, S. (2019). Leadership 4.0: How Ready Are You to Be A Digital Leader? *Leadership Excellence*, *36*(2), 28–30.

Bayer, R. C., & Ke, C. (2013). Discounts and consumer search behavior: The role of framing. *Journal of Economic Psychology*, *39*, 215–224. doi:10.1016/j.joep.2013.08.003

Beauprez, C. (2010). *Consumer behavior and buying profile in the Wooden Housing Industry in France* [Unpublished bachelor's thesis]. Turku University of Applied Sciences.

Becker, T. E. (2005). Potential problems in the statistical control of variables in organizational research: A qualitative analysis with recommendations. *Organizational Research Methods*, *8*(3), 274–289. doi:10.1177/1094428105278021

Beckford, C. L., Jacobs, C., Williams, N., & Nahdee, R. (2010). Aboriginal environmental wisdom, stewardship, and sustainability: Lessons from the Walpole island first nations, Ontario, Canada. *The Journal of Environmental Education*, *41*(4), 239–248. doi:10.1080/00958961003676314

Ben-Hur, S., & Kinley, N. (2016). Intrinsic motivation: The missing piece in changing employee behavior. *Perspectives for Managers*, *192*, 1.

Bennett, J., & Carter, C. (2014). Adopting virtual production for animated filmmaking. In *Proceedings of the 7th Annual International Conference on Computer Games, Multimedia and Allied Technology* (pp. 81-86). Global Science and Technology Forum (GSTF).

Benton, D., & Hazell, J. (2013). *Resource resilient UK: A report from the Circular Economy Task Force*. Green Alliance.

Beuren, F. H., Ferreira, M. G. G., & Miguel, P. A. C. (2013). Product-service systems: A literature review on integrated products and services. *Journal of Cleaner Production*, *47*, 222–231. doi:10.1016/j.jclepro.2012.12.028

Bezuidenhout, M. (2011). *The development and evaluation of a measure of graduate employability in the context of the new world of work* (Doctoral dissertation). University of Pretoria.

Bhattacharyya, S. S., & Nair, S. (2019). Explicating the future of work: Perspectives from India. *Journal of Management Development*, *38*(3), 175–194. doi:10.1108/JMD-01-2019-0032

Bibi, P., Ahmad, A., & Majid, A. H. A. (2018). The impact of training and development and supervisor support on employees retention in academic institutions: The moderating role of work environment. *Gadjah Mada International Journal of Business*, *20*(1), 113. doi:10.22146/gamaijb.24020

Bigum, M., & Oposa, A. (2020, November 17). *A circular economy for a sustainable plastic future*. Retrieved from https://www.adb.org/news/features/circular-economy-sustainable-plastic-future

Bilal, A. R., Naveed, M., & Anwar, F. (2017). Linking distinctive management competencies to SMEs' growth decisions. *Studies in Economics and Finance*, *34*(3), 302–330. doi:10.1108/SEF-10-2015-0236

Bilan, Y., Hussain, H. I., Haseeb, M., & Kot, S. (2020). Sustainability and economic performance: Role of organizational learning and innovation. *The Engineering Economist*, *31*(1), 93–103. doi:10.5755/j01.ee.31.1.24045

Biswas, A., Licata, J. W., McKee, D., Pulling, C., & Daughtridge, C. (2000). The recycling cycle: An empirical examination of consumer waste recycling and recycling shopping behaviors. *Advertisement and Environmental Issues, 19*(1), 93-115.

Blackwell, R. D., Miniard, P. W., & Engel, J. F. (2006). *Consumer Behavior* (10th ed.). Thomson Higher Education.

Blanco, L., Gonzalez, F., & Ruiz, I. (2011). *The Impact of FDI on CO2 Emissions in Latin America.* Pepperdine University, School of Public Policy Working Papers. Paper 28.

Blodgett, J. G., Bakir, A., & Rose, G. (2008). A test of the validity of Hofstede's cultural framework. *Journal of Consumer Marketing*, *25*(6), 339–349. doi:10.1108/07363760810902477

Bloemer, J., Pluymaekers, M., & Odekerken, A. (2013). Trust and affective commitment as energizing forces for export performance. *International Business Review*, *22*(2), 363–380. doi:10.1016/j.ibusrev.2012.05.002

Bloomberg Businessweek. (2020, Aug. 3). Bollywood Gets a Covid Makeover. *Bloomberg Businessweek.*

Boccaletti, G., Loffler, M., & Oppenheim, J. M. (2008). How IT Can Cut Carbon Emissions. *The McKinsey Quarterly*, (October), 1–5.

Bocken, N. M., de Pauw, I., Bakker, C., & van der Grinten, B. (2016). Product design and business model strategies for a circular economy. *Journal of Industrial and Production Engineering*, *33*(5), 308–320. doi:10.1080/21681015.2016.1172124

Bocken, N. M., Schuit, C. S., & Kraaijenhagen, C. (2018). Experimenting with a circular business model: Lessons from eight cases. *Environmental Innovation and Societal Transitions*, *28*, 79–95. doi:10.1016/j.eist.2018.02.001

Bødker, M., Gimpel, G., & Hedman, J. (2009). *The user experience of smart phones: A consumption values approach.* Paper presented at Global Mobility Roundtable, Cairo, Egypt.

Boes, K., Buhalis, D., & Inversini, A. (2016). Smart Tourism Destinations: Ecosystems for Tourism Destination Competitiveness. *International Journal of Tourism Cities*, *2*(2), 108–124. doi:10.1108/IJTC-12-2015-0032

Bohlinger, S. (2008). Competences as the Core Element of the European Qualifications Framework. *European Journal of Vocational Training*, *42*(1), 96–112.

Bokpin, G. A. (2017). Foreign direct investment and environmental sustainability in Africa: The role of institutions and governance. *Research in International Business and Finance*, *39*, 239–247. doi:10.1016/j.ribaf.2016.07.038

Bondarouk, T., & Brewster, C. (2016). Conceptualising the future of HRM and technology research. *International Journal of Human Resource Management*, *27*(21), 2652–2671. doi:10.1080/09585192.2016.1232296

Bondarouk, T., Parry, E., & Furtmueller, E. (2017). Electronic HRM: Four decades of research on adoption and consequences. *International Journal of Human Resource Management*, *28*(1), 98–131. doi:10.1080/09585192.2016.1245672

Bondarouk, T., & Ruël, H. J. M. (2009). Electronic human resource management: Challenges in the digital era. *International Journal of Human Resource Management*, *20*(3), 505–514. doi:10.1080/09585190802707235

Bondarouk, T., Ruël, H. J. M., & van der Heijden, B. (2009). E-HRM Effectiveness in a Public Sector Organization: A Multi-Stakeholder Perspective. *International Journal of Human Resource Management*, *20*(3), 578–590. doi:10.1080/09585190802707359

Bonham, C., Gangnes, B., & Zhou, T. (2009). Modeling Tourism: A Fully Identified VECM Approach. *International Journal of Forecasting*, *25*(3), 531–549. doi:10.1016/j.ijforecast.2008.11.014 PMID:32287620

Bonini, S., & Oppenheim, J. (2008). Cultivating the Green Consumer. *Stanford Social Innovation Review*, *6*(4), 56–61.

Boon, C., & Kalshoven, K. (2014). How high-commitment HRM relates to engagement and commitment: The moderating role of task proficiency. *Human Resource Management*, *53*(3), 403–420. doi:10.1002/hrm.21569

Borensztein, E., De Gregorio, J., & Lee, J. W. (1998). How Does Foreign Direct Investment Affect Economic Growth? *Journal of International Economics*, *45*(1), 115–135. doi:10.1016/S0022-1996(97)00033-0

Bossen, C., Jensen, L. G., & Udsen, F. W. (2013). Evaluation of a comprehensive EHR based on the DeLone and McLean model for IS success: Approach, results, and success factors. *International Journal of Medical Informatics*, *82*(10), 940–953. doi:10.1016/j.ijmedinf.2013.05.010 PMID:23827768

Bossler, M., & Grunau, P. (2020). Asymmetric information in external versus internal promotions. *Empirical Economics*, *59*(6), 2977–2998. doi:10.100700181-019-01749-7

Bostan, I., & Onofrei, M., Gavriluţă (Vatamanu), A. F., Toderaşcu, C., & Lazăr, C. M. (2019). An Integrated Approach to Current Trends in Organic Food in the EU. *Foods*, *8*(5), 144. doi:10.3390/foods8050144 PMID:31035453

Bowman, S. (2013). *Impact of Electronic Health Record Systems on Information Integrity: Quality and Safety Implications.* Perspectives in Health Information Management. Retrieved February 13, 2019, from https://www.ncbi.nlm.nih.gov/pmc/articles/PMC3797550/pdf/phim0010-0001c.pdf

Box, S., & Lopez-Gonzalez, J. (2017). The future of technology: Opportunities for ASEAN in the digital economy. In S. S. C. Tay & J. P. Tijaja (Eds.), *Global megatrends: Implications for the ASEAN economic community* (pp. 37–60). ASEAN Secretariat.

Boyd, R., & Richerson, P. (1985). *Culture and the Evolutionary Process*. Univ. of Chicago Press.

Boyer, L., Samuelian, J. C., Fieschi, M., & Lancon, C. (2010). Implementing electronic medical records in a psychiatric hospital: A qualitative study. *International Journal of Psychiatry in Clinical Practice*, *14*(3), 223–227. doi:10.3109/13651501003717243 PMID:24917324

Boztepe, A. (2012). Green marketing and its impact on consumer buying behavior. *European Journal of Economic and Political Studies*, *5*(1), 5–21.

Bradbury, K. E., Balkwill, A., Spencer, E. A., Roddam, A. W., Reeves, G. K., Green, J., Key, T. J., Beral, V., & Pirie, K. (2014). Organic food consumption and the incidence of cancer in a large prospective study of women in the United Kingdom. *British Journal of Cancer*, *110*(9), 2321–2326. doi:10.1038/bjc.2014.148 PMID:24675385

Branca, T. A., Colla, V., Algermissen, D., Granbom, H., Martini, U., Morillon, A., Pietruck, R., & Rosendahl, S. (2020). Reuse and recycling of by-products in the steel sector: Recent achievements paving the way to circular economy and industrial symbiosis in Europe. *Metals*, *10*(3), 345. doi:10.3390/met10030345

Braungart, M., McDonough, W., & Bollinger, A. (2007). Cradle-to-cradle design: Creating healthy emissions–a strategy for eco-effective product and system design. *Journal of Cleaner Production*, *15*(13-14), 1337–1348. doi:10.1016/j.jclepro.2006.08.003

Brewer, M. B. (1991). The social self: On being the same and different at the same time. *Personality and Social Psychology Bulletin*, *17*(5), 475–482. doi:10.1177/0146167291175001

Brida, J. G., Risso, W. A., & Carrera, E. J. S. (2008). A Long-Run Equilibrium Demand Function: Tourism in Mexico. *Tourismos*, 3.

Brooks, L. M., & Fenner, C. (2018). The Effect of Materialistic Behavior on the Workplace Motivation in Business Managers. *Academy of Business Research Journal*, *4*, 26–41.

Brown, T. A. (2015). *Confirmatory factor analysis for applied research* (2nd ed.). Guilford Press.

Brudirect. (2018, December 31). *The No Plastic Bag Everyday Initiative Begins On 31 December 2018*. Retrieved from https://www.brudirect.com/news.php?id=60531

Brunei Ministry of Development. (2019). *Strategic planning 2018 – 2023*. Retrieved on 08/12/2019, from http://www.mod.gov.bn/_layouts/15/osssearchresults.aspx?u=http%3A%2F%2Fwww%2Emod%2Egov%2Ebn&k=strategic%20plan%202018%2D2023

Brunei Prime Minister's Office. (2009). *Line manager self-service booklet*. Retrieved August 11, 2018, from http://www.gems.gov.bn/gemshelpcentre/Resource/GEMS BD_TR_Line%20Man ager%20Booklet%20Content_v0.15.pdf

Brunei Vision 2035. (2018). Retrieved October 17, 2018 from Embassy of Brunei Darussalam to the United States of America: https://www.gov.bn/SitePages/Wawasan%20Brunei%202035.aspx

Brunsson, N. (2007). *The consequences of decision making*. Oxford University Press.

Bryman, A. (2012). *Social Research Methods* (4th ed.). Oxford University Press.

Buchholz, K. (2020, June 2). Asia produces half the plastic in the world. *Statista*. Retrieved from https://www.statista.com/chart/17564/annual-per-capita-production-of-plastic-by-region/

Bueno, C., & Sass, T. R. (2018). The effects of differential pay on teacher recruitment and retention. *Andrew Young School of Policy Studies Research Paper Series*, (18-07).

Buhalis, D. (2015). *Working definitions of smartness and smart tourism destination*. Available at: http://buhalis.blogspot.co.uk/2014/12/working-definitions-of-smartness-and.html

Buhalis, D. (2000). Marketing the competitive destination of the future. *Tourism Management*, *21*(1), 97–116. doi:10.1016/S0261-5177(99)00095-3

Buhalis, D., & Amaranggana, A. (2014). Smart tourism destinations. In Z. Xiang & L. Tussyadiah (Eds.), *Information and Communication Technologies in Tourism 2014* (pp. 553–564). Springer.

Buil, I., Catalán, S., & Martínez, E. (2019). Encouraging intrinsic motivation in management training: The use of business simulation games. *International Journal of Management Education*, *17*(2), 162–171. doi:10.1016/j.ijme.2019.02.002

Bujang, S. D. A., Selamat, A., Krejcar, O., Maresova, P., & Nguyen, N. T. (2020). Digital Learning Demand for Future Education 4.0—Case Studies at Malaysia Education Institutions. *Informatics (MDPI)*, *7*(2), 13. doi:10.3390/informatics7020013

Bullmore, J. (2000). Alice in Disneyland, a creative view of international advertising. In J. P. Jones (Ed.), *International Advertising, Realities and Myths*. Sage. doi:10.4135/9781452231334.n4

Bunce, D., & West, M. A. (1995). Self perceptions and perceptions of group climate as predictors of individual innovation at work. *Applied Psychology*, *44*(3), 199–215. doi:10.1111/j.1464-0597.1995.tb01076.x

Burcu, C., & Seda, Y. (2013). Investigating the relationship between consumption values and personal values of green product buyers. *International Journal of Economics and Management Sciences*, *2*(12), 29–40.

Burns, D. (2018). A connected South-East Asia. In *Asia Society, Disruptive Asia 2018* (pp. 43–45). Asia Society Australia.

Burt, S. (1989). Trends and management issues in European retailing. *International Journal of Retailing*, *4*(4), 2–22. doi:10.1108/EUM0000000002924

Business Wire. (2020). *Global organic fresh food market 2019-2023: Evolving Opportunities*. Retrieved February 3, 2020, from https://www.businesswire.com/news/home/20200107005947/en/Global-Organic-Fresh-Food-Market-2019-2023-Evolving

Callero, P. L., Howard, J. A., & Piliavin, J. A. (1987). Helping behavior as role behavior: Disclosing social structure and history in the analysis of prosocial action. *Social Psychology Quarterly*, *50*(3), 247–256. doi:10.2307/2786825

Camilleri, M. A., & Camilleri, A. (2018). The performance management and appraisal in higher education. In Driving Productivity in Uncertain and Challenging Times. British Academy of Management.

Campbell, D. T., & Fiske, D. W. (1959). Convergent and discriminant validation by the multitrait-multimethod matrix. *Psychological Bulletin*, *56*(2), 81–105. doi:10.1037/h0046016 PMID:13634291

Cankar, S. S., & Petkovšek, V. (2013). Private and public sector innovation and the importance of cross-sector collaboration. *Journal of Applied Business Research*, *29*(6), 1597–1606. doi:10.19030/jabr.v29i6.8197

Capgemini. (2018). *Understanding digital mastery today*. Digital Transformation Institute.

Caragliu, A., Del Bo, C., & Nijkamp, P. (2011). Smart cities in Europe. *Journal of Urban Technology*, *18*(2), 65–82. do i:10.1080/10630732.2011.601117

Carbonell, X., & Panova, T. (2017). A critical consideration of social networking sites' addiction potential. *Addiction Research & Theory, 25*(1), 48–57.

Carbonell, X., Chamarro, A., Oberst, U., Rodrigo, B., & Prades, M. (2018). Problematic use of the internet and smartphones in university students: 2006–2017. *International Journal of Environmental Research and Public Health*, *15*(3), 475. doi:10.3390/ijerph15030475 PMID:29518050

Carbonell, X., Fuster, H., Chamarro, A., & Oberst, U. (2012). Internet and mobile cell phone addiction: A review of Spanish empirical studies. *Papeles del Psicólogo*.

Carbonell, X., Guardiola, E., Beranuy, M., & Bellés, A. (2009). A bibliometric analysis of the scientific literature on Internet, video games, and cell phone addiction. *Journal of the Medical Library Association: JMLA*, *97*(2), 102–107. doi:10.3163/1536-5050.97.2.006 PMID:19404500

Carlucci, D., & Schiuma, G. (2006). Knowledge Value Spiral: Linking Knowledge Assets to Company Performance. *Knowledge and Process Management*, *13*(1), 35–46. doi:10.1002/kpm.243

Caselli, G., Marino, C., & Spada, M. M. (2021). Modelling Online Gaming Metacognitions: The Role of Time Spent Gaming in Predicting Problematic Internet Use. *Journal of Rational-Emotive & Cognitive-Behavior Therapy*, *39*(2), 172–182. doi:10.100710942-020-00365-0

Castrogiovanni, G. J., Urbano, D., & Loras, J. (2011). Linking corporate entrepreneurship and human resource management in SMEs. *International Journal of Manpower*, *32*(1), 34–47. doi:10.1108/01437721111121215

Cavalli-Sforza, L., & Feldman, M. (1981). *Cultural Transmission and Evolution*. Princeton Univ. Press.

Cavana, R., Delahaye, B., & Sekeran, U. (2001). *Applied business research: Qualitative and quantitative methods*. John Wiley & Sons.

Cekik, R., & Telceken, S. (2018). A new classification method based on rough sets theory. *Soft Computing*, *22*(6), 1881–1889. doi:10.100700500-016-2443-0

Chamberlin, R., Wragg, T., Haynes, G., & Wragg, C. (2002). Performance-related pay and the teaching profession: A review of the literature. *Research Papers in Education*, *17*(1), 31–49. doi:10.1080/02671520110102534

Chandarana, A. (2011). *Crossroads of Culture – How to do business effectively in the global marketplace.* Available online at https://www.slideshare.net/prturner/avinash-chandaranacrossroads-of-culture-cesse-2011

Changing Market Foundation. (2020). *Talking trash, the corporate playbook of false solutions to the plastic crisis.* Changing Market Foundation.

Chan, R. Y. K., & Lau, L. B. Y. (2000). Antecedents of Green Purchases: A survey in China. *Journal of Consumer Marketing*, *17*(4), 338–357. doi:10.1108/07363760010335358

Chan, W. (1996). External recruitment versus internal promotion. *Journal of Labor Economics*, *14*(4), 555–570. doi:10.1086/209822

Chao, W. C., Hu, H., & Ung, C. O. (2013). Benefits and Challenges of Electronic Health Record System on Stakeholders: A Qualitative Study of Outpatient Physicians. *Journal of Medical Systems*. Retrieved November 5, 2018 from https://www.researchgate.net/profile/Hao_Hu11/publication/249321144_Benefits_and_Challenges_of_Electronic_Health_Record_System_on_Stakeholders_A_Qualitative_Study_of_Outpatient_Physicians/links/00b4952dc8dd7b02ee000000/Benefits-and-Challenges-of-Electroni

Chaston, I., Badger, B., Mangles, T., & Sadler-Smith, E. (2001). Organisational learning style, competencies and learning systems in small, UK manufacturing firms. *International Journal of Operations & Production Management*, *21*(11), 1417–1432. doi:10.1108/EUM0000000006224

Chatterjee, R. (2020). Confessions of Indian cinema's first woman superstar: Kanan Devi's memoirs, film history and digital archives. *Indian Film Stars: New Critical Perspectives*, 31.

Chen, A., & Peng, N. (2012). Green hotel knowledge and tourists' staying behavior. *Annals of Tourism Research*, *39*(4), 2211–2216. doi:10.1016/j.annals.2012.07.003

Chen, R., & Hsiao, J. (2012). An investigation on physicians' acceptance of hospital information system: A case study. *International Journal of Medical Informatics*, *81*(12), 810–820. doi:10.1016/j.ijmedinf.2012.05.003 PMID:22652011

Chen, W.-J. (2016). The model of service-oriented organizational citizenship behavior among international tourist hotels. *Journal of Hospitality and Tourism Management*, *29*, 24–32. doi:10.1016/j.jhtm.2016.05.002

Chen, X.-P., Eberly, M. B., Chiang, T.-J., Farh, J.-L., & Cheng, B.-S. (2014). Affective trust in Chinese leaders: Linking paternalistic leadership to employee performance. *Journal of Management*, *40*(3), 796–819. doi:10.1177/0149206311410604

Chen, Y. S., & Chang, C. H. (2012). Enhance green purchase intentions: The roles of green perceived value, green perceived risk, and green trust. *Management Decision*, *50*(3), 502–520. doi:10.1108/00251741211216250

Chen, Y., Jaw, Y., & Wu, B. (2016). Effect of digital transformation on organisational performance of SMEs. *Internet Research*, *26*(1), 186–212. doi:10.1108/IntR-12-2013-0265

Chen, Y., Tang, G., Jin, J., Xie, Q., & Li, J. (2014). CEO s¢ transformational leadership and product innovation performance: The roles of corporate entrepreneurship and technology orientation. *Journal of Product Innovation Management*, *31*, 2–17. doi:10.1111/jpim.12188

Cheong, C. W. H., Lee, M. H., & Weissmann, M. A. (2020). Credit access, tax structure and the performance of Malaysian manufacturing SMEs. *International Journal of Managerial Finance*, *16*(4), 433–454. doi:10.1108/IJMF-08-2019-0308

Chereau, P., & Meschi, P. (2019). The performance implications of the strategy–business model fit. *Journal of Small Business and Enterprise Development*, *26*(3), 441–463. doi:10.1108/JSBED-04-2018-0122

Chiappetta Jabbour, C. J., Sarkis, J., Lopes de Sousa Jabbour, A. B., Scott Renwick, D. W., Singh, S. K., Grebinevych, O., Kruglianskas, I., & Filho, M. G. (2019). Who is in charge? A review and a research agenda on the 'human side' of the circular economy. *Journal of Cleaner Production*, *222*, 793–801. doi:10.1016/j.jclepro.2019.03.038

Ching, S. M., Hamidin, A., Vasudevan, R., Sazlyna, M. S., Wan Aliaa, W. S., Foo, Y. L., Yee, A., & Hoo, F. K. (2017). Prevalence and factors associated with internet addiction among medical students-A cross-sectional study in Malaysia. *The Medical Journal of Malaysia*, *72*(1), 7–11. PMID:28255133

Chiva, R., Alegre, J., & Lapiedra, R. (2007). Measuring organisational learning capability among the workforce. *International Journal of Manpower*, *28*(3/4), 224–242. doi:10.1108/01437720710755227

Choi, E., Heshmati, A., & Cho, Y. (2010). An Empirical Study of the Relationships between CO_2 Emissions, Economic Growth and Openness. *IZA Discussion Papers*, (5304), 1–27.

Choudhury, R. R., & Dixit, S. K. (2018). Prospect and Challenges in Smart Tourism in India: Case Study of Smart City Bhubaneswar. *International Journal of Creative Research Thoughts*, *6*(I), 242–248.

Cho, Y. J., & Park, H. (2011). Exploring the relationships among trust, employee satisfaction, and organizational commitment. *Public Management Review*, *13*(4), 551–573. doi:10.1080/14719037.2010.525033

Christensen, C. (2013). *The innovator's dilemma: when new technologies cause great firms to fail*. Harvard Business Review Press.

Christensen, C. M., Raynor, M. E., & McDonald, R. (2015). What is disruptive innovation. *Harvard Business Review*, *93*(12), 44–53. PMID:17183796

Chugan, P. K., & Singh, S. (2015). Export Commitment and Its Impact on Firm-level Export Performance: Evidence from SMEs Cluster of Ahmedabad, India, *Journal of Behavioural Economics, Finance, Entrepreneurship. Accounting and Transport*, *3*, 90–95.

Chun, G. (2016, October 31). KT added to carbon management honors club. *Energy Economy*. https://www.ekn.kr/news/article.html?no=246713

Chung, H., Ding, Z., & Ma, X. (2019). Organisational learning and export performance of emerging market entrepreneurial firms. *European Journal of Marketing*, *53*(2), 257–278. doi:10.1108/EJM-08-2017-0496

Churchill, G. A. Jr. (1979). A paradigm for developing better measures of marketing constructs. *JMR, Journal of Marketing Research*, *16*(1), 64–73. doi:10.1177/002224377901600110

Chusmir, L. (1985). Motivation of managers: Is gender a factor? *Psychology of Women Quarterly*, *9*(1), 153–159. doi:10.1111/j.1471-6402.1985.tb00868.x

Circulair, N. (2015). *The Potential for High Value Reuse in a Circular Economy*. Academic Press.

Cohen, B. (2012). *What exactly is a Smart City?* Retrieved from: https://www.fastcoexist.com/1680538/what-exactly-is-a-smart-city

Cohen, J. (2013). *Statistical power analysis for the behavioral sciences*. Academic press. doi:10.4324/9780203771587

Colbert, A., Yee, N., & George, G. (2016). The digital workforce and the workplace of the future. *Academy of Management Journal*, *59*(3), 731–739. doi:10.5465/amj.2016.4003

Cole, M. A. (2004). Trade, the pollution haven hypothesis and the environmental Kuznets curve: Examining the linkages. *Ecological Economics*, *48*(1), 71–81. doi:10.1016/j.ecolecon.2003.09.007

Collin, J., Hiekkanen, K., Korhonen, J. J., Halen, M., Itala, T., & Helenius, M. (2015). IT Leadership in Transition-The Impact of Digitalization on Finnish Organizations. *The Academy of Management Annals*, *9*(1), 393–482.

Comrey, A. L., & Lee, H. (1992). *A first course in factor analysis*. Lawrence Erlbaum Associates, Inc.

Cooper, D., & Schindler, P. (2014). *Business Research Methods* (12th ed.). McGraw-Hill/Irwin.

Corbley, M. (2019, June 27). Students Design Beach Vacuum That Can Suck Up Microplastics While Leaving All the Sand. *Good News Network*. https://www.goodnewsnetwork.org/students-design-beach-vacuum-cleaner-for-plastic/

Cordano, M., Welcomer, S., Scherer, R. F., Pradenas, L., & Parada, V. (2011). A cross-cultural assessment of three theories of pro-environmental behavior: A comparison between business students of Chile and the United States. *Environment and Behavior*, *43*(5), 634–657. doi:10.1177/0013916510378528

Cordell, D., Rosemarin, A., Schröder, J. J., & Smit, A. L. (2011). Towards global phosphorus security: A systems framework for phosphorus recovery and reuse options. *Chemosphere*, *84*(6), 747–758. doi:10.1016/j.chemosphere.2011.02.032 PMID:21414650

Corum, J., Wee, S., & Zimmer, C. (2020). Coronavirus vaccine tracker. *New York Times*. Available online as of 23 September 2020: https://www.nytimes.com/interactive/2020/science/coronavirus-vaccine-tracker.html

Costa, L. A., Cool, K., & Dierickx, I. (2012). The competitive implications of the deployment of unique resources. *Strategic Management Journal*, *34*(4), 445–463. doi:10.1002mj.2018

Crampon, L. J., & Tan, K. T. (1973). A Model of Tourism Flow into the Pacific. *Tourism Review*, *28*(3), 98–104.

Creswell, J. W. (2012). *Educational research: Planning, conducting and evaluating quantitative and qualitative research* (4th ed.). Pearson Education.

Cropley, D. H., Cropley, A. J., Kaufman, J. C., & Runco, M. A. (Eds.). (2010). *The dark side of creativity*. Cambridge University Press. doi:10.1017/CBO9780511761225

Cull, R., Li, W., Sun, B., & Xu, L. C. (2015). Government Connections and Financial Constraints Evidence from a Large Representative Sample of Chinese Firms. *Journal of Corporate Finance*, *32*(June), 271–294. doi:10.1016/j.jcorpfin.2014.10.012

Cunningham, L. X., & Rowley, C. (2007). Human resource management in Chinese small and medium enterprises. *Personnel Review*, *36*(3), 415–439. doi:10.1108/00483480710731356

Dabic, M., Ortiz-De-Urbina-Criado, M., & Romero-Martínez, A. M. (2011). Human resource management in entrepreneurial firms: A literature review. *International Journal of Manpower*, *32*(1), 14–33. doi:10.1108/01437721111121206

Dahlstrom, P., Desmet, D., & Singer, M. (2017). *The seven decisions that matter in a digital transformation: a CEO's guide to reinvention*. McKinsey.

Danish, M., Ali, S., Ahmad, M. A., & Zahid, H. (2019). The influencing factors on choice behavior regarding green electronic products: Based on the green perceived value model. *Economies*, *7*(4), 99. doi:10.3390/economies7040099

Danish, R. Q., Ali, N., Ali, H., Afzal Humayon, A., Bilal Ahmed, M., & Gohar, A. (2019). Spirit and Innovation at Work in Software Houses of Pakistan: How Does Job Satisfaction Intervene the Relationship? *European Online Journal of Natural and Social Sciences*, *8*(1), 66–78.

Darling-Hammond, L. (1997). Doing what matters most: Investing in quality teaching. National Commission on Teaching & America's Future.

Davenport, T., & Kirby, J. (2016). *Only humans need apply: Winners and losers in the age of smart machines*. Harper Business.

Davidson, T., & De Stobbeleir, K. E. (2011). Shaping environments conducive to creativity: the role of feedback, autonomy and self-concordance. *Academy of Management Proceedings*. 10.5465/ambpp.2011.65869660

Davies, A., Fidler, D., & Gorbis, M. (2011). *Future work skills 2020*. Institute for the Future for University of Phoenix Research Institute.

Davoudi, S. M. M., & Fartash, K. (2012). Electronic human resource management: New avenues which leads to organizational success. *Journal of Multidisciplinary Research, 1*(2), 75–87.

De Mello, L. (1999). Foreign Direct Investment-Led Growth: Evidence from Time Series and Panel Data. *Oxford Economic Papers, 51*(1), 133–151. doi:10.1093/oep/51.1.133

De Mooij, M. (2004). *Consumer behavior and culture: Consequences for global marketing*. Sage.

De Mooij, M. (2009). *Global marketing and advertising: Understanding cultural paradoxes* (3rd ed.). Sage.

De Mooij, M., & Hofstede, G. (2002). Convergence and divergence in consumer behavior: Implications for international retailing. *Journal of Retailing, 78*(1), 61–69. doi:10.1016/S0022-4359(01)00067-7

de Vries, M. F. R. K. (2001). Creating authentizotic organizations: Well-functioning individuals in vibrant companies. *Human Relations, 54*(1), 101–111. doi:10.1177/0018726701541013

Dearnaley, P. (2013). Competitive advantage in the new contrived social care marketplace: Do we need a new theoretical framework? *Housing. Care and Support, 16*(3/4), 126–135. doi:10.1108/HCS-08-2013-0013

Delery, J. E., & Doty, D. H. (1996). Modes of theorizing in strategic human resource management: Tests of universalistic, contingency, and configurational performance predictions. *Academy of Management Journal, 39*(4), 802–835. doi:10.5465/256713

Deloitte (2020). *Edges of southeast asia*. The Deloitte Center for the Edge US-ASEAN Business Council, and the Singapore Economic Development Board (EDB).

Deloitte. (2018). *Consulting*. Telecommunications Industry Outlook.

DeLone, W. H., & McLean, E. R. (2016). *Foundations and Trends in Information System*. Retrieved February 10, 2019 from https://www.nowpublishers.com/article/DownloadSummary/ISY-005

Deluga, R. J. (1994). Supervisor trust building, leader-member exchange and organizational citizenship behaviour. *Journal of Occupational and Organizational Psychology, 67*(4), 315–326. doi:10.1111/j.2044-8325.1994.tb00570.x

Demailly, D., & Novel, A. S. (2014). The sharing economy: make it sustainable. *Studies, 3*(14.1).

Demircioglu, M. A., & Audretsch, D. B. (2017). Conditions for innovation in public sector organizations. *Research Policy, 46*(9), 1681–1691. doi:10.1016/j.respol.2017.08.004

Demming, C. L., Jahn, S., & Boztug, Y. (2017). Conducting mediation analysis in marketing research. *Marketing ZFP, 39*(3), 76–98. doi:10.15358/0344-1369-2017-3-76

Department of Economic Planning and Development. (2017). Statistics on micro small and medium enterprises (MSMEs). Seminar presented at Department of Economic Planning and Development, Brunei Darussalam, Bandar Seri Begawan.

De-Pelsmacker, P., Driesen, L., & Rayp, G. (2003). Are fair trade labels good business? Ethics and coffee buying intentions. *The Journal of Consumer Affairs*, *2*, 39.

Dervojeda, K., Verzijl, D., Rouwmaat, E., Probst, L., & Frideres, L. (2014). *Clean technologies circular supply chains.* EU report, 248-274.

Dettmann, R. L., & Dimitri, C. (2010). Who's buying organic vegetables? Demographic characteristics of US consumers. *Journal of Food Products Marketing*, *16*(1), 79–91. doi:10.1080/10454440903415709

DeVaro, J., Maxwell, N., & Morita, H. (2017). Training and intrinsic motivation in nonprofit and for-profit organizations. *Journal of Economic Behavior & Organization, 139*, 196–213.

Dhar, R. L. (2016). Ethical leadership and its impact on service innovative behavior: The role of LMX and job autonomy. *Tourism Management*, *57*, 139–148. doi:10.1016/j.tourman.2016.05.011

Diamantidis, A. D., & Chatzoglou, P. D. (2014). Employee post-training behaviour and performance: Evaluating the results of the training process. *International Journal of Training and Development*, *18*(3), 149–170. doi:10.1111/ijtd.12034

Dickey, D. A., & Fuller, W. A. (1979). Distribution of the Estimators for Autoregressive Time Series with a Unit Root. *Journal of the American Statistical Association*, *74*(366), 427–431. doi:10.2307/2286348

Dickey, D. A., & Fuller, W. A. (1981). Likelihood Ratio Statistics for Autoregressive Time Series with a Unit Root. *Econometrica*, *49*(4), 1063. doi:10.2307/1912517

Dick, G., & Metcalfe, B. (2001). Managerial factors and organisational commitment-A comparative study of police officers and civilian staff. *International Journal of Public Sector Management*, *14*(2), 111–128. doi:10.1108/09513550110387336

Dickson, M. (2001). Utility of no sweat labels for apparel consumers: Profiling label users and predicting their purchases. *The Journal of Consumer Affairs*, *35*(1), 96–119. doi:10.1111/j.1745-6606.2001.tb00104.x

Dinar Standard. (2020). *State of the global islamic economy report 2020/2021*. Dinar Standard, Dubai Islamic Economic Development Center, and Salam Gateway.

Dinard Standard. (2014). *State of the Global Islamic Economy Report 2014/2015*. Dinar Standard, Dubai Islamic Economic Development Center, and Salam Gateway.

Dinard Standard. (2015). *State of the Global Islamic Economy Report 2015/2016*. Dinar Standard, Dubai Islamic Economic Development Center, and Salam Gateway.

Dinard Standard. (2016). *State of the Global Islamic Economy Report 2016/2017*. Dinar Standard, Dubai Islamic Economic Development Center, and Salam Gateway.

Dinard Standard. (2017). *State of the Global Islamic Economy Report 2017/2018*. Dinar Standard, Dubai Islamic Economic Development Center, and Salam Gateway.

Dinard Standard. (2018). *State of the Global Islamic Economy Report 2018/2019*. Dinar Standard, Dubai Islamic Economic Development Center, and Salam Gateway.

Dinard Standard. (2019). *State of the Global Islamic Economy Report 2019/2020*. Dinar Standard, Dubai Islamic Economic Development Center, and Salam Gateway.

Ding, C. G., & Tseng, T. H. (2015). On the relationships among brand experience, hedonic emotions, and brand equity. *European Journal of Marketing*, *49*(7/8), 994–1015. doi:10.1108/EJM-04-2013-0200

Dominguez, N., & Mayrhofer, U. (2017). Internationalization stages of traditional SMEs: Increasing, decreasing and re-increasing commitment to foreign markets. *International Business Review*, *26*(6), 1051–1063. doi:10.1016/j.ibusrev.2017.03.010

Donnellan, J., & Rutledge, W. L. (2019). A case for resource-based view and competitive advantage in banking. *Managerial and Decision Economics*, *40*(6), 728–737. doi:10.1002/mde.3041

Dont, E. (2021). *Why EHRs are not disruptive?* Available online at http://captaindont.blogspot.com/2014/05/why-ehrs-are-not-yet-disruptive.html?m=1

Dritsakis, N., & Gialetaki, K. (2004). Cointegration Analysis of Tourism Revenues by the Member Countries of European Union to Greece. *Tourism Analysis*, *9*(3), 179–186. doi:10.3727/1083542042781258

Drucker, P. F. (1998). The Coming of the New Organization. In *Harvard Business Review on Knowledge Management*. Harvard Business School Press.

Du, F., Yang, F., Liang, L., & Yang, M. (2016). Do service providers adopting market segmentation need cooperation with third parties?: An application to hotels. *International Journal of Contemporary Hospitality Management*, *28*(1), 136–155. doi:10.1108/IJCHM-01-2014-0014

Dummett, K. (2006). Drivers for corporate environmental responsibility. *Environment, Development and Sustainability*, *8*(3), 375–389. doi:10.100710668-005-7900-3

Dumont, J., Shen, J., & Deng, X. (2017). Effects of green HRM practices on employee workplace green behavior: The role of psychological green climate and employee green values. *Human Resource Management*, *56*(4), 613–627. doi:10.1002/hrm.21792

Durmuş, A. (2019). Endustri 4.0 Egitim 4.0 Liderlik 4.0 Toplum 5.0 (1st ed.). İstanbul: Efe Akademi Yayınları.

Dutta, S., Geiger, T., & Lanvin, B. (2015). *The Global Information Technology Report 2015: ICTs for Inclusive Growth*. Geneva: World Economic Forum and INSEAD. Available at: http://www3.weforum.org/docs/WEF_Global_IT_Report_2015.pdf

Dysvik, A., & Kuvaas, B. (2008). The relationship between perceived training opportunities, work motivation and employee outcomes. *International Journal of Training and Development*, *12*(3), 138–157. doi:10.1111/j.1468-2419.2008.00301.x

EC. (2010). *European Commission – Joint Research Centre – Institute for Environment and Sustainability: International Reference Life Cycle Data System (ILCD) Handbook – General Guide for Life Cycle Assessment – Detailed Guidance, first edition*. March 2010. EUR 24708 EN. Luxembourg. Retrieved from https://publications.jrc.ec.europa.eu/repository/bitstream/JRC48157/ilcd_handbook-general_guide_for_lca-detailed_guidance_ 12march2010_isbn_fin.pdf

EC. (2015). *Communication from the commission to the parliament, the council and the European economic and social commitee and the commitee of the regions: Closing the loop – An EU action plan for the Circular Economy*. COM (2015) 614 final.

Economy, C. (2017). *Business Imperative for India*. Retrieved from https://www.teriin.org/sites/default/files/2018-03/TERI-YES_BANK_Circular_Economy_Report.pdf

EEA. (2016). *Developments in indicators: Total Material Requirement*. TMR.

E-Government national centre. (2019). *One government network*. Retrieved 27 June, 2019, from http://www.egnc.gov.bn/SitePages/OGN.aspx

Eisele, L., Grohnert, T., Beausaert, S., & Segers, M. (2013). Employee motivation for personal development plan effectiveness. *European Journal of Training and Development*, *37*(6), 527–543. doi:10.1108/EJTD-02-2013-0015

Eisenberger, R., Huntington, R., Hutchison, S., & Sowa, D. (1986). Perceived organizational support. *The Journal of Applied Psychology*, *71*(3), 500–507. doi:10.1037/0021-9010.71.3.500

Eisenhardt, K. M., & Martin, J. A. (2000). Dynamic capabilities: What are they? *Strategic Management Journal*, *21*(10-11), 1105–1121. doi:10.1002/1097-0266(200010/11)21:10/11<1105::AID-SMJ133>3.0.CO;2-E

El Sawy, O. A., Kræmmergaard, P., Amsinck, H., & Vinther, A. L. (2016). How LEGO Built the Foundations and Enterprise Capabilities for Digital Leadership. *MIS Quarterly Executive*, *15*(2), 141–166.

Ellen MacArthur Foundation. (2012). *Towards the circular economy vol. 1: An economic and business rationale for an accelerated transition.* Retrieved from https://www.ellenmacarthurfoundation.org/publications/towards-the-circular-economy-vol-1-an-economic-and-business-rationale-for-an-accelerated-transition

Ellen MacArthur Foundation. (2013). *Towards the circular economy vol. 1: Opportunities for the consumer goods sector.* Retrieved from https://www.ellenmacarthurfoundation.org/assets/ downloads/publications/TCE_Report-2013.pdf

Ellen MacArthur Foundation. (2016, January 19). *The new plastics economy: Rethinking the future of plastics*. Retrieved from https://www.ellenmacarthurfoundation.org/publications/the-new-plastics-economy-rethinking-the-future-of-plastics

Ellen MacArthur Foundation. (2017). *Priority Research Agenda*. Available at Error! Hyperlink reference not valid.

Ellen MacArthur Foundation. (2017, January 20). *The new plastics economy catalysing action.* Retrieved from https://www.ellenmacarthurfoundation.org/publications/new-plastics-economy-catalysing-action

Elliott, R., & Shimamoto, K. (2008). Are ASEAN Countries Havens for Japanese Pollution-Intensive Industry? *World Economy*, *31*(2), 236–254. doi:10.1111/j.1467-9701.2007.01088.x

Elsalanty, L. E. (2011). The Mediating Methods of Leadership Development in the Relationship between Talent Management and Job Performance. *International Journal of Innovation & Human Resources Management, 1*(1).

Emerson, R. M. (1976). Social exchange theory. *Annual Review of Sociology*, *2*(1), 335–362. doi:10.1146/annurev.so.02.080176.002003

Emmerik, I., Gardner, W., & Wendt, H. (2010). Associations of Culture and Personality with McClelland's Motives: A Cross-Cultural Study of Managers in 24 Countries. *Group and Organization Management, 35*(3), 329-367.

Engle, R., & Granger, C. W. J. (1987). Cointegration and Error Correction: Representation, Estimation and Testing. *Econometrica*, *55*(2), 251–276. doi:10.2307/1913236

Epetimehin, F. M. (2013). Cross-border insurance marketing and the corporate implications. *European Scientific Journal*, *9*(1), 152–162.

Espinosa, D. J., & Lujan, S. M. (2010). *Putting e-HR into practice: The case of the University of Alicante*. Retrieved 27 April, 2019, from http://www.egnc.gov.bn /SitePages/OGN.aspx.http://ceur-ws.org/Vol-570/paper020.pdf

Esposito, M., Tse, T., & Soufani, K. (2018). Introducing a Circular Economy: New Thinking with New Managerial and Policy Implications. *California Management Review*, *60*(3), 5–19. doi:10.1177/0008125618764691

European Commission. (2019). *A circular economy for plastics: Insights from research and innovation to inform policy and funding decisions*. European Commission.

Eva, N., Meacham, H., Newman, A., Schwarz, G., & Tham, T. L. (2019). Is coworker feedback more important than supervisor feedback for increasing innovative behavior? *Human Resource Management*, *58*(4), 383–396. doi:10.1002/hrm.21960

Eysenck, H. J. (1966). Personality and experimental psychology. *Bulletin of the British Psychological Society*.

Falk, R. F., & Miller, N. B. (1992). *A Primer for Soft Modeling*. University of Akron Press.

Farmer, S. M., Tierney, P., & Kung-Mcintyre, K. (2003). Employee creativity in Taiwan: An application of role identity theory. *Academy of Management Journal*, *46*(5), 618–630.

Farren, C. (2000). Mastery: The critical advantage. Management C, 21, 95–105.

Felício, J. A., Meidutė, I., & Kyvik, Ø. (2016). Global mindset, cultural context, and the internationalization of SMEs. *Journal of Business Research*, *69*(11), 4924–4932. doi:10.1016/j.jbusres.2016.04.054

Fernandes, C., & Karnik, A. V. (2010). Estimating Elasticity of Demand for Tourism in Dubai. *Tourism Analysis*, *15*(1), 57–69. doi:10.3727/108354210X12724734223630

Ferrari, A. (2012). *Digital competence in practice: an analysis of frameworks. JRC Technical Reports, European Commission, Joint Research Centre.*

Figlietti, C. D. (2016). *Developing an Electronic Health Record Training Program for New Employees*. Retrieved November 5, 2018 from Doctor of Nursing Practice (DNP) Projects: https://repository.usfca.edu/cgi/viewcontent.cgi?article=1105&context=dnp

Filkins, B. L., Kim, J. Y., Roberts, B., Armstrong, W., Miller, M. A., Hultner, M. L., & Steinhubl, S. R. (2016). Privacy and security in the era of digital health: What should translational researchers know and do about it? *American Journal of Translational Research*, *8*(3), 1560–1580. PMID:27186282

Findikli, M. A., & Bayarcelik, E. B. (2015). Exploring the outcomes of Electronic Human Resource Management (E-HRM). *Procedia: Social and Behavioral Sciences*, *207*, 424–431. doi:10.1016/j.sbspro.2015.10.112

Fischer, A., & Pascucci, S. (2017). Institutional incentives in circular economy transition: The case of material use in the Dutch textile industry. *Journal of Cleaner Production*, *155*, 17–32. doi:10.1016/j.jclepro.2016.12.038

Fisher, C., Bashyal, S., & Bachman, B. (2012). Demographic impacts on environmentally friendly purchase behaviors. *Journal of Targeting. Measurement and Analysis for Marketing*, *20*(3), 172–184. doi:10.1057/jt.2012.13

Fisher, T. (1997). The Designer's Self-Identity—Myths of Creativity and the Management of Teams 1. *Creativity and Innovation Management*, *6*(1), 10–18. doi:10.1111/1467-8691.00044

Floren, H., Rundquist, J., & Fischer, S. (2016). Entrepreneurial orientation and human resource management: Effects from HRM practices. *Journal of Organizational Effectiveness: People and Performance*, *3*(2), 164–180. doi:10.1108/JOEPP-03-2016-0029

Follows, S. B., & Jobber, D. (2000). Environmentally responsible purchase behaviour: A test of a consumer model. *European Journal of Marketing*, *34*(5/6), 723–746. doi:10.1108/03090560010322009

Fonkeng, C. (2018). *Effects of job-stress on employee performance in an enterprise. A microfinance institution in Cameroon*. Centria University of Applied Sciences.

Fornell, C., & Larcker, D. F. (1981). Evaluating structural equation models with unobservable variables and measurement error. *JMR, Journal of Marketing Research*, *18*(1), 39–50. doi:10.1177/002224378101800104

Forsgren, M. (2002). The concept of learning in the Uppsala internationalization process model: A critical review. *International Business Review*, *11*(3), 257–277. doi:10.1016/S0969-5931(01)00060-9

Frederiks, E. R., Stenner, K., & Hobman, E. V. (2015). Household energy use: Applying behavioural economics to understand consumer decision-making and behaviour. *Renewable & Sustainable Energy Reviews*, *41*, 1385–1394. doi:10.1016/j.rser.2014.09.026

Frishammar, J., & Parida, V. (2019). Circular business model transformation: A roadmap for incumbent firms. *California Management Review*, *61*(2), 5–29. doi:10.1177/0008125618811926

Gabriel, A. S., Frantz, N. B., Levy, P. E., & Hilliard, A. W. (2014). The supervisor feedback environment is empowering, but not all the time: Feedback orientation as a critical moderator. *Journal of Occupational and Organizational Psychology*, *87*(3), 487–506. doi:10.1111/joop.12060

Gagné, M., Forest, J., Vansteenkiste, M., Crevier-Braud, L., van den Broeck, A., Aspeli, A. K., Bellerose, J., Benabou, C., Chemolli, E., Güntert, S. T., Halvari, H., Indiyastuti, D. L., Johnson, P. A., Molstad, M. H., Naudin, M., Ndao, A., Olafsen, A. H., Roussel, P., Wang, Z., & Westbye, C. (2015). The Multidimensional Work Motivation Scale: Validation evidence in seven languages and nine countries. *European Journal of Work and Organizational Psychology*, *24*(2), 178–196. doi:10.1080/1359432X.2013.877892

Gandolfo, G. (1998). *International Trade Theory and Policy: With 12 Tables*. Springer. doi:10.1007/978-3-642-61680-8

Garaika, G. (2019). The Effects Of Fatigue, Role Overload And Stress On Farmer'S Work Safety. *Journal of Management*, *36*(6), 1699–1724.

García-Barragán, J. F., Eyckmans, J., & Rousseau, S. (2019). Defining and measuring the circular economy: A mathematical approach. *Ecological Economics*, *157*, 369–372. doi:10.1016/j.ecolecon.2018.12.003

Garcia, G., Woolley, E., Rahimifard, S., Colwill, J., White, R., & Needham, L. (2017). A methodology for sustainable management of food waste. *Waste and Biomass Valorization*, *8*(6), 2209–2227. doi:10.1007/s12649-016-9720-0 PMID:32010409

García-Granero, A., Llopis, Ó., Fernández-Mesa, A., & Alegre, J. (2015). Unraveling the link between managerial risk-taking and innovation: The mediating role of a risk-taking climate. *Journal of Business Research*, *68*(5), 1094–1104. doi:10.1016/j.jbusres.2014.10.012

Gardner, A. (2021). The importance of creating the right 'culture' in Industry 4.0. *Business Insights: Essentials*. Available online at http://bi.gale.com.ezproxy.lib.uwf.edu/essentials/article/GALE%7CA616135591/a122f7264ff04c67475a42a51429c96b?u=pens49866

Gardner, S. D., Lepak, D. P., & Bartol, K. M. (2003). Virtual HR: The impact of information technology on the human resource professional. *Journal of Vocational Behavior*, *63*(2), 159–179. doi:10.1016/S0001-8791(03)00039-3

Gardner, W. L., Lowe, K. B., Moss, T. W., Mahoney, K. T., & Cogliser, C. C. (2010). Scholarly leadership of the study of leadership: A review of the leadership quarterly's second decade, 2000–2009. *The Leadership Quarterly*, *21*(6), 922–958. doi:10.1016/j.leaqua.2010.10.003

Garin-Munoz, T., & Montero-Martin, L. F. (2007). Tourism in the Balearic Islands: A Dynamic Model for International Demand Using Panel Data. *Tourism Management*, *28*(5), 1224–1235. doi:10.1016/j.tourman.2006.09.024

Gartner. (2016). *Market Share Analysis: Consulting Services, Worldwide, 2015*. Available at. https://www.gartner.com/doc/3317117/market-share-analysis-consulting- services.

Gaur, S. S., Vasudevan, H., & Gaur, A. S. (2011). Market orientation and manufacturing performance of Indian SMEs: Moderating role of firm resources and environmental factors. *European Journal of Marketing*, *45*(7), 1172–1193. doi:10.1108/03090561111137660

Geissdoerfer, M., Pieroni, M. P., Pigosso, D. C., & Soufani, K. (2020). Circular business models: A review. *Journal of Cleaner Production*, *277*, 123741. doi:10.1016/j.jclepro.2020.123741

Gelhard, C., & Von Delft, S. (2016). The role of organizational capabilities in achieving superior sustainability performance. *Journal of Business Research*, *69*(10), 4632–4642. doi:10.1016/j.jbusres.2016.03.053

General, R. (2019). Supermarkets in Asia are Now Using Banana Leaves Instead of Plastic Packaging. *Nextshark*. https://nextshark.com/banana-leaves-asia-plastic-packaging/

Gershoff, A. D., & Johar, G. V. (2006). Do You Know Me? Consumer Calibration of Friends' Knowledge. *The Journal of Consumer Research*, *32*(4), 496–503. doi:10.1086/500479

Ghali, Z., & Hamdi, R. (2015). The purchase and consumption motivations of an organic product by the Tunisian consumer: An application on the prickly pear seed oil (PPS). *Journal of North African Research in Business*, *11*, 211–233. doi:10.5171/2015.220428

Gharakhani, D., & Mousakhani, M. (2012). Knowledge management capabilities and SMEs organizational performance. *Journal of Chinese Entrepreneurship*, *4*(1), 35–49. doi:10.1108/17561391211200920

Ghassemzadeh, L., Shahraray, M., & Moradi, A. (2008). Prevalence of Internet addiction and comparison of Internet addicts and non-addicts in Iranian high schools. *CyberPsychology & Behavior, 11*(6), 731–733.

Ghavifekr, S., & Rosdy, W. A. W. (2015). Teaching and learning with technology: Effectiveness of ICT integration in schools. *International Journal of Research in Education and Science*, *1*(2), 175–191. doi:10.21890/ijres.23596

Ghisellini, P., Cialani, C., & Ulgiati, S. (2016). A review on circular economy: The expected transition to a balanced interplay of environmental and economic systems. *Journal of Cleaner Production*, *114*, 11–32. doi:10.1016/j.jclepro.2015.09.007

Ghosh, S., & Das, N. (2013). New model of performance management and measurement in higher education sector. *Management*, *2*(8), 267–274.

Giles, D. (2011, April 29). *Testing for Granger Causality*. Retrieved from http://davegiles.blogspot.in/2011/04/testing-for-granger-causality.html

Gilson, L. L., & Shalley, C. E. (2004). A little creativity goes a long way: An examination of teams' engagement in creative processes. *Journal of Management*, *30*(4), 453–470. doi:10.1016/j.jm.2003.07.001

Gilster, P. (1997). *Digital literacy*. Wiley.

Goe, L., Bell, C., & Little, O. (2008). *Approaches to evaluating teacher effectiveness: A research synthesis*. National Comprehensive Center for Teacher Quality.

Goldhaber, D. (2002). The mystery of good teaching. *Education Next*, *2*(1), 50–55.

Gomes, G., & Wojahn, R. M. (2017). Organizational learning capability, innovation and performance: Study in small and medium-sized enterprises (SMES). *Revista ADM*, *52*(2), 163–175. doi:10.1016/j.rausp.2016.12.003

Gontarek, W. (2016). Risk governance of financial institutions: The growing importance of risk appetite and culture. *Journal of Risk Management in Financial Institutions*, *9*(2), 120–129.

Google. (2020). *COVID-19 Community Mobility Reports*. As of 23 September 2020:https://www.google.com/covid19/mobility/

Gormus, S., & Gocer, I. (2010). The Socio-economic Determinants of Tourism Demand in Turkey: A Panel Data Approach. *International Research Journal of Finance and Economics*, *55*, 88–99.

Gorra, A. (2007). *An analysis of the relationship between individuals' perceptions of privacy and mobile phone location data - a grounded theory study* [PhD thesis, Leeds Metropolitan University]. https://www.academia.edu/6331343/Chapter_3_-Methodology_PhD_thesis_Andrea_Gorra_Chapter_3_Research_Methodology

Gorzeń-Mitka, I. (2013). Risk Identification Tools – Polish MSMES Companies Practices. *Problems of Management in the 21stcentury*, *7*, 6-11.

Gossling, S., Scott, D., & Hall, C. M. (2020). Pandemics, tourism and global change: A rapid assessment of COVID 19. *Journal of Sustainable Tourism*, *29*(1), 1–21. doi:10.1080/09669582.2020.1758708

Government of Sikkim (GoS). (2019a). *4th Anniversary of Smart City Project*. Retrieved from: https://www.sikkim.gov.in/media/press-release/press-info?name=Video+conference+organised+to+mark+4th+anniversary+of+Smart+City+Project

Government of Sikkim (GoS). (2019b). *Namchi Smart City Mission*. Retrieved from: https://www.sikkim.gov.in/media/press-release/press-info?name=Press+Conference+at+the+office+of+Namchi+Smart+City+Mission

Goyal, S., Esposito, M., & Kapoor, A. (2018). Circular economy business models in developing economies: lessons from India on reduce, recycle, and reuse paradigms. *Thunderbird International Business Review, 60*(5), 729-740.

Grabchak, E.P., Medvedev, E.A., & Vasilyeva, I.G. (2018). How to make digitalization successful. *Energetic Keskaya Politika, 5*, 25-29.

Grant Thornton (GT). (2019). *Smart Cities Mission- A Story of Unique Interventions*. Retrieved from: https://www.grantthornton.in/globalassets/1.-member-firms/india/assets/pdfs/smart_cities_compendium_final.pdf

Greener, S. (2008). *Business research methods*. BookBoon.

Greenhalgh, T., Hinder, S. K. S., Bratan, T., & Russell, J. (2010). Adoption, non-adoption, and abandonment of a personal electronic health record: case study of HealthSpace. *BMJ*. Retrieved November 5, 2018 from http://sci-hub.tw/https://doi.org/10.1136/bmj.c5814

Greenstein, S., Zhu, F., & Herman, K. (2017). *Korea Telecom: Building a GiGAtopia (A) and (B)*. https://store.hbr.org/product/korea-telecom-building-a-gigatopia-a/617014?sku=617014-PDF-ENG

Greenwald, A. G., & Banaji, M. R. (1995). Implicit social cognition: Attitudes, self-esteem, and stereotypes. *Psychological Review*, *102*(1), 4–27. doi:10.1037/0033-295X.102.1.4 PMID:7878162

Gremler, D. D., Gwinner, K. P., & Brown, S. W. (2001). Generating positive word-of-mouth communication through customer-employee relationships. *International Journal of Service Industry Management*, *12*(1), 44–59. doi:10.1108/09564230110382763

Gretzel, U., Werthner, H., Koo, C., & Lamsfus, C. (2015). Conceptual Foundations for Understanding Smart Tourism Ecosystems. *Computers in Human Behavior*, *50*, 558–563. doi:10.1016/j.chb.2015.03.043

Griffith, D. A., Noble, S., & Chen, Q. (2006). The performance implications of entrepreneurial firm performance. *Strategic Management Journal*, *30*(8), 909–920.

Griffiths, M. (2000). Internet addiction-time to be taken seriously? *Addiction Research*, *8*(5), 413–418. doi:10.3109/16066350009005587

Groening, C., Sarkis, J., & Zhu, Q. (2018). Green marketing consumer-level theory review: A compendium of applied theories and further research directions. *Journal of Cleaner Production*, *172*, 1848–1866. doi:10.1016/j.jclepro.2017.12.002

Gronseth, S., Gronseth, S., Dalton, E., Alvarez, B., Iglesias, I., Vergara, P., Ingle, J. C., Pacheco-Guffrey, H., Bauder, D., Cooper, K., Anderson, C., Anderson, K., Intatano, V., Semingson, P., Pole, K., Armstrong, K., Boreham, B., Mack, T., Harris, L., . . . Yearta, L. (2019). Using UDL-related methods in education, teacher training, and job-development. *Society for Information Technology & Teacher Education International Conference, 2019*(1), 245–249.

Grossman, G. M., & Krueger, A. B. (1991). *Environmental Impacts of a North American Free Trade Agreement. NBER Working Paper Series,* 3914.

Gruber, M., Heinemann, F., Brettel, M., & Hungeling, S. (2010). Configurations of resources and capabilities and their performance implications: An exploratory study on technology ventures. *Strategic Management Journal*, *31*(12), 1337–1356. doi:10.1002mj.865

Gruman, G. (2016). What digital transformation really means. *InfoWorld.* Available online at: https://www.infoworld.com/article/3080644/what-digital-transformation-really-means.html

Gruman, A., & Saks, A. M. (2011). Performance management and employee engagement. *Human Resource Management Review*, *21*(2), 123–136. doi:10.1016/j.hrmr.2010.09.004

GSMA. (2017). *KT MEG: Korea's Smart Energy System.* GSMA.

Guagnano, G. A., Stern, P. C., & Dietz, T. (1995). Influences on Attitude-Behavior Relationships: A Natural Experiment with Curbside Recycling. *Environment and Behavior*, *27*(5), 699–718. doi:10.1177/0013916595275005

Guiso, L., Sapienza, P., & Zingales, L. (2006). Doeas culture affect economic outcomes. *The Journal of Economic Perspectives*, *20*(2), 23–48. doi:10.1257/jep.20.2.23

Guizzardi, A., Emanuele, F., & Ranieri, E. (2017). Advance booking and hotel price variability online: Any opportunity for business customers? *International Journal of Hospitality Management*, *64*, 85–93. doi:10.1016/j.ijhm.2017.05.002

Gunarekha, B. S., & Binly, T. A. (2018). Digital marketing Transformation for the Smart Tourism Ecosystem: A Study. *Journal of Emerging Technologies and Innovative Research*, *5*(2), 216–222.

Gunawan, H., & Amalia, R. (2015). Wages and employees performance: The quality of work life as moderato. *Journal of Economics and Financial Issues*, 234-248.

Gunningberg, L., Fogelberg-Dahm, M., & Ehrenberg, A. (2009). Improved quality and comprehensiveness in nursing documentation documentation of pressure ulcers after implementing an electronic health record in hospital care. *Journal of Clinical Nursing*, *18*(11), 1557–1564. doi:10.1111/j.1365-2702.2008.02647.x PMID:19220607

Guo, N., Luk, T. T., Wang, M. P., Ho, S. Y., Fong, D. Y. T., Wan, A., Chan, S. S., & Lam, T. H. (2021). Self-Reported Screen Time on Social Networking Sites Associated With Problematic Smartphone Use in Chinese Adults: A Population-Based Study. *Frontiers in Psychiatry*, *11*, 614061. doi:10.3389/fpsyt.2020.614061 PMID:33519554

Gupta, A., Saha, S. K., Sharma, N. D., & Jha, A. (2021). Perceptual Differences Across Various Stakeholder Groups: A Study of Challenges for Skill Development in Sikkim, India. *International Journal of Asian Business and Information Management*, *12*(3), 43–66. doi:10.4018/IJABIM.20210701.oa4

Guzy, N., & Hirtenlehner, H. (2015). *Trust in the German police: determinants and consequences for reporting behavior. In Trust and legitimacy in criminal justice*. Springer.

Habeeb, N. J., & Weli, S. T. (2020). Relationship of Smart Cities and Smart Tourism: An Overview. *Hightech Innovation Journal, 1*(4), 194–202. doi:10.28991/HIJ-2020-01-04-07

Hadji, B., & Degoulet, P. (2016). Information system end-user satisfaction and continuance intention: A unified modeling approach. *Journal of Biomedical Informatics, 61*, 185–193. doi:10.1016/j.jbi.2016.03.021 PMID:27033175

Hagist, C., & Kotlikoff, L. (2009). *Who's going broke? Comparing growth in public healthcare expenditure in ten OECD countries*. Hacienda Pública Española.

Hair, J. (2014). Partial Least Squares Structural Equation Modeling (PLS-SEM): An Emerging Tool for Business Research. *ResearchGate*, 106-121.

Hair, J. F., Black, W. C., Babin, B. J., & Anderson, R. E. (2010). *Multivariate data analysis* (7th ed.). Pearson.

Hair, J. F., Black, W., Babin, B., & Anderson, R. (2010). *Multivariate Data Analysis* (7th ed.). Pearson.

Hair, J. F., Hult, G., Ringle, C., & Sarstedt, M. (2014). *A Primer on Partial Least Square Structural Equation Modeling (PLS - SEM)*. SAGE.

Hair, J. F. Jr, Hult, G. T. M., Ringle, C., & Sarstedt, M. (2016). *A primer on partial least squares structural equation modeling (PLS-SEM)*. Sage Publications.

Hair, J. F. Jr, Ringle, C. M., & Sarstedt, M. (2013). Partial least squares structural equation modeling: Rigorous applications, better results and higher acceptance. *Long Range Planning, 46*(1-2), 1–12. doi:10.1016/j.lrp.2013.01.001

Hair, J. F., Ringle, C. M., & Sarstedt, M. (2011). PLS-SEM: Indeed a silver bullet. *Journal of Marketing Theory and Practice, 19*(2), 139–151. doi:10.2753/MTP1069-6679190202

Hair, J. F., Risher, J. J., Sarstedt, M., & Ringle, C. M. (2019). When to use and how to report the results of PLS-SEM. *European Business Review, 31*(1), 2–24. doi:10.1108/EBR-11-2018-0203

Hair, J. F., Sarstedt, M., Ringle, C. M., & Mena, J. A. (2012). An assessment of the use of partial least squares structural equation modeling in marketing research. *Journal of the Academy of Marketing Science, 40*(3), 414–433. doi:10.100711747-011-0261-6

Hair, J., Wolfinbarger, M., & Money, A. (2011). *Essentials of Business Research Methods* (2nd ed.). M.E. Sharpe.

Halid, H., Yusoff, Y. M., & Somu, H. (2020, May). The Relationship Between Digital Human Resource Management and Organizational Performance. In *First ASEAN Business, Environment, and Technology Symposium (ABEATS 2019)* (p. 96-99). 10.2991/aebmr.k.200514.022

Hall, E. T. (1966). *Hidden Dimension*. Doubleday & Company Inc.

Hall, E. T. (1976). *Beyond Culture*. Anchor Books.

Hall, E. T. (1983). *The Dance of Life*. Anchor Books.

Halliburton, C., & Hunerberg, R. (2005). Pan-European marketing ten years after 1993—A current appraisal and proposed conceptual framework. In E. Kaynak & F. Jallat (Eds.), *Marketing issues in Western Europe —Changes and developments* (pp. 16–29). Routledge. doi:10.1300/J037v14n01_02

Hammadi, F. A., & Hussain, M. (2019). Sustainable organizational performance. *The International Journal of Organizational Analysis*.

HammerJ. (2014). Available online at https://www.youtube.com/watch?v=wKydlMWHwSc

Hammermann, A., & Stettes, O. (2017). Does digitization make new demands on leadership and performance management? *IW Trends Quarterly on Empirical Economic Research, 44*(4), 93-111.

Handayani, E., Ferdinand, A. T., & Sugiono, S. (2017). Analysis of Factors Affecting the Performance of SME Exports in Central Java through Export Marketing Strategies. *Jurnal Sains Pemasaran Indonesia, 16*(2), 103–116. doi:10.14710/jspi.v16i2.103-116

Handayani, P. W., Hidayanto, A. N., & Budi, I. (2017). User acceptance factors of hospital information systems and related technologies: Systematic review. *Informatics for Health & Social Care*. Retrieved February 6, 2019, from sci-hub.tw/10.1080/17538157.2017.1353999 PMID:28829650

Han, H., Hsu, L. T. J., & Lee, J. S. (2009). Empirical investigation of the roles of attitudes toward green behaviors, overall image, gender, and age in hotel customers' eco-friendly decision-making process. *International Journal of Hospitality Management, 28*(4), 519–528. doi:10.1016/j.ijhm.2009.02.004

Hanim, N., Osman, R., Noor, A. H. A. M., & Hasim, M. S. (2010). Malaysian Tourism Demand from the Middle East Market: A Preliminary Analysis. *Journal Antarabangsa Kajian Asia Barat, 2*(1), 37–52.

Hanscheke, I. (2018). *Digitization and Industry 4.0 – simple and effective: Mastering the digital transformation systematically and lean*. Carl Hanser Verlag.

Hansen, S. D., Dunford, B. B., Boss, A. D., Boss, R. W., & Angermeier, I. (2011). Corporate social responsibility and the benefits of employee trust: A cross-disciplinary perspective. *Journal of Business Ethics, 102*(1), 29–45. doi:10.100710551-011-0903-0

Hansmann, R., Baur, I., & Binder, R. (2020). Increasing organic food consumption: An integrating model of drivers and barriers. *Journal of Cleaner Production, 275*, 123058. doi:10.1016/j.jclepro.2020.123058

Hanushek, E. A., Kain, J. F., & Rivkin, S. G. (2004). Why public schools lose teachers. *The Journal of Human Resources, 39*(2), 326–354. doi:10.2307/3559017

Harrison, T., & Bazzy, J. D. (2017). Aligning organizational culture and strategic human resource management. *Journal of Management Development, 36*(10), 1260–1269. doi:10.1108/JMD-12-2016-0335

Harvard Business Review Analytic Services. (2017). *Operationalizing Digital Transformation: New Insights into Making Digital Work*. Available online at: https://hbr.org/sponsored/2017/05/operationalizing-digital-transformation-new-insights-into-making-digital-transformation-work

Hasaballah, A. H. A., Genc, O. F., Mohamada, O., & Ahmed, Z. U. (2019). How do relational variables affect export performance? Evidence from Malaysian exporters. *Asia Pacific Journal of Marketing and Logistics, 31*(1), 128–156. doi:10.1108/APJML-12-2017-0345

Hassan, M., Toylan, N. V., Semerciöz, F., & Aksel, I. (2012). Interpersonal trust and its role in organizations. *International Business Research, 5*(8), 33. doi:10.5539/ibr.v5n8p33

Hawkins, D., & Mothersbaugh, D. (2010). *Consumer Behavior: Building Marketing Strategy* (11th ed.). McGraw-Hill Irwin.

Hay Group. (2003). *Picture Story Exercise (PSE): Technical manual*. The McClelland Center for Research and Innovation, Hay Group.

Hayes, A. F., & Preacher, K. J. (2010). Quantifying and testing indirect effects in simple mediation models when the constituent paths are nonlinear. *Multivariate Behavioral Research, 45*(4), 627–660. doi:10.1080/00273171.2010.498290 PMID:26735713

Heinonen, K., & Strandvik, T. (2020). Reframing service innovation: COVID-19 as a catalyst for imposed service innovation. *Journal of Service Management.*

Heinrich Böll Foundation and Break Free From Plastic. (2019). *The plastic atlas 2019.* Druckhaus Kaufmann.

HeinrichÃ, S (2014). Socio-Economic Consequences of Digital Transformation: Socio-ekonomske posledice digitalne transformacije. *Socioeconomica – The Scientific Journal for Theory and Practice of Socio-economic Development. Procia CIRP, 3*(6), 179-202. Doi:10.12803/SJSECO.369814

Henseler, J. (2009). *The Use of Partial Least Squares Path Modeling in International Marketing.* JAI Press.

Henseler, J., Dijkstra, T. K., Sarstedt, M., Ringle, C. M., Diamantopoulos, A., Straub, D. W., Ketchen, D. J. Jr, Hair, J. F., Hult, G. T. M., & Calantone, R. J. (2014). Common beliefs and reality about PLS: Comments on Rönkkö and Evermann (2013). *Organizational Research Methods, 17*(2), 182–209. doi:10.1177/1094428114526928

Henseler, J., Ringle, C. M., & Sinkovics, R. R. (2009). *The use of partial least squares path modeling in international marketing New challenges to international marketing.* Emerald Group Publishing Limited.

Henseler, J., Ringle, C., & Sarstedt, M. (2015). A new criterion for assessing discriminant validity in variance-based structural equation modeling. *Journal of the Academy of Marketing Science, 43*(1), 115–135. doi:10.100711747-014-0403-8

He, P., Sun, Y., Zhang, Y., & Li, T. (2020). COVID–19's impact on stock prices across different sectors—An event study based on the Chinese stock market. *Emerging Markets Finance & Trade, 56*(10), 2198–2212. doi:10.1080/1540496X.2020.1785865

Herder-Wynne, F., Amato, R., & Uit de Weerd, F. (2017). *Leadership 4.0 A review of the thinking.* Oxford Leadership.

Hertin, R. D., & Al-Sanjary, O. (2018). Performance of Hospital Information System in Malaysian Public Hospital: A Review. *IACSIT International Journal of Engineering and Technology, 7*(4), 24–28. doi:10.14419/ijet.v7i4.11.20682

Herzberg, F. (1966). *Work and the nature of.* World Publishing.

Herzberg, F., Mausner, B., & Snydermann, B. (1959). *The motivation to work.* Wiley.

Hessami, H. Z., & Yousefi, P. (2013). Investigation of major factors influencing green purchasing behavior: Interactive approach. *European Online Journal of Natural and Social Sciences, 2*(4), 584–596.

Hess, R., Bryce, C. L., Paone, S., Fischer, G., McTigue, K. M., Olshansky, E., & Siminerio, L. (2007). Exploring Challenges and Potentials of Personal Health Records in Diabetes Self-Management: Implementation and Initial Assessment. *Telemedicine Journal and e-Health, 13*(5), 509–517. doi:10.1089/tmj.2006.0089 PMID:17999613

Hidayat, S. E., & Musari, K. (2022). ASEAN towards a global halal logistics through the digitally-enabled community. *International Journal of Asian Business and Information Management, 13*(2).

Hill, K., & Boyd, R. (2021). Behavioral convergence in humans and animals. *Science, 271*(6526), 235–236. doi:10.1126cience.abf7572 PMID:33446544

Hilson, G. (2003). Defining "cleaner production" and "pollution prevention" in the mining context. *Minerals Engineering, 16*(4), 305–321. doi:10.1016/S0892-6875(03)00012-8

Hindasah, L., & Nuryakin, N. (2020). The relationship between organizational capability, organizational learning and financial performance. *The Journal of Asian Finance, Economics, and Business*, *7*(8), 625–633. doi:10.13106/jafeb.2020.vol7.no8.625

Hisham, M., & Florent, Z. (2019). Briefing note ASEAN inter-parliamentary assembly: Overview of plastic issues in ASEAN, focusing on marine debris and microplastics in the region. Phnom Penh: Parliamentary Institute of Cambodia (PIC).

Hitam, M. B., & Borhan, H. B. (2012). FDI, Growth and the Environment: Impact on Quality of Life in Malaysia. *Procedia: Social and Behavioral Sciences*, *50*, 333–342.

Hitt, M. A., Xu, K., & Carnes, C. M. (2016). Resource-Based View in operations management research. *Journal of Operations Management*, *100*(41), 77–94. doi:10.1016/j.jom.2015.11.002

Hjalager, A.-M. (2010). Progress in Tourism Management: A Review of Innovation Research in Tourism. *Tourism Management*, *31*(1), 1–12. doi:10.1016/j.tourman.2009.08.012

Hobson, K., & Lynch, N. (2016). Diversifying and de-growing the circular economy: Radical social transformation in a resource-scarce world. *Futures*, *82*, 15–25. doi:10.1016/j.futures.2016.05.012

Hoerr, T. (1998). A case for merit pay. *Phi Delta Kappan*, *80*(4), 326–327.

Hofstede, G. (1991). Cultures and Organizations, Software of the Mind. London: McGraw Hill.

Hofstede, G. (2001). *Culture's Consequences* (2nd ed.). Sage.

Hofstede, G., & McCrae, R. (2004). Personality and Culture Revisited: Linking Traits and Dimensions of Culture. *Cross-Cultural Research*, *38*(1), 52–88. doi:10.1177/1069397103259443

Hollands, R. G. (2008). Will the real smart city please stand up? Intelligent, progressive or entrepreneurial? *City*, *12*(3), 303–320. doi:10.1080/13604810802479126

Hollands, R. G. (2015). Critical Interventions into the Corporate Smart City. *Cambridge Journal of Regions, Economy and Society*, *8*(1), 61–77. doi:10.1093/cjres/rsu011

Hollins, O. (2011). *Study into the feasibility of protecting and recovering critical raw materials through infrastructure development in the south east of England.* Oakdene Hollins Ltd.

Holmes, K., Clement, J., & Albright, J. (2013). The complex task of leading educational Change in schools. *School Leadership & Management*, *33*(3), 270–283. doi:10.1080/13632434.2013.800477

Homans, G. (1961). Social behavior: Its elementary forms. New York: Harcourt, Brace.

Hooi, L. W., & Ngui, K. S. (2014). Enhancing organizational performance of Malaysian SMEs. *International Journal of Manpower*, *35*(7), 973–995. doi:10.1108/IJM-04-2012-0059

Hopewell, J., Dvorak, R., & Kosior, E. (2009). Plastics recycling: Challenges and opportunities. *Philosophical Transactions of the Royal Society of London. Series B, Biological Sciences*, *364*(1526), 2115–2126. doi:10.1098/rstb.2008.0311 PMID:19528059

Hoppe, F., May, T., & Lin, J. (2018). *Advancing towards ASEAN digital integration empowering SMEs to build ASEAN's digital future.* Report of Bain & Company.

Hosamane, M. D., & Alroaia, Y. V. (2009). Entrepreneurship and development of small-scale industries in Iran: Strategic management tools and business performance assessment. *The IUP Journal of Entrepreneurship Development*, *6*(1), 27.

Hossain, A. (2014). An overview on effective employee training systems of private sector commercial banks in Bangladesh. *International Journal of Ethics in Social Sciences*, *2*(1), 33–44.

Ho, T. C. F., Ahmad, N. H., & Thurasamy, R. (2013). Learn and thou shall thrive: Advancing a model of workplace familism and organizational learning capability in small and medium enterprise (SMEs) manufacturers in Malaysia. *Business Strategy Series*, *14*(5/6), 151–159. doi:10.1108/BSS-08-2012-0045

Hoyle, R. H., & Robinson, J. C. (2004). Mediated and moderated effects in social psychological research. Handbook of methods in social psychology, 213-233.

Hsu, S. Y., Chang, C. C., & Lin, T. T. (2016). An analysis of purchase intentions toward organic food on health consciousness and food safety with/under structural equation modeling. *British Food Journal*, *118*(1), 200–216. doi:10.1108/BFJ-11-2014-0376

Huang, H. (2016). Media use, environmental beliefs, self-efficacy, and pro-environmental behavior. *Journal of Business Research, 69*(6), 2206–2212. doi:.031 doi:10.1016/j.jbusres.2015.12

Huang, T. C. (2001). The effects of linkage between business and human resource management strategies. *Personnel Review*, *30*(2), 132–151. doi:10.1108/00483480110380316

Hu, L., & Bentler, P. M. (1999). Cutoff criteria for fit indexes in covariance structure analysis: Conventional criteria versus new alternatives. *Structural Equation Modeling*, *6*(1), 1–55. doi:10.1080/10705519909540118

Hulin, C., Netemeyer, R., & Cudeck, R. (2001). Can a Reliability Coefficient Be Too High? *Journal of Consumer Psychology*, *10*(1), 55–58. doi:10.1207/S15327663JCP1001&2_05

Human Capital Development Blueprint. (2019). *National Workforce Human Capital Development Blueprint 2018 – 2025.* Available online at: https://www.hrdf.com.my

Hung, K.-P., Chen, A. H., Peng, N., Hackley, C., Tiwsakul, R. A., & Chou, C.-L. (2011). Antecedents of luxury brand purchase intention. *Journal of Product and Brand Management*, *20*(6), 457–467. doi:10.1108/10610421111166603

Hussein, R., Selamat, H., & Abdul Karim, N. S. (2005). The impact of technological factors on information systems success in the electronic government context. *The Second International Conference on Innovations in Information Technology*, 6-7. Retrieved February 6, 2019 from https://pdfs.semanticscholar.org/3051/fe1d66792683073bc0f6eafe63e4a95de48f.pdf

Hutchinson, K., Quinn, B., & Alexander, N. (2006). SME retailer internationalisation: Case study evidence from British retailers. *International Marketing Review*, *23*(1), 25–53. https://doi.org/10.1108/02651330610646287

Iacobucci, D. (2010). Structural equations modeling: Fit indices, sample size, and advanced topics. *Journal of Consumer Psychology*, *20*(1), 90–98. doi:10.1016/j.jcps.2009.09.003

IBEF. (2018). *Foreign Direct Investment (FDI).* Retrieved from www.ibef.org

IBM. (2014). *Smartercities*. Retrieved from: www.ibm.com/smarterplanet/us/en/smarter_cities/overview/?lnk1/4fkt-scit?lnk1/4fkt-smci-uken

IBM. (2015). *A smarter planet.* Retrieved from: www.ibm.com/smarterplanet/uk/en/overview/ideas/index.html

Ibrahim, H., & Yusoff, Y. (2013). *Satisfaction towards E-HRM in government organisations of Malaysia: A proposed model based on field theory*. Retrieved August 11, 2018, from https://pdfs.semanticscholar.org/779d/152a79c2763072028c022416f49a3d5c0954.Pdf?_ga=2.174827874.1187198535.1561975056-741735385.1561975056

Ibrahim, F., & Ali, D. N. (2021). Evaluating Knowledge Management Practices in Higher Education Institutions (HEIs): Towards KMPro Framework Guidelines. In S. Zyngier (Ed.), *Handbook of Research on Knowledge Management Tools in Higher Education* (pp. 221–245). IGI Global.

Ibrahim, F., Edgar, D., & Reid, V. (2009). Assessing the role of knowledge management in adding value: Moving towards a comprehensive framework. *Journal of Information & Knowledge Management*, *8*(4), 275–286. doi:10.1142/S0219649209002397

Ibrahim, F., & Reid, V. (2009). What is the Value of Knowledge Management Practices? *Electronic Journal of Knowledge Management*, *7*(5), 567–574.

Ibrahim, F., & Reid, V. (2010). Integrated Use of Information Technology and People Involvement for Knowledge Management. *International Journal of Technology, Knowledge and Society*, *6*(2), 163–180. doi:10.18848/1832-3669/CGP/v06i02/56086

Ibrahim, I., Ali, D. N. H., & Besar, N. S. A. (2020). Accounting information system (AIS) in SMEs: Towards an integrated framework. *International Journal of Asian Business and Information Management*, *11*(2), 51–67. doi:10.4018/IJABIM.2020040104

ICD-11 - ICD-11 for Mortality and Morbidity Statistics. (n.d.). Retrieved July 2, 2021, from https://icd.who.int/browse11/l-m/en#/http://id.who.int/icd/entity/1448597234

Ikiz Kaya, D., Pintossi, N., & Dane, G. (2021). An empirical analysis of driving factors and policy enablers of heritage adaptive reuse within the circular economy framework. *Sustainability*, *13*(5), 2479. doi:10.3390u13052479

Ilomaki, L., Paavola, S., Lakkala, M., & Kantosalo, A. (2016). Digital competence–an emergent boundary concept for policy and educational research. *Education and Information Technologies*, *21*(3), 655–679. doi:10.100710639-014-9346-4

Imran, M., Hamid, S. N. B. A., Aziz, A. B., & Wan, C. Y. (2019). *The Effect of Performance Appraisal Politics on Employee Performance in Emergency Services of Punjab*. Academy of Strategic Management Journal.

Indian Government. (2014). *Smart City Guidelines*. Retrieved on 7 Dec - 2019, http://smartcities.gov.in / writereaddata/SmartCityGuidelines.pdf

Industrial Revolution. (2021). Retrieved online at https://www.britannica.com/event/Industrial-Revolution

Inkeles, A., & Levinson, D. J. (1969). National character: The study of modal personality and sociocultural systems. The Handbook of Social Psychology, 4, 418-506.

Inkeles, A., & Levinson, D. J. (1969). National character: The study of modal personality and sociocultural systems. In G. Lindzey & E. Aronson (Eds.), *The handbook of social psychology IV* (pp. 418–506). McGraw-Hill. (Original work published 1954)

Innovation & Growth. (2013). *Talent Management: Process Guide*. Retrieved from: http://novascotia.ca/psc/pdf/ hrCentre/resources/talentManagement/TM_Process_Guide.pdf

Interactive, M. (2018). *Study finds that only 3% of Malaysian businesses are digital leaders*. Available online at: https://www.marketing-interactive.com/study-finds-that-only-3-of-malaysian-businesses-are-digital-leaders

IPCC. (1996). Second Assessment on Climate Change. International Panel on Climate Change. Cambridge, UK: Cambridge University Press.

Ishajaya. (2012). *Bru-HIMS will bring better efficiency to Brunei Healthcare*. Retrieved June 23, 2019, from http://www.ishajaya.com/index.php?option=com_content&view=article&id=70:06-june-2012-bru-hims-will-bring-better-efficiency-to-brunei-healthcare&catid=8&Itemid=115

Ishibashi, Y., & Kottke, J. (2009). Confucianism, personality traits, and effective leaders in Japan and the United States. *Annual Conference of the Association for Psychological Science*.

Islam, R., & bin Mohd Rasad, S. (2006). Employee performance evaluation by the AHP: A case study. *Asia Pacific Management Review, 11*(3).

Islam, A., Jerin, I., Hafiz, N., Tali Nimfa, D., & Abdul Wahab, S. (2021). Configuring a blueprint for Malaysian SMEs to survive through the COVID19 crisis: The reinforcement of Quadruple Helix Innovation Model. *Journal of Entrepreneurship. Business Economics (Cleveland, Ohio)*, *9*(1), 32–81.

Ismail, N. (2017). *The game has changed: adapting to digitalisation necessary to stay ahead of the pack*. Assess on 10.4.2020. https://www.information-age.com/game-changed-adapting-digitalisation-necessary-stay-ahead-pack-123466799/

Ismail, N. I., Abdullah, N. H., & Shamsuddin, A. (2015). Adoption of Hospital Information System (HIS) in Malaysian Public Hospitals. *Procedia: Social and Behavioral Sciences*, *172*, 336–343. doi:10.1016/j.sbspro.2015.01.373

Issock-Issock, P. B., Mpinganjira, M., & Roberts-Lombard, M. (2019). Modelling green customer loyalty and positive word of mouth. *International Journal of Emerging Markets*, *15*(3), 405–426. doi:10.1108/IJOEM-09-2018-0489

Ivanov, S., & Zhechev, V. (2012). Hotel revenue management-a critical literature review. *Tourism (Zagreb)*, *60*(2), 175–197.

Jackson, C. K. (2012). Recruiting, retaining, and creating quality teachers. *Nordic Economic Policy Review*, *3*(1), 61–104.

Jalagat, R. (2017). Determinants of Job Stress and Its Relationship on Employee Job Performance. *American Journal of Management Science and Engineering*, *2*(1), 1–10. doi:10.11648/j.ajmse.20170201.11

Jalali, S. H. (2012). Export Barriers and Export Performance: Empirical Evidence from The Commercial Relationship Between Greece and Iran. *South-Eastern Europe Journal of Economics*, *1*, 53–66.

Jambeck, J. R., Geyer, R., Wilcox, C., Siegler, T. R., Perryman, M., Andrady, A., Narayan, R., & Law, K. L. (2015). Plastic waste inputs from land into the ocean. *Science*, *347*(6223), 768–771. doi:10.1126cience.1260352 PMID:25678662

Jameson, J. (2013). e-leadership in higher education: The fifth "age" of educational technology research. *British Journal of Educational Technology*, *44*(6), 889–915. doi:10.1111/bjet.12103

Jamsandekar, S. S., & Mudholkar, R. R. (2013). Performance evaluation by fuzzy inference technique. *International Journal of Soft Computing and Engineering*, *3*(2), 158–164.

Jang, S. (2017, February 6). "Difficult to grow with telecommunications only" Telcos reach out to new businesses. *Economy Chosun*. http://economychosun.com/special/special_view.php?boardName=C05&t_num=11200

Janosov, M., Battiston, F., & Sinatra, R. (2020). Success and luck in creative careers. *EPJ Data Science*, *9*(1), 9. doi:10.1140/epjds13688-020-00227-w

Janssen, O., Van de Vliert, E., & West, M. (2004). The bright and dark sides of individual and group innovation: A special issue introduction. *Journal of Organizational Behavior*, *25*(2), 129–145. doi:10.1002/job.242

Jansson, J., Marell, A., & Nordlund, A. (2010). Green consumer behavior: Determinants of curtailment and eco-innovation adoption. *Journal of Consumer Marketing*, *27*(4), 358–370. doi:10.1108/07363761011052396

Jasrotia, A., & Gangotia, A. (2018). Smart Cities to Smart Tourism Destination: A Review Paper. *Journal of Tourism Intelligence and Smartness*, *1*(1), 47–56.

Jaussi, K. S., Randel, A. E., & Dionne, S. D. (2007). I am, I think I can, and I do: The role of personal identity, self-efficacy, and cross-application of experiences in creativity at work. *Creativity Research Journal*, *19*(2-3), 247–258. doi:10.1080/10400410701397339

Jawahir, I. S., & Bradley, R. (2016). Technological Elements of Circular Economy and the Principles of 6R-Based Closed-Loop Material Flow in Sustainable Manufacturing. *Procedia CIRP*, *40*, 103–108. doi:10.1016/j.procir.2016.01.067

Jeong, D., Kim, H., & Yoo, S. (2013). KT Smartgrid implementation. *Information and Communications Magazine*, *30*(2), 59–65.

Jeong, M., & Shin, H. H. (2019). Tourists' Experiences with Smart Tourism Technology at Smart Destinations and Their Behaviour Intentions. *Journal of Travel Research*, *59*(8), Pp1464–Pp1477. doi:10.1177/0047287519883034

Jeyakumar-Nathan, R., Soekmawati, Victor, V., Popp, J., Fekete-Farkas, M., & Oláh, J. (2021). Food Innovation Adoption and Organic Food Consumerism—A Cross National Study between Malaysia and Hungary. *Foods*, *10*(2), 363. doi:10.3390/foods10020363 PMID:33562411

Joe, Y. F.L. (2011). *An introduction to critical thinking and creativity: Think more, think better.* John Wiley & Sons.

Johansen, S. (1988). Statistical Analysis of Cointegration Vectors. *Journal of Economic Dynamics & Control*, *12*(2), 231–254.

Johansen, S., & Juselius, K. (1990). Maximum likelihood estimation and inference on cointegration- with applications to the demand for money. *Oxford Bulletin of Economics and Statistics*, *52*(2), 169–210.

Johari, S., & Jha, K. N. (2020). Impact of Work Motivation on Construction Labor Productivity. *Journal of Management Engineering*, *36*(5), 04020052. doi:10.1061/(ASCE)ME.1943-5479.0000824

Johnson, D., & Grayson, K. (2005). Cognitive and affective trust in service relationships. *Journal of Business Research*, *58*(4), 500–507. doi:10.1016/S0148-2963(03)00140-1

Johnson, D., & Turner, C. (2010). *International Business: Themes and Issues in the Modern Global Economy* (2nd ed.). Routledge, Taylor & Francis Group.

Johnson, R. D., Stone, D. L., & Lukaszewski, K. M. (2021). The benefits of eHRM and AI for talent acquisition. *Journal of Tourism Futures*, *7*(1), 40–52. doi:10.1108/JTF-02-2020-0013

Johnson, S. M., & Papay, J. P. (2009). *Redesigning teacher pay: A system for the next generation of educators* (Vol. 2). Economic Policy Institute.

Jones, S. (2002). The Internet Goes to College. Pew Internet & American Life. *USDLA Journal*, *16*(10).

Jonkers, H., Lankhorst, M. M., ter Doest, H. W. L., Arbab, F., Bosma, H., & Wieringa, R. J. (2006). Enterprise architecture: Management tool and blueprint for the organisation. *Information Systems Frontiers*, *8*(2), 63–66. doi:10.100710796-006-7970-2

Joo, B. K., & Park, S. (2010). Career satisfaction, organizational commitment, and turnover intention: The effects of goal orientation, organizational learning culture and developmental feedback. *Leadership and Organization Development Journal*, *31*(6), 482–500. doi:10.1108/01437731011069999

Jorgenson, A. K., Dick, C., & Mahutga, M. C. (2007). Foreign Investment Dependence and the Environment: An Ecostructural Approach. Society for the Study of Social Problems, Oxford University Press.

Joshi, Y., & Rahman, Z. (2015). Factors Affecting Green Purchase Behaviour and Future Research Directions. *International Strategic Management Review, 3*(1), 128–143.

Joshi, J. B. D., Ghafoor, A., Aref, W. G., & Spafford, E. H. (2002). Security and Privacy Challenges of a Digital Government. In W. J. McIver & A. K. Elmagarmid (Eds.), *Advances in Digital Government. Advances in Database Systems* (Vol. 26). Springer. doi:10.1007/0-306-47374-7_7

Joshi, Y., & Rahman, Z. (2015). Factors Affecting Green Purchase Behaviour and Future Research Directions. *International Strategic Management Review*, *3*(1), 128–143. doi:10.1016/j.ism.2015.04.001

JRC. (2011b). *Supporting Environmentally Sound Decisions for Waste Management - A technical guide to Life Cycle Thinking (LCT) and Life Cycle Assessment (LCA) for waste experts and LCA practitioners.* JRC Scientific and Technical Reports. https://tinyurl.com/zwen5p2

Judge, T. A., Bono, J. E., Ilies, R., & Gerhardt, M. W. (2002). Personality and leadership: A qualitative and quantitative review. *The Journal of Applied Psychology*, *87*(4), 765–780. doi:10.1037/0021-9010.87.4.765 PMID:12184579

Jusoh, R., & Parnell, J. A. (2008). Competitive strategy and performance measurement in the Malaysian context: An exploratory study. *Management Decision*, *46*(1), 5–31. doi:10.1108/00251740810846716

Kalmuk, G., & Acar, A. Z. (2015). The mediating role of organizational learning capability on the relationship between innovation and firm's performance: A conceptual framework. *Procedia: Social and Behavioral Sciences*, *210*, 164–169. doi:10.1016/j.sbspro.2015.11.355

Kandpal, V. (2016, April 7). *Challenges In Financing Smart City Projects In India.* Retrieved November 18, 2019, from http://swarajyamag.Com/smart-cities/chall-enges-in-financing-smart-city-projects-in-india

Kang, H., Park, H., Yun, S., & Jung, H. (2014). Ambidextrous organization of COSMAX. *Korea Business Review*, *18*(1), 177–199.

Kang, Y., Ryu, M.-H., & Kim, S. (2010). Exploring sustainability management for telecommunications services: A case study of two Korean companies. *Journal of World Business*, *45*(4), 415–421.

Kaplan, R. S., & Norton, D. P. (1996). Using balanced scorecard as a strategic management system. *Harvard Business Review*, *74*(1), 75–85.

Kaplan, R. S., & Norton, D. P. (2004). The strategy map: Guide to aligning intangible assets. *Strategy and Leadership*, *32*(5), 10–17. doi:10.1108/10878570410699825

Kapoor, N., Jauhari, D. S., & Maheshwari, D. D. (2021). Understanding of Circular Processes and Its Impact on Indian Economy. *Journal of Contemporary Issues in Business and Government*, *27*(3), 2076–2084.

Kapoor, N., Jauhari, S., & Maheshwari, D. (2021). Policies for Promoting the Circular Economy in India. In Examining the Intersection of Circular Economy, Forestry, and International Trade (pp. 68-82). IGI Global.

Kapoor, H., & Kaufman, J. C. (2020). Meaning-making through creativity during COVID-19. *Frontiers in Psychology*, 11. PMID:33391115

Karam, A. A. (2019). The Impact of Training and Development on Different Cultural Employees Performance through Interaction Employees Motivation in Erbil Public and Private Banks. *Mediterranean Journal of Social Sciences*, *10*(1), 193–206. doi:10.2478/mjss-2019-0017

Karami, A., Analoui, F., & Cusworth, J. (2004). Strategic human resource management and resource-based approach: The evidence from the British manufacturing industry. *Management Research News*, *27*(6), 50–68. doi:10.1108/01409170410784202

Karavdic, M., & Gregory, G. (2005). Integrating e-commerce into existing export marketing theories: A contingency model. *Marketing Theory*, *5*(1), 75–104. doi:10.1177/1470593105049602

Karimi, R., Omar, Z., Alipour, F., & Karimi, Z. (2014). The influence of role overload, role conflict, and role ambiguity on occupational stress among nurses in selected Iranian hospitals. *International Journal of Asian Social Scienece*, *4*, 34–40.

Karwowski, M., Lebuda, I., Wisniewska, E., & Gralewski, J. (2013). Big five personality traits as the predictors of creative self-efficacy and creative personal identity: Does gender matter? *The Journal of Creative Behavior*, *47*(3), 215–232. doi:10.1002/jocb.32

Kassim. (2015). *MoH staff trained to file health data*. Retrieved Jun 4, 2019, from The BT Archive: https://btarchive.org/news/national/2015/08/08/moh-staff-trained-file-health-data

Kataria, A., Aakanksha, K., & Ruchi, G. (2013). Factors Affecting Green Buying Behavior: An In-Depth Study of Indian Consumers. *Journal of Management Research*, *1*(2), 3–17.

Katsikeas, C. S., & Morgan, R. E. (1994). Differences in perceptions of exporting problems based on firm size and. *European Journal of Marketing*, *28*(5), 17–35.

Katt, F., & Meixner, O. (2020). A systematic review of drivers influencing consumer willingness to pay for organic food. *Trends in Food Science & Technology*, *100*, 374–388. doi:10.1016/j.tifs.2020.04.029

Katz, R. L. (1974). Skills of an Effective Administrator. *Harvard Business Review*, (Sep-Oct), 91–93.

Kaufmann, H. R., Pann, İ. M., Khan, F. A., & Orphanıdou, Y. (2012). Factors Affecting Consumers' Green Purchasing Behavior: An Integrated Conceptual Framework. *Amfiteatru Economic*, *15*(31), 50–56.

Kaur, A. (2000). Internet facility at GNDU: A survey. *National Seminar on Academic Libraries in the Modern Era*, 119–124.

Kaur, P., Dhir, A., Talwar, S., & Ghuman, K. (2021). The value proposition of food delivery apps from the perspective of theory of consumption value. *International Journal of Contemporary Hospitality Management*. doi:10.1108/ijchm-05-2020-0477

Kaur, A., & Kaur, R. (2015). Electronic human resource management. *International Journal of Business and Management*, *2*(2), 1118–1125.

Kaur, P. (2013). E-HRM: A Boon or Bane? *Journal of Management*, *1*(1), 35–38.

Kaya, N. (2015). Corporate entrepreneurship, generic competitive strategies, and firm performance in small and medium-sized enterprises. *Procedia: Social and Behavioral Sciences*, *207*(20), 662–668. doi:10.1016/j.sbspro.2015.10.136

Kaynak, E., & Jallat, F. (2005). *Marketing in Western Europe: A monolith or a multidimensional market?* In E. Kaynak & F. Jallat (Eds.), *Marketing issues in Western Europe—Changes and developments* (pp. 4–9). Routledge.

Kazaz, A., Manisali, E., & Ulubeyli, S. (2008). Effect of basic motivational factors on construction workforce productivity in Turkey. *Journal of Civil Engineering and Management*, *14*(2), 95–106. doi:10.3846/1392-3730.2008.14.4

Kearny, A. T. (2018). *The 2018 A.T. Kearney Foreign Direct Investment Confidence Index*. Retrieved from www.atkearney.com

Kedia, B. L., & Mukherji, A. (1999). Global managers: Developing a mindset for global competitiveness. *Journal of World Business*, *34*(3), 230–251. doi:10.1016/S1090-9516(99)00017-6

Kekec, P., Thongpapanl, N., & Auh, S. (2015). Unveiling the Influence of the consumer wine appreciation dimension on purchasing behavior. In K. Kubacki (Ed.), *Ideas in marketing: Finding the new and polishing the old--developments in marketing science. Proceedings of the Academy of Marketing Science*. Springer. 10.1007/978-3-319-10951-0_242

Kelchner, L. (2013). *Strengths and weaknesses of cross-functional teams*. Retrieved from: https://smallbusiness.chron.com/strengths-weaknesses-cross-functional-teams-24653.html

Keller, M. E., Kelling, S. E., Cornelius, D. C., Oni, H. A., & Bright, D. R. (2015). *Enhancing Practice Efficiency and Patient Care by Sharing*. Perspective in Health Information Management. Retrieved February 20, 2019 from https://www.ncbi.nlm.nih.gov/pmc/articles/PMC4632871/

Khan, M. R., & Wajidi, A. (2019). Role of leadership and team building in employee motivation at workplace. *GMJACS, 9*(1), 11.

Khan, N., Khan, S., Tan, B. C., & Loon, C. H. (2021). Driving Digital Competency Model Towards IR 4.0 In Malaysia. *Journal of Physics: Conference Series, 1793*(1), 12–49. doi:10.1088/1742-6596/1793/1/012049

Khurshid, R., & Darzi, M. A. (2016). Go green with green human resource management practices. *Clear International Journal of Research in Commerce & Management, 7*(1).

Kim, C. Y., Lee, J. H., & Shin, S. Y. (2019). Why Are Your Employees Leaving the Organization? The Interaction Effect of Role Overload, Perceived Organizational Support, and Equity Sensitivity. *Sustainability, 11*(3), 657. doi:10.3390u11030657

Kim, W., Han, S., & Park, J. (2019). Is the Role of Work Engagement Essential to Employee Performance or 'Nice to Have'? *Sustainability, 11*(4), 1050–1067. doi:10.3390u11041050 PMID:30809384

Kim, Y. J., Kim, W. G., Choi, H.-M., & Phetvaroon, K. (2019). The effect of green human resource management on hotel employees' eco-friendly behavior and environmental performance. *International Journal of Hospitality Management, 76*, 83–93. doi:10.1016/j.ijhm.2018.04.007

Kim, Y., & Choi, S. M. (2005). Antecedents of green purchase behavior: An examination of collectivism, environmental concern, and PCE. *Advances in Consumer Research. Association for Consumer Research (U. S.), 32*, 592.

Kim, Y.-M., Jung, D., Chang, Y., & Choi, D.-H. (2019). Intelligent micro energy grid in 5G era: Platforms, business cases, testbeds, and next generation applications. *Electronics (Basel), 8*(4), 468.

Kinjerski, V., & Skrypnek, B. (2006). Measuring The Intangible: Development Of The Spirit At Work Scale. *Academy of Management Best Conference Paper*, A1-A6.

Kin, T. M., & Kareem, O. A. (2019). School leaders' Competencies that make a difference in the Era of Education 4.0: A Conceptual Framework. *International Journal of Academic Research in Business & Social Sciences, 9*(4). Advance online publication. doi:10.6007/IJARBSS/v9-i4/5836

Kirkland, R. (2014). Artificial Intelligence Meets the C-suite. *McKinsey Quarterly*. Available onlineat: https://www.mckinsey.com/insights/strategy/artificial_intelligence_meets_the_c-suite

Klarmann, M., & Feurer, S. (2018). Control Variables in Marketing Research. *Journal of Research and Management, 40*(2), 26–40.

Klein, K. J., & Sorra, J. S. (1996). The Challenge of Innovation Implementation. *Academy of Management Review, 21*(4), 1055–1080. doi:10.5465/amr.1996.9704071863

Kline, R. B. (2011). *Principles and practice of structural equation modeling (3. Baskı)*. Guilford.

Kline, R. B. (2011). *Principles and practice of structural equation modeling*. Guilford Press.

Knox, J. L. (2020). *Mitigating Perceived External Export Barriers for Small and Medium-Sized Enterprises that Manufacture and Sell "Made in the USA" Consumer Apparel Products in Washington State* (DBA dissertation). City University of Seattle.

Kofler, T. (2018). Digitale Transformation in Unternehmen. In N. Hohne, D. Méndez, K. B. Zimmer (Ed.), ZD. B Digital Dialogue Positions papier.

Kohli-Khandekar. (2021, Apr. 26). The Covid effect: Pandemic has enhanced creative output Indian cinema. *Business Standard.*

Kollmuss, A., & Agyeman, J. (2002). Mind the gap: Why do people act environmentally and what are the barriers to pro-environmental behavior? *Environmental Education Research, 8*(3), 239–260. doi:10.1080/13504620220145401

Konietzko, J., Baldassarre, B., Brown, P., Bocken, N., & Hultink, E. J. (2020). Circular business model experimentation: Demystifying assumptions. *Journal of Cleaner Production, 277*, 122596. doi:10.1016/j.jclepro.2020.122596

Kooganurmath, M. M., & Jange, S. (1999). Use of Internet by social science research scholars: A study in academic libraries in the Internet era. *National Convention Academic Libraries in the Internet Era*, 478–483.

Koopman, J. (2015). Pulling the Sobel test up by its bootstraps. In C. E. Lance & R. J. Vandenberg (Eds.), *More Statistical and Methodological Myths and Urban Legends* (pp. 224–244). Routledge.

Kordab, M., Raudeliūnienė, J., & Meidutė-Kavaliauskienė, I. (2020). Mediating Role of Knowledge Management in the Relationship between Organizational Learning and Sustainable Organizational Performance. *Sustainability, 12*(23), 10061. doi:10.3390u122310061

Korn Ferry Institute. (2018). *Digital Leadership in Malaysia*. Available online at: https://focus.kornferry.com/wp-content/uploads/2015/02/Korn-Ferry-Digital-leadership-in-Malaysia.pdf

Kossman, S. P. (2006). Perceptions of Impact of Electronic Health Records on Nurses' Work. *Consumer-Centered Computer-Supported Care for Healthy People*, 337-341. Retrieved November 5, 2018 from https://ebooks.iospress.nl/publication/9218

Kostic, M. (2017). Challenges of Agile Practices Implementation in The Medical Device Software Development Methodologies. *European Project Management Journal., 7*(2), 36–44.

Kouzes, J. M., & Posner, B. Z. (2006). *The leadership challenge* (Vol. 3). John Wiley & Sons.

Krejcie, R. V., & Morgan, D. W. (1970). Determining sample size for research activities. *Educational and Psychological Measurement, 30*(3), 607–610. doi:10.1177/001316447003000308

Krook, J., & Eklund, M. (2010). The strategic role of recycling centres for environmental performance of waste management systems. *Applied Ergonomics, 41*(3), 362–367. doi:10.1016/j.apergo.2009.06.012 PMID:19691952

Kulkarni, R., Chauhan, S., Patil, A., Shivkumar, P., Tayade, S., Dohate, N., Patil, A., Deshpande, A., & Karnataki, M. (2019). Impact of Training on Awareness and Knowledge of Service Providers About Maternal Near-Miss Events in Maharashtra, India. *Journal of Obstetrics and Gynaecology of India, 69*(6), 529–534. doi:10.100713224-019-01259-7 PMID:31844368

Kumar, M. D., & Vats, A. (2016). Mapping animation and visual effects in Indian media and entertainment industry opportunities and threats. *International Journal of Humanities, Art and Social Studies, 1*(2).

Kumar, R., & Kaur, A. (2005). Internet and its use in the engineering colleges of Punjab, India: A case study. *Webology, 2*(4), 1–22.

Kuznets, S. (1995). Economic Growth and Income Inequality. *The American Economic Review*, *45*, 1–28.

Kuzozumi, E., & Yamamoto, T. (2000). Modified lag augmented autoregressions. *Econometric Reviews*, *19*, 207–231.

Kyvik, O., Saris, W., Bonet, E., & Augusto Felício, J. (2013). The internationalization of small firms: The relationship between the global mindset and firms' internationalization behavior. *Journal of International Entrepreneurship*, *11*(2), 172–195.

L'Ecuyer, F., & Raymond, L. (2017). Aligning the e-HRM and strategic HRM capabilities of manufacturing SMEs: A "gestalts" perspective. In *Electronic HRM in the Smart Era (The Changing Context of Managing People, Volume)* (pp. 137–172). Emerald Publishing Limited. doi:10.1108/978-1-78714-315-920161006

Laconi, S., Kaliszewska-Czeremska, K., Gnisci, A., Sergi, I., Barke, A., Jeromin, F., Groth, J., Gamez-Guadix, M., Ozcan, N. K., Demetrovics, Z., Király, O., Siomos, K., Floros, G., & Kuss, D. J. (2018). Cross-cultural study of Problematic Internet Use in nine European countries. *Computers in Human Behavior*, *84*, 430–440. doi:10.1016/j.chb.2018.03.020

Lacy, P., Gupta, P., & Hayward, R. (2019). From incrementalism to transformation: Reflections on corporate sustainability from the UN global compact-Accenture CEO study. In *Managing sustainable business* (pp. 505–518). Springer. doi:10.1007/978-94-024-1144-7_23

Lages, L. F., & Montgomery, D. B. (2004). Internet resources and capabilities: Japanese SME risk-taking, industry and performance. *European Journal of Marketing*, *38*(9/10), 1186–1214. doi:10.1108/03090560410548933

Lai, O. K. (2000). *Greening of Hong Kong: Forms of manifestation of environmental movements. In the dynamics of social movement in Hong Kong*. City University Press.

Lal, K. (2004). E-Business and Export Behavior: Evidence from Indian Firms. *World Development*, *32*(3), 505–517. doi:10.1016/j.worlddev.2003.10.004

Lal, P., Malhotra, R., Ahuja, C., & Ingle, G. K. (2006). Internet use among medical students and residents of a medical college of North India. *Indian Journal of Community Medicine*, *31*(4), 293–294.

Lancaster, G. (2005). *Research Methods in Management. A Concise Introduction to Research in Management and Business Consultancy, Jordan Hill*. Elsevier Butterworth-Heinemann Linacre House.

Lancaster, S., Di Milia, L., & Cameron, R. (2013). Supervisor behaviours that facilitate training transfer. *Journal of Workplace Learning*, *25*(1), 6–22. doi:10.1108/13665621311288458

Lander, J. (2020). *The relationship between principals' pillars of digital leadership aligned values and actions and teacher technology use*. St. John's University.

Lane, G. W., & Wagner, T. P. (2013). Examining recycling container attributes and household recycling practices. *Resources, Conservation and Recycling*, *75*, 32–40. doi:10.1016/j.resconrec.2013.03.005

Lankford, H., Loeb, S., & Wyckoff, J. (2002). Teacher sorting and the plight of urban schools: A descriptive analysis. *Educational Evaluation and Policy Analysis*, *24*(1), 37–62. doi:10.3102/01623737024001037

Lanvin, B. & Passman, P. (2008). *Building E-skills for the Information Age*. Academic Press.

Larsen, E., Fong, A., Wernz, C., & Rarwani, R. (2017). Implications of Electronic Health Record Downtime: An Analysis of Patient Safety Event Reports. *Journal of the American Medical Informatics Association: JAMIA*, 1–5. Retrieved February 20, 2019, from https://www.researchgate.net/publication/317335260_Implications_of_electronic_health_record_downtime_An_analysis_of_patient_safety_event_reports PMID:28575417

Larsson, A., & Lindfred, L. (2019). Digitalization, circular economy and the future of labor: How circular economy and digital transformation can affect labor 1. In The Digital Transformation of Labor (p. 280-315). Academic Press.

Latour, B. (2005). *Reassessing the Social: An Introduction to Actor-Network Theory*. Oxford University Press.

Lawal, F. A., Adegbuyi, O. A., Iyiola, O. O., Ayoade, O. E., & Taiwo, A. A. (2018). Nexus Between Informal Networks and Risk-Taking: Implications for Improving the Performance of Small and Medium Enterprises (SMEs) In Nigeria. *Academy of Strategic Management Journal*, *17*(2), 1–13.

Lawler, E. J. (2001). An affect theory of social exchange. *American Journal of Sociology*, *107*(2), 321–352. doi:10.1086/324071

Lazarova, V., Sturny, V., & Sang, G. T. (2012). Relevance and Benefits of Urban Water Reuse in Tourist Areas. *Water (Basel)*, *4*(1), 107–122. doi:10.3390/w4010107

Lazzarini, S. G. (2015). Strategizing by the Government: Industrial Policy and Sustainable Competitive Advantage. *Strategic Management Journal*, *36*(1), 96–112. https://doi.org/10.1002/smj.2204

Leeflang, P. S. H., & van Raaij, W. F. (1995). The changing consumer in the European Union: A "metaanalysis. *International Journal of Research in Marketing*, *12*(5), 373–387. doi:10.1016/0167-8116(95)00031-3

Lee, H., Kim, G., & Kim, M. (2016). Understanding disruptive innovation in the perspective of the market. *Korea Business Review*, *20*(1), 43–67.

Lee, I. (2011). Modeling the benefit of e-recruiting process integration. *Decision Support Systems*, *51*(1), 230–239. doi:10.1016/j.dss.2010.12.011

Lee, J., & Cho, M. (2019). The Effects of Consumers' Media Exposure, Attention, and Credibility on Pro-environmental Behaviors. *Journal of Promotion Management*. Advance online publication. doi:10.1080/10496491.2019.1699629

Lee, K. (2008). Opportunities for green marketing: Young consumers. *Marketing Intelligence & Planning*, *26*(6), 573–586. doi:10.1108/02634500810902839

Lee, S. (2009). Manage your customer's experience - CEM Marketing. *Marketing*, *43*(2), 73–76.

Lee, W. R., Choi, S. B., & Kang, S.-W. (2021). How Leaders' Positive Feedback Influences Employees' Innovative Behavior: The Mediating Role of Voice Behavior and Job Autonomy. *Sustainability*, *13*(4), 1901. doi:10.3390u13041901

Lee, Y. Y., Hsieh, M. J., & Fan, K. K. (2013). Study on Development of Indian Film Industry. *Applied Mechanics and Materials*, *311*, 544–549. doi:10.4028/www.scientific.net/AMM.311.544

Legner, C., Eymann, T., Hess, T., Matt, C., Bohmann, T., Drews, P., Madche, A., Urbach, N., & Ahlemann, F. (2017). Digitalization: Opportunity and Challenge for the Business and Information Systems Engineering Community. *Business & Information Systems Engineering*, *59*(4), 301–308. doi:10.100712599-017-0484-2

Lemire, L., & Rouillard, C. (2005). An empirical exploration of psychological contract violation and individual behaviour. *Journal of Managerial Psychology*, *20*(2), 150–163. doi:10.1108/02683940510579786

Lemmens, A., Croux, C., & Dekimpe, M. G. (2005). The European consumer: United in diversity? ERIM Report Series Research in Management. Reference No. ERS- 2005-022-MKT, Erasmus University, Rotterdam, The Netherlands.

Lengnick-Hall, M. L., & Moritz, S. (2003). The impact of e-HR on the human resource management function. *Journal of Labor Research*, *24*(3), 365–379. doi:10.100712122-003-1001-6

Leonidou, C. L. (2004). An analysis of the barriers hindering small business export development. *Journal of Small Business Management*, *42*(3), 279–302.

Leonidou, L. C., Leonidou, C. N., & Kvasova, O. (2010). Antecedents and outcomes of consumer environmentally friendly attitudes and behaviour. *Journal of Marketing Management*, *26*(13-14), 1319–1344. doi:10.1080/0267257X.2010.523710

Lepp, A., Li, J., Barkley, J. E., & Salehi-Esfahani, S. (2015). Exploring the relationships between college students' cell phone use, personality and leisure. *Computers in Human Behavior*, *43*, 210–219. doi:10.1016/j.chb.2014.11.006

Lersch, K. M., & Mieczkowski, T. (2005). Violent police behavior: Past, present, and future research directions. *Aggression and Violent Behavior*, *10*(5), 552–568. doi:10.1016/j.avb.2004.10.002

Lester, S. W., Turnley, W. H., Bloodgood, J. M., & Bolino, M. C. (2002). Not seeing eye to eye: Differences in supervisor and subordinate perceptions of and attributions for psychological contract breach. *Journal of Organizational Behavior*, *23*(1), 39–56. doi:10.1002/job.126

Leung, S. L., & Bozionelos, N. (2004). Five-factor model traits and the prototypical image of the effective leader in the Confucian culture. *Employee Relations*, *26*(1), 62–71. doi:10.1108/01425450410506904

Levitt, T. (1983). The globalization of markets. *Harvard Business Review*, *61*(3), 92–102.

Lewis, R. (2006). *When Cultures Collide: Leading Across Cultures*. Nicholas Brealey International. Retrieved online at http://www.utntyh.com/wp-content/uploads/2011/11/When-Cultures-Collide.pdf

Lewis, R. (2019). The cultural imperative: Global trends in the 21st century. *Training*. *Language and Culture*, *3*(3), 8–20. doi:10.29366/2019tlc.3.3.1

Liang, G. (2013). Performance-related pay for teachers: An updated review. *Journal of Postdoctoral Research*, *1*(1), 99–117. doi:10.14304/SURYA.JPR V1N1.10

Liao, S. H., Chen, C. C., Hu, D. C., Chung, Y. C., & Liu, C. L. (2017). Assessing the influence of leadership style, organizational learning and organizational innovation. *Leadership and Organization Development Journal*, *38*(5), 590–609. doi:10.1108/LODJ-11-2015-0261

Liao, S. H., Chen, C. C., Hu, D. C., Chung, Y. C., & Yang, M. J. (2017). Developing a sustainable competitive advantage: Absorptive capacity, knowledge transfer and organizational learning. *The Journal of Technology Transfer*, *42*(6), 1431–1450. doi:10.100710961-016-9532-1

Liao, Y. S. (2005). Business strategy and performance: The role of human resource management control. *Personnel Review*, *34*(3), 294–309. doi:10.1108/00483480510591444

Liao, Y., Ho, S. S., & Yang, X. (2016). Motivators of pro-environmental behavior: Examining the underlying processes in the influence of presumed media influence model. *Science Communication*, *38*(1), 51–73. doi:10.1177/1075547015616256

Liberato, P., Alen, E., & Liberato, D. (2018). Smart Tourism Destinations Triggers Consumers Experiences Case of Porto. *European Journal of Management and Business Economics*, *27*(1), 6–25.

Liberato, P., Alen, E., & Liberato, D. (2018). Smart Tourism Destinations Triggers Consumers Experiences Case of Porto. *European Journal of Management and Business Economics*, *27*(1), 6–25. doi:10.1108/EJMBE-11-2017-0051

Liebenberg, P. (2015). *Identifying Factors that Influence Green Purchasing Behaviour in South Africa*. North-West University.

Liebowitz, J. (2010). The role of HR in achieving a sustainability culture. *Journal of Sustainable Development*, *3*(4), 50–57. doi:10.5539/jsd.v3n4p50

Lien, C. Y., Huang, C. W., & Chang, H. J. (2012). The influence of green consumption cognition of consumers on behavioral intention: A case study of the restaurant service industry. *African Journal of Business Management*, *6*(26), 7888.

Lim, S. (2017, July 11). KT replaces its corporate vehicles with electric vehicles. *Maeil Economy*. http://news.mk.co.kr/newsRead.php?year=2017&no=465080

Li, M., & Hsu, C. (2017). Customer participation in services and its effect on employee innovative behavior. *Journal of Hospitality Marketing & Management*, *26*(2), 164–185. doi:10.1080/19368623.2016.1215946

Li, M., & Hsu, C. H. (2016a). Linking customer-employee exchange and employee innovative behavior. *International Journal of Hospitality Management*, *56*, 87–97. doi:10.1016/j.ijhm.2016.04.015

Li, M., & Hsu, C. H. (2016b). A review of employee innovative behavior in services. *International Journal of Contemporary Hospitality Management*, *28*(12), 2820–2841. doi:10.1108/IJCHM-04-2015-0214

Li, M., & Hsu, C. H. (2018). Customer participation in services and employee innovative behavior. *International Journal of Contemporary Hospitality Management*, *30*(4), 2112–2131. doi:10.1108/IJCHM-08-2016-0465

Lim, C., & McAleer, M. (2002). A Cointegration Analysis of Annual Tourism Demand by Malaysia for Australia. *Mathematics and Computers in Simulation*, *59*(1-3), 197–205. doi:10.1016/S0378-4754(01)00408-6

Lim, C., Min, J. C. H., & McAleer, M. (2008). Modelling Income Effects on Long and Short Haul International Travel from Japan. *Tourism Management*, *29*(6), 1099–1109. doi:10.1016/j.tourman.2008.02.012

Lim, D. S. K., Celly, N., Morse, E. A., & Rowe, W. G. (2012). Rethinking the effectiveness of asset and cost retrenchment: The contingency effects of a firm's rent creation mechanism. *Strategic Management Journal*, *34*(1), 42–61. doi:10.1002mj.1996

Lim, F. W., Ahmad, F., & Abdul-Talib, A. N. (2019). Behavioural Intention towards Using Electronic Wallet: A Conceptual Framework in the Light of the Unified Theory of Acceptance and Use of Technology (UTAUT). *Imperial Journal of Interdisciplinary Research*, *5*(1), 79–86.

Lin, P., Huang, Y., & Wang, J. (2010). Applying the theory of consumption values to choice behavior toward green products. *Management of Innovation and Technology (ICMIT), 2010 IEEE International Conference on IEEE*, 348-353. 10.1109/ICMIT.2010.5492714

Lin, C., Lin, P., Song, F. M., & Li, C. (2011). Managerial incentives, CEO characteristics and corporate innovation in China's private sector. *Journal of Comparative Economics*, *39*(2), 176–190. doi:10.1016/j.jce.2009.12.001

Lindner, D., & Greff, T. (2019). Fuhrung im Zeitalter der Digitalisierung–was sagen Fuhrungskrafte? *HMD Praxis der Wirtschaftsinformatik*, *56*(3), 628–646. doi:10.136540702-018-00447-9

Linh, D. H., & Lin, S. M. (2015). Dynamic Causal Relationships Among CO_2 Emissions, Energy Consumption, Economic Growth and FDI in the Most Populous Asian Countries. *Advances in Management and Applied Economics*, *5*(1), 69–88.

Lin, J., Guo, J., Turel, O., & Liu, S. (2020). Purchasing organic food with social commerce: An integrated food-technology consumption values perspective. *International Journal of Information Management*, *51*, 102033. doi:10.1016/j.ijinfomgt.2019.11.001

Lin, P. C., & Huang, Y. H. (2012). The influence factors on choice behavior regarding green products based on the theory of consumption values. *Journal of Cleaner Production*, *22*(1), 11–18. doi:10.1016/j.jclepro.2011.10.002

Lippert, S. K., & Swierez, P. M. (2005). Human resource information system and technology trust. *Journal of Information Science*, *31*(5), 340–353. doi:10.1177/0165551505055399

Liu, R., Pieniak, Z., & Verbeke, W. (2013). Consumers' attitudes and behavior towards safe food in China: A review. *Food Control*, *33*(1), 93–104. doi:10.1016/j.foodcont.2013.01.051

Liu, T., & Potenza, M. N. (2007). Problematic Internet use: Clinical implications. *CNS Spectrums*, *12*(6), 453–466. doi:10.1017/S1092852900015339 PMID:17545956

Li, W., Liu, K., Belitski, M., Ghobadian, A., & O'Regan, N. (2016). E-Leadership through Strategic Alignment: An Empirical Study of Small and Medium-Sized Enterprises in the Digital Age. *Journal of Information Technology*, *31*(2), 185–206. doi:10.1057/jit.2016.10

Li, X., & Liu, X. (2005). Foreign Direct Investment and Economic Growth: An Increasingly Endogenous Relationship. *World Development*, *33*(3), 393–407.

Li, Y., Beeton, R. J., Sigler, T., & Halog, A. (2016). Modelling the transition toward urban sustainability: A case study of the industrial city of Jinchang, China. *Journal of Cleaner Production*, *134*, 22–30. doi:10.1016/j.jclepro.2015.10.053

Lopez-Cabrales, A., & Valle-Cabrera, R. (2020). Sustainable HRM strategies and employment relationships as drivers of the triple bottom line. *Human Resource Management Review*, *30*(3), 100689. doi:10.1016/j.hrmr.2019.100689

Lorenzen, M., & Täube, F. A. (2008). Breakout from Bollywood? The roles of social networks and regulation in the evolution of Indian film industry. *Journal of International Management*, *14*(3), 286–299. doi:10.1016/j.intman.2008.01.004

Lorenzi, N. M., Kouroubali, A., Detmer, D. E., & Bloomrosen, M. (2009). How to successfully select and implement electronic health records (EHR) in small ambulatory practice settings. *BMC Medical Informatics and Decision Making*, *9*(15), 1–13. doi:10.1186/1472-6947-9-15 PMID:19236705

Lorenz, M., Rubmann, M., Strack, R., Lueth, K. L., & Bolle, M. (2015). *Man and Machine in Industry 4.0. How Will Technology Transform the Industrial Workforce Through 2025?* The Boston Consulting Group.

Lüdeke-Freund, F., Gold, S., & Bocken, N. M. (2019). A review and typology of circular economy business model patterns. *Journal of Industrial Ecology*, *23*(1), 36–61. doi:10.1111/jiec.12763

Luomala, H., Puska, P., Lähdesmäki, M., Siltaoja, M., & Kurki, S. (2020). Get some respect – buy organic foods! When everyday consumer choices serve as prosocial status signaling. *Appetite*, *145*, 104492. doi:10.1016/j.appet.2019.104492 PMID:31654656

Lu, S., Wang, X., & Bendle, N. (2020). Does Piracy Create Online Word of Mouth? An Empirical Analysis in the Movie Industry. *Management Science*, *66*(5), 2140–2162. doi:10.1287/mnsc.2019.3298

Lusch, R. F., & Vargo, S. L. (2014). *Service Dominant Logic: Premises, Perspectives, Possibilities*. Cambridge University Press. doi:10.4324/9781315699035

Lu, V. N., & Julian, C. C. (2007). The internet and export marketing performance: The empirical link in export market ventures. *Asia Pacific Journal of Marketing and Logistics*, *19*(2), 127–144. doi:10.1108/13555850710738480

Lynn, M. (2000). National Personality and Tipping Customs. *Personality and Individual Differences*, *28*(2), 395–404. doi:10.1016/S0191-8869(99)00109-9

Lynn, R. (1971). *Personality and national character*. Pergamon Press.

Lynn, R. (1981). Cross-cultural differences in neuroticism, extraversion and psychoticism. In R. Lynn (Ed.), *Dimensions of personality: Papers in honour of H. J. Eysenck* (pp. 263–286). Pergamon Press.

Lynn, R. (1991). *The secret of the miracle economy: Different national attitudes to competitiveness and money*. The Social Affairs Unit.

Lynn, R., & Hampson, S. L. (1975). National differences in extraversion and neuroticism. *The British Journal of Social and Clinical Psychology*, *14*(3), 223–240. doi:10.1111/j.2044-8260.1975.tb00175.x PMID:1182404

Lynn, R., & Martin, T. (1995). National differences for 37 nations in extraversion, neuroticism, psychoticism and economic, demographic and other correlates. *Personality and Individual Differences*, *19*(3), 403–406. doi:10.1016/0191-8869(95)00054-A

Ma Prieto, I., & Pilar Perez-Santana, M. (2014). Managing innovative work behavior: The role of human resource practices. *Personnel Review*, *43*(2), 184–208. doi:10.1108/PR-11-2012-0199

Maamuon, M. A., Satria, M. H., Supriyanto, E., & Yunus, J. (2015). *Exploring Factors Influencing 'Perceived Usefulness' and Its Relationship on Hospital Information System End User Satisfaction*. Retrieved February 14, 2019 from https://pdfs.semanticscholar.org/196f/57f014c06b2bd1db61bfcd37aaee4c9a128a.pdf

MacArthur, E. (2015). *Towards a circular economy: business rationale for an accelerated transition*. Academic Press.

MacArthur, E. (2013). *Towards the circular economy, economic and business rationale for an accelerated transition*. Ellen MacArthur Foundation.

Macke, J., & Genari, D. (2019). Systematic literature review on sustainable human resource management. *Journal of Cleaner Production*, *208*, 806–815. doi:10.1016/j.jclepro.2018.10.091

Macwan, N., & Sajja, D. P. S. (2013). Performance appraisal using fuzzy evaluation methodology. *International Journal of Engineering and Innovative Technology*, *3*(3), 324–329.

Madrid-Guijarro, A., Garcia, D., & Van Auken, H. (2009). Barriers to innovation among Spanish manufacturing SMEs. *Journal of Small Business Management*, *47*(4), 465–488.

Ma, E., & Qu, H. (2011). Social exchanges as motivators of hotel employees' organizational citizenship behavior: The proposition and application of a new three-dimensional framework. *International Journal of Hospitality Management*, *30*(3), 680–688. doi:10.1016/j.ijhm.2010.12.003

Mago, R. (2016). E-HRM Electronic human resource management. *International Journal of Business and Scientific Research*, *23*, 41–47.

Maguad, B. A., & Krone, R. M. (2009). Ethics and moral leadership: Quality linkages. *Total Quality Management*, *20*(2), 209–222. doi:10.1080/14783360802623043

Mahajan, S. G., & Patil, S. K. (1999). Internet: Its use in university libraries in India. *National Convention on Academic Libraries in the Internet Era*, 483–488.

Mahapatro, B. B. (2010). New age human resource management. New Delhi: New Age International (P) Ltd.

Maheshwari, S., & Vohra, V. (2015). Identifying critical HR practices impacting employee perception and commitment during organizational change. *Journal of Organizational Change Management*, *28*(5), 872–889. doi:10.1108/JOCM-03-2014-0066

Mahfod, J., Noof, Y., Khalifa, Y., & Faisal, A. M. (2017). Electronic Human Resource Management (E-HRM) System. *International Journal of Economic Research*, *14*(15), 563–575.

Mahmood, M. A., Burn, J. M., Gemoets, L. A., & Jacquez, C. (2000). Variables Affecting Information Technology End-User Satisfaction: A Meta-Analysis of the Empirical Literature. *International Journal of Human-Computer Studies*, *52*(4), 751–771. doi:10.1006/ijhc.1999.0353

Mainemelis, C., Kark, R., & Epitropaki, O. (2015). *Creative Leadership: A Multi-Context*. Academic Press.

Mainieri, T., Barnett, E., Valdero, T., Unipan, J., & Oskamp, S. (1997). Green buying: The influence of environmental concern on consumer behavior. *The Journal of Social Psychology*, *137*(2), 189–204. doi:10.1080/00224549709595430

Maity, S. (2019). Identifying opportunities for artificial intelligence in the evolution of training and development practices. *Journal of Management Development*, *38*(8), 651–663. doi:10.1108/JMD-03-2019-0069

Ma, L., & Ye, M. (2015). The Role of Electronic Human Resource Management in Contemporary Human Resource Management. *Open Journal of Social Sciences*, *3*(04), 71–78. doi:10.4236/jss.2015.34009

Małachowski, B., & Korytkowski, P. (2016). Competence-based performance model of multi-skilled workers. *Computers & Industrial Engineering*, *91*, 165–177. doi:10.1016/j.cie.2015.11.018

Malaysia, D. (2013). *Empowering Malaysia towards a digital economy*. Available online at: http://www.digitalmalaysia.my/ebook/

Malaysian Communications and Multimedia Commission. (2017). https://skmm.gov.my/skmmgovmy/media/General/pdf/InternetUsersSurvey2016.pdf

Maletic, M., Maletic, D., & Gomiscek, B. (2018). The role of contingency factors on the relationship between sustainability practices and organizational performance. *Journal of Cleaner Production*, *171*, 423–433. doi:10.1016/j.jclepro.2017.09.172

Malik, M., Sajjad, M., Hyder, S., Ahmad, M., Ahmed, J., & Hussain, S. (2013). Role overload: A cause of diminishing employee retention and productivity. *Middle East Journal of Scientific Research*, *18*, 1573–1577.

Mandip, G. (2012). Green HRM: People management commitment to environmental sustainability. *Research Journal of Recent Sciences*, 244–252.

Manrai & Manrai. (2001). Cultural issues in the cross-cultural and cross-national consumer research in the new millennium. *Journal of East West Business*, *7*(1), 1–10.

Manzoor, F., Wei, L., Bányai, T., Nurunnabi, M., & Subhan, Q. A. (2019). An examination of sustainable HRM practices on job performance: An application of training as a moderator. *Sustainability*, *11*(8), 2263. doi:10.3390u11082263

Marchini, P. L., Mazza, T., & Medioli, A. (2018). Related party transactions, corporate governance and earnings management, *Corporate Governance. The International Journal of Business in Society*, *18*(6), 1124–1146. doi:10.1108/CG-11-2017-0271

Marín, L. S., & Roelofs, C. (2017). Promoting Construction Supervisors' Safety-Efficacy to Improve Safety Climate: Training Intervention Trial. *Journal of Construction Engineering and Management*, *143*(8), 04017037. doi:10.1061/(ASCE)CO.1943-7862.0001330

Marler, J. (2009). Making human resources strategic by going to the Net: Reality or myth? *International Journal of Human Resource Management*, *20*(3), 515–527. doi:10.1080/09585190802707276

Marler, J. H., & Parry, E. (2015). Human resource management, strategic involvement and e-HRM technology. *International Journal of Human Resource Management*, 1–21. doi:10.1080/09585192.2015.1091980

Martilla, J. A., & James, J. C. (1977). Importance-performance analysis. *Journal of Marketing*, *41*(1), 77–79. doi:10.1177/002224297704100112

Martin, J. (2018). *Skills for the 21st Century: Findings and Policy Lessons from the OECD Survey of Adult Skills*. Working Papers 201803, Geary Institute, University College Dublin.

Martinson, M., & Leon, J. D. (2018). Testing horizontal and vertical alignment of HR practices designed to achieve strategic organizational goals. *Journal of Organizational Effectiveness: People and Performance*, *5*(2), 158–181. doi:10.1108/JOEPP-10-2016-0057

Maskuriy, R., Selamat, A., Ali, K. N., Maresova, P., & Krejcar, O. (2019). Industry 4.0 for the construction industry—How ready is the industry? *Applied Sciences (Basel, Switzerland)*, *9*(14), 2819. doi:10.3390/app9142819

Maslow, A. H. (1943). A theory of human motivation. *Psychological Review*, *50*(4), 370–396. doi:10.1037/h0054346

Mat Said, A., Ahmadun, F. R., Hj Paim, L., & Masud, J. (2003). Environmental Concerns, Knowledge and Practices Gap Among Malaysian Teachers. *International Journal of Sustainability in Higher Education*, *4*(4), 305–313. doi:10.1108/14676370310497534

Mathews, S. W., Maruyama, M., Sakurai, Y., Bebenroth, R., Luck, E., Chen, H. L., & Franco, E. (2018). Internet resources and capabilities: Japanese SME risk-taking, industry and performance. *Asia Pacific Business Review*, *24*(5), 675–692. https://doi.org/10.1080/13602381.2018.1492690

Matlay, H., Khandekar, A., & Sharma, A. (2005). Organizational learning in Indian organizations: A strategic HRM perspective. *Journal of Small Business and Enterprise Development*, *12*(2), 211–226. doi:10.1108/14626000510594610

Matthews, R. L., MacCarthy, B. L., & Braziotis, C. (2017). Organisational learning in SMEs: A process improvement perspective. *International Journal of Operations & Production Management*, *37*(7), 970–1006. doi:10.1108/IJOPM-09-2015-0580

Matzler, K., Schwarz, E., Deutinger, N., & Harms, R. (2008). The Relationship between Transformational Leadership, Product Innovation and Performance in SMEs. *Journal of Small Business & Entrepreneurship*, 21(2): 139–151. Available online at: . doi:10.1080/08276331.2008.10593418

Mazzarol, T. (2015). SMEs engagement with e-commerce, e-business and e-marketing. *Small Enterprise Research*. Advance online publication. doi:10.1080/13215906.2015.1018400

Mc Quaid, L., Breen, P., Grimson, J., Normand, C., Dunne, M., Delanty, N., & Fitzsimons, M. (2010). Socio-technical considerations in epilepsy electronic patient record implementation. *International Journal of Medical Informatics*, *79*(5), 349–360. doi:10.1016/j.ijmedinf.2010.01.013 PMID:20181511

McAdams, D. P. (1995). What do we know when we know a person? *Journal of Personality*, *63*(3), 365–396. doi:10.1111/j.1467-6494.1995.tb00500.x

McClelland, D. C. (1976). The achieving society. New York: Irvington.

McClelland, D., Winter, D. (1971). *Motivating Economic Achievement*. Free Press-Collier-Macmillan.

McClelland, D. (1961). *A scoring manual*. Cambridge University Press. doi:10.1017/CBO9780511527937.011

McClelland, D. C. (1951). *Personality*. Sloane. doi:10.1037/10790-000

McClelland, D. C. (1985). *Human motivation*. Scott, Foresman.

McDule-Ra, D., & Chettri, M. (2019). Himalayan Boom Boom: Rural urban transition in Namchi, Sikkim. *Development and Change*, *49*(6), Pp1471–Pp1494. doi:10.1111/dech.12450

McEachern, M., & McClean, P. (2002). Organic purchasing motivations and attitudes: Are they ethical? *International Journal of Consumer Studies*, *26*(2), 85–92. doi:10.1046/j.1470-6431.2002.00199.x

McEvoy, G. M., & Buller, P. F. (2013). Human resource management practices in mid-sized enterprises. *American Journal of Business*, *28*(1), 86–105. doi:10.1108/19355181311314789

MDEC. (2021). *MDEC Confident Growth of Digital Economy Will Continue to Strengthen, In Line with GDP Performance.* https://mdec.my/news/mdec-confident-growth-of-digital-economy-will-continue-to-strengthen-in-line-with-gdp-performance/

Meehl, P. E. (1971). High School Yearbooks: A Reply to Schwarz. *Journal of Abnormal Psychology*, *77*(2), 143–148. doi:10.1037/h0030750

Mehraj, H. K., Bhat, A. N., & Mehraj, H. R. (2014). Impacts of media on society: A sociological perspective. *International Journal of Humanities and Social Science Invention*, *3*(6), 56–64.

Mehta, P. S. (2002). The Indian Mining Sector: Effects on the Environment & FDI Inflows. *CCNM Global Forum on International Investment, Conference on Foreign Direct investment and the Environment.*

Meijer, A., & Bolívar, M. P. R. (2015). Governing the Smart City: A Review of the Literature on Smart Urban Governance. *International Review of Administrative Sciences*, *82*(2), 392–408. doi:10.1177/0020852314564308

Melville, N. (2010). Information Systems Innovation for Environmental Sustainability. *Management Information Systems Quarterly*, *34*(1), 1–21. doi:10.2307/20721412

Menon, S., Narayanan, L., & Kahwaji, A. T. (2018). Internet addiction: A research study of college students in India. *Journal of Economics and Business*, *1*(1), 100–106. doi:10.31014/aior.1992.01.01.9

Meral, Y. (Ed.). (2019). Tools and techniques for implementing international e-trading tactics for competitive advantage. Academic Press.

Meyer, J. P., & Allen, N. J. (1991). A three-component conceptualization of organizational commitment. *Human Resource Management Review*, *1*(1), 61–89. doi:10.1016/1053-4822(91)90011-Z

Micheli, P., Schoeman, M., Baxter, D., & Goffin, K. (2012). New business models for public-sector innovation: Successful technological innovation for government. *Research Technology Management*, *55*(5), 51–57. doi:10.5437/08956308X5505067

Mingjun, W., Zhen, Y., Wei, Z., Xishang, D., Xiaofei, Y., & Chenggang, S. (2012). A Research on Experimental System for Internet of Things Major and Application Project. In *System Science, Engineering Design and Manufacturing Informatization.* 10.1109/ICSSEM.2012.6340722

Minh, N. (2021). Vietnam ranks second in world Covid-19 response. *VietnamExpress.* Available online at https://e.vnexpress.net/news/news/vietnam-ranks-second-in-world-covid-19-response-4227749.html

Ministry of Finance. (2017). *Budget speech financial year 2015/2016.* Retrieved on 06-03-2017, from http://www.mof.gov.bn/attachments/article/223/BUDGET%20SPEECH%20FY%202015%202016.pdf

Ministry of Health Brunei Darussalam. (n.d.). *Introduction Bru-HIMS.* Retrieved October 30, 2018 from http://www.moh.gov.bn/SitePages/Bru-HIMS%20Introduction.aspx

Ministry of Housing and Urban Affairs (MHUA). (2020). *City Ranking 2020.* Retrieved from: https://eol.smartcities.gov.in/dashboard

Ministry of Housing and Urban Affairs (MHUA). (2021). *Smart City: Gangtok.* Retrieved from: https://smartcities.gov.in/node/191

Ministry of International Trade and Industry. (2019). *Industry 4wrd.* Assess on 19.4.2020. https://www.miti.gov.my/index.php/pages/view/industry4WRD?mid=559

Ministry of Urban Development (MUD). (2016). *India Smart City Mission- Gangtok.* Retrieved from: https://smartcitygangtok.com/images/SCP%20Gangtok.pdf

Minunno, R., O'Grady, T., Morrison, G. M., & Gruner, R. L. (2020). Exploring environmental benefits of reuse and recycle practices: A circular economy case study of a modular building. *Resources, Conservation and Recycling, 160*, 104855. doi:10.1016/j.resconrec.2020.104855

Mishra, R., Pareek, G., & Chakrabarti, T. (2020). Green HRM Practices Effectiveness on the Psychological Contract: The Changing Nature of Employee-Employer. *International Journal of Recent Advances in Multidisciplinary Topics, 1*(1), 37–39.

Misra, R., Singh, S., & Mahajan, R. (2020). An analysis on consumer preference of ayurvedic products in Indian market. *International Journal of Asian Business and Information Management, 11*(4), 1–15. doi:10.4018/IJABIM.2020100101

Mitchell, T. R. (1982). Motivation: New directions for theory, research, and practice. *Academy of Management Review, 7*(1), 80–88. doi:10.5465/amr.1982.4285467

Mitrovic, Z. (2015). Strengthening the evidence-base for open government in developing countries: Building Open Data Capacity through e-Skills Acquisition. (March):1–38.

Mittal, M., & Bhakkar, D. (2018). Examining the Impact of Role Overload on Job Stress, Job Satisfaction and Job Performance-A study among Married Working Women in Banking Sector. *International Journal of Management Studies, 5*(2), 7–19. doi:10.18843/ijms/v5i2(7)/01

Moen, Ø., Heggeseth, A. G., & Lome, O. (2016). The Positive Effect of Motivation and International Orientation on SME Growth. *Journal of Small Business Management, 54*(2), 659–678. https://doi.org/10.1111/jsbm.12163

Mohamad, S. S., Rusdi, S. D., & Hashim, N. H. (2014). Organic food consumption among urban consumers: Preliminary results. *Procedia: Social and Behavioral Sciences, 130*, 509–514. doi:10.1016/j.sbspro.2014.04.059

Mohamed, E. S. A. (2020). The Role of Employee's Innovative Behavior in Strengthening the Impact of Customer Participation on Customer Engagement. *International Journal of Customer Relationship Marketing and Management, 11*(4), 1–19. doi:10.4018/IJCRMM.2020100101

Mohrman, A. M. Jr, Mohrman, S. A., & Odden, A. R. (1996). Aligning teacher compensation with systemic school reform: Skill-based pay and group-based performance rewards. *Educational Evaluation and Policy Analysis, 18*(1), 51–71. doi:10.3102/01623737018001051

Molinillo, S., Vidal-Branco, M., & Japutra, A. (2020). Understanding the drivers of organic foods purchasing of millennials: Evidence from Brazil and Spain. *Journal of Retailing and Consumer Services, 52*, 101926. doi:10.1016/j.jretconser.2019.101926

Moreau, V., Sahakian, M., van Griethuysen, P., & Vuille, F. (2017). Coming Full Circle: Why Social and Institutional Dimensions Matter for the Circular Economy. *Journal of Industrial Ecology, 21*(3), 497–506. doi:10.1111/jiec.12598

Morgan, N. A., Vorhies, D. W., & Mason, C. H. (2009). Market orientation, marketing capabilities, and firm performance. *Strategic Management Journal, 30*(8), 909–920. doi:10.1002mj.764

Moser, G., & Uzzell, D. L. (2003). Environmental Psychology. In T. Millon & M. J. Lerner (Eds.), *Comprehensive Handbook of Psychology: Personality and Social Psychology* (Vol. 5, pp. 419–445). John Wiley & Sons. doi:10.1002/0471264385.wei0517

Mostafa, M. M. (2007). Gender differences in Egyptian consumers green purchase behavior: The effects of environmental knowledge, concern and attitude. *International Journal of Consumer Studies, 31*, 220–229.

Moşteanu, N. R., Faccia, A., & Cavaliere, L. P. L. (2020, August). Digitalization and green economy-changes of business perspectives. In *Proceedings of the 2020 4th International Conference on Cloud and Big Data Computing* (p. 108-112). 10.1145/3416921.3416929

Mulgan, G., & Albury, D. (2003). Innovation in the public sector. *Strategy Unit. Cabinet Office*, *1*(1), 40.

Munton, A. G., & West, M. A. (1995). Innovations and personal change: Patterns of adjustment to relocation. *Journal of Organizational Behavior*, *16*(4), 363–375. doi:10.1002/job.4030160407

Mu, R., & Wang, H. (2020). A systematic literature review of open innovation in the public sector: Comparing barriers and governance strategies of digital and non-digital open innovation. *Public Management Review*, 1–23. doi:10.1080/14719037.2020.1838787

Murray, A., Skene, K., & Haynes, K. (2017). The Circular Economy: An interdisciplinary exploration of the concept and its application in a global context. *Journal of Business Ethics*, *140*(3), 369–380. doi:10.100710551-015-2693-2

Murthy, C. S. H. N. (2013). Film remakes as cross-cultural connections between North and South: A case study of the Telugu film industry's contribution to Indian filmmaking. *Journal of International Communication*, *19*(1), 19–42. doi:10.1080/13216597.2012.739573

Murthy, C. S. H. N. (2015). Rethinking what is special about Indian Cinema. *Media Asia*, *42*(1-2), 36–38. doi:10.1080/01296612.2015.1100377

Musari, K., and Zaroni. (2021). Reverse logistics in the age of digital transformation for circular economy and halal logistics through the leadership of Asia. In P. O. de Pablos, X. Zhang, & M. N. Almunawar (Eds.), *Handbook of research on disruptive innovation and digital transformation in Asia* (pp. 83-103). Hershey, PA: IGI Global. . doi:10.4018/978-1-7998-6477-6

Muster, V., & Schrader, U. (2011). Green work life balance: A new perspective for green HRM. *German Journal of Human Resource Management*, *25*(2), 140–156. doi:10.1177/239700221102500205

N., & Rani, S. (2019). Effectiveness of Training on Food Processing among Women in Haryana, India. *Current Journal of Applied Science and Technology, 33*(6), 1–6. doi:10.9734/cjast/2019/v33i630103

Nadda, V., Chaudhary, H. S., & Arnott, I. (2020). *Cloud Computing in Tourism*. doi:10.4018/978-1-5225-9783-4.ch007

Nadeem, M. T., Zia-uD-din, M., Riaz, W., Shafique, M. Z., & Sattar, A. (2018). The Effects of Employees Empowerment on Organizational Performance: A Case of Hotel Industry in Pakistan. *International Journal of African and Asian Studies, 47*.

Nadler, D., & Tushman, M. (1980). A model for diagnosing organizational behavior. *Organizational Dynamics*, *9*(2), 35–51. doi:10.1016/0090-2616(80)90039-X

Nagin, D. S., Rebitzer, J. B., Sanders, S., & Taylor, L. J. (2002). Monitoring, motivation, and management: The determinants of opportunistic behavior in a field experiment. *The American Economic Review*, *92*(4), 850–873. doi:10.1257/00028280260344498

Namchi Smart City Ltd. (2020). *Project List: Namchi Smart City Ltd.* Retrieved from: https://namchismartcity.co.in/wp-content/uploads/2020/03/Project-List-NSCL.pdf

Nandana. (2020, July 6). Do producers make less money on OTT compared to box office collections? *Business Line*.

NaseerD. R. (Producer). (2018, February 3rd). *Tribune*. Retrieved from https://tribune.com.pk/story/1625223/seven-minutes-rescue-1122-maintains-average-response-time

Nason, R. S., & Wiklund, J. (2018). An assessment of resource-based theorizing on firm growth and suggestions for the future. *Journal of Management*, *44*(1), 32–60. doi:10.1177/0149206315610635

Nayananjalee, W. T., & De Alwis, A. (2017). *HR Professionals Perception towards Electronic Human Resource Management*. Retrieved from https://www.researchgate.net /publication /320163215_HR_Professionals_Perception_towards_Electronic_ Human_ Resource_Management

Naz, F., Aftab, J., & Awais, M. (2016). Impact of human resource management practices (HRM) on performance of SMEs in Multan, Pakistan. *International Journal of Management. Accounting & Economics*, *3*(11), 699–708.

Nazim, A., & Ahmad, S. (2013). Assessing the unidimensionality, reliability, validity and fitness of influential factors of 8th grades student's mathematics achievement in Malaysia. *International Journal of Advanced Research*, *1*(2), 1–7.

Neogi, A., Mondal, A. C., & Mandal, S. K. (2011). A cascaded fuzzy inference system for university non-teaching staff performance appraisal. *Journal of Information Processing Systems*, *7*(4), 595–612. doi:10.3745/JIPS.2011.7.4.595

Neumeier, M. (2005). *The Brand Gap* (Revised Edition). Peachpit Press.

Newbert, S. L. (2008). Empirical research on the resource-based view of the firm: An assessment and suggestions for future research. *Strategic Management Journal*, *28*(2), 121–146. doi:10.1002mj.573

Newman, A., & Sheikh, A. Z. (2014). Determinants of best HR practices in Chinese SMEs. *Journal of Small Business and Enterprise Development*, *21*(3), 414–430. doi:10.1108/JSBED-05-2014-0082

Nguyen, H. V., Nguyen, N., Nguyen, B. K., Lobo, A., & Vu, P. A. (2019). Organic food purchases in an emerging market: The influence of consumers' personal factors and green marketing practices of food stores. *International Journal of Environmental Research and Public Health*, *16*(6), 1037. Advance online publication. doi:10.3390/ijerph16061037 PMID:30909390

Nguyen, L., Bellucci, E., & Nguyen, L. T. (2014). Electronic health records implementation: An evaluation of information system impact and contingency factors. *International Journal of Medical Informatics*, *83*(11), 779–796. doi:10.1016/j.ijmedinf.2014.06.011 PMID:25085286

Ng, Y. N., & Salamzadeh, Y. (2020). The Impact of Ethical Leadership on the Intention to Stay among the Generation-Y Workforce of MNCs in Penang, Malaysia: Mediating Role of Employee Rewards. *International Journal of Business Science and Applied Management*, *15*(2).

Nhamo, G., Dube, K., & Chikodzi, D. (2020). *Counting the cost of COVID-19 on the global tourism industry*. Springer Nature. doi:10.1007/978-3-030-56231-1

Nhamo, G., Dube, K., & Chikodzi, D. (2020). Implications of COVID-19 on gaming, leisure and entertainment industry. In *Counting the Cost of COVID-19 on the Global Tourism Industry* (pp. 273–295). Springer. doi:10.1007/978-3-030-56231-1_12

Niehoff, B. P., & Moorman, R. H. (1993). Justice as a mediator of the relationship between methods of monitoring and organizational citizenship behavior. *Academy of Management Journal*, *36*(3), 527–556.

Niehoff, B. P., Moorman, R., Blakely, G., & Fuller, J. (2001). The Influence of Empowerment and Job Enrichment on Employee Loyalty in a Downsizing Environment. *Group & Organization Management*, *26*(1), 93–113. doi:10.1177/1059601101261006

Nilsson, L., Persson, P. O., Rydén, L., Darozhka, S., & Zaliauskiene, A. (2007). *Cleaner Production: Technologies and Tools for Resource Efficient Production*. Baltic University Press.

Nissen, M. E. (2014). Organization design for dynamic fit: A review and projection. *Journal of Organization Design*, *3*(2), 30–42. doi:10.7146/jod.8196

Nivlouei, F. B. (2014). Electronic Human Resource Management System: The Main Element in Capacitating Globalization Paradigm. *International Journal of Business and Social Science*, *5*(2), 147–159.

Njegovan, N. (2005). A Leading Indicator Approach to Predicting Short-Term Shifts in Demand for Business Travel by Air to and from the UK. *Journal of Forecasting*, *24*(6), 421–432. doi:10.1002/for.961

Njegovan, N. (2006). Elasticities of Demand for Leisure Air Travel: A System Modelling Approach. *Journal of Air Transport Management*, *12*(1), 33–39. doi:10.1016/j.jairtraman.2005.09.003

Noonan, C. (2020). Public funding in a time of crisis: Film funds and the pandemic. *Baltic Screen Media Review*, (8), 10–17.

Noor, R. (2020). *Percepatan pembangunan ekosistem industri halal di Indonesia melalui intervensi teknologi.* A presentation material at Webinar 'Digitalisasi New Normal Industri Halal di Indonesia' held by Sucofindo.

Nunkoo, R., & Ramkissoon, H. (2012). Power, trust, social exchange and community support. *Annals of Tourism Research*, *39*(2), 997–1023. doi:10.1016/j.annals.2011.11.017

Nunnally, j. c., & Bernstein, I. H. (1994). The Capability Approach and Evaluation of the Well-Being in Senegal: An Operationalization with the Structural Equations Models. *The Assessment of Reliability. Psychometric Theory,* 248-292.

O'cass, A., & Frost, H. (2002). Status brands: Examining the effects of non-product-related brand associations on status and conspicuous consumption. *Journal of Product and Brand Management*, *11*(2), 67–88. doi:10.1108/10610420210423455

O'Cass, A., & Siahtiri, V. (2013). In search of status through brands from Western and Asian origins: Examining the changing face of fashion clothing consumption in Chinese young adults. *Journal of Retailing and Consumer Services*, *20*(6), 505–515. doi:10.1016/j.jretconser.2013.05.005

O'Malley, A. S., Grossman, J. M., Cohen, G. R., Kemper, N. M., & Pham, H. H. (2009). Are Electronic Medical Records Helpful for Care Coordination? Experiences of Physician Practices. *Journal of General Internal Medicine*, *25*(3), 177–185. doi:10.100711606-009-1195-2 PMID:20033621

O'Riordan, J. (2017). *The practice of human resource management.* State of public service research paper. Retrieved August 11, 2018 from https://www.ipa.ie/_ fileUpload/Documents /the_practice _of_hrm.pdf

Oberer, B., & Erkollar, A. (2018). Leadership 4.0: Digital Leaders in the Age of Industry 4.0. *International Journal of Organizational Leadership*, *7*(4), 404–412. doi:10.33844/ijol.2018.60332

Odden, A. (2001). Defining Merit. *Education Matters*, *1*(1), 16–24.

Odden, A., Odden, A. R., & Kelley, C. (2002). *Paying teachers for what they know and do: New and smarter compensation strategies to improve schools*. Corwin Press.

Oelze, N., Hoejmose, S. U., Habisch, A., & Millington, A. (2016). Sustainable development in supply chain management: The role of organizational learning for policy implementation. *Business Strategy and the Environment*, *25*(4), 241–260. doi:10.1002/bse.1869

Office of Government Commerce. (2002). *ICT infrastructure management*. The Stationary Office.

Ojo, A. I. (2017). Validation of the DeLone and McLean Information System Success Model. *Health Informatics Research, 23*(1), 60-66. Retrieved November 5, 2018 from https://www.ncbi.nlm.nih.gov/pmc/articles/PMC5334133/pdf/hir-23-60.pdf

Ojo, A. I., & Popoola, S. O. (2015). Some Correlates of Electronic Health Information Management System Success in Nigerian Teaching Hospitals. *Biomedical Informatics Insights*, *7*, 1–9. doi:10.4137/BII.S20229 PMID:25983557

Ojokoh, B., Akinsulire, V., & Isinkaye, F. O. (2019). An Automated Implementation of Academic Staff Performance Evaluation System based on Rough Sets Theory. *AJIS. Australasian Journal of Information Systems*, *23*, 23. doi:10.3127/ajis.v23i0.2033

Oktariani, A., Tirdasari, N. L., Hasanah, N., & Indrawan, D. (2020). Setting up a business environment to introduce a new material for packaging in Indonesia. *Indonesian Journal of Business and Entrepreneurship*, *6*(3), 302–310. doi:10.17358/ijbe.6.3.302

Olanipekun, A. O., Xia, B., Hon, C., & Darko, A. (2018). Effect of Motivation and Owner Commitment on the Delivery Performance of Green Building Projects. *Journal of Management Engineering*, *34*(1), 04017039. doi:10.1061/(ASCE)ME.1943-5479.0000559

Ologunde, A. O., Monday, J. U., & James-Unam, F. C. (2015). The impact of strategic human resource management on competitiveness of small and medium-scale enterprises in the Nigerian hospitality industry. *African Research Review*, *9*(4), 264–276. doi:10.4314/afrrev.v9i4.20

Oltra, M. J., & Flor, M. L. (2010). The moderating effect of business strategy on the relationship between operations strategy and firms' results. *International Journal of Operations & Production Management*, *30*(6), 612–638. doi:10.1108/01443571011046049

Omalaja, M. A., & Eruola, O. A. (2011). Strategic management theory: Concepts, analysis and critiques in relation to corporate competitive advantage from the resource-based philosophy. *Strategic Management Theory*, *44*(1-2), 59–77.

Omotosho, S., & Anyigba, H. (2019). Conceptualising corporate entrepreneurial strategy: A contingency and agency collaborative approach. *Journal of Strategy and Management*, *12*(2), 256–274. doi:10.1108/JSMA-05-2018-0046

ONC (The Office of the National Coordinator for Health Information Technology). (2012). *Health Information Technology Patient Safety Action & Surveillance Plan for Public Comment*. Retrieved June 4, 2019, from https://www.healthit.gov/sites/default/files/safetyplanhhspubliccomment.pdf

Ooi, J. M., Kwek, C. L., & Keoy, K. H. (2012). The Antecedents of Green Purchase Intention among Malaysian Consumers. *Asian Social Science Archives*, *8*(13), 248–263. doi:10.5539/ass.v8n13p248

Organisation for Economic Co-Operation and Development. (2008). *Removing Barriers to SME Access to International Markets*. The 30th Small and Medium Enterprises Working Group Meeting, Hong Kong, China.

Organisation for Economic Co-Operation and Development. (2017). *Enhancing the Contributions of SMEs in a Global and Digitalised Economy*. Meeting of the OECD Council at Ministerial Level. Paris.

Osterwalder, A., & Pigneur, Y. (2010). *Business model canvas*. Self Published.

Othman, A. K., Mahmud, Z., Noranee, S., & Noordin, F. (2018). Measuring Employee Happiness: Analyzing the Dimensionality of Employee Engagement. *Proceedings of the 7th International Conference on Kansei Engineering and Emotion Research*, 19-22. 10.1007/978-981-10-8612-0_90

Our World Data. (2021). Available online at https://ourworldindata.org/covid-vaccinations?country=OWID_WRL

Owenvbiugie, R. O. (2017). Role of Finance on the Growth of Small and Medium Scale Enterprises in Edo State of Nigeria. *Journal of Educational and Social Research*, *5*(1), 241. https://doi.org/10.5901/jesr.2015.v5n1p241

Ozdil, S. O., & Kutlu, O. (2019). Investigation of the mediator variable effect using BK, Sobel and Bootstrap methods (Mathematical literacy case). *International Journal of Progressive Education*, *15*(2), 30–43. doi:10.29329/ijpe.2019.189.3

OziliP. K.ArunT. (2020). Spillover of COVID-19: impact on the Global Economy. Available at SSRN 3562570. doi:10.2139srn.3562570

Ozkeser, B. (2019). Impact of training on employee motivation in human resources management. *Procedia Computer Science*, *158*, 802–810. doi:10.1016/j.procs.2019.09.117

Paauwe, J., & Boon, C. (2009). Strategic HRM: A critical review. In D. F. Collings & T. W. Geoffrey (Eds.), *Human resource management: A critical approach* (pp. 38–54). Routledge.

Paco, A. D., & Raposo, M. (2009). "Green" segmentation: An application to the Portuguese consumer market. *Marketing Intelligence & Planning*, *27*(3), 364–379. doi:10.1108/02634500910955245

Pai, C. K., Liu, Y., Kang, S., & Dai, A. (2020). The Role of Perceived Smart Tourism Technology Experience for Tourist Satisfaction, Happiness and Revisit Intentions. *Sustainability*, *12*(16), 6592. doi:10.3390u12166592

Pai, F. Y., & Huang, K. I. (2011). Applying the Technology Acceptance Model to the introduction of healthcare information systems. *Technological Forecasting and Social Change*, *78*(4), 650–660. doi:10.1016/j.techfore.2010.11.007

Panetta, K. (2016). Analyst answers: The CIO's biggest digital transformation challenges. Available online at: https://www.gartner.com/smarterwithgartner/cios-biggest-digital-transformationchallenges/. Assessed on 30.4.2020.

Pangarker, N. A., & Smit, E. M. (2013). The determinants of box office performance in the film industry revisited. *South African Journal of Business Management*, *44*(3), 47–58. doi:10.4102ajbm.v44i3.162

Pardoe, I. (2012). *Applied regression modeling* (2nd ed.). Wiley. doi:10.1002/9781118345054

Parisi, C. (2012). The impact of organizational alignment on the effectiveness of firms' sustainability strategic performance measurement systems: An empirical analysis. *The Journal of Management and Governance*, *17*(1), 71–97. doi:10.100710997-012-9219-4

Park, J. (2017, March 31). KT Smart Energy business gets on track, targets 200B won revenue this year. *Financial News*. https://www.fnnews.com/news/201703311517431179

Parker, P. (1992). Price elasticity dynamics over the adoption life cycle. *JMR, Journal of Marketing Research*, *24*(3), 358–367. doi:10.1177/002224379202900306

Parlow, A., & Wagner, S. (2018). *Netflix and the Demand for Cinema Tickets-An Analysis for 19 European Countries*. Academic Press.

Parnell, J. A. (2010). Strategic clarity, business strategy and performance. *Journal of Strategy and Management*, *3*(4), 304–324. doi:10.1108/17554251011092683

Parry, E., & Tyson, S. (2011). Desired goals and actual outcomes of e-HRM. *Human Resource Management Journal*, *21*(3), 335–354. doi:10.1111/j.1748-8583.2010.00149.x

Patnaik, B., & Padhi, P. C. (2012). Compensation management: A theoretical preview. *TRANS Asian Journal of Marketing & Management Research*, *1*(1), 39–48.

Paul, H. (2000). Creating a mindset. *Thunderbird International Business Review*, *42*(2), 187–200.

Peattie, K. (2001). Golden goose or wild goose? The hunt for the green consumer. *Business Strategy and the Environment*, *10*(4), 187–189. doi:10.1002/bse.292

Pedro, P. L. J., & Lemke, F. (2013). Exploring green consumers' product demands and consumption processes: The case of Portuguese green consumers. *European Business Review*, *25*(3), 281–300. doi:10.1108/09555341311314825

Peng, H. (2018). Global shift of the TV landscape and popular culture in East Asia: From Cultural imperialism to the rise of regionalization. *The 7th Annual International Conference on Journalism and Mass Communications (JMCommm 2018).* doi:10.5176/2301-3710_JMComm18.131

Pesaran, M. H., & Shin, Y. (1999). An autoregressive distributed lag modelling approach to cointegration analysis. In S. Strom (Ed.), *Econometrics and Economic Theory in the 20th Century: The Ragnar Frisch Centennial Symposium.* Cambridge University Press.

Pesaran, M. H., & Shin, Y. (1998). An autoregressive distributed-lag modelling approach to cointegration analysis. *Econometric Society Monographs*, *31*, 371–413. doi:10.1017/CCOL0521633230.011

Pesaran, M. H., Shin, Y., & Smith, R. J. (2001). Bounds testing approaches to the analysis of level relationships. *Journal of Applied Econometrics*, *16*(3), 289–326. doi:10.1002/jae.616

Phau, I., Quintal, V., & Shanka, T. (2014). Examining a consumption values theory approach of young tourists toward destination choice intentions. *International Journal of Culture, Tourism and Hospitality Research*, *8*(2), 125–139. doi:10.1108/IJCTHR-12-2012-0090

Phelps, K. C. (2014). 'So much technology, so little talent'? Skills for harnessing technology for leadership outcomes. *The Journal of Leadership Studies*, *8*(2), 51–56. doi:10.1002/jls.21331

Phillips, P. C. B., & Perron, P. (1988). Testing for unit root in time series regression. *Biometrika*, *75*, 335–346.

Pigosso, D. C., Zanette, E. T., Guelere Filho, A., Ometto, A. R., & Rozenfeld, H. (2010). Ecodesign methods focused on remanufacturing. *Journal of Cleaner Production*, *18*(1), 21–31. doi:10.1016/j.jclepro.2009.09.005

Pimentel, D., Williamson, S., Alexander, C. E., Gonzalez-Pagan, O., Kontak, C., & Mulkey, S. E. (2008). Reducing energy inputs in the US food system. *Human Ecology*, *36*(4), 459–471. doi:10.100710745-008-9184-3

PlasticsEurope. (2019). *Plastics – the Facts 2019*. PlasticsEurope.

PlasticsEurope. (2020). *Plastics – the Facts 2020*. PlasticsEurope.

Podgorodnichenko, N., Edgar, F., & McAndrew, I. (2020). The role of HRM in developing sustainable organizations: Contemporary challenges and contradictions. *Human Resource Management Review*, *30*(3), 100685. doi:10.1016/j.hrmr.2019.04.001

Podgursky, M. J., & Springer, M. G. (2007). Teacher performance pay: A review. *Journal of Policy Analysis and Management*, *26*(4), 909–949. doi:10.1002/pam.20292

Poisat, P., & Mey, M. R. (2017). Electronic human resource management: Enhancing or entrancing? *Journal of Human Resource Management*, *15*, 1–9.

Polit, D. F., & Beck, C. T. (2010). Generalization in quantitative and qualitative research: Myths and strategies. *International Journal of Nursing Studies*, *47*(11), 1451–1458. doi:10.1016/j.ijnurstu.2010.06.004 PMID:20598692

Preacher, K. J., & Hayes, A. F. (2004). SPSS and SAS procedures for estimating indirect effects in simple mediation models. *Behavior Research Methods, Instruments, & Computers*, *36*(4), 717–731. doi:10.3758/BF03206553 PMID:15641418

Preacher, K. J., & Hayes, A. F. (2008). Asymptotic and resampling strategies for assessing and comparing indirect effects in multiple mediator models. *Behavior Research Methods*, *40*(3), 879–891. doi:10.3758/BRM.40.3.879 PMID:18697684

Press Trust of India (PTI). (2020). *Sikkim Suffers Rs. 600 Crore Blow as Covid Cripples Tourism Industry.* Retrieved from: https://www.business-standard.com/article/current-affairs/2020-sikkim-suffers-rs-600-crore-blow-as-covid-cripples-tourism-industry-120122700409_1.html

Prime Minister's Office. (2008). *What you need to know about GEMS.* Retrieved August 11, 2018, from http://www.gems.gov.bn/gemshelpcentre/Resource/GEMS%20Awareness %20 Pamphlet%20v0.6.pdf

Priya, S. & Munivenkatappa. (2017). A study on the satisfaction level of employees towards e-hrm systems. *International Journal of Applied Research, 3*(9), 467–471.

Public Service Department. (2015, Oct. 14). GEMS aplikasi rekod kedatangan. *Pelita Brunei,* p. 13.

Pulley, M. L., & Sessa, V. I. (2001). E-leadership: Tackling complex challenges. Industrial and Commercial Training, 33(6/7). proclivity: a dynamic capabilities approach. *Journal of Retailing, 82*(1), 51–62.

Punjani, K. (2019). Objectives of the Study Chart 1 (Source: Planning Commission India-11th five year plan) " " Skill Development : The Key to Economic Prosperity A Study On The Requirement Of Skills Development For The Success Of "Make In India" Project. *Tactful Management Research Journal.* www.makeinindia.com

Qasim, H., Yan, L., Guo, R., Saeed, A., & Ashraf, B. (2019). The defining role of environmental self-identity among consumption values and behavioral intention to consume organic food. *International Journal of Environmental Research and Public Health, 16*(7), 1106. doi:10.3390/ijerph16071106 PMID:30925666

Qin, A. (2015). China's Love Affair With Irresistible Korean TV. *New York Times Style.* http://cn.nytstyle.com/culture/20150721/t21koreatv/en-us/

Qteishat, M., Alshibly, H. H., & Al-ma'aitah, M. A. (2014). The impact of e-ticketing technique on customer satisfaction: An empirical analysis. *Journal of Information Systems and Technology Management, 11*(3), 519–532. doi:10.4301/S1807-17752014000300001

Qu, Q. S., & Dumay, J. (2011). The qualitative research interviews. *Qualitative Research in Accounting & Management, 8*(3), 238–264. doi:10.1108/11766091111162070

Racela, O. C. (2014). Customer orientation, innovation competencies, and firm performance: A proposed conceptual model. *Procedia: Social and Behavioral Sciences, 148*, 16–23. doi:10.1016/j.sbspro.2014.07.010

Radzi, C. W. J. B. W. M., Jenatabadi, H. S., & Hasbullah, M. B. (2015). Firm Sustainability Performance Index Modeling. *Sustainability, 7*(12), 16196–16212. doi:10.3390u71215810

Rafferty, A. E., & Jimmieson, N. L. (2016). Subjective Perceptions of Organizational Change and Employee Resistance to Change: Direct and Mediated Relationships with Employee Well-being. *British Journal of Management, 28*(2), 248–264. doi:10.1111/1467-8551.12200

Raisch, S., Birkinshaw, J., Probst, G., & Tushman, M. L. (2009). Organizational ambidexterity: Balancing exploitation and exploration for sustained performance. *Organization Science, 20*(4), 685–695.

Rajadhyaksha, A. (2003). The 'Bollywoodization' of the Indian cinema: Cultural nationalism in a global arena. *Inter-Asia Cultural Studies, 4*(1), 25–39. doi:10.1080/1464937032000060195

Rajendran. (2020, Sept. 2). 'C U Soon': Mahesh-Fahadh film is a reminder of what the Malayalam industry does best. *Mollywood Wednesday.*

Raju, K. K. (2016). Growth Driver of an Indian Economy-Make-in-India. *The Indian Journal of Commerce, 68*(5).

Ramanathan, R., Ramanathan, U., & Hsiao, H. L. (2012). The Impact of e-commerce on Taiwanese SMEs: Marketing and operations effects. *International Journal of Production Economics*, *140*, 934–943. https://dx.doi.org/10.1016/j.ijpe.2012.07.017

Raman, B., & Chebrolu, K. (2007). Experiences in using WiFi for rural internet in India. *IEEE Communications Magazine*, *45*(1), 104–110. doi:10.1109/MCOM.2007.284545

Ramasamy, A. (2017). *A study on implications of implementing green HRM in the corporate bodies with special reference to developing nations*. Academic Press.

Ramawickrama, J., & Opatha, H. H. P., & PushpaKumari, M. (. (2017). A Synthesis towards the construct of job performance. *International Business Research*, *10*(10), 66–81. doi:10.5539/ibr.v10n10p66

Ramayah, T., Lee, J., & In, J. (2011). Network collaboration and performance in the tourism sector. *Service Business*, *5*(4), 411–428. doi:10.100711628-011-0120-z

Ramkissoon, H., Nunkoo, R., & Gursoy, D. (2009). How consumption values affect destination image formation. Perspectives on cross-cultural, ethnographic, brand image, storytelling, unconscious needs, and hospitality guest research. *Advances in Culture Tourism and Hospitality Research*, *3*, 143–168.

Rana, R., & Sharma, M. (2019). Dynamic causality testing for EKC hypothesis, pollution haven hypothesis and international trade in India. *The Journal of International Trade & Economic Development*, *28*(3), 348–364.

Rana, R., & Sharma, M. (2020). Dynamic causality among FDI, economic growth and CO_2 emissions in India: With open markets and technology gap. *International Journal of Asian Business and Information Management*, *11*(3), 15–31.

Rao, C. H. G., Doppala, B. P., Swathi, K., & Rao, N. T. (2021). Development of an Automated CGPBI Model Suitable for HEIs in India. In *Machine Intelligence and Soft Computing* (pp. 185–196). Springer.

Rao, C. H. G., Kosaraju, P. K., & Kim, H. J. (2017). Performance Based Incentives Policy: A Geometric Hybrid Model. *International Journal of Advanced Science and Technology*, *102*, 1–16. doi:10.14257/ijast.2017.102.01

Ravesteijn, P., & Ongena, G. (2019). The role of E-leadership in relation to IT capabilities and digital transformation. IADIS Proceedings.

Raza, B. (2016). Leadership 4.0. Module: Management Competencies 1 (MC1) (Master's thesis, Frankfurt University of Applied Sciences, Frankfurt, Germany).

Raza, S. H., & Mehmood, D. B. (2014). Efficiency differences among law enforcing units in Punjab, Pakistan: Application of Data Envelopment Analysis. *Pakistan Journal of Applied Economics*, 17–37.

Reed, A. H., Henry, R. J., & Mason, W. B. (1971). Influence of Statistical Method Used on the Resulting Estimate of Normal Range. *Clinical Chemistry*, *17*(4), 275–284. doi:10.1093/clinchem/17.4.275 PMID:5552364

Rehberger, M., & Hiete, M. (2020). Allocation of environmental impacts in circular and cascade use of resources—Incentive-driven allocation as a prerequisite for cascade persistence. *Sustainability*, *12*(11), 4366. doi:10.3390u12114366

Rensis, L. (1932). Technique for the Measurement of Attitudes. *Archives of Psychology*.

Resources, B. (2005). *The Thrusts and Strategies of the Brunei Darussalam's E-Government Programme*. Retrieved June 23, 2019, from http://www.bruneiresources.com/speeches/pehinhazair_strategiesegovernment.html

Restubog, S. L. D., Bordia, P., & Tang, R. L. (2007). Behavioural outcomes of psychological contract breach in a non-western culture: The moderating role of equity sensitivity. *British Journal of Management*, *18*(4), 376–386. doi:10.1111/j.1467-8551.2007.00531.x

Rezai, G., Mohamed, Z., & Shamsudin, M. N. (2011). *Malaysian Consumer's Perceptive Towards Purchasing Organically Produce Vegetable (2nd International Conference on Business and Economic Research (2nd ICBER 2011) Proceeding, Issues 2011–310).* Conference Master Resources. https://econpapers.repec.org/RePEc:cms:2icb11:2011-310

Richardson, R. (1999). *Performance related pay in schools: An assessment of the green papers: A report prepared for the National Union of Teachers.* London School of Economics and Political Science.

Ringim, K. J., & Reni, A. (2018) Mediating effect of Social Media on the Consumer Buying Behaviour of Cosmetic Products. In *The 3rdInternational Conference on Accounting Management and Economics (ICAME) 1- 23.* Hassanuddin University.

RitchieH.RoserM. (2018, September). *Plastic pollution.* Retrieved from https://ourworldindata.org/plastic-pollution#total-plastic-waste-by-country

Ritter, M., Borchardt, M., Vaccaro, G. L. R., Pereira, G. M., & Almeida, F. (2015). Motivations for Promoting The Consumption Of Green Products In An Emerging Country: Exploring Attitudes Of Brazilian Consumers. *Journal of Cleaner Production, 106*, 507–520. doi:10.1016/j.jclepro.2014.11.066

Rizos, V., Tuokko, K., & Behrens, A. (2017). *The Circular Economy: A review of definitions, processes and impacts.* Academic Press.

Robbins, S. J. (2013). *Organizational Behavior* (15th ed.). Pearson.

Robbins, S. P., & Coulter, M. (2002). *Management* (7th ed.). Prentice Hall.

Roberts, N., & Grover, V. (2011). Investigating firm's customer agility and firm performance. the importance of aligning sense and respond capabilities. *Journal of Business Research, 64*(3), 1–7.

Robinson, R., & Smith, C. C. (2002). Psychosocial and Demographic Variables Associated with Consumer Intention to Purchase Sustainable Produced Foods as Defined by the Midwest Food Alliance. *Journal of Nutrition Education and Behavior, 34*(6), 316–325.

Robinson, S. L., Kraatz, M. S., & Rousseau, D. M. (1994). Changing obligations and the psychological contract: A longitudinal study. *Academy of Management Journal, 37*(1), 137–152.

Roca-Puig, V., & Bou-Llusar, J. C. (2007). Organizational fit and performance in Miles and Snow's configurational Theory: A covariant analysis. *Management Research, 5*(1), 17–28. doi:10.2753/JMR1536-5433050102

Rockoff, J. E. (2004). The impact of individual teachers on student achievement: Evidence from panel data. *The American Economic Review, 94*(2), 247–252. doi:10.1257/0002828041302244

Rockwell, S. (2019). A resource-based framework for strategically managing identity. *Journal of Organizational Change Management, 32*(1), 80–102. doi:10.1108/JOCM-01-2018-0012

Rodriguez, J., & Walters, K. (2017). The importance of training and development in employee performance and evaluation. *World Wide Journal of Multidisciplinary Research and Development, 3*(10), 206–212.

Rodwell, J. J., Kienzle, R., & Shadur, M. (1998). The Relationships Among Work-Related Perceptions, Employee Attitudes, And Employee Performance: The Integral Role Of Communication. *Human Resource Management, 37*(3 & 4), 277–293. doi:10.1002/(SICI)1099-050X(199823/24)37:3/4<277::AID-HRM9>3.0.CO;2-E

Rohila, A., Yadav, K., & Ghanghas, B. (2017). Role of Information and communication technology (ICT) in agriculture and extension. *Journal of Applied and Natural Science, 9*(2), 1097–1100. doi:10.31018/jans.v9i2.1328

Romani, J. (2009). *Strategies to promote the development of e-competencies in the next generation of professionals: European and international trends*. Available online at: http://www.cardiff.ac.uk/socsi/research/researchcentres/skope/publications/monograp hs/monograph13.pdf

Rosnan, H., Saihani, S., Yusoff, N., & Norzaidi, M. D. (2014). Export Readiness Among Small- and Medium-Sized Enterprises in Malaysia. *AAGBS International Conference on Business Management*, 57–64.

Roy, A., & Sekhar, C., & Vyas, V. (2016). Barriers to internationalization: A study of small and medium enterprises in India. *Journal of International Entrepreneurship*, *14*, 513–538. doi:10.100710843-016-0187-7

Rudman, R. (2020). *Performance planning and review: Making employee appraisals work*. Routledge. doi:10.4324/9781003116684

Rudolf, G., Fertner, C., Kramar, H., Kalasek, R., Pichler-Milanovic, N., & Meijers, E. (2007). *Smart Cities-Ranking of European Medium-Sized Cities*. Rapport technique, Vienna Centre of Regional Science. Retrieved from: http://curis.ku.dk/ws/files/37640170/smart_cities_final_report.pdf

Ruel, H. J. M., Bondarouk, T., & van der Velde, M. (2007). The contribution of e-HRM to HRM effectiveness. Results from a quantitative study in a Dutch Ministry. *Employee Relations*, *29*(3), 280–291. doi:10.1108/01425450710741757

Rvo. (2015). *Smart Cities in India*. Retrieved from www.rvo.nl/sites/smart/cities/india: http://www. rvo.nl/ sites/default/files/Smart%20Cities%20India.pdf

Ryan, R. M., & Deci, E. L. (2000). Intrinsic and Extrinsic Motivations: Classic Definitions and New Directions. *Contemporary Educational Psychology*, *25*(1), 54–67. doi:10.1006/ceps.1999.1020 PMID:10620381

Rynes, S. L., Gerhart, B., & Minette, K. A. (2004). The importance of pay in employee motivation: Discrepancies between what people say and what they do. *Human Resource Management*, *43*(4), 381–394.

S., C., V., J., S, K. N., G., R., & V., R. D. (2020). A Study on the Effectiveness of Human Resource Information System (HRIs) on Bureau Veritas Consumer Product Services (India) Pvt. Ltd. *NOLEGEIN-Journal of Human Resource Management & Development*, 1–9. http://mbajournals.in/index.php/JoHRMD/article/view/624

S., K., & Price, C. (2014). *Beyond Performance: How Great Organizations Build Ultimate Competitive Advantage*. New York: Wiley.

Saatcioglu, O. Y. (2007). *What determines user satisfaction in erp projects: benefits, barriers or risks*. Retrieved August 12, 2018, from https://pdfs.semanticscholar.org/02e0/ fd1caef0c5c47c9488dfb952d3f360c0f5d3.pdf

Sachdeva, S., Jordan, J., & Mazar, N. (2015). Green consumerism: Moral motivations to a sustainable future. *Current Opinion in Psychology*, *6*, 60–65. doi:10.1016/j.copsyc.2015.03.029

Saha, N., Chatterjee, B., Gregar, A., & Sáha, P. (2016). The impact of SHRM on sustainable organizational learning and performance development. *International Journal of Organizational Leadership*, *5*(1), 63–75. doi:10.33844/ijol.2016.60291

Saha, S. K. (2015). A study on the Internet Usage Pattern of Doctors. *CBS Journal of Management Practices*, *2*(1), 113–122.

Saha, S. K. (2016). What are Medical Students Doing Online. *A Study in Kolkata, India. Arabian J Bus Manag Review*, *6*(214), 2.

Sahoo, S. S., Mukunda, B. G., & Kanungo, D. (2019). Smart City and Tourism: An Analysis of Development of Bhubaneswar as a Smart City. *International Journal of Research and Analytical Review*, *6*(1), 246–256.

Salahuddin, L., Ismail, Z., Hashim, U. R., Ikram, R., & Ismail, N. H., & Naim, M. H. (2018). Sociotechnical factors influencing unsafe use of hospital information systems: A qualitative study in Malaysian government hospitals. *Health Informatics Journal*. Retrieved February 8, 2019, from sci-hub.tw/10.1177/1460458218759698 PMID:29521162

Saleem, J. J., Russ, A. L., Justice, C. F., Hagg, H., Ebright, P. R., Woodbridge, P. A., & Doebbeling, B. N. (2009). Exploring the persistence of paper with the electronic health record. *International Journal of Medical Informatics*, *78*(9), 618–628. doi:10.1016/j.ijmedinf.2009.04.001 PMID:19464231

Saleki, R., Quoquab, F., & Mohammad, J. (2019). What drives Malaysian consumers' organic food purchase intention? The role of moral norm, self-identity, environmental concern and price consciousness. *Journal of Agribusiness in Developing and Emerging Economies*, *9*(5), 584–603. doi:10.1108/JADEE-02-2019-0018

Samson, A., & Voyer, B. G. (2014). Emergency purchasing situations: Implications for consumer decision-making. *Journal of Economic Psychology*, *44*, 21–33. doi:10.1016/j.joep.2014.05.004

Samuel, O. W., Omisore, M. O., & Atajeromavwo, E. J. (2014). Online fuzzy based decision support system for human resource performance appraisal. *Measurement*, *55*, 452–461. doi:10.1016/j.measurement.2014.05.024

Sanchez, A. A., Marin, G. S., & Morales, A. M. (2015). The mediating effect of strategic human resource practices on knowledge management and firm performance. *Revista Europea de Dirección y Economía de la Empresa*, *24*(3), 138–148. doi:10.1016/j.redee.2015.03.003

Saphores, J. D. M., Ogunseitan, O. A., & Shapiro, A. A. (2012). Willingness to engage in a pro-environmental behavior: An analysis of e-waste recycling based on a national survey of US households. *Resources, Conservation and Recycling*, *60*, 49–63. doi:10.1016/j.resconrec.2011.12.003

Sarumathi, S. (2014). Green Purchase Behavior–A Conceptual Framework of Socially Conscious Consumer Behavior. *Global Journal of Finance and Management*, *6*(8), 777–782.

Saunders, M., Lewis, P., & Thornhill, A. (2009). *Research Methods for Business Students* (5th Edition). Financial Times/ Prentice Hall.

Saunders, M. N. K., Gray, D. E., & Goregaokar, H. (2013). SME innovation and learning: The role of networks and crisis events. *European Journal of Training and Development*, *38*(2), 136–148. doi:10.1108/EJTD-07-2013-0073

Savrul, M., Incekara, A., & Sener, S. (2014). The Potential of E-commerce for SMEs in a Globalizing Business Environment. *Procedia: Social and Behavioral Sciences*, *150*, 35–45.

Scaria, A. G. (2013). Online piracy of Indian movies: Is the film industry firing at the wrong target. *Mich. St. U. Coll. L. Int'l L. Rev.*, *21*, 647. doi:10.2139srn.2175621

Schappe, S. P., & Doran, A. C. (1997). How does fair treatment affect employee commitment to an organization? A field study of financial holding company employees. *The Mid-Atlantic Journal of Business*, *33*(3), 191.

Schaufeli, W. B., Bakker, A., & Salanova, M. (2006). The Measurement of Work Engagement With a Short Questionnaire: A Cross-National Study. *Educational and Psychological Measurement*, *66*(4), 701–716. doi:10.1177/0013164405282471

Schaufeli, W. B., Martínez, I., Marques Pinto, A., Salanova, M., & Bakker, A. (2002). Burnout and Engagement in University Students: A Cross-National Study. *Journal of Cross-Cultural Psychology*, *33*(5), 464–481. doi:10.1177/0022022102033005003

Schembri, P., & Petit, O. (2009). Clean technology transfers and North-South technological gap: An important issue for environmental policies. *Inter Economics*, *120*, 109–130.

Schindler, P. L., & Thomas, C. C. (1993). The structure of interpersonal trust in the workplace. *Psychological Reports, 73*(2), 563–573. doi:10.2466/pr0.1993.73.2.563

Schjoedt, L., & Sangboon, K. (2015). Control Variables: Problematic Issues and Best Practices. In The Palgrave Handbook of Research Design in Business and Management (pp. 239-261). Palgrave Macmillan.

Schmidt, R. A. (1996). Serving the Euro-consumer: A marketing challenge or a case for intervention? *Marketing Intelligence & Planning, 14*(5), 14–19. doi:10.1108/02634509610127527

Schoemaker, P. J., Heaton, S., & Teece, D. (2018). Innovation, dynamic capabilities, and leadership. *California Management Review, 61*(1), 15-42.

Schuler, R. S. (2000). The internationalization of human resource management. *Journal of International Management, 6*(3), 239–260. doi:10.1016/S1075-4253(00)00025-9

Schuler, R. S., & MacMillan, I. C. (1984). Gaining competitive advantage through human resource management practices. *Human Resource Management, 23*(3), 241–255. doi:10.1002/hrm.3930230304

Schuler, R., & Jackson, S. E. (2014). Human resource management and organizational effectiveness: Yesterday and today. *Journal of Organizational Effectiveness: People and Performance, 1*(1), 35–55. doi:10.1108/JOEPP-01-2014-0003

Schwab, K., & Davis, N. (2018). *Shaping the Fourth Industrial Revolution* (1st ed.). Crown Publishing Group.

Sciglimpaglia, D., & Saghafi, M. (2005). Marketing consequences of European internal market unification: An executive perspective. *Journal of Euromarketing, 14*(1/2), 35–57. doi:10.1300/J037v14n01_03

Scott, S. G., & Bruce, R. A. (1994). Determinants of innovative behavior: A path model of individual innovation in the workplace. *Academy of Management Journal, 37*(3), 580–607.

Sekaran, U., & Bougie, R. (2010). *Research Methods for Business: A Skill Building Approach* (5th ed.). John Wiley & Sons.

Sekaran, U., & Bougie, R. (2016). *Research Methods for Busines: A Skill Building Approach* (7th ed.). Wiley.

Sekaran, U., & Bougie, R. (2016). *Research methods for business: A skill building approach.* John Wiley & Sons.

Seker, F., Ertugrul, H. M., & Cetin, M. (2015). The Impact of Foreign Direct Investment on Environmental Quality: A Bounds Testing and Causality Analysis for Turkey. *Renewable & Sustainable Energy Reviews, 52*, 347–356.

Sekhon, A. K., & Kathuria, L. M. (2019). Corporate Social Responsibility: A Case Study of Vardhman Textiles Limited in India. *MANTHAN: Journal of Commerce and Management, 6*(2), 105. doi:10.17492/manthan.v6i2.187351

Selvalakshmi, M., Verma, H., & Jain, N. (2020). Emergence of Indian Film Industry in the International Markets: Facilitators and Impeders. *International Journal of Asian Business and Information Management, 11*(3), 32–44. doi:10.4018/IJABIM.2020070103

Semler, S. W. (1997). Systematic agreement: A theory of organizational alignment. *Human Resource Development Quarterly, 8*(1), 23–40. doi:10.1002/hrdq.3920080105

Seo, H. M., Kim, M. C., Chang, K., & Kim, T. (2016). Influence of interpersonal trust on innovative behaviour of service workers: Mediating effects of knowledge sharing. *International Journal of Innovation Management, 20*(02), 1650026. doi:10.1142/S1363919616500262

Seong, J. Y. (2011). The effects of high performance work systems, entrepreneurship and organizational culture on organizational performance. *Seoul Journal of Business, 17*(1), 3–36. doi:10.35152nusjb.2011.17.1.001

Seoul Newspaper. (2017, March 1). KT Wins Glomo Awards. *Seoul Newspaper*. https://www.seoul.co.kr/news/newsView.php?id=20170302021023&wlog_tag3=naver

Sever, I. (2015). Importance-performance analysis: A valid management tool? *Tourism Management*, *48*, 43–53. doi:10.1016/j.tourman.2014.10.022

Sevkli, M., Zaim, S., Turkyilmaz, A., & Satir, M. (2010, July). An application of fuzzy Topsis method for supplier selection. In *International Conference on Fuzzy Systems* (pp. 1-7). IEEE. 10.1109/FUZZY.2010.5584006

Seymour, T. J., Frantsvog, D., & Graeber, T. (2012). Electronic Health Records (EHR). *American Journal of Health Sciences*, *3*(3), 201–210. doi:10.19030/ajhs.v3i3.7139

Shabani, N., Mahboobeh, A., Mohammad, T., Hamed, B., & Marjan, N. F. (2013). The Study of Green Consumers' Characteristics and Available Green Sectors in the Market. *International Research Journal of Applied and Basic Sciences*, *4*(7), 1880–1883.

Shafik, N., & Bandyopadhyay, S. (1992). Economic growth and environmental quality: time-series and cross-country evidence. World Bank Publications.

Shahbaz, M., Nasreen, S., Abbas, F., & Anis, O. (2015). Does Foreign Direct Investment Impede Environmental Quality in High, Middle and Low-income Countries? *Energy Economics*, *51*, 275–287.

Shah, N. Z. (2008). Are graduates to be blamed? Unemployment of computer science graduates in Malaysia. *Computer Science*, *3*, 19–5.

Shalley, C. E., & Gilson, L. L. (2004). What leaders need to know: A review of social and contextual factors that can foster or hinder creativity. *The Leadership Quarterly*, *15*(1), 33–53. doi:10.1016/j.leaqua.2003.12.004

Shankar, K. S., & Ram, K. R. (2021). *Changing movie viewing patterns of moviegoers and the rise of multiplex theatres in India: Is it the end of the show for single-screen theatres*. Academic Press.

Shao, Y. (2018). Does FDI affect carbon intensity? New evidence from dynamic panel analysis. *International Journal of Climate Change Strategies and Management*, *10*(1), 27–42. https://doi.org/10.1108/IJCCSM-03-2017-0062

Sharaf, M. A., & Perumal, S. (2018). How Does Green Products' Price and Availability Impact Malaysians' Green Purchasing Behavior? *The Journal of Social Sciences Research*, *4*(3), 28–34.

Sharma, B., Saha, S. K., & Jha, A. (2020). Understanding Inter-Relational Dynamics of Different Factors Impacting the Cymbidium Orchids-Based Economy in Sikkim, India Using DEMATAL. In *Handbook of Research on Managerial Practices and Disruptive Innovation in Asia* (pp. 282–299). IGI Global. doi:10.4018/978-1-7998-0357-7.ch016

Sharma, S. (2019). The role of perceived value and gender on customers' purchase intention of ride sharing services. *International Journal of Asian Business and Information Management*, *10*(4), 31–46. doi:10.4018/IJABIM.2019100103

Sharma, Y. (2011). Changing consumer behaviour with respect to green marketing–a case study of consumer durables and retailing. *International Journal of Multidisciplinary Research*, *1*(4), 152–162.

Shavarini, S. K., Salimian, H., Nazemi, J., & Alborzi, M. (2013). Operations strategy and business strategy alignment model (case of Iranian industries). *International Journal of Operations & Production Management*, *33*(9), 1108–1130. doi:10.1108/IJOPM-12-2011-0467

Sheth, J. N., Newman, B. I., & Gross, B. L. (1991). Why we buy what we buy: A theory of consumption values. *Journal of Business Research*, *22*(2), 159–170. doi:10.1016/0148-2963(91)90050-8

Shevlin, H. (2020). Rethinking creative intelligence: Comparative psychology and the concept of creativity. *European Journal for Philosophy of Science, 11*(1), 16. Advance online publication. doi:10.100713194-020-00323-8

Shilpa, V., & Gopal, R. (2011). The implications of implementing electronic- human resource management (E-HRM) systems in companies. *Journal of Information Systems and Communication, 2*(1), 10–29.

Shin, J., Choi, S., & Moon, T. (2009). Empirical study on the flow experience and intention to repurchase of mobile contents service. *Internet E-Commerce Research, 9*(3), 115–132.

Shirokova, G., Vega, G., & Sokolova, L. (2013). Performance of Russian SMEs: Exploration, exploitation and strategic entrepreneurship. *Critical Perspectives on International Business, 9*(2), 173–203. doi:10.1108/17422041311299941

Siddiqui, S., & Rakesh, S. (2018). Digitalization and E-Commerce in India: An Employment Generation Initiative. *Intl. J. Adv. Res. Comm & Mgmt, 4*(2), 1–11.

Sidek, Y. H., & Martins, J. T. (2017). Perceived critical success factors of electronic health record system implementation in a dental clinic context: An organisational management perspective. *International Journal of Medical Informatics, 107*, 88–100. doi:10.1016/j.ijmedinf.2017.08.007 PMID:29029696

Sigala, M. (2020). Tourism and Covid 19: Impacts and Implications for Advancing and Resetting Industry and Research. *Journal of Business Research, 17*, 312–321. doi:10.1016/j.jbusres.2020.06.015 PMID:32546875

Sikora, H. (2017). Digital Age Management: Leadership in the Digital Age. *E & I Electrical Engineering and Information Technology, 134*(7), 344-348.

Silow-Carrol, S., Edwards, J. N., & Rodin, D. (2012). *Using Electronic Health Records to Improve Quality and Efficiency: The Experience of Leading Hospitals.* Retrieved November 5, 2018 from The Commonwealth Fund: https://pdfs.semanticscholar.org/0e75/8272eab4ba74933ed4fdf860362f2365f3d3.pdf

Silva, J. R., Franco, M., & Magrinho, A. (2016). Empirical investigation of the effects of industry type and firm size on export barriers. *Journal of Business. Economics and Management, 17*(6), 1052–1065. doi:10.3846/16111699.2016.1143874

Sims, C. A. (1972). Money, income and causality. *The American Economic Review, 62*, 540–552.

Simsek, Z., Heavey, C., Veiga, J. F., & Souder, D. (2009). A typology for aligning organizational ambidexterity's conceptualizations, antecedents, and outcomes. *Journal of Management Studies, 46*(5), 864–894.

Singh, D. (2017). Police Training in Punjab: An Evaluating Study towards training facilities at PPA, Phillaur. *International Research Journal of Commerce Arts and Science, 8*(9).

Singh, R. (2018). Formal human resource management (HRM) Practices and the performance of small & medium-sized enterprises (SMEs): A study of SMEs in the Caribbean nation of Trinidad. *Journal of Elasticity, 42*(2), 53–80.

Sinkovics, R. R., Kurt, Y., & Sinkovics, N. (2018). The effect of matching on perceived export barriers and performance in an era of globalization discontents: Empirical evidence from UK SMEs. *International Business Review, 27*(5), 1065–1079. https://doi.org/10.1016/j.ibusrev.2018.03.007

Sinnappan, P., & Abd Rahman, A. (2011). Antecedents of green purchasing behaviour among Malaysian consumers. *International Business Management, 5*(3), 129–139. doi:10.3923/ibm.2011.129.139

Slåtten, T., & Mehmetoglu, M. (2011). What are the drivers for innovative behavior in frontline jobs? A study of the hospitality industry in Norway. *Journal of Human Resources in Hospitality & Tourism, 10*(3), 254–272. doi:10.1080/15332845.2011.555732

Small and Medium Industries Development Corporation Malaysia. (2006). *SME Performance Report 2005.* Author.

Smart City Governments (SCG). (2021). *Top 50 Smart City Governments: Introduction*. Retrieved from: https://www.smartcitygovt.com/introduction

Smith Travel Research. (2019). https://www.str.com/

Smith Travel Research. (2021). https://www.str.com/

Smith, B. (2018). Generalizability in qualitative research: Misunderstandings, opportunities and recommendations for the sport and exercise sciences. *Qualitative Research in Sport, Exercise and Health*, *10*(1), 137–149. doi:10.1080/2159676X.2017.1393221

Smith, J. S., Jayaram, J., Ponsignon, F., & Wolter, J. S. (2019). Service recovery system antecedents: A contingency theory investigation. *Journal of Service Management*, *30*(2), 276–300. doi:10.1108/JOSM-01-2018-0026

Smith, K. A., Vasudevan, S. P., & Tanniru, M. R. (1996). Organizational learning and resource-based theory: An integrative model. *Journal of Organizational Change Management*, *9*(6), 41–53. doi:10.1108/09534819610150512

Smith, N. C. (2003). Corporate social responsibility: Whether or how? *California Management Review*, *45*(4), 52–76. doi:10.2307/41166188

Smoliar, S. W., & Sprague, R. (2003). Technology Support for Communication and Understanding. *Journal of Decision Systems*, *2*(2), 123–139. doi:10.3166/jds.12.123-139

Snell, S. A., Stueber, D., & Lepak, D. P. (2001). Virtual HR departments: Getting out of the middle. *Cornell University*. Retrieved August 12, 2018, from https://digitalcommons. Ilr.cornell.edu/cgi/viewcontent.cgi?referer=https://www.google.com/&httpsredir=1&article=1070&context=cahrswp

Sobel, M. E. (1982). Asymptotic confidence intervals for indirect effects in structural equation models. *Sociological Methodology*, *13*, 290–312. doi:10.2307/270723

Sojka, L. (2015). Investigation the relationship between human resource management practices and firm's finance performance. *European Scientific Journal*, *11*(34), 87–105.

Solaiman, M., Halim, M. S. A., Manaf, A. H. A., & Nor Azila, M. N., Noor, & Rana, S. M. S. (2017). Consumption values and green purchase behavior: An empirical study. *International Business Management*, *11*(6), 1223–1233.

Solmon, L. C., & Podgursky, M. (2000). *The Pros and Cons of Performance-Based Compensation*. Academic Press.

Somasundram, C., Razali, Z., & Santhirasegaram, V. (2016). A review on organic food production in Malaysia. *Horticulturae*, *2*(3), 12–18. doi:10.3390/horticulturae2030012

Song, W., Yu, H., Zhang, Y., & Jiang, W. (2015). Goal orientation and employee creativity: The mediating role of creative role identity. *Journal of Management & Organization*, *21*(1), 82–97. doi:10.1017/jmo.2014.64

Son, N. T. X. (2020). Policy on marine plastic waste in ASEAN and Viet Nam. *Environmental Claims Journal*, 1–13. doi:10.1080/10406026.2020.1775347

Soon, C. C., & Salamzadeh, Y. (2021). The impact of Digital Leadership Competencies on Virtual Team Effectiveness in MNC companies in Penang, Malaysia. Journal of Entrepreneurship. *Business Economics (Cleveland, Ohio)*, *8*(2), 219–253.

Sooreh, L. K., Salamzadeh, A., Safarzadeh, H., & Salamzadeh, Y. (2011). Defining and measuring entrepreneurial universities: A study in Iranian context using importance-performance analysis and TOPSIS technique. *Global Business and Management Research*, *3*(2), 182–199.

Sousa, H. P., & Leite, J. C. S. (2014). Modeling Organizational Alignment. In E. Yu, G. Dobbie, M. Jarke, & S. Purao (Eds.), Lecture Notes in Computer Science: Vol. 8824. *Conceptual Modeling*. Springer. doi:10.1007/978-3-319-12206-9_34

Spangler, W. D. (1992). Validity of questionnaire and TAT measures of need for achievement: Two meta-analyses. *Psychological Bulletin*, *112*(1), 140–154. doi:10.1037/0033-2909.112.1.140

Spector, P. E. (2020). Mastering the Use of Control Variables: The Hierarchical Iterative Control (HIC) Approach. *Journal of Business and Psychology*, 1–14. doi:10.100710869-020-09709-0

Springer, M. G., & Taylor, L. L. (2016). Designing incentives for public school teachers: Evidence from a Texas incentive pay program. *Journal of Education Finance*, *41*(3), 344–381. doi:10.1353/jef.2016.0001

Staffen, S., & Schoenwald, L. (2016). *Leading in the Context of the Industrial Revolution*. https://www.capgemini.com/consulting-de/wp-content/uploads/sites/ 32/2017/08/resouces_leader_40_industrial_revolution.pdf

Steininger, K., Stiglbauer, B., Baumgartner, B., & Engleder, B. (2014). Factors Explaining Physicians' Acceptance of Electronic Health Records. In *47th Hawaii International Conference on System Science* (pp. 2768-2777). Retrieved February 10, 2019 from https://ieeexplore.ieee.org/stamp/stamp.jsp?tp=&arnumber=6758948

Stern. (2000). *Stern's Attitude-Behaviour-Context Model*. Retrieved 2019, June 19th, from http://www.cres.gr/behave/pdf/Stern_ABC_model.pdf

Stillitano, T., Spada, E., Iofrida, N., Falcone, G., & De Luca, A. I. (2021). Sustainable Agri-Food Processes and Circular Economy Pathways in a Life Cycle Perspective: State of the Art of Applicative Research. *Sustainability*, *13*(5), 2472. doi:10.3390u13052472

Strand, R. (2011). Exploring the role of leadership in corporate social responsibility: *A review. Journal of Leadership, Accountability and Ethics*, *8*(4), 86–96.

Street, R. Jr, Liu, L., Farber, N. J., Chen, Y., Calvitti, A., Zuest, D., Gabuzda, M. T., Bell, K., Gray, B., Rick, S., Ashfaq, S., & Agha, Z. (2014). Provider interaction with the electronic health record: The effects on patient-centered communication in medical encounters. *Patient Education and Counseling*, *96*(3), 315–319. doi:10.1016/j.pec.2014.05.004 PMID:24882086

Strohmeier, S. (2009). Concepts of e-HRM consequences: A categorisation, review and suggestion. *International Journal of Human Resource Management*, *20*(3), 528–543. doi:10.1080/09585190802707292

Strohmeier, S., & Kabst, R. (2014). Configurations of E-HRM an Empirical Exploration. *Employee Relations*, *36*(4), 333–353. doi:10.1108/ER-07-2013-0082

Styvén, M. E., & Mariani, M. M. (2020). Understanding the intention to buy secondhand clothing on sharing economy platforms: The influence of sustainability, distance from the consumption system, and economic motivations. *Psychology and Marketing*, *37*(5), 1–16. doi:10.1002/mar.21334

Suh, T., & Kwon, L.-W. (2002). Globalization and reluctant buyers. *International Marketing Review*, *19*(6), 663–680. doi:10.1108/02651330210451962

Suki, N. M. (2016). Consumer environmental concern and green product purchase in Malaysia: Structural effects of consumption values. *Journal of Cleaner Production*, *132*, 204–214. doi:10.1016/j.jclepro.2015.09.087

Sultana, R. G. (2009). Competence and competence frameworks in career guidance: Complex and contested concepts. *International Journal for Educational and Vocational Guidance*, *9*(1), 15–30. doi:10.100710775-008-9148-6

Sun, C. C., & Lin, G. T. (2009). Using fuzzy TOPSIS method for evaluating the competitive advantages of shopping websites. *Expert Systems with Applications*, *36*(9), 11764–11771. doi:10.1016/j.eswa.2009.04.017

Su, X. (2007). Intertemporal pricing with strategic consumer behavior. *Management Science*, *53*(5), 726–741. doi:10.1287/mnsc.1060.0667

Swanson, D., Jin, Y. H., Fawcett, A. M., & Fawcett, S. E. (2017). Collaborative process design: A dynamic capabilities view of mitigating the barriers to working together. *International Journal of Logistics Management*, *28*(2), 571–599. doi:10.1108/IJLM-02-2016-0044

Tabachnick, B., & Fidell, L. (2013). Using Multivariate Statistics (6th ed.). Pearson Education Limited.

Takahashi, K. (2006). Effects of wage and promotion incentives on the motivation levels of Japanese employees. *Career Development International*, *11*(3), 193–203. doi:10.1108/13620430610661722

Talluri, K., & Ryzin, G. (2004). The Theory and Practice of Revenue Management. Springer. doi:10.1007/b139000

Tamayo-Torres, I., Gutiérrez-Gutiérrez, L. J., Llorens-Montes, F. J., & Martínez-López, F. J. (2016). Organizational learning and innovation as sources of strategic fit. *Industrial Management & Data Systems*, *116*(8), 1445–1467. doi:10.1108/IMDS-12-2015-0518

Tam, V. W. Y., & Fung, I. W. H. (2012). Behavior, attitude, and perception toward safety culture from mandatory safety training course. *Journal of Professional Issues in Engineering Education and Practice*, *138*(3), 207–213. doi:10.1061/(ASCE)EI.1943-5541.0000104

Tanakasempipat, P. (2019, November 13). *Southeast Asian countries need tougher plastic policies to curb pollution: U.N.* Retrieved from https://www.reuters.com/article/us-asia-plastic-idUSKBN1XN1QL

Tan, B. C., & Lau, T. C. (2010). Attitude towards the environment and green products: Consumers' perspective. *Journal of Management Science and Engineering*, *4*(2), 27–39.

Tan, C. L. T., Smyrnios, K. X., & Xiong, L. (2014). What drives learning orientation in fast growth SMEs? *International Journal of Entrepreneurial Behaviour & Research*, *20*(4), 324–350. doi:10.1108/IJEBR-02-2013-0032

Tang, S. M. (2014). *Factors That Influence Green Purchase Behaviour of Malaysian Consumers* [Masters Thesis]. Universiti Tunku Abdul Rahman.

Tang. (2014). *Factors That Influence Green Purchase Behaviour of Malaysian Consumers* [Masters Thesis]. Universiti Tunku Abdul Rahman. Retrieved 2019, June 19th from http://eprints.utar.edu.my/1299/1/Final_Research_Project_(MBA).pdf

Tang, T. L., & Chiu, R. K. (2003). Income, money ethic, pay satisfaction, commitment, and unethical behavior: Is the love of money the root of evil for Hong Kong employees? *Journal of Business Ethics*, *46*(1), 13–30. doi:10.1023/A:1024731611490

Tang, T. L., Shin-Hsiung, D., & Arocas, R. (2005). Money Profiles: The Love of Money, Attitudes, and Needs. *Personnel Review*, *34*(5), 603–618. doi:10.1108/00483480510612549

Tan, J., & Tan, D. (2004). Environment-strategy co-evolution and co-alignment: A staged model of Chinese SOEs under transition. *Strategic Management Journal*, *26*(2), 141–157. doi:10.1002mj.437

Tan, L. L., Abd Aziz, N., & Ngah, A. H. (2020). Mediating effect of reasons on the relationship between altruism and green hotel patronage intention. *Journal of Marketing Analytics*, *8*(1), 18–30. Advance online publication. doi:10.105741270-020-00067-7

Tapachai, N., & Waryszak, R. (2000). An examination of the role of beneficial image in tourist destination selection. *Journal of Travel Research*, *39*(1), 37–44. doi:10.1177/004728750003900105

Taube, F.A., & Lorenzen, M. (n.d.). *Bollywood and the Banyan Tree Organization: Leveraging Family Interconnectedness in the Indian Film Industry*. Academic Press.

Teeratansirikool, L., Siengthai, S., Badir, Y., & Charoenngam, C. (2013). Competitive strategies and firm performance: The mediating role of performance measurement. *International Journal of Productivity and Performance Management*, *62*(2), 168–184. doi:10.1108/17410401311295722

Teng, Y. M., Wu, K. S., & Liu, H. H. (2015). Integrating altruism and the theory of planned behavior to predict patronage intention of a green hotel. *Journal of Hospitality & Tourism Research (Washington, D.C.)*, *39*(3), 299–315. doi:10.1177/1096348012471383

Teoh, W. C., & Nor Azila, M. N. (2015). The importance of consumers' attitudes towards purchase intention of hybrid car in Malaysia. *Academic Research International*, *6*(4), 111–122.

Testa, F., Pretner, G., Iovino, R., Bianchi, G., Tessitore, S., & Iraldo, F. (2020). Drivers to green consumption: A systematic review. *Environment, Development and Sustainability*. Advance online publication. doi:10.100710668-020-00844-5

Tharenou, P. (2001). The relationship of training motivation to participation in training and development. *Journal of Occupational and Organizational Psychology*, *74*(5), 599–621. doi:10.1348/096317901167541

The ASEAN Post Team. (2019). *Southeast Asia's Internet Economy Booming*. Retrieved from https://theaseanpost.com/article/southeast-asias-internet-economy-booming

The Guardian. (2021). *From Pfizer to Moderna: who's making billions from Covid-19 vaccines?* Available online at https://www.theguardian.com/business/2021/mar/06/from-pfizer-to-moderna-whos-making-billions-from-covid-vaccines

Thomée, S., Härenstam, A., & Hagberg, M. (2012). Computer use and stress, sleep disturbances, and symptoms of depression among young adults—A prospective cohort study. *BMC Psychiatry*, *12*(1), 1–14. doi:10.1186/1471-244X-12-176 PMID:23088719

Thomé, K. M., Cappellesso, G., & Pinho, G. M. (2020). Food consumption values and the influence of physical activity. *British Food Journal*, *123*(3), 943–957. doi:10.1108/BFJ-05-2020-0432

Thompson, A., & Thompson, H. (2010). The Exchange Rate, Euro Switch and Tourism Revenue in Greece. *Tourism Economics*, *16*(3), 773–780. doi:10.5367/000000010792278338

Thornhill, A., Saunders, M., & Lewis, P. (2009). *Research methods for business students*. Prentice Hall.

Tiersky, H. (2017*). 5 top challenges to digital transformation in the enterprise*. Available online at:<https://www.cio.com/article/3179607/e-commerce/5-top-challenges-to-digitaltransformation

Tiraieyari, N., Hamzah, A., & Samah, B. A. (2014). Organic farming and sustainable agriculture in Malaysia: Organic farmers' challenges towards adoption. *Asian Social Science*, *10*(4), 1–7. doi:10.5539/ass.v10n4p1

Tiseo, I. (2020a, June 22). Leading plastic waste importers worldwide 2018. *Statista*. Retrieved from https://www.statista.com/statistics/1127268/plastics-waste-import-shares-by-country-worldwide/

Tiseo, I. (2020b, September 4). Plastic waste worldwide - statistics & facts. *Statista*. Retrieved from https://www.statista.com/topics/5401/global-plastic-waste/

Toda, H. Y., & Phillips, P. C. B. (1993). Vector autoregressions and causality. *Econometrica*, *61*, 1367–1393.

Toda, H. Y., & Yamamoto, T. (1995). Statistical inferences in vector autoregressions with possibly integrated processes. *Journal of Econometrics*, *66*, 225–250.

Toduk, Y. (2014). *2023 Lideri Dijital Çagın Liderlik Sırları* (1st ed.). Dogan Egmont Yayıncılık.

Torres, T. O., & Arias, M. O. (2009). *Human resources information systems: Challenges in e-hrm*. IGI Global.

Tran, X. (2015). Effects of economic factors on demand for luxury hotel rooms in the U.S. *Advances in Hospitality and Tourism Research*, *3*(1), 1–17.

Trepanier, D. (2012). *Define Digital Skills*. Available online at: www.ymcaimpact.ca/content/define-digitalskills#sthash.usCOWpvO.pdf

TripAdvisor. (2017). *Top ten Beaches*. https://tripadvisor.mediaroom.com/press-releases?item=125343

Tripathi, G., & Ahad, M. A. (2017). Impact of excessive use of internet on cognitive development of youngsters. *International Journal of Information Technology (Singapore)*, *9*(3), 281–286. doi:10.100741870-017-0028-5

Tsen, C. H., Phang, G., Hasan, H., & Buncha, M. A. (2006). Going green: A study of consumers' willingness to pay for green products in Kota Kinabalu. *International Journal of Business and Society*, *7*(2), 40–54.

Tseng, K. K. M., & Johnsen, R. E. (2011). Internationalisation and the internet in UK manufacturing SMEs. *Journal of Small Business and Enterprise Development*, *18*(3), 571–593. doi:10.1108/14626001111155571

Tse, T., Esposito, M., & Soufani, K. (2015, November). Why the circular economy matters. *European Business Review*.

Tsoukas, H. (2005). *Complex Knowledge: Studies in Organizational Epistemology*. Oxford Press.

Tucker, L. R., & MacCallum, R. C. (1997). *Exploratory factor analysis*. Retrieved from https://www.unc.edu/~rcm/book/factor.pdf

Tucker, P., & Douglas, P. (2007). *WR0112: understanding household waste prevention behaviour*. Final Report & Technical Reports.

Tuerlinckx, F., De Boeck, P., & Lens, W. (2002). Measuring needs with the Thematic Apperception Test: A psychometric study. *Journal of Personality and Social Psychology*, *82*(3), 448–461. doi:10.1037/0022-3514.82.3.448 PMID:11902627

Tully, S. M., & Winer, R. S. (2014). The role of the beneficiary in willingness to pay for socially responsible products: A meta-analysis. *Journal of Retailing*, *90*(2), 255–274. doi:10.1016/j.jretai.2014.03.004

Turel, O., Serenko, A., & Bontis, N. (2010). User acceptance of hedonic digital artifacts: A theory of consumption values perspective. *Information & Management*, *47*(1), 53–59. doi:10.1016/j.im.2009.10.002

Turner, A. (2017). How does intrinsic and extrinsic motivation drive performance culture in organizations? *Cogent Education*, *4*(1), 1337543. doi:10.1080/2331186X.2017.1337543

Tussyadiah, L. P., & Fesenmaier, D. R. (2009). Mediating Tourist Experience Access to Places Via Shared Video. *Annals of Journal Research*, *36*(1), 24–40.

Tuzunkan, D. (2017). The Relationship between Innovation and Tourism: The Case of Smart Tourism. *International Journal of Applied Engineering Research*, *12*(23), 13861–13867.

Twelfth Malaysia Plan. (2019). *Preparation of the Twelfth Malaysia Plan*. Available online at: http://rmke12.epu.gov.my/

Twomey, D. F., & Harris, D. L. (2000). From strategy to corporate outcomes: Aligning human resource management systems with entrepreneurial intent. *International Journal of Commerce and Management*, *10*(3/4), 43–55. doi:10.1108/eb047408

Uddin, M. A., Priyankara, H. R., & Mahmood, M. (2019). Does a creative identity encourage innovative behaviour? Evidence from knowledge-intensive IT service firms. *European Journal of Innovation Management*, *23*(5), 877–894. doi:10.1108/EJIM-06-2019-0168

UNCRD. (2019). *State of plastics waste in Asia and the Pacific: Issues, challenges and circular economic opportunities.* United Nations Centre for Regional Development (UNCRD).

UNEP & Sida. (2006). Applying Cleaner Production to MEAs – Global Status Report. United Nations Environment Programme, Division of Technology, Industry and Economics.

Uner, M. M., Kose, N., & Gokten, S. (2008). An Econometric Model of Tourism Demand and Room Rates: A Study in Belek, Antalya. *Anatolia*, *19*(1), 41–50. doi:10.1080/13032917.2008.9687052

Unnikrishnan, B., Kulshrestha, V., Saraf, A., Agrahari, A. C., Prakash, S., Samantaray, L., & Parida, A. (2008). Pattern of computer and internet use among medical students in Coastal South India. *South East Asian Journal of Medical Education*, *2*(2), 18–25.

Urban Development and Housing Department (UDHD). (2019). *Techno-Economic Feasibility Report of Cable Car as Public Transport for Gangtok*. Final Report. Urban Mass Transport Company.

Valmohammadi, C. (2011). The impact of TQM implementation on the organizational performance of Iranian manufacturing SMEs. *The TQM Journal*, *23*(5), 496–509. doi:10.1108/17542731111157608

Van Auken, H. E., & Carter, R. B. (1989). Acquisition of capital by small business. *Journal of Small Business Management*, *27*(2), 1.

Van den Branden, M., Wiratunga, N., Burton, D., & Craw, S. (2011). Integrating case-based reasoning with an electronic patient record system. *Artificial Intelligence in Medicine*, *51*(2), 117–123. doi:10.1016/j.artmed.2010.12.004 PMID:21232927

Van Iddekinge, C. H., Aguinis, H., Mackey, J. D., & DeOrtentiis, P. S. (2018). A meta-analysis of the interactive, additive, and relative effects of cognitive ability and motivation on performance. *Journal of Management*, *44*(1), 249–279. doi:10.1177/0149206317702220

Van Laar, E., Van Deursen, A. J. A. M., Van Dijk, J. A. G. M., & De Haan, J. (2017). The relation between 21st-century skills and digital skills: *A systematic literature review. Computers in Human Behavior*, *72*, 577–588. doi:10.1016/j.chb.2017.03.010

van Rooij, T., Ferguson, C. J., de Mheen, D., & Schoenmakers, T. M. (2017). *Time to abandon internet addiction? Predicting problematic internet, game, and social media use from psychosocial well-being and application use.* Clinical Neuropsychiatry.

Van Wart, M., Roman, A., Wang, X., & Liu, C. (2019). Operationalizing the definition of e-leadership: Identifying the elements of e-leadership. *International Review of Administrative Sciences*, *85*(1), 80–97. doi:10.1177/0020852316681446

Van, N.T.T., Vrana, V., Duy, N.T., Minh, D.X.H., Dzung, P.T., Mondol, S.R. & Das, S. (2020). The Role of Human-Machine Interactive Devices for Post Covid 19 Innovative Sustainable Tourism in Ho Chi Minh City, Vietnam. *Sustaiability*, *12*(9523), 1-30.

Vanderstoep, S. W., & Johnson, D. D. (2008). *Research methods for everyday life: Blending qualitative and quantitative approaches* (Vol. 32). John Wiley & Sons.

Vane, J. R. (1981). The Thematic Apperception Test (TAT): A review. *Clinical Psychology Review*, *1*(3), 319–336. doi:10.1016/0272-7358(81)90009-X

Vargas-Hernández, J. G. (2021). Circular-Green Economy: Analysis Based on the Theory of Resources and Capabilities. In Examining the Intersection of Circular Economy, Forestry, and International Trade (pp. 1-17). Academic Press.

Vargo, S. L., & Lusch, R. F. (2004). Evolving a Dominant Logic for Marketing. *Journal of Marketing*, *68*(1), 1–17. doi:10.1509/jmkg.68.1.1.24036

Vasavada, M., & Padhiyar, Y. J. (2016). Smart Tourism: Growth for Tomorrow. *Journal for Research*, *1*(12), 55–61.

Velázquez-Martínez, O., Valio, J., Santasalo-Aarnio, A., Reuter, M., & Serna-Guerrero, R. (2019). A critical review of lithium-ion battery recycling processes from a circular economy perspective. *Batteries*, *5*(4), 68. doi:10.3390/batteries5040068

Veloce, W. (2004). Forecasting Inbound Canadian Tourism: An Evaluation of Error Corrections Model Forecasts. *Tourism Economics*, *10*(3), 262–280. doi:10.5367/0000000041895049

Venkatesh, V., Morris, M. G., Davis, G. B., & Davis, F. D. (2003). User acceptance of information technology: Toward a unified view. *Management Information Systems Quarterly*, *27*(3), 425–478. doi:10.2307/30036540

Verhoest, K., Verschuere, B., & Bouckaert, G. (2007). Pressure, legitimacy, and innovative behavior by public organizations. *Governance: An International Journal of Policy, Administration and Institutions*, *20*(3), 469–497. doi:10.1111/j.1468-0491.2007.00367.x

Vermeir, I., & Verbeke, W. (2006). Sustainable food consumption: Exploring the consumer "attitude – behavioral intention" gap. *Journal of Agricultural & Environmental Ethics*, *19*, 169–194. Retrieved June 11th, 2019, from https://www.eur.nl/sites/corporate/files/Vermeir_and_Verbeke__JAEE__2006.pdf

Vidgen, R., Shaw, S., & Grant, D. B. (2017). Management challenges in creating value from business analytics. *European Journal of Operational Research*, *261*(2), 626–639. doi:10.1016/j.ejor.2017.02.023

Vivekanandan, K., & Rajendran, R. (2006). Export Marketing and The World Wide Web: Perceptions of Export Barriers Among Tirupur Knitwear Apparel Exporters- An Empirical Analysis. *Journal of Electronic Commerce Research*, *7*(1), 27–40.

Vives, A., Jacob, M., & Payeras, M. (2018). Revenue management and price optimization techniques in the hotel sector. *Tourism Economics*, *64*(6), 720–752. doi:10.1177/1354816618777590

Vogel, H. L. (2020). *Entertainment industry economics: A guide for financial analysis*. Cambridge University Press.

Voorbij, H. J. (1999). Searching scientific information on the Internet: A Dutch academic user survey. *Journal of the American Society for Information Science*, *50*(7), 598–615. doi:10.1002/(SICI)1097-4571(1999)50:7<598::AID-ASI5>3.0.CO;2-6

Vu, T. B., Gangnes, B., & Noy, I. (2006). *Is Foreign Direct Investment Good for Growth?: Evidence from Sectoral Analysis of China and Vietnam*. Working Papers 200801, University of Hawaii at Manoa, Department of Economics.

Vui-Yee, K. (2018). Linking training and development to employee turnover intention: are performance management and compensation sequential mediators? *Journal for Global Business Advancement,* 564 - 586.

Wadongo, B., & Abdel-Kader, M. (2014). Contingency theory, performance management and organisational effectiveness in the third sector. *International Journal of Productivity and Performance Management*, *63*(6), 680–703. doi:10.1108/IJPPM-09-2013-0161

Wahid, N. A., Rahbar, E., & Shyan, T. S. (2011). Factors influencing the green purchase behavior of Penang environmental volunteers. *International Business Management*, *5*(1), 38–49. doi:10.3923/ibm.2011.38.49

Waiganjo, E. W., Mukulu, E., & Kahiri, J. (2012). Relationship between strategic human resource management and firm performance of Kenya ' s corporate organizations. *International Journal of Humanities and Social Science*, *2*(10), 62–70.

Walji, M. F., Taylor, D., Langabeer, J. R. II, & Valenza, J. A. (2009). Factors Influencing Implementation and Outcomes of a Dental Electronic Patient Record System. *Journal of Dental Education*, *73*(5), 589–600. doi:10.1002/j.0022-0337.2009.73.5.tb04734.x PMID:19433534

Wambugu, A. W., Gichira, R., Wanjau, K. N., & Mung'atu, J. (2015). The Relationship Between Risk Taking and Performance of Small and Medium Agro-Processing Enterprises In Kenya. *International Journal of Economics. Commerce and Management*, *3*(12), 1–13.

Wang, L., Gao, Y., Yan, J., & Qin, J. (2020). From freemium to premium: the roles of consumption values and game affordance. *Information Technology & People*. doi:10.1108/itp-10-2019-0527

Wang, A. C., & Cheng, B. S. (2010). When does benevolent leadership lead to creativity? The moderating role of creative role identity and job autonomy. *Journal of Organizational Behavior*, *31*(1), 106–121. doi:10.1002/job.634

Wang, C.-J., Tsai, H.-T., & Tsai, M.-T. (2014). Linking transformational leadership and employee creativity in the hospitality industry: The influences of creative role identity, creative self-efficacy, and job complexity. *Tourism Management*, *40*, 79–89. doi:10.1016/j.tourman.2013.05.008

Wang, D., Park, S., & Fesenmaier, D. R. (2010). An examination of information services and smartphone applications. *Proceedings of 16th Annual Graduate Student Research Conference in Hospitality and Tourism.*

Wang, J., Pham, T. L., & Dang, V. T. (2020). Environmental consciousness and organic food purchase intention: A moderated mediation model of perceived food quality and price sensitivity. *International Journal of Environmental Research and Public Health*, *17*(3), 850. doi:10.3390/ijerph17030850 PMID:32013260

Wang, L., Law, R., Hung, K., & Guillet, B. D. (2014). Consumer trust in tourism and hospitality: A review of the literature. *Journal of Hospitality and Tourism Management*, *21*, 1–9. doi:10.1016/j.jhtm.2014.01.001

Wang, X. H., Fang, Y., Qureshi, I., & Janssen, O. (2015). Understanding employee innovative behavior: Integrating the social network and leader–member exchange perspectives. *Journal of Organizational Behavior*, *36*(3), 403–420. doi:10.1002/job.1994

Wang, X., Pacho, F., Liu, J., & Kajungiro, R. (2019). Factors influencing organic food purchase intention in developing countries and the moderating role of knowledge. *Sustainability*, *11*(1), 209. doi:10.3390u11010209

Waugh, R. F. (2002). Creating a scale to measure motivation to achieve academically: Linking attitudes and behaviours using Rasch measurement. *The British Journal of Educational Psychology*, *72*(1), 65–86. doi:10.1348/000709902158775 PMID:11916465

Waugh, W. L. Jr, & Streib, G. (2006). Collaboration and leadership for effective emergency management. *Public Administration Review*, *66*(s1), 131–140. doi:10.1111/j.1540-6210.2006.00673.x

Weaver, T. (1988). Theory M: Motivating with money. *The Cornell Hotel and Restaurant Administration Quarterly*, *29*(3), 40–45. doi:10.1177/001088048802900314

Wee, C. S., Ariff, M. S. B. M., Zakuan, N., Tajudin, M. N. M., Ismail, K., & Ishak, N. (2014). Consumer's perception, purchase intention and actual purchase behaviour of organic food products. *Review of Integrative Business and Economics Research*, *3*(2), 378–397.

Wee, M., Zaki, K. M., Sadik, M. Z., Marmaya, N. H., & Razak, N. A. (2019). The challenges faced by Malaysian Small Medium Entrepreneurs (SMEs) in export initiatives. *ASEAN Entrepreneurship Journal*, *5*(2), 14–19.

Weiskopf, N., Hripcsak, G., Swaminathan, S., & Weng, C. (2013). Defining and measuring completeness of electronic health records for secondary use. *Journal of Biomedical Informatics*, *46*(5), 830–836. doi:10.1016/j.jbi.2013.06.010 PMID:23820016

Wekeza, S., & Sibanda, M. (2019). Factors influencing consumer purchase intentions of organically grown products in shelly centre, Port Shepstone, South Africa. *International Journal of Environmental Research and Public Health*, *16*(6), 956. doi:10.3390/ijerph16060956 PMID:30884921

Wen Lim, H., Li, N., Fang, D., & Wu, C. (2018). Impact of Safety Climate on Types of Safety Motivation and Performance: Multigroup Invariance Analysis. *Journal of Management Engineering*, *34*(3), 04018002. doi:10.1061/(ASCE)ME.1943-5479.0000595

Werner, P. (2004). Reasoned action and planned behaviour. In S. J. Peterson & T. S. Bredow (Eds.), *Middle range theories: Application to nursing research* (pp. 125–147). Lippincott, Williams & Wilkins.

Westerman, G., Bonnet, D., & McAfee, A. (2014). *Leading digital: turning technology into business transformation*. Harvard Business Press.

Whittaker, A. A., Aufdenkamp, M., & Tinley, S. (2009). Barriers and Facilitators to Electronic Documentation in a Rural Hospital. *Journal of Nursing Scholarship, 41*(3), 293-300. Retrieved November 5 5, 2018 from http://sci-hub.tw/https://doi.org/10.1111/j.1547-5069.2009.01278.x

Widiani, N. P., Putri, I., Sari, M. R., & Wirajaya, I. (2019). The Effect of Love of Money and Emotional Intelligence on Employee Performance with Organizational Citizenship Behavior as Mediating Variable. *International Research Journal of Engineering, IT & Scientific Research*, *5*(1), 39–49.

Wijayarathne, J. M. D. S., & Perera, M. P. S. R. (2018). Sri Lankan SMEs and Perceived Export Barriers: Evidence from Manufacturing Sector. *Asian Journal of Economics Business and Accounting*, *7*(3), 1–10.

Williams, B., Onsman, A., & Brown, T. (2010). Exploratory factor analysis: A five-step guide for novices. *Australasian Journal of Paramedicine, 8*(3).

Williamson, B. (2016). Digital education governance: Data visualization, predictive analytics, and 'real-time'policy instruments. *Journal of Education Policy*, *31*(2), 123–141. doi:10.1080/02680939.2015.1035758

Williamson, J. B., & Fleming, J. J. (1996). Convergence theory and the social welfare sector: A cross-national analysis. In A. Inkeles & M. Sasaki (Eds.), *Comparing nations and cultures* (pp. 349–354). Prentice Hall.

Williams, P., & Soutar, G. N. (2009). Value, satisfaction and behavioral intentions in an adventure tourism context. *Annals of Tourism Research*, *36*(3), 413–438. doi:10.1016/j.annals.2009.02.002

Willis, G. (1991). The single market and national marketing thinking. *European Journal of Marketing*, *25*(4), 148–156.

Wilson, A., Lenssen, G., & Hind, P. (2006). *Leadership qualities and management competencies for corporate responsibility*. Academic Press.

Winter, D. (1973). *The Power Motive*. Free Press.

Winter, D. (1982). A motivational model of leadership: Predicting long-term management success from TAT measures of power motivation and responsibility. *The Leadership Quarterly*, *2*(2), 67–80. doi:10.1016/1048-9843(91)90023-U

Winter, D. G., & Stewart, A. J. (1977). Power motive reliability as a function of retest instructions. *Journal of Consulting and Clinical Psychology*, *45*(3), 436–440. doi:10.1037/0022-006X.45.3.436

Winter, D., John, O., Stewart, A., Klohnen, E., & Duncan, L. (1998). Traits and motives: Toward an integration of two traditions in personality research. *Psychological Review*, *105*(2), 230–250. doi:10.1037/0033-295X.105.2.230 PMID:9577238

Winterton, J., Delamare-Le Deist, F., & Stringfellow, E. (2005). *Typology of knowledge, skills and competences: clarification of the concept and prototype.* Office for Official Publications of the European Communities.

Woetzel, J., Tonby, O., Thompson, F., Burtt, P., & Lee, G. (2014). *Southeast Asia at the crossroads: Three paths to prosperity.* McKinsey Global Institute.

Wong, K. H., Chang, H. H., & Yeh, C. H. (2019). The effects of consumption values and relational benefits on smartphone brand switching behavior. *Information Technology & People*, *32*(1), 217–243. doi:10.1108/ITP-02-2018-0064

Woodman, R. W., Sawyer, J. E., & Griffin, R. W. (1993). Toward a theory of organizational creativity. *Academy of Management Review*, *18*(2), 293–321. doi:10.5465/amr.1993.3997517

Woo, E., & Kim, Y. G. (2019). Consumer attitudes and buying behavior for green food products. *British Food Journal*, *121*(2), 320–332. doi:10.1108/BFJ-01-2018-0027

World Bank Data. (2021). Available at https://data.worldbank.org/

World Bank Group. (2016a). *World Development Indicators 2016.* Retrieved from http://databank.worldbank.org/data/reports.aspx?source=2&country=IND#

World Bank Group. (2016b). *Gross Domestic Product 2016.* Retrieved from https://databank.worldbank.org/data/download/GDP.pdf

World Bank Group. (2019). *World Development Indicators 2019.* Retrieved from http://databank.worldbank.org/data/reports.aspx?source=2&country=IND#

World Bank Group. (2020). *Malaysia's experience with the SME Masterplan: Lessons Learnt.* Author.

World Bank Group. (2021). *Market study for Malaysia: Plastics circularity opportunities and barriers.* Marine Plastics Series, East Asia and Pacific Region.

World Data. (2021). Available online at https://ourworldindata.org/covid-vaccinations?country=OWID_WRL

World Economic Forum. (2014). *Reorganize and streamline pure materials flows.* Author.

World Economic Forum. (2018). *Digital Transformation Initiative - Unlocking $100 Trillion for Business and Society from Digital Transformation.* Available online at: http://reports.weforum.org/digitaltransformation/wpcontent/blogs.dir/94/mp/files/pages/files/dti-executive-summary-

World's Best Award. (2017). Available at http://www.danang.intercontinental.com/top-100-hotels-in-the-world-by-travel-leisure-world-s-best-awards-2017

Woschke, T., Haase, H., & Kratzer, J. (2017). Resource scarcity in SMEs: Effects on incremental and radical innovations. *Management Research Review*, *40*(2), 195–217. doi:10.1108/MRR-10-2015-0239

Wright, P. M., & Dyer, L. (2000). *People in the E-Business: New challenges, new solutions.* Ithaca: Cornell university, school of industrial and labor *relations.*

Wuen, C. H., Ibrahim, F., & Ringim, K. J. (2021). Mediating effect of competitive strategy in the relationship between strategic human resource management and performance of small and medium enterprises in Brunei Darussalam. *Middle East Journal Management*, *8*(2/3), 254–277. doi:10.1504/MEJM.2021.114010

Xepapadeas, A. (2005). Economic Growth and the Environment. Handbook of Environmental Economics, 1(2), 1219-1271.

Xerri, M. (2013). Workplace relationships and the innovative behaviour of nursing employees: A social exchange perspective. *Asia Pacific Journal of Human Resources*, *51*(1), 103–123. doi:10.1111/j.1744-7941.2012.00031.x

Xiao, R. X., & Mossig, I. (2017). Co-evolution of institutions, culture and industrial organization in the film industry: The case of Shanghai in China. *European Planning Studies*, *25*(6), 923–940. doi:10.1080/09654313.2017.1300638

Xu, B. (2000). Multinational enterprises, technology diffusion, and host country productivity growth. *Journal of Development Economics*, *62*, 477–493.

Xu, F. Z., & Wang, Y. (2020). Enhancing employee innovation through customer engagement: The role of customer interactivity, employee affect, and motivations. *Journal of Hospitality & Tourism Research (Washington, D.C.)*, *44*(2), 351–376. doi:10.1177/1096348019893043

Yamoah, E. E. (2013). Relationship between compensation and employee productivity. *Singaporean Journal of Business, Economics and Management Studies*, *51*(1115), 1–5.

Yang, C., Lin, H., & Han, C. (2010). Analysis of International Tourist Arrivals in China: The Role of World Heritage Sites. *Tourism Management*, *31*(6), 827–837. doi:10.1016/j.tourman.2009.08.008 PMID:32287732

Yang, O., Park, J., & Lim, S. (2015). Xiaomi: Revolution of a rice grain. *Korea Business Review*, *19*(3), 83–118.

Yang, X. H., Lim, Y. T., Sakurai, Y., & Seo, S. Y. (2009). Internationalization of Chinese and Korean Firms. *Thunderbird International Business Review*, *51*(1), 37–51. doi:10.1002/tie.20243

Yanuarti, D. W., & Murwatiningsih, M. (2019). Mediating role of competitive strategy and marketing capability on the relationship between entrepreneurial orientation and market performance. *Management Analysis Journal*, *8*(2), 188–195.

Yao, F. K., & Chang, S. (2017). Do individual employee's learning goal orientation and civic virtue matter? A micro-foundations perspective on firm absorptive capacity. *Strategic Management Journal*, *38*(10), 2041–2060. doi:10.1002mj.2636

Yap, K.H., & Yap, S.T. (2018). COSO Enterprise Risk Management: Small-Medium Enterprises Evidence. *Asia-Pacific Management Accounting Journal*, *13*(2), 83–111.

Yates, R. (2017). ASEAN as the 'regional conductor': Understanding ASEAN's role in Asia-Pacific order. *The Pacific Review*, *30*(4), 443–461. doi:10.1080/09512748.2016.1264458

Yatim, N. H. M., Rusuli, M. S. C., & Yatim, N. A. M. (2019). The Effect of Government Intervention on The Sustainable Competitive Advantage Among SMEs In Malaysia. *International Journal of Modern Trends in Business Research*, *2*(8), 15–22.

Yau, G. L., Williams, A. S., & Brown, J. B. (2011). Family physicians' perspectives on personal health records: Qualitative study. *Canadian Family Physician Medecin de Famille Canadien*, *57*(5). Retrieved November 5, 2018, from https://www.ncbi.nlm.nih.gov/pmc/articles/PMC3093606/pdf/0570e178.pdf PMID:21642732

Yebowaah, F. A. (2018). Internet use and its effect on senior high school students in Wa municipality of Ghana. *Library Philosophy & Practice*.

Yeo, B. L., Mohamed, R., Hj, N., & Muda, M. (2016). A study of Malaysian customers purchase motivation of halal cosmetics retail products: Examining theory of consumption value and customer satisfaction. *Procedia Economics and Finance*, *37*, 176–182. doi:10.1016/S2212-5671(16)30110-1

Yin, R. K. (2003). *Case Study Research: Design and Methods* (2nd ed.). Sage Publications.

Yin, R. K. (2011). *Qualitative Research from Start to Finish*. The Guilford Press.

Ylä-Mella, J., Keiski, R. L., & Pongrácz, E. (2015). Electronic waste recovery in Finland: Consumers' perceptions towards recycling and re-use of mobile phones. *Waste Management (New York, N.Y.)*, *45*, 374–384. doi:10.1016/j.wasman.2015.02.031 PMID:25797074

Yousaf, Z., & Majid, A. (2016). Strategic performance through inter-firm networks: Strategic alignment and moderating role of environmental dynamism. *World Journal of Entrepreneurship, Management and Sustainable Development*, *12*(4), 282–298. doi:10.1108/WJEMSD-03-2016-0015

Yuan, F., & Woodman, R. W. (2010). Innovative behavior in the workplace: The role of performance and image outcome expectations. *Academy of Management Journal*, *53*(2), 323–342.

Yu, C., Zhang, Z., & Shen, H. (2017). The effect of organizational learning and knowledge management innovation on SMEs' technological capability. *Eurasia Journal of Mathematics, Science and Technology Education*, *13*(8), 5475–5487. doi:10.12973/eurasia.2017.00842a

Yue, B., Sheng, G., She, S., & Xu, J. (2020). Impact of Consumer Environmental Responsibility on Green Consumption Behavior in China: The Role of Environmental Concern and Price Sensitivity. *Sustainability*, *12*(5), 1–16. doi:10.3390u12052074

Yuen, K. F., Wang, X., Ma, F., Lee, G., & Li, X. (2019). Critical success factors of supply chain integration in container shipping: An application of resource-based view theory. *Maritime Policy & Management*, *46*(6), 653–668. doi:10.1080/03088839.2019.1597289

Yuliansyah, Y., Gurd, B., & Mohamed, N. (2017). The significant of business strategy in improving organizational performance. *Humanomics*, *33*(1), 56–74. doi:10.1108/H-06-2016-0049

Yu, S., & Lee, J. (2019). The Effects of Consumers' Perceived Values on Intention to Purchase Upcycled Products. *Sustainability*, *11*(4), 1034. doi:10.3390u11041034

Zaidi, S. M. M. R., Lai, Y., Bhutto, M. Y., Ali, R., & Fahad, A. (2019). The influence of consumption values on green purchase intention: A moderated mediation of greenwash perceptions and green trust. *Pakistan Journal of Commerce and Social Sciences*, *13*(4), 826–848.

Zailani, S., Dahlan, N., & Jallaludin, Y. H. (2009). E-business adoption among SMEs in Malaysia: Investigation from the supply chain perspective. *Problems and Perspectives in Management*, *7*(4), 46–57.

Zailani, S., Iranmanesh, M., Sean Hyun, S., & Ali, M. (2019). Applying the theory of consumption values to explain drivers' willingness to pay for biofuels. *Sustainability*, *11*(3), 668. doi:10.3390u11030668

Zakaria, N. (Ed.). (2016). *Handbook of research on impacts of international business and political affairs on the global economy*. IGI Global. doi:10.4018/978-1-4666-9806-2

Zakaria, N., & Amelinckx, A. (2020). *Transcending Cultural Frontiers*. Springer Singapore. doi:10.1007/978-981-15-4454-5

Zamani, S. N. M., Abdul-Talib, A. N., & Ashari, H. (2016). Strategic orientations and new product success: The mediating impact of innovation speed. International Information Institute Information, 19(7B), 2785-2790.

Zhang, L., & Wang, H. (2006). Intelligent information processing in human resource management: An implementation case in China. *Expert Systems: International Journal of Knowledge Engineering and Neural Networks*, *23*(5), 356–369. doi:10.1111/j.1468-0394.2006.00416.x

Zhang, Y., Luo, Y., Zhang, X., & Zhao, J. (2019). How green human resource management can promote green employee behavior in China: A technology acceptance model perspective. *Sustainability*, *11*(19), 5408. doi:10.3390u11195408

Zhou, J. (1998). Feedback valence, feedback style, task autonomy, and achievement orientation: Interactive effects on creative performance. *The Journal of Applied Psychology*, *83*(2), 261–276. doi:10.1037/0021-9010.83.2.261

Zhou, J., & George, J. M. (2003). Awakening employee creativity: The role of leader emotional intelligence. *The Leadership Quarterly*, *14*(4-5), 545–568. doi:10.1016/S1048-9843(03)00051-1

Zhu, Y., Ritter, S. M., Müller, B. C., & Dijksterhuis, A. (2017). Creativity: Intuitive processing outperforms deliberative processing in creative idea selection. *Journal of Experimental Social Psychology*, *73*, 180–188. doi:10.1016/j.jesp.2017.06.009

Ziyae, B. (2016). Presenting an evaluation model of human resource management's effect on corporate entrepreneurship. *World Journal of Entrepreneurship, Management and Sustainable Development*, *12*(3), 228–242. doi:10.1108/WJEMSD-03-2016-0013

Ziyae, B., Sajadi, S. M., & Mobaraki, M. H. (2014). The deployment and internationalization speed of e-business in the digital entrepreneurship era. *Journal of Global Entrepreneurship Research.*, *4*(15), 1–11. http://www.journal-jger.com/content/4/1/15

About the Contributors

Patricia Ordóñez de Pablos is a professor in the Department of Business Administration in the Faculty of Business and Economics at The University of Oviedo (Spain). She completed her education in The London School of Economics (UK). Her teaching and research interests focus on the areas of strategic management, knowledge management, organizational learning, human resource management, intellectual capital, information technologies, with special interest in Asia (Bhutan, China, Laos, Myanmar). She is Editor-in-Chief of the International Journal of Learning and Intellectual Capital (IJLIC) and International Journal of Asian Business and Information Management (IJABIM), respectively. She has edited books for IGI-Global, Routledge and Springer.

* * *

Asmat-Nizam Abdul-Talib teaches international business and marketing at the Universiti Utara Malaysia. He received his PhD in International Marketing from Aston Business School, Aston University, UK, his MBA in International Business from Cardiff University, UK, and a Bachelors Degree in Economics from Concordia University, Canada. At current, his academic research has received financial support or support in kind from various institutions. His research interests lie primarily in international marketing and strategic marketing, especially in export market intelligence, and the use of export market intelligence in the firm's export decision process.

Sampath Dakshina Murthy Achanta received his B.Tech in Electronics and Communication Engineering Degree in 2013 and M.Tech Degree in Digital Electronics and Communication Engineering 2015. He is working as an Assistant Professor in Department of Electronics and Communication Engineering at Vignan's Institute of Information Technology (A). Pursuing a Ph.D. in Electronics and Communication Engineering from Koneru Lakshmaiah Education Foundation Deemed University in Guntur, Andhra Pradesh. His research interest includes Gait analysis in Pattern Recognition, Image & Video Processing, Fuzzy Logic, and Neural Networks. He has published 36 papers in International Journals. He is having 3 patents; 2 books published and received various 5 International and 5National awards. He is a Life member of I.S.R.S, IEI, C.S.I, and MIET. He is a reviewer and editorial board for journals in Scopus and SCI. He has 4 years of teaching and research experience.

Iqra Akhtar completed her master studies at the Institute of Business Management and Administrative Sciences, The Islamia University of Bahawalpur, Pakistan. She got good marks in research subjects. Currently, she is working on several research projects, this is one of them.

Tehmina Ambreen completed her master's studies at the institute of business management & administrative sciences, The Islamia University of Bahawalpur, Pakistan. She is working on a various research project this one of it.

Hui Nee Au Yong holds a PhD degree from Universiti Sains Malaysia, a graduate of MA Economics from University of Tsukuba and Bachelor of Science (Honours) Resource Economics from Universiti Putra Malaysia. She is an associate professor / Dean of the Faculty of Business and Finance, Universiti Tunku Abdul Rahman. She was sponsored to attend Impact Evaluation Methods by World Bank Group and Women's Director Programme by the Ministry of Women, Family and Community Development. Dr. Au Yong was trained in commercial and investment banks. Prior to joining academia, she held managerial positions at Fortune 500 multinational corporations and a state agency, managing the information system, environment safety & health, supply chain & logistics and compliance risk management. Furthermore, she is journal editor and reviewer, and published over 100 papers and other publications. She has received over USD150,000 of research grants from local and abroad. She was a Monbukagakusho Scholar and awarded the Malaysian Institute of Management Tun Razak Youth Leadership Award, best oral presentation award and best paper awards.

Hari Govinda Rao Chukka has completed his Ph.D. in Housing-Finance and presently working as Professor in Management Studies at Vignan's Institute of Information Technology. He has more than 17 years of experience in teaching and research in the area of Management. His teaching interests include financial Management, International Financial Management, Security Analysis and Portfolio Management, Investment Management and Accounting and Financial Management. His research interests includes Working Capital Management, Housing Finance and Financial Management. Dr. Ch. Hari Govinda Rao has Published a Patent and several articles in the reputed international journals and guided more than 200 academic theses and projects. He has participated and presented various papers in national, international seminars and conferences. He has been associated with reputed international journals as an Editorial Board Member and reviewer as well. He is being recognized with prestigious institute level awards like, Vijeta, Sastra, and Prathiba Puraskar, etc.

Nurhidayatul Gulihana is a Postgraduate student of MSc Management & Technology at UTB School of Business.

Hajah Siti Wardah Haji Abd Rahman is a PhD holder in Economics, awarded by Universiti Putra Malaysia. She is an Economics lecturer at Universiti Teknologi Brunei (UTB). Her research interests include population aging, economic growth, human capital, entrepreneurship and green sustainability. She has experience in consultancy service for UTB's Executive Development Program (EDP) for government officials at senior management level. Her research publication ranges from the areas of economics and population aging to finance and management. She is also a journal reviewer in areas related to economics and finance.

Fahmi Ibrahim (PhD) is Assistant Professor of School of Business, Universiti Teknologi Brunei (UTB), Brunei Darussalam. He gained his PhD from Glasgow Caledonian University, Glasgow, UK and MSc in Business Information Technology Systems (BITS) from University of Strathclyde, Glasgow, UK. He has a wide range of academic experience, gained in further and higher education establishments in the Brunei Darussalam and UK. This experience includes module and programme development, programme leadership, and international collaboration. His current teaching and research areas are in the field of Strategic Management, Knowledge Management, Intellectual Capital Management, Management Information Systems (MIS), Human Resource Management, Operations Management and Tourism Management-Development within public, private and SMEs organisations. His consultancy experience is in the area of Business Transformation particularly in SMEs. The consultancy expertise is supported by and complemented by his research interests. His research output includes book chapters, journal articles and conference papers. In recent years his research interest has evolved to be contextualised around the strategic development of organisations in complex and transitional environments. Also he has developed research interest on learning and teaching drawing from cross-disciplinary initiatives. He is currently on the editorial board of four international journals. In addition, he has been a keynote speaker in international conference, regularly contributes to conference organising committees and acts as a reviewer for a range of conferences.

Muhammad Imran is working as an Assistant Professor, Department of Project and Operations Management, The Islamia University of Bahawalpur, Punjab, Pakistan.

Ajeya Jha is a Professor at the Department of Management Studies at Sikkim Manipal Institute of Technology (SMIT) since February 2000. In addition to having post-graduate and doctoral degrees in Business Administration, he possesses graduation and post graduation in Pharmaceutical Sciences also. fellow of International Society of Management. Has a rich and diverse industrial experience of 15 years (includes launching two green-field projects), teaching 22 years and with NGO 8 months. He is the founder Chief coordinator of Entrepreneurship Development Cell (EDC) at SMIT established with support from Department of Science and Technology, Government of India.

Dongwook Kim is an independent consultant in the telecommunications industry. Prior to his consulting services, he served as a technical specialist at global organizations like the GSM Association, representing more than 750 mobile operators globally and 350 ecosystem players. His research focuses on the industry transformation enabled by next generation mobile networks, economics of network deployment and business models enabled by mobile networks.

Kabiru Maitama Kura is an Assistant Professor of Organisational Behaviour at the UTB School of Business, Universiti Teknologi Brunei. His research interests focus workplace deviance, organisational citizenship behaviour, job attitudes, personality and individual differences, green behaviour at work, and leadership. Prior to joining UTB School of Business, he was a Senior Lecturer/Director School of Remedial and Basic Studies, at the Federal Polytechnic Kaura Namoda, Nigeria. Kabiru earned a Doctor of Philosophy degree (PhD) in Human Resource Management from Universiti Utara Malaysia. Kabiru has published in SCOPUS, Web of Science, ABS Ranking and ABDC Listed journals, such as the Global Business Review, Journal of African Business, International Journal of Public Administration, African Journal of Economic and Management Studies, International Journal of Business and Society, and SAGE Open. He is a member of, American Psychological Association (APA), a member of, Nigerian Institute of Management (Chartered), a Member of, Commodity Brokers Association of Nigeria, member of, Nigerian Institute of Management (Chartered), member, Institute of Management Consultants of Nigeria. Kabiru was the chairman of the Nigerian Institute of Management (Chartered), Zaria Chapter.

Junghwan Lee is an Associate Professor at the Chungbuk National University. His research focuses on the innovation, quantitative data analysis, entrepreneurship, technology commercialization and mobile business model.

Ke Xin Liew is a Master graduate of Universiti Tunku Abdul Rahman.

Selvalakshmi M. has over 20 years of experience in teaching Marketing and Strategy to MBA students. Her area of research interest includes Services Management and Education. She has published cases in Ivey Publishing and The Case Centre. She has held administrative positions in the past and currently serves as the Principal of a popular B-School in India. Earlier she served in the Education services industry in the field of Sales and Marketing for a period of three years and has been recognized with the Award of Excellence. She has trained the executives of Corporate in Marketing and Personal Effectiveness.

Sree Maruthuvellu has worked in several companies in her twelve years of career history. She holds the qualifications of Bachelor of Human Resource Management (Hons) from University of Greenwich, United Kingdom. She is currently pursuing her final year of Master in Business Administration from Graduate School of Business, Universiti Sains Malaysia. Her research interests lie primarily in the area of Global Strategy and Organization Behavior. Sree Gayithri is inspired by Steve Jobs. "Have the courage to follow your heart and intuition. They somehow already know what you truly want to become.

Liana Artini Haji Mohamad Noor is a lecturer at UTB School of Business at Universiti Teknologi Brunei. Currently she is the Programme Leader under the Management Programme Area. Specializing in the area of Management, her areas of interest include Human Resource Management, People Analytics, Knowledge Management and Hospitality Management. She graduated from University of Salford, United Kingdom in 2003 with a Bachelors (Hons) in Hospitality Management and successfully completed her Master of Management in 2013 from Universiti Brunei Darussalam. Growing up abroad for most of her life, Liana is happily residing in Brunei however her love for travelling endures.

Khairunnisa Musari is currently an Assistant Professor at Department of Islamic Economics, Postgraduate Program and Faculty of Islamic Business Economics (FEBI), Kiai Haji Achmad Shiddiq State Islamic University (UIN KHAS), Jember, Indonesia. She is a member of the Indonesian Association of Islamic Economist (IAEI) and a Lead Independent Associate Ambassadors of VentureEthica. She has experience as a Senior Specialist for Islamic Finance of UNDP Indonesia. She was listed as the Top 150 Most Influential Women in Islamic Business & Finance 2020 by Cambridge-IFA.

Khairul Nizam Mahmud is a sessional lecturer at Universiti Utara Malaysia.

Jaya Pandey is currently working as Assistant Professor at Sikkim Manipal Institute of Technology since January 2008. She holds masters degree in Economics and also in Business administration. She has completed her doctoral work on a topic related to Pharmaceutical marketing and awarded with PhD degree. She has 15 papers to her credit and which have been published in peer-reviewed national and international journals. She has co-authored Two books. She is also a co-investigator in a project funded by All India Council for Technical Education.

Kabila Ramanthan is an MBA student of Thiagarajar School of Management, India with specialization in Marketing. She completed her under graduation in Electrical Engineering and has two years of work experience. Her area of research interest includes Bottom of the Pyramid and Consumer Behavior.

Ritu Rana holds a PhD degree from Department of Humanities and Social Sciences, National Institute of Technology Hamirpur, Himachal Pradesh, India. She has also worked with Indian Institute of Foreign Trade (IIFT), New Delhi as Programme Associate. She did her MBA (Finance and Marketing) and B. Com. (Foreign Trade) from Kurukshetra University, Kurukshetra (Haryana), India. Her research interests include International Economics, International Business, Sustainable Development, Entrepreneurship Development and studying about the effects of Foreign Direct Investment on the Economic Growth and Environment of the host country.

Christopher Richardson is a Senior Lecturer at USM's Graduate School of Business, where he also serves as the PhD programme manager. His research interests include firm internationalisation and cross-cultural management and his work has appeared in several notable outlets, such as Journal of World Business, International Business Review, and Management International Review.

Kabiru Jinjiri Ringim is a Senior Lecturer in the ABU Business School, Ahmadu Bello University, Zaria (ABU Zaria). He is specialising in the field of production and operations management, supply chain management, quality and project management. He obtained his PhD from the University Utara Malaysia. His research interest focuses on human resource management, business process reengineering, information technology capability, organisational performance, survey research and quantitative analysis.

Saibal Kumar Saha (UGC NET Qualified) holds a first class Master's degree in MBA and a first class Bachelor's Degree in Electronics and Communication Engineering. He has 10+ years of experience and has worked in MNCs like Cognizant Technology Solutions and Tata Aig Life. He has served National Institute of Technology - Silchar, Jyotirmoy School of Business – Kolkata, University of Technology and Management - Shillong and is presently working as Assistant Professor at Sikkim Manipal Institute of Technology - Majitar, India.

Sangita Saha is an MBA master from Sikkim Manipal Institute of Technology and BCA graduate from Indira Gandhi National Open University. She has specialized in Human Resource and Marketing. She has active interest in academic research and her area of interest includes motivation, consumer behaviour, tourism and digital technologies.

Yashar Salamzadeh is a PhD scholar in Human Resources Management and is a Senior Lecturer in Graduate School of Business at Universiti Sains Malaysia. He has published more than 100 research articles in international and national journals and conferences. He has the experience of eleven years teaching in MBA and Master of management courses in five different universities. He has supervised more than 70 graduate students (On MBA and Master level) in their thesis and dissertation and is supervising 8 PhD and DBA students as well. He has developed many managerial workshops on leadership, social entrepreneurship, HRM, Business models in different countries such as Iran, Turkey, Russia, Malaysia, Hungary and UK. He has worked as a project management in many national and international research projects. He has the experience of five years management consultancy for different public and private organizations on Leadership, Organizational re-structuring, EFQM, Culture, HRM systems, Organizational behavior. He also has cooperated in more than twenty international journals as an editorial board member and review board member. He is also an EFQM auditor. He has served GSB as Head of "Global Strategy and Organizational Behavior" research cluster since 2018. He is leading the micro-credential initiative of GSB as well. His fields of interest include entrepreneurship, Entrepreneurial Universities, Leadership and digital leadership, business models, strategic management, green business and CSR, HRM (HCM) and networked organizations.

Manoj Sharma is working as Assistant Professor (Grade I) in the Department of Humanities and Social Sciences, National Institute of Technology (NIT) Hamirpur, Himachal Pradesh, India. He received his PhD, M.Phil. (Econ.) and MBA from Himachal Pradesh University, Shimla, India. During his fifteen years of teaching and research, he has published more than thirty research papers in journals. He has also served various universities and institutions in different capacities and chaired technical sessions in national and international conferences. His areas of interest are Applied Economics, Environmental Economics, Transportation Economics and Entrepreneurship Development.

Ajay Singh is presently working as Assistant Professor at IIT Jammu.

Hazimah Suhip is a postgraduate student of MSc Management & Technology at UTB Business School.

Heru Susanto is currently Assistant Professor at School of Business, Universiti Teknologi Brunei, Researcher at Research Center for Informatics, the Indonesian Institute of Sciences. At present he is an Honorary Professor, Department of Information Management, College of Management, Tunghai University, Taichung, Taiwan. Dr. Susanto has worked as an IT professional in several roles, including Web Division Head of IT Strategic at Indomobil Group, and Prince Muqrin Chair for Information Security Technologies. His research interests are in the areas of Information Security, 5G Technologies, Grid Application, Big Data, Business Process Re-engineering, and e-Marketing. Dr. Susanto received a BSc in Computer Science; an MBA in Marketing Management; an MSc in Information Systems; and a PhD in Information Security, from IPB University, King Saud University and Tunghai University, respectively. Nowadays, Dr. Heru Successfully authoring more than 35 books published by Francis & Taylor Group; including 8 full authored books and 30 book chapters, and more than 60 international publication in peer review journal and high impact journal; Scopus, Science Direct, Springer, ISI, and Global Indexed, such as: Information Security Management Systems, Business Process Reengineering An ICT Approach, The Emerging Technology of Big Data, Human Capital through ICT, Chemical Technology and Informatics in Chemistry with Applications.

Xuan V. Tran (The University of West Florida,) is a full professor. His papers were published in Annals of Tourism Research, Anatolia, Journal of Vacation Marketing, Tourism Analysis, and other tourism journals.

Hammad Wajid is pursuing his master studies at the Institute of Business Management and Administrative Sciences, The Islamia University of Bahawalpur, Pakistan. He got good marks in research subjects. Currently, he is working on several research projects, this is one of them.

Chin Han Wuen completed his PhD in Management at the Universiti Teknologi Brunei, Brunei Darussalam. His main research areas include strategic management, human resource management, organizational learning and micro, small and medium enterprises (MSMEs).

Index

A

B

C

D

E

G

H

I

K

L

M

N

O

P

R

S

T

U

V

W

www.ingramcontent.com/pod-product-compliance
Lightning Source LLC
LaVergne TN
LVHW080407011026
849161LV00009B/2362